# THE YOUNG CHILD

## Development from Prebirth Through Age Eight

*Second Edition*

**Janet K. Black**
*Texas A & M International University*

**Margaret B. Puckett**
*Texas Wesleyan University*

*Merrill,*
*an imprint of Prentice Hall*
Englewood Cliffs, New Jersey    Columbus, Ohio

Library of Congress Cataloging-in-Publication Data
Black, Janet, K.
   The young child: development from prebirth through age eight /
Janet K. Black, Margaret B. Puckett—[Rev.]
      p. cm.
   Includes bibliographical references and index.
   ISBN 0-02-310241-1
   1. Child development. 2. Infants—Development. 3. Child
psychology. I. Puckett, Margaret B. II. Title.
   [HQ767.9.B56 1996]
   305.23'1—dc20                                          95-8646

Cover photo: © Ted Horowitz/The Stock Market
Editor: Kevin M. Davis
Developmental Editor: Carol S. Sykes
Production Editor: Julia Anderson Tober
Project Management and Text Design: Elm Street Publishing Services, Inc.
Photo Editor: Anne Vega
Cover Design: Patti Ann C. Okuno-Levering
Production Manager: Deidra Schwartz

This book was set in 10/12 Sabon by Elm Street Publishing Services, Inc. and was printed and bound by R. R. Donnelley & Sons Company. The cover was printed by Phoenix Color Corp.

© 1996 by Prentice Hall, Inc.
A Simon & Schuster Company
Englewood Cliffs, New Jersey 07632

Earlier edition © 1992 by Macmillan Publishing Company.

Photos by Nancy P. Alexander, pp. 7, 20, 24, 31, 52, 111, 128, 134, 145, 151, 160, 173, 178, 206, 213, 215, 219, 224, 230, 242, 247, 251, 262, 267, 272, 292, 305, 308, 315, 321, 326, 330, 332, 350, 364, 369, 371, 386, 403, 418, 430, 439, 447, 452, 455, 462, 467, 473, 476, 477, 478; Children's Hospital, Columbus, Ohio, p. 89; Scott Cunningham/Merrill/Prentice Hall, pp. 33, 426; Timothy O'Leary/Merrill/Prentice Hall, p. 346; Margaret B. Puckett, pp. 2, 80, 98, 110, 114, 164, 183, 226; Anne Vega/Merrill/Prentice Hall, pp. 91, 393; Cathy Watterson, p. 50; Ulrike Welsch, p. 408; Vera Wulf, p. 194.

Printed in the United States of America

10 9 8 7 6

ISBN: 0-02-310241-1

Prentice-Hall International (UK) Limited, *London*
Prentice-Hall of Australia Pty. Limited, *Sydney*
Prentice-Hall of Canada, Inc., *Toronto*
Prentice-Hall Hispanoamericana, S.A., *Mexico*
Prentice-Hall of India Private Limited, *New Delhi*
Prentice-Hall of Japan, Inc., *Tokyo*
Simon & Schuster Asia Plo. Ltd., *Singapore*
Editora Prentice-Hall do Brasil, Ltda., *Rio de Janeiro*

To those who helped us with our "roots and wings"...

**Our parents**
Wilson LaMar and Lelah Knisely Knecht
Hugh Bevil and Neutie LeHew Brous

**Our spouses**
Clifford M. Black
John Wesley Puckett

**Our children**
Jonathan Andrew Black
John Wesley Puckett, Jr.
Dan William Puckett
Paula Puckett Jeffers

**Our grandchildren**
Katherine Elaine Puckett
Madeline Kay Jeffers
Macy Clare Jeffers

**And last but not least, our mentors**
Martha L. King, Ph.D.
Velma E. Schmidt, Ph.D.
Marion Wilson Brous, M.D.

# PREFACE

Welcome to the second edition of *The Young Child*. This text was written to provide you with the most important tool possessed by the competent early childhood professional: current theory and knowledge in the field of early childhood growth, development, and learning.

Like the first edition, this text is based on the premise that knowledge about child growth, development, and learning is constantly evolving. This ever-expanding field of research and its resulting knowledge base are reflected throughout the second edition in new and expanded information provided in the following areas:

- Human diversity, with a greater emphasis on inclusion and multicultural perspectives
- Expanded interpretations of *developmentally appropriate practice* into the broader concept of *developmentally appropriate practices*
- A greater emphasis on societal change and its impact on children, families, schools, and communities
- Increased attention to the concept of multiple intelligences and learning styles
- An expanded focus on the role of play in the development and learning of young children
- An increased emphasis on the role of authentic assessment in facilitating the development and learning of young children
- Expanding responsibilities of the early childhood professional
- Increased attention to environmental and health issues affecting the well-being of children and families

The earliest growth and development, from conception through a child's eighth year, are dynamic. The progression from an energetic cell mass to a child of infinite characteristics and abilities at age eight is a journey of such complexity and magnitude that few, if any, authors fully capture its totality.

We recognize that the first eight years are critical to later development and attempt to present a "whole child" perspective, emphasizing that an understanding of the development of infants and young children is a prerequisite to becoming a competent early childhood professional. In this context, we bridge theory and practice by juxtaposing research and theories of early growth and development with the role of the adult in facilitating this development.

This text presents the development of young children from an ecological perspective, addressing the young child in the global context of family, school, community, and society. Major theories are interrelated with all aspects of development, including physical and motor, psychosocial, cognitive, language, and literacy. The text also highlights the long-term benefits of developmentally appropriate practices in the early years. To further help the reader make the association between theory and practice, ongoing vignettes about two children appear throughout the chapters. A unique feature of this text is the interfacing of adult and professional development in the context of the developing child. Ethical responsibility in promoting developmentally appropriate practices and the role of advocacy is emphasized.

## ORGANIZATION OF THE TEXT

The text is divided into seven parts. Part One, An Overview of Early Childhood Development, outlines historical viewpoints and the evolution of the study of early childhood. It presents current theories of early childhood development and emphasizes the importance of this information to the developing professional. Early and classical research in the fields of child development and early education are discussed, as are various approaches and resources for studying young children.

Part Two, The Child's Life Begins, discusses the family before birth with attention to educational, sociocultural, and economic antecedents to parenting. It describes prenatal development with an emphasis on health, nutrition, and medical supervision of pregnancy. Childbirth and the family dynamics of the newborn are also examined.

Parts Three, Four, Five, and Six trace physical and motor, psychosocial, and cognitive, language, and literacy development during infancy, ages 1 through 3, ages 4 through 5, and ages 6 through 8, respectively. This organization facilitates either chronological or topical discussion and study.

Part Seven, A Brief Look Beyond the Early Years, begins with a brief overview of child development beyond the early years and projects the effects of early development on later development. It concludes with a focus on the developing professional's self-understanding, adult developmental patterns, and ongoing professional development, including dimensions of responsibility, developmentally appropriate practices, ethical behavior, interpersonal relationships, advocacy, and continuing study.

At the end of each chapter, the reader will find Review Strategies and Activities, which include relevant, hands-on suggestions. In addition, the Further Reading sections that conclude each chapter have been expanded and updated.

## ANGELA AND JEREMY

Two young children, Angela and Jeremy, are introduced beginning in Chapter 2, and subsequent chapters follow their development and relationships. These vignettes illustrate the uniqueness of growth and development in young children and their families. Angela and Jeremy are composites of many children we have known and are not representative of any particular racial or ethnic group. We caution the reader to avoid viewing these children in a stereotypical or prejudicial manner. While both children and their families experience adversity to varying degrees, the vignettes attempt to illustrate the power of resiliency and potential for learning and development in all individuals.

## ACKNOWLEDGMENTS

We are grateful to the early childhood education students at Southwest Texas State University who have provided us with ongoing feedback and thoughtful critique and suggestions during the past two years. Special thanks to colleagues and students at our universities, Deborah Diffily, Tara Knecht, Susan Cook, Kathy Hoover, Annette Seigler, and Dawn Greenfield, for providing suggestions for content and format. We are grateful to Nancy Alexander, whose expertise in child development and early childhood education provided outstanding photography for this edition. Appreciation is also expressed to Kathy Fite, Southwest Texas State University, for her work on the *Instructor's Manual* that accompanies this text. We also extend appreciation to Joy Edwards, Texas Wesleyan University, for advice and input on inclusion practices for children with disabilities, and to Carlos Martinez, Texas Wesleyan University, for his expertise on human diversity and multicultural considerations. For assistance in library research and resources, we are grateful to Cindy Potter, Paula Sanders, and Sheila Holder, Texas Wesleyan University—Eunice and James L. West Library.

We continue to be grateful to the late Marion Wilson Brous, M.D., for pediatric advice, references, and resources, and to the late Velma E. Schmidt, Ph.D., University of North Texas, for her mentoring and inspiration for our own professional development and for her legacy to the field of early childhood education.

We would like to acknowledge the reviewers of this edition: Kathleen E. Fite, Southwest Texas State University; Barbara Foulks, Radford University; Rey Gomez, Arizona State University; Barbara H. Harkness, San Bernardino Valley College; Cindy Gayle McGaha, University of North Carolina; Paulette E. Mills, Washington State University; Jeanne B. Morris, Illinois State University; Barbara Rodriguez, University of Central Florida; Marcia P. Rysztak, Lansing Community College; and Deborah J. Smith, Appalachian State University.

To our many friends and colleagues around the country whose support and encouragement are so characteristic of early childhood professionals, we say a hearty thank you.

To a delightful and skilled team of editors whose constant support and encouragement made this revision of *The Young Child* an enjoyable project, we express genuine appreciation to Kevin Davis, Carol Sykes, Julie Tober, Anne Vega, and Barbara Campbell.

Janet K. Black, Ph.D.
Margaret B. Puckett, Ed.D.

# CONTENTS IN BRIEF

# CONTENTS

# PART ONE

# An Overview of Early Childhood Development

# CHAPTER ONE

*There are two lasting gifts we can give our children—one is roots; the other is wings.*

**(Author unknown)**

# The What and Why of Early Childhood Development

After studying this chapter, you will demonstrate comprehension by:

- Reflecting on personal goals as a developing early childhood professional.
- Defining *early childhood development*.
- Describing the importance of understanding early childhood development.
- Outlining the historical viewpoints of childhood.
- Describing the evolution of early childhood development study.
- Outlining the current theories in early childhood development.
- Listing emerging issues in the field of early childhood development.

If you are reading this book, you must have noticed young children at some time or another and found them interesting, perhaps even fascinating. Just where and when did *your* interest in young children begin? Perhaps it was while babysitting, helping in classrooms, counseling at summer camps, or parenting your own children. Wherever it was, did you notice young children's general zest for life? Did you find their insatiable curiosity intriguing? Did you find some of their perceptions of the world quite different from yours and at times humorous? Did you receive inner satisfaction in helping young children learn or in providing security and nurturance in their times of need? If you said yes to some of these questions, you are like many others who have chosen to become early childhood professionals.

## THE EARLY CHILDHOOD DEVELOPMENT PROFESSION

**Professionals** learn the knowledge base of their particular field. This knowledge base, coupled with practice in the field, facilitates the development of competent practitioners and professionals.

*Becoming a competent early childhood professional begins with learning about the growth and development of young children, including those from developmentally and culturally diverse backgrounds. It also entails continuously learning about young children and their families throughout one's professional career.*

*professionals: individuals who internalize the evolving knowledge base of their particular fields and implement this knowledge through appropriate practices*

3

The study of children had its beginnings in the late 1700s. Within the last 25 to 30 years, a substantial body of knowledge has been added to this research. These more recent studies increasingly indicate that while similarities may exist among various aspects of development, professionals need to learn about and respect variations in the backgrounds of young children and their families (Bredekamp & Rosegrant, 1992; Mallory & New, 1994). Therefore, professionals who work with young children and their families will continuously evolve in their understanding of **developmentally appropriate** learning environments for all young children.

Currently most of the 50 states require teachers of young children to have specialized training in early childhood development and related areas. In 1982, the National Association for the Education of Young Children (NAEYC) developed guidelines for training professionals who work with young children. These *Early Childhood Teacher Education Guidelines* were subsequently adopted by the National Council for the Accreditation of Teacher Education (NCATE). Considerable research began in 1992 when NAEYC's National Institute for Early Childhood Professional Development launched a nationwide review process in which professional input was sought. A consensus was eventually established and these 1982 guidelines were revised and published as the *NAEYC Guidelines for Preparation of Early Childhood Professionals* (NAEYC, 1995). In addition to NCATE's endorsement in September, 1994, these revised guidelines were also endorsed by the Division of Early Childhood (DEC) of the Council for Exceptional Children (CEC).

These revisions reflect two recent federal laws—the Individuals with Disabilities Education Act (IDEA), passed in 1991, and the Americans with Disabilities Act (ADA), passed in 1992. These laws mandate that persons with disabilities are entitled to equal rights in (1) public accommodations such as child care centers, family child care homes, preschools, and public schools, (2) state and local services, and (3) employment. Specifically, all early childhood programs must provide services to young children with developmental delays or disabilities and to those at risk for developmental delays.

Inclusion refers to theoretical and curricular means for assuring that all children are fully accepted members of the learning communities in which they participate. This practice of **inclusion** benefits *all* children and families. Inclusion helps children appreciate and accept human differences while developing caring attitudes and a recognition of our interdependence. Early childhood professionals need training and practice regarding inclusion. In addition, the changing demographics occurring nationwide require that early childhood professionals become aware of the increasing culturally and linguistically diverse backgrounds of children and their families.

The revision of the guidelines illustrate an ever-expanding knowledge base in child development, early childhood education, and family and community relationships. The revised professional development guidelines emphasize preparing personnel for:

- Full inclusion of children with disabilities in all early childhood settings
- Cultural and linguistic diversity
- Individualization of curriculum and instructional practices
- Working collaboratively with other adults
- Supervisory and administrative roles

*developmentally appropriate:*
*pertains to (1) age appropriateness, the universal and predictable patterns of growth and development that occur in children from birth through age 8; and (2) individual appropriateness, the individual rates and patterns of physical/motor, psychosocial, cognition, language and literacy development, personality and learning style, and family and cultural background of each young child*

*inclusion:*
*the principle of including children who are developmentally and culturally diverse in integrated settings*

- Continual pursuit of central concepts and tools of inquiry in various curriculum content areas
- Understanding the interrelationship among culture, language, and thought
- Understanding the function of the home language
- Supporting the development of, and meeting the needs of individual children
- Appropriate use of technology with children
- Responding to changes in our culture and the life experiences of individual children
- Supporting and maintaining the physical and psychological health and safety of children
- Providing family-centered approaches in family and community relationships
- Assessment and evaluation that is both individualized and performance based
- Applying new methodology in program evaluation
- Continuing professional development including becoming an advocate for children, families, highest quality programs, and the early childhood care and education profession, itself (Bredekamp, 1995; National Association for the Education of Young Children, 1995)

These early childhood professional development guidelines also promote specialized and consistent early childhood licensure standards in every state. Improving professionalism in teacher education could include these components:

- National accreditation of teacher education programs
- Performance-based licensure of teachers requisite to practice
- Certification through the National Board for Professional Teaching Standards (NBPTS) (Wise & Liebbrand, 1993)

Another effort to provide training and credentialing for those who work with young children is the Child Development Associate (CDA) National Credentialing Program. This program was initiated in 1971 for the purpose of enhancing "the quality of child care by defining, evaluating and recognizing the competence of child care providers and home visitors" (Council for Early Childhood Professional Recognition, 1992, p. 1). A person who is awarded a CDA has demonstrated competency in working with young children and their families by successfully completing the CDA assessment process.

The recognition of the importance of training for those who work with young children arises from the results of longitudinal studies on various early childhood programs for both **at-risk** and **low-risk** children (Lazar & Darlington, 1982; Schweinhart & Weikart, 1985; Larsen & Robinson, 1989; Schweinhart, Barnes, & Weikart, 1993).

The emphasis on the training of teachers of young children arises from a growing public awareness of the importance of the early years in the learning process. The Carnegie Corporation of New York report *Starting Points* (1994) clearly demonstrates recent scientific findings indicating that the "quality of young children's environment and social experience has a decisive, long-lasting impact upon their well-being and ability to learn" (p. xiii).

*at-risk:*
*children who have been or are in prebirth or afterbirth environments that do not promote typical physical/motor, psychosocial, cognitive, language, and literacy development*

*low-risk:*
*children who have been and continue to be in settings that facilitate normal physical/motor, psychosocial, cognitive, language, and literacy development*

The Goals 2000 Educate America Act (1994) requires states to develop education reform plans that set voluntary standards for student performance, curriculum, teacher preparation, and the resources and materials to ensure that all children have the opportunity to learn. Goal 1 states, "All children will arrive at school ready to learn." Another example of the growing recognition of the importance of the early years is the passage of the Head Start Reauthorization Act (1994). This legislation provides funding for the expansion of the Head Start program and ensures its continuation through 1998.

Because of the great demand for early childhood classrooms, not enough trained teachers are available. Unfortunately, at times young children are in settings that are **developmentally inappropriate** because the adults working with them are unaware of information pertaining to the children's learning styles, developmental diversity, and cultural backgrounds.

*developmentally inappropriate: pertains to adult expectations that are not age appropriate or individually appropriate for children from birth through age 8*

To promote greater understanding of the development and learning of young children, a number of professional organizations have developed position statements. The National Association for the Education of Young Children has developed two publications to meet this need: *Developmentally Appropriate Practice in Early Childhood Education Programs Serving Children from Birth Through Age 8* (1987) and *Reaching Potentials: Appropriate Curriculum and Assessment for Young Children, Volume 1* (1992).

These publications and the concept of developmentally appropriate practice are viewed from a dynamic perspective. The evolving knowledge base of the field of early childhood development and education will require changes and adjustments in practices. Current initiatives in making early childhood settings more accommodating of culturally and developmentally diverse children and the notion that teachers and parents are coconstructors of knowledge with children are examples of the dynamic nature of the field of early childhood development.

The growing recognition of the unique nature of young children's development and of the importance of the early years for lifelong productivity have created a great demand for trained early childhood professionals. The goal of this text is to provide you with the background information you need to develop into a competent early childhood professional. Such competency requires the perspective that learning about young children and their families is an ongoing, career-long process.

## DEFINITION OF EARLY CHILDHOOD DEVELOPMENT

*early childhood development: the study of the physical/motor, psychosocial, cognitive, language, and literacy development in children from prebirth through age 8 including those from developmentally and culturally diverse backgrounds*

**Early childhood development** is the study of how children from prebirth through age 8, including those from culturally and developmentally diverse backgrounds, grow and develop in the physical/motor, psychosocial, cognitive, language, and literacy domains. For convenience, this book will discuss the various domains separately. Nevertheless, it should be noted that development is interactive and that development in one area affects development or behavior in another area.

This text also recognizes the uniqueness of each individual. Therefore, it focuses on the diverse backgrounds, behaviors, and development of children in early childhood settings whose presence contributes to the richness of those classroom environments.

*All children are unique in their development.*

## THE IMPORTANCE OF UNDERSTANDING EARLY CHILDHOOD DEVELOPMENT

It is important to know about early childhood development for several reasons. First, a knowledge of growth and development in the early years can facilitate your self-understanding. Second, the knowledge of early childhood development by parents and professionals can facilitate the optimal growth and learning in young children. Finally, it is important to recognize that learning about early childhood development is an ongoing process.

## EVOLUTION OF THE STUDY OF YOUNG CHILDREN

John Locke (1632–1704) was one of the first people to advocate more humane treatment of young children. He also was one of the first to suggest that the environmental experience of the child may influence the development of the child's knowledge. Locke described the newborn's mind as a *tabula rasa*, an "empty slate," on which knowledge is written based on children's sensory experiences in their environment.

In 1774, Johann Pestalozzi (1746–1827) published a study of his son that for the first time gave serious attention to the nature of development during the early years of life. Nearly a century later, Charles Darwin (1809–1882) published a day-to-day record of the development of his young son. Darwin's publication of *The Origin of Species* (1859) had far-reaching effects on many aspects of knowledge, including the study of children.

As a biologist, Darwin took a trip to the Galapagos Islands in the South Pacific, where he collected birds and animals that were virtually unknown and therefore had not been classified according to any designated species. Darwin used these birds and animals to disprove the idea of a fixed nature of species. His development of the scientific method and conceptualization that the world is dynamic and not static set the stage for the scientific study of children.

Darwin's notion that animals adapt to their particular environments over time led biologists, psychologists, and others to begin studying the adaptive characteristics of humans. One of these psychologists, G. Stanley Hall (1846–1924), was instrumental in implementing the scientific method to study change and development in children. In 1893, Hall published *The Contents of Children's Minds*. This book was one of the first texts to be used in colleges and universities for training students who wanted to learn about young children. Another of Hall's important contributions to the study of child development was the establishment of the first child development research journal, *The Journal of Genetic Psychology*. Some of Hall's more illustrious students included Arnold Gesell, who developed norms regarding the physical maturation of children; John Dewey, whose democratic ideas concerning the learning process created major educational reform; and Lewis Terman, who developed the idea of the intelligence quotient(I.Q.). Hall's international reputation and influence enabled him to convince Sigmund Freud to come to Clark University to lecture on psychoanalysis.

After World War I, Lawrence K. Frank (1890–1968) was influential in obtaining foundation monies to establish various institutes to study child development. Subsequently, the Society for Research in Child Development was founded in 1933. During World War II, child development research and study declined. The conclusion of World War II, however, brought a substantial increase in the number of investigations concerning the nature of children. This intense interest in learning about young children continues today.

The intellectual and social perspectives just discussed were derived from individuals whose backgrounds reflected Western industrialized societies. These theories have dominated the thinking in the field of child development. Current thought is beginning to recognize the need to expand this body of knowledge to include information about developmental and cultural variations among children and their families. This evolving nature of the field needs to be kept in mind.

*theories:*
*ideas that are organized in a systematic manner based on observations or other kinds of evidence and are used to explain and predict the behaviors and development of young children, older children, and adults*

## THE NATURE OF A THEORY

In the area of early childhood development, a number of individuals have proposed ideas or **theories** that attempt to explain in an organized or systematic manner how young children develop and learn. The personal backgrounds of these theorists, as well as political and sociological events, often influence the development of ideas and the nature of research. At times, radical thinkers propose such new ideas that they change previous accepted theories. Thus, as new information is added, a theory may change. If research and practice continue to support a theory, it will continue to be useful, but if new information does not support a theory, it will be modified or discarded.

## THEORIES IN EARLY CHILDHOOD DEVELOPMENT

A number of theories attempt to explain early childhood development. These include psychoanalytic, behaviorist, cognitive, and ecological systems. Some of these theories attempt to explain only one aspect of development, while others are more comprehensive. All theories can help provide information about the total development of children. The following sections provide an overview of the various theories that have influenced the body of information on early childhood development. In-depth discussion will be presented throughout the text.

## PSYCHOANALYTIC, PSYCHOSEXUAL, PSYCHOSOCIAL, AND RELATED THEORIES

**Psychoanalytic theory** attempts to explain the inner thoughts and feelings, at both the conscious and subconscious levels, that influence behavior (Freud, 1938). Sigmund Freud (1856–1939) laid the foundations for psychoanalytic or **psychosexual theory**. As a physician in Vienna specializing in nervous or mental conditions, he became intrigued with adults' problems that seemed to have begun in childhood. Freud developed a stage theory that suggested that certain drives and instincts emerge at various periods of development through biological systems such as the mouth, the anus, and the sex organs. This theory is presently viewed as simplistic and overly focused on sexual feelings and erogenous zones. However, Freud's basic premise that children's early experiences can influence their later lives has remained viable.

*psychoanalytic theory: the ideas of personality development as presented in Freud's psychosexual and Erikson's psychosocial theories*

*psychosexual theory: Freud's theory that suggests that sexual drives play an important role in personality development*

Erik Erikson (1902–1994) built on Freud's theories and studied with Freud's daughter, Anna. Erikson believed that Freud's exploration of sexuality as the main explanation for behavior was rather limiting. He thought the broader social context of the child and family also influences behavior and incorporated this idea into his **psychosocial theory** (1963). Erikson also developed a stage theory but extended his theory to encompass the total life span.

Erikson provided the impetus for a number of studies focusing on the nature of adult developmental stages. This fairly recent information is discussed in more detail in Chapter 18 and should provide you with information about your own continued development as an adult and that of other adults with whom you will live and work. For a description of Erikson's developmental stages and a comparison with Freud's, see Table 1.1. Erikson's stages as they relate to young children are discussed in depth in Chapters 6, 9, 12, and 15.

Two contemporary theorists whose ideas are rooted in Freud and Erikson are

*psychosocial theory: Erikson's theory that argues that social interactions are more important than sexual drives in personality development*

TABLE 1.1
A Comparison of Freud's Psychosexual and Erikson's Psychosocial Stages of Development

| Freud's Five Stages and Related Conflicts | | Approximate Ages | Erikson's Eight Stages |
|---|---|---|---|
| Oral | Weaning | Birth–1½ | Basic trust vs. mistrust |
| Anal | Toilet learning | 1½–3 | Autonomy vs. shame/doubt |
| Phallic | Oedipal and Electra | 3–5 | Initiative vs. guilt |
| Latency | — | 5½–12 | Industry vs. inferiority |
| Genital | — | Adolescence | Identity vs. role confusion |
| — | — | Young adulthood | Intimacy vs. isolation |
| — | — | Middle adulthood | Generativity vs. stagnation |
| — | — | Late adulthood | Ego integrity vs. despair |

Source: Erikson (1963) and Freud (1938).

*self-actualization:*
*according to Maslow,*
*the process of having*
*basic physical and*
*social/emotional needs*
*met so that individuals*
*can become creative,*
*contributing members*
*of society and feel posi-*
*tive about themselves*

Carl Rogers and Abraham Maslow. Rogers and Maslow believe that individuals have the capacity to be creative in their decisions about life. Therefore, life is not viewed as being determined by negative early events, as in Freud's theory, but can be changed or influenced by the individual's choices.

Unlike Freud, Maslow studied people with healthy personalities. Maslow developed the notion of **self-actualization,** the process of individual growth resulting in the culmination of a fulfilled person (Maslow, 1970). Maslow suggests that feelings and aspirations must be considered to understand behavior. Self-actualized persons are continually in the process of "becoming," are in touch with and accepting of reality, are confident yet aware of their limitations, and have commitment to a meaningful project or goal. Maslow suggests that for self-actualization to occur, certain needs must be met. These needs are in hierarchical order.

Carl Rogers (1902–1987) has notions similar to Maslow's, including the importance of developing a positive self-concept and the interaction of development and environment (Rogers, 1961). Rogers' and Maslow's ideas are discussed in more detail in Chapters 6, 9, 12, and 15.

*behavioral theory:*
*the theory that empha-*
*sizes the importance of*
*directly observable*
*behavior as influenced*
*by the environment*
*rather than genetic fac-*
*tors or other unobserv-*
*able forces such as*
*motivation*

## BEHAVIORAL THEORY

Behaviorists concentrate on observable behavior rather than examining and explaining the internal processes of behavior. They do not classify behavior into stages but suggest that learning is a gradual and continuous process. Experience is considered most important, and heredity is given little or no attention. **Behavioral theory** is generally classified into three types: classical conditioning, operant conditioning, and social learning theory.

*classical conditioning*
*theory:*
*the first idea regarding*
*behavioral theory,*
*based on Pavlov's*
*experiment in which*
*repeated pairing of two*
*events conditioned the*
*same response to either*
*event*

**Classical Conditioning Theory.** The principles of **classical conditioning theory** were developed by Russian Ivan P. Pavlov (1849–1936). He paired two events, the placing of meat powder on a dog's tongue and the ringing of a bell, to create a conditioned stimulus. Over a period of time, these repeated events produced a conditioned response of salivation. In other words, the stimulus of the sound of the bell alone caused the dog to salivate even if no meat powder was present. The dog's association of the meat powder with the sound of the bell stimulated a response.

In this country, E. L. Thorndike conducted numerous animal experiments and is considered the "father of behaviorism." However, John B. Watson (1878–1958) was responsible for implementing the ideas of classical conditioning. Watson's famous experiment with an 11-month-old infant, Albert, was used to justify the notion that certain behavioral responses can be created through conditioning. Watson believed he could take a baby at random and produce "any type of specialist I might select—doctor, lawyer, artist, merchant-chief, and yes beggar-man and thief, regardless of his talents, penchants, tendencies, abilities, vocations and race of his ancestors" (Watson, 1928, p. 104).

In Watson's experiment (Watson & Rayner, 1920), Albert was shown a white rat at the same time a loud noise was made. Initially Albert was not afraid of the rat but was distressed at the loud noise. Eventually Albert's association of the loud noise with the rat produced a fear of many white furry objects such as his mother's muff, rabbits, and Santa's beard. Unfortunately, Albert left the hospital where this experiment was conducted before Watson could **extinguish** his fear.

*extinguish: stopping a behavior or response by not reinforcing it over a period of time*

While Watson is generally associated with the Albert experiment, his notions on child rearing were widespread and are still evident in the behaviors of some parents today. Watson suggested that showing affection for young children would spoil them. He advocated feeding infants every four hours, advised parents against rocking their children, and suggested that a handshake was more appropriate than a goodnight hug and kiss (Watson, 1928).

**Operant Conditioning Theory.**  A later proponent of behaviorism was Harvard psychologist B. F. Skinner. He explained Watson's views in a well-known book, *Walden Two* (1948). Skinner's thoughts and experiments expanded on classical conditioning theory and evolved into the theory of **operant conditioning**, in which the operant is the voluntary action on the part of an individual. Desired behavior is reinforced or rewarded after the behavior occurs. Over a period of time, the reinforcement is expected to make the desired behavior more frequent. Punishment is used to decrease the frequency of undesirable behavior. However, Skinner believed punishment is generally an ineffective way to control undesirable behavior. Instead, he suggested extinguishing behavior or ceasing to reinforce the behavior until it stops. Skinner and his wife decided to try this technique on their 5-year-old daughter, Julie (Skinner, 1979). Skinner reported that it took a month or two to accomplish. At first, Julie behaved in ways that in the past would have brought her punishment, and she watched her parents closely for their reactions. In time, the desired behaviors emerged. Skinner indicated that he and his wife found various reinforcement techniques more effective than punishment (Skinner, 1979, p. 279).

*operant conditioning: Skinner's term for the voluntary change or modification in behavior as a result of reinforcement or punishment*

**Social Learning Theory.**  **Social learning theory** is another adaptation of classical and operant conditioning. This theory emphasizes the importance of role models and significant adults in children's lives. Social learning theorists propose that children learn and imitate behaviors from people who are important to them and that children do not always need reinforcement to learn. This theory was

*social learning theory: a behavioral theory that argues that learning can also occur through observing others, thus emphasizing the role modeling of other persons the child observes directly and in various media* introduced in 1941 by Neil Miller and John Dollard in *Social Learning and Imitation*. However, Albert Bandura is the current leading proponent of social learning theory. His research (1965) demonstrated that children learn behavior from observation. In other words, learning does not depend on direct personal experience. In Bandura's classic research, two different groups of children observed two versions of a film in which a large plastic inflatable doll called a "Bobo doll" was hit by an adult model. In one version, the model's behavior was rewarded with adult praise, candy, and soft drinks. The second version concluded with another adult model hitting the first model with a rolled-up newspaper. After viewing the films, the children who saw the version with the reward were more likely to imitate aggressive behavior than the children who viewed the version in which the model was punished. Bandura concluded that children learn from observing others. Whether they act on what they observe depends on the particular circumstances.

## COGNITIVE THEORY

**cognitive theory:**
*the theory that explains the development of learning in terms of how children think and process information; usually associated with Piaget and, more recently, the information-processing theorists*

**schemata:**
*mental concepts or categories; plural for schema (Piaget)*

**assimilation:**
*the process of incorporating new motor or conceptual learning into existing schemata (Piaget)*

**accommodation:**
*the cognitive process by which patterns of thought (schemata) and related behaviors are modified to conform to new information or experience (Piaget)*

**equilibration:**
*the process of establishing a balance in thinking (Piaget)*

**Cognitive theory** attempts to explain how young children think and process information. Jean Piaget (1896–1980) developed the major theory of cognition in child development. Piaget's theory achieved recognition in the United States during the 1960s for several reasons. First, the insistence of the behaviorists on quantifiable research with large populations was beginning to be questioned. Second, Piaget's theory on the nature of how young children learn came into acceptance during a time of great interest in the development of cognitively oriented experiences for young children. Finally, Piaget's theory readily explained what perceptive parents and teachers of young children had already observed: that young children's processing of knowledge differs from that of older children and adults.

Piaget worked in France to establish norms on Binet's Intelligence Test. In that process, he observed that many young children gave similar incorrect answers. Piaget began to wonder if the development of cognition proceeded in stages. Using the clinical interview, Piaget questioned children to determine their thought processes. This approach, coupled with the detailed observations of his own three children, provided the basis for Piaget's theory (Piaget, 1952).

Piaget suggests that thinking develops sequentially in four stages: sensorimotor, preoperational, concrete operations, and formal operations. Table 1.2 provides an overview of each stage. The first three stages will be more thoroughly discussed later in this book.

Piaget grew up around Lake Neuchatel in Switzerland and became intrigued with the differences in behavior in mollusks at various locations around the lake. This fascination created a lifelong interest in the effects of the environment on living organisms and organisms' subsequent adaptations to the environment.

Piaget proposed that children order their interactions with the environment and then adapt to or change this order if they have new insights or information. The ordering of thought was termed **schemata**. **Assimilation** represents the child's attempts to fit new ideas and concepts into existing schemata. **Accommodation** is the change in schemata that a child makes as a result of new information. As children grow older and have more experiences with their environment, their **equili-**

**TABLE 1.2**
**Piaget's Stages of Cognitive Development**

| Stage | Approximate Age | Characteristics |
|---|---|---|
| Sensorimotor period | Birth to 2 years | Infant develops concepts regarding object identity and object permanence |
| Preoperational period | 2 to 7 years | Reliance on personal perceptions of the environment; egocentric thought |
| Concrete operations | 7 to 11 years | Children can focus on more than one attribute through manipulation of concrete objects |
| Formal operations | 11 years through adulthood | Abstract reasoning; hypothesis testing/experimentation and critical thinking |

**bration,** or balance in thinking, is often disturbed. Piaget says that this dissatis-faction or **disequilibrium** with present ideas motivates the child to accommodate new information and change schemata. Figure 1.1 shows an example of this process.

While Piaget claims that cognitive development influences language development, another theorist, Lev Vygotsky (1899–1934), suggests that thought and language eventually converge into meaning, particularly in those cultures where verbal interaction is important and verbal language is used for problem solving (Vygotsky, 1962).

Recently the work of Vygotsky has received considerable attention in the United States. Vygotsky, a Russian psychologist, produced some major works during a relatively short life. Two of his books, *Thought and Language* (1962) and *Mind and Society* (1978), have been translated into English.

Much of Vygotsky's research looked at children's ability to acquire a concept for a set of characteristics regarding color, shape, and size. He determined that when children are provided with words, they are better able to form concepts than when they are not provided with words.

As young children interact with others, they observe actions, become familiar with objects, and, through the labeling of these objects and actions by older children and adults, learn the **tools of the world**. These tools are organized over a period of time into **concept clusters,** or thought categories. Eventually, these categories become internalized representations, or **signs.** Vygotsky's ideas will be discussed further throughout this text, particularly in the areas of oral language and literacy development.

*disequilibrium:
the imbalance in thinking that leads the child to assimilate or accommodate (Piaget)*

*tools of the world:
the language and objects of the external world (Vygotsky)*

*concept clusters:
organization of the tools of the world into categories or patterns of thinking (Vygotsky)*

*signs:
internalized representations that are later associated with tools of the world (Vygotsky)*

Sometimes you just have to accommodate!

FIGURE 1.1
As young children absorb new information, they often find it necessary to change or accommodate their initial concept. (From *Piaget's Theory of Cognitive and Affective Development* by Barry J. Wadsworth. Copyright © 1989 by Longman Publishers. Reprinted by permission of Longman Publishing Group.)

*information-processing theory:*
*a theory of cognitive development that suggests that the mind is similar to the information-processing system of a computer and, unlike Piaget, emphasizes similarities in the thinking of children and adults*

*intrafamilial:*
*actions and behaviors occurring within the immediate family*

*extrafamilial:*
*actions and behaviors occurring outside the immediate family*

*ecological systems theory:*
*the theory that argues that a variety of social systems influence the development of children (Bronfenbrenner)*

In the early 1970s, dissatisfaction with Piaget's ideas led to the development of the **information-processing theory**. This theory suggests that a child's mind operates on the same principle as a computer (Newell & Simon, 1972). This theoretical approach is also discussed in Chapters 7, 10, 13, and 16.

## ECOLOGICAL SYSTEMS THEORY

In the past, much of child development research focused on parent-child interactions or **intrafamilial** processes. Urie Bronfenbrenner (1979, 1986) argues that the factors influencing development are much more complex in that intrafamilial processes are affected by **extrafamilial** forces. This **ecological systems theory** is represented in Figure 1.2.

Each of the four systems in this figure interacts with the others, and all of them influence the child's development. The child is at the core of the four systems. The system closest to the child is called the *microsystem*. The microsystem focuses on the roles, relationships, and experiences in the child's immediate environment. The *mesosystem* pertains to the interrelationships among various microsystem environments, such as home, school or child care center, neighborhood, and religious groups. The *exosystem* consists of formal and informal social groups that affect children in the microsystem. Formal groups include parents' workplaces and legal and community services. Examples of informal social networks include friends of the parents, neighbors, and extended family. Mass media are also part of the exosystem. The fourth system, the *macrosystem* refers to the attitudes, values, customs, laws, regulations, and rules of the culture at large that influence the child.

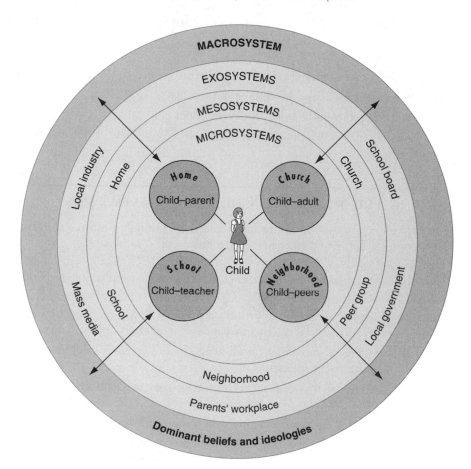

**FIGURE 1.2**
Bronfenbrenner's ecological systems theory emphasizes a variety of influences on the development of children. (From *The Development of Children*, 2/e, by Cole and Cole.  Copyright © 1993 by Michael Cole, Sheila R. Cole, and Judith Boies. Used with permission of W.H. Freeman and Company.)

Recent perspectives recommend that various theories of development be viewed as complementary rather than competing. These theories should be integrated with new viewpoints of development, particularly those pertaining to inclusion. According to Mallory (1994), these models share the following common attributes:

- Independent mastery of tasks
- Adaptation to environmental demands
- The value of a contingently responsive social context
- The aim of achieving social competence in young children
- A concern for individualized intervention (p. 57)

Recommendations are being made that child development research and theory include

- Cultural differences in parental role interpretation
- Cultural structuring of the developmental process
- Cultural interpretations of optimal development
- Variations in child development norms and pedagogy (New, 1994, pp. 69–72)

## EMERGING TRENDS IN EARLY CHILDHOOD DEVELOPMENT

Topics for research about young children and their families continue to reflect a variety of issues. Some of these emerging trends are:

- An increasing emphasis on accreditation of programs and training and credentialing of teachers
- The view of developmentally appropriate practice (DAP) as an evolving and dynamic model currently being redefined as developmentally appropriate practices
- A rapid explosion of knowledge in all areas, including early childhood development and continuing education
- Increasing attention to transcultural perspectives in early childhood care and education
- Increasing attention to developmental differences and the concept of inclusion
- An increasing number of groups and organizations outside the field of early childhood education that are advocating for the needs of children and their families
- A greater awareness of the importance of child and family health issues
- Changing economics and demographics
- Increasing collaboration among business and educational entities at all levels
- An increasing awareness that development and behaviors exhibited in later years are related to development and behaviors in the early years

We authors hope you have discovered that early childhood development is an interesting, important, and complex field of study. The next chapter will provide you with additional information on how researchers study children and on how you can learn about young children through your own study.

Did you notice the quote at the beginning of this chapter? It says, "There are two lasting gifts we can give our children—one is roots; the other is wings." A knowledge of how young children develop and learn helps early childhood development professionals (and parents) to provide the conditions necessary for young children to develop deep roots and strong wings—two prerequisites for leading happy and productive lives. We hope the following chapters will help you learn how to provide both the roots and the wings to facilitate optimal development in young children.

## KEY TERMS

accommodation
assimilation
at-risk
behavioral theory
classical conditioning
  theory
cognitive theory
concept clusters
developmentally
  appropriate
developmentally
  inappropriate
disequilibrium

early childhood
  development
ecological systems
  theory
equilibration
extinguish
extrafamilial
inclusion
information-
  processing theory
intrafamilial
low-risk
operant conditioning

professionals
psychoanalytical
  theory
psychosexual theory
psychosocial theory
schemata
self-actualization
signs
social learning theory
theories
tools of the world

## REVIEW STRATEGIES AND ACTIVITIES

1. Review the key terms individually or with a classmate.
2. Think back to your early childhood years through age 8. Try to recall your ealiest memory. At what age did it occur? What other recollections do you have from your early childhood years?
   a. Chart out a life line. State how old you were at the time of your earliest recollection. Describe that recollection and others that took place during that year. Continue this process up through age 8 or to your current age.
   b. Discuss these recollections with other students in your early childhood development class. Your classmates probably have had similar experiences, or their recollections will help you remember some events you have forgotten.
   c. Relate events in your life to the various developmental theories discussed in the chapter.
   d. Identify personal cultural influences within your life from childhood to the present.
3. Why do you wish to become an early childhood professional?
   a. List those persons or events that have encouraged your interest in the profession.
   b. What are your concerns about becoming an early childhood professional?
   c. What are your short- and long-term professional goals?
   d. Discuss your responses with students in your class.

## FURTHER READINGS

Bredekamp, S. (Ed.). (1987). *Developmentally appropriate practice in early childhood programs serving children from birth through age 8.* Washington, DC: National Association for the Education of Young Children.

Bredekamp, S., & Rosegrant, T. (1982). *Reaching potentials: Appropriate curriculum and assessment for young children* (Vol. 1). Washington, DC: National Association for the Education of Young Children.

Carnegie Task Force on Meeting the Needs of Young Children. (1994) *Starting points*. New York: Carnegie Corporation.

Council for Early Childhood Professional Recognition. (1992). *Child development associate assessment and competency standards*. Washington, DC: Author.

Mallory, B. L., & New, R. S. (Eds.). (1994). *Diversity and developmentally appropriate practices*. New York: Teachers College Press.

National Academy of Early Childhood Programs. (1984). *Accreditation criteria and procedures*. Washington, DC: National Association for the Education of Young Children.

National Association for the Education of Young Children (1995). *NAEYC Guidelines for Preparation of Early Childhood Professionals*. Washington, DC: Author.

# CHAPTER TWO

*More often, teachers find as they study children, they themselves change. Thus (through child study), we often gain insight and understanding not only of the children but of ourselves as well. . . . But "understanding" alone, whether of the children or of ourselves, is not enough. The crucial question is whether such understanding improves the teacher's ability to help children learn, whether it facilitates provision of the experiences children need.*

**Millie Almy and Celia Genishi**

# The Where, When, and How of Early Childhood Study and Assessment

After studying this chapter, you will demonstrate comprehension by:

- Describing the contribution of early childhood development research in the training of the early childhood professional.
- Outlining the various types of child development research studies.
- Identifying ethical considerations in conducting research on young children.
- Describing the importance of developing reflecting-in-action and teacher-as-researcher perspectives when studying young children.
- Justifying the importance of the ongoing study of young children in a variety of contexts and its relationship to authentic assessment.
- Outlining the various approaches the early childhood professional can use in studying young children, including the use of portfolios.
- Identifying related resources that help in the study of young children.
- Describing the process of documenting the growth and development of young children.

It is the first day of kindergarten, and Cathleen seems upset at having her mother leave her at the classroom door. Ms. Schwartz, Cathleen's teacher, invites her mother to stay awhile. This relieves Cathleen's anxiety, and eventually she begins to participate in the sociodramatic (pretend play) area of the classroom. Periodically she returns to her mother and then rejoins other children in the sociodramatic center. Eventually, Cathleen's mother tells her that she has some errands to run and will be back at 11:30 to pick her up. Cathleen seems to accept her mother's departure. This pattern is repeated for three days, with Cathleen's mother spending less and less time in the classroom. On the fourth day, Cathleen enters the classroom without hesitation and gives her mother a confident, "goodbye." Later Ms. Schwartz observes Cathleen in the sociodramatic area. Ms. Schwartz suggests that she "call" her mother on the phone and tell her what she is doing. ■

Juan is 18 months old. His mother is planning to return to her job as a buyer for a large department store. She has enrolled Juan in a child care center. The director, Mr. Hubbard, has encouraged Juan's parents to visit the center with Juan several times a few days before Juan is to begin attending. Mr. Hubbard also suggests that Juan's parents send Juan's favorite stuffed toy and blanket every day. A picture of Juan's mother and father is posted on a low-level bulletin board, along with pictures of the other toddlers' parents. ■

What would you have done had you been Cathleen's or Juan's teacher? Typical responses include telling Cathleen's mother to leave her and not allowing favorite blankets and stuffed animals to be brought into the child care center. Why did Ms. Schwartz and Mr. Hubbard act in the ways they did?

## THE CONTRIBUTION OF RESEARCH LITERATURE IN THE DEVELOPMENT OF THE EARLY CHILDHOOD PROFESSIONAL

Ms. Schwartz and Mr. Hubbard acted on their knowledge of child growth and development research. Their training included many opportunities to read the professional early childhood development research and literature. Their training also provided them with opportunities to observe and study young children's behavior, as well as the responses and behavior of teachers of young children. In addition, their experience with children and families from diverse backgrounds has helped them to become more appreciative and responsive to the uniqueness of all children and their families.

Through their reading and study of young children and observation of other early childhood professionals, Ms. Schwartz and Mr. Hubbard have learned that a major developmental task of young children is to separate from parents and move into other social settings. Both Ms. Schwartz and Mr. Hubbard are familiar with the research on attachment (see Chapters 6 and 9). They have observed the techniques and strategies early childhood professionals have used to facilitate young children's adjustment to a new setting. Therefore, they make appropriate decisions about what to do to help children form new attachments and assist them in the separation from their parents.

*preservice:*
*individuals who are in training to teach or serve young children*

*inservice:*
*individuals who have completed teacher training programs and accepted jobs teaching or serving young children*

Early childhood professionals learn about young children both at the **preservice** and **inservice** levels by reading about the studies of researchers in the area of early childhood development. This is why you are reading this book. You also need to learn about young children through your own observation and study of young children and their family backgrounds. First-hand experiences with young children can reinforce previously read child development information and facilitate further reading about the nature of behavior in young children. This chapter provides information about the study of children through the professional research literature on early childhood development and your own study and investigation of young children and the adults who work with them.

## TYPES OF CHILD DEVELOPMENT RESEARCH STUDIES

Like you, other people find the growth and development of children very interesting. These people may be affiliated with colleges or universities, research centers, public agencies, or private groups. They often have hunches, or **hypotheses**, about the development of young children. They design research studies to determine if their hunches are correct. The results of these studies may be published in journals, books, theses, dissertations, and mass media or presented in papers at professional conferences. Two terms that are used in evaluating the design of a research study are **reliability** and **validity**. Basic definitions of these terms are provided in the margin notes.

A brief overview of some of the more common types of research in the area of childhood development study follows. While presented separately for purposes of discussion, these research methods are not mutually exclusive categories. For example, correlational techniques can be used with longitudinal, cross-sectional, and descriptive studies. If you would like more in-depth information about various research techniques, check the Further Readings section at the end of this chapter.

## DESCRIPTIVE STUDIES

**Descriptive studies** generally attempt to describe behavior. Many early studies in child development, particularly the maturation theory studies, were descriptive in nature. Researchers (e.g., Gesell & Amatruda, 1941) would observe many children at various ages in a particular area of development, such as physical development. This information was then converted into **norms,** or averages, so that teachers, parents, and physicians would have some guidelines as to the approximate age that various aspects of physical development occurred. For example, research of this nature described the average age at which infants would sit, stand, and walk (Gesell & Amatruda, 1941). This research was conducted primarily on children from white, middle-class families and is increasingly being perceived as inappropriate to apply to all children given their diverse family and cultural backgrounds (Mallory & New, 1994).

A more recent trend in descriptive research is to use some of the techniques and approaches from the field of anthropology. Shirley Brice Heath's study (1983) on the nature of oral and written language in three fictitiously named communities is an example of this type of research. Unlike earlier studies, this type of descriptive research examines smaller populations and attempts to describe individual behavior based on the context of the environment. For example, Heath found that families in Roadville, a white, working-class community, used alphabet and number books, Bible stories, real-life stories, and nursery rhymes with their children. Families in Trackton, an African-American, working-class community, told fictional stories incorporating common events into new situations and rarely read books to their children. Parents in Maintown, a mainstream, middle-class community, began reading books to their children during the first year of life, asking

*hypotheses:*
*hunches about the development of young children, usually examined through research*

*reliability:*
*the consistency with which various research methods produce the same or relatively similar results for each individual from one administration assessment to the next*

*validity:*
*the degree to which an instrument or a procedure measures what it is intended to measure*

*descriptive study:*
*research that is collected by observing and recording behavior and providing a description of the observed behavior*

*norms:*
*average age of developmental behaviors or average scores on tests that according to statistical procedures, should be based on large samples representative of the whole population*

*Early childhood professionals learn about young children by reading child develop-
ment research studies.*

questions about the books, relating the books' stories to their children's daily
experiences, and encouraging their children to tell both real and made-up stories.

## CROSS-SECTIONAL AND LONGITUDINAL STUDIES

*cross-sectional study: research that studies subjects of different ages at the same time*

*representative sample: a sample of subjects in approximately the same proportions that are in the population as a whole regarding age, gender, racial and ethnic background, geographic location, and socioeconomic level*

*longitudinal study: research that collects information about the same subjects at different ages over a period of time*

**Cross-sectional studies** look at an aspect of development or behavior at various
ages or stages at the same time. For example, a **representative sample** of children
at ages 2 to 18 had their height and weight recorded at the same time. This information was converted to charts that pediatricians use to predict young children's
weight and height at later ages. Cross-sectional research can provide information
about certain types of development, such as height and weight, within a relatively short period of time. However, this type of study cannot determine exactly
when an individual changes.

One way to study change in the development of individuals is the **longitudinal
study**. This type of study looks at the same individuals over a period of time. An
important example of this type of study is the research conducted on a number of
at-risk young children who were enrolled in early childhood education programs
in the 1960s (Schweinhart, Barnes, & Weikart, 1993; Berrueta-Clement,
Schweinhart, Barnett, Epstein, & Weikart, 1984; Lazar & Darlington, 1982). In
the Perry Preschool Program, subjects from age 4 through 19 years were tested

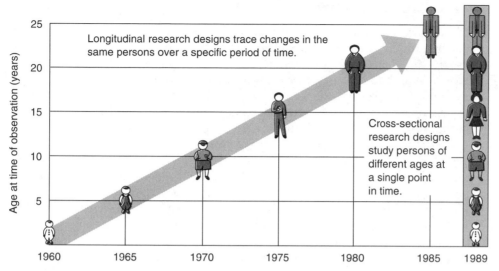

**Figure 2.1**
This graph demostrates the difference between cross-sectional and longitudinal research. (From *The Development of Children* by Michael Cole and Sheila R. Cole. Copyright © 1993 by Michael Cole, Sheila R. Cole and Judith Boies. Reprinted with permission by W. H. Freeman and Company.)

and interviewed to determine if their participation in early childhood programs had long-term effects. They were then compared with children who had not attended any program. Generally, these studies indicated that at-risk **pre-primary** children who were in high-quality early childhood programs were better students and more productive as young adults than at-risk children who were not enrolled in early childhood programs. Chapter 17 discusses these studies in greater detail. See Figure 2.1 for a comparison of cross-sectional and longitudinal studies.

*pre-primary:*
*the time in young children's lives before they enter the primary (first, second, or third) grades*

## CORRELATIONAL STUDIES

**Correlational studies** look at the nature of the relationship between two sets of measurements. For example, in a study by Ackerman-Ross and Khanna (1989), one finding indicated a positive relationship between the language performance of 3-year-old children and the amount of time parents engaged in language activities with their children, as well as the parents' economic status. Correlational studies only indicate relationships; they do not indicate causes. Thus, it *cannot* be said that the higher economic status of parents and more time spent in language activities with their 3-year-olds caused the improved language performance in their children. It can be said only that there is a positive relationship among parental income, parent-child language activities, and the language performance of the 3-year-old children.

*correlational study:*
*research that attempts to determine a relationship between two or more sets of measurements*

## EXPERIMENTAL STUDIES

experimental study:
research that involves
treating each of two or
more groups in different
ways to determine
cause-and-effect rela-
tionships

random:
assigning children to
experimental and con-
trol groups so that each
child has the same
chance of being selected

In **experimental studies,** the researcher usually **randomly** divides the population under study into two groups. One group is designated as the *control group* and usually does not receive any treatment; the second group is called the *experimental group* and does receive special treatment. Sometimes the two groups receive two different types of treatment. The researcher then employs statistical analysis to determine if the differences between the groups were of significance. Subjects are given pre- and posttests to eliminate the possibility of outside influence.

An interesting example of experimental research is the study by Webster, Wood, Eicher, and Hoag (1989) to determine if intensive tutoring would improve the language skills of language-poor children. The children identified as language-poor in a Head Start early childhood program were given the Peabody Picture Vocabulary Test (PPVT) as a pretest. One-half of the children were then randomly assigned to the control group and the other half to the experimental group. The experimental group children were then randomly assigned to university students who provided three to four hours a week of informal experiences that involved constant verbal interaction. The control group did not engage in any of these activities.

At the end of the experiment, the PPVT was administered again. Surprisingly, the control group achieved a mean gain of 4.6 months in language growth, while the experimental group recorded a mean gain of only 2.6 months. The researchers explored possible reasons for this unexpected finding. More in-depth analysis of the children in the experimental group indicated that many of them came from families characterized as disorganized. This family disorganization made it impossible for a number of children in the experimental group to participate in the tutoring experiences on a regular basis. The researchers concluded that family support appears to be essential in such a language tutoring project.

## ETHICS OF EARLY CHILDHOOD DEVELOPMENT RESEARCH

Because of the increasing awareness regarding the rights and feelings of young children, careful attention is now being given to ensure that no psychological or physical damage occurs to children during the research process. Both the American Psychological Association (1992) and the Society for the Research in Child Development (1990) have developed procedures for conducting research with human subjects. These standards outline the rights of children and the responsibilities of researchers and stipulate that parental or guardian permission must be obtained before any research can begin.

Another area of ethics involves the honesty of the researcher in reporting the study. Most researchers plan well-designed studies. However, the unpredictable nature of children and other complications sometimes prevent the researcher from completing the study as originally intended. It is the responsibility of the researcher to acknowledge these limitations when publishing the study. At times, pilot studies or smaller preliminary studies can help identify some potential problems with the research design.

## SOCIOCULTURAL PERSPECTIVES IN STUDYING YOUNG CHILDREN

Much of the early child development research information comes from studies conducted by researchers who have the same economic and sociocultural backgrounds as the children they have studied. Therefore, the universal application of the research to all groups of children must be interpreted with caution. Researchers need to include children from a variety of socioeconomic and cultural groups before attempts at universal application can be made, or they need to acknowledge the lack of broad representation in their study. Researchers also need to be aware of various culturally distinct behaviors when they attempt to design their research or interpret their findings. (Mallory & New, 1994).

One researcher who helped create awareness of the importance of taking sociocultural considerations into account is William Labov. Labov (1970, 1972) examined the effects of a variety of social situations on the nature of language produced by African-American speakers. He determined that in more formal contexts such as testlike settings, some children produced little verbalization. However, in more informal and relaxed situations the children were more verbal. When 8-year-old Leon, his best friend, and an Anglo male sat on the floor eating a bag of potato chips and talking about taboo subjects, Leon demonstrated that he was highly verbal. In contrast, Leon verbalized very little in testlike settings. Thus, certain research contexts can convey that children from various linguistic and cultural groups are nonverbal, when in reality they are highly verbal. Sensitivity to cultural behaviors and the effects of some research designs on certain behaviors can help prevent biased and incorrect information about various cultural groups. Likewise, sensitivity to sociocultural perspectives in behavior facilitates an awareness of the reality that there are many ways of doing and behaving. The following section provides information about how you can learn about young children through your own study and observation.

## YOUNG CHILDREN WITH DISABILITIES AND CHILD DEVELOPMENT STUDY

As the field of early childhood development continues to become more sensitive to the principle of inclusion, new ways of viewing the development of children with disabilities must be taken into account. First, early childhood professionals must be cognizant of both the sequence of the child's development and the "organization within the individual child at that particular point" (McCollum & Bair, 1994, p. 86). Second, development and learning goals may vary for each child. Third, acknowledgment of the differences in development and learning goals may require different strategies or modifications in the strategies that promote the attainment of those learning goals. Thus, as early childhood settings become more inclusive, professionals from the early childhood education field are encouraging a broader interpretation and redefinition of development for children with disabilities. This process then necessitates a more inclusive interpretation of developmentally appropriate practices.

For example, a young boy who lived on a farm in the Midwest lost both his arms in a piece of farm equipment as he was helping his grandfather put crops in storage. The boy was fitted with prostheses for both arms and received extensive physical therapy. Eventually he became very adept at using his feet and toes to draw, write, and do his homework. In fact, he could write and draw even more skillfully using his feet and toes than a number of his classmates could using their fingers and hands. This real-life story demonstrates that there is a wide range of resilient and adaptive behaviors that exists within each individual. Consequently, these differences in behaviors must be accepted and taken into consideration in the strategies used to promote learning and in the assessment process.

## YOUR OWN STUDY AND OBSERVATION OF YOUNG CHILDREN

Along with reading professional child development research and literature, your own study of young children can help you develop a knowledge base regarding the unique nature of young children's development and behavior. This base fosters an awareness of the enormous diversity in behavior and development. It can help you select materials and strategies for working with young children. Informed study can also help you avoid bias and become more objective in looking at children. However, it is important to acknowledge biases and to realize that early childhood professionals bring their own backgrounds, experiences, belief systems, and values to the interpretation of children's behavior. At times, it may be helpful to have other professionals use the same procedures and tools to verify your information and ensure objectivity.

Four behaviors are important for the developing early childhood professional to acquire: perspective taking, reflecting-in-action, teacher-as-learner, and teacher-as-researcher.

*perspective taking: the ability to understand one's own or another's viewpoint and an awareness of the coordinated and interrelated set of ideas that are reflected in behavior*

**Perspective taking** is a process that early childhood professionals use to become more aware of their own perspectives as well as those of children and parents. In-depth discussion of children's and parents' perspectives will occur throughout this text. Attention to one's own perspective taking must begin early in the process of becoming an early childhood development professional. This process requires that early childhood development professionals examine their own viewpoints on children's development, assessment and competence. Recent studies (e.g., Blosch, Tacachnick, and Espinosa-Dulanto, 1993, p. 225) reveal that teachers' perspectives are influenced by the following interrelated factors:

- The teacher's personal and professional experiences and beliefs
- The teacher's and the school's beliefs regarding assessment as it relates to children's age, developmental level, cultural and class background, and beliefs and policies promulgated at the national, state, school district, and individual school setting or campus levels
- The teacher's awareness or lack of awareness of children's competencies and broader social issues that relate to the teacher's attitudes toward children as being "different" with respect to ethnicity, gender, race, language, and class "group" identities or membership.

A second behavior the developing early childhood professional must acquire is **reflecting-in-action**. At the outset of their field-based experiences, developing early childhood professionals need to reflect on their behaviors and how those behaviors affect children and their families, and vice versa. Time needs to be set aside in both preservice and inservice settings for early childhood professionals to engage in reflection, both individually and in collaboration with colleagues.

Such opportunities assist the early childhood development professional in internalizing reflecting behaviors within the classroom settings. These experiences facilitate the concept of **teacher-as-learner**, one who learns continually from children, their families, and other professionals and from the changing professional research and literature. The process of acquiring new ideas, values, and practices demands that teachers restructure their personal and professional knowledge.

In other words, children, parents, and teachers learn from one another. In this process, new hypotheses regarding development and practice emerge. These hypotheses often lead to investigations and experimentation regarding interpretations of behaviors, teaching strategies, and approaches to evaluation and assessment of learning and development. The end result is often new understandings or perspectives about children, families, early childhood development behavior and learning, developmentally appropriate practice, and oneself as a professional and as a person.

From this process emerges an expanded perspective: **teacher-as-researcher**. In other words, early childhood professionals, through perspective taking and reflecting-in-action behavior, continuously learn about themselves and others, thereby acquiring and demonstrating the behaviors of a researcher. If this process is internalized, the early childhood professional often begins to view children not as deficient but as different. In discovering the broad continuum of development and the many ways of behaving and doing, children and their families come to be viewed not as incompetent but as competent. As more and more professionals adopt these behaviors, the study of children will come to focus on what children can do—their strengths and competencies—rather than on their alleged deficiencies.

The lack of child development study on culturally diverse children and their families and the rapidly changing demographics in early childhood classrooms around the country require that behaviors of perspective taking, reflecting-in-action, teacher-as-learner, and teacher-as-researcher be internalized. These skills are prerequisites to becoming a competent professional in the inclusive classroom of the present and of the future.

*reflecting-in-action:* *thinking about and analyzing one's professional behavior and children's or parents' behaviors while engaged or acting in contexts for purposes of assessment and evaluation*

*teacher-as-learner:* *the process by which teachers continue to learn from children, parents, other professionals, and changing professional research and literature throughout their careers*

*teacher-as-researcher:* *the process by which early childhood professionals, through their perspective taking and reflecting-in-action, acquire and demonstrate the behaviors of a researcher*

## THE IMPORTANCE OF THE ONGOING STUDY OF YOUNG CHILDREN IN MANY CONTEXTS: AUTHENTIC ASSESSMENT

Competent early childhood professionals realize the importance of studying children in a variety of situations, including settings within the classroom, in outdoor learning areas, at lunch, and during rest or quiet times, as well as in the wider context of the family and community settings. Complete understanding of young children involves study of their behavior in a variety of contexts, in real-life situations over a period of time, as children's behavior changes from one setting to another. The nature of the setting, the people in the setting, and the time all influence the way children behave. In addition, artificial, unfamiliar, or laboratory-type environments can convey misleading information about children, their behaviors, and their competencies (Ceci & Bronfenbrenner, 1985).

Studying children in a variety of settings over a period of time helps the early childhood professional see the common characteristics of young children as well as individual behaviors. The study of young children can also help the early childhood professional provide specific examples of children's behavior when in conference with parents. The study of young children can also serve as a means of documenting that program goals for facilitating young children's development and learning are being accomplished. Appropriate, reliable, and valid strategies for studying young children are becoming increasingly important as many early childhood programs are dependent on private, state, or federal funding and often require documentation of performance or achievement of goals and objectives.

## AUTHENTIC ASSESSMENT OF EARLY CHILDHOOD DEVELOPMENT AND LEARNING

Recently, futurists have emphasized that the competencies needed to function effectively in the 21st century include problem-solving skills; the ability to communicate orally, through writing and through technology; the ability to view events from a changing and global perspective; and the capacity to work with others (cooperate, collaborate, and negotiate) in group settings (U.S. Department of Labor, 1992). The explosion of knowledge due to rapidly changing information systems suggests that children need to know how to access information rather than focusing on learning bits of information. These realities have been the impetus for curricular reform in a number of disciplines. These reforms, coupled with increasing concern about the inappropriate use of standardized tests, have precipitated the need to find new ways to evaluate learning (U.S. Department of Labor, 1992). One such approach is **authentic assessment**. Authentic assessment is the process of observing and documenting children's learning and behavior and using this information to make educational decisions that promote their learning and development. It is continuous, context bound, and qualitative in nature. According to Puckett and Black (1994, p. 22), the essential components of authentic assessment are as follows:

*authentic assessment: the ongoing, continuous, context-based observation and documentation of children's behavior used to make decisions about extending children's learning and development*

- Authentic assessment celebrates development and learning.
- Authentic assessment emphasizes emerging development.
- Authentic assessment capitalizes on the strengths of the learner.
- Authentic curricula are, first and foremost, developmentally appropriate.
- Authentic assessment is based on real-life events.
- Authentic assessment is performance based.

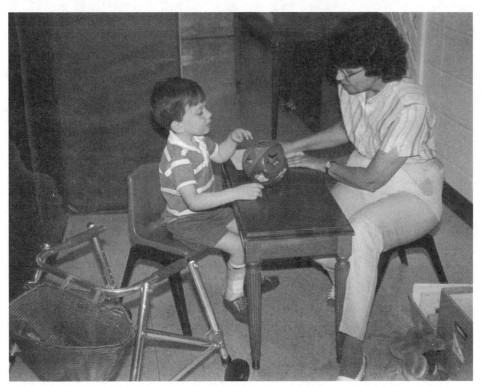

*Controlled laboratory experiments do not always indicate how young children act in real life.*

- Authentic assessment is related to instruction.
- Instruction informed by research on early learning and child growth and development can be valid and can inform continuing instruction.
- Authentic assessment focuses on purposeful learning.
- Authentic assessment is ongoing in all contexts.
- Authentic assessment provides a broad and general picture of student learning and capabilities.
- Authentic assessment is collaborative among parents, teachers, students, and other professionals as needed.

## VARIOUS APPROACHES TO STUDYING YOUNG CHILDREN

A variety of tools and techniques can be of help to the early childhood professional in the study of young children. Generally, these approaches are classified into two types: **formal** and **informal** (see Table 2.1).

*formal approach:*
*refers to information gathered about young children, usually through standardized tests*

*informal approach:*
*refers to information gathered about young children through approaches other than standardized tests*

TABLE 2.1
Formal and Informal Approaches to Studying Young Children

| Formal | Informal |
|--------|----------|
| Achievement tests | Narrative observations: running records, specimen records, anecdotal records |
| Readiness tests | |
| Developmental screening tests | Checklists |
| Diagnostic tests | Rating scales |
| Intelligence tests | Time sampling |
| | Event sampling |
| | Interviews/conferences: child, parents, support staff, resource persons, peers |
| | Children's products: art, writings, class work, projects |

standardized test:
a test that is administered and scored according to set procedures and whose scores can be interpreted according to statistical measures representative of the group for which the test was designed

achievement test:
a test that measures what children have learned as a result of instruction

readiness test:
a test that measures what beginning skills children have to predict whether they will succeed in a new learning task, e.g., reading

developmental screening test:
a test that determines if a child is developing normally

diagnostic test:
a test that identifies a child's strengths or weaknesses in a certain area of development

intelligence test:
a test that measures those abilities that have been designated as a sign of intelligence

## FORMAL APPROACHES TO CHILD STUDY

Formal approaches in the study of young children usually refer to the use of a **standardized test**. Wortham (1990) states, "The increased use of standardized testing at all levels has been criticized, but the testing of young children is of particular concern". According to the NAEYC position statement on testing (1988), increased use of standardized testing with young children is indicative of the "escalating trend toward curriculum . . . that is inappropriate for the age and developmental level of the children." In other words, kindergartens are what used to be first grades and prekindergartens are what used to be kindergartens. Nevertheless, there is no research information to indicate that the way young children learn, or their developmental needs, has changed.

The end result of this curricular escalation is increased school failure among young children. Raising the legal age for school entry, beginning school a year later for those children whose birth dates fall well into the school year, and using standardized tests to more accurately place children in the hope of preventing school failure are some of the inappropriate attempts to solve this problem (Bredekamp & Shepard, 1989; Charlesworth, 1989).

In response to a growing national concern about the inappropriate uses of standardized testing with young children, NAEYC developed its position statement entitled "Testing of Young Children: Concerns and Cautions" (1988). In it, NAEYC states that standardized tests "are designed for a specific purpose and should be used only for the purpose for which they were designed." According to NAEYC, some of the more common types of standardized tests include **achievement tests** and **readiness tests**. These two kinds of tests are designed to provide teachers with information with which they can individualize instruction. These tests should *not* be used to make school entry, promotion, or retention decisions. Other frequently used tests include **developmental screening tests**. It is recommended that these tests be used only as the first step in identifying children who may be in need of further evaluation. **Diagnostic** and **intelligence tests** are also common types of standardized tests. Children should not be placed in special

*Many standardized tests cause stress behaviors and are not appropriate to use with young children.*

education programs solely on the basis of such tests, however. Placement decisions should be made *only* through the use of multiple measures of assessment, both informal and formal, with input by parents.

NAEYC (1988) cites the following reasons standardized testing is "potentially harmful to young children" and their learning:

- Testing narrows the curriculum as teachers begin to focus on specific test items. They begin to "teach the test."

- Many important skills young children need to acquire—self-esteem, social competence, desire to learn, self-discipline—are not easily measured by standardized tests.

- Standardized testing encourages the learning of rote information. Reading for information, composing stories, problem solving, and creative thinking are not emphasized. Yet these are the skills children need to learn if they are "to function in an ever-changing American society."

- Testing can lead to labeling, mislabeling, and inappropriate placement of young children. The end result is that teacher and parent perceptions of children's ability create negative feelings of the child as a competent learner and a negative self-concept in the child.

- Testing puts stress on young children, even those who perform well on tests.

A study by Fleege, Charlesworth, Burts, & Hart (1992) documents the stress behaviors of both able and less competent learners in a kindergarten classroom during the administration of a standardized test. This study indicates that kindergarten teachers may respond to the stress observed in their students by using a variety of techniques that violate standardized testing procedures.

The NAEYC position paper (1988) states that standardized testing of young children is inappropriate for several reasons:

- *Young children are not good test takers.* The younger the child, the more difficult it is to obtain reliable information (consistent over time) and valid (accurate) results from tests. Results are easily influenced by a young child's test-taking skills: the ability to sit down, be quiet, and make a mark in the correct place. Such behavior does not necessarily reflect children's level of learning.

- *Young children are growing and learning rapidly.* Just how quickly children grow and learn is reflected in the fact that a school year constitutes one-fourth of the lifetime of a 4-year-old.

- *There is no such thing as a culture-free test.* Test bias has been well documented. Test developers ignore language and culture variations too often. Any test in English given to non-native English speakers, or children who speak a dialect of English, is first and foremost a language test, regardless of its intent. With young children, language and culture are essential aspects of children's learning and development. For example, when asked on a test, "Where do lions live?", a child who spent his early years in Kenya might answer, "In the park." From his experiences, the answer is correct; however, the test manual says the correct answer is "in the zoo," and the teacher would record his answer as an error.

According to the NAEYC position statement, standardized tests should be administered only by "qualified professionals." These tests need to be "carefully selected and used only for the purposes for which they were designed and for which there are data demonstrating the accuracy of the measures." If beneficial treatment does not exist, standardized tests do not serve a useful purpose.

The NAEYC position statement proposes the following solutions to the standardized testing dilemma:

1. Children should enter school on the basis of their chronological age and legal right to enter, not on the basis of what they already know.

2. In the primary grades, group sizes should be small (preferably no more than 20) and teacher-child ratios low so that teachers can individualize instruction. Not all children should be expected to accomplish the same task at the same time.

3. Groupings of children for individual activities should be flexible and change frequently so that children do not have to conform to rigid group expectations and can work at their own pace.

4. Children's development and learning should be assessed through ongoing and systematic observation by qualified teachers and other professionals. Developmental screening should be used to identify those children who may need further testing to diagnose a specific learning problem and suggest remediation strategies.

5. Curriculum and teaching methods should be appropriate to the age and development of the children. The curriculum should be rich in all content areas, not dictated by the need to produce predetermined test scores.

6. Decisions about promotion to the next grade or placement in special or remedial education should be based on multiple sources of information, including parents' and teachers' observations, and *never* on the basis of a single test score.

The preceding discussion indicates that formal methods of studying young children need to be used with caution. Informal approaches generally are more appropriate techniques.

## INFORMAL APPROACHES TO CHILD STUDY

Informal approaches to child study are more frequently used with children through the kindergarten year. With entry into first grade, more formal approaches are usually used. In light of the previously discussed concerns regarding the use of standardized testing, continued use of informal approaches should be extended into the primary grades (Wortham, 1995).

Most informal approaches to child study can be classified under narrative observation of children's spontaneous behaviors and observation using predefined instruments. Regardless of the technique used, it is important to study and be aware of the child's total development and behavior. This study of the whole child may include self-identity, emotional development, social development and prosocial behavior, gross and fine motor development, cognitive development, communicative competence, written language and print awareness, and creative and aesthetic development (Beaty, 1990).

### NARRATIVE OBSERVATIONS

**Narrative observations** are records of behaviors as they occur. The period of time may vary from several minutes to hours at a time. Notepads and pencil are all that is needed. Running records, specimen records, and anecdotal records are three types of narrative observations (Beaty, 1990).

*narrative observation: a written observation of behavior as it occurs*

**Running Records. Running records** are accounts of *all* behavior as it occurs. See Figure 2.2 for an example of a running record. A collection of these observations can be helpful in describing and documenting young children's behavior and development. This type of observation is used most frequently in preservice settings. If there is only one teacher in a classroom with no aide, running records can be difficult to create because teachers need to be available to young children. However, using parent volunteers or planning for a time when the children are involved in independent activity can give the classroom teacher some time to conduct running records.

*running record: a type of narrative observation that records all behavior as it occurs*

Procedures for using running records include

1. *Description of the setting*—including the time the observation begins and the activity taking place.

---

**FIGURE 2.2**
**A Running Record**

Child's Name: Daniel          Age: 3½          Date: 3/10
Observer: Veronica            Place: Lab       Time: 9:36

| Observation | Comments |
|---|---|
| Daniel is sitting at a table in the class-room rolling out clay. He is making primarily flat shapes with a rolling pin. | Daniel has excellent arm strength and good coordination of his movements. |
| He stands while rolling out the clay and sits to cut the shapes. | The table is evidently too high for Daniel because he had to stand while rolling out the clay. |
| After rolling out each piece of clay completely, he takes a cookie cutter and cuts circles out of the clay. | Daniel is cutting out circles exclusively, because no other shapes are available. Other children working with clay are using other cutters. |
| Taking two of the cut-out circles, he places them over his eyes and says "I have new glasses, like my daddy." | Daniel has used the objects he created to move into fantasy and socialize with the other children. |
| Teacher asks, "What can you see with your new glasses?" | |
| Daniel: "Dark." | |
| Teacher: "No, what can you see?" | Teacher is attempting to draw language from Daniel. His response indicates that he may not be certain of the teacher's intent or the actual meaning of the question. |
| Daniel: "I can't see anything with my new glasses, it's just dark . . . they're just *pretend* glasses!" | |

---

2. *Recording information*—taking down information in a detailed, sequential manner. Information needs to be factual and objective, not biased by personal opinions. Time can be jotted down in the margin at one-minute intervals.

3. *Comments and analysis*—writing down inferences and conclusions. The comments and analysis should be related to child development information.

**Specimen Records. Specimen records** are narrative observations that are more detailed than running records. Specimen records usually focus on a particular time of day, setting, or child. Specimen records can provide *detailed* information to early childhood professionals about the effects of scheduling, the influence of

*specimen record:*
*a type of narrative observation that provides detailed information about a particular event, child, or time of day*

---

**FIGURE 2.3**
**A Specimen Record**

A group of preschool-age boys were beginning an outdoor play activity. There was a disagreement about who was going to enact the more desirable characters. Their language characterizes the overt organizational behaviors of the fantasy theme among the frustrated subjects.

| | |
|---|---|
| John (M1): | There will be three Lukes today. |
| All: | I want to be Luke today! (competing for the role) |
| Jim (M6): | I'll be Luke. |
| Bruce (M4): | There can't be all Lukes. (frustrated) |
| Kevin (M3): | I'll be Chewy. |
| Paul (M5): | Who else is Luke? |
| Chuck (M2): | He is. (pointing to Bruce) |
| Dan (M7): | What? |
| Bruce (M4): | We got our whole game mixed up! |
| Kevin (M3): | Right, I'm Chewy. |
| Bruce (M4): | Two people are Lukes, all right? |
| Jim (M6): | I'm Luke! |
| Bruce (M4): | No, I'm Luke! |
| Chuck (M2): | I wanna . . . |
| Bruce (M4): | All right! |
| Jim (M6): | Let's have a converse (conference?), let's hold hands. Let's hold hands . . . we are having a converse, right? (looking for agreement among the play group members) |
| Paul (M5): | Right now? |
| Bruce (M4): | Hold onto my sleeve. (to Paul) |
| John (M1): | The game's mixed up. (directed to the adult observer) |
| Inv: | The game's mixed up? (responding to John's statement) |
| Bruce (M4): | Yeah, we get it mixed up all of the time. |

The boys formed a circle and held hands during the "converse" (conference). The discussion developed out of frustration and lack of cooperation at the outset of the play activity. This specimen of linguistic behavior provides a source of information regarding play theme management and status hierarchies in play groups.

---

certain curricular and management strategies, and specific children and their behavior. The format used for running records can be used for specimen records. At times, audiotape recorders or video cameras may provide more complete and detailed information. See Figure 2.3 for an example of a specimen record.

**Anecdotal Records.** **Anecdotal records** differ from running and specimen records in that they are usually written *after* the incident occurs. They are brief and describe only one incident at a time that the early childhood professional believes is significant. Anecdotal records are cumulative and describe in a factual manner what happened, how it happened, when and where it happened, and what was

*anecdotal record:*
*a type of narrative*
*observation that*
*describes in detail an*
*incident after it occurs*

FIGURE 2.4
An Anecdotal Record

**Date:** February 19, 1995
**Observer:** Schwartz
**Child:** Ann S.
**Time:** 8:38 a.m. During center time this morning, Ann was playing in the dramatic play center with a rag doll. While sitting on the floor, Ann began to repeatedly beat the floor with the head and upper torso of the doll while holding on to the doll's legs and feet. At first she hit the floor lightly and sporadically. Then the intensity and frequency of the activity increased to the extent that the doll's arm began to tear away. I intervened at this point and redirected Ann to another activity with the teacher assistant.
**Time:** 9:20 a.m. During the transition from centers to story time, Ann walked past the block area and knocked down Daniel's tower of blocks that he had built during today's center time. Daniel screamed as the tower fell, and Ann watched passively as he called for me. Ann was unable to verbalize what had happened, but did manage to apologize to Daniel for this "accident."
**Time:** 10:30 a.m. On the playground, I observed Ann push her way past children on three separate occasions. Twice she pushed past children to gain access to the slide and once she pushed a child from behind to get a tricycle. The latter incident caused the child to skin her knee, requiring a trip to the school nurse. Ann was unable to verbalize what had happened and denied any responsibility for the incident.
**Time:** 11:15 a.m. As the children were washing their hands and getting drinks of water, I saw Ann purposefully tear her painting as it was hanging on the drying rack. Her expression was passive, a blank stare, as she tore the wet painting in two pieces. As both halves hung on the rack, she had no explanation for how the "accident" occurred.
**Summary:** While observing Ann throughout this morning, it was clear that something was bothering her. The aggressive incidents were uncharacteristic of Ann and appeared to occur without premeditation. Despite efforts by the classroom teaching team to involve Ann in guided group activities this morning, she tended to lose interest and find solitary activities. Typically, when she was working or playing independently this morning, she had difficulty or acted aggressively. Further attention must be given to these behaviors for the next several days. A closer observation may be warranted. If this continues, I may need to contact Ann's parents.

said and done. Commentaries can be written in the margin or at the conclusion of the anecdote. Anecdotal records can be particularly helpful to the busy classroom teacher who finds it somewhat difficult to do the more time-consuming running record and the more detailed specimen record. Ms. Schwartz, a kindergarten teacher, became concerned about 5-year-old Ann's periodic aggressive behavior. Ms. Schwartz began to take anecdotal records after these episodes occurred. These notes were then analyzed according to time, activity, and children involved.

## FIGURE 2.5
## Frost-Wortham Developmental Checklist

### Motor Development: Preschool (Small Movement)

| Level III (approx. age 3) | Introduced | Progress | Mastery |
|---|:---:|:---:|:---:|
| 1. Places small pegs in pegboards | ___ | ___ | ___ |
| 2. Holds a paintbrush or pencil with the whole hand | ___ | ___ | ___ |
| 3. Eats with a spoon | ___ | ___ | ___ |
| 4. Buttons large buttons on his or her own clothes | ___ | ___ | ___ |
| 5. Puts on coat unassisted | ___ | ___ | ___ |
| 6. Strings beads with ease | ___ | ___ | ___ |
| 7. Hammers a pound toy with accuracy | ___ | ___ | ___ |
| 8. Works a three- or four-piece puzzle | ___ | ___ | ___ |

| Level IV (approx. age 4) | | | |
|---|:---:|:---:|:---:|
| 1. Pounds and rolls clay | ___ | ___ | ___ |
| 2. Puts together a five-piece puzzle | ___ | ___ | ___ |
| 3. Forms a pegboard design | ___ | ___ | ___ |
| 4. Cuts with scissors haltingly and pastes | ___ | ___ | ___ |
| 5. Eats with a fork correctly | ___ | ___ | ___ |
| 6. Holds a cup with one hand | ___ | ___ | ___ |
| 7. Puts a coat on a hanger or hook | ___ | ___ | ___ |
| 8. Manipulates large crayons and brushes | ___ | ___ | ___ |
| 9. Buttons buttons and zips zippers haltingly | ___ | ___ | ___ |

| Level V (approx. age 5) | | | |
|---|:---:|:---:|:---:|
| 1. Cuts and pastes creative designs | ___ | ___ | ___ |
| 2. Forms a variety of pegboard designs | ___ | ___ | ___ |
| 3. Buttons buttons, zips zippers, and ties shoes | ___ | ___ | ___ |
| 4. Creates recognizable objects with clay | ___ | ___ | ___ |
| 5. Uses the toilets independently | ___ | ___ | ___ |
| 6. Eats independently with a knife and fork | ___ | ___ | ___ |
| 7. Dresses and undresses independently | ___ | ___ | ___ |
| 8. Holds and manipulates pencils, crayons, and brushes of various sizes | ___ | ___ | ___ |
| 9. Combs and brushes hair | ___ | ___ | ___ |
| 10. Works a twelve-piece puzzle | ___ | ___ | ___ |

*Source:* From "Frost-Wortham Developmental Checklist," *Play and Playscapes* (Albany, NY: Delmar, 1992a). Reprinted with permission of the authors.

## OBSERVATION WITH PREDEFINED INSTRUMENTS
Predefined instruments frequently used in studying young children include checklists, rating scales, time sampling, event sampling, and interviews. Like narrative observations, these techniques have advantages and disadvantages.

---

**FIGURE 2.6**
**Rating Scale**

**Your Child's Sleep Behaviors**
(Circle the appropriate response)

1. **My child always sleeps through the night:**
   Little body movement; regular breathing; no response to mild stimulation.

2. **My child often sleeps through the night:**
   Increased body movements; irregular breathing; more easily aroused by external stimuli.

3. **My child sometimes sleeps through the night:**
   Between regular and irregular sleep, accompanied by muscle movements, rapid breathing, and then short periods of calm activity.

4. **My child seldom sleeps through the night:**
   Wakefulness; scans the environment; large motor activity (head, trunk, arms, and legs), alert but relaxed.

5. **My child never sleeps through the night:**
   Intense motor activity may signal physiological need; whimpering, crying states, becoming louder as distress increases.

*Source:* Application of Wolff, P. H. (1966). *Causes, Controls, and Organization of Behavior in the Neonate.* (Table 5.2, p.119) Madison, CT: International Universities Press, Inc.

*checklist:*
*a list of developmental behaviors that the observer identifies as present or absent*

**Checklists.** A **checklist** is a list of developmental behaviors that have been identified as important to look for in young children. They are helpful tools in studying children when many easily specified behaviors need to be observed and recorded. Checklists are usually used with one child at a time and need to be prepared in an objective manner. See Figure 2.5 (p. 39) for an example of a checklist.

*rating scale:*
*a scale with various traits or categories that allows the observer to indicate the importance of the observed behaviors*

**Rating Scales.** **Rating scales** are similar to checklists in that they include large numbers of traits or behaviors to observe. They provide more detailed information about the quality of traits or behaviors than checklists. However, the use of rating scales is dependent on the observer's judgment, so objectivity must be maintained. See Figure 2.6 for an example of a rating scale.

*time sampling:*
*an observation technique for recording how often certain behaviors occur over time*

**Time Sampling and Event Sampling.** Two other techniques used to observe and record behavior in young children are time sampling and event sampling. **Time sampling** records how often certain behaviors occur over a period of time. The observed behavior needs to be obvious and frequent in occurrence for this type of observation to be effective.

*event sampling:*
*an observation technique for recording when certain events occur*

In **event sampling,** the observer decides on an event to study, waits for the event to occur, and then records it. If narratives or time sampling do not seem to be appropriate ways to get information, event sampling can be helpful to the early childhood professional. See Figures 2.7 and 2.8 for examples of time sampling and event sampling.

---

## FIGURE 2.7
## Time Sampling

| Behavior: | Biting other children |
|---|---|
| Subject(s): | Jimmy (2 years, 6 months) |
| Observer: | Ms. Gilliam |
| Observation Begins: | 8:00 a.m. |
| Observation Ends: | 4:00 p.m. |
| Date: | 6/7/95 |

| Hour of the Day | Time of Incident | Observer Notes |
|---|---|---|
| 8:00 | | Observation begins |
| | 8:09 | |
| | 8:35 | |
| 9:00 | | Morning snack |
| | | Group time |
| 10:00 | | Centers |
| | 10:32 | |
| 11:00 | | Begin lunch routine |
| 12:00 | | |
| 1:00 | | Nap time begins 12:30 |
| | | Nap time |
| 2:00 | | Nap time |
| | | Child awake: 2:36 p.m. |
| 3:00 | 3:02 | Selected centers |
| | 3:48 | |
| 4:00 | | Observation ends |

**Findings:** 5 biting incidents during observation period

---

# OTHER METHODS OF GATHERING INFORMATION ABOUT YOUNG CHILDREN

At times, **interviews** can be helpful in obtaining information about young children. During an interview, an adult verbally questions or interacts with a child on a one-to-one basis using predetermined questions. The purpose of an interview is to find out how and why children think the way they do. It is important for a successful interview that the interviewer spend time establishing rapport with the young child.

When using this technique, several other preconditions are necessary: (1) children must be able to express themselves verbally; (2) children must be comfortable with the interviewer; (3) the interviewer must be sensitive to the child's level of receptive language and cognitive development, as many responses may not be incorrect but in reality be developmentally appropriate; and (4) interviews are best conducted in familiar settings without other distractions.

*interview:*

*asking the child predetermined questions on a one-to-one basis to find out more about the child*

---

### FIGURE 2.8
### Event Sampling

| Behavior: | Biting other children |
|---|---|
| Subject(s): | Jimmy (2 years, 6 months) |
| Observer: | Ms. Koth |
| Observation Begins: | 8:00 a.m. |
| Observation Ends: | 4:00 p.m. |
| Date: | 6/7/95 |

| Time | Observed Behavior | Observer Comments |
|---|---|---|
| 8:09 a.m. | Jimmy and Josh are pulling on a large unit block. Both are kneeling facing each other. Each is using two hands to hold on to the block. Jimmy has lowered his head as a wedge between Josh's body and the block. After a brief pause, Josh screams, releases the block, and grasps his left forearm. Josh runs to the classroom teacher, still grasping his arm, crying, and unable to speak. | The physical behavior of biting appears to be Jimmy's strategy for gaining materials and objects that are held or claimed by other children.<br><br>No audible language was observed during the confrontation. |
| 8:35 a.m. | Jimmy repeats a similar conflict with Kenneth over a pair of headphones in listening center. Same physical posture and strategy to gain control of a disputed object. | Similar circumstances—no language observed, physical posture was similar, confrontation was brief with no amiable solution. |

---

Other methods of gathering information about young children include samples of children's products such as artistic creations, writings, and daily class work; informal and formal meetings, including conferences and home visits with the child's parents; school records, if objective and factual; and other teachers, **support staff, resource persons,** and **peers.**

Technology can be helpful in recording various types of information. Audiotapes can help teachers study children's oral language, including oral reading. Videotapes can be helpful in documenting and analyzing a wide range of behaviors. Videotapes can also be used to aid discussion about a child with parents and other support personnel who find it difficult to observe the child on a regular basis. Computers can be useful for storing and quickly retrieving information about children. See Figure 2.9 for guidelines for conducting observations.

*support staff:*
*other persons within the educational setting who support the learning and development of young children, e.g., nurses, social workers, diagnosticians, psychologists, secretaries, cooks, and custodian*

## FIGURE 2.9
## Effectively Observing Young Children's Behavior

An observer of young children has two responsibilities: (1) not to interfere with the normal operations of the early childhood setting they are studying and (2) to accurately characterize the children's behavior in any reports, term papers, or academic reports. The following guidelines will help observers fulfill these responsibilities.

**Be quiet.** Any behavior that draws children's attention will upset the classroom routine and will affect the behavior of the children, thus influencing any observation procedures. Good observers are able to move about the early childhood setting without drawing attention to themselves while still getting a good view of activities.

**Sit low and to the side of activities.** Unobtrusiveness is essential to good observations in early childhood settings. Observers should sit with their backs to exterior walls or in corners so that all activities are easily observable.

**Honesty is the best policy.** When observers are approached by children in the classroom, classroom assistants or children's parents respond to their questions with honesty and simplicity. Children are sensitive to evasive or vague answers to their questions, and they will insist on clear answers. Observers should try to avoid prolonged or unnecessary conversations with children and adults in the observation site; thus, they should give simple, clear, and honest answers to any questions about their activities.

**Don't let your emotions get the best of you.** Sometimes young children make amusing statements, and it is natural to respond with a laugh or a chuckle. Observers should remember that they are technically not a part of the social climate in the classroom and should avoid "normal" emotional responses. However, observers should respond to statements or activities that are specifically directed to them. Observers should always remember to be polite.

**Be quick on your feet.** Observers will be asked to move from their observation position to make room for children's activities or to follow the group of children out to the play area. Observers should bring minimal materials that can be easily and quickly packed and moved to another observation location. Observers of young children should remember not to "lose themselves in their work." Any guest in an early childhood setting should be sensitive to the needs and well-being of the adults and the children and be alert and ready to respond quietly if necessary.

## RELATED RESOURCES THAT HELP IN THE STUDY OF YOUNG CHILDREN

A number of other resources can be helpful in studying young children. These include:

1. Child development research journals such as *Early Childhood Research Quarterly, Journal of Research in Childhood Education, Child Development, Developmental Psychology, Society for Research in Child Development Monographs, American Educational Research Journal, Research in the Teaching of English,* and *Journal of Experimental Psychology.*

*resource persons:*
*persons outside the educational setting, usually from health-related fields, who can provide information about young children's development and learning*

*peers:*
*other children who are the same age as a particular child*

2. Journals from professional organizations and related groups such as *Young Children, Childhood Education, Dimensions, The Reading Teacher, Language Arts, Science and Children, Mathematics Teacher, Arithmetic Teacher, Teaching Exceptional Children, Journal of Special Education, Gifted Child Quarterly, Elementary School Journal, Journal of Negro Education, Journal of Ethnic Studies, Journal of Children in Contemporary Society, Phi Delta Kappan, Educational Leadership*, and *Journal of Teacher Education*.

3. Professional magazines such as *Day Care and Early Education, Child Care Information Exchange, Learning, Instructor, Prekindergarten, Early Years*, and *School-Age Notes*.

4. Professional organization position statements. (See the Further Readings section at the end of this chapter.)

## RECORDKEEPING TO DOCUMENT AND RECORD BEHAVIOR AND DEVELOPMENT

All quality early childhood programs have some recordkeeping process to document the behavior and development of young children. All approaches, including those developed by the early childhood professional, need to be evaluated for (1) developmental appropriateness, (2) objectivity, and (3) usefulness to early childhood professionals and parents in helping them understand and facilitate the child's growth and development.

Child study and appropriate recordkeeping at the preservice level help future professionals learn more about children and ways to document children's behavior. Both of these skills will help the beginning teacher develop into a competent early childhood professional.

Early childhood professionals need to continue their child study and observation skills. NAEYC states in its position statement, "Testing of Young Children: Concerns and Options" (1988), that "the systematic observations of trained teachers and other professionals in conjunction with information obtained from parents and other family members are the best sources of information." At times, competent early childhood professionals may need to revise or work to eliminate the use of certain assessment or reporting techniques that are not developmentally appropriate. Additional methods of studying and documenting the behavior and development of children may need to be designed and used. The use of **portfolios**, which contain a variety of materials, including children's products with dates written on them, can be helpful in documenting the ongoing development of young children (Grace, Shores, Brown, Arnold, Graves, Jambor, & Neill, 1991).

Early childhood professionals are very busy, and not all teachers have an aide or a teaching team. Consequently, they may need to be creative in devising ways that help them learn more about children in their own environment. There is no single correct way to study children. However, following are some guidelines for early childhood professionals to facilitate child study and observation:

*portfolio:*
*a collection of children's products, e.g., art, written work, and related materials, all of which are dated and used to document development and learning over a period of time*

1. In addition to conducting ongoing assessment, try to identify times when observations might be conducted.

2. Try to identify how you can conduct observations. Parent volunteers, student teachers, or child development students can supervise young children occasionally, giving the classroom teacher the opportunity to do some observing.

3. Wear clothing with a pocket so that small note pads or cards and pencil are available for recording information as it occurs.

4. Keep all information confidential, and do not talk about the children in their presence.

Remember the quote at the beginning of this chapter? Take a look at it again. More than any other factor, your ability to study young children will be the key to understanding their behavior as well as your own. Child study is not to be looked upon lightly or grudgingly. Child study, coupled with your knowledge of child development, provides the foundation for your development into a competent early childhood professional.

Observing children can be a key to understanding ourselves. People who develop observational skills notice human behavior more accurately. They become skilled at seeing small but important facets of human personality. They learn to differentiate between what is fact and what is inference. This increases an awareness of how one's biases affect the perceptions of children. The values and benefits of observations are long-lasting. Only by practicing observations— what it takes to look, to see, to become more sensitive—will teachers be able to record children's behavior fully and vividly, capturing the unique qualities and personality of each child. (Gordon & Browne, 1985, p. 138)

## KEY TERMS

| | | |
|---|---|---|
| achievement test | informal approach | readiness test |
| anecdotal record | inservice | reflecting-in-action |
| authentic assessment | intelligence test | reliability |
| checklist | interview | representative sample |
| correlational study | longitudinal study | resource persons |
| cross-sectional study | narrative observation | running record |
| descriptive study | norms | specimen record |
| diagnostic test | peers | standardized test |
| developmental | perspective taking | support staff |
|   screening test | portfolio | teacher-as-learner |
| event sampling | preprimary | teacher-as-researcher |
| experimental study | preservice | time sampling |
| formal approach | random | validity |
| hypotheses | rating scale | |

## REVIEW STRATEGIES AND ACTIVITIES

1. Review the key terms individually or with a classmate.

2. After reading this chapter, develop a list of questions that you would like to ask early childhood professionals who teach in developmentally appropriate classrooms. These questions should focus on:
   - Techniques used in assessing children's development and learning
   - Inclusion practices
   - An antibias climate

3. Experiment with one of the assessment techniques described in this chapter.
   a. Discuss with your class what you learned about children through using your child study technique.
   b. Discuss what you learned about this child study technique with your class. What did you find difficult to do? What seemed easy? What are the drawbacks and benefits of certain techniques? When would it be most appropriate to use each technique?

4. Read a child development research study in one of the research journals listed in the chapter.
   a. Would you categorize the research as descriptive, longitudinal, correlational, or experimental?
   b. Was the study conducted in an ethical manner?
   c. Did the study take sociocultural factors into consideration?

5. Choose one child to observe for an extended period of time. Note how the child's behavior changes depending on the context of the setting, the people in the setting, and the time of day.

6. Read several articles in various professional journals. What did you learn about the development of young children that will help you?

## FURTHER READINGS

Borich, G. D. (1994). *Observation skills for effective teaching* (2nd ed.). New York: Merrill.

Bredekamp, S., & Rosegrant, T. (Eds.). 1992. *Reaching potentials: Appropriate curriculums and assessment for young children* (Vol. 1). Washington, DC: NAEYC.

Genishi, C. (Ed.). (1992). *Ways of assessing children and curriculum: Stories of early childhood practice*. New York: Teachers College Press.

Grace, K., Shores, E. F., Brown, M., Arnold, F. D., Graves, S. B., Jambor, T., Neill, M. (Eds.). (1991). *The portfolio and its use: Developmentally appropriate assessment of young children*. Little Rock, AR: Southern Early Childhood Association.

Kamii, C. (Ed.). (1990). *Achievement testing in the early grades: The games grown-ups play*. Washington, DC: National Association for the Education of Young Children.

Marsden, D. B., Meisels, S. J., & Jablon, J. R. (1993). *The work sampling system: Preschool through grade three*. Ann Arbor, MI: University of Michigan, Center for Human Growth and Development.

McAfee, O., & Leong, D. (1994). *Assessing and guiding young children's development and learning.* Boston: Allyn and Bacon.

Perrone, V. (1991). *On standardized testing.* The Association for Childhood Education International, 11141 Georgia Avenue, Suite 200, Wheaton, MD 20902, (800) 423–3563.

Puckett, M. B., & Black, J. K. (1994). *Authentic assessment of the young child: Celebrating development and learning.* New York: Macmillan.

Wortham, S. C. (1995). *Tests and measurement in early childhood education.* 2/e Columbus, OH: Merrill.

## Position Statements from Professional Organizations

*Developmentally appropriate assessment.* The Southern Association on Children under Six, P. O. Box 5403 Brady Station, Little Rock, AR 72215, (501) 663–0353.

*Developmentally appropriate practice in early childhood programs, serving children from birth through age 8.* (1987). The National Association for the Education of Young Children, 1834 Connecticut Avenue N.W., Washington, DC 20009, (800) 424–2460.

National Association for the Education of Young Children (1995). NAEYC Guidelines for Preparation of Early Childhood Professionals. Washington D.C: author.

*Quality child care.* The Southern Association on Children under Six (see address above).

*Quality programs for five year olds.* The Southern Association on Children under Six (see address above).

*Quality programs for four year olds.* The Southern Association on Children under Six (see address above).

*School readiness.* (1990). The National Association for the Education of Young Children (see address above).

*Testing of young children: Concerns and cautions.* (1988). The National Association for the Education of Young Children (see address above).

# PART TWO

# The Child's Life Begins

# CHAPTER THREE

*A parent has the potential to gain what is without a doubt the highest satisfaction a human being can enjoy—the gratification of nurturing the development of a child into an emotionally stable and mature young man or woman. There is no greater reward for the adult; there is no greater gift to the child.*

**Richard A. Gardner**

# The Family Before Birth

After studying this chapter, you will demonstrate comprehension by:

- Explaining why it is important that early childhood professionals understand the role of parents in the development of children from prebirth through age 8.
- Describing the status of the family.
- Outlining the possible implications of the presence or absence of choice for parenting.
- Identifying the impact of the sociocultural and economic factors in becoming parents.
- Identifying emotional and psychological aspects of preparing for parenting.
- Describing prenatal development.
- Describing quality prenatal care.
- Describing education for childbirth and parenting.
- Explaining the importance of preparing siblings for birth.
- Identifying sociocultural influences in prenatal care.

## The Importance of Early Childhood Professionals in Understanding the Role of Parents

Throughout this text, much attention is given to the role of parents in the development of young children. It is important that early childhood professionals be aware of this information for several reasons. First, the behaviors and attitudes of parents directly influence the development of the young child even prior to birth. For example, as discussed later in this chapter, parents' use of chemical substances and the mother's nutritional habits can affect the growth and development of the baby before it is born. These parental behaviors can have consequences for the later development and learning of young children. Second, the behaviors and attitudes of the parents after birth and throughout the early childhood years continue to influence the development and learning of the young child. Third, parents' knowledge of their young child can be helpful to early

51

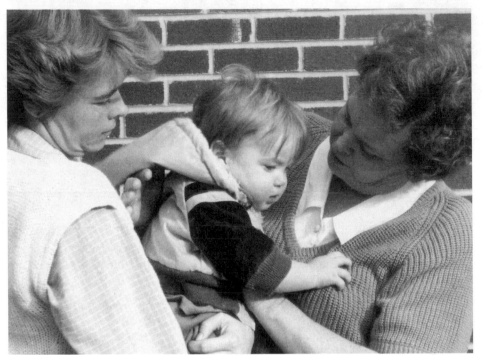

*For partnerships to be effective, early childhood professionals must have an empathetic understanding of the challenges and demands of parenting.*

childhood professionals. Thus, parents and early childhood professionals must be partners if optimal learning and development are to occur in young children. For this partnership to be effective, early childhood professionals must have an empathetic understanding of the challenges and demands of parenting. For instance, third-grade teacher Sharon Smith was upset with Joe's mother because she did not make him learn his multiplication tables. Through talking with the school counselor, Ms. Smith found out that Joe's mother was a single parent working at two jobs, one of which was during the evening hours. There were five children in the family, and they lived in a two-room apartment. An awareness of the demands on Joe's mother helped Ms. Smith adopt a more empathetic attitude toward her. Tutoring by a sixth-grade boy during school and help from an older brother provided more support for Joe and his learning needs.

Early childhood professionals can also help parents understand the development of their young children and learn appropriate parenting techniques. Remember in Chapter 2 how Mr. Hubbard helped Juan's parents become aware of the importance of their behavior in helping Juan adjust to the child care center? Mr. Hubbard encouraged Juan's parents to bring him to the center and stay with him for several short periods before he began to attend full time and to bring Juan's favorite toy and blanket every day.

Finally, an increased understanding of parental roles not only enhances the effectiveness of early childhood professionals in working with young children in their classrooms but can also benefit early childhood professionals in their own parenting roles. Occasionally, students who are parents of older children wish they had had early childhood development information when their own children were young, but they may find it helpful in their role as grandparents. It is important to remember that all parents do the best they can and that many parents have never had a course in child development or parenting. An awareness of the importance of the parental role and its impact on the development and learning of young children is necessary for the early childhood professional to effectively relate to young children and their families.

## THE STATUS OF FAMILIES

The current status of families has been described as a "quiet crisis" (Carnegie Corporation, 1994, p. 12). Changing values and growing economic pressures are frequently the reasons given for this crisis.

More and more mothers, including those with infants and toddlers, find it necessary to work outside the home to meet family economic needs. The general lack of support for family needs, including child care, places increased stress on parents. Another stressor is the resulting decrease in the time parents have to attend to their children and to home-related tasks. Many parents report feeling overwhelmed and exhausted.

Another reason for this "quiet" crisis is the dramatic increase in single-parent families. One out of four American children now lives in a single-parent home, and 90 percent of these families are headed by women. Only 50 percent of divorced families receive financial support from the father.

Studies of the negative effects on children of these single-parent families transcend issues such as economics, education of the mother, and minority status. The effects include lower scores on health, education, and emotional and behavioral measures. These children are more likely to drop out of school, become single parents themselves, and experience lower socioeconomic status as adults.

The increase in single-parent families is particularly prevalent among African Americans (Sawhill, 1992). Reasons include restrictive policies of government assistance programs that penalize two-parent families and the lack of employment opportunities. Frequently, children in single-parent families are cared for by extended-family members who in the process may jeopardize their own employment opportunities. A related phenomenon is the increasing number of adolescent pregnancies. This topic will be addressed later in this chapter.

Because of work demands and greater mobility, families are experiencing increased isolation from extended families, friends, and community life. Furthermore, violence has become commonplace in many neighborhoods and now infiltrates formerly safe areas of the community. Very young children either experience violence directly or witness violence against others in the home, the neighborhood, or the media (Craig, 1992).

While the poverty rate overall is the same as it was two decades ago, fewer elderly and more young children live below the poverty line today (Danziger and Danziger, 1993). Poverty has many severe consequences, including homelessness (Linehan, 1992).

---

**FIGURE 3.1**
**America Lags Behind**

---

The United States:

- Is *not* one of 150 nations that have signed or ratified the UN Convention on the Rights of the Child (Cambodia, Iran, Iraq, Libya, and South Africa have also not signed).
- Is *not* one of 127 nations that permit employees to take paid parental leave after the birth of a baby (as do Canada, France, Germany, and Japan, among others).
- Has a *worse* low-birthweight rate than 30 other nations.
- Has a *smaller* proportion of babies immunized against polio than 16 other nations.
- Has one of the *worst* adolescent pregnancy rates in the developed world—twice as high as England and seven times as high as the Netherlands.

Our policies contrast sharply with those of most other industrialized countries, particularly those in Europe. European child care for children under age three varies significantly from country to country, but generally speaking, the Europeans are moving toward paid leaves for new parents and a range of subsidized child care options for toddlers.

Here are some examples of countries that offer job protection and paid leaves to employed parents (usually, but not always, mothers) who have sufficient work histories:

- In Germany, a new parent can receive modest financial support while staying at home for up to one and a half years, or she can work part-time at her previous workplace.
- In France, she can count on modest compensation at home for as long as three years, or she can go back to work and take advantage of subsidized child care.
- In Sweden, she receives full pay while staying at home with a new baby for a year and a half, or she can opt to work part-time for a longer period and receive full pay.
- In Finland, she can stay home until her child is three, knowing that her job (or a comparable job) will be waiting for her when she returns. She receives her full salary for one year and a lesser amount for the next two years. Or she can take advantage of subsidized child care.
- In Austria, she can stay at home throughout her child's first two years, or work part-time until the child's third birthday, while receiving financial support equivalent to the wage of an unskilled worker.

*Source:* Reprinted from *Starting Points: Meeting the needs of our children* (April, 1994), with permission from the Carnegie Corporation of New York.

Even if parents work, poverty is not always eliminated. Housing, transportation, health care, and child care cost more today than they did two decades ago. Furthermore, real wages have decreased disproportionately for younger workers relative to older workers.

The "quiet" crisis will have a profound impact on the well-being of families in this country as it faces the economic and technological challenges of the 21st century. As a result, the Carnegie Task Force on Meeting the Needs of Young Children has recommended a national commitment and investment in children and their families. The nation must

- Promote opportunities for responsible parenthood
- Guarantee quality child care choices for children under age 3
- Ensure good health and protection for infants and toddlers

---

**FIGURE 3.2**
**The Costs of Societal Neglect**

---

Each year, American taxpayers reach deep into their pockets to meet the costs, both direct and indirect, of policies that are based on remediation rather than prevention.

- In the six years between 1985 and 1990, estimated public outlays related to teenage childbearing totaled more than $120 billion. More than $48 billion could have been saved if these births had been postponed until the mother was 20 or older.
- Of teens who give birth, 46 percent will go on welfare within four years; of unmarried teens who give birth, 73 percent will be on welfare within four years.
- In 1991, federal and state expenditures for Aid to Families with Dependent Children, the largest entitlement program for poor families, totaled $20 billion plus administrative costs of $2.6 billion.
- In 1991, the estimated annual cost of treating fetal alcohol syndrome was $74.6 million.
- Initial hospital care for each low-birthweight infant averages $20,000. Total lifetime medical costs for a low-birthweight infant average $400,000.

---

*Source:* Reprinted from *Starting Points: Meeting the needs of our children* (April, 1994), with permission from the Carnegie Corporation of New York.

- Mobilize communities to support young children and their families (Carnegie Corporation, 1994, p. 22)

Figures 3.1 and 3.2 document the fact that America lags behind many other countries in addressing the needs of families and the commitment to providing funding to meet these needs.

**Meet Jeremy**—Ann and Bill Johnson live in a large metropolitan area in the South. Ann is a technical illustrator for a publisher, and Bill is an accountant. Bill grew up in a suburban area, where his father was an accountant and his mother was a child development specialist. Both parents were active in community affairs. Bill feels fortunate to have grown up with loving parents.

Ann's parents divorced when she was 7. While her relationship with her father was close, he was transferred to another company on the West Coast. As a result, she saw him only a few times each year. Ann's mother was a somewhat distant person, and Ann never felt emotionally close to her.

After college graduation, Ann and Bill married. They worked hard to establish themselves in their respective careers. They traveled, saved their money, and eventually bought a home in the suburbs. When several of their friends began to start their families, Bill and Ann felt privileged to share in the discussions about pregnancy, childbirth, and becoming parents. They began to talk about having children of their own. Bill wanted several children, but Ann was not so sure. Her own unhappy childhood made her question her ability to be a good parent. Eventually, Ann went to a counselor to work through her feelings. During this time she and Bill read many books about pregnancy, childbirth, and parenting. This process helped Ann resolve her fears, and she decided that she could provide a safe and secure childhood for her children.

Bill and Ann analyzed their family finances. Between the two of them, they had a comfortable income. Ann's company provided paid maternity leave, and Bill's accounting firm would grant him parental leave. Ann and Bill began to investigate possible types of child care for infants. About this time, Bill's firm, along with several other businesses, decided to establish a child care center, which included an infant room.

Ann and Bill had always been health conscious. They exercised regularly and paid attention to their diets. Neither smoked or abused drugs or alcohol. Both had annual checkups. They consulted with their doctors and told them they would like to begin their family. The doctors asked for a brief family history and inquired about possible genetic defects. Ann and Bill requested the names of several obstetricians whose practice focused on family-centered maternity care.

Three months later, Ann missed her menstrual period. She made an appointment with one of the recommended obstetricians, Dr. Susan Windle. Bill went with Ann to see Dr. Windle. They were ecstatic when Dr. Windle confirmed that Ann was pregnant. Dr. Windle took a detailed medical history of both Bill and Ann, and shared information with them regarding the early stages of pregnancy. She described the care she would be providing for Ann and asked for questions. Dr. Windle also discussed various fees and hospital procedures and encouraged Ann and Bill to visit the birthing center. She told them about two childbirth classes, the first on general information regarding pregnancy and the development of the baby and the second on Lamaze prepared childbirth, to be taken near the end of Ann's pregnancy. As they left Dr. Windle's office, Ann and Bill were given a number of brochures and booklets to read. They celebrated at one of their favorite restaurants. Over a candlelit dinner, they decided to name the baby Jeremy if it was a boy. They were not quite sure about a girl's name. Bill liked Elizabeth, while Ann liked Julia, the name of a favorite aunt.

During the beginning of her pregnancy, Ann's moods varied from elation to mild depression. At times these mood swings were difficult for Bill to understand. At their first future parents' class, they found that other couples were experiencing similar problems. Jane, the instructor, explained that these mood swings were caused by the hormonal changes of pregnancy. Ann, like some of the other women, also reported increased fatigue and nausea. Jane told the class that usually by the end of the first three months, most of these discomforting but normal effects of pregnancy would subside.

Bill and Ann made regular trips to Dr. Windle throughout the pregnancy. Ann ate nutritious and well-balanced meals, increased her intake of fruits, vegetables, and dairy products, and took no medication without the approval of Dr. Windle. Bill and Ann attended childbirth classes, visited the hospital, bought furniture and clothes for the baby, and compromised on a girl's name, Julia Elizabeth. They enjoyed talking with other new parents and reading books about parenting, finding that this helped relieve some of their normal feelings of anxiety. They followed the development of their baby with **ultrasound** tests, which indicated that the fetus was developing normally and would probably be a boy—Jeremy.

*ultrasound:*
*a technique using sound frequencies that can detect structural disorders in the fetus and the approximate week of pregnancy*

Bill and Ann finalized their plans for the baby's care after Ann returned to work. They discussed their parental leaves with their employers. Bill wanted to take at least a week off after the baby was born. Ann decided to return to work when the baby was 6 weeks old. But as the baby's birth drew near, Ann decided she did not want to leave her young baby in a group care situation, even though Bill's firm had implemented an excellent program for infants and toddlers. Ann and Bill felt more comfortable having someone care for their baby in their home. Ann contacted an agency that provided trained nannies. After several interviews, Ann and Bill chose Phyllis. She was 23, had worked for several other families who provided excellent references, had a good knowledge of young children's development, and demonstrated a love of young children. Ann and Bill fixed up a bedroom and bath in another wing of their home for Phyllis. Since Phyllis was completing her position with another family, she would be able to join the Johnsons about two weeks before Ann was to return to work.

Ann's mother wanted to come to help. Bill and Ann had learned from their parenting classes that each couple has to decide if they want family help with their new baby. Some people can be a great help to new parents, giving them information about the habits of babies as well as helping with household chores. However, some extended families are not very supportive and take control at a time when the new parents should be in charge. Ann finally decided that, given the somewhat tense relationship she had with her mother, it would be best to invite her mother for a visit after the new Johnson family had a week or two together. Bill and Ann had taken the time to prepare for the optimal development of their baby and to inform themselves about pregnancy and parenting. Now all they had to do was practice the exercises they had learned in the childbirth classes and wait. ■

**Meet Angela**—Cheryl Monroe is 15 years old. She lives in an urban area with her mother and four brothers and sisters. Her grades are barely passing and she has considered dropping out of school, but her mother tells her it is important to get an education. Every afternoon Cheryl's mother takes the bus downtown, where she works until midnight cleaning corporate offices. Cheryl does not know who her father is.

Cheryl's dream is to be a movie star or a singer with a rock group. Like most adolescent girls, she is very interested in boys and has been seeing James for about seven months. They have been sexually active and spend their evenings watching TV, listening to music, and eating junk food.

It has been four months since Cheryl has had a menstrual period, and her changing body is now reinforcing the idea that she is indeed pregnant. Finally, she shares her suspicions with several of her teenage friends. They generally respond that she is lucky because she will have a cute baby to love her. Eventually, Cheryl tells her mother she is going to have a baby. Her mother reacts with concern, anger, and disappointment. She knows this will probably mean an end to Cheryl's high school education. She doubts that James will be able to support Cheryl and believes Cheryl's baby will be another mouth to feed in their already economically stressed household.

James is proud of his impending fatherhood and brags about it to his friends. He does care for Cheryl and intends to help support the baby from his occasional part-time work.

One day, Cheryl's mother shares her concern about her daughter with one of the women in their church, Linnie Hudson. Ms. Hudson tells her it is important for Cheryl to receive prenatal care as soon as possible. She tells her to talk to their minister about getting Cheryl into a clinic that provides care and services for unwed mothers. Cheryl's mother gets the information from Reverend Brown and schedules an appointment for Cheryl at the clinic.

During her first visit to the prenatal clinic, an examination reveals that Cheryl is six to seven months pregnant. She is counseled on nutrition, told how to sign up for WIC (Women, Infants, and Children), a federally funded program that provides various dairy and other food products for pregnant and nursing women and their young children, and is scheduled for follow-up visits.

Cheryl spends the last two to three months of her pregnancy working on her studies at home, watching TV, helping out around the apartment, seeing James and her other friends, and visiting the clinic for prenatal checkups. Medical personnel feel encouraged from their exams that the baby seems to be developing normally. Ultrasound tests indicate the baby will probably be a girl. Cheryl convinces James to name their daughter Angela. Cheryl and James await Angela's birth. ■

These two vignettes describe two very different situations into which babies will be born. One is planned and optimal. The other is by chance and at risk for a variety of reasons. This chapter discusses the importance of planning for a family, of good health in both parents, and of quality prenatal care throughout the pregnancy in promoting the optimal development of young children.

## THE PRESENCE OR ABSENCE OF CHOICE IN PARENTING

During the 1960s, several events stimulated a great deal of research on the early years of life. The translation of Piaget's (1952) work indicated that the early years of life are critical in the development of intelligence. Benjamin Bloom's (1964) research on human intelligence revealed that the capacity for the development of intellectual potential is greatest during the first three years of life. The studies of J. McVicker Hunt (1961) documented the importance of environments and early experience in the development of intelligence.

This interest in the early years of life encompasses the study of the development and behavior of infants at birth and even before, and is demonstrated by the publication of many research articles on infants in journals such as *Infant Behavior and Development* and the *Infant and Mental Health Journal*. The research findings have increased awareness of the importance of what happens before pregnancy, during pregnancy, and in the early years of life to long-term development. Consequently, many adults consider the choice of having a child a serious decision, one that entails education and preparation before the baby is born and even before conception.

According to the Carnegie Task Force on Meeting the Needs of Young Children (Carnegie Corporation, 1994), the United States has one of the highest rates of unintended pregnancy in the industrialized world. Fifty-six percent of all pregnancies are unplanned. This report also indicates that women with unintended pregnancies are also less likely to reduce or cease smoking, obtain **prenatal care,** or see that their infants receive immunizations. Research also indicates that the potential for child abuse and neglect, low birthweight, and infant mortality is greater for children who were unplanned than for those who were actively planned (Zuravin, 1987).

*prenatal:*
*the time from conception until birth, an average of 266 days or 38 weeks*

Increased recognition of the long-term emotional and financial commitment to child rearing, the availability of natural and artificial methods of birth control, and the growing social acceptance of small, one-child, or no-children families have provided many options for family planning. Ideally, the prospective mother and father will both decide they want to become parents because they (1) enjoy children, (2) want to share their love and lives with children as they continue to grow and mature, and (3) are committed to providing opportunities for their children to become well-adjusted and productive members of society (Earls & Carlson, 1993).

Unfortunately, many children are conceived under less than desirable circumstances. The relationship between the mother and father may be casual or unstable rather than based on a loving, supportive commitment. Many people may not realize the extent of responsibility involved in parenting. Others have children in an attempt to satisfy their own emotional needs, to please parents, or in response to pressure from friends. People who fail to take parenting seriously or examine their motives for becoming parents are often frustrated and disappointed with the expense and the loss of flexibility, privacy, and freedom. If their lives are already stressful, a child adds to the pressure. The result is unhappy parents whose children do not feel wanted or loved. Children in these families can become victims of neglect or physical and emotional abuse. Overwhelmed parents often fail to introduce their children to the excitement of learning about the world as they grow and develop. These factors can set the stage for at-risk children, children who fail to develop and learn in optimal ways.

Conversations with parents who are considered excellent mothers and fathers indicate that while they believe parenting brings many joys, it is also the most challenging and demanding job in the world. Becoming competent parents requires commitment and education. For the most part, good parents do not just happen, and the decision to have a child should not be made lightly. It is a long-term commitment requiring emotional maturity and adequate financial resources. The Carnegie Task Force on Meeting the Needs of Young Children (Carnegie Corporation, 1994, p. 26) determined that prospective parents would benefit from education, services, and support in three key areas: planned childbearing, prenatal care and support, and parent education and support.

## SOCIOCULTURAL AND ECONOMIC FACTORS

A number of sociocultural and economic factors affect the quality of life for newborn children and their families. Some of these include teenage pregnancy, the number and spacing of children in the family, cultural differences in prenatal care, and family income. A number of these factors are common to all cultural and economic groups. For example, teenage pregnancy transcends virtually all social and economic groups. In addition, a comprehensive analysis of the literature (Frymier, 1992) revealed that academic failure is precipitated by personal pain, family tragedy, family socioeconomic situation, and family instability.

## TEENAGE PARENTING

Many children today are born to adolescents, some younger than 12 years. This epidemic of "children having children" has become one of the major concerns of a number of groups, including the Children's Defense Fund. The Carnegie Task Force on Meeting the Needs of Young Children (Carnegie Corporation, 1994) revealed the following information about teenage pregnancy:

- Eighty percent of teenage pregnancies are unplanned.

- From 1985 to 1990, public costs related to adolescent childbearing totaled $120 billion. More than $48 billion could have been saved had the mothers been at least 20 years of age.

- The children of teenage parents are more apt to have poor health, have reduced performance in school, experience behavioral problems, and become adolescent parents themselves.

*fetus:*
*the developing human from 9 weeks after conception until birth*

Children of teenage parents are often at risk for a number of reasons. Many teenagers eat a poorly balanced diet, and good nutrition is critical to the development of a healthy baby. Smoking or drug abuse by a pregnant teenager can also threaten the development of the **fetus**. Many teenagers do not receive prenatal care for a variety of reasons. Biological immaturity of the developing teenager can also contribute to the onset of complications during pregnancy (Children's Defense Fund, 1994).

According to Children's Defense Fund data (1994), many teenage mothers do not marry the fathers of their babies. Teenagers often do not understand the reproductive process and lack reliable information about birth control. Some teenage girls want a baby to provide them with the love they feel they have never received from their parents, but they do not understand that it is very difficult to be a single parent. At times, the father may want to be involved with his baby, but lack of job security may prevent the couple from marrying. Thus, many teenage mothers must rely on their parents for social and economic support. Often the parents of teenage girls resent having to sacrifice their time, financial resources, and jobs to help care for their grandchildren. These grandparents may also be caring for their own aging parents. The end result is that many teenage mothers and their children become dependent on public assistance.

To reduce the rate of teenage pregnancy, the Children's Defense Fund and other groups are helping to make teenagers aware of the risks and realities of teenage pregnancy. They are encouraging teenagers to postpone pregnancy through abstinence or the practice of safe sex. Teenagers need to be helped to understand the quality-of-life issues related to adolescent pregnancy. They need to understand that delaying parenthood by completing schooling and seeking job training and improved economic opportunities provides long-term benefits. In the event of pregnancy, teenagers are being made aware of the importance of good prenatal care. A number of programs have been implemented to encourage teenage girls to complete their high school education by providing on-site child care (Children's Defense Fund, 1989, p. 96).

Research suggests that teenage mothers who stay in school, limit the number of additional children, and have a successful marriage are similar to mothers who had their first child in their twenties or later (Furstenburg, Brooks-Gunn, and Chase-Lansdale, 1989). However, children of teenage mothers show reduced cognitive development, lower school achievement, and higher rates of school dropout. They also demonstrate less self-control and more drug use and delinquency (Nord, Moore, Morrison, Brown, and Myers, 1992).

## SIZE OF FAMILY

Another sociocultural factor is the number of children already in the family and their ages relative to the anticipated baby. Some child development experts suggest a spacing of three years between children as optimal for effective parenting and child rearing (Dunn, 1984; Dunn & Kendrick, 1982a,b). If there are several young children quite close in age, the addition of an infant can impose additional stress on the family, since caring for and nurturing young children is demanding and time consuming. While some parents can handle a large family with children close in age, others cannot.

## ATTITUDES OF THE EXTENDED FAMILY

Another sociocultural factor affecting prospective parents is the attitudes of extended family and friends. The responses of family members toward the pregnancy also influence the perceptions and feelings of the prospective father and mother. Unsolicited advice and "information" can encourage and support or create anxiety about approaching parenthood (Shapiro, 1987).

## ECONOMIC CONSIDERATIONS IN HAVING A CHILD

Many parents probably believe they are less financially secure than they would like to be, but the cost of adequately clothing and feeding a child should be considered when making a decision about having a baby. Can the family's financial resources realistically support the child, or will the addition of a child create an undue economic hardship? Ideally, these questions should be considered in family planning. Families that are too large for the financial resources available can lead to stress and resentment in parents, and the children come to feel they are not wanted and are a burden to their parents (Garbarino, 1977).

In addition, lack of adequate economic resources can adversely affect the prenatal health care of the mother and the developing child. Unfortunately, within American society there are many families who do lack access to adequate nutrition and prenatal care. While some programs, such as WIC (Women, Infants, and Children), provide milk and other essential foods to low-income pregnant women and new mothers, their infants, and their young children, they do not serve all eligible people. People are often unaware of medical services, and those services that are available may be underfunded and understaffed.

The consequences of poor nutrition and poor prenatal care are reflected in babies who have **low birthweight**. If these at-risk babies survive, the financial cost of possible extended hospital care and the social cost of long-term developmental

*low birthweight:*
*a weight at birth of less*
*than 5½ pounds or*
*2,500 grams*

problems are major concerns. Solutions to these problems include establishing a network of services that will provide appropriate education and health care to families during and after pregnancy.

## EMOTIONAL AND PSYCHOLOGICAL ASPECTS OF PREPARING FOR PARENTHOOD

Ideally, the newborn child has a mother and a father whose relationship is stable, mature, and based on mutual love and support. In reality, not all marriages are so fortunate, and the idea that a baby can help a troubled marriage is a myth. The demands of adjusting to another family member may only add to an already stressful situation. Couples who have an unstable relationship are wise to seek professional counseling before they decide to become parents.

Prospective parents react individually to pregnancy depending on the choices and the social and economic factors discussed earlier. Some prospective parents feel elated and overjoyed; others are fearful or resentful. Mixed emotions are not uncommon.

### REACTION OF THE PROSPECTIVE MOTHER

*trimester:*
*the first, second, or*
*third three months of*
*pregnancy*

Anthony and Benedek (1975) propose that future mothers go through three emotional stages at either a conscious or unconscious level. During the first **trimester,** or three months of pregnancy, the mother-to-be finds it difficult to accept the idea of a fetus within her body. She begins to think about the impending change in her lifestyle and family structure. These concerns, coupled with hormonal changes, can create mood swings. During the second trimester, the future mother begins to think of the baby as a separate being. In the third trimester, she comes to terms with the actual birth process and impending motherhood. Anthony and Benedek (1975) also indicate that developmental conflicts during the mother's life are often relived during pregnancy. These past events influence a woman's perspective of motherhood and her attitude toward her child. If these conflicts arise, they can best be resolved through professional counseling.

Some studies indicate that maternal stress can have adverse effects in terms of medical complications and birth abnormalities (Omer & Everly, 1988). Nevertheless, a strong social support system can help prevent prenatal complications.

### REACTION OF THE PROSPECTIVE FATHER

In the past, attention has been focused primarily on the prospective mother, but recently the emotional reactions and feelings of the prospective father have also been examined. Prospective fathers are now observed to be more involved in preparing for the birth, helping with the birth, and sharing in the child care (Shapiro, 1987). However, their common feelings of anxiety, anger, sadness, and fear are often viewed as unacceptable. A study by Shapiro (1987) discovered that at least 40 percent of prospective fathers had some major fears and concerns, including (1) queasiness about the actual birth process, (2) concern about increased financial responsibility, (3) feeling put down by obstetrical-gynecological staff, (4) questioning about their paternity, (5) fear of loss of spouse and/or child, (6) feeling left out as the mother-to-be begins turning inward and bonding with the growing fetus, and (7) an increased awareness of life and death in general. The study indicated that these concerns generally were not communicated with others, but when future fathers did share their concerns with their wives, the marriage relationship strengthened and the couples felt closer. Shapiro suggests that these natural and normal feelings need to be recognized by the prospective father, his wife, the family, and society in general.

The prospective mother's emotional and psychological states affect the prospective father, and vice versa. Thus, the emotional reactions of both mother and father need to be acknowledged and accepted, and if special problems develop, professional counseling is advised. As will be discussed in Chapter 6, the emotional climate created by the prospective parents' relationship will be largely responsible for the psychological well-being of the newborn child.

## PRENATAL DEVELOPMENT

You have probably noticed that all children differ from one another in the way they look and the way they act. These differences are due to the fact that everyone has a different set of inherited characteristics, or **heredity**. In addition, everyone has a different **environment**, that is, different relationships, physical settings, and educational experiences. Even within the same family, everyone has a different set of inherited characteristics as well as different environmental experiences. Children are born in different order, and as new family members are added, relationships change.

For many years, people have debated the influence of heredity and environment on the development of an individual. In certain situations, the influence of heredity or environment may be obvious, but more often behavior is best explained by the combination or interaction of both heredity and environment. In any case, optimal development of an individual depends on both healthy genetic traits and a healthy environment (Mange & Mange, 1990).

## CHROMOSOMES AND GENES

At conception, the sperm from the father penetrates the egg, or ovum, from the mother. The ovum can be fertilized by a sperm approximately every 28 days during a period of about 24 hours. At the point of fertilization, the **chromosomes** of the mother and father unite. Chromosomes are located in the nucleus of a cell and contain thousands of **genes**. This combination of genes from the mother and

*heredity:*
*the inherited characteristics of humans carried by genes*

*environment:*
*the experiences, conditions, objects, and people that directly or indirectly influence the development and behavior of a child*

*chromosomes:*
*ordered groups of genes within the nucleus of a cell*

*genes:*
*molecules of DNA that store and transmit the characteristics of past generations*

the father determines a person's genetic potential, or **genotype**. Genotype also includes **recessive genes**. These genes are not evident if they are paired with dominant genes. Genes, which are composed of **DNA**, make the blueprint that codes the complex information that causes the development of tissues, organs, and physiological functions (Thompson & Thompson, 1986).

## CAUSES OF CONGENITAL MALFORMATIONS

At times, numerical or structural abnormalities of chromosomes can result in incomplete or imperfect cell formation. Many of these abnormalities result in spontaneous **abortion** early in the pregnancy. If the baby is born, these defective chromosomes can result in **congenital malformations** and/or mental retardation. These physical abnormalities may be obvious at birth, or they may be internal. Table 3.1 provides a brief overview of some of the more common congenital malformations.

One example of numerical chromosome abnormality is Down's syndrome. Down's syndrome characteristics vary in degree but usually include mental retardation, certain physical characteristics, and congenital heart defects. Other disorders associated with abnormal genes include cystic fibrosis, Tay-Sachs disease, thalassemia, dwarfing condition, and sickle cell anemia. These disorders can be evident when both parents' chromosomes carry the defective gene. Thus, the baby receives an abnormal gene from each parent.

Some congenital malformations result when two or more combinations of abnormal genes and environmental agents cause a defect. Spina bifida (an opening in the spinal column), anencephaly (little or no brain development), cleft lip and palate, club feet, congenital heart disease, and dislocation of the hips are some of the disorders caused by genetic and environmental factors (Jones, 1988).

Another condition that can cause congenital malformation and even stillbirth is the Rh factor. The **Rh factor** (detected in the rhesus monkey after which this condition is named) is caused when the fetus of a mother who has Rh negative blood inherits Rh positive blood from the father. Usually this condition does not harm the first baby. At present there are two types of treatment for the Rh factor. The first involves changing the blood of the fetus in the uterus before birth or immediately after. In the second, a serum, RhoGam, is administered to the mother during pregnancy or within several days after the delivery of her first Rh baby. This treatment prevents the formation of antibodies.

## GENETIC COUNSELING AND TESTING

**Genetic counseling** can be helpful to couples whose background indicates possible genetic defects or whose fetus has been diagnosed as at risk. As indicated, problems can occur if a child is born to parents who both carry the same harmful trait.

While genetic counselors cannot accurately predict if a child will be born with a disorder, they can provide information to couples, who can then decide whether to have a child. In situations where conception has already occurred, various tests

TABLE 3.1
Common Genetic Diseases and Conditions

| Disease or Condition | Description | Mode of Transmission | Incidence | Prognosis | Prenatal Detection | Carrier Detection |
|---|---|---|---|---|---|---|
| Cleft palate, cleft lip | The two sides of the upper lip or the palate are not joined | Causes include genetic defects, prenatal injury, drugs, and malnutrition | 1 in 700 births | Correctable by surgery | Yes | No |
| Cystic fibrosis | Lack of enzyme causes mucous obstruction, especially in the lungs and digestive tract | Recessive gene | 1 in 21,000 live births in U.S.; most common in people of Northern European descent | Few victims survive to adulthood | No (possible in near future) | No |
| Diabetes melitus (juvenile form) | Deficient metabolism of sugar because body does not produce adequate insulin | Thought to be polygenic | 1 in 25 to 40 of all diabetics | Fatal if untreated; controllable by insulin and a restricted diet | No | No |
| Down's syndrome | Physical and intellectual retardation; distinctive physical appearance | Chromosomal abnormality; extra chromosome 21 | 1 in 600 to 700 births | Moderate to severe mental retardation; eye, ear, and heart problems | Yes | Possible in cases of chromosomal rearrangement (only 5% of cases) |
| Hemophilia (bleeding disease) | Blood does not clot readily | X-linked gene; also spontaneous mutation | 1 in 21,500 live births of males | Possible crippling and death from internal bleeding; transfusions are used to ameliorate effects | No | Yes |
| Huntington's chorea | Deterioration of the central nervous system and body in middle age | Dominant gene | Rare | Fatal | Yes | Yes |
| Klinefelter's syndrome | Affects males; failure to mature sexually at adolescence; sterility | Chromosomal abnormality; an extra X chromosome (XXY) | 1 in 1,000 white males in U.S. | Emotional and social problems; treated by administering testosterone | Yes | No |

TABLE 3.1
*(continued)*

| Disease or Condition | Description | Mode of Transmission | Incidence | Prognosis | Prenatal Detection | Carrier Detection |
|---|---|---|---|---|---|---|
| Muscular dystrophy (Duchenne's type) | Weakening and wasting away of the muscles | X-linked gene | 1 in 200,000 males under the age of 20 | Crippling; often fatal by age of 20 | Yes | Sometimes |
| Neural tube defects (anencephaly and spina bifida) | In anencephaly, part of the brain and skull is missing; in spina bifida, part of the spine is not closed over | Uncertain | 1 in 1,000 live births in U.S. | Babies with anencephaly die shortly after birth. Those with spina bifida may survive with surgery; their prognosis depends on the defect's severity | Yes | No |
| Phenylketonuria (PKU) | Lack of enzyme causes abnormal digestion of certain proteins | Recessive gene | 1 in 15,000 white births; lower in blacks and Ashkenazi Jews | Mental retardation and hyperactivity; controllable in many through diet | Yes | Often |
| Sickle-cell anemia | Abnormal red blood cells | Recessive gene | 1 in 625 births among U.S. blacks | Possible heart and kidney failure; many survive into adulthood | Yes | Yes |
| Tay-Sachs disease | Lack of an enzyme causes waste build-up in the brain | Recessive gene | 1 in 3,600 for Ashkenazi Jews in U.S. | Neurological degeneration leading to death before the age of 4 | Yes | Yes |
| Thalassemia (Cooley's anemia) | Abnormal red blood cells | Recessive gene | 1 in 100 births in populations from subtropical and tropical areas of Europe, Africa, and Asia | Listlessness, enlarged liver and spleen, occasionally death; treatable by blood transfusions | Yes | Yes |
| Turner's syndrome | Affects females; short stature, webbed neck, and broad chest; failure to produce the hormone estrogen; sterility | Chromosomal abnormality; single X chromosome (XO) | 1 in 10,000 female births | Physical defect may lead to social and emotional problems; treated with hormone therapy | Yes | No |

can provide information regarding the condition of the fetus. While this information cannot always predict the extent of the disorder, it may be helpful to parents in making the very difficult decision about whether to complete or terminate the pregnancy (American Academy of Pediatrics Committee on Genetics, 1994).

There are several techniques for determining genetic defects. Testing the blood of the prospective parents can help determine several possible problems. The gene for sickle cell anemia is present in 8 percent of African Americans. Tay-Sachs, an enzyme deficiency seen more commonly in Ashkenazi Jewish descendants, causes neurological degeneration and early death. Blood analysis can determine the presence of both sickle cell anemia and Tay-Sachs. Another blood test, the **alphafetoprotein test**, is used to detect disorders in the brain or spinal column. Another procedure, **amniocentesis**, can aid in identifying all chromosomal disorders and over 100 biochemical disorders. This procedure involves analysis of the fetal cells in the amniotic fluid from the uterus. Amniocentesis is recommended when the mother is of advanced age or family history indicates the fetus may be at risk. It is usually done approximately 14 to 16 weeks into the pregnancy, when there is sufficient amniotic fluid surrounding the fetus. Analysis takes about two weeks, and the results are sometimes not available until the fifth month of pregnancy (Vogel & Motulsky, 1979).

A third method of determining chromosomal disorders is the **chorionic villus test (CVT)**. A sample of cells is taken from the hairlike projections (villi) on tissue (chorion) in the placenta. The CVT has some advantages over amniocentesis, as it can be done as early as the ninth week of pregnancy and the results are usually available in several days.

A fourth technique helpful in determining possible problems with the fetus is ultrasound. Ultrasound exams are often used to confirm results of the tests just described. The uterus is scanned with high-frequency sound waves to create an outline of the fetus.

The Human Genome Project identifies genes associated with specific genetic disorders. The information gleaned from this research will allow scrutiny of preembryos for a wider range of physical conditions from rare, inherited ailments to more common diseases such as cancer. This process involves the identification of a gene in the cell of a preembryo through a technique called **polymerase chain reaction (PCR)**. If the PCR of a single cell from the eight-cell preembryo results in many copies of a target DNA sequence, the preembryo has the disease-causing gene. This process currently is very expensive and sometimes has to be repeated before a definitive diagnosis can be made. As a result, PCR will not become readily available in the near future.

Questions of medical ethics have arisen regarding who should actually decide whether a disorder is pervasive enough to prevent a birth. In addition, the identification of the responsible gene does not indicate how severely an individual will be affected. Also, treatments for some genetic disorders are being developed so rapidly that PCR may become obsolete. Nevertheless, PCR can provide information to prospective parents to help them make the decision to avoid passing on a genetically based disease.

While these techniques can help detect problems, a number of disorders cannot be determined before birth. Nevertheless, recent medical advances provide new

*alphafetoprotein test (AFP):*
*a blood test that can identify disorders in the brain or spinal column in the fetus*

*amniocentesis:*
*a technique that involves extracting amniotic fluid from the uterus for the purpose of detecting all chromosomal and over 100 biomedical disorders*

*chorionic villus test (CVT):*
*a test that analyzes samples of the hairlike projections (chorionic villi) of tissue in the placenta to determine chromosomal disorders (can be done earlier than amniocentesis)*

*polymerase chain reaction (PCR):*
*the process used to identify disease-causing genes in an eight-cell preembryo*

intervention procedures for some conditions. Blood transfusions, special diets, fetal surgery, and other treatments before and after birth can greatly reduce the severity of some conditions. Advances in genetics and genetic programming will continue to provide more information and improved treatments for these and other disorders.

## STAGES OF PRENATAL DEVELOPMENT

**Implantation Stage: Conception to Week 3 of Pregnancy.** The fertilized cell of a developing human is called a **zygote**. The **gender** of the zygote is determined at conception by the sperm type. In simple terms, if the sperm cell carries an X chromosome, the zygote will develop into a female; if the sperm cell carries a Y chromosome, the zygote will develop into a male.

During the week after fertilization, the zygote has traveled to the Fallopian tube, where cell division begins. By about the fifth or sixth day, cell division has created two different parts. Inside is the cell mass that gradually develops into a human being. The complex outside cell mass becomes the **placenta**. The placenta transmits nutrients from the mother's bloodstream to the developing embryo and fetus. The placenta also filters out waste from the fetus through the mother's bloodstream. By the end of the second week, the zygote has moved through the Fallopian tube and become implanted in the uterus.

Sometimes a zygote divides into two identical halves that develop separately, creating **identical twins**. These monozygotic, or one zygote twins will look alike, since they have the same genetic code. If two ova (eggs) are fertilized by two sperm, the result is **fraternal** (dizygotic, or two zygotes) **twins**. These twins do not share the same genetic code.

**Embryonic Stage: 3 to 8 Weeks.** The **embryonic stage** is critical to the healthy development of the fetus. It is during the first eight weeks that the major organ systems develop. Exposure to **teratogens**, such as chemical substances, viruses, alcohol, drugs, or other environmental factors, can cause congenital malformations or birth defects.

**Fetal Stage: Week 9 to Conclusion of Pregnancy.** By week 9, the embryo has a humanlike appearance and is now a fetus. The **fetal stage** continues until birth. During the fetal stage, growth and differentiation in organs and tissues takes place. In addition, the weight and size of the fetus increase considerably.

See Figure 3.3 for a general description of growth from fertilization to birth.

## QUALITY PRENATAL CARE

It is important that the expectant mother seek prenatal care as soon as she suspects she is pregnant. Signs of pregnancy include one or several of the following symptoms: a missed menstrual period, a need for more rest, nausea, and swollen, sensitive breasts. As mentioned previously, the first eight weeks of pregnancy are

---

**zygote:**
*the first cell resulting from the fertilization of the ovum by the sperm*

**gender:**
*the maleness or femaleness of the zygote as determined by the kind of sperm fertilizing the ovum (Y sperm—genetically male; X sperm—genetically female)*

**placenta:**
*the organ that is attached to the wall of the uterus and transmits nutrients from the mother to the embryo/fetus and filters wastes from the embryo/fetus to the mother*

**identical twins:**
*twins whose development began when the zygote splits into two identical halves, thus ensuring that both twins have the identical genetic code*

**fraternal twins:**
*twins whose development began by the fertilization of two ova (eggs) by two sperms, causing both twins to have different genetic codes*

**embryonic stage:**
*weeks 3 through 8 of pregnancy, during which the major organ systems are formed*

**teratogens:**
*environmental factors, such as viruses and chemical substances, that can cause abnormalities in the developing embryo or fetus*

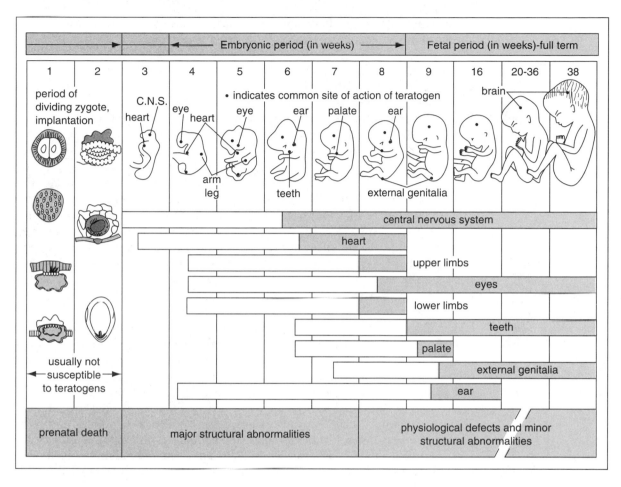

**Figure 3.3**
There are critical periods during fetal growth for the development of each major body part and system. (From *Before We Are Born*, 4th ed., by Dr. Keith L. Moore and Persand, T.V.N., © 1993. Philadelphia: Sauders. Reprinted by Permission.)

critical to the developing fetus, since this is the time that all major organ systems develop. Early detection of problems is important in ensuring the development of a healthy baby.

At the first prenatal visit, medical personnel will run one of several available tests to determine pregnancy. An examination provides basic information about the overall health of the mother-to-be. Blood tests are taken to determine if the prospective mother is anemic, has syphilis, or has had rubella, or if there could be Rh blood incompatibility. Questions about the prospective mother's and father's past medical history, family history, and personal health habits attempt to identify nutritional state, possible substance abuse, and the need for genetic screening. Prospective mothers are usually counseled about the importance of proper diet and avoiding drugs and X rays, and are advised to check with their doctors before

*fetal stage:*
*the stage that begins after the first eight weeks of pregnancy and continues until birth*

taking any medication. It is important that prospective mothers have medical checkups at regular intervals throughout pregnancy.

## NUTRITION

Research demonstrates that mothers-to-be at all economic levels may not eat the nutritious diet necessary to ensure the healthy development of a baby. Daily calorie intake from junk food and/or alcohol can endanger the baby's development. Likewise, excessive dieting and overuse of vitamins can put the developing fetus at risk (Wyden, 1971). Balanced diets of proteins, complex carbohydrates, grains, fruits and vegetables, and dairy products should be a priority of every prospective mother. See Figure 14.3 for information on the USDA Food Guide Pyramid.

*critical period:*
*a time of physiological and/or psychological sensitivity, during which the normal development of a major organ or structural system must take place or permanent damage to body structure and/or behavior will result*

Werner's investigation (1979) documented that undernutrition can interfere with the healthy development of the fetal central nervous system during two **critical periods** of development. The first major period of brain growth occurs between the tenth and twentieth weeks of pregnancy. The second important period for brain growth takes place from the twentieth week of prenatal development to four to six months after birth (Winick, 1981).

Undernutrition during these times can impair brain growth, which ultimately affects intellectual performance and physical development (Winick, 1976). If undernutrition occurs at these critical times, young children do not catch up with their peers, even if provided with nutritional diets later on. However, there is some evidence (e.g., Tanner, 1973) to suggest that children who were deprived during other than critical times can catch up on growth if they are fed proper diets. Dietary deficiencies can also cause anemia, poorly developed bones and teeth, physical abnormalities, low birthweight, and complications during pregnancy and labor. Nutritional and diet disorders such as **anorexia** and **bulimia,** which occur most often in teenage girls, can adversely affect the development of the fetus, particularly late in pregnancy.

*anorexia:*
*a severe disorder, usually seen in teenage girls, characterized by self-starvation*

*bulimia:*
*a severe disorder, usually seen in teenage girls, characterized by binging and then self-induced vomiting*

Recent research among the grandchildren of Dutch women who were starved during World War II indicates that the effects of malnutrition during the third semester of pregnancy led to small babies. When these children became adults, their offspring were of normal size. However, when these babies matured into women, they produced underweight infants. In other words, the grandmothers' malnutrition was programmed in utero so that the grandchildren would be affected. This research suggests that long-term effects of malnutrition may appear over several generations or more (Diamond, 1990).

## CHEMICAL SUBSTANCES

Just as malnutrition can have delayed effects on offspring, delayed effects can occur in the children of women who used certain drugs (Tyler, 1992). For example, delayed effects of diethylstilbestrol (DES), a synthetic hormone used to prevent miscarriage, can appear in the adolescent female children of users in the form of vaginal abnormalities and cancer of the cervix (Nevin, 1988).

Recent research indicates that other substances can cause genetic abnormalities in sperm leading to permanent defects, including heart abnormalities and mental retardation. Many researchers conjecture that environmental toxins such as lead and industrial pollution may play a significant role in the 60 to 80 percent of birth defects of unknown cause (Needleman, 1992). There is also some evidence that alterations in sperm may cause childhood cancer and learning disorders. Consequently, health and occupational safety officials are beginning to reevaluate safety regulations for the purpose of extending them to men whose jobs may be considered harmful to sperm (Davis, 1989, Merewood, 1991).

In general, use of chemical substances should be avoided during pregnancy. Use of any medications should first be cleared with a physician. However, certain medications prescribed by the physician may be necessary for the mother's well-being during pregnancy.

Use of chemical substances during pregnancy can contribute to a number of abnormalities in the developing fetus. Several factors contribute to the degree of the abnormality, including (1) the amount of the substance, (2) the stage of development of the embryo or fetus, and (3) the amount of time the prospective mother was exposed to or used the substance.

Various substances appear to have the potential to harm the developing embryo or fetus (Yaffee, 1980). These include some drugs used in the treatment of cancer, thyroid malfunction, the common cold (tetracycline), emotional stress (Valium, Librium, Miltown, phenobarbital), seizures (Dilantin, phenobarbital), and acne (Accutane). Caffeine (found in coffee, tea, cola drinks, chocolate, and certain medications), if taken in excess, may produce problems in the developing fetus, particularly if accompanied by cigarette smoking (Linn et al., 1982).

From numerous reports and media attention, there is no doubt that smoking during pregnancy increases the risk of spontaneous abortion, fetal and newborn deaths, and smaller babies. Interestingly, there is some evidence (e.g., Evans, 1981) that smoking on the part of the father-to-be can produce abnormal sperm and increased death and birth defects compared to nonsmoking fathers. Thus, the overwhelming evidence suggests that it is best for the healthy development of the baby that the prospective mother and father do not smoke.

Many physicians also advise prospective mothers not to consume alcoholic beverages. Studies indicate that alcohol abuse can contribute to **fetal alcohol syndrome (FAS)**. FAS can cause mental retardation, physical deformities of the limbs, muscle damage, heart disorders, dysfunction of the central nervous system, miscarriages, sleep disturbances in the newborn, and abnormalities of the face and head (Harlap & Shlono, 1980; Rosctt et al., 1979). One study (Streissgoth, Martin, Barr, & Sandman, 1984) examined 4-year-old children of moderate (one glass of wine or beer per day) drinkers and nondrinkers. Children of the moderate drinkers had longer response times and shorter attention spans than children of the nondrinkers. At present, no safe level of alcohol consumption has been determined for pregnant women. Several drinks taken at a critical time may cause severe damage to an unborn baby. Therefore, it is best that all pregnant women refrain from consuming alcohol.

*fetal alcohol syndrome (FAS):*
*the physical and mental abnormalities found in babies whose mothers consumed excessive amounts of alcohol during pregnancy*

Burgess and Streissgoth (1992) suggest that to meet the needs of children with FAS, it is necessary to "confront the issues at home, classroom, school and district levels" (p. 28). These efforts include the following steps:

- Include (nonjudgmental) questions about prenatal alcohol and drug exposure in the health screening process.
- Develop a plan for distribution and use of information gathered from health screening.
- Provide educational opportunities for distribution and use of information gathered from health screening.
- Provide educational opportunities for district personnel regarding FAS and fetal drug effects.
- Develop a referral system for students identified as having possible alcohol- or drug-related problems.
- Develop a districtwide plan for meeting the needs of students with known or suspected effects. (Burgess & Streissgoth, 1992, p. 28)

Substance abuse is also dangerous to the developing fetus and can cause fetal death, premature birth, and retarded fetal growth. At birth, these children face severe symptoms of withdrawal from the drug. Possible long-term effects include hyperactivity, brain damage, and other behavioral and physical abnormalities (Householder et al., 1982; Vorhees & Mollnow, 1987).

The harmful effects of maternal use of cocaine on children is causing increasing concern among educators. Symptoms include attention deficit disorder, hyperactivity, poor coordination, a low stimulation tolerance level, unpredictable behavior, poor memory, and indications of drug abuse in the home (Gregorchik, 1992).

However, Tyler (1992) cautions that early childhood professionals must be careful when referring to children with prenatal drug exposure as "drug babies" or "crack babies." While drug exposure creates high-risk developmental concerns for children, environmental influences determine long-range outcomes. A stable and nurturing environment can make all the difference for an at-risk child. Depending on the environment, drug-related effects lie on a broad continuum from minimal to severe. Griffith (1992) reassures teachers that the problems of "crack babies" are problems that creative teachers have handled in the past. He emphasizes that the most successful tool teachers can use for developing intervention strategies is the behavior log and that teachers need to help children develop new coping strategies before eliminating existing ones.

## OTHER TERATOGENS

**rubella:**
*a virus that can cause birth disorders if the mother contracts it during the first three months of pregnancy (also known as* German measles*)*

Physicians also usually caution mothers-to-be not to have X rays during pregnancy and to be aware of environmental pollutants that may affect the developing fetus. Viruses can also cross the placenta and infect the fetus. If **rubella**, also known as *German measles*, is contracted during the first trimester, serious birth defects such as mental retardation, blindness, and deafness can result. A blood test can determine if the mother-to-be has had rubella. If she has, antibodies will prevent the fetus from being affected if she is exposed to rubella again. Rubella inoculation of children is required in all states.

Physicians also may ask prospective mothers if they have cats as pets. **Toxoplasmosis** is a parasitic infection caused by contact with cat droppings or raw or undercooked meat. While this disease does not affect prospective mothers, it can cause serious damage to the central nervous system or eyes of the fetus. Pregnant women who have cats are advised not to change litter boxes, to seek innoculation, and to eat well-cooked meat.

Other infectious diseases that can affect pregnancy include mumps, rubeola (red measles), chicken pox, polio, syphilis, and **acquired immunodeficiency syndrome (AIDS)**. Syphilis can be detected by a blood test, which is required in many states. This disease can be treated successfully, even during pregnancy. AIDS in babies seems to be caused by the presence of the virus in the uterus, with the first indications usually appearing around 6 months of age. The symptoms are similar to a number of diseases, making accurate diagnosis difficult. Most babies live five to eight months after the symptoms first appear (Minkoff et al., 1987). At present, there is no known cure for AIDS.

Current estimates suggest that for every child with AIDS, there are several times as many children infected with **human immunodeficiency virus (HIV)** (Seidel, 1992). HIV attacks the central nervous system during prenatal development and results in neuropathological deviations in cognitive, motor, psychosocial, and sensory/perceptual development. Frequently the appearance of developmental delays is one of the first signs of the neurological abnormalities associated with a child with HIV infection. HIV has become the greatest infectious cause of retardation in young children.

Seidel (1992, p. 40) cautions that important modifications to the usual special education procedures are necessary when dealing with children with HIV infection and their families. These include the following:

* Records containing HIV-related information should be kept confidential.

* Diagnostic reevaluations to detect changes in development should be made three times a year for children up to age 4 and twice a year for older children.

* Procedures that permit flexibility in providing a variety of educational and programmatic services need to be established.

* According to law, no school employee has the "right to know" about a student's HIV status, and parental consent must be given when school personnel need to be consulted in decisions regarding treatment. School attorneys need to be involved in the establishment of disclosure procedures.

* Special inservice training should be available to teachers who work with children infected with HIV.

The diagnosis of HIV infection creates a set of complex dynamics for the child, the family, and those who provide services. Psychological reactions include denial, anger, guilt, anxiety, and distress. A primary concern for families is confidentiality of HIV diagnosis. If the child's health status is revealed, jobs, homes, access to care, and treatment options may be jeopardized. Children over age 3 fall under the protection of the Individuals with Disabilities Education Act (PL 101-476) of

*toxoplasmosis:
an infection that can be transmitted from cat droppings or raw meat to the mother and to the fetus or embryo via the placenta, causing birth disorders*

*acquired immunodeficiency syndrome (AIDS):
a virus that can be transmitted from the mother to the fetus/embryo via the placenta; attacks the immune system, causing death from illnesses that the immune system cannot prevent*

*human immunodeficiency virus (HIV):
a virus that attacks the central nervous system and is particularly harmful to the fetus when contracted through the infected mother*

1990. Infants and toddlers receive support under Part H of the IDEA amendments of 1991 (PL 102-119). Part H provides for early intervention programs.

Another incurable disease that can be transmitted across the placenta is genital herpes. Herpes infection is usually transferred to the newborn during the birth process and can cause blindness, brain damage, and even death. Prospective mothers with active herpes are advised not to have vaginal deliveries.

Regular prenatal visits ensure that the mother-to-be will be monitored for **toxemia** of pregnancy and diabetes. Toxemia usually affects women in the last trimester of pregnancy, and the causes are unknown. Symptoms of this condition include high blood pressure, water retention as indicated by swelling of the legs and ankles, and protein in the urine. This disease can cause death in both mother and child, so early detection and treatment are important. Women with diabetes also need monitoring during pregnancy.

*toxemia:*
*a disease of unknown cause that occurs in the last trimester of pregnancy and can cause death to both mother and child*

## PRENATAL LEARNING

In investigating whether learning occurs in utero, DeCasper and Fifer (1980) discovered that infants are able to vary their sucking patterns to activate a recording of their mothers' voices in preference to another woman's voice. In another study (DeCasper & Spence, 1986), mothers read *The Cat in the Hat* to their fetuses twice a day six weeks before the due date. After birth, the infants were read both *The Cat in the Hat* and *The King, the Mice and Cheese*. The infants demonstrated through their sucking that they preferred *The Cat in the Hat*. This study and others suggest that prenatal auditory experiences influence postauditory preferences.

## EDUCATION FOR CHILDBIRTH AND PARENTING

In the past, women had control over where they gave birth and who assisted them. With the increased use of anesthetics to relieve pain, physicians began to play the dominant role in directing the birth process, and fathers were usually relegated to the waiting room. Over a period of time, many parents became frustrated over their lack of involvement in one of the most important events in their lives. In addition, the increasing number of research studies documenting the negative effects of medication during labor and delivery caused increasing concern among many health care professionals (Sepkoski, 1985; Wilson, 1977). Over time, parents and health care professionals became advocates for educated childbirth and for more active involvement of the parents in the pregnancy, delivery, and care of the newborn in the hospital setting.

*Lamaze method:*
*a method developed by Fernand Lamaze that involves training the prospective mother and a partner/coach in breathing and relaxation techniques to be used during labor*

One of the better-known educated childbirth approaches is the **Lamaze method** (Karmel, 1959). The Lamaze technique instructs the mother-to-be and her coach, usually the father-to-be, in various breathing patterns that help to control the pain and discomfort during the different stages of labor. The prospective mother and her coach practice these techniques during the last months of pregnancy.

Prospective parents are given information about the various types of medication and their effects on the fetus and the mother. They are encouraged to discuss their preferred medications with their physicians in advance of delivery. Many Lamaze classes are preceded by a course dealing with general pregnancy and childbirth information. These classes usually occur earlier in the pregnancy and inform the prospective parents about physiological and psychological aspects of pregnancy, childbirth, and parenting.

Some parents-to-be are now opting to have their babies born at home with the assistance of a physician or midwife. While home births provide the prospective parents with more control over the birthing process and can involve family or friends, some risks are involved. If complications arise, the lack of hospital equipment and trained specialists can put mother and infant in danger. In response to consumer demand, many hospitals now provide birthing rooms that allow the mother to remain in one room throughout labor and delivery with husband and family members often present. Birthing rooms usually are furnished in a homelike setting, yet provide all of the necessary medical support services.

Ideally, prospective parents select their obstetrician and hospital with care. An obstetrician who is comfortable with the father's active involvement throughout the pregnancy and who recognizes the value of educated childbirth provides valuable support to the prospective parents. Likewise, a hospital that offers family-involved birthing experiences, allows the father, other children, and close relatives extended visitation privileges, permits the baby to "room in" with the mother, and has classes for new parents on the care and feeding of the newborn provides helpful services to new parents. Such experiences help parents learn about and get to know their baby and thus develop confidence in their parenting abilities.

## THE IMPORTANCE OF PREPARING SIBLINGS FOR THE BIRTH

Preparing brothers and sisters for the arrival of a new baby helps create positive sibling relationships from the beginning. Less jealousy and decreased sibling rivalry later on are the benefits of thoughtful attention to the needs of existing children within the family.

For children younger than 3, parents need to plan some special activities or time spent alone with them after the birth of a new brother or sister. Thinking about how and when this will occur can prevent the children from feeling neglected. A doll and various accessories used in the care of young babies can help during times when parents are busy with the newborn. Older brother and sister can feed, bathe, and change the baby just as mother or father does. Siblings can help in preparing the baby's room or bed, gathering clothes, and choosing the baby's name.

Some hospitals have special programs for siblings. Prospective brothers and sisters can visit the hospital to see where their mother and the new baby will stay. Hospital staff members talk to the children about what babies are like and what their care entails. Discussion of the range of feelings about being a brother or sister can also help children deal with their emotions.

Careful thought must be given to who will care for the siblings during the mother's hospital stay. Those who care for them need to be nurturant and understanding of their expressions of distress at separation from their mother and other anxieties. Careful planning for siblings can reduce stress for the entire family and promote positive sibling relationships.

## SOCIOCULTURAL PERSPECTIVES

Due to the lack of universal health care, some of the health services described in this chapter have not been available to all socioeconomic groups. The provision of more extensive coverage to all segments of the population will be an ongoing effort in the years to come. As services expand to meet the needs of an increasingly diverse population, programs must be sensitive to the cultural backgrounds of various groups that will use them (Fleishman, no date).

As discussed in the previous chapters, perceptions of what constitutes optimal development, developmental norms, and aberrations in development differ across cultures (New, 1994). Yet the developmental psychology literature still fails to address these variations, possibly because of the belief that people are all basically the same (Rowe, Vazonyi, & Flannery, 1994). Other reasons for not attending to cross-cultural differences include the belief that research and replication of research must be conducted under controlled conditions and the belief that there is one best process of development. A growing awareness of broader cultural interpretations of behavior based on human diversity indicates that future child development literature will include an expanding interpretation of development.

This chapter has addressed a number of issues regarding optimal conditions preceding the birth of a child. Nevertheless, not all children born to advantaged families have advantaged circumstances as adults. Likewise, not all children born into less than desirable settings remain disadvantaged. The existing studies indicate that the forces that create inequality in families are complex and interact in a synergistic process (Garrett et al., 1994). Werner and Smith (1982) studied adolescents who were classified as resilient. These children seemed to have been "protected" by the following factors: good temperament, small family size, positive parenting patterns, a relationship with a caring adult other than a parent, low levels of family conflict, fewer stressful experiences, and access to counseling and remediation services. Werner (1989) also found that early responsibility in caring for a sibling, grandparent, or an ill or incompetent parent was another factor in the lives of resilient adolescents.

In his transcultural study of individual competence, Heath (1977) identified a core set of behaviors including (1) an ability to anticipate consequences; (2) calm and clear thinking; (3) potential fulfillment; (4) orderly, organized approaches to life's problems; (5) predictability; (6) purposefulness; (7) realism; (8) reflectiveness; (9) strong convictions; and (10) implacability. Finally, self-esteem, coupled with the perception of the individual as one who can cope successfully by the family and others in the culture, was important.

Ann and Bill Johnson, like Cheryl Monroe and James, are awaiting the births of their babies. These babies will have been affected by very different sets of circumstances before their births. Chapter 4 will show how these circumstances influence the development of the babies and their family contexts at birth and soon after.

## Role of the Early Childhood Professional

### Working with Families with Young Children

1. Understand how cultural background and parental behaviors and attitudes directly influence the development of the young child even before birth.
2. Understand that behaviors and attitudes of the parents influence development and learning after birth and throughout the early childhood years.
3. Be aware of the challenges and demands of the parenting role.
4. Work with parents to understand the development of young children.
5. Work with young parents in developing appropriate parenting skills.
6. Understand that parents are valuable sources of information about their children and that early childhood professionals must work in partnership with parents if optimal learning and development are to occur in young children.  ■

## KEY TERMS

abortion
acquired immuno-
  deficiency syndrome
  (AIDS)
alphafetoprotein test
  (AFP)
amniocentesis
anorexia
bulimia
chorionic villus test
  (CVT)
chromosomes
congenital
  malformations
critical period

DNA
embryonic stage
environment
fetal alcohol syndrome
fetal stage
fetus
fraternal twins
gender
genes
genetic counseling
genotype
heredity
human immuno-
  deficiency virus (HIV)
identical twins

Lamaze method
low birthweight
placenta
polymerase chain
  reaction (PCR)
prenatal
recessive gene
Rh factor
rubella
teratogens
toxemia
toxoplasmosis
trimester
ultrasound
zygote

## REVIEW STRATEGIES AND ACTIVITIES

1. Review the key terms individually or with a classmate.

2. Interview your classmates who are parents. Ask them to share with you some of the following:
   a. Their reactions upon finding out they were going to be a parent
   b. Their feelings and reactions throughout the pregnancy
   c. Reactions of the baby's other parent and of family and friends
   d. The nature of their prenatal care
   e. The kinds of care their children required at various times: birth, toddlerhood, 2 to 8 years of age
   f. A typical day as a parent
   g. The joys and challenges of becoming a parent
   h. How becoming a parent has changed their lives

3. Find out what support services your community provides to prospective parents (e.g., local hospitals, public health centers, prenatal clinics, prenatal classes on pregnancy and parenting, related support groups).

4. Identify cultural tendencies and dispositions associated with pregnancy, birth, and parenting.

5. Read some articles about teenage pregnancy. Then
   a. Develop a list of possible solutions to this problem.
   b. Develop a list of strategies that can help the teenage mother, the father, and the baby.

6. Describe how you think heredity and environment influenced your development. Share with your classmates in small groups.

7. Invite the following speakers to your class:
   a. A genetic counselor to discuss the importance of genetic counseling
   b. A Lamaze instructor to describe the Lamaze method
   c. A LaLeche League representative to explain the advantages of breast feeding
   d. A pharmacist to discuss the effects of drugs during pregnancy

8. Make a list of practices that help ensure the birth of a healthy baby.

## FURTHER READINGS

The local chapter of the March of Dimes provides pamphlets on genetic counseling, prenatal development, and ways to prevent birth defects.

Ambert, A. M. (1992). *The effect of children on parents*. Binghampton, NY: Hayworth Press.

Burns, A. (1994). *Mother-headed families and why they have increased*. Hillsdale, NJ: Lawrence Erlbaum Associates, Inc.

Carnegie Corporation. (1994). *Starting points: Meeting the needs of our youngest children: The report of the Carnegie Task Force on Meeting the Needs of Young Children*. New York: Author.

Cowan, C. P., & Cowan, P. A. (1993). *When partners become parents: The big life change for couples*. New York, NY: Basic Books.

Griswold, R. L. (1993). *Fatherhood in America*. New York, NY: Basic Books.

Hofferth, S. L., & Hayes, C. D. (Eds.). (1987). *Risking the future: Adolescent sexuality, pregnancy and childbearing (Vol. 2)*. Washington, DC: National Academy Press.

Nilsson, L., Sundberg, A., & Wirsen, C. (1981). *A child is born*. New York: Dell/Seymour Lawrence.

Swick, K. J., & Grave, S. (1993). *Empowering at-risk families during the early childhood years*. Washington, DC: National Education Association.

# CHAPTER FOUR

*To be a child is to know the fun of living. To have a child is to know the beauty of life.*

(Author unknown)

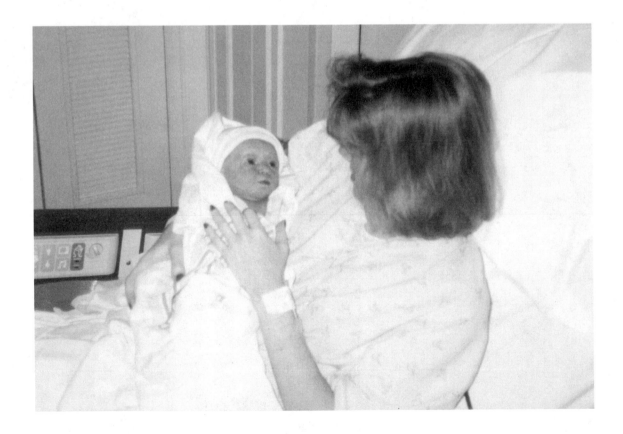

# The Child and Family at Birth

After studying this chapter, you will demonstrate comprehension by:

- Describing the stages of labor.
- Identifying the various types of deliveries.
- Describing the assessment and care of newborns.
- Outlining the change in family dynamics at birth, including bonding and reactions of the newborn, parents, siblings, and extended family.
- Identifying sociocultural factors regarding the birth experience.
- Describing the needs and care of special infants and their families.

## STAGES OF LABOR

 **Labor** is divided into three stages: dilation to delivery, the birth itself, and the expulsion of the placenta.

### STAGE 1: DILATION TO DELIVERY

It is 6:25 in the morning. Ann Johnson feels a slight snap in her abdominal area. Amniotic fluid empties from her uterine cavity and soaks the bed linen. Ann quickly realizes she is in labor and Jeremy's birth will soon be a reality. **Dilation,** the first stage of labor, actually began two days earlier. On Friday, Ann's checkup with Dr. Windle indicated that her **cervix** was dilated to 3 centimeters. By the time her baby is born, Ann's cervix will have dilated to 10 centimeters (4 inches). This opening is usually wide enough to allow most babies to be born.

Bill and Ann have learned from their childbirth education classes that each labor and delivery is unique. Nevertheless, one or more of the following signs usually indicates that labor is in process: lower backache, indigestion, diarrhea, abdominal cramps, the expulsion of the mucous plug, and the discharge of amniotic fluid. They have also learned that if the "water breaks" during the early part of labor, the fetus can be subject to infection.

*labor:*
*the three stages of the birth process: dilation, birth of the baby, and discharge of the placenta*

*dilation:*
*the gradual opening of the cervix, which occurs in the first stage of labor*

*cervix:*
*the opening of the uterus*

81

Ann awakens Bill and tells him what has happened. He excitedly phones Dr. Windle. She tells Bill that since Ann's water has broken, it is best that they go to the hospital immediately. Dr. Windle says she will meet them there in about 45 minutes. Ann and Bill dress, gather up their bags (which have been packed for several weeks), and drive to the hospital.

contraction:
the movement of the
muscles of the uterus
that forces the baby
through the cervical
opening and into the
birth canal

Ann's **contractions** have been relatively short, lasting about 30 to 45 seconds, and have occurred about every 15 to 20 minutes. During the drive, she uses some of the Lamaze breathing exercises and records the time and duration of each contraction. Ann and Bill are greeted at the hospital by obstetrical nurse Maria Lopez. She helps Ann into a wheelchair and takes her to the birthing room, while Bill checks Ann into the hospital. Maria is familiar with Lamaze techniques, so she temporarily takes over as Ann's coach as the contractions occur.

The birthing room looks very much like a bedroom, attractively furnished in mauves and grays. In addition to the birthing bed are a sofa, several comfortable chairs, and a table with four chairs. Unlike the traditional hospital setting where mothers are moved to the delivery room before the birth, Ann will remain in the birthing room for both labor and delivery. She is free to move about, eat, and drink. Friends and family can visit, according to Ann and Bill's wishes. Dr. Windle and Maria will be on hand to help Bill and Ann and provide specialized medical assistance if needed.

The birthing bed is very different from the traditional delivery table on which women lie down with their feet propped up in stirrups. It allows Ann to recline slightly, and there is a place to rest her legs to help in pushing during the final stage of labor. The position of the birthing bed will relieve pressure on Ann's back and allow the force of gravity to assist in the birth process.

Dr. Windle soon arrives. She checks Ann and determines that labor is progressing normally. Bill enters the birthing room and resumes coaching Ann and timing her contractions. During this first stage of labor, Ann's contractions become more frequent and intense. Ann adapts her Lamaze breathing patterns to the intensity of contractions. She walks around the room or sits in the birthing bed, depending on what feels more comfortable. Since she seems to be experiencing intense pain in her lower back, Bill rubs her back with a tennis ball to relieve the pressure. Throughout labor, Dr. Windle and Maria check in on Bill and Ann. It is now 10:00 A.M., and Ann has been in labor at least four hours—possibly longer, since she was asleep when her water broke. Jeremy is on his way into this world.

Let's see what is happening to Cheryl Monroe and James.

It is four weeks before Cheryl Monroe's due date. She and James are watching TV. Cheryl does not feel well; she has indigestion and diarrhea. While she is in the bathroom, she notices a mucuslike, blood-tinged discharge on her undergarments. The social worker who has been helping Cheryl told her about the signs of labor. She walks to the living room and tells James and her sister that she thinks the baby is coming.

Cheryl's sister calls the emergency room to tell them of Cheryl's condition. Because it is a month before Cheryl's estimated due date, the emergency room nurse says Cheryl needs to come to the hospital as soon as possible. James goes to a neighbor who has a car to see if he will drive them to the hospital.

Shortly after midnight, Cheryl's mother arrives home from her evening job to find the house in an uproar. She quickly gathers clothes and cosmetics into a bag for Cheryl. Cheryl is afraid, and her mother does her best to calm her while they walk to the neighbor's car for the short drive to the hospital. Cheryl's mother and James help her into the large hospital complex, which also has a medical school. Preliminary paperwork about Cheryl has been forwarded by the social worker. It is pulled from the file, and various forms are completed while Cheryl is placed in a wheelchair and taken to an examining room. The examination indicates that labor is well under way. Cheryl is then wheeled to a large room, where she is prepared for labor and delivery. There are other women in the room; one woman is screaming with labor pains. This increases Cheryl's anxiety.

Because of Cheryl's family's income level, she does not have access to a birthing room. Hospital and personal economics require that Cheryl share a room and medical personnel with a number of other pregnant women. Due to staff limitations, family and friends are not allowed in the labor or delivery room. Cheryl's mother, James, and the neighbor are asked to go to the waiting room. A nurse tells them he will keep them informed of Cheryl's progress.

A specialist comes in to assess the condition of the fetus. He uses an **electronic fetal monitor** and places electrodes on the scalp of the fetus through Cheryl's cervix. The monitor indicates that the fetus is in stress. The specialist calls to the delivery room and tells them to prepare immediately for a **cesarean** delivery. Since Cheryl's baby will be **preterm** (born three weeks or more before the due date), the doctor orders an **isolette** to be brought to the delivery room. An isolette is a small crib that provides a controlled environment for the newborn. It monitors the physiological condition of the infant and provides nutrients to it through a tube that runs from the infant's nose to the stomach.

## STAGE 2: BIRTH

Stage 2 of labor begins when the cervix has dilated to 10 centimeters and the head of the fetus pushes through the cervical opening into the vagina. After some time, Ann Johnson has the urge to push. However, Lamaze training has prepared Ann to know what to do during this part of labor. She begins a Lamaze breathing technique to help her control the urge to expel the baby. The pains from the contractions become intense, and Ann mentions to Bill that she would like some medication. In their Lamaze class, Bill and Ann learned that at times medication can be necessary and helpful in the birth process. However, it can also have some negative effects, the extent of which is determined by the type of medication, the amount given, and the stage of labor during which it is administered. Discussion with Dr. Windle and Maria reminds Ann that the most difficult part of labor is almost over and the baby will soon be born. Along with Bill, they encourage her to continue without any medication because the fetal head has already numbed the vaginal opening. Medication at this point might reduce Ann's contractions and make her awareness less effective in pushing during the final part of delivery. Bill also reminds her that continuing without medication will help the baby be more alert not only at birth but also for some time after (Brackbill, 1979; Smolak, 1986). Buoyed by their encouragement, Ann decides to proceed without medication.

*electronic fetal monitor:*
*a device used during labor that is attached to the abdomen of the pregnant woman or the scalp of the fetus to determine the fetal heart rate*

*cesarean:*
*a surgical procedure during which an incision is made through the abdominal and uterine walls of the mother to deliver the baby*

*preterm:*
*infants born several weeks before the full term (38 weeks) of pregnancy*

*isolette:*
*a small crib that provides a controlled environment for newborns who are considered at risk*

*episiotomy:*
*an incision made in the opening of the vulva to prevent it from tearing during birth*

Ann's last ultrasound had indicated that the baby may be large, 8 to 9 pounds. For this reason, Dr. Windle decides to do an **episiotomy**. An episiotomy is a small incision that helps prevent the opening of the vulva from tearing during birth.

It is now close to 3:00 P.M., and it is time for Maria's nursing shift to end. She decides to stay longer, since it is almost time for Ann to give birth. The intense contractions are about a minute apart and last for almost 60 seconds. Dr. Windle and Maria now tell Ann to push. As she squeezes Bill's hand, Ann pushes and the baby's head begins to appear. Shortly, with another push, the head emerges. Dr. Windle removes the mucus from the baby's nose and mouth. From the mirror above the birthing bed, Bill and Ann have their first look at Jeremy. With the next contraction, Ann gives another big push and Jeremy's full body appears. He begins to cry softly. (For an illustration of the first two stages of labor, see Figure 4.1.)

The birthing room has been kept a comfortable 78 degrees, with relaxing music playing in the background. This provides a soothing setting for Jeremy's entrance into the world from the protective environment of the uterus. Dr. Windle and Maria quickly evaluate Jeremy for any signs of complications. He appears fine and is gently wiped off and placed on Ann's abdomen. Ann and Bill talk gently to Jeremy and begin cuddling him. He has dark hair like Ann's father. Jeremy stops crying and looks directly into their eyes. Ann and Bill are truly in awe of this miracle of life. They examine his hands and feet. Bill decides he looks like one of his brothers. Ann places Jeremy at her breast, and he begins to nurse. "You smart little thing," says Ann. After awhile the blood in the blood vessels in the umbilical cord stops throbbing, and Dr. Windle cuts the umbilical cord. Bill then takes Jeremy and places him into a warm bath. This concept of "gentle birth" is the **Leboyer method**, based on the ideas of Frederick Leboyer (1975), a French obstetrician. Creating a calm, relaxed environment and placing the baby in warm water similar to the amniotic fluid are believed to help the baby adjust to life outside the uterus.

*Leboyer method:*
*a technique used during childbirth to help the baby in the transition from life inside to outside the uterus; characterized by warm delivery rooms, muted lighting, soothing music, a warm bath, etc.*

*afterbirth:*
*the placenta after it moves from the uterus and is expelled through the cervix*

## STAGE 3: EXPULSION OF THE PLACENTA

The third stage of labor involves the expulsion of the placenta and umbilical cord, or **afterbirth**, through the cervix. Ann's afterbirth appears. Dr. Windle and Maria examine it to be sure everything has been completely discharged from the uterus. A very calm and relaxed Jeremy has been enjoying his first bath. Jeremy is dried, then weighed and measured. He weighs 8 pounds, 14 ounces and is 21 inches long. An identification bracelet matching Ann's bracelet is placed around his wrist.

Jeremy has arrived! What about Angela?

*anoxia:*
*the condition caused by the lack of oxygen in the brain of an infant during labor and delivery; can cause brain damage*

Cheryl is prepared for surgery. Because of her nervous state, the anesthesiologist administers medication to prevent her from observing Angela's birth. The doctor makes an incision and pulls away layers of skin and abdominal muscle. As Angela is lifted from the uterine cavity, the doctor discovers the umbilical cord is wrapped around her neck, depriving her of oxygen and creating a condition called **anoxia**. Angela does not begin breathing on her own. Quickly, a team of pediatric specialists is called. Angela is placed in the isolette and taken immediately to the neonatal care unit.

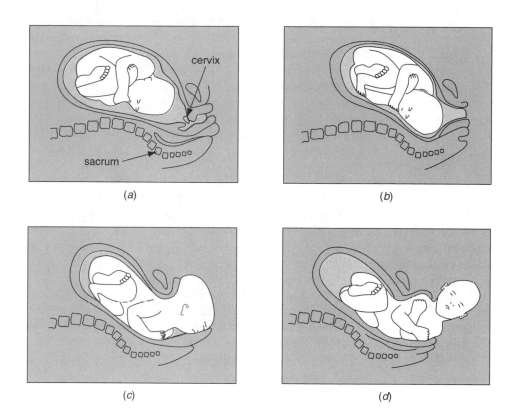

**FIGURE 4.1**
During the first stage of labor (a, b), the uterus contracts, causing the cervix to dilate. In stage 2 (c, d), the baby moves down the birth canal and is pushed out. (Reprinted by permission from Laura E. Berk, *Child Development* 3rd ed. © 1994. Needham Heights, MA: Allyn & Bacon.)

Anoxia can also occur if the placenta detaches too soon during prenatal development; if the prospective mother smokes, has **anemia**, is Rh incompatible; or for other unknown reasons. Mild anoxia can destroy or damage some of the baby's brain cells. Oxygen deprivation can cause babies to cry more than normal and can lead to learning and behavior problems, but these problems usually decrease as the child grows older (Stechler & Halton, 1982). Severe anoxia can cause cerebral palsy, mental retardation, and death. Electronic fetal monitoring devices are frequently used during labor if there is concern about anoxia. Controversy has arisen about the overuse of fetal monitors in healthy pregnancies, their interference with the normal process of labor, and the mistaken identification of fetal stress that often precipitates cesarean deliveries (Samuels & Samuels, 1986).

In addition to fetal stress, another common reason for doing a cesarean delivery is **breech birth**. This complication occurs when a part of the body—usually the

*anemia:*
*a condition caused by a lack of red blood cells*

*breech birth:*
*a birth in which a body part other than the head presents itself for delivery first, usually the buttocks, feet, or in some cases the umbilical cord*

buttocks, feet, or umbilical cord—other than the head is positioned to emerge first from the cervix. If the mother's pelvic bone structure is too small to accommodate the birth of a large baby, a cesarean delivery may be performed.

Some doctors and other interested persons (Rosen, 1981; United States Congress, Senate Committee on Human Resources Research, 1978) have questioned the increase in the number of cesarean births. Explanations for this increase include possible lawsuits if the baby is at risk, fetal exposure to genital herpes, convenience for the obstetrician, and increased obstetrician earnings for cesarean deliveries. Since this procedure is considered major surgery and prolongs the recovery of the mother, it is important to use it only when necessary for the well-being of mother and child.

Studies indicate that there are few long-term cognitive and neurological effects on a cesarean-delivered infants (Entwisle & Alexander, 1987). While initial mother-child interaction may be affected by anesthetics and the mother's recovery from major surgery (Reilly, Entwisle, & Doerling, 1987), fathers may take a more active role in caring for their cesarean-delivered babies than fathers of traditionally delivered infants (Pederson, Zaslow, Cain, & Anderson, 1981).

At times **forceps** are used to speed up delivery when there is danger to the fetus. In a forceps delivery, the doctor fits forceps around the baby's head and pulls the fetus through the vagina. This procedure should be used only during the second stage of labor and with great caution, or brain damage can result.

*forceps:*
*a surgical instrument, similar to tongs, that is applied to the head of the fetus to speed delivery*

## ASSESSMENT AND CARE OF NEWBORNS

Dr. Virginia Apgar (1953) invented a process to evaluate the ability of newborns to cope with the stress of delivery and adjust to breathing independently. The **Apgar score** is usually obtained by observing the newborn at 1, 5, and sometimes 15 minutes after birth. Five areas of appearance or performance are evaluated: the *a*ppearance (skin color), *p*ulse (heart rate), *g*rimace (reaction to slight pain), *a*ctivity (motor responsiveness and tone), and *r*espiration (breathing adequacy). These five categories spell APGAR, which helps to make them easy to remember. Each category receives 0, 1, or 2 points. Generally a score of 7 or above indicates the newborn is doing well. If the newborn's score is between 5 and 7, there usually is a need for some type of additional care. Infants with a score of 4 or below require immediate medical attention, as such a score indicates a life-threatening situation. (See Table 4.1.)

A second evaluation procedure used to examine a variety of behaviors in newborns was developed by pediatrician T. Berry Brazelton in 1973. The **Brazelton Neonatal Behavioral Assessment Scale (NBAS)** assesses 26 behavioral items and 16 reflexes that newborns possess. This assessment technique requires training, since it tries to elicit the infant's highest level of performance and is most commonly used in research settings and on preterm or at-risk infants. The Brazelton Scale helps parents to become aware of the infant's competencies. Parents who have been trained to administer the Brazelton were, after four weeks, more knowledgeable about their infants, had more confidence in handling the infants, and had more satisfactory interactions with their infants than parents who had not learned

*Apgar score:*
*a score that rates the physical condition of newborns in the areas of appearance, pulse, grimace, activity, and respiration*

*Neonatal Behavioral Assessment Scale (NBAS or Brazelton Scale):*
*an assessment of 16 reflexes, responsiveness, state changes, and ability to calm itself in the newborn*

**TABLE 4.1**
**Apgar Scale**

| Sign | Score | | |
|---|---|---|---|
| | 0 | 1 | 2 |
| Heart rate | Absent | Less than 100/min. | More than 100/min. |
| Skin tone | Blue, pale | Body pink, limbs blue | Completely pink |
| Muscle Tone | Limp | Some flexing of limbs | Active motion |
| Reflexes | No response | Grimace or cry | Startled, loud cry |
| Respiratory effort (breathing) | Absent | Slow, irregular | Strong, regular breath |

*Sources:* Adapted from Apgar, V. (1953). A proposal for a new method of evaluation in the newborn infant. Current research in Anesthesia and Analgesia, 32, 260–267. Also Berman, R.E., M.D., & Vaughn, V.C. III, M.D. (1987). Evaluation of the newborn infant (Table 8-3, p. 363). *Nelson Textbook of Pediatrics, 13/e.* With permission of W.B. Saunders Company.

the Brazelton (Myers, 1982). Fathers who learned how to administer the Brazelton were more actively involved with their infants than fathers who had not received the training (Myers, 1982).

The NBAS also helps identify infants who are not able to control or regulate the various states ranging from deep sleep to crying. Ill or premature infants and those with immature central nervous systems may cry often, lack the ability to settle themselves, and refuse to be cuddled. Such behaviors can be upsetting and frustrating to new parents. These parents can be provided with continued medical assistance in coping with their infants.

Jeremy's Apgar scores were 9 and 9. A third evaluation was not needed, since he was doing well. Angela scored 3, 4, and 5 and required immediate attention due to her lack of ability to breathe independently. Dr. Jones, Angela's pediatrician, plans to return to the neonatal care unit later in the day to see if her condition has stabilized. That afternoon he reads her charts and examines her. After several days, Dr. Jones and the neonatal staff decide to conduct the NBAS, as he notes that Angela seems to have difficulty calming herself when she is in a fussy state. Dr. Jones thinks he may have to provide Cheryl with some techniques for helping Angela learn to comfort herself. ■

## FAMILY DYNAMICS: A NEW SOCIAL SYSTEM

The birth of a baby into a family unit establishes a new social system as different relationships and roles are created. According to Bronfenbrenner's ecological systems theory (1979, 1986), reactions on the parts of all members of this new social system vary depending on the nature of the pregnancy and birth experience, the baby's position in the family unit, various sociocultural factors, the state of health of various family members, and the nature of support from the medical profession and community health services.

## BONDING

bonding:
a complex psychobio-
logical connection
between parent and
infant

Marshall H. Klaus and John H. Kennell are two pediatricians who have conducted research on bonding. They define **bonding** as the establishment of a complex psychobiological connection from parent to infant (Klaus & Kennel, 1982). The connection from infant to parent is called *attachment*. Bonding and attachment will be discussed in greater detail in Chapter 6.

## REACTIONS OF THE NEWBORN

Reactions of newborns vary according to prenatal care, the labor and delivery experience, the nature of parental interactions, and the infant's own personal temperament. The uterus has provided a consistent temperature and constant nourishment. After the arduous birth process, the infant must adjust to breathing independently and take an active role in the feeding process. Fortunately, most infants are resilient in nature and possess many capabilities that help them adjust. These competencies will be discussed in Part Three. Nevertheless, good prenatal care, a normal labor and delivery process, positive interaction with parents, and quality care from the medical profession can promote optimal adjustment for the newborn.

## REACTIONS OF THE MOTHER

Good prenatal care, educational preparation for childbirth and parenting, a normal labor and delivery, and a supportive husband and family all help the mother adjust to her new role. However, even new mothers who enjoy optimal pregnancy and delivery conditions feel overwhelmed, tired, and depressed at times.

In most instances, giving birth is a very rigorous event demanding a great deal of physical and emotional energy. After delivery, the mother's body begins to undergo a tremendous hormonal adjustment to the nonpregnant state. These changes can create mood swings and depression. In addition, caring for a newborn who needs to be fed every few hours around the clock can be an exhausting experience.

The need to deal with the realities and responsibilities of parenting following the emotional high of anticipation of the baby's birth can be overwhelming to some mothers. In addition, many mothers think they should feel instant maternal love for their babies. If they do not, they feel guilty. Contrary to early research on bonding, human relationships take time to develop. One study (Robson, 1968) indicated that 59 percent of first-time mothers did not feel intense attachments to their infants at birth. Strong feelings began to develop between babies and their mothers between four and six weeks after birth.

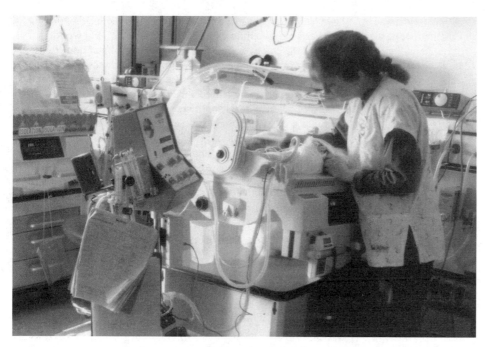

*Parents are encouraged to caress, touch, and care for their children as soon as possible.*

New mothers often have many questions about their babies' behavior, particularly eating and crying. Books and advice from family, friends, and the medical profession can be helpful. At times, however, the mother's reading of her baby and her "maternal instinct" may be the best way to handle situations.

Ann had been advised by the nurses at the hospital to bathe Jeremy when he awakened from his afternoon nap and then feed him after his bath. Hungry, Jeremy cried more and more intensely during his bath. Ann became fearful that Jeremy would come to dislike bathtime. On her own, Ann decided to feed Jeremy first. She could see Jeremy relax as his tummy became full. After a time for burping and cuddling, Ann gave a relaxed and happy Jeremy his bath.

After several days in the neonatal care unit, Angela seems to be breathing easier. Her skin tone has improved, and the usual weight loss after birth has not been as great as the doctors feared. However, the doctors tell Cheryl they want to keep Angela in the neonatal care unit for a week or two just to be sure she is breathing independently.

Upon Dr. Jones's direction, Cheryl and James have been visiting Angela in the neonatal care unit several times a day. Angela cries frequently, which can be expected of preterm babies with anoxia. The nurses tell Cheryl it is important to respond to Angela's cries since she is trying to communicate hunger, discomfort, or boredom. Cheryl replies that one of her hospital roommates told her that picking up crying babies can spoil them. The nurses reassure Cheryl that this is not the case. Cheryl feels confused. She has noticed that when she visits Angela and Angela has been crying, touching her and talking to her in a soothing voice do seem to calm her. Maybe the nurses are right.

Cheryl and James have felt extremely stressed by Angela's special needs. Visiting the neonatal care unit has been a frightening experience for them. Cheryl wonders if Angela will cry as much when she comes home. She is glad she will be at home without her for awhile, but these thoughts make her feel guilty. The nurses tell her she can visit Angela during the week or two that she needs to remain in the neonatal care unit. Cheryl wonders how she will get there, since her family has no car and little money for public transportation. Cheryl's minister talks with her social worker to try to work out some times when neighbors and friends in their church can take Cheryl and James to visit Angela. Cheryl notices that she too feels like crying much of the time. Her mother is concerned about her and wonders how they will manage when Angela leaves the neonatal care unit. ■

*postpartum depression: a period of depression that affects most mothers for a few days and in some cases for weeks and months after childbirth*

One study (Zaslow & Pedersen, 1981) indicated that 89 percent of mothers struggle with some degree of **postpartum depression.** As their bodies return to the prepregnancy state, their energy level increases, and they begin to develop confidence in their mothering abilities, most new mothers' depression disappears. A few mothers become severely depressed to the point where they cannot function in the maternal role and may even be a danger to their own or the baby's well-being. Hormonal readjustment, lack of support from the father or other family members, and severe past emotional conflict in the mother are possible reasons for deep postpartum depression. Friends, relatives, and the medical profession need to be sensitive to severe postpartum depression and seek treatment for the new mother, who may be incapable of obtaining help for herself (Hopkins, Marcus, & Campbell, 1984).

## REACTIONS OF THE FATHER

Recently more attention has been given to the reactions of prospective fathers and new fathers (see Chapter 3). New fathers worry about whether they will be good fathers, whether they will please their wives, added financial responsibility, changes in their relationship with their wives, and lack of freedom. If there are siblings, fathers wonder how they will react to the new brother or sister (Shapiro, 1987). A study by Zaslow and Pedersen (1981) indicated that 62 percent of the fathers who actively participated in childbirth classes and in the delivery of their children also experienced some degree of postpartum depression.

The increasing need for two incomes to support a family and family-centered maternity care have encouraged many fathers to become more involved in the birth and care of their children (Palkovitz, 1984). Studies indicate that a father's participation in the preparation for the birth, delivery, and early care of the baby leads to later positive interaction patterns with his child (Klaus & Kennell, 1982; Parke & Sawin, 1981). The new mother, the medical profession, and friends and family need to be supportive of new fathers.

 As Bill watches Ann breast-feed Jeremy in the hospital, he sometimes feels left out. In some ways, he wishes Ann had not decided to nurse Jeremy. He knows breast-fed babies have more immunity to illness and a mother's milk is more nutritious than formula, but if Jeremy were bottle fed, Bill could be a part of the feeding.

Bill mentions these feelings to Ann. She jokingly says he will be glad that she is breast-feeding when he realizes she has to get up to nurse Jeremy several times during the night. Ann thinks about Bill's comments. She asks Bill if he would like to burp Jeremy and cuddle him after feeding. ■

*Parents can help their older children adjust to a new brother or sister by talking with them about the needs of the baby, pointing out the baby's interest in them, and planning a time alone with them.*

## REACTIONS OF SIBLINGS

A study by Stewart, Mobley, Van Tuyl, Salvador (1987) indicated that even though parents prepare children for the birth of a new brother or sister, many adjustments must be made. Stewart studied middle-class families with a firstborn child of 2, 3, or 4 years of age over a 15-month period. Findings indicated that these firstborns spent much time trying to get their mothers' full attention and that their strategies followed similar patterns regardless of age.

During the first four months after the birth of a brother or sister, the firstborns engaged in such behaviors as baby talk, using baby table manners, demanding a bottle or pacifier, and regression in toilet training. Another tactic included verbal and physical confrontations with the infant, parents, and even inanimate objects. At times, the firstborn children were whiny, withdrawn, and clingy and had a need for a security blanket or toy. By the fourth month after the birth of the baby, displays of imitation or confrontation usually disappeared. Anxiety behaviors continued, however. Four months later, when new brother or sister was around 8 months old, the older siblings again used confrontational strategies. According to the researchers, these behaviors were explained by the baby's increasing mobility and responsiveness.

The brothers and sisters said they helped care for the new baby. Ninety-five percent of the mothers confirmed this behavior. Over half said they liked to cuddle the new baby. During the last visit, when the new baby was just over a year old, 63 percent of the firstborns said they were ready for a new baby.

Siblings of the same gender were reported to show a higher incidence of all types of behaviors. Fathers seemed to help out and give the firstborns needed attention. By the end of the study, the fathers were talking and playing with their firstborns as much as the mothers were. This study indicates that at least in some middle-class families, the attention-getting behaviors of firstborns are normal, that fathers can help meet their need for attention, and that in spite of the obvious negative feelings of firstborns, they also have positive attitudes toward the new baby.

A study by Dunn and Kendrick (1982a) suggests that parents can help their older children adjust to a new brother or sister if they talk about the baby's needs and involve the older sibling in making decisions regarding the infant. Explaining the infant's behaviors and pointing out his or her interest in the older sibling can also facilitate positive interactions.

## REACTIONS OF EXTENDED FAMILY

Reactions of extended family can vary and also affect the immediate family of the newborn. Grandparents are usually thrilled. However, comments sometimes suggest mixed or negative feelings about the birth of a grandchild. Grandparents often view the birth of a grandchild as a sign that they are getting older. Adjusting to the aging process can be difficult for some. At times, feelings of failure or inadequacy that the grandparents experienced as parents can surface and create tension.

Ann's mother had not been successful at breastfeeding, and she kept telling Ann that Ann's breasts were too small to feed Jeremy. Fortunately, Ann's childbirth classes had given her background information regarding the physiological process of nursing. She calmly responded to her mother's concerns, explaining that the glands and not the size of the breasts stimulated milk production. Ann also pointed out that the baby's sucking increased the supply of milk. This information seemed to relieve Ann's mother. ■

Because a number of prospective parents today attend childbirth classes, they have new and up-to-date information. At times this may threaten some of the ideas about parenting held by grandparents. Grandparents may feel unsure about what they should do. This insecurity may be viewed as a lack of interest in the grandchild or the new parents. In addition, some grandparents find it difficult to allow their children to become parents. The grandparents have been in control in their role as parents, and they feel a need to stay in control rather than allowing their child to take charge of his or her new family.

At times, the new parents' siblings may feel jealousy over all the attention the new parents are receiving. Becoming a new aunt or uncle also involves adjusting to a new role. If there has been a great deal of competition between the new parent and his or her siblings, old feelings of rivalry can surface and persist even when the sibling becomes a parent, and cousins can be pitted against one another.

Nevertheless, many extended family members can provide information, needed support, and encouragement to the new parents. The reactions of the extended family add to the complexity of relationships surrounding the birth of a baby. An awareness of some of these feelings and their possible causes can help new parents better understand and cope with these behaviors and feelings.

## SOCIOCULTURAL PERSPECTIVES

Different cultural groups have different attitudes toward pregnancy, the birth process, and the care of newborns. An awareness of these differences and a knowledge of the reasons for them can help early childhood professionals understand that there are many ways of behaving in the process of starting a family. Throughout this text, cultural differences in development will be presented to help the early childhood professional gain a broader perspective on the variety of child and adult behaviors.

## INFANTS WITH SPECIAL NEEDS AND THEIR FAMILIES

By 28 weeks, the physical systems of the fetus are sufficiently developed that if birth occurs, chances of survival are improved. However, with the resources available in neonatal nurseries, even infants who weigh under 2 pounds can survive.

A number of programs and technologies have been developed to meet the needs of preterm and low-birthweight infants. These programs often involve stimulation of conditions in utero or replication of experiences of full-term infants. Studies indicate that these stimulation programs demonstrate short-terms gains (Korner, 1989). However, not all infants need stimulation, so individual differences must be taken into consideration regarding the purpose, type, and duration of the stimulation program.

Parenting a preterm infant can create a great deal of stress in the parents' relationship during the child's first two years of life, particularly in families experiencing economic hardship. Thus, intervention programs must attend to the entire family system (Resnick et al., 1990).

Children born into families with limited economic resources may need additional assistance to ensure their continued growth and development. Infants with special physical or health needs and their families may need continued support from the medical profession and local community, state, or federal health services. Early identification and treatment of problems can reduce the cost of health care and increase human potential. These are two important reasons for providing private and public services for young children and their families.

We hope this chapter has made you more aware of the complex set of circumstances which affect newborns and their families. An awareness of these factors and dynamics can facilitate a more complete understanding of young children and their families. A positive birth experience and adjustment of all family members to the newborn can pave the way for a child to "know the joy of living" and for the parents to enjoy and celebrate "the beauty of life" (see the quote at the beginning of this chapter).

Bill, Ann, and Jeremy Johnson have had optimal circumstances for beginning their lives as a family. Cheryl Monroe, James, and Angela have not been so fortunate. The following chapters continue the story of the growth and development of Jeremy and Angela.

---

 *Role of the Early Childhood Professional*

## Working with Families with Newborns

1. Be aware of the possible relevance of special circumstances surrounding the pregnancy and birth of young children whose development appears atypical.
2. Help parents understand the reactions of siblings to a new baby.
3. Help parents with suggestions for preparing siblings for a new baby.
4. Be aware of possible changes in classroom behavior in young children during the weeks after the birth of a sibling.
5. Be aware of programs and services available to infants wih special needs and their families.  ■

---

## KEY TERMS

afterbirth
anemia
anoxia
Apgar Scale
bonding
breech birth
cervix
cesarean

contraction
dilation
electronic fetal
  monitoring
episiotomy
forceps
isolette
labor

Leboyer method
Neonatal Behavioral
  Assessment Scale
  (NBAS)
postpartum
  depression
preterm

## REVIEW STRATEGIES AND ACTIVITIES

1. Review the key terms individually or with a classmate.
2. Interview several parents of newborns. Ask them to share with you
   a. The delivery and hospital experience
   b. Opportunities for and experiences with bonding
   c. The first two months after the baby's birth
   d. Reactions of immediate and extended family to the baby's birth
3. Invite an obstetrical or pediatric nurse to your class to discuss
   a. The care of a newborn infant
   b. The care of an at-risk infant
   c. The care of the mother
   d. Support for the family
   e. Evaluation of the newborn, including the Apgar and Brazelton scales and other assessment tools
   f. Follow-up support
4. Discuss the short-term and long-term implications of quality prenatal and neonatal care worldwide.

## FURTHER READINGS

Arlip, M. A., Arlip, J. A., and Saltzman, E. S. (1993). *The new American family.* Lancaster, PA: Starbursts, Inc.

Campion, M. J. (1994). *Who's fit to be a parent?* London: Routledge.

Galinski, E. (1990). *The six stages of parenthood.* Reading, MA: Addison-Wesley.

Skolnick, A. S., and Skolnick, J. H. (1994). *Family in transition.* New York: HarperCollins College.

# PART THREE

# Infancy

# CHAPTER FIVE

*Infancy conforms to nobody—all conform to it.*
**Ralph Waldo Emerson**

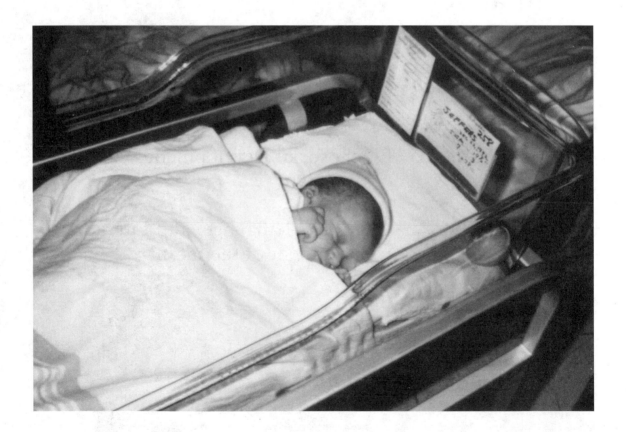

# Physical and Motor Development of the Infant

After studying this chapter, you will demonstrate comprehension by:

- Outlining principles of development related to the physical and motor development of infants from birth to the end of the first year.
- Identifying sociocultural influences on growth and development.
- Describing major neonatal reflexes and their developmental implications.
- Explaining expected patterns of physical and motor development during the first year.
- Identifying major factors influencing physical and motor development.
- Suggesting strategies for promoting and enhancing physical and motor development during the first year.
- Describing contemporary infant health and well-being issues.

Extended family members and friends gather eagerly in Cheryl's hospital room to share in the joy of Angela's birth. Since Angela was receiving special attention in the neonatal intensive care unit, they are also concerned for her well-being. Family and friends stroll quietly in and out of Angela's room to view the newborn and return to Cheryl's room to comment on their observations. "She's so beautiful, so tiny." "I believe she has James's eyes; I always thought James and his brother had those same beautiful eyes." "She sure is calm and quiet, even with all those nurses fussing over her." "Cheryl, that's the way you were when you were a baby." "I don't remember Cheryl being so calm," chirps one of her siblings. "Well, I was until you came along," quips Cheryl goodnaturedly. Many such musings go on among Cheryl and her friends and family: Will Angela be musically inclined or skilled in mathematics, as Cheryl seems to be? Will she have James's personality and charm, his energy, or his athleticism: Most of all, will she be normal and healthy? ■

## PRINCIPLES OF GROWTH, DEVELOPMENT, AND BEHAVIOR

Imbedded in all of the questions about Angela are assumptions regarding Angela's inherited traits and concerns about her future. Are heredity or environmental factors more influential in a child's growth, development, and behavior? Over the last 100 years, this topic has aroused lively debate among students of child growth and development and continues to emerge in scholarly discussion and literature today. For instance, we can all agree that eye color is genetically determined and cannot be altered by environmental influences. But could we all agree that an infant's motor agility is genetically determined and unalterable through environmental influences? What does theory tell us about this issue?

Over the years, theorists on both sides of the heredity-environment debate have provided numerous perspectives regarding various behaviors and growth and development outcomes. On the one hand is the point of view that growth and development are controlled primarily by nature (heredity) and are governed by an inborn, unalterable blueprint that defines what, when, and to what extent, each aspect of growth and development will occur. This point of view proposes that all growth, development, thinking, and behavioral changes in an organism result from maturation from within represented by an "unfolding" of traits along predictable time lines (Anastasi, 1958; Hall, 1893; Gesell & Amatruda, 1941; Gesell & Ilg, 1949).

On the other hand is the assertion that the environment is the more critical determinant of the outcomes of growth and development. This theory suggests that the human being is quite malleable and therefore growth and development are facilitated or impeded by forces in the individual's environment (Watson, 1924, 1970; Bandura, 1977, 1986; Bijou & Baer, 1961; Skinner, 1974). This view asserts that the environment shapes developmental outcomes regardless of genetic makeup. Consequently, where the environment provides positive influences, the outcomes for the individual are also positive.

*interactionist perspective:*
*derived primarily from the works of Jean Piaget, refers to the interactive influences of heredity and environment*

Piaget's (1952) **interactionist perspective** challenged these opposing views by suggesting that neither heredity nor environment is more important. Rather, they should be viewed as complementary, each playing a distinct and necessary part in growth and development and each interacting with the other. These interactions occur through direct experiences (physical and social) and result in *equilibration*, or a balanced state. The individual remains in this state until maturity and further experience upset the balance, causing change (or growth and development) to follow. Thus, the interactive perspective became an overriding point of view.

*transactional model:*
*the give-and-take model of hereditary and environmental influences on growth and development*

Still another theoretical perspective postulated a **transactional model** (Sameroff & Chandler, 1975), in which one's inherited constitution and environmental experiences influence each other through an ongoing interplay between heredity and environment. This interplay proceeds in a mutual give-and-take manner throughout the life span of the individual.

This text proposes that growth and development are largely predictable and that wide variations occur within and among all cultures (though some growth and developmental patterns transcend race and locale). It also proposes that powerful interactions and transactions occur between and among hereditary and environmental factors. This text therefore provides an eclectic approach to understanding this very complex topic.

We believe that growth, development, and behavior emerge as a result of factors within each of these categories of influence:

1. Biological influences (physical characteristics, rate of growth, health, and disease)

2. Psychological influences (feelings, emotions, and attitudes)

3. Cognitive influences (intelligence, language, and thought processes)

There is mutual dependency and interrelatedness in all growth and development, as a continuous thrust toward change proceeds throughout the life span.

In addition, all growth, development, and behavior must be considered within specific contexts, or environments (Bronfenbrenner, 1979, 1986; see Chapter 1). For example, different contexts (family and culture group, guided by their values and belief systems) encourage early walking by providing infants with greater freedom of movement within the safe confines of an "at-large" environment. Others keep infants tightly swaddled, perhaps carried about on their mothers' sides or backs during most of the early months. Still others restrict infants' explorations to designated spaces. These simple differences in early child rearing result in slightly different timetables for the onset of walking.

In the process of formulating an eclectic framework for understanding child growth and development, early childhood professionals are guided by very basic principles of growth, development, and behavior. These principles are thought to be generally true for all growth and development and to transcend, at least to some degree, race and locale. These principles are as follows:

1. *Growth and development follow a* **cephalocaudal** *and* **proximodistal** *direction*. That is, growth and development proceed from the head downward and from the central axis of the body outward. This is evident in the bodily proportions of the newborn. The newborn is quite top-heavy, with the head comprising one-quarter of the total body length. At birth, the newborn's head is 70 percent of its eventual adult size. These proportions are illustrated in Figure 5.1.

    This law of developmental direction applies not only to body proportions but also to other forms of development. It is most significant in the development and coordination of large and small muscles. Coordination of the large muscles of the upper body, including the neck, shoulders, upper trunk, and upper arms, precedes coordination of the smaller muscles in those body regions. Also, throughout infancy and early childhood, the muscles of the upper body will become more mature and coordinated than those of the lower body, with the large muscles of the hips and upper legs developing before the smaller muscles of the lower legs, ankles, and feet.

2. *Most children follow a similar developmental pattern*. As a rule, one stage of the pattern lays the foundation for the next. In motor development, for instance, a predictable sequence of developments precedes walking. The infant lifts and turns its head before it can turn over and is able to move its arms and legs before grasping an object.

3. *Growth and development proceed from general to specific*. In motor development, the infant first makes very generalized, undirected movements, waving arms or kicking before reaching or creeping toward a desired object. The infant will be able to grasp an object with the whole hand before using only the thumb and forefinger.

*cephalocaudal:*
*refers to the head to tail or long axis of the body*

*proximodistal:*
*refers to the direction from the body's center outward to the extremities*

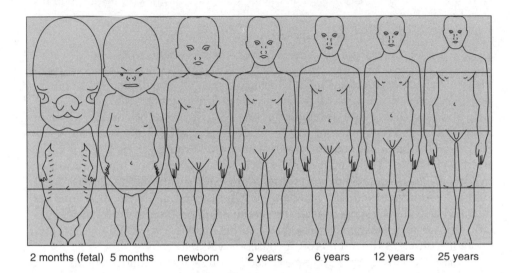

2 months (fetal)  5 months     newborn     2 years     6 years     12 years     25 years

**FIGURE 5.1**
At birth, the newborn's head is 70 percent of its eventual adult size. (From *Biology* by William A. Jensen, Bernd Heinrich, David B. Wake, and Marvalee H. Wake. © 1979 by Wadsworth, Inc. All rights reserved. Reprinted by permission of the publisher.)

4. *There are individual rates of growth and development.* While the patterns or sequences for growth and development usually remain the same, the rates at which individual children reach specific developmental milestones vary. For example, one child may begin walking unassisted at 9 months; another may begin walking at 15 months. Also, most children grow in spurts, but some grow in what appear to be steady increments.

5. *There are critical periods or optimal stages during growth and development in which the child is most sensitive to experiences.* During these periods, the child is susceptible to both positive and negative events, and mastery of certain developmental capabilities can occur with greater ease.

   Likewise, rates of development are not uniform within an individual child. For instance, a child's intellectual development may outpace his emotional or social development. Another child may show precocious language development, but be less motorically coordinated than many of his age-mates. As a rule, girls precede boys in the progression toward maturation.

6. *Growth and development result from a combination of maturation, learning, and environmental influences.* Maturational patterns are innate; they are genetically programmed. Learning occurs as a result of experiences, and the environment sets the stage for maximizing or impeding optimal growth and development.

Rates of physical and motor development are primarily the result of heredity. However, opportunities to explore the world when crawling, along with a rich and varied environment in which to explore, enhance both physical and motor skills and cognitive development in infancy. In contrast, an infant in the crawling stage who is confined to a playpen has limited opportunities to practice motor skills and limited environmental stimulation for learning. Fullest realization of inherited growth and development potential may be thwarted in such instances.

7. *Human growth, development, and behavior are influenced by one's cultural and societal contexts and occur over the entire life span.*

## SOCIOCULTURAL PERSPECTIVES ON GROWTH, DEVELOPMENT, AND BEHAVIOR

Since physical and motor development are for the most part readily observable and seem to emerge in similar and predictable fashion for all children, many assume this aspect of growth and development is biologically driven with little, if any, influence from the environment. However, studies of physical and motor development in infants and children of various cultures in the United States and around the world challenge this assumption.

Recent cross-cultural studies are yielding more precise understandings of specific cultural contributions to individual developmental outcomes. Studies of cultures provide a much broader and empathic perspective on individual growth and development and lead us away from a monocultural point of view. Berk (1994, p. 29) expresses the requirements of this broader perspective:

A cross-cultural perspective reminds us that the majority of child development specialists reside in the United States, and their subjects of study are only a small minority of humankind. We cannot assume that the developmental sequences observed in our own children are "natural" or that the experiences fostering them are "ideal" without looking around the world. (Laboratory of Comparative Human Cognition, 1983)

Around the world and within the United States are many and varied child-rearing practices, socioeconomic conditions, values and belief systems, education levels, and health care opportunities that exert enormous influences on child growth and development. Knowledge, appreciation, and acceptance of cultural uniqueness is essential in the child development and early childhood education professions. Optimal growth and development are best facilitated by those who demonstrate understanding of individual uniqueness.

Following is but a sampling of a wide range of belief systems regarding child growth and development and child-rearing practices. These examples illustrate the variety of physical/motor and interactive environments that children in different cultures experience. They show us that there are many pathways to growth and development and point out the uniqueness of our own development.

## THE BIRTHING PROCESS

Birthing procedures range from no or limited assistance from family and friends to high-technology hospitals with professionally educated and trained physicians, nurses, and other health care professionals and preparation classes for parents-to-be, followed by encouragement of spouse and family support during the birthing process. An example of minimal assistance is found among the Siriono of South America. The mother lies in a hammock, delivers the baby unassisted, and allows the newborn to fall from the hammock to the ground—a procedure thought to stimulate the birth cry. While many of the women in the community gather around to keep the birth mother company, they make no attempt to assist her. This practice differs appreciably from hospital or at-home deliveries assisted by a certified nurse-midwife, or possibly a nonprofessional midwife and other family members. Home deliveries are popular in a number of countries, such as England, Holland, and Sweden.

## CARRYING, CUDDLING, AND TRANSPORTING THE INFANT

In Africa, Asia, South America, and some other cultures, infants are carried about all day on their mothers' backs or in a sling or pouch at their mothers' sides while the mothers go about their daily chores. Infant and mother are virtually inseparable, and the infant is breast-fed on demand throughout the day. Some babies are carried this way until ages 2, 3, and 4 years; the arrival of a sibling usually necessitates the separation (Weisner, 1982).

In contrast, in Western cultures, babies are carried upright peering over the shoulders of their parents or caregivers, and often transported in a variety of devices such as strollers, baby carriages, and carrying seats of various types, such as pouches strapped across the shoulders and around the waist of the adult.

## INFANT CRYING

In some cultures, infants' cries are perceived as distress signals and are responded to readily with food, a pacifier, patting, or holding. In others, such as the United States, adults often take a wait-and see stance to determine the extent of the infant's distress and whether the baby is able to comfort itself and return to sleep. Japanese mothers often let their babies nestle in bed with them and cuddle and hold them until they fall back to sleep.

## NONMATERNAL CHILD CARE

North Americans and Europeans in the mid-20th century believed mothers should not work but devote their time and energies to child rearing. Yet for many cultures today, particularly in industrialized countries, nonmaternal child care and employed mothers are the norm (Lamb & Sternberg, 1992). Nonmaternal child care is provided by the grandmother or another older female in the extended family for Chinese infants whose mothers return to work soon after the first month. Home care is preferred during the first year (Chance, 1984).

In some Native American tribes, all members of the family are expected to contribute to the maintenance and well-being of the family or group, regardless of the absence or presence of the mother. Grandmothers, aunts, male relatives, and other children may share responsibility for infants. Sometimes very young children (4 and 5 years old) are expected to care for babies and toddlers (Locust, 1988).

An even further departure from European-American culture is the kibbutz, frequently found in Israel. *Kibbutz*, which means "group" in Hebrew, is a socially and economically independent society in which members live and work together. Children are often reared in the "children's" house under the care and tutelage of a *metapelet* (infant nurse or caregiver). Infants (usually from birth to 18 months) receive care from the mother and the *metapelet* during most of the day and night. Toddlers (18 months to age 3) live in the "toddlers'" home, and children ages 3 to 7 live in the "kindergarten." Parents are thus freed from child care duties while they perform their individual tasks for the maintenance and welfare of the kibbutz. In some kibbutzim, children stay with their parents in their living quarters at night; in others, the children remain in the children's house around the clock and are visited at specified times during the day and on weekends and holidays. At visiting times, parents are expected to provide undivided attention to their children.

## BEGINNINGS: PHYSICAL AND MOTOR COMPETENCE OF THE NEWBORN

The newborn enters the world with impressive abilities. From intrauterine to extrauterine life, the newborn must make a number of physiological adjustments, including breathing, taking in nourishment, and eliminating body wastes. The newborn makes adjustments from being surrounded by the warm amniotic fluid of the uterine environment to being surrounded by air, which may be cool and fluctuating in temperature. The newborn also adjusts from an environment of minimal sensory stimulation to an environment of varied stimuli that quicken all of the sensory mechanisms, including sight, sound, smell, touch, and taste. Despite seemingly overwhelming demands on the previously profoundly dependent organism, the infant emerges as a remarkably competent individual. How might the newborn be described, and just what competencies are present in very young infants?

## THE NEONATE

The **neonatal period** is usually defined as the first four weeks of life and is a critical period in infant development. Many physiological adjustments required for extrauterine existence are taking place. During this period, all bodily functions and psychological states are monitored to ensure a healthy beginning.

*neonatal period: the first four weeks of extrauterine life*

Physically, the newborn may be a frightful sight, though the infant's parents may disagree with this generalization. The skin is wrinkled, red, and covered with a cheeselike, greasy substance called **vernix caseosa**, which protects the skin during uterine development. In addition, the head is large in proportion to the rest of the body; the chest circumference is smaller than that of the infant's head. Sometimes the neonate's head has become temporarily misshapen during a lengthy delivery. Following the struggle to enter the world, some infants fall into a deep sleep and for the first day or so may even have difficulty staying awake long enough to nurse.

*vernix caseosa:*
*the oily covering that*
*protects the skin of the*
*fetus*

## REFLEXES

The full-term neonate is quite prepared for life and is equipped with a number of inborn movement patterns that help it adapt to new surroundings and new demands. These movement patterns, many of which are present prior to birth, are reflexes. **Reflexes** are unlearned, automatic responses to stimuli resulting from earliest neuromuscular development. Both Jeremy and Angela display infant reflexes of rooting and sucking. For the most part, these early reflexes are a function of **subcortical** (brainstem and spinal cord) mechanisms, though some cortical control is evident. The **cerebral cortex** is the part of the brain that is responsible for perception, memory, and thinking.

*reflex:*
*an unlearned, involun-*
*tary response to stimuli*

*subcortical:*
*the portion of the brain*
*just below the cerebral*
*cortex that is responsi-*
*ble for controlling*
*unlearned and reflexive*
*behavior*

Some reflexes are called **survival reflexes** because they are necessary for the infant to sustain life. The obvious example is breathing. The birth cry, which sometimes occurs before the infant is fully delivered, sets the respiratory mechanisms in motion, oxygenating the red blood cells and expelling carbon dioxide from the lungs.

*cerebral cortex:*
*the outer layer of the*
*cerebral hemisphere,*
*made up of gray tissue*
*that is mostly responsi-*
*ble for higher nervous*
*functions*

Most subcortical or **primitive reflexes** gradually disappear as the cerebral cortex matures and begins to direct and control bodily movements and behaviors. Some reflexes, such as breathing and other involuntary functions, such as bladder and bowel control, may continue to have elements of both subcortical and cortical control. The developmental course of the individual reflexes varies; some disappear in the first few days, others vanish within the first 12 to 18 months, and still others persist throughout life, becoming more precise and organized.

*survival reflexes:*
*reflexes that are essen-*
*tial to sustaining life*

In preterm infants, subcortical reflexes are frequently not evident at birth but will appear soon thereafter. Premature infants often exhibit weak rooting and sucking responses. Continued absence or weakness of these early reflexes suggests delayed development or dysfunction in the central nervous system. In premature infants, these early reflexes disappear somewhat more slowly than they do in full term infants. Table 5.1 lists some major reflexes observed in early infancy. In addition, gagging, sneezing, and hiccuping are present before and after birth.

*primitive reflexes:*
*reflexes, controlled by*
*subcortical structures*
*in the brain, that*
*gradually disappear*
*during the first year*
*of life*

In addition to an impressive array of reflexes, what other beginnings might be described? To answer this question, three additional characteristics—psychological states and activity levels, sensory capabilities, and expected growth and development patterns—are of interest.

TABLE 5.1
**Major Reflexes Present in Infancy**

| Reflex | Description |
|---|---|
| **Survival Reflexes** | |
| Breathing reflex | Inhales/exhales, oxygenating the red blood cells and expelling carbon dioxide. |
| Rooting reflex | Turns in direction of touch on the cheek as though searching for a nipple. Serves to orient the infant to breast or bottle. |
| Sucking and swallowing reflex | Stimulated by nipple placed in mouth; allows the infant to take in nourishment. |
| Eyeblink and pupillary reflex | Eyes close or blink; pupils dilate or constrict to protect the eyes. |
| **Primitive Reflexes** | |
| Grasping reflex | Holds firmly to an object touching the palm of the hand. Disappearance around the fourth month signals advancing neurological development. |
| Moro reflex | Often referred to as the *startle reflex;* a loud noise or sudden jolt will cause the arms to thrust outward, then return to an embrace-like position. Disappearance around the fifth or sixth month signals advancing neurological development. |
| Babinski reflex | Toes fan outward, then curl when the bottom of the foot is stroked. Disappearance by end of first year signals advancing neurological development. |
| Tonic neck reflex | A "fencing pose," often assumed when sleeping—head turned to one side, arm extended on the same side, and opposite arm and leg flexed at the elbow and knee. Disappearance around 7 months signals advancing neurological development. |

# PSYCHOLOGICAL STATES, TEMPERAMENT, AND ACTIVITY LEVELS

Jeremy, now 48 hours old, is cradled in his mother's arms and sleeping quite soundly. His face is scrunched into a tight expression—eyes tightly closed, mouth puckered into an overbite position, chin almost buried in his chest. He is swaddled snugly under the soft baby wrap, arms folded comfortably against his chest, knees bent slightly upward, and toes pointed inward.

Ann attempts to rouse her sleeping baby by gently rubbing her fingers across his soft cheek. He squirms slightly, stretching his legs and turning his head toward the touch; his mouth opens slightly, but he resists waking, and returns to his previous comfortable sleeping state. His mouth makes faint sucking movements briefly before he lapses into a fairly deep sleep.

> Angela, now 2 weeks old and home from the neonatal care unit, is crying vigorously. Her legs stretch stiffly, and her arms and hands flail in the air. Her blanket is in disarray, and her mother is hurriedly preparing a bottle to feed her. As the nipple of the bottle brushes against her lips, Angela frantically and clumsily searches and struggles to grasp it. Her sucking response is somewhat weak, and she whimpers until the hunger pains subside and the warmth and comfort of nourishment soothe her. ■

*psychological state: pertains to conditions of arousal and alertness in infancy*

Psychologists use the term **psychological state** when describing the infant's relationship to the outside world. States are characterized in terms of the degree of arousal and alertness the infant exhibits.

**Sleep Behavior.** An eagerly awaited milestone in infant development is "sleeping through the night." Sleeping patterns of infants are often the subject of discussion by proud (or tired) parents. Researchers also are interested in infant sleep patterns. Patterns, characteristics, and problems of sleep in young children comprise a large body of literature and a broad field of study.

Sleep patterns change as the infant matures. Newborn infants can be expected to sleep approximately 18 out of 24 hours (Berg, Adkinson, & Strock, 1973). The longest period of sleep may be 4 to 4½ hours during the first days. By 4 to 6 weeks of age, the infant may be sleeping 12 to 14 hours a day, taking as many as seven "naps" during a 24-hour period.

Some infants sleep a six-hour night by the fourth week after birth, but some will not sleep through the night until they are 7 or 8 months old. Some infants sleep more during the day and others at night, though most infants seem to sleep for longer periods at night. There is great variation in both the amount and type of sleep exhibited in infants. In his study of states of arousal in infancy, Wolff (1966) identified six states, summarized in Table 5.2.

By observing eye movements beneath the eyelid during sleep, one can ascertain the infant's sleep phase. There are two sleep phases, *rapid eye movement (REM)* and *non-rapid eye movement (NREM)* sleep. REM sleep is characterized by closed eyes; uneven respiration; limp muscle tone; intermittent smiles, grimaces, sighs, and sucking movements; and rapid eye movement beneath the eyelids as though the infant is dreaming. NREM sleep ranges from eyes partially open or still closed and a very light activity level with mild startles, to alertness but minimal motor activity, to eyes open with increased motor activity and reactions to external stimuli, to crying, sometimes quite intense.

Sleep researchers believe REM sleep is vital to growth of the central nervous system. Observations of infant sleep states and patterns help physicians identify central nervous system abnormalities. For instance, preterm infants generally display a greater amount of REM sleep. There is some evidence that infants suffering from brain damage or birth trauma may exhibit disturbed REM/NREM sleep patterns.

> Jeremy, now 4 months old, is usually quite content at bedtime. His mother usually holds him in her lap for awhile after the evening feeding, while he drifts into drowsiness and then into irregular sleep. Her soft voice hums to him while he languishes in her arms. Sensing his readiness for the crib, she carries him to his room. Placing him quietly in his crib, she continues to hum. She rubs his back softly and then leaves the room after observing that he will soon fall soundly to sleep.

TABLE 5.2
**Classification of Infant States**

| State | Characteristics |
|---|---|
| Regular sleep | Little body movement; regular breathing; no response to mild stimulation. |
| Irregular sleep | Increased body movements; irregular breathing; more easily aroused by external stimuli. |
| Periodic sleep | Occurs between regular and irregular sleep and is accompanied by muscle movements and rapid breathing, then short periods of calm inactivity. |
| Drowsiness | Little motor activity, yet sensitive to external stimuli. |
| Alert inactivity | Visually and/or auditorially scans the environment; large motor activity (head, trunk, arms and legs), alert and relaxed. |
| Waking activity | More intense motor activity may signal physiological need. |
| Crying | Motor activity passes into a whimpering, crying state, becoming louder as distress increases. Thrashing; twisting of torso and kicking vigorously. |

*Source:* Reprinted from *Psychological Issues,* "Causes, Controls and Organization of Behavior in the Neonate" by P. H. Wolff. By permission of International Universities Press, Inc. Copyright 1966 by International Universities Press.

However, on this particular evening Jeremy resists sleep. His eyes are open and scanning his surroundings, though he appears tired and cries sporadically. Tonight he is what most parents would call "cranky." His mother, also tired, wishes some magic formula would soothe him and help him rest. Nevertheless, after determining that Jeremy is not hungry, his diaper does not need changing, and his clothing is comfortable, she follows her established routine with him, sustaining each phase slightly longer. After being placed in his crib, he rouses somewhat and cries resistively while Ann strokes his back gently. Though he has not fallen into sound sleep, she leaves the room. ■

Predictable, unhurried bedtimes with regular routines help the reluctant infant to separate from the family and fall asleep more readily. Routines may include a relaxed bathtime during which the interaction between parent and child is satisfying to both, followed by being held in the parent's lap, rocked, and sung to softly. Cuddling a soft stuffed toy while being held focuses attention away from more stimulating activities occurring around the infant. This routine is followed by being placed in bed with a moment of slow back rubbing and a kiss on the cheek, a spoken "good night," and then departure from the room.

A recent study of night waking among 9-month-old infants (Adair et al., 1991) found that infants whose parent or caregiver routinely remained present with them at bedtime until they fell asleep were more likely to wake during the night. This finding suggests that putting infants to bed when they are at least partially awake elicits their own internal devices for falling asleep. If the infant wakes during the night, barring no problems such as hunger, discomfort, or impending illness, she or he can learn to

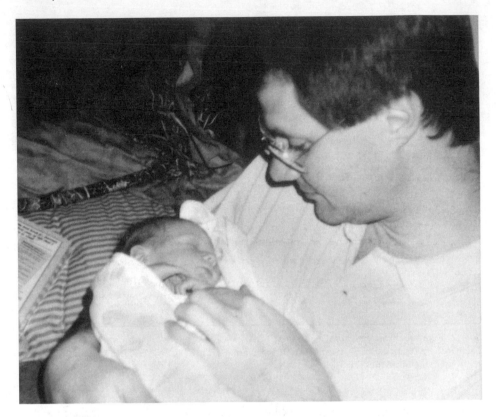

*Infants exhibit great variation in both amount of sleep and types of sleep behavior.*

employ the same internal devices rather than soliciting parental intervention. While this study did not establish true cause and effect, the researchers suggested that infant temperament and parental difficulty in separating from the infant may be factors associated with frequent night waking in some babies. Other reasons for night waking include being too cold or too warm and needing appropriate covers, colic, an unfamiliar bed or new surroundings, disturbing sensory stimuli such as loud or startling noises, and sudden bright light. Some infants signal that they are awake; others do not unless they are in some form of distress such as hunger or a wet diaper. Infants generally sleep through the night by age 3 months, typically from five to eight hours.

Such routines vary from family to family; however, the intent is to provide unhurried yet interactive bedtime rituals that reassure and comfort the infant. There is no need to insist that the household be abnormally quiet, as infants readily adjust to routine noises in their environments. Nor should siblings be expected to be particularly quiet—though rowdy play, of course, disturbs anyone's rest. Some infants may be soothed by usual household noises, which may provide a sense of security and an auditory sense of the permanence of people and the predictability of routines.

Similar routines in out-of-home child care arrangements facilitate naptime for infants and reassure them of the support of their other caregivers. As with noise

*Infants' behavior styles influence reciprocal interactions between infants and parents and other caregivers.*

levels at home, rest times can be scheduled during periods of the day when noise levels are at a minimum; yet there is no need to expect that all noise can be curtailed during group care naptimes.

**Temperament.** **Temperament** is an individual's biologically based behavior style which helps us to describe the infant's responses (Chess, 1967; Thomas & Chess, 1977; Thomas, Chess, & Birch, 1968). While this dimension of infant development will be discussed more fully in Chapter 6, it is mentioned here as one of the psychological states in infancy. Chess and Thomas (1987) identified several dimensions of temperament, including activity level, rhythms, approach and withdrawal behaviors, adaptability, responsiveness, intensity of reaction, quality of mood, distractability, and attention span and persistence. Using these activity classifications, the researchers delineated three basic temperament patterns: *easy*, *difficult*, and *slow to warm up*. These behavior styles influence the reciprocal interactions between infants and their caregivers. There are wide variations in temperaments among infants. Some infants are less able to calm themselves than others; some are easily comforted by their caregivers.

*temperament: an individual's behavior style that is both biologically and environmentally derived*

Angela is less easily soothed than Jeremy. At bedtime, she is quite fretful and restless. Inferring from the usual afternoon and evening family routines that bedtime is drawing near, she begins to whimper and cry and will not sustain her grasp on a soft toy offered to her. She resists being held or comforted.

Since birth, Angela has had a variety of caregivers, from hospital neonatal care nursing staff in her first two weeks to a home with extended family, including her grandmother and her own mother's siblings, some young children, and some teenagers. Each has assumed responsibility for her care when needed. Thus, Angela's care has been neither predictable nor consistent.

Angela's grandmother, sensing a difficult bedtime, intervenes. She carries Angela on her shoulder as she walks about the house giving cleanup and bedtime instructions to the other children. Patting a fretful Angela, she continues to walk, talk, and hush the baby. Unsuccessful, she proceeds to a back bedroom where, separated from the rest of the family, she places Angela across her lap and begins to sing and talk softly to her. For a time Angela still wiggles, lifts her head and frets, and is easily distracted by the sound of children playing inside the house. Her grandmother continues to sing and talk or hum until at last Angela begins to rest and finally dozes. ■

Temperament is readily observable in infancy, expressing itself through various behaviors such as modulated and unmodulated emotions. In the preceding vignette, Angela seems unable to modulate her emotions at this point and thus becomes more and more agitated as others attempt to comfort her.

While individual styles of behaving endure over time, the behavior itself is expressed in age-related forms. For instance, Angela's resistance to comforting efforts may at a later age manifest itself in self-comforting strategies such as associating a particular person, place, chair, pillow, or blanket with restful sleep.

The activity levels of neonates have been positively correlated with activity levels at ages 4 and 8 (Korner et al., 1985). Activity levels have recently been associated with birth order (Eaton, Chipperfield, & Singbeil, 1989). A study of 7,000 children ranging in age from 4 days to 7 years, including first- through sixth-born children, found that earlier-born children were more active than later-born children. Heredity seems to play a role in determining individual temperament, as does a child's environment. However, the relative influence of each has not been established.

## SENSORY CAPABILITIES IN INFANCY

The newborn's sensory equipment is remarkably operative at birth. Neonates are capable of seeing, hearing, tasting, smelling, and responding to touch. The neonate takes in and processes information to a much greater extent than we might expect. **Perceptual** development begins as the infant seeks and receives information through the senses.

*perception: the physiological process by which sensory input is interpreted*

**Touch.** Scientists believe the sense of touch emerges between 7½ and 14 weeks of embryonic development (Hooker, 1952). Skin, muscular, and inner ear (vestibular) senses are more mature at birth than are the other senses (Gottfried, 1984). The sense of touch, particularly around the mouth area, is especially acute and facilitates infant rooting and nursing. Certain other parts of the body are sensitive to touch. These include the nose, skin of the forehead, soles of the feet, and genitals. Most of the reflexes listed in Table 5.1 are stimulated by touch. In addition to touch, the skin is sensitive to temperature, pressure, and pain.

For obvious ethical reasons, little research exists on sensitivity to pain. Contrary to the previous notion that neonates do not experience great pain, we now know they do. Recent studies of pain associated with infant circumcision procedures have helped to advance knowledge about infant pain. By analyzing the recorded vocalizations of newborn males during circumcision, researchers identified significant differences in vocalizations as each step of the procedure became more invasive (Porter, Miller, & Marshall, 1986). Some surgical procedures previously thought to be painless for newborns are now accompanied by analgesia or anesthesia whenever possible (American Academy of Pediatrics, 1989; Ryan & Finer, 1994).

Studies of preterm infants have found that touch plays a very significant role in their development. Many neonatal care units encourage parents of preterm infants in particular to gently hold and caress them (when the infant's physical condition permits). When the infant cannot be held, gently caressing the infant in the isolette is encouraged. In some hospitals volunteers hold, rock, and softly stroke these small and vulnerable babies. A study by Field and her colleagues (1986) found that preterm infants who were gently touched and caressed several times each day gained weight faster than preterm infants who did not receive this regular stimulation. These infants also exhibited advanced mental and motor development at the end of the first year compared to the control group infants.

The importance of touch and the infant's need for it have been of interest to researchers for years. Lack of soothing tactile sensations during infancy has been associated with delays in cognitive and affective development (Ainsworth, 1962; Yarrow, 1961). Thus, in addition to the sheer pleasure experienced by both infant and caregiver when hugging, rocking, caressing, patting, and so on, these experiences provide the infant with tactile stimulation essential to perceptual and sensory development.

**Vision.**  The neonate's vision functions well at birth, though visual acuity is imperfect, with a tendency toward nearsightedness (Cornell & McDonald, 1986). Neonates can follow a moving light and fixate on an object at a distance of about 9 inches. In his pioneering studies of infant visual preferences, Fantz (1961) found that infants prefer human faces and enjoy bold patterns such as checkerboards or bull's-eye patterns, but do not attend well to solid colors. Infants tend to look at the edges of the designs or at the point where two contrasts come together. Other researchers have found that infants watch more intently a face that is active, smiling, talking, blinking, or laughing (Haith, 1966; Samuels, 1985). Others have found that infants attend longer to a face that imitates their own facial movements and expressions (Winnicott, 1971). Bornstein (1984, 1985) found that infants respond to differences in colors and suggested that later ability to categorize by color, thought to be a result of cognitive development, has its origins in the earliest visual perceptual processes. Whereas vision improves rapidly over the first few months of life, mature 20/20 vision is not achieved until about age 5 (Bornstein, 1988).

**Hearing.**  Though the passages of the ear (Eustachian tubes and external canal) may still contain amniotic fluids for the first few days after birth, the newborn hears fairly well. After the fluids are absorbed, the neonate responds vigorously to

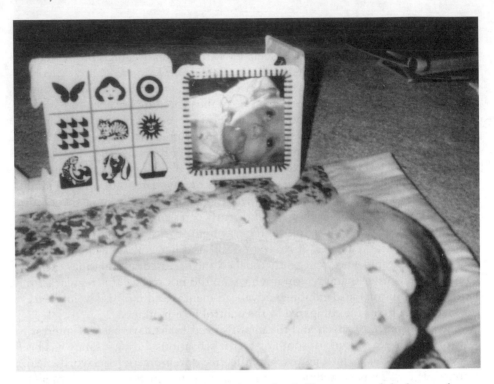

*Studies of infants' visual preferences indicate that bold patterns and the human face sustain the infant's gaze.*

various sounds in the environment. The infant is startled by loud noises and soothed by soft sounds. It has been suggested that neonates can discriminate between loud and soft sounds but do not respond to variations in pitch (Bench, 1978). Researchers have also demonstrated that neonates are capable of discriminating among sounds that differ in duration, direction, and frequency as well as loudness (Bower, 1982).

Neonates seem particularly responsive to the human voice (Caron, Caron, & MacLean, 1988). The neonate will often stop crying when spoken to, visually scan when it hears voices, and attempt to vocalize (Rosenthal, 1982). Could it be that human infants are genetically "programmed" to react to human speech?

**Taste.** Newborns are very responsive to variations in taste. The taste of milk seems to elicit a reaction of satisfaction in infants. Infants prefer sweet tastes and usually react negatively to sour, bitter, or salty tastes (Steiner, 1979).

**Smell.** Infants sense a variety of odors and will turn away from noxious odors such as vinegar or alcohol. Interestingly, they seem able to recognize the smell of their mothers within the first few days of life (MacFarlane, 1977; Makin & Porter, 1989) and will turn away from an unused breast pad or the breast pad of another mother. Musick and Householder (1986) suggest that the early bonding process might be facilitated if the mother left her breast pad or another small article of her clothing in the bassinet to reinforce the infant's sensory attachment to her.

## PHYSICAL AND MOTOR DEVELOPMENT DURING THE FIRST YEAR

Growth and development during this first year are both dramatic and significant. According to Sandra Anselmo (1987, p. 148), "In no other one-year period until puberty are there so many physical changes. The changes in infancy are measured in terms of days and weeks rather than in terms of months and years."

### PHYSICAL CHARACTERISTICS

Birthweight and birth length are always of interest to parents, grandparents, and health care professionals. While birthweight and birth length often make for proud conversation, physical measurements are quite significant in the context of infant health and development. Low birthweight, for instance, has serious implications for survival and for subsequent normal development. Contemporary studies indicate that there are race-specific influences on birthweight distributions (Yi, Zhu, & Chong, 1991; Wilcox & Russell, 1990; Shiono et al., 1986).

The average birthweight for full-term infants is 7½ pounds, with a range from 5½ to 10 pounds. Boys usually are slightly heavier than girls at birth. Birth length ranges from 18 to 22 inches, with an average of 20 inches. The neonate frequently loses weight in the first few days due to loss of body fluids and the inability to adequately take in nourishment, but will gain at a rate of 6 to 8 ounces per week, and by 5 to 6 months may have doubled the birthweight. The infant's length also will have increased, by 6 to 7 inches.

During the second half of the first year, gains in pounds and inches decelerate somewhat, though growth continues at a rapid pace. Weight may increase by 4 to 6 ounces weekly and height by 3 to 4 inches. By the first birthday, infants may have tripled in weight and grown 10 to 12 inches since birth. If growth were to proceed at such pace, an 18-year-old would measure more than 15 feet tall and weigh several tons! Fortunately, growth slows appreciably after the first two years.

Weight and height are observable characteristics. While this outward growth is readily observable, significant internal growth is taking place as the central nervous system matures and bones and muscles increase in weight, length, and coordination. The soft bones of early infancy gradually **ossify** as calcium and other minerals harden them. The bones are soft and pliable and are difficult to break. They do not support the infant's weight in sitting or standing positions. The skull bones are separated by **fontanelles** (often called "soft spots"), which may compress to facilitate passage through the birth canal. These fontanelles tend to diminish after 6 months and may close between 9 and 18 months.

Interestingly, the bones of the skull and wrists ossify earliest, with the wrists and ankles developing more bones as the child matures. Girls may be several weeks ahead of boys in bone development at birth. Physicians may use X rays of

*ossify:*
*to convert cartilage or membrane to bone*

*fontanelles:*
*membranous space between the cranial bones of the fetus and infant*

skeletal age:
a measure of physical
development based on
examination of skeletal
X rays

the wrists to determine the **"skeletal age"** of individual children. Such X rays reveal the number of bones in the wrist along with the extent of ossification. This information assists in assessing expected growth progress and diagnosing growth disorders and disease.

Though infants are born with all the muscle cells they will ever have (Tanner, 1989), there is a large amount of water in muscle tissue. Gradually, as protein and other nutrients replace this cellular fluid, the strength of the muscles increases.

Neurological development exhibits a growth spurt in the last trimester of prenatal development and during the first two years of life. During this period, more than half of the brain's mature weight is added. Since brain growth is rapid during prenatal development and the first year, head circumference measures provide the best indication of brain growth. Small-for-age head circumference measurements at 8 months to 2 years of age may indicate developmental delay. As is true of other organs, not all parts of the brain develop at the same rate. At birth, the brainstem and the midbrain are the most highly developed. These areas of the brain control consciousness, inborn reflexes, digestion, respiration, and elimination.

The cerebrum and the cerebral cortex surround the midbrain and are significant in the development of primary motor and sensory responses. Following the law of developmental direction, the nerve cells that control the upper trunk and arms mature before those that control the lower trunk and legs. Observation of infant motor activity reveals a growing number of skills that utilize the muscles of the neck, arms, and hands, skills that precede the abilities to turn over, sit up, or crawl. By 6 months of age, the cerebral cortex has matured sufficiently to control most of the infant's physical activity. At this point in growth and development, many of the reflexes of early infancy should be disappearing, signaling the maturation of the neurological system.

## EXPECTED PATTERNS AND DEVELOPMENTAL MILESTONES

Recall the examples at the beginning of the chapter drawn from cross-cultural studies of variations in child growth and development. Both timing and sequence of development can vary among and within cultures and racial groups. In addition, current thinking regarding the expected patterns of growth and development calls for a consideration of national, racial, and socioeconomic factors that influence the economic conditions that facilitate or impede growth and development. These factors include the quality of home environments, parental competence, growth- and health-promoting nutrition, health care and immunizations, and educational and recreational opportunities. Diverse parental goals and expectations influence growth and development through the types of "training" imposed on children, play opportunities, and other experiences provided for them (Bronfenbrenner, 1986; Garrett et al., 1994; Ogbu, 1981). Therefore, in studying Table 5.3, consider the ages as approximations rather than absolutes, and recognize that the sequence may indeed vary. For instance, some children scoot in a seated position rather than crawl. This represents a variation, but not a developmental "abnormality."

**TABLE 5.3**
**Developmental Milestones in Motor Control During the First Year**

| Age | Motor Development |
|---|---|
| Birth to 3 months | Supports head when in prone position<br>Lifts head<br>Supports weight on elbows<br>Hands relax from the grasping reflex<br>Visually follows a moving person<br>Pushes with feet against lap when held upright<br>Makes reflexive stepping movements when held in a standing position<br>Sits with support<br>Turns from side to back |
| 3 to 6 months | Slaps at bath water<br>Kicks feet when prone<br>Plays with toes<br>Reaches but misses dangling object<br>Shakes and stares at toy placed in hand<br>Head self-supported when held at shoulder<br>Turns from back to side<br>Sits with props<br>Makes effort to sit alone<br>Exhibits crawling behaviors<br>Rocks on all fours<br>Draws knees up and falls forward |
| 6 to 9 months | Rolls from back to stomach<br>Crawls using both hands and feet<br>Sits alone steadily<br>Pulls to standing position in crib<br>Raises self to sitting posture<br>Successfully reaches and grasps toy<br>Transfers object from one hand to the other<br>Stands up by furniture<br>Cruises along crib rail<br>Makes stepping movements around furniture |
| 9 to 12 months | Exhibits "mature" crawling<br>Cruises holding on to furniture<br>Walks with two hands held<br>Sits without falling<br>Stands alone<br>May walk alone<br>Attempts to crawl up stairs<br>Grasps object with thumb and forefinger |

## RELATION OF PHYSICAL AND MOTOR DEVELOPMENT TO PSYCHOSOCIAL DEVELOPMENT

Ever-increasing physical and motor abilities during the first year expand the infant's psychosocial horizons. By providing hunger, pain, and happiness cues through crying, cooing, and other vocalizations, infants learn that they can lead others to interact with them. When these interactions are positive and supportive, infants learn to trust both parents/caregivers and themselves to meet their needs. Each new physical milestone—prone, sitting, crawling, standing, and so on—brings about new sets of behaviors and new types of interactions between infant and caregivers. For most infants, each new ability elicits encouragement, praise, and joy, supporting an emerging sense of self. As motor abilities increase, parents, siblings, and caregivers begin to perceive the infant as more "grown up" and may unwittingly attribute greater self-sufficiency to the infant than is really the case: holding a bottle, feeding self, understanding distances and depths, and so on. Of course, these misattributions can compromise the infant's safety and deflates an emerging sense of confidence.

As the infant becomes more mobile, concerns about safety bring about new forms of communicating through facial expressions, voice tone and pitch, and verbal cautions and commands. Undue restraint and excessive restrictions, particularly if delivered in impatience and anger, frighten and confuse the infant. Such interactions can reduce children's emerging self-confidence and willingness to explore, learn, and express themselves (Comer & Poussant, 1992). While it may be necessary to say "no" and "don't touch" often, overuse of such restrictions can cause infants to associate negative and disapproving responses with the people who mean the most to them. Attempts to explore and investigate and to try out emerging skills will thus be impeded, as will the confidence and independence that new skills bring. It is better to establish safe, "child-friendly" environments than to impose constant verbal restrictions (Meyerhoff, 1994).

## RELATION OF PHYSICAL AND MOTOR DEVELOPMENT TO COGNITION

Motor experiences in infancy form the basis of meaning in earliest cognitive development as physical movements emerge. At first the movements are unintentional (as with many reflexes); later most of them become purposeful. Piaget's (1952) stages of cognitive development begin with the *sensorimotor* stage, from birth to age 2. This sensorimotor stage of cognitive development follows a pattern from random, involuntary reflex activity, in which cognition is dominated by sensory input, to anticipatory and intentional behaviors facilitated by increasing mobility and emerging large and fine motor controls.

An environment rich in sensory input—sights, sounds, tastes, aromas, textures, and movement—enhances cognitive development in infants. In addition, talking, singing, sharing books, and interacting socially with the infant provide needed input for a rapidly developing mind. An environment that encourages social interactions and freedom to explore is essential to a well-integrated cognitive system.

# FACTORS INFLUENCING PHYSICAL AND MOTOR DEVELOPMENT

## GENETIC MAKEUP

Each infant is a unique individual with a special genetic endowment. This genetic endowment is really observable in physical features such as eye, hair, and skin color, shape and size of facial features, body build, activity levels, and so on. It is also related to mental and psychosocial characteristics such as temperament, some forms of mental retardation, and certain psychological disorders. Contemporary research in genetics is beginning to pinpoint the influence of heredity on less observable characteristics such as size and functioning of the internal organs, susceptibility to disease, psychological strengths and disorders, and numerous other facets of human individuality. Screening tests during pregnancy to detect genetic abnormalities have broadened this knowledge base and allow early identification of and intervention in potential mental and physical disabilities.

## INTEGRITY OF PRENATAL DEVELOPMENT

Chapter 3 described the rapid development of the human organism during prenatal development. To the extent that this critical period in growth and development is protected from hazard, the integrity of the fetus is ensured. Studies of the vulnerability of the fetus during various prenatal stages indicate that there are both immediate and long-term "sleeper" effects of unhealthy intrauterine environments (Bornstein & Lamb, 1992). Infants who benefit from a healthy prenatal journey, one free of drugs, toxins, poor nutrition, maternal stress, and other environmental hazards, are less likely to experience the myriad and sometimes devastating health, growth, and developmental outcomes associated with poor or inadequate intrauterine environments.

## PRETERM AND LOW-BIRTHWEIGHT INFANTS

Prematurity is measured by *gestational age*, which ranges from 23 weeks or less to a full term of 38 to 42 weeks. Gestational age is an important predictor of survival and developmental outcomes. Infants born at full term but weighing less than expected for a full-term baby are considered *small for gestational age (SGA)*. Usually these infants are healthy, but they are immature and small and have insufficient body fat to assist in regulation of body temperature. Weight gain is usually their primary challenge; however, there may be other, more serious reasons for the infant's failure to gain sufficient weight in utero. Low-birthweight (LBW) infants range from 3.5 to 5.5 pounds. Infants in this birthweight range not only must build fat stores but, perhaps more critical, may face respiratory distress syndrome (RDS) due to immature lungs and breathing mechanisms. Low-birthweight infants are also at risk for mental retardation, cerebral palsy, convulsions, delayed speech, blindness, and deafness.

Very-low-birthweight (VLBW) infants weigh less than 3 pounds. These infants are extremely immature and need intensive neonatal care immediately following birth to help them survive. They are at higher risk of dying in the first 28 days— some estimate 40 times more likely— than "mature" newborns (Brecht, 1989). Sometimes their care requires lengthy and costly hospitalization. Many of these infants do not survive.

It is estimated that 7 percent of infants born in 1991 weighed less than 5.5 pounds (Children's Defense Fund, 1994). Preventing prematurity and low birth-weight in neonates is a complex challenge involving issues such as poverty, poor nutrition, lack of adequate health care, teenage pregnancy, delayed childbearing choices, genetic research, in utero medical treatment, emerging medical technology, ethics, and education.

## GENERAL HEALTH AND FREEDOM FROM DISEASE

**Regular Health Checkups and Immunizations.**  Regular visits to the pediatrician or family health care specialist are necessary to monitor the infant's progress in growth and development, assess nutritional needs, treat infections, allergies, and illness, and administer disease-preventing immunizations. The American Academy of Pediatrics recommends preventive health care visits for healthy infants and children at 1, 2, 4, 6, 9, 12, 15, and 18 months, then annually from ages 2 through 6, and then every two years through adolescence. More frequent visits may be necessary for children with special needs and between regular checkups as the need arises. In addition to checking growth progress through weight, height, and head circumference measurements, the physician and parent have an opportunity to discuss the child's health, preventive health care measures, how to meet individual nutritional requirements, how to deal with allergies and other treatment needs, and other parenting concerns.

Fortunately, infant immunizations now prevent many life-threatening diseases in infants and children, and many promising new vaccines are on the horizon. The chicken pox vaccine became available in 1995.

But despite great strides in immunizing infants and children, reports of failure to immunize seem to be on the rise. The Children's Defense Fund (1994) reports that in 1991, only 55.5 percent of all 2-year-olds were adequately immunized. Many of these children are from families that lack the resources and the knowledge to obtain health care for their children. Low rates of immunizations sometimes result in an alarming resurgence of serious communicable diseases that spread among other unimmunized children and adults. For example, in 1983 there were fewer than 1,500 cases of measles in the United States (Center for Disease Control, 1992). In 1992 this number escalated to nearly 26,500 cases, with 89 measles-related deaths. The alarming increase in cases of mumps, rubella, German measles, whooping cough, and polio has provoked a variety of campaigns and programs, both national and international, to educate and provide immunizations. The American Academy of Pediatrics Recommended Schedule of Immunization of Healthy Infants and Children was revised in 1994 (American Academy of Pediatrics, 1994). This schedule for immunizations appears on the following page.

**Dental Health.** The first teeth begin to erupt between 5 and 9 months of age. The first teeth to erupt are usually the two lower middle incisors, followed in a few months by the four upper middle incisors. By the end of the first year, most infants have these six teeth. The complete set of 20 teeth does not erupt until around 2 1/2 years. Pain associated with the eruption of teeth varies among infants. Some infants cry, are sleepy and fretful, seem to want to chew on anything, and drool considerably. Others appear to feel no pain or discomfort and may, to the surprise of their parents, present a "toothed" smile.

Care of teeth during the first year involves relieving the discomfort accompanying eruptions of new teeth and providing adequate proteins and minerals, particularly calcium and fluoride, in the infant's diet. Fluoride is usually available in adequate amounts in community water supplies; in some cases, however, fluoride supplements are prescribed. Now is the time for parents to begin limiting refined carbohydrates such as cookies, candies, soft drinks, and sweetened dry cereals. Curtailing indiscriminate use of the bottle will also protect the infant's teeth. "Nursing bottle" caries, or decay, occurs when sweetened water and juices are consumed from baby bottles taken to bed or carried about by the infant as a "constant companion" (Nizel, 1977).

**Nutrition.** The role of nutrition in ensuring optimal growth and developmental outcomes is paramount during prenatal development and infancy. During this period of very rapid growth, brain growth is particularly dramatic. Studies have linked impaired functioning of the central nervous system to poor nutrition in the early months of life (Dobbing, 1984; Galler, Ramsey, & Solimano, 1984, 1985). Adequate nutrition helps to prevent illnesses and ensures the developmental integrity of the individual.

*Breast or Formula Feeding.* One of the first decisions regarding feeding the newborn is whether to breast- or formula-feed. This decision is a personal one and is best made in consultation with one's obstetrician and pediatrician prior to the time of delivery. While in recent years the number of mothers choosing to breast-feed has declined slightly, the medical profession continues to encourage it (American Academy of Pediatrics, 1993). The choice not to breast-feed, however, does not preclude good healthy infant nutrition and sound infant-parent relationships.

Because of its biochemical composition, breast milk is best suited to the infant's immature digestive system. It provides initial immunologic advantages through **colostrum,** a substance that precedes mature breast milk in the first days of breast feeding. Mature breast milk is secreted between the third and sixth day after childbirth. Colostrom provides immunity to a number of infections when the mother carries the immunities. Human milk is also less likely to trigger allergies or gastrointestinal distress and is more easily digested and metabolized than cow's milk. To complete its superior nutritional composition, vitamin D supplements are often recommended. Vitamin C is recommended when the nursing mother's diet is deficient in it. Fluoride supplements may also be advised.

*colostrum:*
*the first liquid secreted*
*by the mammary glands*
*soon after childbirth*

Contemporary studies of human milk and the practice of breast feeding have revealing additional advantages (Duncan et al., 1993; Association for Childhood Education International Exchange, 1990).

☐☐☐  **BOX 5.1**    RECOMMENDED CHILDHOOD IMMUNIZATION SCHEDULE
UNITED STATES-JANUARY 1995

Vaccines are listed under routinely recommended ages. Shaded bars indicate range of acceptable ages for vaccination.

| Age ►  Vaccine ▼ | Birth | 2 months | 4 months | 6 months | 12[5] months | 15 months | 18 months | 4-6 years | 11-12 years | 14-16 years |
|---|---|---|---|---|---|---|---|---|---|---|
| Hepatitis B[1] | HB-1 | | | | | | | | | |
| | | HB-2 | | HB-3 | | | | | | |
| Diphtheria,Tetanus, Pertussis[2] | | DTP | DTP | DTP | DTP or DTaP at 15+ m | | | DTP or DtaP | Td | |
| H. influenzae type b[3] | | Hib | Hib | Hib | Hib | | | | | |
| Polio | | OPV | OPV | OPV | | | | OPV | | |
| Measles, Mumps, Rubella[4] | | | | | MMR | | | MMR or MMR | | |

[1]**Infants born to HBsAg-negative mothers** should receive the second dose of hepatitis B vaccine between 1 and 4 months of age, provided at least 1 month has elapsed since receipt of the first dose. The third dose is recommended between 6 and 18 months of age.
**Infants born to HBsAg-positive mothers** should receive immunoprophylaxis for hepatitis B with 0.5 ml Hepatitis B Immune Globulin (HBIG) within 12 hours of birth, and 0.5 ml of either Merck Sharpe & Dohme vaccine (Recombivax HB) or of SmithKline Beecham vaccine (Engeriz-B) at a separate site. In these infants, the second dose of vaccine is recommended at 1 month of age and the third dose at 6 months of age. All pregnant women should be screened for HBsAg in an early prenatal visit.
[2]The fourth dose of DTP may be administered as early as 12 months of age, provided at least 6 months have elapsed since DTP3. Combined DTP-Hib products may be used when these two vaccines are to be administered simultaneously. DTaP (diptheria and tetanus toxoids and acellular pertussis vaccine) is licensed for use for the 4th and/or 5th dose of DTP vaccine in children 15 months of age or older and may be preferred for these doses in children in this age group.
[3]*Three H. influenzae* type b conjugate vaccines are available for use in infants: HbOC [HibTITER] (Lederle Praxis); PRP-T [ActHIB; OmniHIB] (Pasteur Mérieux, distributed by SmithKline Beecham; Connaught); and PRP-OMP [PedvaxHIB] (Merck Sharp & Dohme). Children who have received PRP-OMP at 2 and 4 months of age do not require a dose at 6 months of age. After the primary infant Hib conjugate vaccine series is completed, any licensed Hib conjugate vaccine may be used as a booster dose at 12-15 months.
[4]The second dose of MMR vaccine should be administered EITHER at 4-6 years of age OR at 11-12 years of age.
[5]Vaccines recommended in the second year of life (12-15 months of age) may be given at either one or two visits.

*Source:* Approved by the Advisory Committee on Immunization Practices (ACIP), the American Academy of Pediatrics, and the American Academy of Family Physicians (AAFP).

- Infants who are breast-fed are less likely to develop ear infections during their first year.

- Breast feeding appears to lower low-density lipoproteins (LDL), or "bad" cholesterol, in an infant's blood.

- Human milk may contain a substance that protects against some childhood cancers, particularly cancers of the lymph systems.

- Breast feeding reduces the risk of breast cancer in premenopausal women.

- Breast feeding contributes to family planning (child spacing) by suppressing ovulation.

Few health care professionals today would not encourage breast feeding. However, some mothers with certain health or physical problems should not breast-feed, and others simply choose not to do so. For these mothers, the choice to provide formula feeding is best. Research to improve the nutritional content, quality, and digestibility of commercial formulas has evolved over many decades and is ongoing. The Food and Drug Administration bases its regulations of infant formula on standards for infant formulas developed by the American Academy of Pediatrics Committee on Nutrition. Today's formulas are designed to simulate human milk and provide essential proteins, fats, carbohydrates, vitamins, and minerals. Thus, the choice to provide formula instead of human milk during the first months is a viable option. Formula can also be used as a supplement for breast milk when the mother must be away or chooses to omit a breast feeding, or when the mother's breast milk is inadequate. In addition, there are special-purpose formulas for specific nutritional or medical needs.

To ensure optimal benefit from formula feeding, formula must be mixed according to the directions supplied by the manufacturer and prescribed by the infant's pediatrician. Overdiluted formula has less nutritional value, may fill the infant's stomach but not satisfy the infant's hunger, and thus fail to provide enough nutrients and calories to sustain growth. Overdilution is often a problem in economically disadvantaged areas where the formula is diluted to make it last longer and thus reduce its cost. In addition to failing to meet the infant's nutritional needs, overdiluting can lead to water intoxication, a very serious condition that can cause brain swelling and convulsions in infants. Underdiluted formula may also cause problems. Due to water loss through urine, feces, regurgitation, fever, or vomiting, underdiluted formula can fail to meet the infant's need for fluid intake, leading to dehydration and other complications.

Other precautions need to be taken when bottle-feeding infants. Bottle-fed infants must be held in a comfortable position during feeding. The bottle should never be propped; lacking the motor skills necessary to move the bottle, the infant can choke on the formula. Propping the bottle has other risks as well. Tooth decay can result when formula stays in the mouth too long, coating the teeth with sugars. Also, when the infant is lying down while bottle feeding, bacteria grow in the pooled liquid in the mouth and cheeks, then make their way to the eustachian tubes, resulting in painful ear infections.

The psychological need of infants to be held when being fed is also important. Whether breast- or bottle-fed, infants experience both physical and emotional closeness to their parent or caregiver while being held and cuddled during feeding. Calm, unhurried feeding times contribute to the infant's sense of well-being and trust.

satiety:
the feeling of having
had sufficient food to
statisfy hunger

Sensitivity to the infant's hunger and **satiety** cues also enhances infants' trust in both themselves and their caregivers. Overfeeding or underfeeding result when adults fail to recognize these cues. Turning the head away from a nipple, facial expressions of distaste, and other bodily attempts to refuse food are the infant's way of communicating satiety. Allowing infants to eat what they need without insisting on further intake helps infants to recognize their own feelings of hunger or fullness. Adults must also avoid giving food indiscriminately in an attempt to curtail crying. Not all crying is hunger-related. Providing food or drink every time the child cries establishes a pattern of satisfying discomforts, regardless of what they are, by eating. The obvious outcome of this psychological behavior is obesity and poor physical and psychosocial health.

For most healthy infants, feeding schedules break into four-hour intervals. Some infants may need to be fed every three hours; smaller infants will need food every two hours. Caregivers soon learn to adjust to these rhythms, knowing that as the infant grows and matures, the schedule will become more predictable.

*Solid Foods.* On the advice of the pediatrician, solid foods are usually introduced sometime between the fourth and sixth months. The decision to introduce solid foods is based on sociocultural, psychological, and economic considerations, as well as the infant's developmental progress (American Academy of Pediatrics, 1993).

Taking in solid foods is a different developmental task than sucking and swallowing liquids. Now the infant must mouth or chew the food to soften it, experience its texture as well as its taste, move it to the back of the mouth, and successfully swallow it. This task is not always well coordinated, as demonstrated by the infant's need for a bib.

Contrary to an often held belief, early introduction of solid foods does not assist the infant in sleeping through the night. Hunger does awaken infants in the night, but nutritionists advise that the decision to introduce solid foods must be based on the infant's need for the nutrients provided by solid foods and on the infant's physiological readiness to handle solid foods.

The introduction of solid foods usually begins with iron-fortified cereals. New foods are introduced one at a time, and usually once a week, to accustom the infant to this new experience and to detect any allergic reaction to specific foods. As the intake of solid foods increases, the need for milk or formula decreases. Neither sugar nor salt should be added to foods given to infants; their immature digestive systems do not handle added seasonings well.

As the infant grows and learns to eat a variety of foods, care must be given to providing a balanced diet consisting of foods selected from the vegetable, fruit, meat, grain, and cereal groups. Foods selected for the youngest eaters should be appealing in color, flavor, texture, and shape. Self-feeding foods, foods that can be held in the hand or grasped from a tray, must be easy to chew and swallow. Mealtimes should be unhurried and pleasant.

When providing solid foods to an infant, several precautions must be taken. Foremost is avoiding food contamination. Foods should be fresh and properly stored. Adults must observe scrupulously hygienic procedures for preparing and serving baby meals: washed hands, clean utensils, foods kept at appropriate hot or cold temperatures, and covered, sanitary, and refrigerated storage of unused portions. It is best not to reheat leftover baby food, since illness is caused by microorganisms that grow in foods at room temperature.

Some foods cause particular problems for infants and young children. For instance, honey and corn syrup have been found to contain **clostridium botulinum,** the organism responsible for **botulism.** In infants under a year old, the immature gastrointestinal tract allows this organism to become active and potentially lethal (Christian & Gregor, 1988). Foods that have caused choking include hot dogs, candy, peanuts, grapes, large chunks of meat, hard or chewy cookies, carrots, popcorn, and chewing gum. Selection of nutritional substitutes for these foods and close supervision as the infant learns to handle new foods are imperative. Infants and small children should not be given foods to eat in a moving vehicle or as they are toddling about, as this increases the risk of choking.

*clostridium botulinum: bacterium that causes botulism*

*botulism: an often fatal form of food poisoning*

Contemporary concerns about obesity, cholesterol, and other diet-related health problems have led some parents to mistakenly believe that reducing fat and calories in the infant's diet is necessary. Quite the contrary is true. Body size, proportions, and composition are in a period of very rapid change. The infant's calorie needs per unit of body weight far exceed that of older children and adults to maintain rapid growth. In the absence of teeth, infants depend on consuming sufficient amounts of breast milk or formula to meet their increased caloric needs. In addition, during the last trimester of prenatal development and during the first few years of postnatal development, rapid **myelination** of the nervous system takes place. Fat is a major component of myelin (the tissue that surrounds the nerves as they mature) and as such is an essential part of the infant's diet if optimal neurological integrity is to be obtained (Eichorn, 1979). The American Academy of Pediatrics, Committee on Nutrition (1993) advises against practices that limit the diets of infants.

*myelination: the process of covering the nerve cells within the central nervous system with fatty tissue (myelin), which promotes efficient transmission impulses along the neurons*

**Colic.** *Colic* is abdominal discomfort that occurs in infants 2 weeks to 3 months of age. It is characterized by irritability, fussing, or crying sometimes for more than three hours a day and occurring as often as three days a week. It can be quite painful for the infant and distressing to parents. Why colic begins to appear at this age is unclear. Some suggested causes are swallowed air, high-carbohydrate foods, overfeeding, intolerance for cow's milk, intestinal allergy, a stressful environment, or impending illness (Pilliteri, 1992). Some infants seem more prone to colic than others, and no universal treatment exists since the causes vary. Physical examination by a pediatrician may be needed to detect more serious problems.

Some preventive measures can be taken to reduce the incidence of colic. These include feeding in an unhurried and calm manner, burping at regular intervals during feeding, avoiding either overfeeding or underfeeding, and identifying possible food allergies with the physician. When colic occurs, holding the baby upright or lying the baby prone across the lap may be helpful. Sometimes changing caregivers helps. A tired and frustrated parent or caregiver whose attempts to soothe the infant have met with failure may, if these efforts continue, exacerbate the problem.

## SAFETY

Environments for infants must always be kept sanitary and safe. Awareness of the infant's growing mobility and inclination to put things in the mouth is critical in providing a clean and safe environment. The infant's surroundings must be examined for potential dangers—objects on the floor that could scratch, cut, or go into the mouth; electrical outlets and wires that could be pulled or mouthed; furnishings that topple easily; poisonous substances within easy reach; swimming pools and bathtubs of water; hot water faucets, unsanitary toilet bowls; and so on.

All baby equipment and clothing should be selected according to current safety standards. These standards apply to bassinets, cribs, carrying seats, swings, playpens, baby carriages, walkers, jogging strollers, pacifiers, toys, and other baby equipment. The Consumer Products Safety Commission regularly publishes information about safe products for children and items that have been recalled because of the hazards they pose. This information can prevent unnecessary accidents and injuries to infants and children.

Beginning in infancy, automobile child safety seats must be consistently used when transporting an infant or young child in a motor vehicle. Proper use of infant safety seats helps to prevent death and injury. The Federal Motor Vehicle Safety Standard Act 213 mandates that passenger safety seats manufactured after January 1981 must meet certain standards for design and use. However, this law did not prohibit the sale of infant passenger seats manufactured before this date. Consequently, some unsafe infant passenger seats may still be on the market through "hand-me-downs" and garage sale sources. Effective September 1, 1995, The National Highway Traffic Safety Administration will require that all manual safety belts have a lockable feature to lock them securely around child safety seats.

## OPPORTUNITIES TO INTERACT, EXPLORE, AND PLAY

Each new motor skill extends the infant's ability to interact with people and objects in the environment. Infants enjoy looking at colorful objects in the environment. They enjoy listening to the human voice and to recordings of pleasing or familiar sounds and music and experiencing different textures such as soft toys, bedding, carpeting, and so on. Toys and focused interactions in which infant and parent or caregiver talk, laugh, imitate each other, play peek-a-boo and pat-a-cake, explore the surroundings, label objects and events, and share pictures and cloth or board books all provide opportunities to play. Play is essential to all facets of growth and development: physical/motor, psychosocial, cognitive, language, and literacy. We will discuss play and play behaviors in the context of these developmental areas throughout the text.

## SOCIOECONOMIC INFLUENCES

Adequate food, clothing, and shelter depend on socioeconomic factors. Availability of and access to medical and preventive health care, good nutrition, child care, educational opportunities, and other community resources are essential to a quality life and, more important, to healthy growth and development.

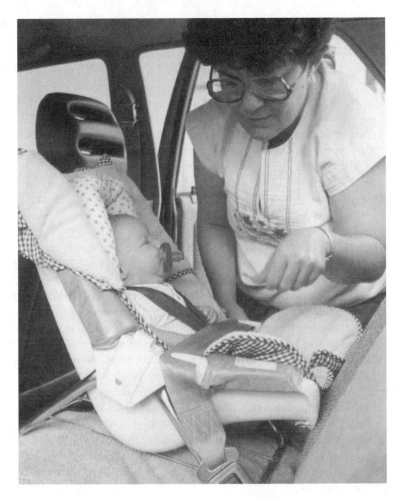

*Proper use of approved infant safety seats helps to prevent death or serious injuries.*

Unfortunately, many American families live in poverty today. Infants and children in these families are far more at risk for poor growth and developmental outcomes than other children (National Center for Children in Poverty, 1994; Children's Defense Fund, 1994).

## HEALTH AND WELL-BEING ISSUES IN INFANT DEVELOPMENT

### INFANT MORTALITY RATES AND RISKS

**Infant mortality** rates (deaths during the first year of life) in the United States are alarmingly high for a modern industrialized and technologically advanced nation. Despite great strides in medical and child health protection over the years, the

*infant mortality: deaths during the first year of life*

*syndrome:*
*a group of combined symptoms that characterize a physiological or psychological disorder*

1991 infant mortality rate for all races in the United States was 8.9 per 1,000 live births. In the United States, an African American infant is more than twice as likely to die during the first year as an Anglo infant (Children's Defense Fund, 1994). The causes of neonatal and infant deaths among all races relate to poor prenatal and newborn care, low birthweight, congenital malformations and diseases, factors associated with certain **syndromes**, including fetal alcohol syndrome, chemical withdrawal syndrome, and sudden infant death syndrome (SIDS).

Sudden infant death syndrome is the sudden and unexpected death of an apparently healthy infant during the first year. An estimated 12.6 percent of infant deaths are attributed to this mysterious syndrome (Colon & Colon, 1989). In the past, it was thought that infants who died in their cribs had smothered in their covers (thus the term *crib death*). However, since its identification as a syndrome in the 1960s, this perplexing phenomenon has commanded considerable research, and its actual cause or causes are still difficult to pinpoint.

In their rigorous yet elusive search for causes over the past three decades, scientists have identified a number of factors associated with SIDS. While these factors are not causes in themselves, they have helped researchers identify high-risk populations. The following factors have been associated with SIDS: prematurity, **apnea**, low birthweight, multiple births, cold weather, young mothers who have had poor prenatal care, low socioeconomic status, a maternal history of smoking, anemia, or drug abuse (particularly methadone), and siblings who died of SIDS.

*apnea:*
*absence of breathing for a period of up to 20 seconds*

A number of theories have attempted to explain SIDS. Some have implicated heredity; others have suggested upper respiratory viruses or a bacterium such as botulism; still others have proposed **metabolic** disorders, allergies, hyper- and hypothermia, and central nervous system abnormalities. One popular explanation relates to the infant's cardiovascular system. Studies have found, in a number of cases, an abnormality in the way the brain regulates breathing and heart rate (Hunt & Brouillette, 1987). However, not all infants studied exhibited this abnormality, so this theory needs additional research. SIDS probably has multiple causes (Kelly & Shannon, 1982).

*metabolic:*
*pertains to the body's complex chemical conversion of food into substances and energy necessary for maintenance of life*

Physicians today attempt to identify infants who may be at risk. For some of these infants, monitoring their respiration and heart rate during sleep is recommended. Monitoring machines that alert adults if apnea (suspended breathing) occurs are available; however, these machines are quite expensive and complicated and may cause more anxiety than relief. There is no evidence to date that these machines help prevent SIDS deaths (Hunt & Brouillette, 1987). Physicians today advise placing infants on their sides (with a rolled blanket for a prop), or on their backs to sleep rather than on their stomachs. Parents who have experienced this tragedy may benefit from support groups such as those sponsored by the National Foundation for Sudden Infant Death. They will need accurate information and supportive friends and professionals to help them cope effectively and avoid undue feelings of guilt, which often accompany the loss of a child.

Fortunately, most infants are born healthy and robust. Most illnesses during the first year are of short duration, lasting only a few days. Nevertheless, education, quality prenatal care, and medical supervision during the infant's earliest development are crucial.

## ABUSE AND NEGLECT

Legally, abuse and neglect are defined as "the physical or mental injury, sexual abuse, negligent treatment, or maltreatment of a child under the age of eighteen by a person who is responsible for the child's welfare under circumstances which indicate that the child's health or welfare is harmed or threatened thereby" (Child Abuse Prevention and Treatment Act of 1975, 42 U.S. Code 5101).

Abuse takes many forms: physical, in which bodily injury is inflicted; psychological, in which a child is cursed, berated, ignored, or rejected; and sexual abuse, which ranges from exposure and fondling to incest and rape. The victims of sexual abuse are sometimes infants. Infants and children under 3 are particularly susceptible to child abuse (Mayhall & Norgard, 1983). Frustrations over infant crying, colic, diaper soiling, eating, sleeping, and other stresses, as well as lack of knowledge about child development, may provoke an abusive adult.

**Failure to thrive** in infancy due to maternal deprivation or neglect has been documented. Studies have shown that children who are raised in impoverished and neglectful conditions during the first year of life show signs of severe developmental retardation (Province & Lipton, 1962). These infants exhibit delayed physical growth and skeletal development, resulting in heights and weights far below those expected for their ages (Barbero & Shaheen, 1967). Neglected children are more susceptible to disease, have more gastrointestinal upsets, and are particularly vulnerable emotionally.

*failure to thrive: a condition in which an apparently healthy infant fails to grow normally*

Neglect may take different forms, such as inadequate dietary practices, which impede growth, and failure to provide other necessities such as clothing, shelter, supervision, and protection. Sometimes neglect includes denial of medical attention. Intellectual stimulation and emotional support may also be absent. Some infants are simply abandoned.

Abuse and neglect occur at all socioeconomic levels, in all ethnic groups, and in all types of families—one-parent, two-parent, extended, large, and small. The incidence of abuse and neglect in families can be cyclical. Children who have been abused may become abusive adults (Gelles & Edfeldt, 1990), though intervention such as counseling and therapy, education, support groups for families, and subsequent positive life experiences may break such a cycle. In some cases, children need to be removed from situations of neglect or abuse. Today all states have child abuse reporting laws under which suspected child abuse must be reported to appropriate authorities.

## INFANTS WITH SPECIAL NEEDS

Infants with special needs require special sensitivity and knowledge. Sometimes the challenges of caring for an infant with special needs can be daunting for parents, family members, and nonparental caregivers. Families that need child care either in or out of the home find qualified services difficult to obtain and sometimes unaffordable. Often these families encounter a seemingly insensitive bureaucracy of social and educational services. Public Law 99-457 (which amended PL 94-142 in 1986) provides financial assistance to states for developing and implementing intervention services for infants and toddlers with disabilities. This law made services available to infants with disabilities from birth through age 2. It also mandates that intervention services be provided in the types of settings in which infants and toddlers without disabilities would participate. This mandates child care programs, nursery schools, public schools, and family care settings to make provisions to successfully integrate infants and toddlers with special needs into their programs. This includes providing additional and sometimes specialized training for adults who are responsible for the children, developing appropriate communicative and interactive skills, adapting physical environments, integrating remediation and intervention strategies into a developmentally appropriate curriculum, and working effectively with parents (Sexton, 1990; Ross, 1992).

## INFANT NONPARENTAL CARE

Today more and more mothers are employed outside the home, and families of all types and circumstances need nonparental care for their children for all or part of the day or night. Quality nonparental child care can be an enormous source of comfort to parents who need it. However, many of these families lack knowledge about how to choose "quality" child care, and the cost of quality care often exceeds the family's ability to pay for it. Selecting nonparental care for infants is particularly problematic, due to both its high cost and the need for adults who are genuinely sensitive to infants' needs at different stages of their development. As for all childhood ages and stages, the cornerstone of quality care and education is the adult who has direct responsibility for the infant. Wise selection of quality care depends on the ability to assess one's own child's needs and the knowledge, capabilities, and sensitivity of the caregiver. The National Association for the Education of Young Children and numerous other professional groups publish and disseminate pamphlets and articles on how to choose child care. Efforts to educate parents in this regard must be strong and ongoing. The Child Care Aware program, launched in 1992 and cosponsored by a number of child advocate organizations, is one such program designed to help parents understand how to recognize quality child care (NAEYC, July 1992). Parents who are knowledgeable in this regard are in a position to demand high-quality, appropriate programs for their children.

On the other hand, those who provide infant care have a moral and ethical responsibility to be knowledgeable about infants' needs and development and to provide healthy, safe, and supportive environments for infants and well-trained, qualified, sensitive personnel. Through state licensing laws and standards, accreditation standards of the National Association for the Education of Young Children, and standards such as those set by the joint efforts of the American Public Health Association and the American Academy of Pediatrics (1992), providers can assess their own facilities, programs, and interactive environments and make continuous efforts to improve and enrich their programs so that parents who enlist their services can be confident in the choices they have made.

 *Role of the Early Childhood Professional*

## *Facilitating Physical and Motor Development in Infants*

1. Provide adequate food, clothing, shelter, and medical attention.
2. Provide safe and secure surroundings for the growing and curious infant.
3. Provide sensorimotor stimulation through enriching interactions, sensory-rich environments, and opportunities to explore.
4. Provide an encouraging, supportive, and predictable atmosphere of love, acceptance, and satisfying human interactions.
5. Provide guidance that is positive and facilitative, helping the increasingly mobile infant to discover his or her capabilities in an atmosphere of both physical and psychological protection and safety.
6. Establish cooperative and supportive relationships with parents of infants.
7. Stay abreast of health and safety issues surrounding infant development.

## KEY TERMS

apnea
botulism
cephalocaudal
cerebral cortex
clostridium
  botulinum
colostrum
failure to thrive
fontanelles
infant mortality

interactionist
  perspective
metabolic
myelination
neonatal period
ossify
perception
primitive reflexes
proximodistal
psychological state

reflex
satiety
skeletal age
subcortical
survival reflexes
syndrome
temperament
transactional model
vernix caseosa

## REVIEW STRATEGIES AND ACTIVITIES

1. Review the key terms individually or with a classmate.
2. Compare infant formulas and baby foods available at your local supermarket. What nutrients are listed on the labels? How do these foods differ? How are they alike? What considerations are essential in the selection of a formula or solid food for individual infants?
3. Invite a child protective services professional from your state or regional human resources department to talk to the class about child abuse and neglect. What is the responsibility of the early childhood professional in dealing with abuse and neglect of young children?

4. Visit an accredited infant care center or a family day home that cares primarily for infants. Make a list of health and safety precautions practiced by the child caregivers and staff in these settings.

5. Identify and investigate support services and infant care programs for infants with special needs and their families.

6. With a classmate of a race or cultural group different than your own, discuss your early life experiences, family expectations, and cultural traditions.

## FURTHER READINGS

American Public Health Association and American Academy of Pediatrics (1992). *Caring for our children: National health and safety performance standards: Guidelines for out-of-home child care programs*. Washington, DC, and Elk Grove Village, IL: Authors.

Division for Exceptional Children Task Force on Recommended Practices (1993). *Division for Exceptional Children recommended practices: Indicators of quality in programs for infants and young children with special needs and their families*. Reston, VA: Council for Exceptional Children.

Godwin, A., & Schrag, L. (1988). *Setting up for infants: Guidelines for centers and family day care homes*. Washington, DC: National Association for the Education of Young Children.

Lindsay, J. W. (1992). *Teens parenting: Your baby's 1st year*. Buena Park, CA: Morning Glory Press.

Lynch, E. W., and Hanson, M. J. (1992). *Developing cross-cultural competence: A guide for working with children and their families*. Baltimore: Brooks Publishing Co.

*Pediatrics for Parents Newsletter*. P. O. Box 1069, Bangor, ME 04402-1069.

Surbeck, E., and Kelly, M. R. (Eds.). (1990). *Personalizing care with infants, toddlers, and families*. Wheaton, MD: Association for Childhood Education International.

# CHAPTER SIX

*The first cry of a newborn baby in Chicago or Zamboango, in Amsterdam or Rangoon, has the same pitch and key, each saying, I am! I have come through! I belong! I am a member of the Family!*

**Carl Sandburg**

# Psychosocial Development of the Infant

After studying this chapter, you will demonstrate comprehension by:

- Describing the psychosocial development of the infant during the first year.
- Identifying major social and emotional milestones in infancy.
- Describing contexts through which psychosocial development emerges.
- Describing the role of adults in facilitating healthy psychosocial development in the infant.

 Listen to the musings of parents as they attempt to ascribe personality characteristics to their newborns:

"He has such a peaceful look on his face."

"She is very squirmy."

"When he cries, he really wants to be heard!"

"She is such an easy baby."

"He is much more alert than his sister was."

What do these early observations foretell of infant personality, emotions, and future social interactions? What are the influences of heredity and environment on psychosocial development? How do infants respond to their experiences and interactions with others? Answers to such questions give us numerous insights into psychosocial development during the first year of life.

## FREUD'S THEORY OF PSYCHOSEXUAL DEVELOPMENT

Recall that Freud (1933) was the first to propose a theory of personality based on underlying psychological structures and needs. His theory focused on psychosexual development. Freud proposed that we are born with psychosexual instincts that change over the years from infancy to maturity. The focus of psychosexual energy relating to these instincts shifts from one part of the body to another as the

135

**TABLE 6.1**
Freud's Psychosexual Stages of Development

| Oral stage (1st year) | The primary focus of stimulation is the mouth and oral cavity, and the primary source of gratification is eating, sucking, and biting. The mother (or primary caregiver) is the source of satisfaction of the basic needs of this period. |
|---|---|
| Anal stage (2nd to 4th year) | Elimination and retention of fecal material become the focus of the child's attentions and energies. The child must learn appropriate time and place for elimination. This is the time when the child first learns to conform to social expectations. |
| Phallic stage (4th to 6th year) | Psychic energy is focused on the genital organs and pleasure received through organ manipulation. The realization that one is biologically and psychologically separate from others occurs, and the resolution of conflicts relating to appropriate sex roles becomes an issue. Children are said to develop incestuous desires for the parent of the other sex during this stage. |
| Latency stage (middle childhood) | Energy formerly directed toward sexual concerns becomes channeled in other directions, mainly that of forming affectional and social relationships with parents and other children (usually same-sex friends). |
| Genital stage (adolescence) | Physical sexual changes and development become the center of attention. Sex-role identity becomes a major issue. |

*Source:* Freud (1933).

individual matures. Development is characterized as a series of five stages revealing the shift in psychosexual energy. Table 6.1 describes this sequence.

## ERIKSON'S THEORY OF PSYCHOSOCIAL DEVELOPMENT

The psychosexual stages of development suggested by Freud provide a backdrop for our understanding of Erik Erikson's theory of personality development. Erikson's psychosocial theory derives from but enlarges on Freud's theory. Like Freud, Erikson explored crucial interactions between children and their caregivers and emphasized the importance of early experiences to later personality development. But Erikson was interested in the larger societal and cultural context in which psychosocial development occurs. By expanding on Freudian theory, Erikson identified eight stages of life that amplify our understanding of the significant encounters between children and their social world.

The eight stages of personality development Erikson proposed are characterized by basic life conflicts to be resolved. These conflicts result from both biological mat-

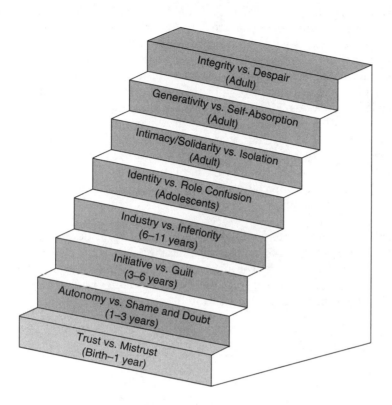

**FIGURE 6.1**
Erikson divided human development into eight psychosocial stages.

uration and societal expectations. Erikson suggests that critical periods, or developmental crises, are associated with each stage of healthy personality development.

According to Erikson, the first year of life is a critical period for the development of a sense of trust. The conflict for the infant involves striking a balance between trust and mistrust. This primary psychosocial task of infancy provides a developmental foundation from which later stages of personality development can emerge. It is represented in Figure 6.1 as the first stage in Erikson's eight-stage theory.

Infants learn to trust when their caregiving is characterized by nurturance, warmth, and predictability. Needs for food, comfort, and satisfying interactions with others depend on a responsive and protective environment. The infant's first experiences of being fed when hungry, held and stroked soothingly when fretful, changed when wet, and played with when bored establish the basis for a developing sense of trust. Infants must be able to depend on their caregivers to come when beckoned; to interact with them in warm, supportive and affectionate ways; and to respond appropriately to their various physiological and psychological needs. When caregiving is responsive to infant cues, infants learn to trust their own ability to signal needs and to get responses from caregivers. This helps to establish not only a trust in others but a trust in oneself (Brazelton & Yogman, 1986).

Mistrust arises when the infant's caregivers fail to adequately respond to cues of hunger, discomfort, boredom, and other needs or do so in inconsistent and unpredictable ways. Infants who are subjected to neglect, rejection, or inappropriate expectations, or infants who are repeatedly left to "cry it out," learn that other people cannot be trusted. Equally detrimental is the failure to learn to trust oneself and to gain a sense of self from positive and responsive interactions with others achieved by one's own efforts.

During this first year, the infant comes to realize that persons and objects exist even though they may not be present. Piaget (1952) considered this a major milestone in cognitive development and termed it *object permanence*. Object permanence is discussed in greater detail in Chapter 7 as it relates to cognitive development. The infant's appreciation of object permanence helps him or her to realize that parents or caregivers exist even when they cannot be seen and that they can be trusted to return.

Parents and adults who care for infants need to help them develop a healthy ratio of trust to mistrust, with trust outweighing mistrust. This is the goal of this first stage of psychosocial development. The infant who has established a healthy sense of trust is better equipped for the next stage, developing a sense of autonomy, which emerges during the second and third years. Autonomy is covered in Chapter 9.

## ATTACHMENT THEORY

*attachment:*
*a strong emotional relationship between two persons, characterized by mutual affection and a desire to maintain proximity*

The subject of infant bonding and **attachment** has received considerable attention in both the professional and the popular press in recent years. Recall from Chapter 4 that *bonding* refers to the strong emotional tie between the mother or father (or caregiver) and the infant, usually thought to occur in the early days or weeks after delivery. Attachment emerges gradually during the first year and may be an outgrowth of the parent-infant bond. It is based on the quality of the interactions between the child and the parent or caregiver.

During the 1950s and early 1960s John Bowlby, a psychiatrist and pioneer in the study of attachment, published a series of papers based on extensive research on mother-child attachments and separations. These papers, later enlarged and refined, were published in three volumes (Bowlby, 1969/1982, 1973, 1980) and have provided the impetus for much scholarly research and discussion.

Studying children who had been raised in institutions, Bowlby focused on their inability to form lasting relationships with others. Bowlby attributed this inability to the lack of opportunity to form an attachment to a mother or mother figure during infancy. He also studied children who, after experiencing strong infant-mother attachments, were separated from their mothers for long periods of time. He observed that these children also developed resistance to close human ties. Bowlby was convinced that to understand these behaviors, one should examine infant-mother attachments.

In the institutions in which the subjects of Bowlby's studies lived, staff members tended adequately to custodial responsibilities of feeding, clothing, bathing, and overseeing the infants' safety. They did not necessarily respond to the infants in affectionate and nurturing ways. Staff members did not respond to infants' cries or return their smiles, nor did they coo and babble with them or carry them about. Even though their physical needs were being met, infants in these settings failed or were severely impaired in their ability to relate to caregivers. Studies of attachment highlight the critical need to form these attachments during the early months and years and suggest that failure to do so may have a lifelong effect on healthy personality development (Ainsworth, 1973; Bowlby, 1973; Bretherton & Walters, 1985).

Bowlby (1969/1982, pp. 265–330) proposed a sequence for the development of attachment between the infant and others. The sequence is divided into four phases: indiscriminate responsiveness to humans, focusing on familiar people, active proximity seeking, and partnership behavior.

**Phase 1 (Birth to 8–12 weeks): Indiscriminate Responsiveness to Humans.** During this phase, infants orient to persons in their environment, visually tracking them, grasping and reaching for them, and smiling and babbling. The infant often ceases to cry upon seeing a face or hearing a voice. These behaviors sustain the attentions of others and thus their proximity to the infant, which is the infant's goal.

**Phase 2 (3 to 6 months): Focusing on Familiar People.** The infant's behaviors toward others remain virtually the same except that they are more marked in relation to the mother or perhaps the father. Social responses begin to become more selective, however, with the social smile reserved for familiar people. Strangers receive a long, intent stare. Cooing, babbling, and gurgling occur with familiar people. A principal attachment figure begins to emerge, usually the mother.

**Phase 3 (6 months to 3 years): Active Proximity Seeking.** Infants show greater discrimination in their interactions with people. They become deeply concerned for the attachment figure's presence and cry when that person starts to leave. Infants will monitor the attachment figure's movements, calling out to them or using whatever means of locomotion they have to maintain proximity to them. The attachment figure serves as a base from which to explore and is followed when departing and greeted warmly upon return. Certain other people may become subsidiary attachment figures; however, strangers are now treated with caution and will soon evoke alarm and withdrawal.

During phase 3, two very predictable fears emerge. **Separation anxiety** occurs as the relationship between the infant and the attachment figure becomes more intense and exclusive. The infant cries, sometimes quite vociferously, upon the departure of the attachment figure and exhibits intense joy upon their reunion. Figure 6.2 offers suggestions for caregivers during this difficult phase.

**Stranger anxiety** is another characteristic fear of phase 3. Occurring around 7 to 8 months, the infant's stranger anxiety is characterized by lengthy stares and subsequent crying at the sight of an unfamiliar person. Alarmed, the infant will cling tightly to the attachment figure and resist letting go. Figure 6.3 includes suggestions for dealing with stranger anxiety.

**Phase 4 (3 years to the end of childhood): Partnership Behavior.** Prior to this phase, the child is unable to consider the attachment figure's intentions. For instance, the suggestion that "I will be right back" is meaningless to the child,

*separation anxiety: fear of being separated from the attachment figure*

*stranger anxiety: fear of strangers characterized by avoidance, crying, or other distress signals*

---

**FIGURE 6.2**
**A Sensitive Response Is Most Appropriate When Dealing with Separation Anxiety**

---

- Recognize that new experiences present new challenges for the infant; some of these challenges can be quite unsettling, maybe even alarming.
- Provide predictable, unhurried schedules, particularly when introducing the infant to new experiences.
- Begin to accustom the infant to short separations at home by
  - Maintaining visual and auditory contact by leaving the infant's door open at nap and bedtimes
  - Maintaining voice contact across rooms, and when departing the room of a protesting infant, providing softly spoken verbal assurances
- Ritualize bedtimes and naptimes; e.g., provide a slower pace, softened volume on TV, bath and change of clothing, brush teeth, read a story, rock and sing, kiss goodnight, and tuck in bed.
- Provide prior opportunities for the infant to become familiar with a new baby-sitter or child care arrangement.
- Select caregivers on the basis of their ability to respond to the infant's unique rhythms and temperament.
- Familiarize the caregiver with the infant's routines and preferences.
- Have available for the infant any special blanket, stuffed toy, or other object from which the infant gains comfort.
- Ritualize departure time: hug, kiss, spoken good-byes, wave, and so on. Never slip away when the child is not looking; rather, let the infant develop confidence in the arrangement.
- Anticipate the new experience with pleasure.
- Be dependable. First separations should be brief in duration and reunions unwaveringly predictable.

---

who will insist on going along anyway. By age 3, the child has developed a greater understanding of parental intent and plans and can envision the parent's behavior while separated. The child is now more willing and able to let go and can be more flexible.

Mary Ainsworth has studied differences in attachment behaviors (1967; 1973; Ainsworth, Blehar, Waters, & Wall, 1978; Ainsworth & Wittig, 1969). Using her Strange Situation test, Ainsworth and her colleagues attempted to delineate individual differences in the quality of attachments that infants form. She devised a series of eight episodes (Table 6.2) designed to induce increasing anxiety in the infant. She recorded and analyzed exploratory behaviors, reactions to strangers, reactions to separation, and infant behaviors upon reuniting with the mother after separation.

From her studies, Ainsworth identified three categories of attachment:

1. Insecure attachment—anxious and avoidant

---

**FIGURE 6.3**
**Stranger Anxiety Is Another Normal Part of Development That Calls for a Sensitive Response**

Learning to distinguish mother and father from others is an important task in infancy, and for many of today's infants, adapting to a nonparental caregiver may be an added task. The parent or caregiver must recognize that fears in the first year relate to new learnings and limited experiences.

- Discourage the unfamiliar person from attempting to hold the baby.
- Provide ample time for the infant to assess the stranger and sense your reaction to him or her.
- When introducing the infant to a new caregiver, invite the person to visit. Spend time together, allowing the infant time to accept this new person into his or her world.
- During this session, let yourself serve as the secure base from which the infant can venture forth to make friendly overtures with the new acquaintance.
- Allow the infant to "control" the encounter, deciding when to approach and when to retreat.
- Provide the infant with familiar and comforting objects to hold.
- The confidence of older siblings who are already familiar with the "stranger" may encourage the infant's comfort and acceptance.

---

2. Secure attachment

3. Insecure attachment—anxious and resistant

Securely attached infants were found to be visibly upset upon separation from the mother and greeted her heartily and sought close physical contact with her upon reunion. In her presence, these infants more willingly explored their environments and were friendly with the stranger.

Insecurely attached, anxious/avoidant infants showed little distress when the mother departed and no great joy upon her return, generally avoiding contact with her. With strangers they behaved similarly, tending to avoid or ignore them.

Insecurely attached, anxious/resistant infants were less likely to explore when the mother was present and were distressed when she departed. The reunion was strained as the infant maintained proximity but resisted the mother's efforts at physical contact, displaying apparent anger at her absence. These infants were quite wary of strangers, even with the mother present.

Another classification of attachment, described by Main and Solomon (1990) as "disorganized," suggests that disorganization or conflicted feelings and behaviors expressing stress or anxiety can occur in any of Ainsworth's three categories of attachment. This disorganization occurs frequently among children who are socially at risk for abuse and neglect due to maternal depression or other parental maladaptive behaviors, low socioeconomic status, and little or no intervention by social service agencies. Expressions of these disorganized attachment behaviors

TABLE 6.2
Eight Episodes That Make Up the Strange Situations Test

| Episode Number | Persons Present | Duration | Brief Description of Action |
|---|---|---|---|
| 1 | Mother, baby, and observer | 30 seconds | Observer introduces mother and baby to experimental room, then leaves. (Room contains many appealing toys scattered about.) |
| 2 | Mother and baby | 3 minutes | Mother is nonparticipant while baby explores; if necessary, play is stimulated after 2 minutes. |
| 3 | Stranger, mother, and baby | 3 minutes | Stranger enters. First minute; stranger silent. Second minute; stranger converses with mother. Third minute; stranger approaches baby. After 3 minutes mother leaves unobtrusively. |
| 4 | Stranger and baby | 3 minutes or less | First separation episode. Stranger's behavior is geared to that of baby. |
| 5 | Mother and baby | 3 minutes or more | First reunion episode. Mother greets and/or comforts baby, then tries to settle him again in play. Mother then leaves saying "bye-bye." |
| 6 | Baby alone | 3 minutes or less | Second separation episode. |
| 7 | Stranger and baby | 3 minutes or less | Continuation of second separation. Stranger enters and gears her behavior to that of the baby. |
| 8 | Mother and baby | 3 minutes | Second reunion episode. Mother enters, greets baby, then picks him up. Meanwhile stranger leaves unobtrusively. |

*Source:* Ainsworth, M. D. S., Blehar, M. C., Waters, E., & Wall, S. (1978). *Patterns of attachment: a psychological study of the strange situation* (p. 413). Hillsdale, NJ: Lawrence Erlbaum Associates, Inc. Copyright 1978 by Lawrence Erlbaum Associates, Inc. Reprinted with permission.

increase in frequency as the severity of the social risk factors increases. Some researchers believe that disorganization of attachment patterns may foretell later hostile behaviors in children (Lyons-Ruth, Alpern, & Repacholi, 1993). Avoidant attachments are also thought to predict of later antisocial behaviors (Fagot & Kavanagh, 1990).

On the positive side, a large body of research found that securely attached infants

- Formed early attachments between 1 and 4 months of age as a result of their mothers' sensitive responses to their cues
- Exhibited trust in their mothers' availability
- Progressed toward autonomous behaviors more easily
- Exhibited more confidence in exploratory behaviors
- Played with toys and other objects more than insecurely attached infants do
- Enjoyed greater involvement and success in peer interactions as they got older (Cassidy & Berlin, 1994; Isabella, 1993)

What did these infants experience that their less successfully attached age-mates did not? Do certain parental characteristics facilitate the attachment process? A number of researchers suggest that the mothers (or primary care-givers) of these infants exhibited more sensitive and responsive behaviors toward them. These mothers

- Were more involved with their infants
- Were sensitive to their infants' behavioral cues
- Were readily accessible
- Were predictable
- Responded to their infants in developmentally appropriate ways
- Generally exhibited more positive behaviors and interactions and expressions of affection
- Enjoyed close physical contact with their infants
- Encouraged exploratory play and timed their interactions strategically so as not to intrude in their infants' play
- Had a sense of when to interact (Ainsworth, Bell, & Stayton, 1974; Cassidy & Berlin, 1994; Grossman et al., 1985; Isabella, Belsky, & von Eye, 1989; Isabella, 1993).

Numerous studies over the past decade have explored the role of fathers in the attachment process. Fike (1993) provides suggestions for both meeting fathers' needs for interaction with their children and fostering the very important relationships that develop between infants and fathers. Fathers should

1. Understand the importance of setting positive expectations for their infants and practice a mental attitude of expecting positive relationships to develop
2. Appreciate the importance of holding, cuddling, and playing with their infants

3. Become involved in the daily lives of their infants through routines such as feeding, changing, bedtime and playtime routines, and so on

4. Become aware of the day-to-day events unfolding in their infants' lives

5. Communicate verbally with their infants in tones of approval and acceptance

6. Nurture their infants through attitudes, deeds, and actions that communicate the infants' unique worth

As fathers in our society become an increasing part of their infants' and young children's lives, researchers will explore even further the positive outcomes that can accrue and how best to help fathers become more comfortable in their new and active role in child growth and development and their shared experiences with others who are important in their infant's lives.

Longitudinal studies have documented the long-term results of secure and insecure attachments. Many researchers have found that personality development is either positively or negatively affected by these early secure or insecure attachments. This expanding area of research has been enormously helpful to the early childhood professional by

- Emphasizing the importance of the first year for the development of parent-child bonds

- Affirming the ameliorative potential for subsidiary attachments (family member, child care providers) when other attachments are insecure

- Affirming the importance of nonparental caregivers in complementing and supporting parent-child attachments

- Supporting the need for professional intervention when parent-child relationships are dysfunctional

## INFANT EMOTIONS

In addition to attachment and the early fears of separation and of strangers, other emotions of infancy are worth noting. The infant displays an array of emotions, including affection, joy, surprise, anger, fear, disgust, interest, and even sadness (Campos et al., 1983). The newborn shows interest and surprise when something catches her or his attention (Field, 1982). The newborn smiles at a pleasing sound or when hunger has been satisfied. A sudden jolt or loud noise may evoke surprise and fear. The infant may show anger or even rage at being restrained or uncomfortable.

Earliest emotions are thought to be mostly reflexive, perhaps of a survival nature, assisting the infant in communicating needs and sustaining adult response. Later emotional responses are produced by external stimuli such as frustration with a toy or fear of an animal. A number of scholars have suggested sequences for the emergence of discrete emotions (e.g., Greenspan & Greenspan, 1985; Izard & Buechler, 1986; Stroufe, 1979). For instance, it is believed that distress,

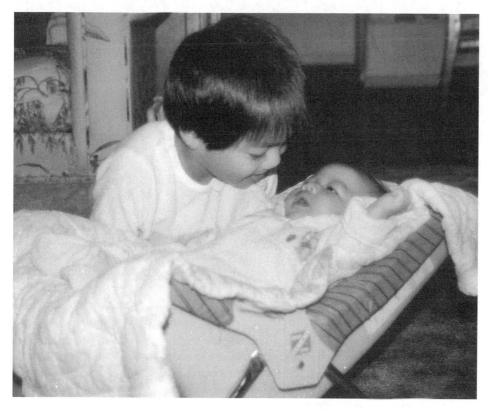

*Social responses become more reciprocal as infants get older.*

disgust, and surprise are expressed by newborns, while anger and joy emerge during the first four months and fear and shyness emerge between age 6 months and a year.

While most emotions seem to be present from birth (Campos et al., 1983), differences in emotional responses occur as the infant gets older. The most significant changes in emotional and social responses in infants occur during the period from 6 to 12 months, due primarily to the dramatic cognitive development taking place during that period. The abilities to recall the past, sense discrepancies, and attend to facial expressions of emotion in caregivers contribute to these differences (Lamb, Morrison, & Malkin, 1987). Thus, the emergence of fear of strangers and of separation is further explained.

## COMMUNICATING THROUGH CRYING

Infants communicate their needs through crying. At first, the cries are reflexive reactions to physiological needs for nourishment, warmth, movement, touch, or relief from various discomforts. Infants have no control over their crying and will not be able to stop crying until a need has been met or they have exhausted themselves. As the infant gets older, the causes of crying change from internal to external stimuli and may be provoked by such things as loud noises, physical restraint, frustration with clothing or toys, and, as mentioned, fear of strangers and of separation.

Infant crying frequently has different tones, rhythms, and intensities. Parents soon learn the nature and the "message" of their infant's various cries and respond accordingly to these various acoustical differences (Green, Jones, & Gustafson, 1987). Shaffer (1971) identified three distinct patterns of crying: the basic cry usually associated with hunger, an angry cry, and a pain cry.

Crying can be quite unsettling to parents and caregivers, particularly when they are unable to determine the infant's needs. Learning to respond appropriately to crying is one of the tasks of parenting and infant caregiving. Bell and Ainsworth (1972) found that infants whose parents responded promptly to their cries and other signals cried less often. When the infants did cry, the crying was of shorter duration. Further, infants who cried and fussed the most after 3 months of age were the ones whose parents did not respond readily to their cries. Another study found that infants who were held and carried about during the day cried less during the night (Hunziker & Barr, 1986).

Parents and other caregivers who are cognizant of the infant's various means of communicating, such as whimpering, facial expressions, wiggling, and vocalizing, are better able to respond before the infant begins to cry. Infants whose caregivers respond to these noncrying signals soon learn to communicate without crying, unless, of course, there is urgent pain, fear, frustration, or exhaustion. These infants will grow in their sense of trust in their caregivers and in themselves as communicators.

Caregivers must also recognize that infants, like anyone else, experience boredom, loneliness, and a need for personal contact. Sometimes crying simply signals a need for companionship, the sound of a familiar voice, and the sensation of a familiar touch or smell. When bored, infants may cry for a change of position or place, or for the nearness and interaction of others. Rocking the infant, holding the infant to one's shoulder to provide opportunities for visual scanning, talking in soft, soothing tones, and gentle caresses are usually successful ways to calm an infant.

Crying has its positive developmental effects. Demos (1986) suggests that one of the developmental tasks of infancy is to learn to modulate emotions. Others suggest that caregivers need not feel they must extinguish all crying. Snow (1989, p. 240) suggests that "crying is necessary for infant behavioral organization and normal physiological functioning." Persistent and unmodulated crying, however, calls for caregiver response.

 Cheryl's mother finds it difficult to work as a housekeeper and help care for Angela. Cheryl goes to school and feels pressured to find other child care arrangements. The older siblings in the family have been called on to help with baby-sitting, but that has not always worked out due to their own childhood needs for play and socialization and desires to succeed in school.

James has tried to be helpful but his visits to his infant daughter are becoming less and less frequent. His own need to work and his desire to stay in school consume his time and his energies. His feelings for both Cheryl and their baby are becoming ambivalent and confused, and sometimes he feels depressed. He isn't sure what his role should be.

Cheryl has experienced mixed feelings as the realities of constantly having to meet an infant's needs become more apparent. She isn't sure of James anymore and anticipates they will probably split up soon. She feels sad, though she does not blame him. She is tired most of the time, since she has returned to school and her classes have become quite demanding. Sometimes she feels like a failure at school and at mothering, and her baby seems cranky much of the time.

Cheryl's mother frequently shares her frustrations with a friend at her church, including the difficulties of making a living and raising a two-generation family. Her friend tells her that some high schools in the area provide on-site child care for teenage mothers. Through a number of inquiries, Cheryl's mother is able to identify one such high school. It isn't the high school in which Cheryl is currently enrolled and will necessitate a family move if Cheryl chooses to take advantage of the child care program.

After several weeks of searching, Cheryl's family locates a small house within walking distance of the new high school. Cheryl doesn't want to move, yet she feels she has no choice. She will miss James and her other friends. James offers to help; he will borrow his brother's pickup truck and will help them prepare the new house for occupancy. Cheryl is pleased at this show of caring and thinks that perhaps her relationship with James will continue.

Meanwhile, Angela has experienced a constant turnover in caregivers. Now 8 months old, her sleeping patterns are still irregular and unpredictable. She is hungry at odd hours and is a finicky eater. She cries easily and often, continuously demands the company of others, and vigorously resists being put to bed. She can be quite playful, however, and enjoys the attention of her school-age aunts and uncles. She responds readily to Cheryl, but her relationship with her grandmother seems stronger and more comforting. She watches the comings and goings of all the family members and frets or cries when left in her playpen as others leave the room. Both Cheryl and her mother care deeply for Angela, and want her to be a happy, cheerful baby.  ■

Jeremy's experiences have been quite different. His psychosocial world has included his mother, his father, Phyllis (his baby-sitter), and an occasional visit from grandparents and trips to the church nursery. Except for periodic bouts of colic, Jeremy's routines of sleeping and eating are generally without incident. Bathing, dressing, playing, and interacting with Phyllis and his parents are, for the most part, relaxed, predictable, and enjoyable.

Ann, now back at work, is making every effort to maintain a sense of order in their lives, though meeting Jeremy's needs has at times overwhelmed her. Ann and Bill talk frequently and frankly about the dramatic change in their lifestyle, daily schedules, social life, and physical stamina.

Bill feels a need and a desire to nurture Jeremy and misses him when he is at work. Jeremy has become his "buddy," and Bill cherishes the smiles, the reaching toward Daddy's face when being held, and the pounding at his legs with uncoordinated hands to get attention or to be held. Dinnertimes are not always serene, nor are bedtimes, yet Bill and Ann both savor the changes they are observing in their growing baby. Indeed, Jeremy has a distinct personality. Does he take after Bill's side of the family or Ann's? Together they anticipate Jeremy's changing looks, behaviors, and interactions with each of them.

Since Jeremy's routines have been mostly predictable and pleasurable, with the adults in his world responding to his cues in caring and nurturing ways, his sense of trust is emerging and he has learned which cues result in which responses from others. At 8 months, however, he is beginning to fret upon separation from his parents and sometimes from Phyllis. He is especially wary of strangers and seems to need more close physical contact than usual. He also cries more frequently than he used to and is especially difficult in the mornings when Ann and Bill are scurrying to dress and leave for work. ■

## INFANT INTERACTIONS WITH OTHERS

In the first few weeks of life, the infant's interaction patterns relate primarily to survival needs, signaling those needs to parents and caregivers through crying, squirming, and fretting. As the infant becomes more alert and begins to study the faces and responses of parents and to discriminate them from others, the infant's responsiveness increases. As experiences with others expand during the first year to include siblings, grandparents, nonparental caregivers, and in some cases other infants and young children, psychosocial development proceeds.

Infants' efforts to interact are characterized by gazing for some time at a face, reaching toward it, imitating facial expressions, and visually and auditorily tracking a person. Socially, the infant enjoys being gently tickled and jostled; responses include cooing, gurgling, babbling, kicking, and wiggling. Such behaviors elicit playfulness, attention, and encouragement from others.

Around age 5 months, interest in other children and siblings increases. The infant engages in prolonged onlooker behavior when placed in the same room with other children. Some consider this to be an early stage of social/play development. Observing others is entertaining in and of itself, and infants derive considerable pleasure from simply being near the action.

Interest in siblings is particularly profound during the latter half of the first year. It is generally thought that playful and responsive siblings increase infant sociability; however, some scholars believe the infant's sociability itself influences the amount of attention received from siblings (Lamb, 1978a). At any rate, infants can be extremely interested in their siblings, following them around, imitating them, actively seeking their attention, and exploring their toys and other belongings. Siblings can be taught to respond to the infant in gentle and playful ways. Around 6 to 8 months, the infant will participate in games such as peek-a-boo and pat-a-cake and infant-initiated reciprocal activities, such as repeatedly dropping a toy to be retrieved, handed back to the infant, and dropped again.

How infants respond to other infants has been the focus of a number of studies (Adamson & Bakeman, 1985; Field, 1979; Fogel, 1979; Hay, Nash, & Petersen, 1983). Infants will react to the sound of another infant's cry and show an awareness of the presence of another infant. At 6 months of age, the infant will reach toward another infant, watch intently, and perhaps smile and make friendly sounds. At this age, infants have been shown to respond positively to one another in groups of two and to generally find other infants intriguing. An infant may crawl into or fall on another infant in clumsy efforts to interact; yet, infant-infant interaction is seen to be positive despite its awkwardness.

## SOCIAL SMILING

Smiles observed in the neonate are thought to be triggered by internal stimuli associated with the immature central nervous system. There seems to be a developmental pattern for smiling (Campos & Stenberg, 1981; Emde & Harmon, 1972) that proceeds from internal to external elicitations.

At first, infants smile at faces regardless of facial expression. Then, from 3 to 7 months, they begin to notice and respond to differences in facial expressions. In the latter part of the first year, infants not only can discriminate differences in facial expressions but may respond to each expression in a different emotional way (Campos & Stenberg, 1981). Infants have also been shown to respond to positive and negative affect in the human voice, smiling more to sounds of approval than to sounds of disapproval (Fernald, 1993).

True social smiling is thought to occur at approximately 6 to 8 weeks. It is believed that when the infant can remember and recognize the face and perhaps the voice of the primary caregiver, smiling becomes more social (Wolff, 1963; Kagan, 1971). As infants get older, they become more discerning in their smiling behavior, choosing to smile at familiar faces, voices, and interactions over unfamiliar ones. Yet the frequency of smiling increases with age. Cognition seems to play a major role in the emergence of smiling that is triggered by external stimuli.

## SOCIAL COGNITION

**Social cognition** is the ability to understand the thoughts, intentions, and behaviors of oneself and of others. As infants develop a basic sense of trust when caregivers are nurturing and responsive, they learn to associate certain behaviors with certain responses from caregivers. This marks the beginning of social cognition. Scholars believe that by the end of the first year, the infant's social understanding is fairly sophisticated (Lamb, 1981).

*social cognition: the ability to understand the thoughts, intentions, and behaviors of oneself and of others*

From experiences during the first year of life, infants become aware of the rhythms, sights, and sounds of the household; feel the warmth of a parent's arms around them; anticipate certain responses to their various cues; recognize the unique aromas of their mothers, fathers, and other caregivers; and perhaps sense the moods of these individuals by the manner in which they respond to them. Infants' responses to facial expressions indicate that they look to others, usually attachment figures, for clues in understanding the sights and sounds around them (Tronick, Cohn, & Shea, 1986).

In adult-infant interactions, the adult typically imitates the infant's facial expressions and vocalizations. As the infant experiences these pleasant interactions, the imitation becomes reciprocal, with the infant imitating the gestures, facial expressions, and vocalizations of the parent or caregiver.

Imitations, then, become a means of interpersonal communication. Imitations seen in games of pat-a-cake and peek-a-boo, and in learning to kiss or wave are behaviors indicative of emerging social cognition. As the infant experiences these social events and finds them pleasurable, the desire to repeat them emerges. These carliest interpersonal communications contribute to social cognition and have far-reaching implications for later language and cognitive development (Clyman et al., 1986).

## FACTORS INFLUENCING PSYCHOSOCIAL DEVELOPMENT

Many factors influence psychosocial development—the infant's own personality and temperament, the quality and consistency of care, the success and quality of attachment behaviors, and the type of nonparental care the infant experiences.

### INFANT PERSONALITY

Infants themselves influence the way others respond to them. Certain personality characteristics seem to affect the quality and quantity of interactions with others. Researchers believe that the primary caregiver's interactions with the infant and subsequent attachments influence and are influenced by infant behaviors (Grossman & Grossman, 1990; Spangler & Grossman, 1993; Stroufe, 1985). It seems that children's own temperaments and personalities affect the development of attachment behaviors, how caregivers respond to their needs, and how the infants will interact with others later. This suggests an interactionist view of psychosocial development that holds that parent or caregiver and infant reciprocally affect each other's personalities.

In studying individuality in children and identifying the components of temperament, Stella Chess and Alexander Thomas (1987) illustrated the effects of certain temperaments of children on their responses to the demands of the environment and their interactions with others. These researchers found that components of temperament (including activity level, rhythmicity, approach and withdrawal behaviors, adaptability, sensory threshold, intensity of response, quality of mood, distractability, persistence, and attention span) tended to cluster around three categories of temperament:

1. The *easy* child is usually easygoing, even-tempered, more tolerant of change, playful, responsive, and adaptable; eats and sleeps with some regularity; is easily comforted when upset; and generally displays a positive mood.

2. The *difficult* child is slower to develop regular eating and sleeping routines, is more irritable, derives less pleasure from playtime activities, has difficulty adjusting to changes in routines, and tends to cry louder and longer than more easily soothed children.

3. The *slow-to-warm-up* child displays only mild positive or negative reactions, resists new situations and people, and is moody and slower to adapt. Interactions such as cuddling may be resisted.

The easy child's behaviors provide positive feedback and reinforcement to caregivers and, in so doing, influence the kinds and amounts of attentions the

*"Goodness of fit" between infants and the personalities and expectations of their caregivers promotes optimal psychosocial development.*

child will receive throughout early development. These children more often than not experience what Chess and Thomas (1987) have called a "goodness of fit" between themselves and the personalities and expectations of their caregivers. *Goodness of fit* is defined as a principle of interaction in which

> the organism's capacities, motivations and styles of behaving and the demands and expectations of the environment are in accord. Such consonance between organism and environment potentiates optimal positive development. Should there be dissonance between the capacities and characteristics of the organism on the one hand and the environment opportunities and demands on the other hand, there is poorness of fit, which leads to maladaptive functioning and distorted development (Chess & Thomas, 1987, pp. 20–21).

Infants described as temperamentally difficult may fail to elicit nurturing and support from their caregivers. Adults who find this temperament hard to respond to may become overly demanding or, conversely, appeasing in their interactions. They may feel helpless and confused, be inconsistent in their responses and expectations, or engage in power struggles for control. One can readily see the "poorness of fit" in this situation and its potential for ineffective and negative adult-child relationships and childhood behavior disorders that may persist into adulthood.

The slow-to-warm-up child generally does not present substantial difficulties in the adult-child relationship. However, this child, being slower to adapt and reticent with new acquaintances and situations, may not receive persistent efforts on the part of caregivers to maintain positive interactions.

Not all children fall neatly into these categories; easy children are not always easy, difficult children are not always difficult, and slow-to-warm-up children are not always reticent. However, these descriptions help us to appreciate wide variations in infant and child behaviors. Recognizing and appreciating individual differences helps adults respond appropriately to these behaviors. Adults must be cautious in applying these categories, however. Self-fulfilling prophecies may occur in which the child behaves according to adult expectations. If adults ascribe labels and misunderstand the infant's cues, they may fail to support the infant's needs for positive and nurturing interactions, regardless of temperament or personality type.

## QUALITY AND CONSISTENCY OF CARE

Whether an infant is cared for by a parent at home or through other arrangements, among the most important qualities of infant care in terms of healthy psychosocial development are consistency, predictability, and continuity of care. Though personalities and adult responses to infants vary greatly, infants need their different caregivers (mother, father, siblings, nonparent caregivers) to respond to their cues in relatively similar and nurturing ways. Also, the infant needs to trust that certain events will occur in a reasonable order and with some predictability. The more predictable the infant's routines and caregiver behaviors, the greater the likelihood of developing a healthy sense of trust in one's world and in one's self.

Continuity of care refers to caregivers' developmental expectations for the infant and knowledge and acceptance of the infant's individual temperament, rhythms, interaction patterns, and other characteristics that make the infant unique. Continuity is maintained when the infant experiences a minimum number of caregivers during the course of a day or a week. Many child care centers today provide a "primary caregiver" to infants in an effort to reduce the number of adults to whom the infant must adapt. This practice enhances the infant's sense of order and facilitates opportunities to form positive relationships and, perhaps, healthy attachments between infant and nonparental caregivers.

The vignettes about Angela and Jeremy earlier in this chapter reveal two very different situations in the quality and consistency of care each infant is receiving. Angela's routines are less predictable; so are her caregivers, as they change frequently. The quality of care she is receiving is not optimal, and the opportunity for her to develop stable, trusting relationships is tenuous.

Jeremy, on the other hand, is experiencing daily schedules and routines that are neither rigid nor inflexible, yet are predictable to him. His caregivers are limited in number, and each responds effectively to his cues for attention and other needs. In both cases, the infants are being provided with **nonparental care** while their parents are away at school or work. What is the relationship between nonparental care and optimal psychosocial development in infants?

*nonparental care: child care provided by someone other than the child's parent*

## NONPARENTAL CHILD CARE

Today an increasing number of infants are receiving nonmaternal child care. It is estimated that in 1990, 6.5 million children younger than 5 whose mothers were employed were cared for by someone other than a parent (Children's Defense Fund, 1994). A large proportion of these young consumers of child care are infants under a year old. The rate of labor force participation of mothers of children under 6 has increased about 50 percent since 1975. Despite the great need for infant nonparental child care, it is not readily available in all communities, and where it is available, it is usually expensive. The quality of infant care programs is also an issue. The types of child care used by families of very young children are as follows: in the home with an unrelated caregiver, 5.1 percent; nonparental relatives, 25.1 percent; **family child care home**, 25.6 percent; child care centers, 37.9 percent; and unspecified other types, 5.1 percent.

*family child care home: a private residence that provides child care for a small number of children*

How well do infants and toddlers adjust to nonparental child care? What impact does nonparental child care have on infant-parent attachments and subsequent psychosocial development? What characteristics of child care providers promote (or impede) optimal development? Given the great disparity in quality of nonparental child care arrangements, knowledge about child care options and the characteristics of quality programs is essential, as is careful consideration of the impact of nonparental child care on infant growth and development.

Recent studies have noted varying adjustment patterns among infants receiving nonparental child care. One study noted that initially, infants showed inhibited behaviors and less positive affect similar to those expected of older children challenged by a new environment. These behaviors, however, were found to diminish over the next six months, after which the children showed more positive affect and positive peer interactions later on (Fein, Gariboldi, & Boni, 1993). This study also found that caregivers were most responsive and comforting to infants at entry, and over the next six months the infants' distress behavior diminished. This study also suggests that it takes three to six months for infants to feel comfortable in child care settings. We can assume that with poor-quality care, the adjustment period could well be longer. However, we would not wish to wait six months to determine infants' adjustment if there is any reason to believe the care is less than optimal.

While some studies propose that long hours (20 or more) in nonparental child care can impede the development of secure attachments between infants and their mothers (Belsky, 1988; Belsky & Rovine, 1988), other studies do not support this perspective. A recent study (Burchinal et al., 1992) found that nonmaternal care had no detrimental effects on the development and maintenance of infant-mother attachments at age 1 year if the age of entry was under 7 months, before attachment patterns begin to emerge, and the quality of the child care arrangement was exemplary. This study also noted that children who received extensive nonmaternal care beginning in early infancy were as likely to develop normal infant-mother attachments as their home-raised peers were. The important point here is the quality of the child care arrangement. Quality of infant care programs is usually defined in terms of involved and developmentally appropriate caregiving, low infant to caregiver/teacher ratios, and small groups (the younger the child, the smaller the group should be).

Earlier in this chapter, we discussed the importance of the mother's and father's sensitivity and responsiveness to their infant's signals. It follows that the infant's nonparental caregivers must also be sensitive and responsive. Stressing the importance of high-quality child care programs, Raikes (1993) focused on how the amount of time an infant spends in the care of a "high-ability" teacher on infant-teacher attachment. Since a secure attachment with a caring and nurturing caregiver can buffer the stress of parental separation, such an attachment can prove to be quite important. It is also thought that such child caregiver attachments may even compensate for insecure parental attachments. Raikes's study was based on the premises that

- High-ability caregivers/teachers support and facilitate the infant's developing sense of trust, predictability, and control.

- Experience with infants allows teachers to become fully acquainted with infants' personalities, that is, what upsets, excites, amuses, and bores infants.

- History in a relationship is required for secure attachments to develop.

- Infants' cognitive, social, emotional, and language development are dependent on quality relationships.

Raikes found that at least 9 months with the same caregiver/teacher provide the best opportunity for the infant to form a secure attachment. She proposes that rather than "promoting" infants at age 6 or 7 months, as is quite common in child care programs, a "new standard for excellence" in the field would keep infants and high-ability teachers together beyond 1 year of age.

Communication between parents and caregivers is also important in nonparental child care. The National Association for the Education of Young Children accreditation standards (Bredekamp, 1991) and other standards set by funding entities encourage frequent interactions and mutual support. The amount of parent-caregiver interactions varies appreciably among child care settings, yet frequent and meaningful communication is predictive of the quality of the child care program itself (Ghazvini & Readdick, 1994).

These findings suggest that developmental outcomes associated with early nonparental child care need not be in jeopardy. Yet the goal of quality programs, high-ability teachers, and a population of informed and conscientious parents remains rather elusive. Early childhood professionals can help by advocating for

---

**FIGURE 6.4**
**Characteristics to Look for in Quality Child Care**

---

1. Trained, knowledgeable, nurturing, and committed caregivers
2. Safe, sanitary, healthy environment for infants and children
3. Low adult-child ratios, with emphasis on providing primary caregivers to individual infants over extended periods of time
4. Cognitively and linguistically enriching, socially stimulating, emotionally supportive environment and caregivers
5. Sensitive, appropriate, antibias interactions and curriculums for all children
6. Sensitivity to parental needs, goals, and concerns
7. Exceeds local and/or state licensing standards
8. Accredited through the National Association for the Education of Young Children

---

high-quality, affordable child care and assisting families in identifying the arrangements that best suit their needs and providing them with current information to help them choose wisely.

Parents need to assess their infants' responses and well-being on an ongoing basis. Are positive and nurturing relationships developing among all who share in the care and nurturing of the infant? Does the infant need the routine at home to be more like that of the infant care program, or vice versa? Is the infant overtired or overstimulated from the day's experiences? What is the parent doing to ensure consistency, predictability, and continuity in the infant's life at home? Are the infant's health and safety paramount to all caregivers? Is the infant exhibiting a basic sense of trust, secure attachments, healthy emotional development, and enjoyment of parents and other caregivers?

Employers are beginning to recognize the increased productivity of employees who feel comfortable about their child care arrangements and are supported in their efforts to provide sound parenting. Some employers provide parental leave opportunities for both mothers and fathers during the earliest weeks and months of their infants' development. Some provide leave opportunities without penalty for parents whose infants or children are ill. Employers of the future may well find other ways to encourage and support effective childrearing practices. Employer policies that support child and family development go a long way in facilitating healthy psychosocial development in children and should be encouraged for the long-term benefit such healthy beginnings may have on society in general.

Qualities to assess in seeking appropriate infant care are listed in Figure 6.4. Parents should make informed choices for themselves and their infants, choosing according to the infant's unique developmental needs and the caregiver's ability to adequately and appropriately meet those needs.

## SOCIOCULTURAL CONTEXTS INFLUENCING PSYCHOSOCIAL DEVELOPMENT

Parents who are knowledgeable about child growth and development tend to be more confident with their children, be more positive and nurturing, and exhibit more developmentally appropriate expectations. In doing so, they facilitate the healthy psychosocial development of their children. This is particularly critical during infancy as the antecedents of healthy personality development are occurring.

However, in some (though certainly not all) families of low socioeconomic status (SES), survival needs often supersede the social and emotional needs of children and the physiological needs for food and medication. In such situations, opportunities to learn about children and child development are limited or not realized. The difficulties of surviving may be so overwhelming that they interfere with healthy parent-parent and parent-child interactions. Children in such families may be hungry, be cold, suffer more illnesses, and even be neglected or abused. Parental efforts to provide food, clothing, shelter, and transportation for the family may be thwarted. Providing psychosocial nurturance to the children is precluded by fatigue, frustration, anxiety, and sometimes resentment or a sense of futility. Personality development of infants in these situations can be at risk.

For such families, high-quality child care is imperative. The professionals involved may provide access to needed social and health care services, job counseling, and parenting education. Along with a full day of quality nurturing and psychosocially sound interactions, the infant is given a better chance at healthy development. The relief from the stress associated with childrearing and the assurance that the infant is well cared for during a number of hours of the day (or night) should provide some relief for the parents in this potentially unhealthy situation.

Cultural contexts also influence psychosocial development in both positive and negative ways. Expressions of emotions, expectations, and encouragement of infant responses, tolerance for infant behaviors, and perceived parental roles vary among families and among cultures. Attitudes toward feeding, crying, holding, and clothing, in the nature and amount of language to which the infant is exposed, and family values and goals provide the cultural contexts through which infant psychosocial development emerges (Garcia-Coll, 1990).

## HEALTH OF INFANT AS AN INFLUENCE ON PSYCHOSOCIAL DEVELOPMENT

Certainly we can assume that healthy infants are better equipped to deal emotionally and socially with their environments. Obstetric and pediatric supervision during prenatal development and infancy provides preventive and corrective measures to facilitate healthy development. Proper nutrition and socially and emotionally satisfying interactions are essential to this health.

Infants who experience chronic illnesses, birth defects, injury, violence, emotionally unstable caregivers, or inconsistent or contradictory childrearing practices are most likely to develop negative emotionality and psychosocial problems later. As we have seen throughout this chapter, manifestation of these problems in infants depends on factors such as age, temperament, past experiences, and bonding and attachment success. Factors relating to the intensity and duration of the problems the infant encounters, including the temperaments and coping abilities of various family members and the willingness and/or ability of the family to seek and benefit from professional help, also influence developmental outcomes.

Infants tend to exhibit signs of stress through physiological functions, such as changes in sleeping and waking patterns, feeding disturbances, heightened emotionality, frantic crying, depressive behaviors, withdrawing, and avoidant behaviors. When these behaviors are evident, parents and professionals might examine the family or child caregiving situation to determine causes and look for solutions. Again, professional counseling may be needed to help the family cope with their difficulties and respond appropriately to the infant.

 *Role of the Early Childhood Professional*

## Promoting Psychosocial Development in Infants

1. Provide predictable, consistent, and continuous care.
2. Respond readily to the infant's cues for food, comfort, rest, play, and social interaction.
3. Recognize that crying is the infant's way of communicating his or her needs.
4. Be aware of sensitive periods relating to attachment behaviors, separation and stranger anxiety, and respond in supportive and empathic ways.
5. Provide stimulating and satisfying social and emotional interactions.
6. Recognize and accept the infant's unique ways of interacting with others.
7. Recognize and accept the infant's various emotional responses as another way in which the infant communicates.

## KEY TERMS

| | | |
|---|---|---|
| attachment | nonparental care | social cognition |
| family child care home | separation anxiety | stranger anxiety |

## REVIEW STRATEGIES AND ACTIVITIES

1. Review the key terms independently or with a classmate.

2. Discuss with classmates the differences in the early lives of Angela and Jeremy. In terms of psychosocial development, what kinds of experiences are these infants having? What are the characteristics of the environmental contexts in which each child is developing? What suggestions can you make to enhance the psychosocial development of each child?

3. Review the qualities of a good infant care center. Visit an NAEYC-accredited child care center in which infants are enrolled.
   a. What are the outstanding qualities of this center?
   b. Would you feel comfortable obtaining the professional services of this center?
   c. Observe the interactions between adults and infants and between infants and other infants.
   d. Do you observe evidence of infant-teacher attachment?
   e. How did the infants respond to you as a stranger? What was the response? How old were the infants whose responses you observed?
   f. How are parents' needs and concerns integrated into the program?
   g. How do the early childhood professionals nurture the psychosocial development of developmentally challenged infants?

4. Interview a working parent to find out how she or he juggles work and parenting. Does this person feel generally positive about his or her lifestyle? What has this person found to be most frustrating? Most rewarding?

5. How might parents and/or primary caregivers ensure that infants develop a healthy sense of basic trust? Develop a list of "dos and don'ts."

## FURTHER READINGS

Bassett, M. M. (1995). *Infant and child care skills.* Albany, NY: Delmar.

Bowe, F. G. (1995). *Birth to five: Early childhood special education.* Albany, NY: Delmar.

Brazelton, T. B. (1994). *Touchpoints: Your child's emotional and behavioral development.* Reading, MA: Addison-Wesley.

Brazelton, T. B. (1987). *Working and caring.* Menlo Park, CA: Addison-Wesley.

Children's Defense Fund. (1992). *Helping children by strengthening families.* Washington, DC: Author.

Comer, J. P., and Poussaint, A. F. (1992). *Raising black children.* New York: Penguin Books.

Curry, N. W. and Johnson, C. N. (1990). *Beyond self-esteem: Developing a genuine sense of human value.* Washington, DC: National Association for the Education of Young Children.

Fike, R. D. (1992). "Personal relationship-building between fathers and infants." Association for Childhood Education International Focus on Infancy 5(4), 1-2.

Kontos, S. (1992). *Family day care: Out of the shadows and into the limelight.* Washington, DC: National Association for the Education of Young Children.

Phillips, D. (Ed.). (1987). *Quality in child care: what does research tell us?* Washington, DC: National Association for the Education of Young Children.

Swick, K. J., and Graves, S. (1993). *Empowering at-risk families during the early childhood years.* Washington, DC: National Education Association.

Weissbourd, B., & Musick, J. S. (Eds.). (1981, 1991, 4th printing). *Infants: Their social environments.* Washington, DC: National Association for the Education of Young Children.

# CHAPTER SEVEN

*The goal of infant and early education should not be to increase the quantity of knowledge, but to help the child—through guiding her experience and creating possibilities—to construct, invent, and discover.*

Judith S. Musick and Joanne Householder

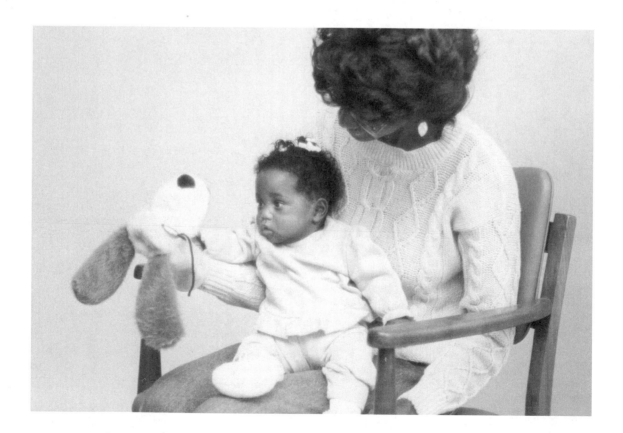

# Cognitive, Language, and Literacy Development of the Infant

After studying this chapter, you will demonstrate comprehension by:

- Describing cognitive development during the infant's first year.
- Outlining language development during the infant's first year.
- Relating cognitive, language, and literacy development to other developmental areas.
- Identifying major factors influencing cognitive, language, and literacy development during the infant's first year.
- Suggesting strategies for promoting and enhancing cognitive, language, and literacy development in infancy.

## COGNITIVE DEVELOPMENT

 Recent research has heightened our awareness of **cognitive development** in infancy. Researchers are studying how and to what stimuli infants respond. Some interesting topics are

*cognitive development: the aspect of development that involves thinking, problem-solving, intelligence, and language*

- Reflexive behaviors as indicators of healthy cognitive development
- Motor behaviors as indicators of healthy cognitive development
- The role of cognition
- Imitative behaviors
- Memory capabilities
- Cognitive development in the absence of certain sensory or motor capabilities
- The social/emotional context in which learning occurs
- Sociocultural influences on cognitive development
- Earliest language
- The genesis of literacy

From this cursory list of current infant research topics, one can see that cognitive development is a dynamic process that is ongoing throughout the life span. It is that area of development in which the child acquires information, expands and modifies it, and stores, retrieves, and uses it. Mental activities may be exhibited through the infant's vocal, social, and physical/motor behaviors and activities.

## PIAGET'S THEORY OF COGNITIVE DEVELOPMENT

Cognitive development is that aspect of development that deals with thinking, problem solving, intelligence, and language. The most familiar theory of cognitive development is that of Jean Piaget (1952). Piaget's studies of cognitive development have dominated the fields of child study, psychology, philosophy, pediatrics, and education since the 1920s. He is perhaps the best-known and most widely quoted of the contemporary cognitive theorists. As we will see later in the chapter, while other theorists have challenged or modified Piaget's theory, he nevertheless has made an astounding impact on knowledge and practice in early childhood education.

Foremost among Piaget's contributions to early childhood education is the recognition that the thinking processes and problem-solving abilities of infants and young children are quite different than those of older children and adults. As you read about the stages of cognitive development that follow, think about the implications of these differences for caregiving and teaching or learning experiences during the infant's first year.

**Four Stages of Cognitive Development.**  Piaget's theory proposes four major stages of cognitive development: the sensorimotor period (birth to age 2), the preoperational period (ages 2 to 7), the concrete operations period (ages 7 to 11), and the formal operations period (age 11 and beyond).

According to Piaget, all children proceed through these stages, with development at each stage benefiting from the accomplishments of the previous stage. Piaget viewed these stages as invariant; that is, one stage always follows another in a predictable sequence. All individuals proceed through the invariant sequence, but they do so at their own rates of development. These differences in rates of entering and exiting the stages are attributed to differences in individual genetic timetables and in cultural and environmental influences.

*sensorimotor:*
*learning that occurs through the senses and motor activities*

The **sensorimotor** period extends from birth to the onset of gestures and language at around age 2. During this period, the infant's cognitive development depends on direct sensory experiences and motor actions; hence the term *sensorimotor*. Recall the reflexive activities of the newborn described in Chapter 5. These genetically programmed reflexes provide a basis for later cognitive development. Piaget believed that all mental processes are rooted in and are a continuation of the earliest reflexive and motor activities. As the infant gains control over his or her reflexes, movement (motor) behaviors become more purposeful. Purposeful motor activities facilitate the infant's explorations and, hence, the infant's awareness of and interactions with objects and people in the environment.

From birth on, through interactions with the environment, the infant begins to form mental structures, which Piaget termed *schemata*. These schemata help the infant organize and interpret experiences. Each additional experience brings new schemata or perhaps a modification of old schemata. The infant's knowledge of the environment grows through direct actions on objects and experiences with others. Piaget describes the infant at this stage as *egocentric*, or able to perceive only from his or her own perspective, not from the perspective of others.

**Assimilation, Accommodation, and Equilibration.** According to Piaget, **adaptation** to environmental demands involves two complementary processes: assimilation and accommodation. As infants attempt to fit new ideas and concepts into existing ones, they *assimilate* additional schemata. At first, the infant visually gazes and tracks, and the infant's hands and arms respond to environmental stimuli by reflex. Later these activities become integrated into "whole" activities of looking and grasping simultaneously, or coordinated eye-hand movements. This higher-order functioning increases the infant's interaction with the world, which in turn increases the infant's schemata, building new learning upon previous actions, events, or experiences.

*adaptation:*
*the process by which one adjusts to changes in the environment*

*Accommodation* is a process by which a previous schema (experience or concept[s]) is modified to include or adapt to a new experience. The breast-fed infant who is changed from breast feeding (existing schema) to bottle feeding (new experience) must alter sucking behaviors to "succeed" with the bottle. This alteration of sucking behavior is an example of accommodation, in this case to a new environmental demand. Each assimilation of an experience is complemented by accommodation to that experience, and this leads to adaptation. Adaptation to an event or experience brings about equilibrium between the individual and her or his environment.

Equilibrium is said to occur when assimilation and accommodation are in balance with each other, that is, the infant has adapted to the demands of the environment. However, this state is usually short-lived, as the infant is constantly acquiring and incorporating new information that requires additional assimilations and accommodations.

**Development During the Sensorimotor Stage.** The sensorimotor period of cognitive development is divided into six substages. Development through these substages is both rapid and dramatic. During the first year, the infant proceeds through the first four of these substages.

1. **Reflexive stage** (*birth to 1 month*). During this period, **reflexes** dominant since birth are modified over time as the infant experiences various sensory stimuli and interacts with the environment. Piaget believed the infant constructs schemata from the numerous sensory and reflexive experiences of these first weeks. The human face or voice, the positioning in the mother's arms prior to breast feeding, and the sounds and rhythms of the household are examples of possible early schemata.

*reflexes:*
*unlearned, involuntary responses to stimuli*

2. **Primary circular reactions** (*1 to 4 months*). At this time, infant reactions center on bodily responses. For example, the infant can now purposefully bring the

*primary circular reactions:*
*simple, pleasurable, repetitive acts centered on the infant's body*

*Emerging coordination of motor skills facilitates exploration, discovery, and a budding sense of autonomy.*

thumb to the mouth to suck. Previous thumb sucking occurred as a result of accidental and uncoordinated reflexive activity. During this stage, the infant will engage in other purposeful motor activity. This period is called *primary* because of its focus on bodily responses; it is called *circular* because the infant repeats the activities over and over again. This repetition may be the first indication of infant memory.

*secondary circular reactions: simple, pleasurable, repetitive acts centered on external objects*

3. **Secondary circular reactions** (*4 to 8 months*). This period is characterized by the infant's enlarging focus on objects and events in the environment. It is called *secondary circular* because it involves the infant's growing awareness of objects and events outside his or her own body. Through chance events, the infant learns he or she can make things happen to external objects. For example, the infant hits the bath water and a big splash results. This novel experience generates a desire to repeat it; and repeat it the infant does, presumably just for the pleasure such activity brings. These behaviors represent early experimentation and may become means/ends behaviors. During this substage, infants imitate sounds and actions that they have previously produced and currently hold in their own repertoires. Infants will now search for a hidden

object, which in previous stages was not pursued if not within their visual field. Piaget believed that for the infant, an object not seen did not exist.

4. **Coordination of secondary schemata** (*8 to 12 months*). This is the period in which the infant's behaviors are clearly evident. Imitative behaviors signal the infant's growing ability to learn through observing the behavior of others. Play becomes more clearly differentiated from other means/end activities and is enjoyed for its own sake. **Object permanence**, the realization that an object exists even though it cannot be touched or seen, is beginning to emerge.

*object permanence: the realization that objects and people continue to exist even though they may not be visible or detected through other senses*

## BROADENING THE PIAGETIAN PERSPECTIVE

Some researchers have challenged Piaget's assumptions regarding cognitive development. The *neo-Piagetians*, as they are called, have proposed theories challenging various aspects of Piaget's theory. For instance, Bower (1982) and Wishart and Bower (1985) challenged the notion of object permanence in the infant at 6 to 8 months. Whereas Piaget proposed that an infant will not search for an object hidden behind a screen because the infant believes the object no longer exists, Bower believes immature space perception may explain the infant's failure to search. He suggests that for the infant, the screen has replaced the hidden object, and two objects cannot occupy the same space. Bower believes that Piaget underestimated what infants come to know about objects and that their failure to search for or locate a hidden object may represent a lack of spatial knowledge rather than a lack of knowledge of object permanence. Bower suggests that infants as young as 5 months old will not only anticipate the reappearance of an object that has been moved to a position behind the screen but will attempt to look for it when a different object or no object appears.

Other researchers have challenged Piaget's notion that infants must do something to or with objects or people in the immediate environment for cognitive development to occur. These neo-Piagetians have proposed theories suggesting that there may be other pathways through which cognition emerges. Studying infants and young children with impaired vision, hearing, and/or motor abilities, they have demonstrated that cognitive development proceeds nonetheless (Bebko, et al., 1992; Mandler, 1988, 1990, 1992; Furth, 1992a, 1992b, 1992c). These theorists argue that infants, through their perceptual abilities and mental imagery, form concepts earlier than Piaget proposed.

In an attempt to explain the adaptive nature of cognitive development, Siegler (1991) proposes that "All current theories recognize that people are biologically prepared to perceive the world in certain ways, that many important perceptual capabilities are present at birth, and that others emerge in the first few months of infancy given all but the most abnormal experience" (p. 92). Siegler further asserts that we all perceive the world through our senses, yet learning inevitably depends on three functions:

- Attending—determining what object, event, or action will be mentally processed
- Identifying—establishing what a perception is through relating a current perception to perceptions already held in one's memory
- Locating—determining where the object of one's perception exists and in what location relative to the observer (p. 93)

Additional theories of cognitive development are described as behavioristic, social learning, information-processing, and contextualistic theories. Behaviorists (Bijou & Baer, 1961; Skinner, 1938; Watson, 1924) place little emphasis on developmental stages, stressing instead that cognition is shaped primarily by the individual's experiences. Greater importance is given to external factors such as reward and punishment in influencing learning than to innate abilities or biological processes. Since behavior is thought to be a result of its consequences, the consequences of trial-and-error behaviors are considered critical to thinking and learning.

Social learning theory (Bandura, 1977), an outgrowth of behaviorist philosophy, emphasizes the role of imitation in cognitive development. Many behaviors are learned simply by watching others, and much learning occurs in social situations. It is believed that very young infants can imitate the facial expressions of others (Meltzoff & Moore, 1983) and that infants may have an innate ability to compare information received through different modalities—e.g., vision, hearing, and their own body movements. They then use this information to coordinate imitative behaviors based on actions observed in others.

The information-processing theory of cognitive development (Sternberg, 1985; Case, 1985, 1987; Klahr & Wallace, 1976) likens it to the modern-day computer's inputs, throughputs, and outputs. *Input* refers to the individual's gathering of information from sensory stimuli: vision, hearing, tasting, smelling, tactile sensations, and sensorimotor activity. Input information is then acknowledged, compared to other "data" already stored in memory, categorized, and stored for future use. This process represents *throughput*. Subsequent verbal and/or nonverbal responses represent *output*. Studies of information processing with older children are described in Chapters 10, 13, and 16.

Contextualistic theories (Bronfenbrenner, 1977, 1986) are among the most contemporary. They describe cognitive development as an integral part of the social and cultural context in which an individual grows and develops. Cognitive development is viewed as an interactive process between the individual and a variety of social and cultural contexts. Cognition continually changes, as does the context in which it occurs. It is determined by many factors, including direct instruction, exploration, discovery, observation, and imitation. From this perspective, cognition is also viewed as developing in many and varied directions simultaneously; for instance, motor, language, and social learning may all be proceeding at the same time. As you will see in the following vignettes, the child both influences and is influenced by the context in which he or she exists. Thus, the context and the infant both play a role in shaping cognitive development.

Jeremy, lying in his crib, is intently watching a yellow soft-sculpture airplane dangling from the mobile above him. He kicks and squeals with glee, then stops and stares at the object bouncing above his crib. Lying still, he seems to notice that the object stopped swinging; kicking some more, the object begins to swing again. The entertainment is quite exhilarating and is repeated several times.

Phyllis, Jeremy's baby-sitter, noticing his playfulness and his interest in the mobile, recognizes that Jeremy has discovered the link between his own bodily movements and the subsequent jiggling of the colorful airplane. She approaches, detaches the airplane from the mobile, and holds it within Jeremy's reach while saying to him, "Do you want to hold the airplane? I think you like this bright toy, Jeremy."

Distracted from his previous activity, Jeremy's kicking subsides. He stares at the soft toy, looks at Phyllis (a bit puzzled), then back again at the soft toy. His eyes then travel to the mobile above where the airplane had been, then back to Phyllis and the toy in her hand. He reaches for the soft toy, grasps it and brings it to his mouth momentarily, then drops it, only to return to the original activity of kicking and watching the mobile. Somehow it isn't the same, and he immediately tires of the effort and begins to fret. ■

Which of Piaget's sensorimotor substages does Jeremy's behavior exhibit? Approximately how old is Jeremy? If your answer is substage 3, secondary circular reactions, you are correct. If you recalled the approximate age range for this substage, you guessed Jeremy's age to be somewhere between 4 and 8 months. Jeremy is now 6 months old. His own motor activity and the resulting movements of the mobile were entertaining in and of themselves. Possibly Jeremy was discovering that his actions could make the airplane wiggle.

However, playful infants attract their caregivers' attention. Phyllis could not resist getting in on the "action," but when she did, Jeremy was presented with a choice that was perhaps difficult for him to make: reach for and hold the toy airplane, interact with Phyllis, or continue the pleasurable activity of kicking and watching the mobile move.

While her timing might have been a little out of synchronization with his, Phyllis was supporting Jeremy's cognitive development by noticing what held his attention, naming the object, and bringing it within touching reach. Observant adults soon learn to synchronize their interactions with the infant's, recognizing when to enter an activity and when to leave the infant to her or his own explorations.

Angela, now 8 months old, is in her high chair. She still has some difficulty sitting alone and slides under the tray, only to be restrained by the high chair safety strap between her legs. Cracker crumbs are in her hair, on her eyebrows, between her fingers, clinging to her clothing, and sprinkled about on the floor on both sides of her. James and Cheryl, seated at the table nearby, have just finished their take-out fast-food burgers and are arguing over James's dating activities. It seems James is seeing some other girls now, and Cheryl is angry.

Angela slides under the high chair tray and frets in discomfort. James offhandedly pulls her back into a seated position and continues arguing with Cheryl. Angela begins to cry intermittently. Cheryl places another cracker on her high chair tray, still arguing with James. Quieted momentarily, Angela bangs the cracker on the tray, holds what is left of it over the floor, then releases her grasp and watches the cracker fall to the floor. Sliding under her tray again, she begins to cry, this time more forcefully. She is pulled back to a seated position by Cheryl, but this does not comfort or quiet her. James, tired of arguing and a bit distracted by the baby's crying, decides to leave.

Frustrated and angry, Cheryl picks up Angela, scolds her about the mess, takes her to the sink to wash her face and hands, then puts her in her playpen even though Angela is fretful. Unable to respond to Angela's needs—her own are more overwhelming at this time—Cheryl turns on the TV, props her feet up on the coffee table, and lapses into sadness.

Unable to elicit her mother's attention, Angela cries awhile longer. Defeated and tired, she picks up her blanket, puts her thumb in her mouth, watches her mother, and listens to the sounds of the television set until she finally falls asleep. ■

Angela's predicament involves psychosocial, physical/motor, and cognitive aspects. At 8 months old, what are Angela's cognitive needs? Is the manner in which her physical/motor and psychosocial needs are being handled in this particular episode conducive to development? What constraints to furthering her cognitive development seem apparent in this vignette? What does her inability to sit comfortably in the high chair tell about her physical and motor development? Still in the sensorimotor stage, what strategies are needed to promote her cognitive development? What neo-Piagetian perspectives can you apply to each of these two scenarios? Let's continue to explore these and other facets of cognitive development.

## SENSORY AND PERCEPTUAL ABILITIES IN INFANCY

Recall from Chapter 5 the sensory capabilities of infants. For most infants vision is reasonably acute, with an ability to visually track an object or a person moving within the infant's visual field. Infants (sometimes within the first few weeks) recognize and respond to the sight, sound, and smell of their mothers. Hearing, taste, and touch are also quite functional. Infants may distinguish their own mothers' voices from other female voices (DeCasper & Fifer, 1980) and can respond differently to infant-directed vocal affect, that is, approving and disapproving tonal qualities and other emotional expressions. It is believed that the infant can make these distinctions in infant-directed speech of several languages (Fernald, 1993). Tactile and kinesthetic sensations complete the sensory repertoire. Thus, the sensory capabilities of infants facilitate reception of environmental stimuli from which perceptions are formed. Perceptions dominate learning in the earliest stages of cognition.

Specific perceptions such as size, shape, weight, distance, and depth, if present at all in early infancy, are imperfect. In efforts to determine specific perceptual abilities of infants, researchers have studied infant responses to facial patterns, geometric patterns, targets that approach and recede from their visual field, looming objects, and depth awareness when placed on an elevated platform. Generally, these perceptions develop over the course of the first year and remain dependent on the maturation of all sensory modalities. Experience also contributes to refinement of perceptions. One can imagine the potential for accidents and mishaps during infancy due to faulty perceptions.

While perceptions dominate infant learning in the first months, infant responses to the same stimuli become less noticeable over time as the events occur repeatedly and become familiar to the infant. Vaughn and Litt (1987) refer to the infant's "orienting response," in which the infant is observed to suppress body movements, exhibit alertness, and turn the head toward the stimulus. (Recall Jeremy and the yellow soft-sculpture mobile.) Heartbeat accelerates during this orienting response, and as the stimulus becomes repetitive and familiar, the orienting response habituates; that is, the infant's response is less dramatic. Additional stimuli or events elicit this orienting response.

During the first year, infants become aware of their own bodies and body parts, noticing and gazing at their hands, clasping them together, sucking on fists and fingers, and playing with feet, toes, and genitalia. Emerging coordination of motor skills leads infants to use their bodies and their abilities to explore, experi-ence, and discover, thus opening up infinite avenues for learning. The ability to grasp and let go leads to handling, mouthing, and experimenting with a variety of playthings. As the infant manipulates a variety of objects, knowledge is being con-structed. The ability to sit, pull to a standing position, cruise, and return to a seated position provides variety to the infant's visual fields and sources of knowl-edge. Mobility through crawling and walking further extends the infant's sources for new explorations, discoveries, and experiences.

During the first year, infants also develop self-awareness, the awareness that certain actions on their part result in certain responses from caregivers. Thus, infants learn they can have some control over events and others. Recall from Chapter 6 that positive responses to the infant's cues result in positive feelings about self and feelings of security and trust, qualities that lead to confidence and eagerness to explore the environment and its many possibilities. Success in obtain-ing caregivers' attentions to needs contributes to the infant's sense of self and sup-ports a growing sense of competence.

## LANGUAGE DEVELOPMENT

One of the most remarkable cognitive achievements of early childhood is the acquisition of language. From beginnings characterized by communication through crying to a variety of interpretable vocal utterances, the infant begins to cognitively construct a very complex communicative system. This system includes focusing attention on another person, gazing and gesturing at sources of sounds, associating certain sounds and voices with particular events and people, developing reciprocity in verbal interactions (as when adult and infant coo back and forth to each other), and learning to use communicative systems to convey needs, feelings, and new learnings. In addition, parents around the world seem to adjust their speech styles when talking to infants, using the simplest words and exaggerating certain vocal sounds and expressions (Fernald & Morikawa, 1993). Thus coaxing language along.

From the moment of birth, infants seem to be "preprogrammed" to commu-nicate. Infants respond readily to the sound of the human voice and have been shown to distinguish the voices of their mothers from other female voices (Mehler, 1985). Infant crying communicates a variety of messages—hunger, discomfort, distress, anger, or boredom—and does so through different intona-tions and patterns, which become recognizable to the infant's parents and other caregivers.

As with cognitive development, a number of theoretical approaches have attempted to explain language development. Some theorists have proposed an inborn capacity for learning language called the **language acquisition device** (LAD) (Chomsky, 1968, 1980). The LAD is a set of innate skills that enable children to infer phoneme patterns, word meanings, and syntax from the language they hear. This skill facilitates the child's own attempts to communicate. This theory repre-sents a nativistic point of view, wherein heredity is believed to play a major role in language development.

*language acquisition device (LAD):*
*an innate mental mech-anism that some theo-rists believe make language development possible*

A behavioristic point of view, in contrast, holds that infants gradually learn languages through imitation of the sounds and speech they hear. When the infant spontaneously, and often accidentally, creates or repeats a sound and the parents respond with glee and encouragement, vocal productions become pleasurable experiences worth repeating (Skinner, 1957). Language is believed to be taught through reinforcement in the form of attention and approval.

The social interactionist point of view emphasizes the importance of the infant's interactions with caregivers in which vocal exchanges occur (Bruner, 1975, 1983; Clark-Stewart, 1973; Golinkoff, 1983). These researchers recognize the communicative aspects of these early vocal exchanges and the emotional satisfaction that accrues from successful exchanges between caregiver and child.

## LANGUAGE DEVELOPMENT IN THE FIRST YEAR

The development of speech in the first year of life varies from child to child. A few children speak in sentences by the end of the first year. Others use only one-word "sentences" that can be understood only by those who participate consistently in the infant's everyday world. Piaget (1923/1926) thought that cognition influences language. Since he viewed infants and young children as egocentric, Piaget therefore concluded that earliest speech is egocentric. He observed that the speech of infants and young children appears to be addressed to no one in particular.

Vygotsky (1934/1962) suggested that language influences cognition and that the speech of infants and young children is not egocentric but is communication with the self. These ideas are explored in more depth in Chapters 10, 13, and 16.

Under normal circumstances, infants follow similar, predictable sequences in the development of language. This seems to be true regardless of culture. As with other areas of development, most children follow a predictable pattern, but not all children proceed through the sequences at the same rate. The sequence for language development during the first year is illustrated in Table 7.1.

As noted earlier, crying conveys a variety of messages, and caregivers soon learn to interpret the sounds and intensities of the infant's cries and respond appropriately. Around age 4 weeks, infants make small, throaty noises that are perhaps precursors to the vowel sounds that will begin to appear around 8 weeks. Infants discover their own voices around 12 weeks and enjoy gurgling and cooing, repeating the same vowel sound over and over, with perhaps some variation in tone. The infant is content to play with his or her voice alone or in "concert" with a parent or caregiver. Laughing aloud also occurs about this time. Infants are thought to view this exchange as a noise-making activity in which infant and others "speak" at the same time (Rosenthal, 1982).

Around 6 months, babbling begins to occur in which the vowel sounds are combined with some consonants: *m, p, b, k, g*. Babbles such as *baba* are repeated over and over in succession, producing **echolalia**. It is believed that regardless of culture or locale, children all over the world produce similar babbles (Olney & Scholnick, 1976). As infants get older, linguists are able, through the use of tape-recorded infant vocalizations, to distinguish subtle differences in the babbles of

*echolalia:*
*the infant's repetitive babbling of one sound*

**TABLE 7.1**
Milestones in Language Development

| Age | Phonology | Morphology and Semantics | Syntax | Pragmatics |
|-----|-----------|--------------------------|--------|------------|
| Birth | Crying | | | |
| 1 month | Attends and responds to speaking voice | | | |
| 2 months | Cooing, distinguishes phoneme features | | | |
| 3 months | Vocalizes to social stimulus | | | |
| 4 months | Chuckles | | | Pointing and gestures |
| 6 months | Babbling | | | |
| 9 months | Echolalia | Understands a few words | | Understands gestures: responds to "bye-bye" |
| 12 months | Repeated syllables, jabbers expressively | First word | | Waves "bye-bye" |
| 18 month | | Comprehends simple questions, points to nose, eyes, and hair, vocabulary of 22 words | Two-word utterances, telegraphic speech | Uses words to make wants known |
| 24 months | | Vocabulary of 272 words | Uses pronouns and prepositions; uses simple sentences and phrases | Conversational turn-taking |

children in different environments (DeBoysson-Bardies, Sagart, & Durand, 1984). This is possible at around 6 to 7 months, when babbling becomes more varied in intonation, loudness, and rhythm and additional consonants are produced. Infants at this age begin to take turns in their vocalizations with a parent or caregiver (Rosenthal, 1982).

During the latter half of the first year, infants are learning about the sounds of their native language and begin to make distinctions between their native language and other languages (Juscyzk, Culter, & Redanz, 1993). Around 8 to 10 months, the infant may vocalize with toys, as though talking to them. Streams of babbles that sound like a conversation occur, yet no meaningful words emerge in this rich array of sounds. The infant may use sounds that approximate words or that are his or her own creation to represent objects or events. These sounds are called **vocables** (Ferguson, 1977). Later in this period, the infant may have learned a few isolated words. These words may or may not have true meaning for the infant, and probably are not associated with actual objects or people. Sometimes the streams of babbles include the interjection of an occasional word, creating a kind of pseudolanguage.

By the end of the first year, the infant may use one or two words correctly and comprehend simple commands and phrases, such as *no-no* and *bye-bye*, and some nonverbal language in the form of gestures, like *come to Daddy* and *peek-a-boo*. Infants respond to their own name and know the names of a few objects, though they may not speak these names. **Holophrasic** words, in which one word or syllable represents a whole sentence, may emerge (e.g., *baba*, means "I want my bottle").

Of interest to researchers and parents alike is the emergence of first words. Katherine Nelson (Nelson, 1973, 1979; Nelson & Lucariello, 1985) refers to the infant's growing awareness of two different worlds: objects and people. During the latter half of the first year, infants begin to realize that these different entities provide different experiences. Nelson argues that coordination of these two worlds is essential for the development of language. First words, **overgeneralized speech**, represent one or the other category; for instance, *ball* may come to represent all toys, not just the child's ball. *Mama*, on the other hand, may come to imply a full message to someone about the infant's need. Nelson places some emphasis on the interactive experiences infants have with adults who are aware of and "in tune" with the child's emerging language. Adults who provide names of objects and events promote optimal language development during this first word acquisition period.

*vocables:*
*early sound patterns, used by infants, that approximate words*

*holophrasic:*
*refers to the infant's use of one word to convey a phrase or a sentence*

*overgeneralized speech:*
*the use of a single word or label to represent an entire category of objects similar in use or appearance*

## LITERACY DEVELOPMENT

Based on the belief that the origins of literacy occur in infancy, researchers in language and literacy development now suggest that infants benefit from and enjoy sharing chants, songs, and books with their parents and caregivers. Hearing softly spoken language with the rich intonations that accompany stories and songs is an enriching and enjoyable auditory experience for infants. These pleasurable auditory experiences set the stage for the enjoyment of visual enrichment through pictures and infant picture books. Contemporary studies of infant language and literacy development emphasize the importance of sharing appropriate picture books with infants (Arnold, et al., 1994; Crain-Thoreson & Dale, 1992; Genishi, 1988).

Linda Lamme (1980) describes five categories of literature for infants: musical literature; point-and-say books; touch-and-smell books; cardboard, cloth, and plastic books; and early stories. Establishing routines in the infant's day that include shared time with such literature enhances parent-child relationships, facilitates language development, and lays the foundation for later reading abilities.

## FACTORS INFLUENCING COGNITION, LANGUAGE, AND LITERACY DEVELOPMENT

Think again about Jeremy and Angela. From the descriptions of their lives so far, several factors influencing development in all areas are beginning to become evident. Compare the lives of Jeremy and Angela in terms of the factors that influence cognition, language, and literacy.

*The origins of literacy occur during the infant and toddler periods.*

1. Full-term infants get off to a healthier, less vulnerable start in life. Optimal health from the beginning facilitates all development—physical and motor, psychosocial, cognitive, language, and literacy.

2. Proper nutrition is essential to good health and supports optimal brain and neurological development. There is some evidence that appropriate and adequate nutrition during the earliest months is critical for brain growth, and in severe cases of malnutrition during the first six months, the deleterious effects can be irreversible.

3. Environments that support the infant's cognitive needs and motivations with enriching sensory stimuli, opportunities for motor exploration, appropriate toys, and enlarging and enriching experiences promote optimal development.

4. Interactions with others who are responsive, supportive, and stimulating enhance not only the psychosocial development of the infant but cognition, language, and literacy development as well.

Adults may facilitate and enhance infant cognition, language development, and emerging literacy in a number of ways. Development cannot be hurried, and any efforts should first take cues from the behaviors of the infant. Bombarding the infant with too much stimuli, inappropriate toys, visually and auditorially overstimulating environments, and developmentally inappropriate expectations can be disconcerting to the infant and can impede optimal psychosocial and cognitive development. Infants thus become irritable and stressed, sometimes become depressed, and may exhibit problems with eating, sleeping, attending, and playing. An appreciation of the infant's own developmental timetable guides parents and caregivers.

## Role of the Early Childhood Professional

### Promoting Cognitive, Language, and Literacy Development in Infants

1. Provide rich, interactive environments that include opportunities for the infant to watch, interact with, feel and be a part of the family or child care group.

2. Provide a safe, supportive and nurturing environment that encourages exploration beyond the crib or playpen.

3. Provide a sensory-rich environment, including vocal and verbal interactions with the infant, soft singing, story reading, bright and cheerful surroundings, visual access to windows, simple, uncluttered pictures on the wall, and other visual interests.

4. Provide appropriate auditory stimuli, including sharing talk and laughter, reading aloud, or playing taped music, voices, pleasing household sounds, and other sources of interesting sounds, such as wind chimes.

5. Vary tactile stimuli with appropriate stuffed toys and soft sculptured items made from a variety of textures.

6. Alter the child's "scenery" periodically: Move the crib to another side of the room, move the high chair to another side of the table, and occasionally change the visuals on the wall around the crib or play areas.

7. Provide simple, satisfying, age-appropriate toys and crib items, and replace them when the infant no longer uses them.

8. Explore the surroundings with the infant, carrying him or her about, looking in the mirror, pointing to a photograph on the wall, looking out the window, finding the lowest kitchen drawer, and so on.

9. Take older infants on brief outings with you. Talk about where you are going, what you are doing, what you are seeing. Name objects, places, and people as you go.

10. Place an older infant's toys on low, open shelves for easy access and clean-up.

11. Recognize the infant's attempts to initiate playfulness and interaction. Respond with enthusiasm.  ■

## KEY TERMS

adaptation
cognitive development
echolalia
holophrasic
language acquisition
  device (LAD)

object permanence
overgeneralized speech
primary circular
  reactions
reflexes

secondary circular
  reactions
sensorimotor
vocables

## REVIEW STRATEGIES & ACTIVITIES

1. Review the key terms individually or with a classmate.

2. This book has introduced a variety of theories of child growth and development and sequences of development in the first year. Angela and Jeremy have provided examples of development during the first year. Reread the stories of Angela and Jeremy. Based on what you have learned so far about child development, make a list of your observations about Angela's and Jeremy's development and their potential. Discuss and compare your lists with those of your classmates.

3. Describe a child care program that offers optimal opportunities for cognitive, language, and literacy development. What types of interactions do you observe?

4. Tape-record the vocalizations of an infant between ages 5 and 12 months. With pencil in hand, listen to the various sounds the infant makes and record the vowels and consonants you think you hear. Which ones occur most often? Describe the tonal quality of the vocalizations. How long did each last? What events stimulated and/or prolonged the vocalizations? Compare your findings with the descriptions in this chapter.

---

## FURTHER READINGS

Bloom, L. (1993). *The transition from infancy to language: Acquiring the power of expression.* New York: Cambridge University Press.

Bredekamp, S. (Ed.). (1987). *Developmentally appropriate practice in early childhood programs serving infants.* Washington, DC: National Association for the Education of Young Children.

Cryer, D., Harms, T., & Bourland, B. (1987). *Active learning for infants.* Menlo Park, CA: Addison-Wesley.

Doake, D. B. (1988). *Reading begins at birth.* Ontario, Canada: Scholastic Canada Ltd.

Fisher, John J. (Ed.). (1988). *From baby to toddler.* New York: Pergee Books.

Garner, B. P. with E. Morsund (Illustrator) (1993). *Room to grow: The physical environment for infants and toddlers.* Little Rock, AR: Southern Early Childhood Association.

Hodge, S. with E. Morsund (Illustrator) (1993). *Caring for infants and toddlers with special needs.* Little Rock, AR: Southern Early Childhood Association.

Neuman, S. B., & Roskos, K. A. (1993). *Language and literacy learning in the early years: An integrated approach.* Fort Worth, TX: Harcourt Brace Jovanovich.

Slonin, M. B. (1991). *Children, culture and ethnicity: Evaluating and understanding the impact.* New York: Garland Publishing.

Stern, D. N. (1992). *Diary of a baby.* New York: Basic Books.

Vaughn, E. with E. Morsund (Illustrator) (1993). *Books for babies: Using books with infants and toddlers.* Little Rock, AR: Southern Early Childhood Association.

# PART FOUR

# The Young Child
# Ages 1 Through 3

# CHAPTER EIGHT

*Little children are not logical—they are motor. To give a child joy, give him something to do.*

**Lucy Gage**

# Physical and Motor Development Ages 1 Through 3

After studying this chapter, you will demonstrate comprehension by:

- Outlining expected patterns of physical and motor development from ages 1 through 3.
- Identifying developmental landmarks in large and small muscle development.
- Identifying developmental landmarks in perceptual motor development.
- Describing the beginnings of body and gender awareness.
- Delineating major factors influencing physical and motor development.
- Suggesting strategies for enhancing physical and motor and perceptual motor development from ages 1 through 3.

## PHYSICAL AND MOTOR COMPETENCE IN THE 1-TO-3-YEAR-OLD

By the end of the first year, the infant has made dramatic developmental strides in all areas of development—physical, social, emotional, cognitive, and language. Of special interest to parents and child development observers is the physical growth that proceeds quite readily, and its accompanying repertoire of motor skills. Indeed, some of the first large motor skills—pulling up, standing alone, and taking the first steps—evoke excitement, praise, and celebration. These milestones signal the beginning of a new period in child development, typically referred to as the *toddler period*. This period extends from age 1 through age 2 and into the third year.

### GENERAL PHYSICAL CHARACTERISTICS

The rapid growth rate of infancy decelerates somewhat during the second year. For example, while the infant's birthweight typically tripled during the first year, the toddler's weight gain will be around 5 to 6 pounds during the second year. Likewise, the infant's length, which increased by about 10 to 12 inches during the first year, is followed by growth of about 5 inches during the second year.

Body proportions begin to change from the short, rounded characteristics of the 1-year-old to a leaner and more muscular configuration by age 3. However, the head is still large in proportion to the rest of the body (comprising one-fifth of the total body length at age 1) and gives the toddler a top-heavy appearance (Figure 5.1, page 102). The toddler's early attempts to walk result in a posture characterized by a protruding abdomen, arms held upward and feet spread wide apart for balance (not always successfully), and a "leading" forehead. Awkward and unsure locomotion, body proportions, and characteristic posture make the term *toddler* quite appropriate for this period in child growth and development. By age 3, the changes in body build and proportions lower the center of gravity from the upper regions of the body to the midsection, facilitating more coordinated locomotion and a leaner and more upright body profile.

It is estimated that by the end of the first year, the brain is two-thirds of its adult size, and by the end of the second year it will be about four-fifths of its adult size (Restak, 1984). When examining infants and toddlers, pediatricians often measure the circumference of the child's head, though this is not done routinely after age 3. Head circumference during these first three years is significant in physical examinations because it assists the physician in assessing ossification of the cranial bones as the fontanelles begin to close and brain growth, which is most rapid during the period from birth to age 3. Whereas the head circumference at birth was greater than that of the chest, it is about equal to the chest circumference when the child is about a year old.

Facial proportions are also changing. The infant and young child have rather high, rounded, and prominent foreheads, resulting from early and rapid brain and cranial growth. Due to this early growth pattern, facial features comprise a smaller portion of the facial area than they will as the child gets older. The face is round with a small jaw and a small, flat nose. The eyes are set close together, and the lips are thin. Over the course of the next few years, facial proportions will change, and the child will lose the "baby face" appearance.

The eruption of teeth contributes to changes in facial proportions. By age 1, six to eight teeth may have appeared, though in some children teeth appear at a much slower rate, with some children having no more than three or four teeth by their first birthday. By age 2½ to 3, most children have all 20 of their **deciduous** ("baby") **teeth** (McDonald & Avery, 1983) (see Figure 8.1). Deciduous teeth, also called *primary* teeth, tend to appear sooner in boys than in girls. However, girls, generally thought to progress toward maturity more rapidly than boys in most areas of development, will be slightly ahead of boys in the eruption of permanent teeth.

*deciduous teeth: the first set of teeth, which erupts during infancy; often called* temporary *or* baby teeth; *will later be replaced by a set of 36 permanent teeth*

Changes in other body proportions are also evident. Look again at Figure 5.1, and notice the changes in body proportions from fetal development to adulthood. Notice that the arms of the newborn seem long and the legs quite short in proportion to the trunk. Then compare the arm and leg lengths with those of the 2-year-old: as the legs grow longer, the arms appear shorter, and the head comprises a much smaller proportion of the body length.

Skeletal development is characterized not only by an increase in size but also by the number and composition of bones. Beginning in the fetal period with soft, pliable cartilage, which begins to ossify around the fifth prenatal month, bones

| Primary Teeth | Upper Teeth | Erupt | Shed |
|---|---|---|---|
| | Central incisor | 8–12 months | 6–7 years |
| | Lateral incisor | 9–13 months | 7–8 years |
| | Canine (cuspid) | 16–22 months | 10–12 years |
| | First molar | 13–19 months | 9–11 years |
| | Second molar | 25–33 months | 10–12 years |
| | Lower Teeth | Erupt | Shed |
| | Second molar | 23–31 months | 10–12 years |
| | First molar | 14–18 months | 9–11 years |
| | Canine (cuspid) | 17–23 months | 9–12 years |
| | Lateral incisor | 10–16 months | 7–8 years |
| | Central incisor | 6–10 months | 6–7 years |

FIGURE 8.1

Sequence of Eruption of Primary Teeth (From American Dental Association (1995). CDT-1, *First Edition (1990–1995); A user's manual*. With permission.)

gradually harden as calcium and other minerals are absorbed. Not all bones grow and develop at the same rate. The cranial bones and long bones of the arms and spine exhibit earliest ossification. The bones of the hands and wrists tend to mature early and serve as valuable indicators of general growth progress in the child (Tanner, 1978).

The amount of **adipose** (fatty tissue) children have depends on a number of factors, including heredity, body type, nutrition and eating habits, activity levels, and exercise opportunities. During infancy, adipose develops more rapidly than muscle. However, children tend to lose adipose tissue toward the end of the first year and continue to do so during the next few years as they become upright and more mobile. The decrease will continue until about age 5, when increases in weight will result from skeletal and muscle growth.

*adipose:*
*the name for tissue in which there is an accumulation of connective tissue cells, each containing a relatively large deposit of fat*

**Locomotor** development refers to the growing ability to move independently from place to place. Like other areas of development, motor development follows the "law of developmental direction," that is, a head-to-foot direction with control over muscles of the upper regions of the body preceding control over muscles in the lower regions. This development parallels neural development, which also proceeds in a head-downward pattern. Brain development, particularly of the cerebellum, which is involved in posture and balance, is rather rapid between 6 and 18 months of age. Thus, neural and muscular development in tandem with changing body proportions facilitate locomotion, and do so in a fairly predictable pattern.

*locomotor:*
*the ability to move independently from place to place*

## DEVELOPMENTAL MILESTONES

By the end of the first year, the child has mastered such motor skills as rolling over, sitting alone, crawling, pulling up, and perhaps standing alone. Between ages 10 to 15 months, the child may walk when held by one hand or may pull to a standing position and "cruise" by holding on to furniture. These activities are referred to as *large motor* activities because they enlist the use and coordination of the large muscles of the arms, trunk, and legs. Because these muscles generally mature earliest, children master large motor skills sooner than small muscle skills such as handling a spoon, a crayon, or buttons.

Large motor development follows predictable patterns. Table 8.1 identifies **developmental milestones** of the period from 1 to 3. Review Table 5.3 (p. 117), and notice how motor development progresses from birth to age 1 and from ages 1 through 3. Notice the impressive array of large motor coordinations and skills that emerge during this first 36 months. However, there are individual differences in rates and sometimes sequences of development in all aspects of child growth and development. Any such sequence of developmental events can provide only approximations with which to observe and understand emerging abilities. Understanding of the sequence is generally more helpful to us than any attempt to apply strict age/stage placements.

*developmental milestones: significant events during the course of growth and development*

## SMALL MOTOR DEVELOPMENT

Equally dramatic, but probably not always as obvious, is the emergence of small motor development. Small muscle development and motor skills also follow the law of developmental direction, proceeding from the head downward and from the central axis outward. This means the coordination of the smaller muscles of the wrists, hands, and fingers is preceded by, and for the most part dependent on, the coordination of the large muscles of the upper trunk, shoulders, and upper arms.

The abilities to reach, grasp, manipulate, and let go of an object become more precise during the second year. Coordination of eyes and hands improves rapidly during the toddler period, and with ever-increasing locomotor skills, new explorations emerge. Locomotion, coupled with improving eye-hand coordination, becomes a primary vehicle for learning. Successful exploration is facilitated by the coordination of large muscles, small muscles, vision, and hearing.

*prehension: the coordination of fingers and thumb to permit grasping*

*flexors: muscles that act to bend a joint*

*extensors: muscles that act to stretch or extend a limb*

By age 1, **prehension**, the ability to use the thumb and fingers in opposition to each other, has become reasonably efficient. Recall that during the first year of development, the grasping muscles (**flexors**) are stronger than the releasing muscles (**extensors**). During the toddler period, grasping and letting go become more efficient. The activities of pouring objects from a container and then, putting them back into the container one by one can be an absorbing activity, requiring both grasping and releasing.

## PERCEPTUAL-MOTOR DEVELOPMENT

Perception is a neurological process by which sensory input is organized. It involves various sensory abilities: visual, auditory, and tactile-kinesthetic. For instance, visual perception involves the ability to recognize and discriminate faces, patterns, sizes, shapes, depth, distance, and so on. Auditory perception involves abilities to use auditory clues to identify people, objects, and events and to discern distance, speed, space, and so on. Tactile-kinesthetic perception provides infor-

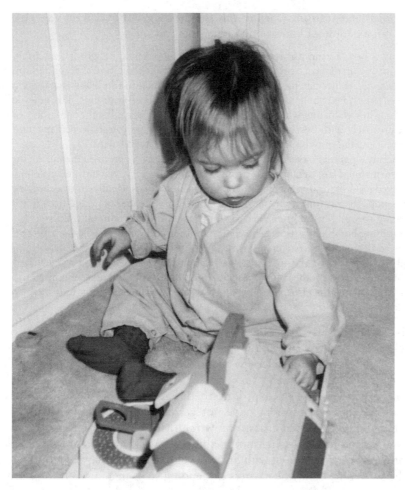

*Eye-hand coordination is enhanced with developmentally appropriate manipulative objects.*

mation relating to touch, textures, temperature, weight, pressure, and one's own body position, presence, or movements.

**Perceptual-motor** development refers to the interrelationship between the child's perceptions and his or her emerging motor abilities. Since perceptions derive from the senses and underlie awareness and understanding, motor development and perception are interdependent, and each influences development and learning.

Such abilities as space perception, depth perception, and weight perception depend heavily on locomotor experiences for their development. Thus, child development observers are interested in the effective integration of perceptual and motor development. When perceptual and motor abilities are integrated, the child uses visual, auditory, tactile, or other sensory data to plan and carry out motor activities. Imitating another child's scribbles is an example of visual-motor integration. Responding to the rhythms of music from the stereo is an example of

*perceptual-motor: interrelationship between perception and motor abilities* audio-motor integration. Curling into one's own cubbyhole at the child care center is an example of kinesthetic-motor integration.

🦋 Jeremy is now 13 months old. He is aware of his parents' delight in watching him attempt his first steps. Feet widespread, arms bent at the elbows, reaching upward for balance, he lifts one foot to step, loses his balance, and tumbles sideways. On the next attempt, he is able to toddle two or three steps before falling. His new skill is thrilling but also somewhat frightening. His parents clap, laugh, coax, and praise him profusely with every attempt. Tiring, he reverts to a more expedient mode of locomotion and crawls easily to his mother's outstretched arms.

Jeremy's parents have attempted to provide space for Jeremy's increasing mobility. Furnishings are arranged to provide obstacle-free movement and to eliminate sharp edges or items over which he might trip. Jeremy especially enjoys climbing the three steps to the front door upon returning from an excursion, and now that he is learning to walk, his mother "experiments" with his stair-climbing skills.

Holding both hands from behind him, mother and Jeremy walk toward the three steps to descend. At first Jeremy thrusts one foot forward into the air, bringing it back to the level of the first step, as though he were walking on a level plane. Consequently, his mother must "rescue" him, or he will tumble down the steps. Not too happy with this effort, Jeremy returns to a crawling position and proceeds to back his way down the steps. ■

This vignette illustrates some aspects of perceptual-motor development. Jeremy's parents are aware that his space and speed perceptions are faulty, so they have arranged their living spaces to accommodate his poorly coordinated movements. Also, Jeremy's mother's "experiment," reveals Jeremy's lack of depth perception. Perhaps Jeremy's visual, kinesthetic, and/or depth perceptions are still immature, or these perceptions have not yet become coordinated with existing motor capabilities. In such cases, one would assert that Jeremy, at 13 months, needs more time for his visual-motor abilities to become integrated. While this integration is occurring along with other developments during these toddler years, it will be some time before he masters descending steps in an upright-forward position. Typically, children do not descend stairs smoothly and unassisted until around age 4.

Visual-motor development is enhanced through opportunities to use developing locomotor abilities and small motor skills. Body awareness, balance, rhythm, space, and temporal awareness are increasing as toddlers explore their surroundings and experience their own body movements and abilities.

🦋 Angela is also 13 months old. Her motor development is somewhat, though not dramatically, delayed. (Recall that Angela was a premature delivery, complicated by anoxia.) Measured against the usual age ranges for emergence of motor skills, Angela has performed approximately four to six months behind expectations for full-term infants. Nevertheless, her development appears to be quite normal, though she exhibits more excitability, restlessness, and frustration, which is not unusual for preterm babies. Her excursions about the house are far reaching when she is allowed to explore beyond the playpen or crib.

Cheryl, now 16 years old, has had a happy and successful year in her new school. With help from the child care center on her high school campus, Cheryl is learning to juggle parenthood and education. She is taking a child development course and is thrilled to learn about the different stages and abilities Angela is exhibiting. She has learned to provide an environment at home in which Angela can safely explore. Yet Cheryl's siblings' activities tend to create a less than safe environment, so Angela is often relegated to the playpen, sometimes for lengthy periods. She cruises around the playpen, watches the other children, listens to the television, and cuddles her soft toys. She enjoys dropping small blocks into a bucket and then dumping them out. The older children bring her other items to play with, and when she gets fussy they increase their verbal interactions with her, playing games like peek-a-boo or "which hand is the toy in?" Angela's environment is verbally rich and interactive.

The limited visual and tactile-kinesthetic environment of the playpen, however, has further delayed Angela's perceptual-motor integration. Delayed perceptual-motor integration could place Angela at risk for learning difficulties later on. How might Angela's motor development be enhanced? ■

## EXPECTED PATTERNS AND DEVELOPMENTAL MILESTONES

Tables 8.1 and 8.2 illustrate expected patterns and developmental milestones from ages 1 through 3. Keep in mind that multiple biological and environmental influences affect both the sequence and timing of motor abilities. These influences have origins in prenatal and infant developmental histories, cultural expectations and backgrounds, nutritional status, general health and well-being, and opportunities to use emerging abilities.

## RELATIONSHIP BETWEEN PHYSICAL/MOTOR AND PSYCHOSOCIAL DEVELOPMENT

In Chapter 5, we pointed out that physical/motor development and psychosocial development are interrelated. Each new motor skill contributes to the child's emerging self-concept. The toddler's early definitions of self are based on the types of interactive experiences he or she has had with parents, primary caregivers, and important others. These relationships and the toddler's increasing awareness of his or her own capabilities and personal qualities form the basis for an emerging self-concept. Self-concept development is a gradual process that continues throughout one's life and changes as experiences and relationships expand.

Older infants and toddlers demonstrate an emerging self-concept by focusing on certain aspects of their own bodies and emerging abilities. Pointing to and naming their own body parts, telling their names, holding the appropriate number of fingers to convey their ages, saying "Look at me!" as they demonstrate a new skill, and insisting on doing things for themselves such as pulling off socks and shoes, holding their own spoon or cup, and preferring to walk rather than being carried are all indications of the child's emerging body awareness. In addition to body awareness, other important aspects of the self-concept during the toddler period are self-help efforts, gender awareness, and toilet learning.

## TABLE 8.1
## Developmental Milestones in Large Motor Controls from Ages 1 through 3

| Age | Motor Development |
|---|---|
| 12 to 18 months | Pulls to standing position holding onto furniture |
| | Throws objects from crib |
| | Cruises while holding onto furniture |
| | Walks with two hands held |
| | Crawls up steps |
| | Rolls a large ball, nondirected, using both hands and arms |
| | Attempts to slide from lap or high chair |
| | Begins to make shift from crawling to walking |
| | Stands alone |
| | Climbs onto a chair |
| | Takes two or three steps without support with legs widespread and arms held upward for balance |
| | Gets into a standing position unassisted |
| | Squats to pick up an object |
| | Reverts to crawling when in a hurry rather than attempting to walk |
| | Cannot yet make sudden stops or turns |
| | "Dances" in place to music |
| 18 to 24 months | Bends to pick up objects |
| | Walks without falling |
| | Pulls, drags toys |
| | Seats self in a child's chair |
| | Walks up and down stairs assisted |
| | Walks backward |
| | "Dances" to music moving about |
| | Mimics household activities: bathing baby, sweeping, dusting, talking on telephone |
| 24 to 36 months | Runs |
| | Walks on toes |
| | Jumps in place |
| | Kicks a large ball |
| | Imitates rhythms and animal movements; e.g., gallops like a horse, waddles like a duck |
| | Throws a ball, nondirected |
| | Catches a ball rolled to her or him |
| | Jumps in place |
| | Rides a tricycle |
| | Walks stairs one step at a time |
| | Jumps from lowest step |
| | Attempts to balance standing on one foot |
| 36 to 48 months | Balances on one foot |
| | Hops, gallops, runs with ease |
| | Avoids obstacles |
| | Stops readily |
| | Walks on a line |
| | Jumps over low objects |
| | Throws a ball, directed |
| | Enjoys simple dances and rhythms |

**TABLE 8.2**
**Developmental Milestones in Small Motor Development from Ages 1 through 3**

| Age | Motor Development |
|---|---|
| 12 to 18 months | Picks up small object with pincer movement |
| | Drops and picks up toys |
| | Releases toy into a container |
| | Knocks over tower with wave of hand |
| | Throws objects to the floor |
| | Finger-feeds efficiently |
| | Uses a spoon awkwardly |
| | Stacks two cubes after demonstration |
| | Pours objects from container |
| | Builds tower of three or four cubes |
| | Holds two cubes in one hand |
| | Takes off shoes, socks |
| | Points to things |
| | Uses cup for drinking |
| | Feeds self efficiently |
| 18 to 24 months | Manages spoon and cup awkwardly |
| | Turns pages of book, two and three pages at a time |
| | Places large pegs in peg board |
| | Holds crayon in fist |
| | Scribbles |
| | Squeezes a soft squeak toy |
| 24 to 36 months | Builds tower of five to seven cubes |
| | Strings three or four large beads |
| | Turns pages one page at a time |
| | Imitates demonstrated vertical and circular scribbles |
| | Manages spoon and cup with increasing efficiency |
| | Lines up object in "train" sequence |
| 36 to 48 months | Builds tower of eight to ten cubes |
| | Imitates variety of shapes in drawings |
| | Feeds self with few spills |
| | Unbuttons front clothing |
| | Zips, handles velcro fasteners |
| | Works puzzles of three to six pieces |
| | Handles books efficiently |
| | Exhibits hand preference |
| | Spreads butter and jam on toast |
| | Dresses and undresses with assistance |

## SELF-HELP EFFORTS

The desire to do things for themselves emerges early when infants choose to hold their own bottles, use their hands and fingers to feed themselves, retrieve and relinquish toys and other belongings, and efficiently (vocally, verbally, or through body language) communicate their needs to others. The toddler's increasing sense of self occurs in tandem with a growing desire for independence or autonomy (self-government).

Mobility facilitated by refinement of large motor abilities and increasingly skilled use and coordination of eyes and hands through small motor development facilitate the child's emerging self-help skills. Awkward yet determined attempts at dressing and undressing (usually starting with the removal of shoes and socks), following simple directions, the enjoyment of "fetch-and-carry" activities, using a wash cloth to wash face after meals, washing hands, bathing self, brushing teeth, and reporting simple events ("I broke it.") are examples of early self-help abilities. Patience, support, and encouragement are needed during these often tedious and sometimes frustrating early efforts. As toddlers become more successful in their attempts at self-help, their sense of positive self-regard grows, and they are encouraged to continue these efforts, becoming more and more efficient with practice and experience.

## BODY AND GENDER AWARENESS

*body awareness:*
*one's cognizance of one's own body and its parts and one's internal and external controls over the body's capabilities*

Toddler **body awareness** emerges with the acquisition and repetition of each new motor activity. Motor behaviors, once discovered, are repeated over and over. Throwing an object from the crib, pulling to a standing position beside furniture and dropping back to a seated one, dumping toys from a container, climbing a staircase, and opening a drawer all become activities to be repeated and mastered. Such activities provide the toddler with a sense of power and control over self and the environment. For the toddler, this is an exhilarating time. It is also a time for close adult supervision!

Through these types of activities, toddlers form mental images and concepts of themselves and their increasing physical/motor abilities. During this age period, children learn to identify themselves according to gender. They begin to name their body parts: eyes, nose, mouth, feet, tummy, and so on. Naming body parts often becomes a game, with the adult asking for identification and delighting in the toddler's answers.

*gender awareness:*
*one's understanding that one is (biologically) male or female*

Discriminations between *male* and *female* emerge during the first year (Brooks-Gunn & Lewis, 1982). Children's awareness of their own gender (**gender awareness**) is usually established by age 2½ to 3 years. The toddler may demonstrate emerging body and gender awareness through curiosity about their own and others' anatomies. The toddler may touch the mother's breasts, watch intently as the father urinates, become intrigued with the body parts of siblings, and explore their own genitalia. These behaviors reflect normal curiosity, are harmless, and represent the child's growing body awareness. Parents should respond in a manner that does not convey shock or embarrassment. Simply naming the body parts is all that is required at this time. It is appropriate to use correct terms such as urinate, bowel movement, breasts, and so on, as this assists the toddler's understanding and helps prevent the development of misconceptions.

Questions often accompany the toddler's curiosity about gender—questions regarding why girls and boys are different, why they use the toilet in different ways, how babies get in a mommy's tummy, why girls don't have a penis, and the like. Parents and caregivers must be matter-of-fact in answering these questions, factual yet simplistic enough for the young child to understand. The child should feel psychologically safe in asking anatomical questions. Adults need to be approachable on topics relating to gender and human anatomy; yet there is little need at this age for elaborate technical or value-laden discussion. Answering questions as they arise is always preferable to postponement to a later time (or age), deferring to the other parent or another adult, or preplanning a selected time for a formal discussion. Such strategies convey confusing messages to children who have asked what to them are reasonable and logical questions.

## TOILET LEARNING

In infancy, the elimination of body wastes occurs involuntarily as a reflexive activity when bladder or bowels need emptying. During the first year or so, the infant must develop a conscious awareness of the feelings of bowel and bladder fullness and develop some control over anal and urethral sphincters. Such control cannot occur until certain nerve pathways have developed and matured. The infant must have developed some language and locomotor skills to signal a need to others, get to the toilet in due time, manage clothing, and then manage toileting itself. This is not a small order.

**Toilet learning** is a gradual maturational process that extends over a period of several years. It is not, as the term *toilet training* implies, something that can be taught at some predetermined age. Parents and caregivers must learn to respond to readiness cues from the child. Efforts to impose toileting schedules are usually unsuccessful and can result in undue stress for parents and unnecessary strain on the toddler-parent relationship.

*toilet learning: a gradual maturational process in which the child gains control over elimination*

Between 18 and 20 months, the toddler begins to indicate toileting needs to caregivers. Usually bowel control precedes bladder control. The toddler may have a toileting expression, such as "poo poo" or "potty," to signal a need for assistance. Verbally expressing the need indicates the child's growing mental awareness of discomfort prior to toileting. For some children, this is only the beginning, since the other skills of voluntarily controlling the sphincters, getting to the toilet in time, managing clothing, and so on are imperfect. The child must experience adult patience and assistance as this process of toilet learning begins.

Some children may have control over their toileting needs by age 2, others may lack such control until age 3, and still others may go beyond age 3. Once control seems to be established, children will have relapses for a variety of reasons: impending illness, diarrhea, bladder infections, sound sleep, being too busy to notice the need, excitement, anxiety, or psychological trauma, to mention a few. Toddlers sometimes revert to precontrol stages when family life is altered in some manner: a family move, a new baby, a family member going to the hospital, a death or divorce in the family, or even an unusually exciting and happy event such as a birthday party. Adults should expect uneven development in toilet learning and should not show disappointment when the toddler is unsuccessful; nor should the adult punish or shame the toddler for relapses, as this prolongs the process of developing control. The positive and supportive manner in which adults handle toilet learning will be instrumental in ensuring continued control and healthy attitudes toward the human body and elimination.

Theorists have related healthy gender awareness experiences and toilet learning to psychosocial development. Erikson, for instance, has related toileting to the child's developing sense of autonomy during the toddler period and suggests that its healthy management is critical to this stage of personality development.

## RELATIONSHIP BETWEEN PHYSICAL/MOTOR AND COGNITIVE DEVELOPMENT

Recall from earlier chapters the discussions of rapid brain development during the prenatal period and the first year. This rapid brain growth continues into the preschool years. The human brain is made up of billions of nerve cells known as **neurons**. These nerve cells begin developing during the embryonic period, when the primitive neural tube begins to emerge and develop. Unlike other cells in the body, the neurons are not packed closely but have spaces between them that allow nerve fibers to connect or "communicate" with one another through a contact process known as **synapse**. During infancy and the toddler period, growth of neural fibers and synapses increases rapidly (Nowakowski, 1987; Volpe, 1987).

As neurons develop, their continued growth and survival depend on environmental stimulation. Input from the child's surrounding environment prompts new synapses. Neurons that are not stimulated tend to die. Appropriate early stimulation thus has long-term implications for cognitive development. Environments rich in visual, auditory, and tactile information (stimulation) facilitate brain growth in this manner.

Brain growth, mostly in weight (rather than in the number of neurons), continues during early childhood as **glial cells**—cells that support and nourish the neurons—increase in number and weight and as myelination occurs. *Myelination* is a process in which nerve fibers are coated with a fatty sheath called *myelin*, which facilitates the transfer of messages across synapses. By the time a child is 2 years old, the growth of glial cells and myelination have brought the brain to almost three-fifths of its adult weight; however, myelination continues into adult life.

It is important to recognize this early neurological development to appreciate the influence of early stimulation and enriching experiences. Rapid brain growth influences first motor abilities, then sensory perceptions (Volpe, 1987). Thus, one can expect that healthy large and small motor development and sensory experiences promote cognitive development. The adult's role, then, is to provide opportunities to explore, enriching sensory experiences, appropriate language and labels, and clarification of events surrounding the child. The toddler's increasingly sophisticated mobility—walking, running, climbing, reaching—and boundless curiosity propel the child

*neuron:*
*a nerve cell responsible for transmitting information in the brain*

*synapse:*
*the point of contact between nerve fibers*

*glial cell:*
*a supporting and connecting cell in the nervous system*

into an ever-enlarging world of explorations, experimentations, and discoveries. The toddler is an insatiable explorer. Needless to say, constant supervision is paramount!

## FACTORS INFLUENCING PHYSICAL AND MOTOR DEVELOPMENT, AGES 1 THROUGH 3

This section elaborates on topics begun in Chapter 5 and includes some additional topics. You may wish to review those factors before reading this section.

### GENERAL HEALTH AND FREEDOM FROM DISEASE

The rapid growth during the preschool years makes ongoing and regular health assessment checkups imperative. In general, children need to be examined two to three times during the second year and one or two times a year thereafter. This schedule helps ensure that immunizations are kept current and that emerging health care needs are addressed as they arise.

Immunizing the nation's children against deadly and debilitating but preventable diseases continues to be a concern to all who work with and care for young children. It is estimated that in 1991, only 55.3 percent of America's 2-year-olds were appropriately immunized. Among 2-year-old children living in poverty, only 38 percent were up to date on their immunizations (Children's Defense Fund, 1994). These are alarming statistics. There certainly is a need, as well as a moral and ethical obligation, to carefully monitor childhood immunizations in all programs that serve young children.

In addition to the lack of immunizations among young children in the United States and around the world and the consequent reemergence of diseases once thought to be under control, other health issues are arousing concern among health care and early childhood professionals. Three of these issues will be discussed later in this chapter: (1) the increasing incidence of tuberculosis in the United States, (2) the continuing exposure of young children to lead contamination, and (3) the rise in human immunodeficiency virus and acquired immunodeficiency syndrome (HIV/AIDS). A new issue for child care programs and schools is the establishment of guidelines for the admission and care of children infected with the HIV virus.

In their manual *Caring for Our Children: National Health and Safety Performance Standards: Guidelines for Out-of-Home Child Care Programs*, the American Public Health Association and the American Academy of Pediatrics (1992) have set forth policies and procedures to follow in maintaining and protecting the health of young children. Based on these guidelines, the National Association for the Education of Young Children published *Keeping Healthy: Parent, Teachers, and Children*, a brochure summarizing important issues relating to avoiding the spread of infectious diseases among children in out-of-home groups (McCracken, 1992). Guidelines for determining when and if a child is well enough to attend an early childhood program are listed in Figure 8.2.

## FIGURE 8.2
## Guidelines for Illnesses Requiring Exclusion

**Exclude children and adults with these illnesses or symptoms:**

**Fever,** defined by the child's age as follows; until medical evaluation indicates inclusion

> **Infants 4 months old and younger:** rectal temperature greater than 101°F., or axillary (armpit) temperature greater than 100°F., even if there has not been a change in their behavior

> **Infants and children older than 4 months** (accompanied by behavior changes or other signs or symptoms of illness): rectal temperature 102°F. or greater oral temperature 101°F. or greater axillary (armpit) temperature 100°F. or greater

**Signs of possible severe illness,** including unusual lethargy, irritability, persistent crying, difficult breathing

**Uncontrolled diarrhea,** defined as an increased number of stools compared with the child's normal pattern, with increased stool water and/or decreased form that is not contained by the diaper or toilet use

**Vomiting** two or more times in the previous 24 hours unless the vomiting is determined to be due to a noncommunicable condition and the child is not in danger of dehydration

**Mouth sores** with drooling unless the child's physician or local health department authority states the child is non-infectious

**Rash** with fever or behavior change until a physician has determined the illness not to be a communicable disease

**Purulent conjunctivitis,** defined as pink or red conjunctiva with white or yellow eye discharge, often with matted eyelids after sleep, and including a child with eye pain or redness of the eyelids or skin surrounding the eye

**Infestation** (e.g., scabies, head lice), until 24 hours after treatment was begun

**Tuberculosis,** until the child's physician or local health department authority states the child is non-infectious

**Impetigo,** until 24 hours after treatment was begun

**Streptococcal pharyngitis,** until 24 hours after treatment as been initiated, and until the child has been afebrile for 24 hours

**Ringworm infection** (tinea capitis, tinea corporis, tinea cruris, and tinea pedis) until 24 hours after treatment was begun

**Varicella** (chicken pox) until 6 days after onset of rash or until all lesions have dried and crusted

**Shingles,** only if the sores cannot be covered by clothing or a dressing, until the sores have crusted

**Pertussis,** which is laboratory confirmed, or suspected based on symptoms of the illness, or suspected because of cough onset within 14 days after having face-to-face contact with a laboratory-confirmed case of pertussis in a household or classroom, until 5 days of appropriate chemoprophylaxis (currently, erythromycin) has been completed

**Mumps,** until 9 days after onset of parotid gland swelling

**Hepatitis A** virus infection, until 1 week after onset of illness or until after immune serum globulin has been given to appropriate children and staff in the program, as directed by the responsible health department

**Measles** until 6 days after the rash appears

**Rubella** until 6 days after the rash appears

Adapted from American Academy of Pediatrics, & American Public Health Association. (1992). *Caring for our children— National health and safety performance standards: Guidelines for out-of-home child care programs.* McCracken, J. B. (1992). Keeping Healthy (brochure). Washington, DC: NAEYC.

## NEED FOR SLEEP

Toddlers are social beings, and resistance to bedtime may well arise. Ages 1 through 3 are marked by an emerging sense of autonomy and a lingering fear of separation. These psychological issues complicate bedtime and naptime rituals. Bedtime difficulties may arise from a low sensory threshold, which causes the young child to be easily distracted by environmental noise, motion, and light; parental overconcern for and difficulty in separating from the child; inappropriate expectations on the part of the adults who may believe that a child can fall asleep on-demand; ambivalence over regular versus child initiated routines; and a variety of physiological problems associated with growth, such as comfort in one's bed, impending illness, overfatigue or overstimulation, hunger, thirst, and toileting needs.

The need for sleep decreases as children get older. Toddlers may take one or two short naps or one long nap during the day and sleep anywhere from 8 to 12 hours at night. Many toddlers are ready to give up the crib in favor of a bed, preferably one with sturdy side rails to prevent falls. Insisting on continued use of the crib may complicate nap- and bedtimes if the child feels she or he has outgrown that sleeping arrangement. Regular and predictable routines (bath, bedtime story, brushing teeth, saying "good night" to everyone, a few moments of quiet with a parent, and finally lights out or night-light on) help toddlers to accept the separation and to meet their own sleep needs more effectively.

## DENTAL HEALTH

As mentioned earlier, all of the child's primary teeth usually have appeared by age 3. Primary teeth usually follow a predictable sequence of eruption, with the lower incisors appearing first. During the second and third year, a total of 20 primary teeth will erupt. The American Academy of Pediatric Dentists recommends a visit to the dentist by the time a child is 1 year old and thereafter every six months. In addition to examining for cavities, the dentist can determine the health of the child's teeth and gums and estimate when new teeth will erupt. The dentist will also counsel parents about nutritional needs and foods to avoid to ensure healthy teeth, and the need for fluoride or vitamin supplements.

Dental health begins in infancy. Regular cleaning of the infant's gums and new teeth after meals with a soft, damp gauze pad begins the process of instilling good oral cleaning habits and avoiding cavities in primary teeth. Avoiding use of the bottle as a "pacifier" is also necessary to prevent "baby bottle decay." With increasing eye-hand and hand-mouth coordination, the toddler can soon learn to use a brush and a small amount of toothpaste. Encouraging brushing after meals and before bedtime begins an essential self-help habit.

## NUTRITION

Nutrition is perhaps the most critical environmental factor relating to optimal growth and development. The visible effects of prolonged malnutrition on young children are seen almost daily on television newscasts and in advertisements soliciting help for children in underdeveloped countries. Yet malnutrition affects

*Optimal growth and development are often compromised of children of poverty.*

alarming numbers of American children as well. In America, at least 5.5 million children younger than 12 experience hunger each year. The Food Research and Action Center reports that in 1993, 1 in 10 Americans participated in the U.S. food stamp program (Children's Defense Fund, 1994).

Hollow eyes, protruding abdomens, and skeletal bodies are compelling characteristics of severely malnourished children. In addition to impaired body growth, prolonged malnutrition has been associated with retarded brain growth, impaired intellectual development, anemias, susceptibility to illnesses, and vulnerability to environmental toxins. Malnutrition is among the leading causes of childhood mortality worldwide (Children's Defense Fund, 1994).

Short-term malnutrition usually is not as devastating. Some researchers are unwilling to attribute all of the developmental problems just listed to malnutrition alone. Ricciuti (1980) suggests that inadequate housing, sanitation, medical care, and child care practices, limited educational opportunities, and increased exposure to disease all contribute to growth and developmental **anomalies**.

When children in less than optimal circumstances are provided the essentials for healthy growth and development, many of the effects of poor nutrition may be reversed. A "catch-up" phenomenon in growth and development sometimes causes poorly nourished children who have subsequently been provided with adequate diets to experience faster than normal growth for a time. This catch-up

**anomaly:**
*a deviation from the norm*

growth seems to be the body's attempt to follow its own genetically programmed growth schedule. Catch-up growth may also follow certain lengthy illnesses. Once back on schedule, the growth rate returns to its expected pace. Permanent physical and intellectual damage seems to result from malnutrition when (1) it occurs early in life, (2) it has been prolonged, and (3) it is left untreated (Ricciuti, 1980).

## SAFETY

Toddlers are particularly vulnerable to mishaps. Their impulsive behaviors, lack of experience and judgment, curiosity, and quest for independence place them at risk for accident and injury. Table 8.3 outlines important measures for adults to take during the toddler period to prevent accidents and injury.

## OPPORTUNITIES TO INTERACT, EXPLORE, AND PLAY

Opportunities to interact with caring, supportive adults and compatible playmates, to explore safe and inviting environments, and to do what children do so well—play—provide motivation to use emerging skills and play behaviors in growth-enhancing ways. Toddlers need environments, toys, and materials that encourage and facilitate

- *Large motor coordination* (wheeled toys; low crawling and climbing equipment; large balls to roll, kick, throw, and bounce; large blocks and construction-type toys; tricycles, wagons; etc.)
- *Small motor coordination* (fill-and-pour toys; connecting blocks and manipulative items; stacking toys; items that snap, button, zip; etc.)
- *Perceptual-motor development* (graduated stacking toys; puzzles with four to five parts; shape-sorting boxes; color-matching games; beanbag toss; sound-identifying games; texture-matching games; etc.)
- *Imitative behaviors and pretend play* (dolls; small vehicles such as trucks, cars, airplanes; household items such as plastic dishes; dress-up clothes and costumes of familiar characters; toy telephone; etc.)
- *Language and literacy* (books and pictures; puppets, dolls, stuffed toys; tape-recorded sounds, tunes, songs, poems, stories; shared-book experiences; conversation; field trips; etc.)

## APPROPRIATE AND INAPPROPRIATE EXPECTATIONS

As infants grow into toddlers and toddlers become preschoolers, their rapid growth and development suggest greater maturity and capability than is actually present. This assumption often leads to inappropriate expectations. Such expectations place young children at both physical and psychological risk. Knowledge of expected patterns and sequences of physical and motor development helps

**TABLE 8.3**
Important Accident Prevention Measures for Families to Observe during the Toddler Period

| Potential Accident Situations | Prevention Measures for Health Teaching |
| --- | --- |
| Motor vehicles | Maintain child in car seat, not just seat belt; do not be distracted from safe driving by a child in a car. Do not allow child to play outside unsupervised. Do not allow to operate electronic garage doors. Supervise toddler too young to be left alone on a tricycle. Teach safety with pedaling toys (look before crossing driveways; do not cross streets). |
| Falls | Keep house windows closed or keep secure screens in place. Place gates at top and bottom of stairs. Supervise at playgrounds. Do not allow child to walk with sharp object in hand or mouth. Raise crib rails and check to make sure they are locked before walking away from crib. |
| Aspiration | Examine toys for small parts that could be aspirated, remove those that appear dangerous. Do not feed a toddler popcorn, peanuts, etc.; urge children not to eat while running. Do not leave a toddler alone with a balloon. |
| Drowning | Do not leave toddler alone in a bathtub or near water (including buckets of cleaning water). |
| Animal bites | Do not allow the toddler to approach strange dogs. Supervise child's play with family pets. |
| Poisoning | Never present medication as candy. Buy medications with child-proof safety caps; put away immediately after use. Never take medication in front of child. Place all medications and poisons in locked cabinets or overhead shelves where child cannot reach. Never leave medication in parents' purse or pocket, where child can reach. Always store food or substances in their original containers. Use nonlead-based paint throughout the house. Hang plants or set them on high surfaces beyond toddler's grasp. Post telephone number of nearest poison control center by the telephone. In all first-aid boxes, maintain supply of syrup of ipecac, an emetic, with proper instructions for administering if poisoning should occur. |
| Burns | Buy flame-retardant clothing. Turn handles of pots toward back of stove to prevent toddler from reaching up and pulling them down. Use cool-mist vaporizer or remain in room when vaporizer is operating so that child is not tempted to play with it. Keep screen in front of fireplace or heater. Monitor toddlers carefully when they are near lit candles. Do not leave toddlers unsupervised near hot-water faucets. Do not allow toddlers to blow out matches (teach that fire is not fun); store matches out of reach. Keep electric wires and cords out of toddler's reach; cover electrical outlets with safety plugs. |
| General | Know whereabouts of toddlers at all times. Toddlers can climb onto chairs, stools, etc., that they could not manage before; can turn door knobs and go places they could not go before. Be aware that the frequency of accidents increases when the family is under stress and therefore less attentive to children. Special precautions must be taken at these times. Some children are more active, curious, and impulsive and therefore more vulnerable to accidents than others. |

*Source:* Pillitteri, A. (1992). *Maternal and Child Health Nursing.* New York: J. B. Lippincott (p. 899). Reprinted with permission by the author.

---

**FIGURE 8.3**
**Healthy Environments for Young Children**

---

Healthy home and child care environments for young children are characterized by
1. **Adequate space.** Toddlers need sufficient space in which to try out their emerging and uncoordinated motor skills. Tumbles and collisions with and furniture are minimized when adequate space is provided.
2. **Clean, sanitary surroundings.** Toddlers put their hands, toys and other objects into their mouths. All necessary precautions must be taken to protect toddlers from infections and disease.
3. **Safe space and play materials.** Reaching, grasping, and mobility skills tempt toddlers to satisfy their natural curiosity. The toddler's environment must be kept free from obstacles, poisons, sharp edges, small objects, unstable furnishings and play equipment, exposed electrical cords and outlets, and so on.
4. **Developmentally appropriate play items and equipment.** Developmentally appropriate play items help ensure safety and provide satisfying and engaging experiences that enhance physical, motor, and perceptual development, and enrich play activities.
5. **Unrelenting supervision.** While toddler mobility and curiousity enhance physical, motor, and perceptual growth and cognitive development, constant vigilance is essential. Safety concerns are paramount at this age.
6. **Supervised health care.** To maintain healthy bodies, health care must be supervised by appropriate medical and dental professionals. Proper diet, immunizations, rest and exercise, and specialized medical attention as needed enhance chances for optimal growth and development.

adults to appreciate each child's unique capabilities and interest and gives direction to providing growth-enhancing experiences for children.

The concept of "miseducation of young children" has been advanced by David Elkind (1987), and warns us of a growing number of misguided notions about what and when children learn. For instance, attempts to teach infants and toddlers to swim reveal adult expectations that are developmentally inappropriate. According to Elkind, swimming lessons for infants and toddlers places them at risk for middle ear infections and possible hearing loss, for asphyxiation from swallowing water, and for diarrhea from urine-contaminated water, since young children may not have bladder control yet. Elkind also admonishes that the added risk of false security the adult acquires and then comes to trust—that the swimming lessons will protect the child from drowning—is a serious misapplication of adult responsibility.

Expecting small children to use writing tools or scissors or to "color within the lines" is equally inappropriate and potentially damaging. Following the developmental cues provided by the interests and emerging capabilities of individual children helps to ensure that the opportunities and practice provided for them will serve fruitful purposes.

---

FIGURE 8.4
Examples of Conditions That May Be Identified on Screening and Benefited by Early Intervention Services

---

Children at biologic risk (i.e., graduates of neonatal intensive care units, survivors of illnesses such as meningitis)
Children at environmental risk
    Impoverished home
    Maladaptive community
    Maladaptive home situation
Chromosomal malfomations and other congenital syndromes
Chronic body illness
    Endocrine disorders (i.e., hypothyroidism)
    Major disease of cardiovascular, renal, pulmonary, hepatic, gastrointestinal, or other systems
    Severe infections (i.e., consequences of human immunodeficiency virus infection)
Defined neurologic disorder
    Central nervous system malformation
    Mental retardation
    Motor disorders (i.e., cerebral palsy)
    Neuromuscular disorders
Developmental disorders
    Autism and other pervasive developmental disorders
    Disorders of attention and activity
    Infants and toddlers at risk for learning disabilities
    Language delays
    Motor delays
Metabolic disorders
Orthopedic problems (i.e., limb reduction)
Sensory impairment (i.e., vision, hearing, pain)

*Source:* Katcher, A. L. & Haher, J. S. (1991). "The pediatrician and early intervention for the developmentally disabled or handicapped child." *Pediatrics in Review,* 12 (10), 306. Reprinted with permission by the American Academy of Pediatrics.

## TODDLERS WITH SPECIAL NEEDS

Many disabling conditions, when recognized and identified early in the child's development, can be treated and often ameliorated. Regular physical examinations and ongoing observations of growth and developmental trends in individual children help to ensure that any unusual developmental events are not overlooked and are responded to in an appropriate and timely way.

Children with special needs often experience diverse health and developmental problems, including chronic illnesses, disabilities and developmental delays, abuse (sexual abuse, substance abuse, neglect, or abandonment), homelessness, malnutrition, and psychological disturbances. An estimated one-fourth to one-third of U.S. children suffer one or more of these problems (Perrin, 1990). Figure 8.4 lists conditions warranting early screening, diagnosis, and intervention.

---

**FIGURE 8.5**
**Early Intervention Service Models**

---

Child-focused approaches
    Manipulate environment and experience
    Arouse central nervous system through effective communication
    Seek active participation of the child
    Strengthen child's ability to tolerate environmental factors
    Offer specific therapies (i.e., speech, physical, occupational)
    Coordinate with other medical therapies
    Offer structure in the form of developmental day care, preschool classroom,
       or center-based, less frequent periodic encounters
Caregiver-focused approaches
    Enable parent or other caregiver to facilitate development
    Range from provision of information through periodic group sessions to indi-
       vidual therapy
    Parent or caregiver seen as therapist
    Structure may be center-based or via home visitor service
Combined approaches
    Utilize elements of both
Early intervention service locations
    A health facility, such as hospital or ambulant care center
    A school
    A public health facility
    A poverty agency
    A nonprofit voluntary community agency for the handicapped

*Source:* Katcher, A. L. & Haher, J. S. (1991). "The pediattician and early intervention for the developmentally disabled or handicapped child." *Pediatrics in Review*, 12 (10), 306. Reprinted with permission by the American Academy of Pediatrics.

Some key physical and motor concerns for toddlers in these categories are related to early identification, assessment, and appropriate treatment of:

1. General health and nutritional needs
2. Ongoing assessment of physical and motor abilities, with special attention to movement competence and emerging large and small motor abilities, including but not limited to

- Posture
- Reflexive reactions
- Equilibrium
- Flexibility
- Voluntary movements
- Transitional movements as in moving from sitting to standing
- Mobility preference patterns
- Eye-hand, eye-foot, hand-mouth coordination

- Prehensor and grasping/releasing abilities
- Chewing and swallowing efficiency

3. Avoiding muscle contractures and structural deformities resulting from prolonged use of abnormal movement patterns

4. Providing appropriate physical and occupational intervention and therapies

5. Providing ongoing assessment, guidance, instruction, and, where needed, adaptive equipment to assist and facilitate emerging motor and self-help abilities

6. Providing purposeful activities and daily routines to facilitate and enhance physical and motor development

7. Providing quality, inclusive early childhood education programs and skilled professionals to ensure optimal developmental progress (Sexton, 1990)

Many types of intervention programs and services are available for children and families with special needs. These programs focus on individual children or specific needs categories, on parent and caregiver skills and knowledge, and/or on family systems and integrated school and community services. Figure 8.5 (See p.199) illustrates these various models.

## SOCIOECONOMIC INFLUENCES

Poverty represents a major impediment to sound growth and development. According to data gathered by the National Center for Children in Poverty (1991) and the Children's Defense Fund (1994), poverty continues to rise in the United States. In 1992, more children were living in poverty than in any year since 1965. The Children's Defense Fund reports that 27 percent of children of all races under age 3 live in poverty. These children are more likely than nonpoor children to die from infections and parasitic diseases, drowning and suffocation, car accidents, and fires. Poor children are more likely to suffer deleterious outcomes associated with prematurity and low birthweight and to exhibit low weight for height, which in turn affects brain growth and development and hence cognitive and psychosocial development. Poor children are also more likely to live in polluted environments, drink water contaminated with lead or breathe lead-contaminated paint dust, and have parents and other family members who are struggling to meet family survival needs and thus are less effective in meeting the special needs of infants and children. Families of these children are also likely to have limited resources for safe and stimulating toys, learning materials, and experiences; be less able to access quality child care; be more likely to live in high-crime neighborhoods; and be less able to access and afford regular, ongoing health care.

Poverty impedes healthy growth and development in myriad ways. Early childhood professionals must be sensitive to the needs of children and families living in poverty. These needs include assistance through various community, state, and federal agencies and early childhood intervention programs, such as Head Start; community immunization and other health care programs; family counseling services; and other resources. Early childhood professionals need to be nonjudgmental, supportive, and helpful. These physically and psychologically vulnerable children need adults who plan for and support their growth needs, accept and respect them, provide developmentally appropriate programs and expectations, and help connect these children and their families with appropriate intervention services.

## HEALTH AND WELL-BEING ISSUES IN TODDLER DEVELOPMENT

### NONPARENTAL CHILD CARE

Because the toddler period is one of rapid physical, psychosocial, and cognitive development, early childhood professionals are particularly concerned that non-parental child care be of the highest quality possible and provide surroundings, interactions, education, and care that best meets toddlers' unique needs.

Two studies of family need for and use of child care found that among families with employed mothers, 32 percent relied on grandparents, 21 percent relied on other relatives, 22 percent used family day care, 20 percent enrolled their children in child care centers, 3 percent provided in-home care for their children, and 2 percent used other forms of child care (Hofferth et al., 1991; Kisker et al., 1991). Regardless of the type of child care arrangement, parents need both knowledge of toddlers' developmental needs and strategies for selecting quality child care to meet both their child's needs and their family situation. Parents should be encouraged to visit, interview, and inquire of those knowledgeable about community child care resources well in advance of their need. Too often parents are forced to make hurried choices, choices that may prove to be injurious.

Monitoring, regulating, and accrediting out-of-home child care programs is a concern of policymakers and early childhood professionals. While these efforts do not guarantee highest-quality child care, they can provide assurances to the parents that would otherwise not be possible.

With more than one-half of mothers of children younger than 3 working outside the home, the need for high-quality, affordable child care is urgent. Research over the past decade has consistently identified certain essential qualities parents should look for to ensure positive developmental outcomes for their children (Phillips & Howes, 1987; Bredekamp, 1987; Galinsky et al., 1994; Carnegie Corporation, 1994):

- Small group size (the younger the child, the smaller the group should be)
- High adult-child ratios (the younger the child, the higher this ratio should be)
- Educated, well-trained caregivers
- Stability in child-caregiver relationships over time
- Developmentally appropriate curriculum and expectations.

We must all become both educators and advocates for quality child care services for families and their children. The emergence in recent years of Child Care Resource and Referral Systems is helping to connect families with child care providers and other community resources.

## RISE IN INCIDENCE OF TUBERCULOSIS AMONG CHILDREN

From 1985 to 1992, the incidence of tuberculosis (TB) in children increased over 36 percent from 789 to 1,074 cases nationwide (Clark, 1994). This rise has been attributed to overcrowding in family dwellings due to increased poverty among Americans; the AIDS epidemic, which reduces AIDS patients' resistance to TB; increased numbers of immigrants arriving from countries in which TB is epidemic; fewer dollars for public health programs to control the disease; and prevailing myths that TB was about to be eradicated (Clark, 1994). Children most likely at risk for TB are those who:

- Are immigrant children
- Have had a tuberculosis contact
- Live in cities with populations of 250,000 or more
- Are or have been homeless
- Have been exposed to an HIV-infected person
- Have contact with someone who has spent time in jail
- Live in indigent areas.

The incubation period for tuberculosis can be as short as two months or as long as 80 years (Clark, 1994). Prevention and treatment of the disease are tricky, since not all tests for TB are always reliable, and not all strains of the disease respond to drug treatment. As this book goes to press, the federal government and several medical groups are developing guidelines for the diagnosis, treatment, and prevention of the spread of tuberculosis. In the meantime, available drugs, regular medical check-ups for high-risk children, encouragement of more hygienic living conditions, and health care policies in schools and child care programs that address this issue should help alleviate this crisis. School and child care policies are best developed in consultation with area health professionals.

## HIV/AIDS

Acquired immunodeficiency syndrome (AIDS) was first described in 1983 (Ammann, 1983). During the ensuing decade, significant advances in recognition, diagnosis, and treatment emerged. HIV/AIDS is transmitted to infants and children through blood transfusions, breast feeding by infected mothers, and sexual abuse. The role of the placenta during prenatal development in facilitating or inhibiting transmission is yet unclear. Diagnosis is now possible in newborns with 50 percent accuracy and in 3-month-olds with 95 percent accuracy. As with other diseases in infancy, early diagnosis is critical. Diagnosis of HIV/AIDS in the expectant mother is recommended by health care professionals to provide timely treatment and appropriate counseling (Ammann, 1994). Currently, however, routine prenatal screening is not available; consequently, many infants and possibly their mothers are not being diagnosed and receiving medical attention.

What guidelines are available to early childhood professionals in accepting and caring for HIV-infected children? The American Public Health Association and the American Academy of Pediatrics (1992) provide helpful information for practices in early childhood programs and are considering additional guidelines as research provides further information. Two important concepts are proposed in their *Guidelines for out-of-home child care programs*. The first relates to the transmission of HIV:

> Studies examining transmission of HIV support the concept that HIV is not a highly infectious agent. The major routes of transmission are through sexual contact, through contact with blood, and from mother to child during the birth process. Several studies have shown that HIV-infected persons do not spread the HIV virus to other members of their households except through sexual contact. HIV has been isolated in very low volumes in saliva and urine. Transmission of Hepatitis B virus (a virus very similar to HIV but more infectious) through saliva appears to be very uncommon. Isolated cases suggest that contact with blood from an HIV-infected individual is a possible mode of transmission. In these situations transmission is most likely to have occurred through contact between nonintact skin and blood or blood-containing fluids (American Public Health Association & American Academy of Pediatrics, 1992, p. 232).

Another important issue is the need to protect the HIV-infected child:

Children who are infected with HIV often have immune systems that do not function properly to prevent infections. Children with immuno-suppression for multiple other reasons are at increased risk for severe complications from infections with chicken pox, CMV, TB, and measles virus. Available data indicate that measles infection is a more serious illness in HIV-infected children than in noninfected children. The first deaths due to measles in the United States reported to the Center for Disease Control (CDC) after 1985 were in HIV-infected children (MMWR, 1988). (American Public Health Association & American Academy of Pediatrics, 1992, p. 233).

## LEAD POISONING

Lead is a toxin known to cause brain and nervous system disorders, kidney damage, and growth retardation. Its prevalence is quite widespread, particularly in large, urban areas. Infants and toddlers are more likely than adults to ingest lead, due to their inclination to put things in their mouths, and to suffer its effects due to their immature digestive and nervous systems.

Lead is found in certain paints, soil, sometimes food, water from old plumbing, batteries, colored newsprint, toys, ceramics, folk remedies, cosmetics, jewelry, workplace dust particles (transported on clothing), and petroleum products. It is possible that high lead levels in the mother's blood cause placental transmission to the fetus. Prevention of lead poisoning in children requires thorough and careful evaluation of and modifications in the environment, avoiding lead-contaminated objects and places, and screening for blood lead levels through blood tests (Klerman, 1991).

 *Role of the Early Childhood Professional*

### Promoting Physical and Motor Development in Children Ages 1 Through 3

1. Create and maintain a safe and healthy environment.
2. Provide for proper nutrition and for ongoing health care.
3. Know and utilize developmentally appropriate activities and expectations.
4. Encourage exploration, discovery, and independence.
5. Provide positive, supportive, and protective guidance.
6. Encourage positive body and gender awareness.
7. Provide a variety of materials to encourage both large and small motor development.
8. Provide toys and experiences that facilitate perceptual-motor development. ■

## KEY TERMS

| | | |
|---|---|---|
| adipose | developmental | neuron |
| anomaly |   milestones | perceptual-motor |
| body awareness | extensors | prehension |
| deciduous teeth | flexors | synapse |
| developmentally | gender | toilet learning |
|   delayed | locomotor | |

## REVIEW STRATEGIES AND ACTIVITIES

1. Review the key terms individually or with a classmate.

2. Observe two children in a child care setting for approximately one hour during outdoor and indoor activity times. Using the physical and motor milestone lists in this chapter, record all motor behaviors observed. Record both large and small motor observations. Compare your lists with those of a classmate. How are the children the same? How do they differ? To what might the differences in motor abilities be attributed?

3. Invite a nutritionist to talk with your class. What dietary plan would she recommend for a 1 year old? 2 year old? 3 year old? How and why do these diets change as the child gets older?

4. Discuss with a classmate safe ways to encourage toddler exploration, discovery, and independence. List your suggestions. What physical/motor or perceptual development will your suggestions enhance?

5. Visit a nursery school in which toddlers (ages 1 to 3) are enrolled. How are children's health and physical well-being protected or enhanced? What precautions are taken to prevent the spread of infection or disease?

6. Throughout this course, compile a folder of child health and safety alerts provided through the media, parenting literature, fliers from physicians, reports of the U.S. Product Safety Commission, and other sources. Discuss prevention strategies with your classmates.

7. Given what you now know about physical and motor development in toddlers, what suggestions would you make to parents and caregivers to protect children from unintentional injury and threats to their health?

## FURTHER READINGS

American Public Health Association & American Academy of Pediatrics (1992). *Caring for our children: National health and safety performance standards: Guidelines for out-of-home child care programs.* Washington, DC, and Elk Grove Village, IL: Authors.

Bailey, D. B., Jr. & Wolery, M. (1989). *Assessing infants and preschoolers with handicaps.* Columbus, OH: Merrill.

Berezin, J. (1990). *The National Association of Child Care Resource and Referral Agencies in cooperation with Child Care, Inc.: The complete guide to choosing child care.* New York: Random House.

Children's Defense Fund (1994). *Wasting America's future: The Children's Defense Fund Report on the costs of child poverty.* Washington, DC: Author.

Deiner, P. L. (1993). *Resources for teaching children with diverse abilities: birth through eight.* Fort Worth, TX: Harcourt Brace College Publishers.

Endres, J. B., & Rockwell, R. E. (1985). *Food, nutrition and the young child* (2nd ed.). St. Louis: Times Mirror/Mosby College Publishing.

Hauser, R. (1989). *Children & the AIDS virus: A book for children, parents, and teachers.* New York: Houghton Mifflin Co. Imprint.

Kendrick, A. S., Kaufmann, R., & Messenger, K. P. (Eds.). (1991). *Healthy young children: A manual for programs.* Washington, DC: National Association for the Education of Young Children.

Metzger, M., & Whittaker, C. P. (1988). *The childproofing checklist: A parent's guide to accident prevention.* New York: Doubleday.

National Safety Council. (1993). *First aid and CPR: Infants and children.* Boston: Jones and Bartlett.

Pediatrics for Parents Inc. Newsletter: *Pediatrics for Parents,* P. O. Box 1069, Bangor, ME 04402-1069.

Shelov, S. P., & Hannemann, R. E. (Eds.). (1993). *Caring for your baby and young child: Birth to age 5: The complete and authoritative guide.* New York: Bantam Books.

# CHAPTER NINE

*Our words should be like a magic canvas upon which a child cannot help but paint a positive picture of himself.*

Haim G. Ginott

# Psychosocial Development Ages 1 Through 3

After studying this chapter, you will demonstrate comprehension by:

- Describing the psychosocial development of the young child from ages 1 through 3.
- Relating selected theories of psychosocial development to the study of the toddler period of development.
- Describing contexts through which psychosocial development emerges.
- Describing the role of adults in healthy psychosocial development of the young child from ages 1 through 3.

The toddler period of child growth and development presents new challenges for parents and caregivers. The formerly dependent, compliant infant now exhibits a striving for independence and for ever-widening opportunities to interact, explore, and learn. Increasingly refined motor capabilities and communication skills are emerging, leading to new and unexpected behaviors. These new behaviors can, at the same time, thrill, perplex, frustrate, and intrigue parents and caregivers.

## ATTACHMENTS

From about ages 6 months to 3 years, the toddler, having grown through phase 1, indiscriminate responsiveness, and phase 2, focusing on familiar people, is now passing through phase 3, active **proximity seeking** of Bowlby's attachment sequence (Bowlby, 1969/1980). During this phase, the child becomes very aware of and monitors the presence or absence of his or her attachment person, which is usually the mother. The child actively seeks to be near and to be held, and cries upon separation. When the attachment person is present, the toddler will at first remain quite close, perhaps in the lap of the adult, then will tenuously venture forth and away, but will return periodically to the attachment person for assurance and interaction. As a sense of trust and self-confidence grows, these ventures will

*proximity seeking: the child's attempts to maintain nearness and contact with the attachment figure*

207

be sustained over longer periods of time. As we learned in Chapter 6, the success of these ventures is thought to relate to the quality of infant-caregiver attachments, particularly the mother's sensitivity and responsiveness to infant/toddler cues. (Isabella, 1993).

As toddlers get older, the ability to visually and auditorally remain "attached," even though the attachment person may not be near, emerges. The toddler learns to "feel attached" from a distance by looking, listening, and vocally communicating (Greenspan & Greenspan, 1985). The child becomes more exploratory as feelings of security with the attachment person and with the environment increase. The toddler begins to rely on self-comforting behaviors such as thumb sucking or fondling a soft toy or blanket, and may begin to find comfort through interactions with persons other than the one with whom they have formed an attachment.

## EXTRAFAMILIAL ATTACHMENTS

Forming secure attachments and trusting relationships with parents and family members is among the first and most important psychosocial tasks of the infant/toddler period. As the toddler gets older, successfully forming attachments to others beyond the family becomes another psychosocial task. **Extrafamilial relationships** include people outside the immediate or extended family, such as a neighbor, family friend, or **primary child caregiver**. Infants and toddlers can and do develop strong feelings for and attachments to others outside the family. Positive interactions and successful experiences with extrafamilial relationships enhance the child's psychosocial development (Pianta, 1992).

*extrafamilial relationships: those relationships that include people outside the immediate or extended family*

*primary child caregiver: the person from whom the child receives essential nonparental care and with whom a warm relationship can form*

Angela's high school–based child care center is, by most standards, state of the art. Situated in its own separate building on the high school campus, it is readily accessible to the young mothers whose children are enrolled. Its program and management are guided by a director with skills and knowledge in early child care and education. The center exceeds local and state licensing requirements and is accredited by the National Association for the Education of Young Children. Child caregivers are educated in child development and early education and are warm, nurturing, and effective teachers. The setting is aesthetically appealing and rich with developmentally appropriate materials and activities. The daily pace is unhurried, comfortable, yet appropriately stimulating.

Two-year-old Angela is active, alert, and eager to explore, and has become reasonably secure in the child care center. She has developed a strong attachment to her primary child caregiver, Ms. Ruiz, who has equally strong feelings for Angela.

Upon arrival today, Angela visually and auditorily scans the playroom for the sight and sounds of Ms. Ruiz. Her facial expression shows both anticipation and anxiety. Locating Ms. Ruiz, she runs eagerly toward her, reaching up for Ms. Ruiz to acknowledge her presence with a hug. Ms. Ruiz greets Angela with a wide smile and obliges with a hug, then offers to help Angela with her coat. Angela resists, however, wanting to do this herself. Ms. Ruiz reminds Angela to say good-bye to her departing mother, as Cheryl must leave to attend her algebra class. While removing her wraps, Angela stops and watches tentatively as Cheryl leaves. Rushing to the door, she calls to her mother, who returns, kisses her good-bye, tells her to have a good time, and then goes on to class. Perhaps Angela still feels some separation anxiety, for her facial expression shows signs of impending tears.

However, Ms. Ruiz, sensitive and reassuring, directs Angela's attention to the large classroom aquarium, points to the fish, and begins to name the items in the aquarium: *gravel, light, water*. She talks with Angela about the fish: "Yes, that is a fish, Angela. This one is an angelfish. Let's put some food in the aquarium for the fish." This interaction has become somewhat routine each morning and, though quite brief, helps Angela make the transition from home to center and from mother to child caregiver.

Once at ease, Angela asserts "No more fish," and proceeds to another part of the room to play. Very soon she will approach her friend Leah, and a different interaction will ensue as the girls proceed to the sand table. ■

The child care center Jeremy attends is also judged to be of high quality. Jeremy's parents visited a number of child care centers and preschool programs, asked many questions, and discussed their options before making their final selection.

Jeremy enjoys attending the child care center. However, in recent weeks separation has become a particular problem for him and for his parents and caregivers. The parents' inquiry to the center director reveals an unusual amount of staff turnover in recent months, and as a consequence, Jeremy has encountered three different primary child caregivers in less than six months.

Unable to comprehend where the child caregivers go and why they are not present, Jeremy demonstrates his confusion and anxiety by clinging to his mother and crying loudly. On this particular day, he has created quite a scene with an angry and fearful tantrum. He vigorously resists the attempts of Ms. Bell to comfort him.

Presently, his special friend Josh arrives and, noticing Jeremy crying, makes his way to where Jeremy and Ann are standing. Josh stares with some concern, as though he sympathizes but isn't sure what is happening. Ann coaxes Jeremy: "Hi, Josh. Jeremy, here is Josh. Josh wants to play with you." Jeremy soon stops crying and, reluctantly and slowly, reaches toward his mother in a quest for a hug. Thus, he signals that he will kiss her good-bye. Mother and child hug and kiss, and Ann begins to lead Jeremy and Josh toward the block center. Once the two are involved, Jeremy's mother says a firm yet reassuring goodbye and departs without further incident. ■

These examples show that attachments can be formed with individuals, both adults and children, beyond the home and family. These attachments can be quite strong and can provide another source of security for the toddler. It is clear that both Angela and Jeremy have found a sense of security and well-being in their child care center relationships. For Angela, the adult child caregiver has become a reliable and trusted source of security in the absence of her mother. For Jeremy, his young friend and playmate Josh has become a trusted friend, a big help in the absence of a continuous relationship with a child caregiver.

Wisely selected child care arrangements offer an expanded circle of friends and healthy, supportive relationships for young children. However, in Jeremy's situation, we can see that staff changes create temporary stress for some children, returning them to earlier and less mature forms of coping, and reduced social competence with peers (Howes, 1987; Howes & Hamilton, 1993). Howes (1987) further cautions that continuity of caregiving is related to the development of secure attachments in out-of-home settings. This continuity helps the child make a smooth transition between the home and the child care setting. Howes also asserts that the child who experiences many different caregivers may fail to become attached to any of them.

## TODDLER/TODDLER FRIENDSHIPS

Past studies of toddler friendships and play behaviors characterized the toddler as engaging in onlooker and/or **parallel play** (Parten, 1933). In parallel play, the toddler enjoys being near and playing beside other children, but pursuing her or his own play interest. In parallel play little, if any, interaction occurs between children. It was previously thought that onlooker and parallel play represent the least mature levels of social interaction. More recent studies of toddler interactions suggest that while parallel play occurs frequently during the toddler period, it is not limited to that period and changes in form as cognition matures and interaction skills emerge. Thus, parallel play has been described as "parallel-functional," "parallel-constructive," "parallel-dramatic," and "parallel-games," each representing different forms and purposes (Rubin, 1982; Rubin, Watson, & Jambor, 1978).

Young children today spend more time in out-of-home child care situations than did children of past generations. Therefore, infants and toddlers have encountered other children from a very early age. Studies have demonstrated that genuine friendships can develop between children in toddler play groups (Greenspan & Greenspan, 1985; Vandell & Mueller, 1980). While first attempts at interaction are clumsy and perhaps antagonistic, they nevertheless can be a source of pleasure and represents earliest attempts to initiate friendships.

As Greenspan and Greenspan (1985) described a sequence of attempts at interaction beginning with the toddler first noticing something about another toddler that attracts him or her—the color of clothing, long, curly hair, or a pretty ribbon, for example. This is followed by mutual explorations between the two children in which the child touches or pulls at the attraction—the ribbon, pretty hair, or whatever. Usually the other child passively allows the explorations to take place—the ribbon to be pulled, for instance. Following this level of interaction, the toddlers may seek a nearby adult, who then becomes an assistant to the interaction. The toddler hands an object to the adult, and the adult in turn hands it to the other toddler, who hands it back to the adult to begin the sequence again. Greenspan calls these exchanges *collaborative interactions*, as the toddlers use the adult as a conduit for the sharing of objects, toys, or food. He further describes toddlers as exhibiting humor in these encounters, laughing together as a block tower collapses or another playful event ensues. Then the toddlers go off to play together, during which time they will continue to interact through facial expressions and gestures.

Toddler friends will imitate one another, laugh with and at one another, and share activities such as looking at books together or filling and dumping objects from a container (Press & Greenspan, 1985). These friendships may be transitory and short-lived, yet their importance to early extrafamilial attachment behaviors and to emerging social development should not be underestimated. One study of separation of nursery school infants and toddlers when they were being "promoted" to new classrooms found that when the children were moved to new classrooms with a close friend, they adapted more readily (Field, Vega-Lahr, & Jagadish, 1984).

The types and availability of toys also influence the quality and success of toddler interactions. Developmentally appropriate toys ensure reasonably successful toddler play. A truck with a missing wheel cannot be successfully rolled back and forth. One pull-toy instead of two creates frustration and tears, whereas pulling toys about the room together can be a joyous social encounter.

## FEARS AND ANXIETIES OF TODDLERS

In addition to attachments and friendships, the preceding vignettes demonstrate the continuing presence of stranger and separation anxieties, which persist from infancy into the toddler period. The occurrence of these anxieties, as we discussed earlier, parallels the development of attachments, influencing and being influenced by the quality of the attachment relationships. These anxieties begin to wane around age 2½ to 3 years.

However, around 18 months, additional fears begin to emerge. This indicates increasing social/emotional and cognitive development. Because all development is interrelated, a discussion of fears must recognize the interrelated role of cognition. As the child can manipulate mental images and mentally elaborate on past events and experiences, new understandings and concepts—and misunderstandings and misconceptions—can bring about new fears. As the toddler begins to imagine, fantasy and reality are not separated.

Fears are normal. Fears are quite real to the child, can be very disturbing, and can be difficult to allay. In addition to separation and stranger fears, common toddler fears include fear of the dark, the bathtub drain, animals, some storybook or media characters, monsters and ghosts, loud noises, lightning and thunder, and vacuum cleaners or other noisy equipment.

Toddlers may acquire some of their fears through social learning. Parents who become fearful during a thunderstorm or who discuss frightening or painful experiences relating to accidents or illnesses, visits to the physician or hospital, or other adult fears may inadvertently instill these fears in their young children. When fear tactics are used to discipline, they create unhealthy and inappropriate fears in the child. For instance, imploring the toddler to "be quiet or Aunt Marti will get you" creates an unfortunate wariness of Aunt Marti and hampers her efforts to establish her own positive relationship with the toddler.

Helping the toddler to understand and cope with fears requires sensitivity and patience. Because fears can be quite real to the child, adults should neither laugh, ridicule, nor minimize them. Very young children will not understand logical explanations; instead, toddlers need adults to help them find ways to deal with their fears. A child who is afraid of the bathtub drain, for instance, can be given "control" over it by being the person who opens or closes the drain or by getting out of the tub before the drain is opened.

Fears are necessary for survival, since they signal dangers to be avoided. However, the toddler may not yet have the necessary survival fears for most potentially dangerous situations. The toddler neither has the judgment nor the background of experiences and understanding to avoid such hazards as the street, "friendly" strangers, fire, poisons, heights, and a host of others. Toddlers lack the space, speed, depth, and other types of perception needed to perceive risks accurately. Toddlers need to be protected from dangers through close supervision and must be taught about dangers in ways that instill knowledge, caution, and skills but do not frighten them unnecessarily. Adults cannot assume toddlers are aware of dangerous situations. In the event of the child's self-endangerment, adults should not react with physical punishment for the child's lack of experience and knowledge. It is the adult's responsibility to monitor and maintain the child's safety and well-being and to teach the child about unsafe objects and situations.

## SELF-COMFORTING BEHAVIORS

### THUMB SUCKING

Most infants find their fists and thumbs sooner or later and derive pleasure and solace from sucking on them. Brazelton (1984) suggests that parents should expect their infants to suck their thumbs, fingers, or fists, and attributes few consequences to this behavior. Thumb sucking can be the child's source of self-comfort when tense or frightened or when simply trying to relax or fall asleep. Brazelton advises adults to expect a great deal of thumb or finger sucking in the first year, somewhat less in the active second year, and even less after the third and fourth years.

While infants are sometimes given pacifiers to satisfy the sucking need, most often pacifiers are provided to calm a fussy child. For some infants and toddlers, the pacifier becomes their self-comforting device; other infants reject it or find little pleasure in it. Whether thumb or pacifier has provided the source of self-comfort to the child, either is usually given up at about the same age. Children may fall back on one or the other during periods of illness, stress, or fear.

### TRANSITIONAL OBJECTS

*transitional object: an object, usually a soft, cuddly item, to which a child becomes attached*

Another self-comforting strategy the toddler uses is the **transitional object,** so named because it assists the child in making the transition from the dependency and protection of infancy to the independence and uncertainty of the toddler period. Attachment to an object such as a teddy bear, special blanket, swatch of soft fabric, doll, or favorite piece of clothing is common and begins in the latter part of the first year, usually around 8 or 9 months. Because these objects have been invested with certain meanings and comforting associations, the child forms an emotional tie to them (Winnicott, 1953, 1971, 1977). The child's attachment to the object can last to age 7 or 8 and sometimes beyond.

Adults often provide "soft name" labels for these objects, such as "loveys" or "cuddlies"; the child also provides a name, for example, "banky" or "bear-bear." These attachments are usually quite strong and extremely important to the child. Children often perceive these objects as extensions of themselves.

Transitional objects serve a variety of comforting roles. Some believe they provide a security link with the home, mother, or other attachment figure during times of separation. In this sense, they serve to ease separation anxiety and other fears. The transitional object provides a sense of security in new, strange, frightening, or stressful situations. Children often treat their transitional objects with love and caring, exhibiting their own abilities to express affection. Sometimes these objects are the child's substitution for the thumb or pacifier and replace these earlier forms of self-comfort. Other children use the transitional object and the thumb or pacifier in combination as a self-comforting strategy.

How should parents and caregivers respond to these objects? Most authorities agree that they fulfill some natural need and provide the child with a source of

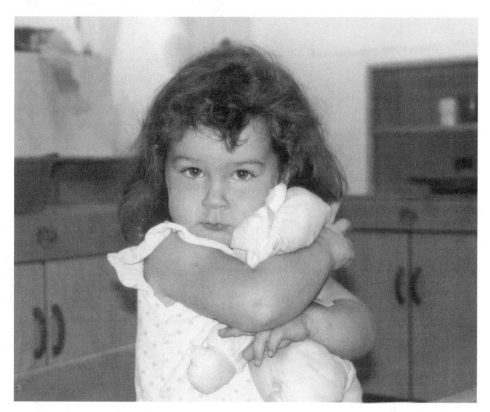

*Attachment to an object such as a soft toy or blanket is a common behavior, beginning in the latter part of the first year and frequently extending into the primary years and beyond.*

security. Interference with these attachments is strongly discouraged; rather, adults are encouraged to expect, accept, acknowledge, and appreciate the child's new attachment. Brazelton (1984, p. 65) writes:

> If a thumb or a beloved object can help a child to grow up, it seems obvious to me that we should treasure them. As children mature, other loves and interests will replace these, but the inner sense of competence they will have learned early from such self-reliant patterns will serve them well.*

## ERIKSON'S THEORY: AUTONOMY VERSUS SHAME AND DOUBT

As toddlers come to trust their environments, the people within them, and themselves, they begin to grow in independence and a sense of autonomy (Erikson, 1963). The toddler's efforts to buckle a seat belt, turn the light switch on or off,

*T. B. Brazelton, M.D. (1984) *To Listen to a Child.* Reprinted by permission of Addison-Wesley.

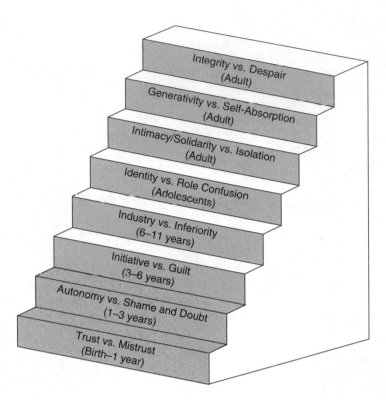

**FIGURE 9.1**
Development of a healthy sense of trust paves the way for successful resolution of the next stage of psychosocial development: autonomy.

open a door, and take off socks, shoes, or other clothing are intensely and personally important at the moment and can result in tears and tantrums when thwarted by an unsuspecting or impatient adult. Previously dependent behaviors are now being superseded by the toddler's efforts to be independent. Locomotion encourages this independence as the toddler gains confidence in walking, climbing, running, moving, and manipulating. Language reveals a striving for independence as the toddler asserts, "Me do it!", "No", and "Mine." While these behaviors tax adult patience and understanding, they are viewed as indicators of positive and healthy psychosocial development.

According to Erik Erikson's (1963) stage theory of psychosocial development, the toddler is entering a period in which the psychological "conflict" to be resolved is that of autonomy versus shame and doubt. **Autonomy** means self-government or independence. Its development extends from about 15 months to 3 years (see Figure 9.1).

*autonomy:*
*a sense of independence*
*or self-government*

During infancy, from birth to about 18 months, developing a sense of trust (versus mistrust) is the critical psychosocial task. A healthy sense of trust, derived from consistent and predictable nurturing, is perhaps the most important stage in psychosocial development. Its healthy development paves the way for successful resolution of subsequent stages.

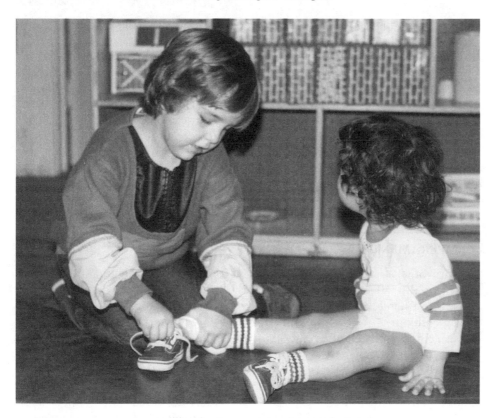

*As autonomy emerges, toddlers begin to resist assistance from others.*

The development of a sense of autonomy in the toddler is facilitated and enhanced by a strong sense of trust developed during infancy. The psychosocial opposite of autonomy is shame or doubt. Adults assist toddlers in their strivings for autonomy when they recognize that the toddler needs to feel independent, self-sufficient, and capable. When this does not occur, shame and doubt may override the sense of autonomy. When this occurs, children may exhibit an array of negative feelings and inappropriate behaviors, including feelings of guilt and penitence, self-consciousness, reluctance to try new things, and overdependence on adults.

The challenge for adults who care for the toddler is to find that important balance between meeting the toddler's needs for both dependence and independence and satisfying the needs for freedom and control. On the one hand, toddlers need and want to do things for themselves. On the other hand, they want and need the security-building presence, protection, and guidance of a nurturing and supportive adult. Successes in locomotion and other motor efforts, the feeding process, toileting, playing, choice making, imitations of more mature behaviors and activities, interactions with others, and so on enhance the toddler's sense of autonomy.

As with other areas of development, adult responses to the toddler's efforts to be autonomous that are overrestrictive, overprotective, or too permissive, or that expect behavior or performance beyond the toddler's developmental capacities, interfere with the developing sense of autonomy. When autonomy exceeds feelings of shame and doubt, the child develops a sense of adequacy, competence, security, worthiness, and healthy self-acceptance.

Because toilet learning is a developmental milestone during this period, Erikson has included it in the developing sense of autonomy. The toddler soon learns to use emerging physical skills of "holding" and "letting go" in bowel and bladder control. For the toddler, this ability imparts a sense of self-government. However, recall that bowel and bladder control are not sufficiently biologically developed for the toddler to always succeed. Yet, the toddler's desire to please caregivers is genuine. Adults who shame or exhibit frustration or anger at the child's inabilities or relapses will undermine the developing sense of autonomy. Instead, adults should encourage, praise, and take cues from the child.

## TEMPERAMENT

As with other aspects of growth and development, the individual child's temperament also influences the outcome of the stage of personality development. As we saw in Chapter 6, each child has a unique way of feeling, thinking, and interacting with others. *Temperament* is the term generally used to reflect this uniqueness. Temperament is probably genetically determined, though certainly it influences and is influenced by the environment (Thomas, Chess, & Korn, 1982). Think of your own brothers, sisters, cousins, or other relatives. What are the similarities and differences in their temperaments? Differences in temperament among individual children within the same family are often noted with surprise and wonder. Yet mothers and fathers themselves exhibit unique temperaments.

Parents and other family members represent an amalgam of differing temperaments. In addition to temperament, each member brings to the family different age-stage needs and reactions that influence the manner in which members respond to one another and to the unique temperaments of the infant and toddler (Dunn, 1993). Further, a recent study of parental interactions during the second year indicates that parents respond differently to their toddlers (18-month-olds) than to their 1-year-olds (Fagot & Kavanagh, 1993). Mothers were shown to provide more positive responses and reported greater satisfaction in parenting at 1 year, and both parents gave more instructions and directions to their children at 18 months. This finding quite likely indicates the unique characteristics of toddlers: their mobility and exploratory behavior and their striving for autonomy. It also indicates the parents' felt need to supervise and control toddler behaviors.

Earlier chapters describe the backgrounds of experience that the parents of Angela and Jeremy bring to the parent-child relationship. The quality of their own childhood experiences, the relationships with their parents and other family members, and the role models that were available to them influence the perceptions they have of themselves and of their roles as parents. Knowledge of child growth and development plays a critical role in this regard. The interplay of all of these factors influences the interactions of parents and children.

Cheryl—young, single, and still an adolescent—is confronting her own developmental needs typical of most adolescent girls. In addition to her need to obtain and maintain support networks to assist her in nurturing Angela, she has needs relating to learning about and gaining satisfaction in the role of mother and single teen parent, completing her education, participating in the social life of her age-mates, and working through Erikson's fifth psychosocial stage, that of developing a sense of identity versus role confusion (Erikson, 1963). Participating in an extended family and projecting a future beyond high school are also tasks before her.

Jeremy's family also has their own needs. His parents, now in their 30s, are striving for success in demanding careers. They seek social and economic upward mobility, a demanding quest in terms of time, energy, and allocation of family resources. Their needs at this age-stage relate to maintaining an intellectually, emotionally, and physically satisfying relationship with one another; meshing career, civic, religious, and social desires and responsibilities; relating to extended family members; providing for an economically stable existence; and integrating all of this with their plans for Jeremy and possibly additional children.

James, low-key and affectionate, enjoys holding Angela on his lap and talking to and reading books with her. His manner has an enjoyably calming effect on Angela, and she responds by seeking to be held by him the moment he arrives for his visits. Knowing that he enjoys reading to her, Angela scurries off to obtain a book—any book—to offer to him. Sometimes James greets her with "Go get a book," whereupon she promptly and happily obliges.

Angela is outgoing, affectionate, observant, and quite verbal; she names many objects and people in her environment. Though unable to focus her attention for more than a few minutes, she seems to need and enjoy the sustained interactions with James and with the books they share. In anticipating her interest, James encourages Angela's autonomy by sending her to fetch a book. Angela, on the other hand, has learned how to seek and hold James's attention. Thus, her developing sense of autonomy, along with her own temperament, is becoming enmeshed with the temperament and personality of her father.

Cheryl, on the other hand, is more inclined to engage in physically active interactions with Angela. She may chase Angela about the house, play hide and seek, take her on outings, walk about the neighborhood with her, and dance and sing with her to music from the television. They especially enjoy playing "copycat" games with each other. Angela has learned when and how to engage her mother in these playful moments, which are quite emotionally satisfying to both of them. James and Cheryl relate to Angela in different ways, each bringing to the interactions their unique personalities and skills. Yet, while quite different in their interactions with Angela, they are complementary. ▪

## EGOCENTRISM

The toddler's behavior is punctuated with assumptions, faulty though they may be, that others feel, see, and hear the same things he or she does. Inability to share is related to this thinking and is expected behavior at this stage. A coveted toy possessed by another child may be proclaimed "Mine!" The toddler who says to his mother, when observing her nursing a younger sibling, "Does her have a mommy?", is demonstrating a lack of perspective beyond his own experiences.

The 3-year-old who attempts to console a crying nursery school friend with her own fuzzy blanket assumes her friend can be comforted as she is by this particular transitional object.

*egocentrism:*
*the tendency to view the world from one's own perspective; the inability to see another point of view*

**Egocentrism** characterizes both the cognitive abilities of toddlers (Piaget, 1952) and their psychosocial development (Erikson, 1963). Piaget theorized that during the preoperational period of cognitive development, children can view the world only from their own perspectives and are unable to appreciate another's point of view. While it is true that egocentrism characterizes the toddler's way of thinking, a growing body of evidence now suggests that young children may be less egocentric than was once believed (Black, 1981). Studies of prosocial behaviors and empathy in young children have begun to modify our thinking about egocentrism.

## PROSOCIAL BEHAVIORS

Kindness, sympathy, generosity, helpfulness, and distress at injustice or cruelty are fairly typical behaviors in young children. Psychologists refer to them as **prosocial behaviors**, since they are intended to benefit or help others without expectation of reward.

*prosocial behavior:*
*behavior that benefits others, such as helping, sharing, comforting, and defending*

Children under age 3 have been observed demonstrating prosocial behaviors through sharing, helping, and cooperating (Leung & Rheingold, 1981; Zahn-Waxler, Radke-Yarrow, & King, 1979). Researchers have studied comforting, defending, and protective behaviors in preschool children (Zahn-Waxler et al., 1979). These and other studies have led psychologists to believe that very young children are not as egocentric as Piaget's theory suggests.

Prosocial behaviors in toddlers are most likely to occur during pretend play (Bar-Tal, Raviv, & Goldberg, 1982) and occur with greater frequency as the child's opportunities for interactions with others increase (Rubin & Everett, 1982). Growing cognitive abilities contribute to the child's ability to view situations from the perspectives of others. More mature levels of thinking enhance **perspective-taking** abilities and **empathy**.

*perspective taking:*
*the ability to understand another's point of view*

*empathy:*
*experiencing the feelings or emotions that someone else is experiencing*

Prosocial behaviors are also influenced by behaviors modeled by others. Parents and caregivers who demonstrate helpfulness, altruism, cooperation, sympathy, and other prosocial attributes provide powerful examples for the toddler. Guidance and disciplinary strategies with young children also affect the development of prosocial behaviors. Guidance that is empathic, supportive, reasonable, and explained to the child assists toddlers in their understanding of social interactions.

Jeremy's teacher asked him to sit by her and talk about the unfortunate encounter he just had with a playmate over the use of a puzzle. Both children wanted to work the puzzle, but not together. The teacher asked Jeremy how he thought his friend felt when he hit her. She also asked him to think about what he might do about the situation now that his friend was crying and hurt. His response was not exactly what the teacher sought, but revealing nevertheless: "I think you better watch me, 'cause I think I'm going to hit her again." ■

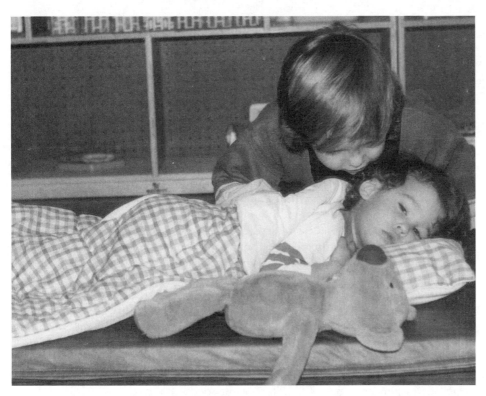

*Toddlers often exhibit an awareness of others' feelings, although they may lack sufficient knowledge and experience to understand those feelings.*

Like Jeremy, toddlers need adults to help them control their impulses. An adult who says, "I can't let you hit Shannon; hitting hurts people," helps the still egocentric toddler to think about the other person. This guidance should be supportive of each child in the encounter. Blaming and punishing only serve to reinforce negative behaviors and neither provide the child with alternative prosocial options nor assist in the development of perspective taking and empathy.

Toddlers' spontaneous attempts to share, help, or cooperate should be reinforced through positive recognition and responses: "Bobby feels better now that you are friends again." "That was kind of you to get Tamara a puzzle like yours." "That was very helpful of you to put the blocks away with Josh." Such verbal responses, while providing positive feedback and reinforcement, also provide labels for expected prosocial behaviors. With these labels, the child's understanding and appreciation of the views and needs of others grow.

## DEVELOPMENT OF SELF-CONCEPT AND SELF-ESTEEM

The **self-concept** is the summary definition one devises of oneself; it represents an awareness of oneself as a separate and unique individual. The self-concept derives

*self-concept: one's sense of oneself as separate and unique from others* from interactions with others, the child's interpretation of those interactions, and the child's ability to accept or negate positive or negative feedback from them. For the most part, the manner in which others respond to and relate to the child determines the self-concept the child will devise.

The self-concept is dynamic in that it changes over time and through additional experiences and understandings. Generally, the development of the self-concept is composed of four accomplishments: (1) self-awareness, (2) self-recognition, (3) self-definition, and (4) self-esteem.

**Self-awareness** *self-awareness:* *refers to infants' perceptions of themselves as distinct and separate from other people and objects*

**Self-awareness** occurs as infants begin to realize that they are distinct and separate from others and that an object is not an extension of themselves. Margaret Mahler (1968), a Freudian psychologist, refers to the emerging independence of the infant and toddler as *separation and individuation*. This process takes place around the fourth and fifth month and continues to age 3. Its first stages reflect the infant's growing awareness of separateness, and the latter stages are characterized by the toddler's ambivalence about dependence and a desire for independence. Mahler proposes that mother-child interactions during this process are critical to the self-concept that will emerge.

*self-recognition:* *the infant's ability to recognize his or her image in a mirror, photograph, or other representation*

**Self-recognition** refers to infants' ability to recognize themselves in a mirror, photograph, or other form (Lewis & Brooks, 1978). This ability seems to parallel the cognitive achievement of object permanence, when the child can form and hold mental images. It is usually evident by age 18 months, and by age 2 most children can distinguish their own photo from someone else's (Lewis & Brooks-Gunn, 1979).

*self-definition:* *the criteria by which the self is defined, such as age, size, and physical and mental abilities*

**Self-definition** emerges as children begin to use language to describe themselves. The toddler's growing awareness of his or her age, size, gender, and skills assist the child in this definition. This development is observed when young children take pride in telling you how old they are. Holding up two, three, or four fingers and exclaiming, "I am 3" is an attempt to define oneself. Also, when children invite attention with "Watch me!" they are demonstrating the skills by which they define themselves. "I can reach it," "Watch me jump," "I am big," and so on are verbal indications of an emerging self-concept.

Toddlers develop positive self-concepts when adults respond to them in affirmative ways. When efforts at independence, self-help, and social interactions are facilitated by sensitive adults, the toddler's self-concept is enhanced. Adult words and interactions that convey acceptance and respect for the developing person encourage a positive sense of self.

*self-esteem:* *one's positive or negative self-evaluation*

Children who perceive themselves as loved, valued, worthy, and competent develop healthy **self-esteem**. As children's interactional opportunities expand, self-evaluations naturally occur. Healthy self-esteem ensures that these evaluations weigh more heavily on the positive than on the negative side.

## GENDER IDENTITY

Most children are able to proclaim that they are a boy or a girl by age 2½ to 3, having constructed what psychologists call *gender schemata* (Liben & Signorella,

1980, Bauer, 1993). Gender identity has both biological and environmental origins. Biological determinants at conception predetermine whether the child will be male or female. Environmentally, the images and hopes of mothers, fathers, and other relatives set the stage for gender identity and for gender role expectations.

Environmental influences on gender identity often begin during prenatal development, when sonogram examinations reveal the sex of the fetus. Parents begin to "think pink or blue" and anticipate and prepare for the expected boy or girl baby. Name, clothes, toys, crib, nursery, and other preparations suggest the baby's gender. Conversations reveal anticipated behaviors and **gender role** expectations as parents project their roles as parents of a boy or a girl. The newborn is thus subjected to preexisting gender-related expectations.

*gender role: the public expression of one's gender identity*

But despite all the gender-specific planning on the part of parents, there is very little difference in the behaviors of girls and boys during the first year (Fagot & Kronsberg, 1982). During the second year, play behaviors begin to reveal differences between boys and girls, much of which is stereotypical and perhaps derived from gender-specific experiences provided by the parents. Parents may tend to be gentler and more cuddling with girls and more "rough and tumble" with boys; parents may talk more softly and gently to girls and more directly to boys. Toy preferences are particularly indicative by 18 to 20 months, as boys tend to play with transportation toys, blocks, and manipulatives and girls tend to choose soft toys and dolls and enjoy dressing up and dancing (Fagot, 1974, 1978). Perhaps these play choices reflect the types of toys parents have provided for their boys or girls, as well as the child's increasing gender schemata.

It is not unusual for toddlers to assume their biological sex can change, that is, that boys can grow up to become mothers and girls can grow up to be fathers. This thinking demonstrates a lack of gender constancy. **Gender constancy** is the realization that one's sex does not change over time or as a result of changes in hairstyle, clothing, or other outward characteristics. Gender constancy is not expected to occur until age 5 to 7 (Kohlberg, 1966).

*gender constancy: the realization that one's gender remains the same regardless of age or changes in clothing, hairstyles, or other outward characteristics*

While gender itself is biologically determined, both gender identity and gender role are strongly influenced by important people in the child's life. Parents, siblings, child caregivers, and others impose certain gender standards and expectations on young children. Parents seem to impose more stringent gender role expectations on boys than on girls (Forman, Hatznecker, & Dunn, 1983). Toddlers tend to imitate the parent of the same sex, and when gender role behaviors are deemed to be appropriate, parents provide positive feedback. On the other hand, when the behavior is deemed to be gender inappropriate, parents tend to intervene. Many a preschool teacher has been approached by an anxious father wanting to know why his young son is playing with dolls in the dramatic play center. Yet few, if any, mothers inquire about their daughters' play with trucks in the block center. From a developmental perspective, either play choice is sound and in no way threatens the child's gender identity.

The fact that boys are often allowed to be more active and aggressive than girls has both environmental and possibly biological antecedents. Are boys just naturally more active and aggressive than girls? Or do standards for and expectations of certain behaviors vary for boys and girls, resulting in different treatment? Again, studies (Fagot, 1982; Fagot & Kronsberg, 1982) suggest that gender differences are a factor in responding to aggressive behaviors of boys and girls. At the same time, the difference in assertiveness and aggressiveness in boys and girls at age 2 to 2½ may well be related to constitutional and temperamental differences in boys and girls at that age (Forman, Hetznecker, & Dunn, 1983).

Psychologists and educators are encouraging less gender stereotyping in the child's early experiences with children's books, toys, television programming, and adult expectations. Boys can certainly be allowed to show feelings, to nurture and be nurtured, and to participate in a range of activities from "gentle" to "rough." Girls can be encouraged to pursue physical activities and to assert themselves in constructive and positive ways. Neither of these efforts need be viewed as endangering gender role behaviors at later ages. Congruence, though never absolute between gender identity and gender role expectations, occurs as children experience a broad range of both "feminine" and "masculine" situations and as role models provide healthy and satisfying gender acceptance.

## AWARENESS OF DIVERSITY AND INDIVIDUAL DIFFERENCES

A number of processes must be examined in the study of childhood responses to racial differences. Ramsey (1987) delineates these processes as perceptual awareness, valuative concepts, racial identification, racial preferences, behaviors toward other races, and knowledge of racial differences.

Ramsey's categories illustrate that the development of racial awareness, understanding, and acceptance is complex. Researchers have attempted to address racial awareness from these various perspectives, though research on infant and toddler racial awareness is limited. There is evidence that racial awareness has its origins before age 3 (Katz, 1976, 1982). Further evidence exists that earliest experiences with and learnings about race result in attitudes that persist into later years (Katz, 1982).

During the toddler period, racial awareness is dominated by perceptions of outward features. Children begin to make distinctions between darker and lighter skins as early as age 3, though labeling is often inaccurate (Williams & Moreland, 1976). By ages 3 to 4, children apply conventional labels of *black* and *white* to pictures, dolls, and people (Katz, 1976). Young children also attend to facial features, hair color, texture, and style, clothing, and voice and speech patterns. However, racial group–referenced identities do not develop until between ages 3 and 8 (Ramsey, 1987). Mature forms of racial awareness, which do not rely on superficial features but depend on deeper understandings of ethnicity, do not emerge until age 9 or 10 (Aboud, 1988).

The toddler's primary source of information about race is the family. Within the family, racial pride is fostered and racial attitudes are transmitted. Children learn about race when their child care arrangements provide experiences with children and adults of other races and cultural groups. Toys, books, and television programs also impart knowledge of and attitudes toward race. While recent years have seen improvements in the accuracy with which diverse races and cultural groups are portrayed in children's books, toys, school curricula, and the media, there is still a need to monitor these sources of information to ensure accurate, positive, and nonbiased portrayals. The toddler's own racial identity and valuative and preferential behaviors depend on accurate information and sensitive guidance.

## MORAL DEVELOPMENT

**Moral behavior** is most often described as the ability to consider the needs and well-being of others. People who are thought to be "moral" exhibit such behaviors as honesty, dependability, helpfulness, and fairness. These individuals do not steal from others or physically hurt or emotionally abuse others. They do not betray trusts and are loyal to their family, friends, and commitments. In short, these people have a personal morality that guides their behaviors. These behaviors represent moral values, reasoning, judgments, and actions.

*moral behavior: the ability to consider the needs and well-being of others and exhibit appropriate behaviors consistent with a set of standards or value orientation*

Cognitive and social development and experiences are necessary for the development of moral reasoning and judgment. The conscience also plays a role in moral development. Moral values, reasoning, judgment, and conscience rely on certain levels of maturity and experience for their realization.

Piaget (1965) and Kohlberg (1968) have proposed developmental sequences for moral reasoning and judgment. These theorists based their conclusions on studies of children beyond the infant/toddler period, but their theories can offer insight into this period. These theories are described more fully in Chapters 12 and 15.

Moral development has origins in (1) infant intellectual development; (2) social cognition, or the manner in which children perceive the behaviors of others and their own interactions with others; (3) adult socialization efforts, whereby adult values, standards and expectations are imposed on the child; and (4) the positive results of prosocial behaviors. Piaget (1965) emphasized both cognitive development and social experiences as precursors to moral thinking, reasoning, and judgments. Piaget associates moral development in children with emerging abilities to interpret rules.

For very young children, notions of right or wrong are just being formulated, and most "rules" are first being introduced. Since moral values are learned, infants and toddlers are thought to be **premoral**. The premoral child is guided by external rules and expectations of obedience rather than by an internal system of values, beliefs, or understandings. The premoral child comes to think of "good" or "bad" in terms of doing what one is told to do. "Moral behaviors" (obedience) are motivated by the expectation of rewards (praise and attention) or the avoidance of punishment (having a toy or privilege taken away).

*premoral: the period in early childhood when the child is unaware of moral rules or values*

Hoffman (1988) has advanced a theory that provides further insights into the beginnings of moral behavior. Hoffman projects an "empathy scheme" in which motivation to behave in moral ways is prompted by empathic feelings, particularly "empathic distress." Hoffman defines *empathy* as "a vicarious affective response that is more appropriate to someone else's situation than to one's own" (p. 509). Empathy includes both affective and cognitive aspects, with the level of empathy depending to some extent on the child's level of cognition. Toddlers, for instance, may respond empathically to another's distress but lack sufficient knowledge and experience to fully grasp the whole situation.

*The social interactions of toddlers are awkward and tend to be more physical than verbal.*

Hoffman describes four developmental levels of empathic distress: global empathy, egocentric empathy, empathy for another's feelings, and empathy for another's life condition. The first three levels have implications for the study of infant/toddler behaviors. The following description of these stages is adapted from Hoffman (1988, pp. 497–548).

Global empathic distress is observed in infants during the first year. Because of the infant's inadequate self-other distinction, the child will respond to distress cues from others, such as another child's crying, as though the discomfort were his or her own. Self-comforting strategies such as seeking mother or thumb sucking are employed; such behaviors would have been employed anyway had the distress truly been the child's own.

Egocentric empathy occurs in the second year, during which a sense of the other emerges as distinct from the self. At this level, the toddler is aware that the other person is in distress, but is not capable of understanding the person's internal states. The toddler, then, inaccurately assumes the distressed person's feelings and needs are his or her own. Hoffman cites an 18-month-old boy who fetched his own mother to comfort a crying friend although the friend's mother was present.

Around age 2 or 3, the child becomes aware that others' feelings differ from his or her own and thus exhibits the third level of Hoffman's scheme, empathy for another's feelings.

The fourth level, empathy for another's life condition, does not occur until later in childhood. At this level, the child can appreciate the larger life contexts in which distress occurs.

This sequence seems particularly helpful in understanding psychosocial origins of moral development. The adult's role in the socialization process should be to recognize the egocentric perspective of the toddler as she or he attempts to address the "welfare of others"—not an easy task given the child's limited cognitive abilities and social experience.

## DEVELOPMENT OF SELF-CONTROL

An important goal in child growth and development is **self-control**. This is a long-term goal, for self-control develops over a period of many years. For the most part, self-control is learned behavior. It is dependent on external controls at first; then the individual gradually assumes more and more responsibility for his or her own behaviors. In very young children, this process is not a smooth one; self-control emerges haltingly. Marion (1991) lists the following indicators of self-control in children: (1) control of impulses, (2) tolerance of frustration, (3) the ability to postpone immediate gratification, and (4) the initiation of a plan that is carried out over a period of time.

*self-control: the ability to govern one's own behavior*

As with other areas of psychosocial development, cognition and social experiences both play a role in the development of self-control. Marion (1991, pp. 198–199) provides a sequence for the development of self-control. A summary of that sequence follows:

*Birth to approximately 12 months:* Voluntary motor acts evolve from earlier reflexive activity. This activity can be modulated, but not always consciously.

*12 months to about 24 months:* Control of walking, running, and other motor activities makes it possible for the child to respond to the demands of adults ("Come here"; "Stop running"; "Take this to Mommy"). More sophisticated communication skills facilitate the child's understanding of adult instructions and modeling. Children at this age are "susceptible" to control by others.

*Approximately 24 months:* This age marks the actual beginnings of self-control due to the ability to recall instructions and behaviors; however, self-control is quite limited at this age.

*Approximately 36 months:* With age, the ability to delay gratification begins to emerge. This is one of the characteristics of self-control.

Toddlers can be assisted in their development of self-control if adults use developmentally appropriate teaching and guidance techniques. Following are suggestions for maximizing self-control in very young children:

1. Provide an environment in which the child's growing sense of autonomy can flourish; this includes
   - Play items and experiences that are engaging and enriching

- Low, open shelves for personal and play items
- Adequate space for use, storage, and retrieval of personal and play items
- Safe and sturdy furnishings and toys
- Dangerous and off-limit items out of sight and reach

2. Provide an atmosphere that encourages the toddler to explore and discover but is in keeping with the child's developmental capacities and is free of inappropriate expectations and pressures to perform.

3. Provide a daily schedule that is predictable so that the toddler can sense its rhythms and anticipate and respond appropriately to regular events: mealtime, bathtime, naptime, storytime, and so on.

4. Set limits for behavior that are consistent, reasonable, and fair and are enforced in supportive but predictable ways.

5. Meet the toddler's needs for food, clothing, rest, and attention expeditiously. Adults who impose undue delays on toddlers fail to recognize their inability to delay gratification and tolerate frustration.

*Pretend play during the toddler period tends to increase, more inclusive of others, and be enhanced by props and conversation.*

## FACTORS INFLUENCING PSYCHOSOCIAL DEVELOPMENT

It is clear that a number of factors influence psychosocial development in children. The child's unique temperament and personality affect and are affected by others. The quality and quantity of these early interactions affirm or discredit the child's emerging sense of self and self-esteem.

The manner in which parents and caregivers respond to the toddler's need for autonomy is critical to healthy psychosocial development. Guidance and discipline techniques should be consistent, predictable, logical, and supportive. Toddlers need the security of a guidance system that nurtures their growing independence while recognizing their continuing need for rules, limits, and protection.

Interactions with siblings and age-mates provide social experiences that lead to social understandings and a grasp of the feelings and intentions of others. Although age-mate friendships between toddlers are transitory and short-lived, they provide experiences for the development of self-other distinctions.

Play interactions with adults or children and with developmentally appropriate toys enhance psychosocial development in toddlers. Through play, the toddler tries out a variety of social roles and emerging social skills. Language and cognition are enhanced, thus furthering the quality and quantity of social interactions. Play enables toddlers to grow in their sense of competence and to resolve a number of fears and anxieties. Play also introduces toddlers to rules from which later behaviors may be self-regulated.

Television and other media can be powerful influences in the development of race and gender attitudes and gender roles. Media programming should be carefully monitored and selected so that positive and appropriate role models and prosocial and moral values are portrayed, for very young toddlers learn from and imitate the media.

Sociocultural factors in psychosocial development help children learn to appreciate their own and others' uniqueness. Racial awareness has its origins in these very early years. Feelings of self-esteem, family pride, acceptance, and respect for others are fostered in the home and in sensitive, responsive child care programs.

Children with delayed development, chronic disease, or disabilities are especially in need of sound and supportive emotional and social interactions. Because these children can be more vulnerable to prolonged attachment behaviors, fears, anxieties, frustrations, and disappointments, self-concept development and healthy self-esteem can be at risk. Adults must be particularly sensitive to the child's needs for assistance and encouragement in social situations and for opportunities to develop autonomy.

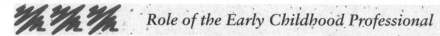

## Role of the Early Childhood Professional

### Enhancing Psychosocial Development in Children Ages 1 Through 3

1. Recognize the role of the adult model in directing the course of psychosocial development in young children.
2. Understand toddler egocentrism.
3. Facilitate autonomy by providing safe surroundings and reasonable limits.
4. Provide positive, predictable, supportive discipline.
5. Understand the toddler's continuing dependency and need for security and protection.
6. Encourage and facilitate play opportunities with other children.
7. Promote self-esteem through sensitive and accurate responses to questions about race and gender.
8. Provide developmentally appropriate books, toys, and media programming to enhance the child's understanding of self and others. ■

## KEY TERMS

autonomy
egocentrism
empathy
extrafamilial
  relationships
gender constancy
gender role
moral behavior

parallel play
perspective taking
premoral
primary child
  caregiver
prosocial behavior
proximity seeking
self-awareness

self-concept
self-control
self-definition
self-esteem
self-recognition
transitional object

## REVIEW STRATEGIES AND ACTIVITIES

1. Review the key terms individually or with a classmate.
2. Survey your classmates about the transitional objects they had as young children. How many recall ever having a transitional object? What was the object? For how long did the attachment to the transitional object persist? What does this survey illustrate about transitional objects?
3. Volunteer to assist in a program for toddlers for at least one day. In a journal, describe instances of prosocial behaviors. What preceded the prosocial response? How did the recipient respond? What followed the prosocial encounter?

4. Engage a 3-year-old in conversation. What clues does the child give about his or her self-perceptions regarding age, size, abilities, gender, race, friends, family, and so on? Be careful not to prompt or suggest expected answers.

5. Observe arrival and departure times at a child care center. How do toddlers respond to their parents when they drop them off and arrive to take them home? How do parents respond? How do caregivers/teachers respond? Ask the instructor to discuss what these behaviors mean in terms of attachments and separation anxiety.

---

## FURTHER READINGS

Ambert, A. (1992). *The effect of children on parents*. Binghampton, NY: Haworth.

The Child Care Careers Institute. (1993). *Integrating children with special needs into preschool settings: A resource handbook*. Cambridge, MA: Author.

Furman, E. (1993). *Toddlers and their mothers: Abridged version for parents and educators*. Madison, CT: International Universities Press.

Galinsky, E. (1990). *The six stages of parenthood*. New York: Addison-Wesley.

Jones, E., & Reynolds, G. (1992). *The play's the thing: Teachers' roles in children's play*. New York: Teachers College Press.

Kostelnik, M. J., Stein, L. C., Whiren, A., & Soderman, A. K. (1993). *Guiding children's social development* (2nd ed.). Albany, NY: Delmar.

Lieberman, A. F. (1993). *The emotional life of the toddler*. New York: The Free Press.

Lindsay, J. W. (1992). *Teens parenting: The challenge of toddlers*. Buena Park, CA: Morning Glory Press.

Lynch, E. W., & Hanson, M. J. (1992). *Developing cross-cultural competence: A guide for working with young children and their families*. Baltimore, MD: Brookes Publishing Co.

Marion, Marian (1991). *Guidance of young children* (3rd ed.). Columbus, OH: Merrill.

Powell, G. J., Yammamoto, J., Romero, A., & Morales, A. (Eds.). (1983). *The psychosocial development of minority group children*. New York: Brunner/Mazel.

# CHAPTER TEN

*Using their sensorimotor capacities and their abilities to master first-order symbol systems, young children develop a vast array of intuitive understandings even before they enter school. Specifically they develop robust and functional theories of matter, life, the minds of other individuals and their own minds and selves. They are aided in this task of theory construction by various constraints, some built into the genome, others a function of the particular circumstances of their culture, and still others a reflection of their own, more idiosyncratic styles and inclinations.*

Howard Gardner

# Cognitive, Language, and Literacy Development Ages 1 Through 3

After studying this chapter, you will demonstrate comprehension by:

- Describing the need for a more inclusive perspective on cognitive, language, and literacy development.
- Describing the cognitive development of children ages 1 through 3.
- Describing the oral language development of children ages 1 through 3.
- Describing the development of literacy of children ages 1 through 3.
- Identifying the factors influencing cognitive, language, and literacy development of children ages 1 through 3.
- Describing the role of the early childhood professional in promoting cognitive, language, and literacy development in children ages 1 through 3.

## THE NEED FOR A MORE INCLUSIVE PERSPECTIVE ON COGNITIVE, LANGUAGE, AND LITERACY DEVELOPMENT

As the quote that opens this chapter indicates, young children demonstrate an enormous capacity to learn even before entering school. This process is facilitated by what Gardner calls *constraints* (Gardner, 1991b, p. 250). These constraints are positive in nature and include the child's genetic legacy, the child's cultural background, and the child's own "idiosyncratic styles and inclinations" (p. 250). This suggests that attention must be given to the uniqueness of *all* children, including their unique individual development and the distinctive contexts that promote cognitive, language, and literacy development. The changing demographics in our communities and schools and the increasingly inclusive nature of classrooms require that early childhood professionals address this uniqueness to promote development and learning in *all* young children.

A major theory of cognitive development in young children is that proposed by Piaget (1952). Within the past few years, a number of child development researchers have begun to question the universal application of Piaget's theories (Bowman & Stott, 1994). These authorities take issue with Piaget's invariant sequence of cognitive development, the focus on logical mathematical and verbal knowledge valued by our Western culture, and the resulting emphasis on assessment in these two areas. If children do not perform well in these areas, their development is often viewed as abnormal.

A more culturally inclusive view of intelligence is that proposed by Howard Gardner (1983, 1991). He suggests that intelligence is the ability to solve problems or create a product that is valued by one's culture or community. Thus, he proposes a theory of *multiple intelligences* (Gardner, 1983, p. 239). These multiple intelligences include

1. *Intrapersonal intelligence* — the ability to "detect and symbolize complex and highly differentiated sets of feelings"
2. *Interpersonal intelligence* — the capacity to recognize distinctions among other people's moods, temperaments, motivations, and intentions
3. *Spatial intelligence* — the ability to transform one's perception of visual stimuli and reconstruct components of these perceptions with the removal of the visual stimuli
4. *Bodily-kinesthetic intelligence* — the capacity to direct one's bodily motions and manipulate objects in a skillful fashion
5. *Musical intelligence* — exceptional awareness of pitch, rhythm, and timbre
6. *Linguistic intelligence* — sensitivity to meaning, order, sounds, rhythms, and inflections of words
7. *Logical-mathematical intelligence* — the ability to attend to patterns, categories, and relationships

A major proponent of Gardner's theory is Armstrong (1994). He provides the following overview of Gardner's theory (Armstrong, 1994, pp. 11–12):

1. Every individual possesses all seven intelligences to a lesser or greater degree.
2. Most individuals are capable of developing each intelligence to an adequate level of competency.
3. The seven intelligences usually work together in complex ways.
4. Intelligence within each category can be demonstrated in a variety of ways.
5. Intelligences other than those currently defined by Gardner probably exist.

This chapter describes the general cognitive, language, and literacy development of children ages 1 through 3 from several perspectives. First, it addresses Piaget's ideas, followed by some revisionist perspectives concerning his theories. Then the chapter discusses recent viewpoints on understanding and facilitating cognitive, language, and literacy development in children from diverse learning and cultural backgrounds.

## PIAGET'S STAGES OF COGNITIVE DEVELOPMENT

Between ages 1 and 2, children are still in the sensorimotor period of cognitive development. Around the end of the second year, children move into what Piaget calls the stage of *preoperational intelligence*. This section discusses the last two substages in the sensorimotor period and the beginnings of preoperational thought (see Table 10.1).

## SENSORIMOTOR SUBSTAGES 5 AND 6

Substage 5 usually occurs at 12 to 18 months of age (Piaget & Inhelder, 1969). This substage is characterized by toddlers' use of **tertiary circular reactions,** or experimentation, more systematic imitation, and further development of object permanence.

*tertiary circular reactions: reactions in children between 12 and 18 months of age that indicate that the toddlers are experimenting to develop knowledge of the environment around them (Piaget's substage 5 in the sensorimotor period)*

Substage 6 usually occurs between 18 months and 2 years of age. This substage is characterized by the development of true object permanence, which also includes person permanence and representational intelligence.

True object permanence indicates that toddlers can search for objects that they did not see hidden. Following is a frequently cited example of true object permanence as demonstrated by Piaget's daughter, Jacqueline:

> Observation 64.–AT 1;7(20) Jacqueline watches me when I put a coin in my hand, then put my hand under a coverlet. I withdraw my hand closed; Jacqueline opens it, then searches under the coverlet until she finds the object. I take back the coin at once, put it in my hand and slip my closed hand under a cushion situated at the other side (on her left and no longer on her right); Jacqueline immediately searches for the object under the cushion. I repeat the experiment by hiding the coin under a jacket; Jacqueline finds it without hesitation.
>
> II. I complicate the test as follows: I place the coin in my hand, then my hand under the cushion. I bring it forth closed and immediately hide it under the coverlet. Finally, I withdraw it and hold it out, closed, to Jacqueline. Jacqueline then pushes my hand aside without opening it (she guesses that there is nothing in it, which is new), she looks under the cushion, then directly under the coverlet where she finds the object. . . .
>
> I then try a series of three displacements: I put the coin in my hand and move my closed hand sequentially from A to B and from B to C: Jacqueline sets my hand aside, then searches in A, in B and finally in C.*

Thus, according to Piaget, children in this stage of development now realize that objects and people have an identity of their own and continue to exist even when the toddler is not present. As mentioned in Chapter 7, Bower (1982) suggests that it is maturing spatial perception rather than the development of object permanence

*From *The Construction of Reality in the Child*, by Jean Piaget, translated by Margaret Cook. Copyright 1954 by Basic Books, Inc. Reprinted by permission of Basic Books, Inc., Publishers, New York.

**TABLE 10.1**
**Piaget's Sensorimotor Stage during the Second Year of Life**

| | Substage | Age | Accomplishments |
|---|---|---|---|
| 5: | Tertiary circular reactions | 12–18 months | Experiments with objects<br>Imitates accurately, needing little "trial and error"<br>Thinks of objects as having permanence and searches for them where last seen |
| 6: | Object permanence | 18–24 months | Works out solutions to problems mentally<br>Defers imitation<br>Comprehends object permanence and can visualize movements of unseen objects |

that causes children in this age range to search for objects. In any event, most young children around 2 years of age develop the ability to think about events, physical objects, and people that are not immediately in their presence. This ability sets the stage for rapid cognitive and language development, described later in this chapter.

Young children in this substage can now solve problems in their minds (representational intelligence) without the aid of sensorimotor trial and error. The following vignette indicates that Jeremy does not always have to experiment to find a solution.

> Jeremy tries to place a triangular shape into the corresponding opening in a three-dimensional puzzle. The puzzle slips, and Jeremy misses the opening. He immediately uprights the puzzle and holds it with one hand while using the other hand to insert the piece into the opening. Jeremy's ability to upright the puzzle and secure it with one hand indicates that through his actions on objects during the sensorimotor stage, he internalized information about what to do in various situations. He uses this representational intelligence to help him complete his goal of putting the puzzle piece through the opening. ■

*deferred imitation:*
*the child's ability to imitate behaviors observed at an earlier time or another place; occurs near the end of the sensorimotor stage*

Children at this stage of development are also able to imitate behavior they have observed at another time. Piaget called this ability **deferred imitation** (Piaget, 1952, 1962). For example, Angela picks up the remote control for the TV and pretends she is talking on the phone. She does this when no one has been talking on the phone for several hours.

## TRANSITION TO PREOPERATIONAL STAGE

By the end of the sensorimotor period, children generally understand that objects have certain basic characteristics and that they continue to exist even when they are out of sight. Children at this point are able to carry a mental image of an object. This development sets the stage for learning more advanced concepts about the social and physical world. These abilities, coupled with the increasing use of symbols through language and play, facilitate the child's transition into Piaget's next period of cognitive development, the preoperational stage.

## PREOPERATIONAL STAGE

The **preoperational stage** of cognitive development extends from 2 to approximately 8 years of age. This section focuses on 2- and 3-year-olds at the beginning of this stage. Part Five of this text addresses later preoperational behaviors.

According to Piaget (1952), preoperational children are not capable of operational, or logical, thinking. Logical operational thinking involves the ability to reverse a mental action. For example, the process of addition is reversible through subtraction. While most older children and adults understand this process, preoperational children do not. However, this inability to reverse thought does not suggest that young children are deficient in their thinking. They are not; they are *different* in their thinking from older children and adults.

Piaget's studies suggest that young children's thinking cannot be simply explained as immature or based on lack of experience. He proposed that the young child's thought patterns or cognitive processes are uniquely different from those of older children and adults. Remember how Piaget became intrigued with young children's answers while he was helping Binet norm his intelligence test? Piaget noticed that young children gave markedly similar incorrect answers to the questions. This behavior motivated Piaget to research the idea that young children's thinking is not just immature adult thinking but is qualitatively different. His research and others' research has substantiated his hypothesis.

Young preoperational children continue to develop the ability to use **mental symbols** such as language, play, and dreams (Piaget, 1962). Language and the use of words to represent objects are discussed later in this chapter. The following vignette illustrates imitation of adult roles and the creation and use of mental symbols through play.

> Jeremy has observed city sanitation workers collecting trash around his neighborhood on his walks with Phyllis. One day, after observing this process for several weeks, he begins to dump all his toys on his bunk bed. Between loads, he presses the bolts at the end of his bed to "grind up the trash." Through his play, he imitates the adult behaviors of the sanitation workers and uses the bolts on his bed to represent the buttons the sanitation workers use on their truck. ■

As mentioned earlier, Piaget's studies indicate that the thinking of children in the early preoperational stage differs from that of older children and adults. These differences are reflected in the young child's reasoning, idiosyncratic concepts, and egocentric behaviors (Piaget, 1952).

Maybe you can think of some comments young children have made that illustrate their unique reasoning. Often these remarks are described as "cute," "humorous," or "off the wall." Their **transductive reasoning** can be described as attending to only one of a number of aspects in a situation, or confusing general and specific events. Transductive reasoning can, at times, lead to appropriate conclusions.

*preoperational: the second of Piaget's stages of cognitive development, in which children from ages 2 to approximately 8 develop the ability to internally represent sensorimotor actions, but cannot engage in the operational or logical thinking of older children and adults*

*mental symbols: the behaviors that occur at the beginning of the preoperational stage, including speech, imitation of others, and using one object to represent another*

*transductive reasoning: according to Piaget, reasoning that occurs in the preoperational stage and involves the young child's attention to the specifics of the immediate situation rather than all aspects of it*

However, much of the transductive reasoning of the young preoperational child leads to inappropriate conclusions, as indicated in the following vignette.

✄ Jeremy and his parents visit Bill's relatives for the holidays. Bill's brother's family is also there. After dinner, Aunt Sarah gives the children their gifts. Jeremy's 3-year-old cousin Matthew receives several presents, while Jeremy is given only one. Aunt Sarah has spent approximately equal amounts of money on both children, thinking she was being careful to show no partiality to either child. As is typical of the young preoperational child, Jeremy attends to the specifics—the number of presents—because the more general concept of the cost is not within his range of conceptual development. Jeremy becomes upset because cousin Matthew "gots more presents." Aunt Sarah tells Bill and Ann that next year she will get the boys the same number of presents and make the presents the same or very similar. An awareness of young children's thought processes can prevent such situations from occurring.

*idiosyncratic concepts: ideas of the preoperational child that are based on personal experience and overgeneralized to other situations*

**Idiosyncratic concepts** are concepts relating to personal experience that are often overgeneralized to other contexts. Jeremy was awakening at night with dreams of ghosts and monsters. In her training to become a child caregiver, Phyllis had learned that young children blend fantasy with reality. She knew Jeremy's dreams were real to him. For this reason, she did *not* say, "Jeremy, there are no ghosts or monsters. They are pretend." Instead, she comforted him and reassured him that she and his parents were there at night to keep him safe. Phyllis told Jeremy they would not let the ghosts and monsters hurt him. After these disturbing dreams continued for several more weeks, Phyllis had another idea. She asked Jeremy what he thought could be done to keep the ghosts and monsters out of his room. Jeremy thought for a moment and then said, "Get a sign that says 'Stop. All ghosts and monsters keep out'." Phyllis got some paper and crayons and drew a sign with that message. She and Jeremy then posted the sign on his door.

Jeremy used his past experience with signs in other contexts and overgeneralized its use to meet his personal experiences. Phyllis did not impose adult problem solving and reasoning on Jeremy but allowed him to problem solve at his cognitive level. As Jeremy prepares for sleep, Bill, Ann, and Phyllis remind him that they are there to keep him safe and that there is a sign on his door telling the monsters and ghosts to "keep out." During the next few weeks, Jeremy's sleep is more peaceful and less filled with nightmares. ■

Egocentrism means "centered on self." Piaget (1952, 1962, 1969) found that young children view situations from their own perspectives and do not seem able to consider the thoughts and feelings of others. He suggested that through interactions with other children and adults, egocentric thought becomes more socialized. Piaget also thought conflict is beneficial, as confrontations can force children to see another's point of view.

✄ Angela's teacher takes the 3-year-olds outside to play. Angela and two other children begin to play in the sand pile. Angela grabs a sifter from one of the children. This child stares at Angela and then leaves the sand area. After several minutes, Angela tries to take a large bucket from another child, Cedrick. He firmly grasps the bucket and refuses to let her have it. Angela then begins hitting Cedrick, and he runs crying to the teacher. The teacher calmly asks Cedrick what happened. He takes her hand and leads her to the sand box, telling her that Angela took his bucket and hit him. Angela's teacher asks Cedrick to tell Angela why he was crying, and the teacher repeats what Cedrick tells her. Calmly and objectively, the teacher describes the consequences of Angela's behavior. "Angela hit Cedrick. Hitting hurts. Cedrick feels bad and is crying. He said he had the bucket first. Here is another big bucket for you, Angela. We have lots of big buckets in our sand pile."

Angela's teacher understands that egocentric behavior is normal for 3-year-olds. Therefore, she does not convey to Angela that she is "a bad girl" for hitting Cedrick. Rather, she repeats what Cedrick said, describing Angela's behavior and the consequences of her actions. The teachers have organized the environment so that there are many duplicate materials, including several big buckets in the sand pile. They know children at this age can become easily frustrated if they see and want something another child has. Multiple materials can prevent the interruption in children's concrete activity and can promote problem-solving skills. When it is not possible to duplicate materials, teachers can promote more socialized behavior by reinforcing children's concerns. "Cedrick said he had the big bucket first. He still wants to use it. When he is done, Cedrick will give it to you." The teacher then observes carefully to make sure Cedrick eventually shares the bucket with Angela. ■

## BEYOND PIAGET'S THEORY

Angela is playing in the sociodramatic center of her child care center classroom. She dumps plastic fruit out of a wooden bowl. As she turns the bowl over, its inverted shape suggests that it could become a hat. Angela takes the bowl and, with considerable force, places it on Maria's head, causing Maria to cry. Angela looks very surprised at Maria's reaction. She pats Maria and tries to comfort her. Angela's teacher observes this interaction and tells Maria that Angela did not mean to hurt her. Ms. Ruiz puts Maria on her lap and attempts to calm her. Angela observes Maria and then goes to her cubbyhole, pulls out her "blanky," and gives it to Maria. ■

Similar behaviors by other young preoperational children have caused observant teachers, parents, and researchers to question Piaget's notion of egocentrism. Angela's behavior appears to indicate that she empathized with Maria. She tried to comfort her through gentle patting and bringing her the blanket.

A number of studies have documented that under certain conditions, young children have demonstrated they are not completely egocentric. As indicated in Chapter 8, one of the earliest studies examining Piaget's notion of egocentrism in very young children was by Yarrow and Zahn-Waxler (1977). After examining 1,500 incidents, they determined that children as young as 1 year old demonstrate compassion and other types of prosocial behavior. Other researchers have modified Piaget's well-known mountain experiment (Piaget & Inhelder, 1967) as a basis for demonstrating that young children are not completely egocentric. Piaget's experiment used a three-dimensional model of three mountains. These three mountains differed in appearance. One had snow on it, the second had a house, and the third had a red cross. Children were seated at a table in front of the model. The experimenter then positioned a doll at various locations on the mountains. Children were then asked to select a picture that showed the doll's perspective. Most children usually selected a card that showed their own perspectives rather than the doll's. Piaget reasoned that these behaviors indicated these young children were egocentric because they could not take on the perspective of someone else.

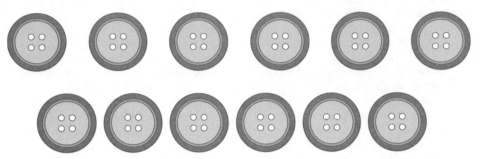

FIGURE 10.1
Piaget's experiments indicated that the preoperational child will say there are more objects in the larger array.  Recent research using more relevant questions and tasks suggests that many 3-year-olds can conserve. (Gelman & Gallistel, 1983).

In several experiments, Hughes and Donaldson (Borke, 1983; Donaldson, 1979; Donaldson, 1983; Hughes & Donaldson, 1983) determined that if tasks were more appropriate and familiar to young children, children are capable of taking the perspectives of other people. Using such props as a toy police officer, Grover from "Sesame Street," a car, boats, and animals, the children were able to take the viewpoint of another. Eighty-eight percent of 3-year-olds (Hughes & Donaldson, 1983) and 80 percent of 3- and 4-year-olds (Borke, 1983) were able to see another's point of view.

In a study involving a "magic task," Gelman and Gallistel (1983) explored young children's conservation of number. Piaget's experiments indicated that if two rows contain the  same number of objects and one row is lengthened, the pre-operational child will say there are more objects in the longer row. In the "magic task," children were not asked to distinguish between *more* and *less*, which are very abstract concepts for young children. Rather, the children were asked to choose a winner or a loser in a number of conservation experiments (see Figure 10.1). Ninety-one percent of the 3-year-olds were able to conserve when presented with various arrays.

Hughes and Grieve (1983) also suggest that the nature of children's answers to bizarre questions often asked in Piaget's experiments demonstrates their attempt to make sense of all situations. They suggest that researchers need to reexamine the underlying assumptions about children's responses when asked these questions. Thus, it appears that if experiments are made more relevant to the real-life experiences of young children, children demonstrate that they are not as egocentric as Piaget indicated.

## SOCIOCULTURAL DIFFERENCES IN PIAGET'S THEORY

Are there sociocultural differences in Piaget's theory? Research on various cultures that engage in planting, harvesting, and cooking grain suggests that children in these groups may acquire the ability to conserve earlier than children who are not a part of such cultures (Ginsburg & Opper, 1979; Rogoff, 1990). In a number of cross-cultural studies, Kagan (1982) found that 2-year-olds begin to demonstrate empathic behavior and the ability to understand the emotions of those around them. Kagan's comprehensive research indicated that very young preoperational children are not completely egocentric, but have the ability to consider the perspective of another person.

After considering the preceding discussion, you may be wondering about the relevance of Piaget's theory. Remember the discussion of theory from Chapter 1. Over time, most theories are modified and some are discarded. As more research is conducted and refined, new or different information and interpretations arise.

More recent research indicates that in some contexts, if children are given appropriate materials with which they can identify, if the tasks involve basic human purposes to which children can relate, and if the questions asked take into account young children's understanding of language and their motivations in answering questions, they can and do demonstrate that they are not totally egocentric (Black, 1981; Flavel, 1985; Sugarman, 1987). These ideas are discussed further in Chapter 13. In addition, alternative explanations as proposed by information-processing theorists are explored.

## LANGUAGE DEVELOPMENT

According to Genishi, Dyson, and Fassler (1994), the pioneering research on language acquisition is restrictive. Much of the prevailing thought in this area is based on investigation of middle-class subjects. Genishi et al. challenge current and future researchers as well as educators to "broaden their scope to include non-white, non-middle class or non-English speaking perspectives . . . to take a sociolinguistic approach that incorporates multiple perspectives to see how language is acquired in different communities and in varied situations within communities and particular social contexts" (p. 253). This section highlights this earlier research and presents background information that highlights the need for more diverse perspectives on language development.

> Angela awakens from her nap at the child care center. She sits up, rubs her eyes, and says, "Waa-waa." Ms. Ruiz fills a cup of water and brings it to her. Angela quickly empties the glass. Ms. Ruiz then allows Angela to play with the empty cup as she changes her diaper and says, "Water all gone, water all gone. Angela drank it all up. Is Angela still thirsty?"

This vignette demonstrates that Angela is learning about **semantics**, or the meaning of language. She indicates that she knows language is used to communicate—to mean something. She vocalizes to Ms. Ruiz that she wants "Waa-waa." Ms. Ruiz responds, reinforcing for Angela the notion that Angela is a meaning maker, that she can control and influence others to meet her needs through language. Ms. Ruiz facilitates this idea for Angela as she changes her diaper and talks with her about the cup, the water, and being thirsty.

*semantics: the meaning of language*

As children attend to the language used in such meaningful interactions, they absorb the speech sounds, or **phonology**, of the language system. Jeremy and

*phonology: the speech sounds of a particular language system*

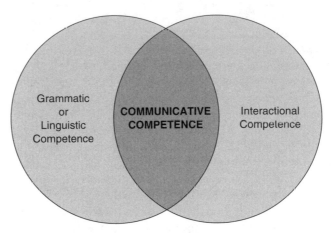

**FIGURE 10.2**
Grammatic and interactional competence interact to form the child's communicative competence.

Angela internalize the basic sounds of the English language system used within the United States, just as French children learn the sounds of the French language. As Jeremy's phonological development continues, he will begin to produce the sounds of language typical of his community and geographic region. Angela will also produce sounds that are typical of her sociocultural context.

As Angela and Jeremy begin to form their first sentences, they demonstrate that they are learning the **syntax**, or structure, of their language system.

*syntax:*
*the grammar or structure of a particular language system*

> It is Saturday, and Bill takes Jeremy with him to run errands. When they return, Ann asks Jeremy, "Where did you eat lunch?" Jeremy replies, "We eated at McDonald's." ∎

Jeremy's response indicates that he has learned how to put words together in a sentence to convey meaning. In addition, his use of *eated* reflects that he had processed the rule of grammar that past tense words end in *-ed*. This ability to form such generalizations is an example of young children's amazing cognitive ability. As Jeremy matures and learns more about the language system, he will come to realize that there are some exceptions to the general patterns of language and will begin to use *ate* instead of *eated*.

Thus, in the first few years of life, young children learn (1) that language conveys meaning, (2) the sound system of the language, and (3) the structure of the language system. In addition to this linguistic or grammatic competence, they begin to learn a repertoire of behaviors that are often called **interactional competence** (Cicourel, 1972). (See Figure 10.2.)

*interactional competence:*
*the repertoire of behaviors that helps young children communicate effectively with others*

Young children acquire interactional competence in the same manner they acquire linguistic competence: by participating with others in meaningful situations. Young children learn appropriate nonverbal behaviors and conversational techniques. These behaviors can vary according to the interactive rule structures of the child's sociolinguistic background. For example, in a number of traditional

Native American cultures, children are expected to listen while adults speak. Rather than providing occasions for children to speak, adults create opportunities for children to listen (Williams, 1994). Thus, children from certain cultural groups view silence as comfortable. In addition, interrupting or speaking too soon after another has spoken is viewed as rude in certain situations (Paul, 1992; Little Soldier, 1992). These interactive behaviors are in contrast to some other cultural groups in which children and adults engage in simultaneous overlapping conversation and interruption is viewed as acceptable behavior (Au & Mason, 1993; Au & Kawakami, 1991). A more inclusive perspective on language development takes into account that while grammatic and interactional competence interact to form the child's communicative competence (Hymes, 1971), communicative competence is culturally specific and "is developed through practice in defined circumstances" (Williams, 1994, p. 161).

## INTERACTION BETWEEN THOUGHT AND LANGUAGE

As discussed in Chapter 7, Piaget believed that young children's thought influences their language (Piaget, 1926). He observed that many children under age 7 frequently talked to themselves. Piaget interpreted this behavior as indicative of young children's egocentric thought. Because Piaget believed young children cannot take the perspectives of others, he regarded their speech as speech for oneself. In addition, he viewed this behavior as the child's way of verbalizing random thinking. Piaget thought that as children mature in their cognitive development, egocentric speech eventually disappears and socialized speech develops.

As mentioned earlier, some of Piaget's ideas are now being reevaluated. The major deviation from Piaget's idea regarding the relationship between thought and language has come from Vygotsky (1962, 1978). Vygotsky noted that young children most often talked to themselves when they were confused or encountered problems. Vygotsky hypothesized that young children talk to themselves for the purpose of solving problems or guiding behavior. He believed that talking to one's self is communication with the self.

It is interesting to note that adults also talk to themselves at certain times. Such behavior is usually viewed with humor. However, research (Berk, 1986b) indicates that adults and older children talk to themselves for the same reasons young children do: to clarify situations, guide behavior, solve problems, or internalize information. Vygotsky (1962) believed that talk to oneself becomes internalized in older children and adults as "inner speech." This inner speech helps guide behavior in our daily lives. However, if problems arise, adults and older children often verbalize this inner speech.

Vygotsky theorized that language and talking to oneself originates in one's early interactions with others. In fact, Vygotsky (1978) thought that all cognitive functioning first evolves in social contexts with others. He believed that adults and more cognitively aware children help less intellectually mature children learn by providing verbal suggestions or information. Without this assistance, or **scaffolding**, children would be unable to accomplish the task or learn the concept. Children then incorporate these suggestions and information into inner speech to aid them in problem solving, guiding behavior, internalizing new information, or

*scaffolding: according to Vygotsky, the process by which adults or more skilled children facilitate concept development or classification in young children by providing verbal information*

*Scaffolding, according to Vygotsky, is an important process during which adults or more skilled children help other children learn by providing verbal suggestions or information.*

clarifying existing concepts. Vygotsky called the level of concept development at which the child cannot accomplish tasks or understand concepts alone but can do so with assistance from adults or more cognitively aware children the **zone of proximal development** (Berk, 1986b; Berk, 1989; Vygotsky, 1978; Wertsch & Tulviste, 1992).

While Piaget (1926) emphasized the idea that children learn or invent primarily through their interactions with objects in the environment, he acknowledged that interactions with peers stimulate children to become more aware of the perspectives of others. Nevertheless, Piaget viewed the development of the human mind as an individual construction; that is, the child individually creates his or her own reality.

Vygotsky, however, points out that social interaction through language with both adults and more astute children facilitates cognitive development. Thus, according to Vygotsky, reality or concept development is viewed more as joint construction between the child and society, parents, other adults, and more astute children.

Dean (1994) expands on Piaget's and Vygotsky's viewpoints regarding the nature of this interaction between children and others. He proposes that the thinking of Hans Loewald (1988) needs to be included to more completely

*zone of proximal development: according to Vygotsky, the level of concept development that is too difficult for the child to accomplish alone but can be achieved with the help of adults or more skilled children*

explain the internalization process of the organizing, synthesizing, and mediating functions of the mind.

Loewald is a contemporary psychoanalyst who is a traditionalist and a radical revisionist of Freud's theory. According to Dean (1994), Loewald adds the dimension of personal motivation of the two participants, child and caring adult, into the internalization process. Simply stated, the subjective instinctual/affective experiences of the child and the significant other both motivate and are motivated by the internalization process. Dean states,

> Ideally, says Loewald, the parent is in an empathic relationship with the child. At the same time that he or she presents to the child a more organized, articulated view of the child's core of being, thus mediating a vision of what the child can become, the parent meets the child at the child's own level. For the child to identify with or internalize the parent's more articulate image, that image must be recognizable to the child as a reflection of him- or herself. The creation of the parents of this optimal environment, this sliding balance, says Loewald, is not merely in the interest of the child's development, but represents a developmental change in the parents (p. 56).

Rosen (1994) extends this idea to the child-teacher relationship:

> This same principle and process can be adapted to the pupil-teacher interaction in the classroom, for so often it is the case that the student has no vision at all of what he or she is capable of becoming, just as the larva emerging from the cocoon does not envision itself as developing into a butterfly. The teacher's heightened awareness of his or her own potential contribution to the child's growth is crucial (p. 60).

Dean's inclusion of Loewald's ideas is an example of how the integration of more than one theory can provide a more complete explanation of development, learning, and behavior.

As Berk (1989) indicated, research during the last several decades tends to support Vygotsky's theory regarding the importance of young children's interactions with both adults and older children in the development of cognition and the relationship between thought and language (Brown, et al., 1983; Kerwin & Day, 1985). As a result of these findings, what Piaget called *egocentric speech* and Vygotsky called *inner speech* are now referred to as **private speech**. Berk (1989) indicates that, contrary to Piaget's ideas, very young children who use private speech have higher rates of social participation and are more socially competent than children who do less "talking to themselves" (Berk, 1984, 1985; Kohlberg, Yaeger, & Hjertholm, 1968). In addition, research suggests that cognitively mature children use private speech at earlier ages (Berk, 1986a; Berner, 1971; Kleiman, 1974; Kohlberg, Yaeger, & Hjertholm, 1968). These findings demonstrate the importance of social interaction and communication in the development of language and cognition in young children. This information provides one of the most important implications for promoting the cognitive development of young children: providing opportunities for children and adults to interact and communicate with each other.

*private speech:* *speech to oneself that helps direct one's own behavior or communication with oneself*

## VOCABULARY DEVELOPMENT

*fast mapping: children's rapid learning of language by relating a word to an internalized concept and remembering it after only one encounter with that word*

Young children's rapid vocabulary development is explained by a process called **fast mapping** (Carey, 1978). Fast mapping refers to the way young children learn and remember an average of nine words a day from the onset of speech until age 6 (Clark, 1983). By that time, young children have acquired approximately 14,000 words (Templin, 1957).

Children's initial understanding of a word during the fast mapping process is often expanded and refined as children continue to learn about the world. The following vignette demonstrates this clarification of vocabulary.

One of Jeremy's favorite early books was Eric Carle's (1979) *The Very Hungry Caterpillar*. Jeremy's first referent for a caterpillar was the tube-shaped animal that crawls. He was somewhat puzzled later on when he had his first encounter with another type of caterpillar, a toy replica of the earth-moving machine. As children refine and extend their vocabulary, they discover that there are words that sound the same but have different meanings. ■

## FIRST SENTENCES

*telegraphic speech: children's early speech, which, like a telegram, includes only words necessary to understanding meaning*

*rich interpretation: acknowledging that young children know more than they can verbally express and use nonverbal behaviors to communicate*

When children are around age 18 to 20 months, they usually have a vocabulary of about 40 to 50 words. At this time, they usually begin to form their first sentences consisting of two words. Two-word sentences are often called **telegraphic speech**, meaning only the most meaningful words are used (Brown & Fraser, 1963). Usually prepositions, articles, auxiliary verbs, conjunctions, plurals, possessives, and past endings are left out of telegraphic speech. An analysis called **rich interpretation** acknowledges that children know more than they can express and are capable of using nonverbal behaviors to facilitate their meaning. Bloom's (1970) classic example of "Mommy, sock" indicated that these two words could convey a variety of meanings: "Mommy's sock," "Mommy, put on my sock," or "Mommy, give me my sock." Thus, context becomes essential to understanding the child's true meaning in these earliest sentences.

Early sentences usually involve questions, descriptions, recurrence, possession, location, agent-action, and negation and wish. Bloom (1970) found that children's first use of *no* conveys nonexistence, for example, "no juice." Next, *no* is used as a negative, as in "no go home." Then *no* is used to convey what the child believes to be not true.

*morpheme: the smallest unit of meaning in oral or written language*

Between ages 2 and 3, simple sentences begin to appear. Cross-cultural research indicates that children begin to incorporate the word order used in their particular linguistic community (Maratsos, 1983). Gradually, children between 1½ and 3½ years of age begin to acquire grammatical **morphemes**, which expand the mean length utterance (MLU) or "sentence." Brown's (1973) research demonstrates that English-speaking children in these age groups acquire grammatical morphemes in a regular order (see Table 10.2).

**TABLE 10.2**
## Order of Acquisition of English Grammatical Morphemes

| Morpheme | Example |
|---|---|
| 1. Verb, present progressive ending (*-ing*) | "She swinging." |
| 2. Preposition *on* | "On Daddy's shoulders." |
| 3. Preposition *in* | "In my car." |
| 4. Noun plural *-s* | "Books." |
| 5. Verb irregular past tense | "Kitty ran." "Chair broke." |
| 6. Noun possessive | "Mommy's shoe." |
| 7. Verb, uncontractible *be* form used with adjective, preposition, or noun phrase | "Are cookies hot?" |
| 8. Articles *a* and *the* | "A book." "The spoon." |
| 9. Verb, regular past tense ending (*-ed*) | "Jessica fixed it." |
| 10. Verb, present tense, third person singular regular ending (*-s*) | "Justin hates it." |
| 11. Verb, present tense, third person singular irregular ending (*-s*) | "He has (from *have*) a hose." "Daddy does (from *do*) make pizza." |
| 12. Auxiliary verb, uncontractible *be* forms | "Are you sleeping?" |
| 13. Verb, contractible *be* forms used with adjective, preposition, or noun phrase | "He's outside." "They're happy." |
| 14. Auxiliary verb, contractible *be* forms | "Mommy's coming." "Caitlin's crying." |

*Source*: Adapted from Brown, D.M. (1979). "Order of acquisition of English grammatical morphemes." (p. 167). *Mother Tongue to English*. NY: Cambridge University Press. With permission by Cambridge University Press.

## YOUNG CHILDREN'S ORAL LANGUAGE APPROXIMATIONS

Most parents and teachers delight in young children's attempts to acquire language. Their **approximations**, or attempts at conventional adult language, are often viewed as cute, charming, or creative. The majority of adults seem to know that given a supportive language environment and time to develop, children's approximations eventually become more conventional (Snow & Ferguson, 1977).

At times, some adults misinterpret young children's developmentally appropriate language behaviors as incorrect and believe it is their duty to correct the language. However, this is not the case. Appropriate teacher and parent responses to young children's language behavior are described later in Chapters 13 and 16. The purpose of this discussion is to provide an understanding of some of the more common oral language approximations young children exhibit.

**Overextension** involves young children's use of a word to refer to a similar but different object, situation, or category. Do you remember the example in Chapter 1 of Jonathan, who pointed to the Goodyear blimp and said, "Truck, truck"?

*approximations: children's attempts at conventional oral or written language, which, when produced, are not quite conventional*

*overextension: occurs when young children use a word to refer to a similar but different object, situation, or category*

Jonathan's use of *truck* indicates that he was overextending the word to refer to other objects. Young children's efforts at cognitive processing are evident in their use of overextensions. Overextensions always apply to a class of similar referents (Clark, 1983). Blimps look similar in shape to trucks.

Interestingly, some researchers suggest that overextension may be a strategy young children use because they have had no opportunity to learn the appropriate word or because they cannot remember the appropriate word. For example, Jonathan had never seen a blimp before, so he attached the label *truck* to the blimp. He had no knowledge of the word *blimp* and to what it referred (Clark, 1978).

In addition, considerable evidence shows that given the correct names in a comprehension task, children can point out specific objects even though they overextend. This may be another example of comprehension of language preceding the production of language (Clark, 1978; Rescorla, 1980).

*creative vocabulary: young children's creation of new words to meet the need for words they have not learned, have forgotten, or for which no word in the language system exists*

Young children use **creative vocabulary** when they create new words to meet the need for a word they have not learned, they cannot remember, or for which no actual word exists in the language system. For example one young child referred to a calculator as a "countulator." Another example occurred when several children in an early childhood classroom were playing "restaurant." They decided that Justin would be the "cooker."

As discussed in Chapter 7, overgeneralization also occurs when young children generalize a grammatical rule to apply to all situations. Interestingly, early in the language acquisition process, very young children seem to use the irregular forms of frequently used words conventionally (Menyuk, 1964). Later, as children begin to unconsciously internalize the general rules for making plurals or past tense, they overgeneralize the rules. For example, the general rule for making past tense is to add *-ed* to a word. In applying this principle, children create *goed, runned, breaked,* and so on. Remember when Jeremy told his mother that they had "eated at McDonald's"?

This discussion indicates that young children's efforts at language development reflect remarkable abilities of cognitive processing. The acquisition of oral language over a relatively short time is one of the most amazing accomplishments in human development.

## SOCIOCULTURAL ASPECTS OF LANGUAGE

As teachers in multicultural schools, our work is to educate children in our care, but not transform them. We must have the courage of our convictions to open up avenues leading into the English language and culture, so that the children of other traditions may enter and move forward in our society, but we must never lose the integrity which enables us to recognize and respect those individual qualities which should remain untouched and unchanged— the rightful heritage of each nationality (Brown, 1979, p. 167).

People who plan to work with young children and who come from mainstream America need to examine their own belief systems regarding possible prej-

*Teachers of young children need to accept all children and their languages.*

udices and negative attitudes toward children who come from families of different cultural, linguistic, and economic backgrounds (Sleeter, 1994). "The long American tradition of negative attitudes toward childhood bilingualism has been fueled by racial and ethnic prejudices, for bilingualism in the United States is strongly associated with low income and minority status" (Berk, 1989, p. 401).

Unless you are a Native American (American Indian), your roots lie in another country, culture, and language system. Reflect on what it must have been like for your ancestors to leave their native land and extended or immediate families to come to this country. Think about their struggle to find shelter, make a living, and learn a new language, new laws, and new ways of doing things. Consider what it would be like if your family decided to move far away to a new country with different foods, housing, clothing, customs, and language. Perhaps some reflection in this area will encourage a more empathic reaction on your part to children and families who come from a background different than yours.

## DIALECTS

Linguists say there are many dialects all over the United States. Consider the variations in sounds and pronunciations of the New England area, the South, and the Midwest. The state of Texas is said to have five regional dialects.

Linguists define **dialects** as speech differences that are unique to various ethnic populations or geographic regions. Dialects vary in pronunciation of words, verb tenses and sound omissions. According to linguists, dialects are *not* inferior forms

**dialects:**
*different forms of language used by various ethnic groups or by people who live in certain geographic regions*

of language but are simply *different* forms. Dialects are rule governed just as standard English is rule governed. *All* young children learn the dialect of the home and community in which they live.

Many young children come from families in which a dialect such as Black English (Ebonics) is routinely spoken. If a dialect has syntactic, semantic, and phological differences from Standard English, children can have difficulty adjusting to Standard English when they enter school.

## BILINGUALISM AND MULTILINGUALISM

*simultaneous bilingual: children who learn two languages at the same time, beginning at birth*

*successive bilingual: children who learn a second language after acquiring proficiency in a first language*

Some children learn two languages at the same time, beginning at birth. These children are referred to as **simultaneous bilingual** and truly have two first languages. Other children learn a second language after acquiring proficiency in a first language. These children are known as **successive bilingual** and often encounter the second language in an intensive context when they enter school.

Increasing numbers of children in the United States come from homes in which English is not the first language. Many young children are in home and school environments where different languages are spoken. Some important background information about learning two or more languages follows:

- Children who do not yet speak English are often very quiet. This lack of verbalization should not be equated with a lack of cognitive ability. Reluctance to speak may indicate that these children are still internalizing the sounds of the new language system, just as infants and toddlers do. If you had no knowledge of the German language but were expected to speak it, write it, and take tests in it, you would not perform well. However, your poor performance would not indicate that you were lacking in intelligence; rather, you would simply be in a language environment that differed from your own. Therefore, you would be unable to express your thoughts so that others could understand them. The same is true for children who are learning a second language.

- There are great differences in the rates and strategies used to acquire a second language just as there are in first-language acquisition (Strong, 1982; Wong-Fillmore, 1976; Wong-Fillmore, 1991).

- Oral language development is not affected in the first language because the child is learning a new language. There does appear to be a slight delay around age 2 or 3 as children learn to separate the phonological and grammar systems. By age 4, children demonstrate normal native ability and good to normal ability in the second language, depending on the amount of exposure (Reich, 1986).

- Second-language acquisition facilitates both cognitive and linguistic skills (Ben Zeev, 1977; Bialystok, 1986; Diaz, 1985). When matched with children who are monolingual, children who are bilingual have outperformed them in areas of verbal and nonverbal intellectual measures, analytic reasoning, concept formation, metalinguistic awareness, and creativity (Ricciardelli, 1993).

- The patterns of second-language development parallel those of first-language development. Second-language acquisition, like first-language acquisition as described earlier in this chapter, is creative (MacLaughlin, 1978; Wong-Fillmore, 1981).

- Input or social interaction with other children and adults is necessary to second-language acquisition just as it is to first-language acquisition (Krashen, 1991).

## SOCIOECONOMIC DIFFERENCES IN LANGUAGE ACQUISITION

Just as children who speak in dialects or have a different first language possess differences, not deficits, in language, linguists and sociolinguists suggest the same is true for children who come from varying socioeconomic backgrounds (Bernstein, 1972; Heath, 1983). Children from lower socioeconomic classes have a language system that is useful within their culture and community. Thus, children who have language differences based on cultural and economic differences need to be respected for possessing viable language systems. They should not be perceived as deficient in either intelligence or language.

Our language and culture are vital to each of us because they help to define who we are and give us our identities. If teachers or other adults who work with young children convey disapproval or nonacceptance of children with cultural and linguistic differences, these children's self-esteem and self-concepts will be severely diminished. A feeling of self-worth is necessary for young children to feel they are competent learners. Early childhood professionals need to accept young children's dialects and respond to the meanings of their language rather than correcting them. The following dialogue provides an example of how a teacher accepts a child's dialect and responds to the meaning of the child's language:

| | |
|---|---|
| Maria: | I be gettin' new shoes. |
| Teacher: | You'll be getting new shoes? Great! What kind do you want? |
| Maria: | Daddy done got me sneakers! |
| Teacher: | Your daddy got you sneakers! What color are they? |
| Maria: | He got me red ones. |

## LITERACY DEVELOPMENT

Cheryl has been doing her homework in front of the TV. She takes a break and walks to the kitchen to get something to eat. As she walks back to the living room, she discovers Angela (now 26 months of age) writing on her notebook. "Angela, that's my homework!" shouts Cheryl. Angela looks up at Cheryl and says, "Angela, homework." ■

It is Saturday. Ann's father has come to visit them, and they decide to go to the mall. As they enter the mall, 2-year-old Jeremy says, "There's Sears." Ann's father cannot believe his ears. "Jeremy is only 2 and he can read *Sears*," the proud grandfather remarks. ■

The above vignettes demonstrate that very young children are learning not only about oral language but also about written language. The idea that very young children learn about literacy is relatively recent.

## INTERACTION AMONG THOUGHT, LANGUAGE, AND LITERACY

In the past, it was thought that children need to spend approximately the first five years of their lives developing a good foundation in oral language before learning to read. When children reached age 6½, they were perceived as generally possessing the maturity and perceptual development required to learn how to read (Morphett & Washburn, 1931). After learning the basic rudiments of reading, children were then ready to begin to learn how to write—to communicate with others via written symbols. This writing for the purpose of communicating with others, as opposed to the perceptual-motor task of handwriting, usually received attention somewhere around the end of the first grade or the beginning of the second. Once introduced to writing, young children were expected to produce interesting stories, with conventional spelling, appropriate grammar, good handwriting, and correct punctuation on their first attempt. If they were not successful, their papers and stories were returned with numerous corrections in red pencil. With such unrealistic expectations as children, it is no wonder many adults do not like to write.

In the 1960s and 1970s, a number of researchers began to question this sequence of literacy development. Their questions, research, and findings have provided some new and fascinating information about how young children develop literacy.

As oral language researchers (Ninio & Bruner, 1978; Snow, 1983) analyzed tapes of young children's verbalizations, they noticed that many young children talked about and were very much interested in print. The vignettes about Jeremy and Angela throughout this chapter indicate these children's awareness of and interest in print.

Reading researchers also recognized that some young children came to first grade already knowing how to read. While some suspected that these children's parents had formally taught them to read, Delores Durkin (1966) undertook a study of early readers and their families to determine exactly how these young children had actually learned to read. The results of this well-known investigation have since been substantiated by other researchers (Clark, 1976; Hall, Moretz, & Statom, 1976; Wells, 1981).

These studies found that the parents did not formally teach their young children how to read. However, these parents displayed a number of other behaviors that seemed to facilitate early reading behaviors. Specifically, they (1) read to their children on a consistent and regular basis when the children were quite young; (2) provided their children with access to a wide range of print materials in the home; (3) read and interacted with print themselves; (4) responded to their children's questions about print; and (5) made writing and drawing tools and paper available to their children.

Observing and participating in meaningful print contexts with parents and the availability of paper and writing tools provided the opportunity for children to express themselves symbolically, explore print, and develop concepts about the nature of print. One of the most interesting findings of Durkin's research was the parents' report that their children did a great deal of writing just before they began to read or that writing and reading seemed to emerge at the same time.

This notion that very young children were interested in writing was rather startling given that children usually were not expected to write communicatively

*Providing children with a wide range of print materials and opportunities to pretend play with them helps children to understand that reading and writing are used to communicate.*

until somewhere around the end of the first grade. Consequently, Durkin's research raised some important questions: Do opportunities to write facilitate learning to read? Should young children be encouraged to write? If the answer is yes, exactly how should adults encourage writing in young children? These questions prompted a flurry of early literacy research, which continues to the present.

Much of the literacy research has focused on the process by which young children develop literacy. Specific details of this development are discussed in Part Five of this text. Several general ideas describe current thinking about the development of literacy in young children:

- Young children learn about literacy (reading and writing) by interacting with others in meaningful print situations (Teale, 1986).

- Learning about print begins quite early in life, certainly during the first year of life (Ninio & Bruner, 1978; Teale, 1984).

- Young children's learning about print differs from the knowledge older children and adults have about print (Ferrerio & Teberosky, 1982; Read, 1971).

- Young children develop an awareness of oral and written language in a holistic and interrelated way rather than in a sequential stage process. In other words, very young children develop simultaneous notions about oral and written language while they are involved with significant others in meaningful situations (Goodman, 1986).

- Virtually all children, regardless of socioeconomic background, learn about literacy early in life (Heath, 1983). Only in those few cultural groups that do not use written language do children lack an awareness of print.

The interaction of meaningful experiences with oral and written language is a very important factor in the development of literacy. Such an awareness suggests it is important that young children have active, meaningful experiences with others involving both oral and written language. These experiences facilitate the child's competence in the development of thought and oral and written communication.

## DEVELOPING AN AWARENESS OF PRINT AS A FORM OF COMMUNICATION

A major concept that all children in literate societies must acquire is that print conveys meaning. Many young children begin to develop this idea as their parents read stories to them (Ninio & Bruner, 1978; Snow & Ninio, 1986; Wells, 1981). Other contexts also help children from a variety of socioeconomic backgrounds understand that print conveys messages. Situations that demand attention to environmental print—religious ceremonies, written directions, writing checks, using the TV guide to select programs—and children's TV programs, like "Sesame Street," also help children develop the understanding that print communicates (Anderson & Smith, 1984; Taylor 1986; Teale, 1986). The two primary sources of young children's learning about the communicative nature of print are environmental print and book print.

## ENVIRONMENTAL PRINT

Remember the vignette about Jeremy and Sears? How did Jeremy come to associate the large building at the mall with the letters S-E-A-R-S on the facade? The answer is through a variety of meaningful experiences that involved both oral and written language. Jeremy had been in the Sears store on numerous occasions. He was with Bill and Ann when they purchased a new washer and dryer. He watched as the Sears truck arrived and the washer and dryer were delivered and installed. Almost every time Bill and Ann are in Sears, they take Jeremy to the toy department to look around. Jeremy has also heard and seen advertisements for Sears on TV. Participating in these meaningful experiences with the accompanying oral and written language helped Jeremy internalize the printed symbols that represent Sears.

As children use and/or observe objects in meaningful contexts, they pay attention to the objects' appearance. Seeing the box of Cheerios every morning on the breakfast table or the tube of Crest toothpaste on the sink, as well as at the grocery store or on TV, helps children become familiar with and internalize certain features about print encountered in the environment. Studies indicate that while young children around age 2 recognize environmental print such as "Coke," "McDonald's," and "K mart," they attend to this print in a very global manner (Goodman, 1980). That is, they pay attention to the whole context and not just the print. For example, very young children attend to the shape of the object, its color, and the design of the print and logo. As their print awareness develops, they begin to focus more directly on the print. Thus, experiences with environmental print are important in facilitating beginning print awareness.

## BOOK PRINT

For the most part, book print differs from environmental print in that it usually consists of more than just one or two words and is organized into one or more lines. Its purpose differs somewhat from that of environmental print, and it requires a more extended focus. Knowledge of book print and how it works is critical for success in the school context (Teale, 1984).

Learning about book print begins at home when parents share books with their children. Many parents introduce their children to books during the first year of life, some even before. Often these experiences involve naming pictures or talking about pictures. During the second or third year, parents usually begin to read the book text to their children. As children hear these stories, they begin to develop the idea that books can bring them information, pleasure, and comfort. This idea seems to foster a love of books and independent reading in children.

Family book reading provides many opportunities for young children to learn a number of important concepts (Schickedanz, 1986). Specifically, they learn

- New information about the world around them
- New vocabulary
- Turn taking (when parents ask questions and children respond)
- The features of print and how to handle books
- The concept of *story*

An important factor in developing an awareness of book print is the parents' behavior. Parents serve as "scaffolders." Remember Vygotsky's zone of proximal development? By responding to their children's behaviors, asking them questions, and making comments, parents facilitate young children's understanding and challenge their thinking. Talking with children about stories read encourages reflective thinking, since the stories are often related to the children's past experiences. Talking about stories also helps children develop **metalanguage**, or the ability to talk about language.

*metalanguage: talk about language itself*

Finally, intimate encounters with books provide time for parent-child communication. Time spent with books not only facilitates literacy development but can promote positive parent-child interactions. Parental behaviors in children's acquisition of literacy have important implications for the role of early childhood professionals in promoting literacy in their classrooms.

## SOCIOCULTURAL INFLUENCES

This chapter has emphasized the need for interaction in young children's development of oral and written language. A review of Heath's (1983) study, presented in Chapter 2, provides information about apparent variations in this social interaction, which occurs in different sociocultural contexts. Heath examined story-reading events in a middle-class, an Anglo working-class, and an African American working-class community in the Piedmont Carolinas. She found distinctive sociocultural differences in children's involvement in literacy events. Heath then documented the effects of these differences on children's success in school.

The middle-class children in the Piedmont area did well in school. Their socialization into literacy events included parents asking questions about books, relating book events to the children's experiences, and encouraging children to tell their own stories based on both reality and fantasy.

The working-class Anglo children were also introduced to books by their parents. Parents centered on children's retelling of factual events rather than thinking about the books in a way that encouraged reflective thinking. These children did well in responding to literal recall questions. However, they had difficulty in the higher grades with analyzing, predicting, and evaluating.

The working-class African American children had few book-reading interactions with their parents. Questions adults asked differed from those asked in the other two communities. Children were asked to compare rather than name or describe. The parents told stories to their children rather than reading them stories. The stories were fictional in nature while often based on familiar events. These children did not do well in school, even though they had advanced skills in fictional narration and analogical reasoning.

In studying African American, Anglo, and Mexican American low-income families, Teale, Estrada, and Anderson (1981) found many differences among these families regarding literacy interactions and events. This research suggests that many variations exist even within cultural and socioeconomic groups. Therefore, it is important to recognize children as unique individuals and accept variations in their home literacy experiences and emerging development.

## FACTORS INFLUENCING COGNITIVE, LANGUAGE, AND LITERACY DEVELOPMENT

We have alluded to some of the factors that influence the early development of young children in the areas of cognition, language, and literacy. This section specifically addresses these factors.

### GENETIC, NUTRITION, AND HEALTH FACTORS

Research by Gardner (1983) indicates that there are seven forms of intelligence based on the child's genetic predisposition. These include linguistic, musical, spatial, interpersonal, intrapersonal, bodily-kinesthetic, and logical-mathematical. Individuals may possess more than one of these "frames of mind." Nelson (1981) has identified differences in young children in the early stages of oral language development that may be a function of brain hemisphere dominance as well as environmental factors. Referential speakers rely mostly on nouns, a few verbs, proper nouns, and adjectives, and they frequently label objects. Expressive speakers use varying forms of speech combinations and frequently use pronouns and compressed one- or two-word sentences. Dyson's (1981) research in the area of young children's writing also documents variation in writing strategies. These differences could be related to individual genetic predisposition as well as to environmental influences.

It is important that children between ages 1 and 3 continue to have proper nutrition and health care. Two-year-olds have developed 70 percent of their adult brain weight, with complete brain weight achieved by age 6 (Kunjufu, 1980). Even mild undernourishment during prenatal development, in infancy, or in childhood can cause cognitive impairment. Undernourished children are apathetic and unresponsive. Very severe malnutrition, as indicated in earlier chapters, results in lower birthweight and smaller brains. In addition, some children appear healthy but actually have iron deficiency anemia. This condition may affect 25 percent of American children from low-income families. Iron deficiency anemia adversely affects the child's ability to concentrate, attention span, and memory with consequences reaching into adulthood (Segan, 1994). Thus, it is critical that young children continue to eat well-balanced diets if their learning potential is to be realized.

Children who do not have regular medical checkups also may have various health needs that are not identified but ultimately can impair cognitive, language, and literacy development. Vision and hearing problems can adversely affect young children's development in these areas.

## THE NATURE OF ADULT-CHILD INTERACTIONS

Another factor influencing cognitive, language, and literacy development in children ages 1 and 3 is the nature of adult-child interactions. Throughout this chapter you have seen the importance of interaction with adults.

As summarized by Genishi and Dyson (1984), research suggests that behaviors of both mothers and fathers influence the nature of young children's language acquisition (Gleason, 1975; Lamb, 1977; Nelson, 1973; Snow & Ferguson, 1977; Wells, 1981). The modifications adults make in their speech to communicate with very young children is called **motherese** and **fatherese**. Motherese by mothers of children whose language developed more rapidly than others involved asking more questions than most, accepting the child's comments, and responding as though the child's talk were meaningful (White, 1985). These mothers also used fewer commands and less directive speech with their young children. Fatherese has not been examined to the extent motherese has. Nevertheless, unique language behaviors on the part of fathers elicit different language responses and behaviors from children than those of mothers. Fatherese has been identified as being more playful (Lamb, 1977), using more direct commands (Gleason, 1975), and eliciting more sophisticated language from young children (Masur & Gleason, 1980) compared with motherese.

The importance of parental responsiveness to the meaning of young children's talk was documented by Cross (1978) and Wells (1981). In a longitudinal study, Wells found that the nature of adult responsiveness to 3-year-old children's speech was associated with rapid oral language development and with reading achievement at age 7. Specifically, the children who did well in language development and

*motherese:*
*modification in the mother's speech when talking with young children*

*fatherese:*
*modification in the father's speech when talking with young children; can differ from motherese*

reading achievement had parents who made "developing responses" to their children's verbalizations. These parents added new information to the topic the child was discussing and encouraged the child to continue talking about the topic, often by asking questions. In addition to the behaviors mentioned, research (Snow & Ferguson, 1977) indicates that when talking to young children, adults use speech that is short and grammatically simple, repeat their speech, and raise and vary the tone and pitch. Adults have also been observed to "scaffold," that is, provide the support children need to advance in their language development (Teale, 1981).

Adults also facilitate the language development of young children through extensions and expansions. **Extensions** are responses that include the essence of children's verbalizations and extend the meaning, while **expansions** provide children with the opportunity to hear the conventional forms of language. Jeremy said, "Get ball." Bill replied, "Oh, you need me to help you get your ball. It rolled under the table." Through this extension, Bill conveys to Jeremy that he understood what Jeremy was verbalizing. Bill also adds more information about the context through his verbalization. Adults use expansions to provide feedback to young children regarding their use of overgeneralizations. Jeremy tells Ann, "We eated at McDonald's." She replies, "Oh, you ate at McDonald's. What did you have to eat?" She does not directly correct Jeremy's *eated* but uses the appropriate form in a conversational context and also extends by asking what Jeremy had to eat. Evidence suggests that adults who use these techniques help children to progress more rapidly in their language development and produce more complex sentences than children who are around adults who do not use extensions and expansions (Cross, 1978; Nelson, Carskaddon, & Bonvillian, 1973; White, 1985).

The effects of various parental behaviors on the development of literacy were discussed earlier in this chapter. Research by Durkin (1966) and others documents the importance of parent interaction with children in print situations. Parents' responses to children's questions about print also document the scaffolding parents can provide to enhance children's literacy development.

## VARIETY OF PRINT CONTEXTS

The nature of adult-child interactions in a variety of print contexts influences the child's awareness of various literacy contexts. Children whose parents actively involve them in reading environmental print and book print, provide them with writing tools so they can explore print, and respond to the children's concerns and questions about print facilitate greater awareness of print than parents who do not respond to children's interests (Bissex, 1980; Durkin, 1966; Heath, 1983).

## BACKGROUND OF EXPERIENCES

The number and kinds of experiences young children have, the nature of the scaffolding role of adults, and the opportunities for young children to play out these experiences all influence the young child's cognitive, language, and literacy development. Around age 3, children begin to demonstrate that they know certain procedures and events, or **scripts**. Scripts are events that are organized in a sequen-

*extensions:*
*responses to children's language that extend the meaning of their language*

*expansion:*
*responses to young children's use of overgeneralizations by using the conventional form in the conversational context*

*scripts:*
*the knowledge of a social procedure or event, which includes sequence of events and of roles, often observed in young children in play contexts*

tial manner (Schank & Abelson, 1977). Knowledge of scripts is demonstrated through verbal and nonverbal behaviors. Once children have internalized a script, they can organize their behavior and language. Jeremy's experiences in observing and participating in the collection of refuse around his neighborhood have provided him with the script about what happens during this event. His knowledge of this script is reflected in his play when he collects his toys, dumps them on his bed (garbage truck), and presses the bolts (buttons) to grind up the "trash." Children whose parents provide a variety of experiences and opportunities for their children to reexperience these events generally develop a greater number of scripts and more elaborate and detailed scripts than those parents who do not (Fivush, 1984; Nelson, 1986).

Children also internalize scripts when hearing or telling stories. Studies indicate that young children can remember more details from stories based on familiar events (Hudson & Nelson, 1983). This information suggests that background of experience is a critical factor when young children are involved in literacy or print settings.

Background experiences and subsequent script formation appear to facilitate "category of concept" formation (Lucariello & Nelson, 1985). It appears that after children have developed a number of scripts involving similar objects, sequences, and functions, they can combine elements of these scripts into larger categories, thus promoting cognitive development.

## PLAY, CONCRETE ACTIVITY, AND DIVERSITY IN PLAY

Most child development experts perceive opportunities for play or concrete activity and the quality of this play as important factors in facilitating the young child's cognitive, language, and literacy development. Most experts on play suggest that sensorimotor play with oneself and with objects facilitates the young child's beginning cognitive development (Piaget, 1962; Smilansky, 1968; Sutton-Smith, 1967). Garvey (1977) indicates that object play often involves a four-step sequence: exploration, manipulation, practice, and repetition. Repetitive play with objects facilitates the development of **physical knowledge** and the eventual development of **logico-mathematical knowledge** (Piaget, 1969).

*physical knowledge: knowledge of physical characteristics of objects and events gained through sensorimotor interaction*

Young children's play with language also encourages language development. Children between ages 1 and 3 often play with sounds, syllables, and words. This play with language can occur when the child is alone, often at bedtime (Garvey, 1977; Weir, 1962).

*logico-mathematical knowledge: knowledge that is constructed primarily from children's actions on and interpretations of objects*

During the child's third year, play with sociodramatic materials and others begins. Sociodramatic play of 3-year-olds usually has no organized theme or plot. Their enactments of play roles are often one-dimensional and change frequently due to the lack of a general theme. Play at this age often involves collecting, hauling, carrying, and dumping objects. Children tend to repeat play over and over. Jeremy's "garbage play" is such an example. Children at this age act out the basics or essentials of certain scripts: eating a meal, visiting the doctor, picking up the trash.

Opportunities for play, the nature of the play, materials available, and adult behaviors during children's play all influence cognitive, language, and literacy development. Teachers need to be aware of differences in play among children from various ethnic or cultural backgrounds. These differences should not be considered deficiencies, and teachers should not try to change play behaviors to that of the dominant culture. Trawick-Smith (1994, pp. 326–329) summarizes culturally diverse play behaviors identified in young children and provides suggested teacher responses:

- Play themes may vary according to cultural background.

  *Teacher response:* Provide play props and encourage themes that reflect cultural diversity.

- Children's activity levels and amount of rough-and-tumble play may vary as a function of culture.

  *Teacher response:* Assist children in modifying the nature of their physical contact or activity level; emphasize that active play is not intended as aggressive behavior; encourage increased activity to meet a variety of developmental needs or outlets.

- European American children tend to be more excluding and independent in their play, while children of African American, Puerto Rican, Mexican American, Native American, and Japanese descent tend to be more cooperative, collective, and inclusive in their play.

  *Teacher response:* Encourage individual initiative; provide optimally competitive games; create opportunities for cooperation; minimize or eliminate competition; clarify individual ownership and the process of asking permission.

## SOCIOCULTURAL AND SPECIAL NEEDS

Throughout this chapter, we have emphasized the differences in children's development in the areas of cognition, language, and literacy. An awareness and an understanding of these differences are essential in promoting the development of young children in these three interrelated areas. It is important that children develop a sense of worth and pride in their identity. This can be difficult to achieve if adults view children who are culturally and economically different as deficient. Understanding young children's differences can help those who work with young children to emphasize their strengths and provide appropriate experiences for them.

An awareness of children's appropriate cognitive, language, and literacy development can help educators provide programmatic assistance to children who have special developmental needs. Regular medical checkups can also help teachers and parents become aware of atypical development. Various health professionals can serve as resources in obtaining needed special services and developing intervention strategies for young children.

In 1986 Congress passed Public Law 99–457, which established a state grant program for children with disabilities from birth through 2 years of age who have been identified as developmentally delayed. By 1992, participating states had to make services available to all infants and toddlers with disabilities. Also by 1992, states applying for funds from the federal government for P.L. 99–457 or

P.L. 101–476 (reauthorization of P.L. 91–142, the Education for All Handicapped Children Act of 1975) had to provide documentation that they are providing "free and appropriate education" to all children with disabilities between ages 3 and 5. In addition to the child's Individual Education Program (IEP), an Individual Family Service Plan (IFSP) must be written. Provisions for offering a variety of program options and services to special-needs children and their families must be included in the IFSP.

## Role of the Early Childhood Professional

### Promoting Cognitive, Language, and Literacy Development in Children Ages 1 Through 3

1. Remember that each child is unique in his or her cognitive, language, and literacy development.

2. Respect sociocultural, linguistic, and socioeconomic differences among young children and their families.

3. Identify cognitive, language, and literacy needs in young children that may require special attention, services, or programs.

4. Remember that in many instances, young children process information differently than older children and adults.

5. Provide safe environments so that young children can explore freely.

6. Provide a variety of interesting materials to promote thinking, talking, reading, and writing.

7. Provide opportunities for young children to interact, talk, read, and write with other children and adults.

8. Demonstrate interest in and curiosity about the world.

9. Use oral and written language in meaningful contexts.

10. Provide scaffolding to help young children expand their cognitive, language, and literacy development. ∎

## KEY TERMS

approximations
creative vocabulary
deferred imitation
dialects
expansion
extension
fast mapping
fatherese
idiosyncratic concepts

interactional
  competence
logico-mathematical
  knowledge
mental symbols
metalanguage
morpheme
motherese
overextension

phonology
physical knowledge
preoperational
private speech
rich interpretation
scaffolding
scripts
semantics
simultaneous bilingual

| successive bilingual | tertiary circular | zone of proximal |
|---|---|---|
| syntax | reactions | development |
| telegraphic speech | transductive reasoning | |

## REVIEW STRATEGIES AND ACTIVITIES

1. Review the key terms individually or with a classmate.
2. Observe parents and caregivers in accredited settings with children ages 1 through 3. With their permission, tape record the language, then analyze it for evidence of scaffolding.
3. Observe caregivers in accredited and inclusive classrooms for 1-, 2-, and 3-year-olds.
   a. Explain how developmental differences and cultural tendencies and dispositions are addressed.
   b. Describe how the environment is organized to promote cognitive, language, and literacy development.
   c. List the materials available and describe how they promote cognitive, language, and literacy development.
   d. Describe how the day is organized. Is the schedule conducive to cognitive, language, and literacy development?
   e. Observe the role of the teacher. List and describe the behaviors that facilitate cognitive, language, and literacy development.

## FURTHER READINGS

Armstrong, T. (1994). *Multiple intelligences in the classroom.* Alexandria, VA: Association for Supervision and Curriculum Development.

Beaty, J. J. (1994). *Observing development of the young child.* Columbus, OH: Merrill/Prentice Hall.

Bentzen, W. R. (1993). *Seeing young children: A guide to observing and recording behavior* (2nd edition). Albany, NY: Delmar.

Eisenberg, A., H. E. Murkoff, & S. E. Hathaway. (1994). *What to expect: The toddler years.* New York: Workman Publishing.

Hiebert, E. H. (Ed.). (1991). *Literacy for a diverse society: Perspectives and policies.* New York: Teachers College Press.

Sawyer, W., & D. E. Comer. (1991). *Growing up with literature.* Albany, NY: Delmar.

Trawick-Smith, J. (1994). *Interactions in the classroom.* New York: Macmillan.

# PART FIVE

# The Young Child
# Ages 4 Through 5

# CHAPTER ELEVEN

*The first and foremost thing you can expect of a child is that he is a child.*

**Armin Grams**

# Physical and Motor Development Ages 4 Through 5

After studying this chapter, you will demonstrate comprehension by:

- Outlining expected patterns of physical and motor development in children ages 4 through 5.
- Describing developmental landmarks in large and small muscle development.
- Describing perceptual-motor development in children ages 4 through 5.
- Describing body and gender awareness in children ages 4 through 5.
- Identifying major factors influencing physical and motor development.
- Identifying and describing health and well-being issues related to children ages 4 through 5.
- Suggesting strategies for enhancing physical and motor and perceptual-motor development in children ages 4 through 5.

## PHYSICAL AND MOTOR COMPETENCE OF CHILDREN AGES 4 THROUGH 5

Physical growth in children seems to follow four stages. From conception to 6 months, growth is dramatic. During the toddler/preschool period, the growth rate tends to level off and proceed at a steady pace until puberty. Then the growth rate increases dramatically for a time and slows again until adult growth is achieved. The growth rate in children ages 4 through 5 is steady, with children gaining 2½ to 3½ inches in height and 4 to 5 pounds in weight each year until around age 6. Each child grows at his or her own rate, although the patterns of growth are fairly predictable. How tall, heavy, or well coordinated a child is depends on heredity, general health, health history, nutrition, emotional well-being, and opportunities for physical and motor activity.

Body proportions change from the chunky, top-heavy look of the toddler to a more lean and upright figure. The child's head, which at age 2 is one-quarter of the total body length, is about one-sixth of the total body length by age 5 to 5½. The brain reaches 90 percent of its adult weight by age 5, and myelination of the brain is fairly complete, making more complex motor abilities possible.

Boys and girls during this age period have similar physiques, both losing the baby fat of earlier years and gaining more bone and muscle. However, boys tend to have more muscle at this age, while girls tend to have more fat. Changing body proportions include a larger chest circumference and a flatter stomach, longer arms and legs, and feet that have lost the characteristic fatty arch pad of baby feet.

General health assessment of children during these growing years requires monitoring their height and weight gains. Regular measurements of height and weight provide a preliminary indication of health and nutritional status. Growth charts developed by the National Center for Health Statistics (NCHS), commonly used by health care professionals, provide a **percentile** measure for children at each age. These percentiles tells us how height and weight compare with those of the same age and sex. For example, if a 4-year-old girl measured 41 inches and weighed 39 pounds, the NCHS growth charts would pinpoint her growth at the 75th percentile. This means this 4-year-old's weight and height measures were equal to or greater than those of 75 percent of 4-year-old girls and lower than those of 25 percent of her same-sex age-mates.

*percentile:*
*a statistical measure that ranks subjects from lowest to highest based on a common characteristic or results of an assessment*

## LARGE MOTOR DEVELOPMENT

By ages 4 through 5 children are quite motoric. Having mastered walking and running, their movements are expansive and include coordination required in climbing, hopping, jumping, sliding, running, and so on. Their large motor skills generally include the following:

| *Age 4* | *Age 5* |
| --- | --- |
| Rides tricycle | Rides bicycle (may need training wheels) |
| Climbs stairs alternating feet | Descends stairs alternating feet |
| Balances on one foot for a short period | Balances on one foot to a count of 5 to 10 |
| Climbs playground equipment with agility | Experiments with playground climbing equipment |
| Enjoys creative responses to music | Enjoys learning simple rhythms and movement routines |
| Skips on one foot | Skips with both feet |
| Jumps easily in place | Hops on one foot in place |
| Throws a ball | Catches a ball |
| Likes to chase | Enjoys follow-the-leader |
| Walks a straight taped line on floor | Walks a low, wide kindergarten balance beam |
| Enjoys noncompetitive games | Enjoys noncompetitive games |

Facility in large motor development enhances the child's total development. Overall health and vitality depend on it, and autonomy and self-sufficiency are encouraged by it. Cognitive development is furthered through an ever-enlarging world in which to explore and discover. When a child experiences mastery over his or her movements, self-concept is enhanced, as is a sense of competence and self-confidence. Self-confidence generally leads to enhanced social interactions.

Opportunities to use, expand, and refine large motor coordination should comprise a significant portion of the child's day. Sufficient large motor activities lead to what Gallahue (1982) described as physical fitness and motor fitness. **Physical fitness** refers to muscular strength, muscular endurance, flexibility, and circulatory-respiratory endurance. **Motor fitness** refers to speed, coordination, agility, power, and balance. In considering children's needs for healthy, sturdy, well-coordinated bodies, it helps to be aware of these different aspects of physical and motor development (see Figure 11.1).

In a study of children enrolled in child care centers and nursery schools, Poest et al. (1989) provided some insights into physical fitness characteristics of preschool-age children. Through questionnaires completed by parents and teachers, these researchers revealed that (1) preschool children were not engaged in physical activity on a year-round basis—they showed more physical activity in spring and summer; (2) boys were more physically active than girls; (3) children whose parents were involved in year-round physical activity were more likely to be involved in physical activity themselves; and (4) children in nursery schools were more physically active than children in child care arrangements.

From their findings, these scholars expressed a number of concerns. The fact that child care and other early childhood programs often emphasize fine motor skills, academics, and social development while limiting opportunities for large motor activities raises concern about the general health of these children, as well as their later ability to participate fully in physical education opportunities. Year-round physical and motor activities provide numerous health benefits; these benefits are not realized if physical activities are forsaken due to seasonal and weather conditions. Teacher training seems to be a factor in recognizing the importance of and providing for large motor activity in preschool experiences. The need for teacher training to include an emphasis on motor development and physical fitness has been identified, as has the need for parents to be better informed about their children's physical and motor status. Physical health and fitness are viewed as prerequisites for healthy development in other domains—cognitive, social, and emotional.

Large motor fitness and physical fitness are enhanced through a variety of opportunities to engage in physically active exploits. Environments that allow children to run, jump, climb, skip, and dance facilitate this development. These environments for young children must be safe yet free of undue restrictions. Wise selection of toys and equipment to enhance motor development is also critical—wheel toys, large balls, bean bags, climbing and balancing apparatus, and music to encourage marching, dancing, and creative movement all encourage the use of large muscles.

*physical fitness:*
*a physical state in which muscular strength, endurance, flexibility, and the circulatory-respiratory systems are all in optimal condition*

*motor fitness:*
*a physical state in which motor coordination facilitates speed, agility, power, and balance*

## SMALL MOTOR DEVELOPMENT

Because motor development follows a head-downward direction, small motor development lags behind large motor controls and coordination. As large motor controls become more refined and coordinated, the muscles of the extremities come under more precise control, and children generally become equipped to perform a variety of small motor tasks (see list on p. 267).

## COORDINATION

The rhythmical integration of motor and sensory systems into a harmonious working together of the body parts.

## SPEED

The ability to move from one point to another in the shortest time possible over a short distance.

## AGILITY

The ability to move from point to point as rapidly as possible while making successive movements in different directions.

## POWER

The ability to perform one maximum explosive force.

## BALANCE

The ability to maintain one's equilibrium in relationship to the force of gravity in both static and dynamic movement situations.

**FIGURE 11.1**
Opportunities to use, expand, and refine motor coordinations enhance motor fitness. (Reprinted with permission from Simon and Schuster, Inc. from the Merrill/Prentice Hall text *Developmental Movement Experience for Children* by David L. Gallahue. Copyright © 1982 by Prentice Hall, Inc.)

*The task of pouring involves eye-hand coordination and kinesthetic sensitivity.*

*Age 4*

Exhibits self-help skills in dressing: some difficulty with zippers, small buttons, tying shoes

Pours from a pitcher

Works a puzzle of several pieces

Exhibits right- or left-handedness; occasional ambidextrous behaviors

Enjoys crayons, paint, clay, and other art media

Uses beads and strings, snap blocks, and various manipulative toys

*Age 5*

Dresses with ease

Ties shoes

Enjoys puzzles with many pieces

Exhibits right- or left-handedness

Enjoys drawing, painting, and using a variety of writing tools

Enjoys a variety of manipulative and construction-type toys

*prehension:*
*the act of grasping and gripping*

The ability to perform these small motor tasks becomes possible due to the maturation and emergence of prehension and dexterity. **Prehension** is the ability to grasp or grip an object and to let go of it. By age 5, grasping and prehension abilities are used to handle crayons, paintbrushes, beads and strings, pegs and peg boards, and other small manipulatives and to manage dressing and undressing with efficiency. Prehension follows a fairly predictable pattern of development, beginning in infancy and becoming more refined as the child gets older (see Figure 11.2).

*dexterity:*
*skill in the use of hands and fingers*

**Dexterity** refers to quick, precise movement and coordination of the hands and fingers. Though less refined at ages 4 and 5, dexterity is exhibited in the child's ability to maneuver small puzzle pieces into place with ease and efficiency; handle small buttons, fasteners, and zippers; sort playing cards; and write legible letters and numerals.

*lateralization:*
*the process whereby certain skills and competencies become localized in one or the other hemisphere of the brain*

Dexterity depends on brain **lateralization**, a neurological process in which certain abilities become located in either the left or the right hemisphere of the brain (Sperry, 1970). Handedness is an outgrowth of this developmental process. It is believed that it begins in infancy, when a preference for a left- or right-facing sleep position and a preferred reaching hand are observed. These infant preferences have been associated with later hand preference (Michel, 1981; Ramsay, 1980). Other behaviors, such as foot, eye, and head turning preferences, also result from lateralization. Foot preference is fairly well established from ages 3 to 5 years, though it sometimes emerges over a longer period of time. Handedness, however, may not be fully dominant until 6, 7, or 8 years of age (Bradshaw, 1989; Cratty, 1986; Gabbard, Dean, & Haensley, 1991; Hellige, 1990).

Handedness, whether right or left, facilitates the use of small motor abilities, leading to more refined coordination and hence dexterity. Some children ages 4 and 5 whose handedness is not clearly established use both hands with facility; some use one hand for one activity, such as eating, and the other for another activity, such as throwing or reaching.

## PERCEPTUAL-MOTOR DEVELOPMENT

Angela has just awakened from her afternoon nap. Hearing the voice of her grandmother visiting with her teacher across the room, she is further aroused. She sits up, rubs her sleepy eyes, clumsily retrieves her shoes, and makes her way toward the area from which she heard grandmother's voice. There she is greeted with hugs and questions about her day in the child care center. ■

Angela has just demonstrated a simple perceptual-motor sequence that involved hearing a sound (auditory sensation), recognizing and identifying the sound as that of her grandmother's voice (perception), and making a decision to walk to the source of the sound (locomotion).

Individuals come into the world equipped with an array of sensory abilities: touch, vision, hearing, smell, and taste. The sense organs provide information about what is going on around us and within us. The ability to make sense of these sensations—to interpret them—is called *perception.*

*kinesthetic:*
*the sensation of body presence, position, and movement*

Perception is dependent on adequate functioning of the sense organs and **kinesthetic** sensitivity (the sensation of body presence, position, and movement), along with

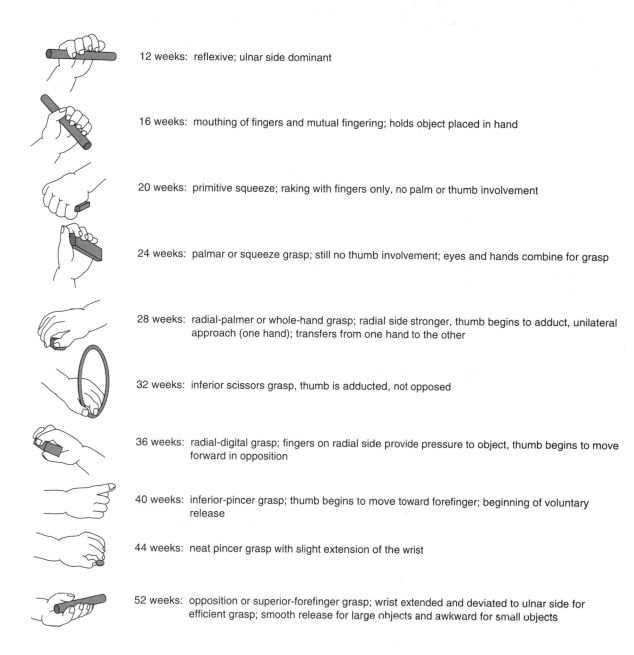

12 weeks:  reflexive; ulnar side dominant

16 weeks:  mouthing of fingers and mutual fingering; holds object placed in hand

20 weeks:  primitive squeeze; raking with fingers only, no palm or thumb involvement

24 weeks:  palmar or squeeze grasp; still no thumb involvement; eyes and hands combine for grasp

28 weeks:  radial-palmer or whole-hand grasp; radial side stronger, thumb begins to adduct, unilateral approach (one hand); transfers from one hand to the other

32 weeks:  inferior scissors grasp, thumb is adducted, not opposed

36 weeks:  radial-digital grasp; fingers on radial side provide pressure to object, thumb begins to move forward in opposition

40 weeks:  inferior-pincer grasp; thumb begins to move toward forefinger; beginning of voluntary release

44 weeks:  neat pincer grasp with slight extension of the wrist

52 weeks:  opposition or superior-forefinger grasp; wrist extended and deviated to ulnar side for efficient grasp; smooth release for large objects and awkward for small objects

**FIGURE 11.2**

Sequential development of grasp.  (Reprinted with permission of Simon and Schuster, Inc. from the Merrill/Prentice *Hall text Assessing Infants and Preschoolers* with Handicaps by Donald B. Bailey and Mark Wolery.  Copyright © 1989 by Prentice Hall, Inc.)

cognitive development and experience. Once a sensation is perceived, one must cognitively decide what to do with that information. Actions that follow are often motoric, for example, turning toward a sound, placing hands over eyes to shield them from a bright light, reaching for an object, and so on. Perceptual motor skills facilitate cognitive abilities, body awareness, spatial and directional awareness, and time-space orientation (Gallahue, 1982).

Perceptual-motor skills are fostered through activities that encourage the child to explore, experiment, and manipulate. Early childhood classrooms, for instance, include a variety of sensory activities: matching fragrance containers (olfactory); mixing and matching fabric patterns (visual) or textures (tactile), and cooking (taste). Musical and rhythmic activities integrate auditory and motor abilities as children respond to such elements as tempo and pitch (kinesthetic).

Children who do not master early sensory, perceptual, and motor skills will have difficulty with more sophisticated cognitive tasks in later school years. Perceiving shapes necessary for forming letters and numbers later on, attending to context cues in picture books, responding adequately to tone of voice as a clue to another's message, and interpreting facial and body language cues of others are tasks that rely on sensory, motor, and perceptual abilities.

## BODY AWARENESS, MOVEMENT, AND SIMPLE GAMES

Children ages 4 through 5 have mastered the basic locomotor skills of crawling, walking, running, jumping, rolling, sliding, and climbing. These skills evolve rapidly from infant reflexive activity, and do so without specific training. Through these unfolding abilities, the child's body awareness also emerges. Body awareness involves how the child perceives and feels about his or her body and what it can be willed to do. Body awareness is furthered through the child's visual, auditory, tactile, and kinesthetic perceptions. Particularly important to body awareness are the child's kinesthetic perceptual abilities, that is, the awareness of the body as a whole that occupies space and how one's body "fits" the available space, functions within it, and adjusts to it. This awareness includes **directionality, left/right dominance,** and **balance.** The ability to move from place to place without running into people or stumbling over objects includes kinesthetic perception, along with vision, hearing, and touch.

Body awareness becomes a powerful and driving force in all areas of the child's development: perceptual-motor, psychosocial, and cognitive. Body awareness is incorporated into the child's emerging sense of self and feelings of competence. Body awareness, which involves a sense of control, motivates the child to attempt increasingly complex physical motor activities and simple games.

Movement activities and simple games help to coordinate and refine fundamental body movements; establish directionality, balance, and left/right orientation; and enhance the development of more complex motor abilities. Movement activities and simple games are especially enjoyed by 4- and 5-year-olds as they continue to discover what they can will their bodies to do. They enjoy responding to music in spontaneous and creative ways, pantomiming, playing follow-the-

*directionality:*
*the perceptual awareness of direction*

*left/right dominance:*
*occurs when one or the other side of the body takes the lead in motor coordination activities such as eating or writing*

*balance:*
*a body awareness component in which postural adjustments prevent one from falling*

leader, and throwing and catching balls and bean bags. Balancing on one foot, jumping over obstacles, reaching the "highest" point, and walking a balance beam forward, sideways, and backwards become challenging and self-affirming activities.

Physically active games at this age are simple, noncompetitive, and often child created, with spontaneously established rules. Games serve important psychosocial functions in child development (as described in Chapters 9 and 12), as well as encouraging and enhancing the physical and motor well-being of the child.

## RELATIONSHIP BETWEEN PHYSICAL/MOTOR DEVELOPMENT AND PSYCHOSOCIAL DEVELOPMENT

### SELF-CONCEPT, SELF-CONFIDENCE, AUTONOMY, AND INITIATIVE

At ages 4 through 5 years, the child's self-concept is intimately associated with an awareness of the child's physical characteristics (hair, eye, and skin color, etc.), gender, capabilities, and feelings of competence. The young child's physical characteristics and emerging capabilities also influence the interactions the child has with others. These interactions provide positive and/or negative feedback that plays a major role in the formation of self-concept. A child viewed as physically or psychosocially "attractive" may receive different feedback than a child viewed as difficult or "unattractive." In turn, the child's interactions with others exhibit various responses ranging from ignoring or chastising to enjoying and affirmation. These interactions influence in both subtle and overt ways subsequent responses, subsequent interactions, and ultimately the child's sense of competence and self-confidence. The more competent a child views herself or himself to be, the more likely the child will become autonomous and eager to take initiative.

This point is particularly poignant in the case of young children with disabilities who sometimes have difficulty finding acceptance by others. Helping these children to develop their physical/motor attributes and self-help skills to the greatest extent possible builds self-confidence, which motivates further efforts and practice. This in turn leads to increased use of physical and motor abilities, building confidence and positive self-regard. When children feel accepted, appreciated, and self-confident and enjoy greater control over their own bodies, their interpersonal relationships are enhanced.

## RELATIONSHIP BETWEEN PHYSICAL/MOTOR DEVELOPMENT AND COGNITIVE DEVELOPMENT

As at earlier ages, children's emerging physical and motor capabilities expand their horizons and afford them new opportunities to learn about the world around them. The 4- to 5-year-old's interest and participation in real-world events that invite the use of motor abilities further cognitive development. A trip to a farm for a pony ride, assisting with selected household chores, responding to music with movement and dance, manipulating books to explore the world of print, performing a broad array of small motor tasks, taking some responsibility for one's own hygiene, health, and safety (discussed in the next section), and participating in the establishment of safety and health maintenance rules and procedures are but a few events that relate physical and motor development to cognitive development.

## LEARNING TO BE RESPONSIBLE FOR OWN HEALTH AND SAFETY

Children at ages 4 through 5 years are coming to understand the importance of such health and safety factors as eating, sleeping, resting, and exercise and can now be taught to assume some responsibility for themselves. Of course, children at this age cannot be expected to protect themselves without adult supervision, teaching, and encouragement. Nevertheless, their cooperation can be elicited in these health and safety areas:

- Regular brushing of teeth
- Predictable naptime and bedtime routines
- Understanding the need for nutritious rather than "junk" food
- Appreciating the need for regular medical and dental check-ups and immunizations
- Recognizing potential hazards (hot items, strangers, electrical items, poisons, unsafe toys, playground and other environmental hazards, streets, driveways, and other traffic hazards, etc.)
- Abiding by household and family rules (e.g., television usage, careful choice of computer and video games, appropriate time and place for certain behavior and activities).
- Consistently using car safety seats or restraints
- Answering the phone or door as instructed
- Understanding where to use or play with certain items, such as tricycles or other wheeled toys, and which toys or equipment require adult assistance
- Learning full name, address (with zip code), phone numbers (with area code), parent's name(s), where to find their work phone numbers; how to call for help; and so on

Cognizance of these issues begins the process of developing good health and safety habits, and taking appropriate precautions. Responsibility for one's own health and safety emerges slowly and sporadically over a course of many years. Children's emerging capabilities and growing sense of responsibility, however, never absolve the adult of responsibility for providing continuing and conscientious supervision and protection. It is easy to assume that young children are more capable in this area than they actually are, but their behaviors are at best inconsistent due to their limited long-term memory, limited or inconsistent opportunities to practice, adult inconsistencies in expectations and routines, distraction by more exciting things to do, and eagerness to explore

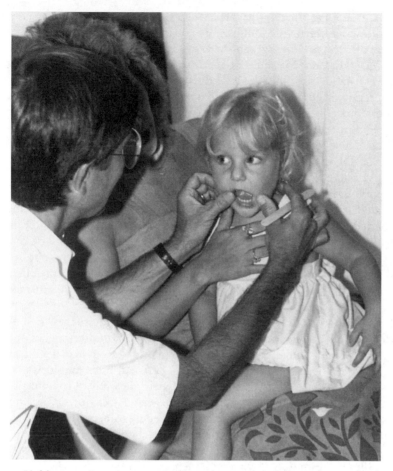

*Children need guidance in developing good dental hygiene.*

and learn about other things. Therefore, the major responsibility to provide safe, hygienic environments and developmentally appropriate experiences and expectations remains with adults. Adults continue to be the child's most powerful role models.

## GENDER CONSTANCY

By age 3, children accurately label themselves as boys or girls. However, gender constancy, the realization that one's gender remains the same regardless of changes in appearance, age, clothing, hairstyles, individual wishes, or other factors, begins to emerge between the ages of 5 and 7 (Kohlberg, 1966). Some scholars have associated this development with the cognitive ability to classify and conserve (Leahy & Shirk, 1984; Marcus & Overton, 1978), an ability that begins to emerge around age 6 or 7 (Piaget, 1952). Development of gender constancy seems to follow a pattern with children attributing gender constancy to themselves before others (Eaton & Von Bargen, 1981). The most frequently observed pattern is (1) gender constancy for self, (2) gender constancy for same-sex others, and (3) gender constancy for individuals of the opposite sex.

Emerging gender constancy brings an awareness that boys and girls, and men and women, differ in a number of ways, not the least of which is anatomy. As children begin to realize that anatomy rather than other factors defines gender, they become interested in the human body. Young children are curious about the physiological differences between boys and girls and between men and women. They observe and compare the anatomies and behaviors of each, forming ideas, some stereotypical, about male and female anatomy, roles, and behaviors. They imitate male/female behaviors in their sociodramatic play, experimenting with "being" either male or female. Some of their behaviors evoke chagrin or consternation on the part of adults: asking direct questions about body parts and their functions, giggling about and teasing or ridiculing members of the opposite sex, engaging in "bathroom talk", and playing "doctor." These normal behaviors indicate a growing awareness and need to find acceptance and satisfaction in one's own gender identity.

Adult responses to these behaviors influence the outcomes of positive or negative gender identity and gender role acquisition. A frank, matter-of-fact approach is certainly preferable to shock, embarrassment, or avoidance. Children need adults to help them learn about the differences between boys and girls and to do so with honest and straightforward answers to their questions. Providing accurate labels, discussing gender roles and behaviors, setting examples, and modeling healthy gender identity and self-acceptance are necessary to building accurate and positive concepts in children. Children must feel comfortable and safe asking questions as they arise. Adults must keep in mind that as children establish gender constancy, they are intensely interested in gender-role behaviors and are particularly interested in and attentive to gender-role models.

## FACTORS INFLUENCING PHYSICAL AND MOTOR DEVELOPMENT

### GENETIC MAKEUP REVISITED

Genes control the child's rate of development, dictating when motor abilities will emerge, growth spurts will occur, teeth will erupt, and adult growth will be achieved. Each individual has inherited a genetic blueprint from his or her parents. This blueprint determines such characteristics as gender, blood type, skin color, hair color and texture, eye color, stature, intellectual potential, temperament, sociability, and a host of other characteristics that make each person unique and explain the enormous array of differences among people. Optimal development relies on healthy genetic traits and supportive, healthy environments.

Because each child grows at her or his own pace, comparisons with siblings or age-mates can be very misleading. Each child's growth occurs according to the child's own biological blueprint. Adults should be cognizant of their expectations and their reactions to individual developmental accomplishments. For instance, a parent or teacher who conveys disappointment to a 4-year-old child who fails to achieve mastery over the use of scissors is exerting unfair expectations on the child, who simply does not have the requisite biological maturity for such mastery. Undue pride in developmental accomplishments over which the child has no control is equally misleading; the child is simply exhibiting observable manifestations of an inner developmental plan.

In the emergence of attributes and skills, the interactions of heredity and environment undoubtedly play a role. Height and weight, for instance, depend on nutrition and other health factors. Motor coordinations relies on opportunities to move about, explore, discover, and practice emerging abilities. Certain personality characteristics, such as activity level, fearfulness, and sociability, which seem to be inheritable traits, are influenced by interactions with others. Adequate health care, proper nutrition, freedom from accidents and stress, appropriate expectations, and sociocultural factors all contribute to the full realization of a person's genetic potential. So we are reminded that while individuals carry blueprints for development when they are born, the development that occurs is intertwined with and dependent on environmental influences.

## SOCIOCULTURAL INFLUENCES REVISITED

Cross-cultural studies have revealed that people from different ethnic groups vary in expected physical height, weight, and motor skills development. While there are always exceptions, children of North American and European ancestry are generally shorter than children of African ancestry. Children of Asian ancestry are usually shorter than North American and European children. Differences in body proportions also reflect cultural differences among groups. For instance, children of African descent develop relatively long legs and arms and narrow hips. In contrast, Asian children usually develop shorter legs and arms and broader hips (Eveleth, 1976).

Higher activity levels and precocious motor abilities are attributed to African American children (Morgan, 1976). In preschool, this higher activity level is often misperceived as "hyperactivity" and can result in inappropriate adult responses.

Adults who are aware of individual differences among children are more accurate in their developmental observations and assessments. Opportunities for enhanced growth and development can be provided when adults are aware of the attributes children bring to the learning situation.

## CHILDREN WITH SPECIAL NEEDS AND INCLUSION PRACTICES

Many types of disabling conditions affect young children, and with varying degrees of severity. Early diagnosis is critical to efforts to intervene and prevent complications and serious developmental problems. With the reauthorization of public laws such as Education for all Handicapped Children Act of 1975, 94–142; Education of the Handicapped Act Amendments of 1986, 99–457; and Education of the Handicapped Act Amendments of 1990, 101–476, which mandate early screening and identification of children with disabilities, early diagnosis has become widespread practice. Children who previously were not served or were poorly served by existing programs may now benefit from stimulating and enriching educational opportunities, with ongoing growth and developmental assessments and the provision of needed medical, nutritional, psychological, or other health care services. These services, along with appropriate and enriching educational and psychosocial experiences, facilitate optimal growth and development.

As screening for at-risk children has become widespread, potential for its abuse has become a concern. Professionals in child development and early childhood education stress the importance of standards in the selection of screening instruments and in the qualifications of individuals who screen and diagnose (Meisels, 1989). Programs to which children are assigned must meet professional standards of quality and developmental appropriateness.

During the assessment and placement process, early childhood professionals must prepare children for their inclusive classrooms and prepare the classroom and curricula to support the inclusion process. To prevent unwanted complications such as poor adjustment and unsuccessful experiences, DeHaas-Warner (1994) suggests three categories of variables to be addressed during the decision-making process:

1. The child's individual characteristics and needs
2. The parents' attitudes and concerns regarding the placement of their child in an inclusionary setting
3. The program's physical and affective characteristics

## GENERAL HEALTH AND FREEDOM FROM DISEASE

Children ages 4 and 5 are more likely to attend prekindergarten and kindergarten programs, and some are enrolled in before- and after-school programs in which they are around other children. Children in groups expose one another to a variety of minor illnesses—ear infections, colds, flu, and an assortment of upper respiratory ailments. Children in preschool programs are at greater risk for contracting gastrointestinal infections with diarrhea.

To ensure continuing good health and freedom from diseases, homes, schools, and child care programs must follow a regimen of frequent and thorough cleaning and observation of all children for signs of illness or infection. Providing children with regular, nutritious meals and snacks, predictable rest and sleep schedules, plentiful exercise, and instruction in hygiene, as well as cutting down on stress-producing events in children's lives, facilitates the maintenance of good health and growth-enhancing environments. This aspect of physical and motor growth and development is expanded on later in this chapter.

## NUTRITION

As with the infant and toddler, the nutritional needs of the child ages 4 through 5 continue to be important. Appetites begin to wane as children get older, and food

---

FIGURE 11.3
DEC Position Statement on Goal One of America 2000

---

*The Division for Early Childhood (DEC) of the Council for Exceptional Children (CEC) developed a position statement on America 2000 and the first goal: "All children will start school ready to learn." They requested NAEYC support for this position statement, and it was given after staff review that confirmed that the statement is congruent with existing NAEYC position statements. The position statement is reproduced below.*

Schools should be ready to accept and effectively educate all children. Schooling will succeed or fail, not children.

When we say *all* children, we do mean all—including children with disabilities, children placed at-risk for school failure, children of poverty, children who are non-English speaking, children with gifts and talents.

Reaching Goal One requires healthy and competent parents, wanted and healthy babies, decent housing, and adequate nutrition.

Quality early education and child care should be a birth right for all children. These services must be comprehensive, coordinated, focused on individual family and child needs, and available to all families that need and choose to use them.

It is not approriate to screen children into or out of early education programs. All children must be given a legitimate opportunity to learn.

Education in the 21st century must attend to children's social and emotional growth and development, not merely focus on academic outcomes.

Early educators must be schooled in and encouraged to use a wide variety of developmentally appropriate curricula, materials, and procedures to maximize each child's growth and development.

Achieving long-term academic goals does not imply that young children be drilled in English, science, and math. These academic goals are best achieved when young children are provided with environments that encourage their eager participation, exploration, and curiosity about the world.

No important social aims are ever achieved by rhetoric. Reaching this goal will require strong and continuing leadership, a wise investment in human and related capital, and collaboration between families, service providers, government, and business.

*Source:* Holder-Brown, L. and H. P., Jr., Parette (1992). Children with Disabilities who use assistive technology: Ethical considerations. *Young Children, 47 (6),* pp 73–77. Reprinted by permission of the National Association for the Education of Young Children.

preferences and aversions begin to emerge. Parents and adults, anxious to provide adequate and nutritious meals and snacks for preschool children, are often perplexed when children show little interest in or even distaste for some foods. There are logical explanations for these behaviors, however.

Children ages 4 through 5 are becoming more verbal, conversational, and social, and enjoying their interactions with others. For them mealtimes, especially when parents and siblings convene to eat together, are coveted times for sharing and talking with family members. Thus, mealtimes should be times when interruptions are kept to a minimum and stresses of the day and squabbling among family members discouraged. For both physical and psychological reasons, mealtimes should be pleasant and stress free.

The eating behaviors of young children reflect their changing growth patterns and physiological and psychological needs. Children at ages 4 and 5 are growing less rapidly than in previous years and thus require less nourishment to support their growth needs. At the same time, food preferences are emerging that reflect the child's growing ability to recognize and differentiate tastes, a desire to make choices, and a growing sense of autonomy and initiative, both at home and in other settings. The ability to help oneself to available foods and snacks at age 4 and 5 fosters a sense of independence and control.

Food preferences change as children experience various food events. Changes in food preferences may reflect the influence of older siblings, or perhaps playmates who share mealtimes in preschool settings. Television advertising also influences the child's food preference. A previous illness may become associated with a certain food, making it aversive for a time. Adults should recognize that fluctuations in appetite and in food preferences are normal and should expect them to occur from time to time. As with most adults, there may also be certain foods that a child may never like.

Children's diets must supply sufficient nutrients to meet the needs of growing bones and muscles, promote healthy formation and eruption of permanent teeth, and sustain continued growth and development of all body tissues and organs. Much energy is needed to sustain the high activity levels typical of young children. In addition, activity levels in children vary; more active children may need more food than less active ones of the same age and size.

Because preschool children have decreased their intake of milk, iron-fortified cereals, and nutrients such as calcium, phosphorous, iron, and vitamins A and C from levels consumed during the infant/toddler period and, as a rule, dislike many vegetables, there may be a need to expand the variety of foods available to them and to provide more nutrient-dense foods. Children ages 4 through 5 continue to expend a large amount of energy and need sufficient calories and nutrients to sustain growth and energy needs.

Recent studies of variability in calorie intake among children ages 2 to 5 years found that the amount of food consumed at individual meals was highly variable from meal to meal, yet the child's daily overall calorie intake was fairly constant (Birch et al., 1991a, 1991b). Meager consumption of food at one meal therefore may be offset by greater consumption at later meals. These findings suggest that children tend to adjust their own calorie needs over a 24-hour period.

---

### □ □ □   BOX 11.1    CHILDHOOD FOOD PREFERENCES

Childhood food preferences reflect
- Cultural practices and preferences
- Peer and sibling influences
- Television and other media advertising
- Naturally occurring fluctuations in the child's interest in certain foods
- Transitory "food jags"
- The child's ability to manage the food—ease in self-feeding, chewing, swallowing
- Food allergy
- A temporary aversion to certain foods associated with an unpleasant experience (e.g., being reprimanded or embarrassed at a time when the food was being consumed; an illness associated with a particular food; same food served too often)
- Associating food with a particularly pleasant memory (e.g., eating at grandparents' or a friend's house; a special occasion; or a holiday dinner)
- Appeal of the food itself based on temperature, texture, color, aroma, size of serving, compatibility with other foods on the plate, cleanliness of eating utensils, dishes, and eating surfaces, aesthetics associated with the table or eating surroundings
- The child's level of cognition and accompanying ability to associate certain foods with good health and feeling good while recognizing food of little nutritional value and learning to reject such foods
- Parental pressure to eat certain foods or "everything on your plate."

---

Two important points need to be made. First, coercing children to eat is of little value and can have psychological as well as physiological consequences. For instance, it can reduce a child's ability to determine satiety, leading to a "clean your plate" syndrome that persists beyond childhood. Second, adults have a responsibility to provide a variety of nutrient-dense foods and to create an environment conducive to food enjoyment. They must also learn to trust children to determine for themselves whether and how much to eat.

Pioneering research on the self-selection of diets by very young children (infants to age 5 years) conducted by pediatrician Clara Davis in the 1920s and 1930s yielded some interesting insights for anxious parents and early childhood professionals. By allowing young orphans who were being housed in a Chicago hospital to select from a "buffet" of assorted nutritious foods, Dr. Davis found that the choices children made over time (though quite variable and unpredictable, such as spinach for breakfast for several days in a row) met their nutritional needs quite well (Davis, 1938). These findings have influenced child-feeding practices and expectations over the past 60 years.

However, before assuming that young children can and will consistently balance their own diets to meet their nutritional needs, note that the menus in Dr. Davis's studies were composed of very basic foods, such as fresh fruits, vegetables, eggs, fish, beef, and oatmeal, that were not combined with other foods or ingredients. Also, unlike today's foods, these foods contained little sugar, salt, spices, preservatives, fat, and so on. Fast food and TV dinners were not options in the era of Davis's research.

A number of issues relating to foods and children have surfaced in recent years, including the relationship between certain foods and behaviors (e.g., sugar and food additives with hyperactivity), cholesterol and later heart disease, obesity in children and its causes and prevention, fast-food diets, and insecticides and cancer. While some hyperactive children may benefit from altered diets (Lipton & Mayo, 1983), well-controlled scientific studies have not been able to substantiate a strong association between food additives and unusual behaviors or mental performance in children.

With regard to cholesterol in children's diets, in recent years the American Academy of Pediatrics Committee on Nutrition (1983, 1986, 1993) set forth recommendations regarding a "Prudent Life Style and Diet." The recommendation proposed that nutritional adequacy is best ensured through a varied diet that limits saturated fat, cholesterol, and salt. This committee and the National Cholesterol Education Program (1992) asserted that dietary fat should not be reduced during the first year of growth and development and reduced only slightly during the second year, in which skim or partly skim milk might be introduced. Thereafter, the fat content of a child's diet should not represent more than 30 to 40 percent of the daily calorie intake.

Recommended food servings for children are shown in Box 11.2. As mentioned earlier, adults are responsible for providing nutritious and adequate diets for children. On the other hand, since hunger can be felt only by the child, the child should exercise control over how much to eat. Helping children to establish regular eating times, avoiding unnecessary snacks that are high in calories but low in nutrients, and encouraging adequate amounts of exercise and activity assist children in developing sound nutritional habits and preferences that will support their growth and ensure health and well-being.

---

❑❑❑  BOX 11.2       WHAT SHOULD YOUNG CHILDREN EAT EACH DAY?

| | |
|---|---|
| Milk, cheese, or yogurt | 2 to 3 servings |
| Bread or cereals | 4 to 6 servings |
| Fruits | 2 to 3 servings |
| Vegetables | 2 to 3 servings |
| Meat, fish, chicken, legumes, eggs, peanut butter | 2 servings |

## SAFETY

The primary causes of injury to children ages 4 through 5 are automobile accidents, falls, burns, choking, poisoning, drowning, and firearms. Automobile accidents are the leading cause; more children are killed by automobiles as passengers or pedestrians than by any other hazard. Auto accidents are also the leading cause of brain damage, spinal cord injury, and mental retardation (Aronson, 1991). Many automobile injuries are preventable through proper use of approved car seats and seat restraints for children. Children with disabilities may need special, crashworthy devices and equipment to be safely transported. Aronson suggests that early childhood professionals need to

1. Advocate safe automobile transportation procedures among parents and others who care for young children
2. Be responsible themselves when transporting children
3. Educate young children about how to be safe passengers and pedestrians

Playground safety is another concern during the early years. Playgrounds have recently come under serious scrutiny as the number and seriousness of playground accidents continue to rise. Joe Frost, an expert on playground design and safety, states:

American public playgrounds are perhaps the worst in the world. They are hazardous. In addition, most playgrounds are designed as though children's play needs are limited to swinging from bars and running across open spaces, as though children cannot think, symbolize, construct, and create. (Frost, 1992, p. 6)

According to Frost, playgrounds have two serious shortcomings. First, they are hazardous. This is due to nonexistent or inadequate regulations and lack of awareness by parents and early childhood professionals of appropriate standards for design and use of playgrounds and playground equipment such as the U. S. Consumer Product Safety Commission's *Handbook for Public Playground Safety* (1981a, 1981b, 1991). These guidelines assist planning and designing safe playgrounds. In addition, early childhood professionals must be trained to use playground time to enhance early growth and development and must take seriously their supervisory role and the need for ongoing surveillance of playground equipment to detect needed repairs.

Second, playgrounds are developmentally sterile, according to Frost. Ongoing research in recent years is yielding more and more insights into the value of well-designed and utilized playgrounds. Appropriate use of playgrounds enhances children's large and small motor skills, cognitive abilities, and social skills and helps meet therapeutic and emotional needs (Frost, 1992b). Frost (1992b, p. 7) admonishes,

Since play time is also learning time, it follows that play leaders should also be trained to assist the learning process. The common practice of using outdoor play time for teacher gossip and coffee break, albeit enjoyable and relaxing, is best reserved for designated breaks.

In addition to playground design and equipment, reports of home exercise equipment injuries are on the increase. Most common sources are entrapment of fingers or toes in stationary bicycle chains or wheel spokes. Eighty-three percent of extremity amputations were reported to have resulted from children touching moving parts of various home exercise equipment. (AAP, Jan., 1995)

Another common injury to young children is burns. Many young children are burned by tipped-over containers of hot food or drink, scalding bathwater, microwave-heated foods (which often have "hot spots"), heating equipment, matches, and cigarette lighters. All of these injuries are preventable. Children generally should not be in a food preparation area unless they are involved in a preparation-related activity that is being very closely supervised. Both formula manufacturers and pediatricians advise against heating foods for infants, toddlers, and young children in the microwave(AAP, 1993). Bathwater temperatures can be regulated by setting hot water heaters on lower temperatures. Heating equipment should be placed safely behind guards or out of child use areas.

Choking in young children can be prevented by making wise decisions about what and how to serve. Infants and toddlers are generally at higher risk for choking because of their tendency to put things into their mouths, their immature chewing and swallowing mechanisms, and their distractibility. Four- and 5-year-olds are also prone to choking, however.

Foods and objects most often associated with choking in young children are any small item less than 1/2 inches in diameter, nuts, seeds, spherical or cylinder-shaped foods and objects, buttons, small toys, rocks, grapes, pieces of hot dog, round hard candies, and items of certain consistencies such as chewing gum, popcorn, corn/potato chips, some uncooked vegetables and fruits, sticky foods (peanut butter, caramel candy, dried fruits, raisins), and hard-to-chew meats. The following suggestions can lower the risk of choking:

- Cook foods to a softness pierceable by a fork.
- Substitute thinly sliced meats and well-cooked hamburger for hot dogs.
- Cut foods into manageable, bite-size pieces; avoid slippery round shapes.
- Be sure to remove all packaging from foods, such as bits of clinging cellophane and paper.
- Remove bones in chicken, meats, and fish.
- Remove seeds and pits from fruits.
- Avoid the snacks and foods listed in the preceding paragraph.

In addition to careful selection and preparation of foods, supervision at mealtimes and snack times is a must. Children should be seated when eating, encouraged to eat slowly, and avoid talking and laughing with food in their mouths. Children should not eat while traveling in a car, since sudden jolts and stops can catapult food into the back of the mouth. Moreover, maneuvering a car out of traffic to tend to a choking child compounds the risk. Every adult should become familiar with the American Red Cross first aid procedures for handling a choking incident.

Poisoning is another major safety hazard for young children. Children can breathe toxins from polluted air, ingest some toxins by mouth, or absorb some poisons through the skin. Hazards exist in many forms: medicines, pesticides, aerosol sprays, gases, dusts, paints and solvents, commercial dyes, various art materials (inks, solvent-based glues, chalk dust, tempera paint dust, some crayons, paints, and clay powders). Toxins are also found in building materials (asbestos, formaldehyde, lead-based paint), lead-containing dishes and ceramics, tobacco smoke, and radon gas in soil.

Prevention of childhood poisoning involves both keeping toxic substances away from children and keeping children away from places where environmental toxins pose a hazard. At home, in child care centers, and at school, medicines, cleaning supplies, fertilizers, pesticides, and so on must all be kept well beyond the child's reach, and some should be stored in locked cabinets. Child care center and school licensing and accreditation standards, city ordinances, and state and federal regulations must be followed, and all potentially poisonous products must be used in strict accordance with physicians', pharmacists', or manufacturers' instructions.

Young children and water create an additional safety concern. Beginning quite early in the toddler period, children must be taught basic water safety. Infants, toddlers, and young children should never be left unattended in bathtubs, wading pools, or swimming areas. Basic water safety includes precautions such as wearing appropriate water safety devices, proper use of water toys such as floats, going into water only when an adult is present, avoiding breakable toys and dishes around bodies of water, and walking carefully on wet surfaces. Adults must establish and enforce water safety rules with children, know rescue techniques and CPR, and be especially vigilant around bodies of water. Providing swimming lessons for young children is somewhat controversial in that adults may develop a false sense of confidence in their children's abilities. For young children, the ability to swim is not accompanied by mature judgments about when and where to swim and what to do in an emergency.

Violence in the lives of children has escalated in recent years prompting many politicians and health care specialists to deem it a national health crisis. We discuss this topic in Chapter 14.

## OPPORTUNITIES TO INTERACT, EXPLORE, AND PLAY

Children have a natural impulse to be active—to run, climb, jump, hop, skip, shout, and ride wheel toys. Opportunities to develop and use these abilities occur when children are provided the space and developmentally appropriate equipment with which to do so. The development of large motor controls and abilities enhances self-concept, self-confidence, social interactions, and emerging small motor controls.

Because children need to be physically active, efforts to restrain and keep them quiet for long periods of time are unhealthy and usually futile. Preschool and kindergarten programs that require children to work at tables or desks or expect children to listen to teacher-directed lessons for extended periods of time are obviously developmentally inappropriate and curtail opportunities for more active and beneficial pursuits. The need for movement, for manipulation of real objects and concrete materials, and for social interactions and pretend play must be respected by adults who work with young children. Each child's day must include opportunities for movement about the classroom and the learning centers, for singing, creative movement and dance, and for use of equipment requiring large motor coordination. Outdoor play should be a daily event in every child's life where running, jumping, skipping, and other large motor activities and games can occur in safe and protected surroundings.

Lack of adequate physical activity impedes physical growth and development and motor coordination. Perceptual-motor abilities are adversely affected, which in turn affects later academic success. Psychological development is affected through reduced self-esteem and decreased social interactions. Both the amount and the quality of social interactions are affected when children do not participate in active play opportunities. Physical fitness—including strength, endurance, balance, and flexibility—is adversely affected. Lack of activity contributes to obesity, poor resting and sleeping habits, poor appetite, and other health problems. One can readily see the importance of opportunities for physical activities to the overall health and well-being of children.

## HEALTH AND WELL-BEING ISSUES RELATED TO CHILDREN AGES 4 THROUGH 5

### ENSURING GROWTH-ENHANCING EXPERIENCES AND ENVIRONMENTS FOR YOUNG CHILDREN

Most children enter some type of formal schooling around age 5; many begin the process of schooling at age 4. Some children enter nursery school and Head Start programs at age 3, and others are introduced to child care and education programs when only a few weeks old. Many children 3 years old and under are served in public schools through special education programs designed to ameliorate developmental anomalies. All of the states now provide public school kindergartens for 5-year-old children, and 32 states offered prekindergarten programs for 4-year-olds during the 1991–1992 school year (Children's Defense Fund, 1994b). Child care has become a basic necessity for many families along with food, clothing, shelter, and health care. In 1993, 54 percent of mothers with children younger than 3 and 64 percent of mothers with children ages 3 to 5 were in the labor force (Children's Defense Fund, 1994a).

These trends in our society have raised numerous health and safety issues and highlight the importance of growth-enhancing environments for young children. Because it is beyond the scope of this text to discuss in depth all aspects of quality, affordable child care, we have chosen three issues that are particularly relevant to this chapter: length of child care day and multiple caregivers, inclusion practices that serve the best interests of young children, and preventing accidents and the spread of disease among children in group settings.

### LENGTH OF CHILD CARE DAY AND MULTIPLE CAREGIVERS

Some public school programs for young children are half-day, (2 1/2 to 3 1/2 hours), some are "all" day (5 1/2 or 6 to 7 1/2 hours), and some range from 9 to

---

☐ ☐ ☐   **BOX 11.3**        **WISE SELECTION OF TOYS, PLAY EQUIPMENT, AND SAFETY GEAR**

1. Know the age, capabilities, and interests of the individual child for whom the item is intended.
2. Scrutinize the toy, play equipment, or safety gear thoroughly, and read labels and instructions carefully.
   a. For what age is the item intended?
   b. Are special skills or knowledge needed to use the item?
   c. Is the item appropriate given the child's large and/or small motor abilities, cognitive abilities, and interests?
   d. Is it made of nontoxic materials (avoid items that carry wording such as "harmful if swallowed," "avoid inhalation," "avoid skin contact," and "use with adequate ventilation").
   e. Is it motorized, electrical, or battery operated?
   f. Is it manufactured by a reputable firm? (Check Consumer Products Safety Commission reports or child health alerts and other publications for recall and safety histories of toys and play equipment).
   g. Does the item do what the manufacturer claims it will do?
   h. Is the item durable?
3. Examine the item for hazards such as lead-based paint, sharp or protruding points or edges, weak construction, small parts that can be swallowed or cause choking (watch for eyes, buttons, bells, and other features on dolls and stuffed toys), and flammable materials.
4. Determine what aspect of development is enhanced through use of the item.
   a. Physical development: large motor; small motor; prehension; pincer movements; eye-hand, hand-mouth, and eye-foot coordination
   b. Cognitive: exploration, curiosity, questions, solving problems, forming concepts, connecting ideas or actions, cause-and-effect understanding, making associations, further inquiry and new ideas
   c. Language and literacy: conversation; labels; new concepts; questions; interest in symbols (signs, letters, numerals); vocabulary and creative use of language through rhymes, storytelling, role playing, songs, and poetry
   d. Psychosocial: pure enjoyment, catharsis and therapy, symbolic play, sociodramatic play, interactions with others, expression of feelings, sense of self-sufficiency and self-confidence, fantasy, imagination, prosocial understandings
5. Determine whether the item can be used in a variety of ways and whether it will sustain interest over an extended period of time.

---

11 hours. Child care programs (center-based day care and family day homes) range from hourly care to 24 hours. The number of hours per setting per child each day varies. Often children of working parents are enrolled in before- and after-school programs resulting in as many as three different sets of nonparental caregivers (before, during, and after school). For some of these children, transportation from one setting to another means additional hours and stress.

The psychosocial impact of these multiple relationships is discussed in later chapters. Concerns for physical and motor development center around stress and fatigue associated with long days, multiple settings, various adult personalities and expectations, changing groups of children, and varying standards and group rules for protecting health and safety. Preventing fatigue and reducing stress entails

- Regularly scheduled and nutritious meals and snacks; ready access to toilet facilities and to fresh drinking water
- Regularly scheduled rest and naptimes, as well as rest periods as needed
- Teachers and staff who have knowledge of and training in child development and understand the effects of multiple settings and caregivers and long days on children
- Provision of outdoor playtimes for children to provide stress-relieving fresh air, sunshine, exercise, and spontaneous play
- Allowing children to make as many choices throughout the day as is reasonable and possible—choices regarding learning centers, materials and activities, playmates, snacks, and so on
- Allowing children to participate in classroom and group rulemaking to decrease the stress of dealing with multiple sets of rules and standards
- Careful observation of and attention to general health characteristics of individual children and prompt attention to signs of stress, fatigue, and/or impending illness

The complexities involved in providing multiple services through multiple settings and programs create a need for collaboration, coordination, and cooperation among all overlapping programs and services for children and their families. Many states have begun such initiatives to bring comprehensive services to children and their families (Task Force on Early Childhood and Elementary Education, 1994; Children's Defense Fund, 1994). Changing patterns of length of day and length of school year in public schools will necessitate serious efforts to establish linkages among child care providers, public schools, health and social services, and families.

## INCLUSION PRACTICES THAT SERVE THE BEST INTERESTS OF YOUNG CHILDREN

Including children with disabilities is both an opportunity and a challenge for early childhood programs and professionals. Planning for the safety of all children and preparing to meet the health-supporting requirements of children with special needs must be the first order of business for successful inclusion practice. Early childhood professionals will need to establish effective and ongoing communication with parents and other professionals involved in the care and education of children with special needs. Classroom layouts and other arrangements may need to be altered to facilitate these children's use and enjoyment of materials and activities. Special dietary requirements will need to be met in classroom food and nutrition lessons, snacks, parties, and so on. Children with visual or hearing difficulties will require making appropriate adjustments in seating and placing classroom visual materials (bulletin boards, charts, art displays, and so on) at comfortable levels and distances. Toileting areas will need to be reassessed, as will shelving and space for personal belongings, wheel chairs, or other equipment.

Special attention must be given to daily health routines of medication, meals and snacks, access to drinking water, toileting, rest and exercise, personal hygiene, and classroom cleanliness and order. The social and intellectual climate of the classroom must be accepting, comfortable, and psychologically safe. The teacher will play an important role in modeling and teaching acceptance and respect for all individuals.

It is imperative that early childhood professionals who have had little or no background in working with children with disabilities and their families seek additional training. This may entail redefining or expanding the perceived role of the early childhood professional. Preservice teachers will need to take advantage of college courses that address this important aspect of child growth, development, and education.

## PREVENTING ACCIDENTS AND SPREAD OF DISEASE AMONG CHILDREN IN GROUPS

In our quest for higher educational standards and performance at all levels of child care and education, cognitive and academic issues have come to overshadow both the teaching of nutrition, health, and safety and the importance of professional planning to meet the nutrition, health, and safety needs of children in group settings. It is thus quite enlightening that in ordering early childhood professional competency goals, the Child Development Associate (CDA) credentialing program places child health and safety first out of six major competency categories (Council for Early Childhood Professional Recognition, 1992): "To establish and maintain a safe, healthy learning environment." This competency is demonstrated by a CDA candidate's ability to

- Provide a safe environment to prevent and reduce injury
- Promote good health and nutrition and provide an environment that contributes to the prevention of illness
- Use space, relationships, materials, and routines as resources for constructing an interesting, secure, and enjoyable environment that encourages play, exploration, and learning (Council for Early Childhood Professional Recognition, Child Development Associate, 1992, p. 5).

Standards for safety and health protection of children in group care have existed since the turn of the century through governmental bodies and professional organizations. Concern over the spread of disease in early childhood settings in recent years has prompted considerable attention and renewed efforts of professional and medical groups to encourage policies and practices that ensure the health and safety of all children in group settings. Standards articulated by the

American Public Health Association and the American Academy of Pediatrics are comprehensive and exemplary (American Public Health Association & American Academy of Pediatrics, 1992).

The most common health-related risks in child care programs serving infants and preschoolers (ages 6 weeks to 5 years) are upper respiratory tract infections often associated with ear infections (otitis media), diarrheal illnesses, chicken pox, hepatitis, and Hemophilus influenza infection, which causes a number of illnesses, including respiratory infections, pneumonia, otitis media, and meningitis (Hurwitz et al., 1991). A number of factors are associated with health risks in children in groups, including the age of the child, the presence of older siblings in the home, duration of exposure, the size of the group or facility, and food handling and housekeeping practices.

In a nationwide study of respiratory illness associated with child care attendance, Hurwitz et al. (1991) concluded that at the time of their study, 7 to 12 percent of all respiratory illnesses in children younger than 5 years of age in the United States may have resulted from attendance in such programs. Interestingly, this study found that among children 3 to 5 years old who had been in child care for 27 or more months, there seemed to be a reduced risk of respiratory illness. Since upper respiratory illness is closely aligned with otitis media and potential associated complications, precautions and prevention are especially important (Wald, Dahefsky, & Byers, 1988; Osterholm et al., 1986; Kendall & Moukaddem, 1992).

Because children in groups share environmental surfaces such as tabletops, shelving and other furnishings, toys, sinks, and toileting areas, and are inclined to share food with unwashed hands, the spread of disease is inevitable if precautions are not taken. Further, young children are still inconsistent in health and hygiene habits such as washing face and hands, using and discarding facial tissue to contain a sneeze or cough or clear a runny nose. Bandages also present problems, as young children love to display this symbol of hurt and bravery. Taking the bandage off, examining the wound beneath it, and attempting to replace the bandage or carelessly leaving it about where others might handle it are common occurrences. To prevent the spread of infectious disease among children in groups, Kendall and Moukaddem (1992) make the following suggestions:

1. Frequent and thorough handwashing by both adults and children with warm water and soap, and drying with a paper towel upon arrival, after outdoor play, after cleanup, before and after food preparation activities and meals, and after a single contact with a possible source of contamination

2. Disinfecting toys and surfaces with a solution of 1/4 cup of bleach to 1 gallon of water, prepared fresh daily

3. Using disposable gloves (discarded after each use in a double plastic bag) when cleaning areas contaminated with blood, vomit, or excretions

4. Dressing children who are in diapers in clothing that fits snugly over the diaper

5. Employing grouping practices that limit the number of children assigned to groups so that infections within a smaller group are not spread to a larger population

6. Enlisting the expertise of health care professionals

To the extent that health protection policies and procedures such as these are followed, the spread of disease among children in groups can be limited. Adhering to guidelines for health and safety such as those mentioned above and those set forth in licensing and accreditation standards can further curtail the spread of infectious disease among children in group settings.

 *Role of the Early Childhood Professional*

## Enhancing Physical and Motor Development in Children Ages 4 Through 5

1. Provide safe and healthy surroundings for children.

2. Provide for the child's nutritional needs.

3. Oversee protection of child's health through immunizations and other protections from disease.

4. Encourage regular dental examinations.

5. Establish healthy routines for rest, sleep, play, and activity.

6. Control the stress-producing events in the child's life.

7. Provide encouragement for emerging large and small motor abilities and body awareness.

8. Provide age- and developmentally appropriate toys, equipment, and materials for the child.

9. Ensure the child's safety through adequate supervision, monitoring the types and condition of toys, materials, and equipment, and removing environmental hazards.

10. Provide opportunities for satisfying and supportive psychosocial interactions with parents, other adults, and other children.

11. Facilitate the child's awareness of health and safety practices.

12. Encourage a sense of responsibility for one's own health maintenance and safety. ■

## KEY TERMS

| | | |
|---|---|---|
| balance | lateralization | percentile |
| dexterity | left/right dominance | physical fitness |
| directionality | motor fitness | prehension |
| kinesthetic | | |

## REVIEW STRATEGIES AND ACTIVITIES

1. Review the key terms in this chapter individually or with a classmate.
2. Visit a school playground during recess for kindergarten and for second or third grade. Compare the types of activities and games in each group, including those used by children who are physically challenged. How do the activities differ? How do the children's large motor abilities in the older, younger, and physically challenged groups compare? How might recess be used to enhance physical and motor fitness in all children?
3. Plan a week of nutritious snacks for young children using a calorie and nutrient guide. What nutrients will children derive from these snacks? How many calories will be supplied?
4. Visit a toy store. Using the information in Box 11.3, make a list of acceptable and unacceptable toys or equipment for 4- and 5-year-old children. Consider culture, gender, and challenges faced by children with special needs.
5. With your classmates, develop a home safety checklist. Inspect your home for health and safety hazards for your own children or children who may visit in your home. What changes will you need to make?
6. Invite a pediatrician or pediatric nurse to speak to the class. Ask about his or her perceptions of the health status of today's children. What are this professional's greatest concerns about child health today? How might parents promote optimal growth and development in their children?

## FURTHER READINGS

American Public Health Association & American Academy of Pediatrics (1992). *Caring for our children: National health and safety performance standards: Guidelines for out-of-home child care programs.* Washington, DC, and Elk Grove Village, IL: Authors.

Aronson, S. (1991). *Health and safety in child care.* New York: HarperCollins.

Division for Exceptional Children Task Force on Recommended Practices (1993). *DEC recommended practices: Indicators of quality in programs for infants and young children with special needs and their families.* Reston, VA: Council for Exceptional Children.

Frost, J. L. (1992). *Play and playscapes.* New York: Delmar.

National Association for the Education of Young Children. (1994). *Child care and ill children and healthy child care practices*. Washington, DC: Author.

National Safety Council. (1993). *First aid and CPR: Infants and children*. Boston: Jones and Bartlett.

Shelov, S. P., and Hannemann, R. E. (Eds.). (1993). *Caring for your baby and young child: Birth to age 5: The complete and authoritative guide*. New York: Bantam Books.

# CHAPTER TWELVE

*And the first step, as you know, is always what matters most, particularly when we are dealing with those who are young and tender. That is the time when they are taking shape and when any impression we choose to make leaves a permanent mark.*

Plato

# Psychosocial Development
# Ages 4 Through 5

After studying this chapter, you will demonstrate comprehension by:

- Describing the psychosocial development of the 4- through 5-year-old child.
- Listing major social and emotional milestones in psychosocial development during this period.
- Identifying factors that influence earliest psychosocial development.
- Discussing the role of play in the development of social competence.
- Describing the role of adults in healthy psychosocial development of 4- and 5-year-olds.

In contrast to children during the turbulent toddler period, 4- and 5-year-olds are composed. Refinements in motor abilities have enhanced self-help and autonomy. Advances in cognitive development have sharpened the child's perceptions and increased understandings. Language development has opened new and more effective communications. An increased ability to delay gratification of needs and desires has led to more patient and negotiable interactions with others. The desire for and enjoyment of age-mates has expanded the child's social circle beyond attachment persons. These developments result in a period during which the child is more amiable, compliant, and socialized.

## EFFECTS OF EARLIER EXPERIENCES ON 4- AND 5-YEAR-OLDS

As the quotation by Plato suggests, for centuries philosophers and psychologists have hypothesized that events in the earliest years of a child's life influence later development, sometimes in critical ways. Centuries since Plato's admonitions, scholars continue to speculate on the relationship between early and later experiences. Sigmund Freud's (1905/1930) psychoanalytic theory, for instance, proposed that experiences and conflicts occurring during early psychosexual stages of development can have lasting effects on later personality development. Freud

293

placed considerable importance on the mother-infant relationship in influencing the child's interpersonal relationships.

Building on Freud's works, Erik Erikson's theory of psychosocial development (1963) supports an early experience/later development hypothesis. Successful outcomes at each of Erikson's eight stages of personality development are thought to prepare the child for subsequent stages.

Studies by Bowlby, Ainsworth, and other ethological theorists have examined the effects of early attachments on later psychosocial development. Securely attached infants have been shown to be more socially competent upon entering preschool and more responsive to their age-mates in kindergarten (Stroufe, 1983; Stroufe Schork et al., 1984). In other studies, securely attached children were found to be less dependent on adults and more curious than were children who had been insecurely attached (Arend, Gove, & Stroufe, 1979; Stroufe, Fox, & Pancake, 1983).

In contrast to the early experience/later development hypotheses, a life-span view of growth and development assures us that single events in early child growth and development do not result in behaviors that are not or cannot be modified as a result of later growth and development or subsequent life experiences. Indeed, throughout life, the potential for both positive and negative influences on growth and development exists. Sociocultural contexts and family interaction patterns influence the course psychosocial development takes (Rizzo, Corsaro & Bates, 1992). Guidance and discipline techniques, adult expectations, unusual or stressful events, individual or family life joys and successes, disappointments and traumas, and various role models influence the course of development over time. Consider these influences as we explore the very complex psychosocial development in 4- through 5-year-old children.

## INITIATIVE VERSUS GUILT

The 4- to 5-year-old has entered Erikson's third stage of psychosocial development (see Figure 12.1). Building on the previous stages of trust and autonomy, the child is now struggling between a sense of **initiative** and a sense of guilt. Of this stage, Erikson (1963) says:

*initiative:*
*The third of Erikson's psychosocial stages, in which the child pursues ideas, individual interests, and activities; when thwarted, the child becomes self-critical and experiences guilt*

There is in every child at every stage a new miracle of vigorous unfolding, which constitutes a new hope and a new responsibility for all. Such is the sense and the pervading quality of initiative. The criteria for all of these senses and qualities are the same: a crisis, more or less beset with fumbling and fear, is resolved in that the child suddenly seems to "grow together," both in his person and in his body. He appears "more himself," more loving, relaxed and brighter in his judgment, more activated and activating. He is in free possession of a surplus of energy which permits him to forget failures quickly and to approach what seems desirable (even if it also seems uncertain and even dangerous) with undiminished and more accurate direction. Initiative adds to autonomy the quality of undertaking, planning, and "attacking" a task for the

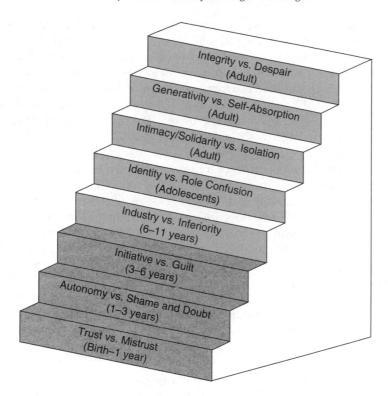

FIGURE 12.1
The child whose sense of initiative is emerging is eager to master new skills.

sake of being active and on the move, where before self-will, more often than
not, inspired acts of defiance or, at any rate, protested independence. (p. 255)

The child whose sense of initiative is emerging is eager to master new skills, use
language to ask questions to seek new meanings, and enlist others in work and
play interactions. The child's social circle is expanding rapidly beyond the attachment persons of earlier years, and interactions with others are vigorously sought.
Mastery of motor skills frees the child to try new feats, such as climbing on playground structures with greater agility or riding the bicycle without training wheels.
The child is eager to learn and genuinely enjoys those events that enlarge and
enrich understandings of an ever-widening world. The child enjoys planning and
cooperating with others and anticipating coming events or activities. Activities like
planning a family outing or cleaning the house or classroom for a special visitor
are pursued with exhilaration and a sense of shared purpose.

Initiative is used to engage others in conversation and to enlist playmates. Play
becomes more social and elaborate. Imitation, imagination, and fantasy lead to
complex and fluid sociodramatic enacting. Extended sociodramatic scenarios,
alone or with playmates, evolve. Sociodramatic scenarios extend, digress, and
diverge with new fantasies as playmates enter and exit the play group.

The developing sense of initiative is not always characterized by positive behaviors, however. Sometimes initiative gets out of bounds. Misdirected energy and enthusiasm can lead children to use physical or verbal aggression. Pushing a playmate aside to be "next" on the balance beam is an example of coercive and negative interactions in which the child attempts to control others. Coercion such as "I won't be your best friend" or "you can't come to my birthday party" are examples of misdirected initiative. In addition, growing facility with language increases the child's use of language to shock or perhaps to deceive, another form of misdirected initiative.

Out-of-bounds initiative can produce feelings of anxiety, embarrassment, and guilt as the child becomes aware that his or her behaviors are unacceptable to others. Unsure and socially unskilled, the child's sense of initiative is placed at risk, unless appropriate alternative behaviors are suggested. Adult guidance is needed to redirect initiative toward positive, more constructive outcomes. Guidance, however, must balance with control and freedom for the child. Failure to guide (undercontrol), or the opposite, overcontrolling, undermines the child's opportunities to succeed with initiating behaviors.

When a sense of guilt exceeds a sense of initiative, children tend to seek undue assurances and permission from adults and peers. They are reluctant to take personal risks, try new activities, or reach out to others for interactions, and often fail to fully enjoy their own emerging capabilities. Both under- and overcontrolling guidance techniques contribute to the development of a sense of guilt. Thwarted in efforts to initiate ideas, interests, and activities, or being teased, ridiculed, or treated as though their many questions are annoying or their pretend play silly, children may develop a lack of self-confidence that persists through later ages.

Initiative is fostered through opportunities to explore and engage in new and challenging activities. Four- and 5-year-old children must have expanded opportunities for social interactions, cooperative endeavors, and mind-engaging projects. They need raw materials from which to create, and space and props for fantasy and imaginative play. Children in this stage of psychosocial development need adults who answer their numerous questions with respect and focused interest. They need adults to encourage and support their unique interests and abilities. At the same time, children need protection from their impulses and help in developing effective social interaction skills. Child guidance must set reasonable limits on behavior, yet encourage children to trust their own ideas.

## EMOTIONAL DEVELOPMENT

Children, like adults, experience an array of emotions from joy and elation to sadness and despair. They express feelings of love, acceptance, frustration, anger, hostility, jealousy, shame, embarrassment, guilt, anxiety, fear, distress, depression, pride, humor, astonishment, yearning, and many more emotions. Expressions of emotion are exhibited in numerous ways: talking about emotional events or feelings, crying, shouting, withdrawing, irritability, pouting, distraction, inattentiveness, verbal exchanges with others, silliness, aggression toward self and others, self-deprecating comments, rejection of others and of efforts to console, destructive behaviors, among many others.

An immensely important developmental task of early childhood is learning about emotions and how to express them. This learning includes *labeling*, *understanding*, and *modulating* emotions. Aspects of this learning include the child's ability to cognitively grasp the concept of emotion, to take into account the types of situations that cause certain emotional reactions, and to understand how their own expressions of emotion affect others.

Labeling occurs as children are given names for emotions in specific situations or descriptors for emotion-evoking events. ("You are really *angry*." "Do you feel *unhappy* when your Dad and Mom are away at work?" "It makes all of us *sad* when someone dies." "When you feel *mad* at someone, let's talk about it." "I can tell that you are very *proud* of yourself." "We are all having such a *joyous* time at the picnic."). Such labeling is an important first step in young children's understanding of emotions.

Labels can go only so far, however. Extended dialogue with children about their feelings is important: what the feelings mean about our shared humanness; what kinds of situations evoke certain behaviors in all of us; how individuals respond in various contexts; while it is appropriate to feel in certain ways and in certain situations, there are appropriate and inappropriate, effective and ineffective, healthy and unhealthy ways to express and deal with feelings; and how the manner in which we express emotions affects others. These dialogues can explore positive and healthful ways to cope with emotional events and the feelings they create. Helping children define and cope with their various emotions is critical to their overall mental health and to their social efficacy, including their ability to relate to and empathize with others.

By the time children are 4 or 5 years old, they have some understanding of their own emotions and the emotions of others. They have the capacity to reflect on their feelings and have some idea that emotions persist for a time after the event that caused them. At this point, though self-control of emotions is far from established, the child is learning when and where certain emotional expressions are acceptable and to modulate expressions of emotion in ways that serve his or her best interests yet are minimally disturbing to others. Children acquire self-comforting strategies to help them cope with negative emotional events: regressing to thumb sucking, withdrawing to a more comfortable place, seeking the proximity of a trusted friend, diverting their own attention and conversations to other topics, and so on. The transitional object of earlier years often persists into early and later childhood. It serves as a very important self-comforting device for young children.

All of these strategies assist children in modulating their emotions, decreasing their intensity and sometimes their frequency. As children get older, they learn, as many adults have, to mask their emotions when they do not want others to be involved or when they realize the context and effects of their behaviors on their own sense of well-being and that of others. Learning to handle emotions and feelings in positive, socially productive, and self-affirming ways is a critical part of the socializing process and has lifelong implications for good mental health and rewarding social interactions.

## FEAR AND ANXIETY

Early studies of fear attributed its evolution to maturation and increasing cognitive development (Gesell, 1930; Jersild & Holmes, 1935a, 1935b; Jones & Jones, 1928). In one of the earliest studies of childhood fears, Jones and Jones wrote, "Fear arises when we know enough to recognize the potential danger in the situation but have not advanced to the point of complete comprehension and control of the changing situation" (p. 143).

Maturation and learning contribute to changes in fear behaviors from the infant/toddler period to ages 4 through 5. The 4- through 5-year-old child experiences a variety of fears due to insufficient experience, incomplete information or knowledge, and a variety of misconceptions:

> After the divorce of her parents, Josie feared her own impulses and behaviors lest she "cause" the other parent to leave her.

Some fears are due to the child's inability to separate fantasy and reality:

> In role playing the *Three Billy Goats Gruff*, Angela became so immersed in the drama that she began to cry and cling to the teacher in fear that the troll would harm her. For a time thereafter, she had nightmares, feared the dark, and resisted retelling the fairy tale.

Still other fears are learned through observation of fears modeled by parents, siblings, relatives, and friends:

> Franky's mother always referred to rain, regardless of amount of precipitation or accompanying elements, as a "storm." Her own childhood experience in a tornado had left a lingering fear of storms and a generalization to all rains as potential storms. Thus, she modeled fear of all rainy weather.

Fears are also learned through one's own experience. For example, a child who is bitten by a dog may fear all dogs, or perhaps all small animals, for a time.

The sources of fear and anxiety are numerous. All children experience fear and anxiety from time to time and in varying degrees of intensity. Yet not all childhood fears are the same. Some children fear the dark, others do not. Also, there are individual differences in the way children respond to fear stimuli. One child may quietly withdraw or hover unobtrusively near a trusted adult; another may cry loudly, cling desperately, and resist being consoled.

Many fears or anxieties serve important adaptive or "self-preservation" functions and, as such, are considered "healthy" fears. Fear of traffic, strange animals, motorized tools and equipment, fires, dangerous elevations, and firearms are healthy because they prompt appropriate avoidance behaviors. Some children do not develop a healthy fear of danger and require guidance and supervision to protect them from avoidable mishaps. Such guidance should be informative without arousing curiosity, which can lead the child into dangerous explorations. On the other hand, explanations should not exaggerate the danger or alarm the child.

Helping young children understand and cope with their fears is a matter of providing appropriate experiences, explanations, and encouragement. Children need age-appropriate dialogue and explanations that provide labels and insights. When

☐☐☐  BOX 12.1          VIOLENCE IN CHILDREN'S LIVES: THE ADULT'S ROLE

A dreadful phenomenon in modern life is the increase in violence in the lives of children. Even a decade ago, few of us could have predicted the prominence of this threat to the health, safety, and well-being of young children. The North American family experiences the highest rates of violence in the world (Gelles & Straus, 1988). Approximately 3.3 million children witness domestic violence every year (American Academy of Pediatrics, 1994c). Many more children witness severe violence in the form of shootings, knifings, and beatings. Many young children are victims of these crimes, with often fatal consequences. A debilitating result of all of this is a phenomenon known as *posttraumatic stress disorder (PTSD)*, a syndrome most often associated with war experiences (McNally & Saugh, 1993; Motta, 1994). Indeed, many children's homes and neighborhoods have become "war zones." Unlike children who live in countries where war is prevalent, American children can make no assumptions that someday the war will end. Hence, many believe that children who live in urban U.S. "war zones" experience more psychological problems than children in the Mideast (Kostelny, AAP News, May 1994, p. 13).

Violence surrounding children inflicts serious damage on children's sense of trust, safety, and well-being and has prolonged effects on their behaviors—effects that often last a lifetime and preclude healthy psychosocial development. Common effects are conduct disorders, antisocial behaviors, self-injurious behaviors, and the potential to become a child abuser as an adult (Wolfe & Korsch, 1994).

How might parents and teachers help children through the traumas perpetuated by violence in their lives? What does one do when children tell gruesome stories of crimes they have witnessed, show "artifacts" from the crime scene, reenact the crime during sociodramatic play, or demonstrate fear that borders on terror? Experts on this topic provide helpful suggestions (Garbarino, Kostelny, & Dubrow, 1991; Garbarino et al., 1992; National Research Council, 1993; Wolfe & Korsch, 1994):

- Encourage children to talk with a sensitive adult (teacher, caregiver, school psychologist/counselor, or relative) about the crime they witnessed or personally experienced.
- Encourage children to fantasize about what they would have had happen instead or what they wish they could have done.
- Help children know they are not at fault.
- Encourage children to draw or write about the experience. Ask what they wish could have happened or what a more civil event might be like.
- Allow children to tell their stories again and again to enhance understanding of the event and promote catharsis.
- Expect and accept regressive behaviors (bed wetting, thumb sucking, proximity seeking, whining, decreased verbalizations, reluctance to play with others), and respond to these behaviors in supportive and encouraging ways. Negative responses or threats of punishment only exacerbate the child's fears and anxieties.
- Be aware that many parents in these situations have exhausted their own physical, psychological, and economic resources and may themselves be coping poorly. Be supportive and nonjudgmental.
- Identify intervention programs and support groups and, when possible, help parents access these services.

(continued)

□ □ □    Box 12.1 (continued)

**How Might Early Childhood Care and Education Programs Help?**

- For young children, teaching about violence, gangs, drugs, and so on is best addressed in day-to-day teacher-child interactions and in the context in which a specific question or issue emerges. More formal approaches are ineffective with younger children and often fail to provide the therapeutic and healing qualities of personal interactions concerning specific experiences, fears, or concerns.

- Developmentally appropriate classrooms and instructional strategies can be particularly helpful for these at-risk children, as the environment should be child friendly, comforting, and aesthetically appealing and teacher behaviors nurturing, supportive, dependable, and predictable. Opportunities to talk, play, interact with adults and peers, utilize the expressive arts, participate in large motor activities and constructive outdoor play, and participate in myriad other growth-enhancing experiences help alleviate at least some of the effects of violence on children's development.

- By providing structure, predictable schedules, clear rules and standards, and socially competent role models early childhood programs can assist children in developing an inner sense of trust, security, and control.

- Placing children in small cooperative groupings help children to focus on tasks to be achieved.

- Providing personal spaces for children that are consistently and unvaryingly theirs until they feel less threatened helps children to find security in the school or child care environment. Demonstrating respect for the child's spaces and personal belongings is especially important.

- A psychologically safe atmosphere in which children can talk, make mistakes, try new ways of solving problems, and learn about conflict resolution helps children develop self-confidence, self-esteem, and more positive regard for others.

- Recognizing when children have experienced particularly stressful times (such as on weekends, when violent episodes seem more prevalent), and altering the curriculum by allowing them to engage in activities already mastered, rather than forcing them to attempt new subject matter or complex skills, helps children to focus and sustain their attention and enhances their sense of achievement, giving them the confidence to tackle new learnings.

- By recognizing that play is both growth and development enhancing and therapeutic for children, developmentally appropriate programs provide children with opportunities to engage in many play modes: talking, pretending, and interacting with others; using music, art, and rhythms to express feelings; and enjoying prosocial story and play themes.

- Advocating for in-school or other caregiving situations, counseling services, support groups, and other intervention programs to assist families at risk is rapidly becoming a responsibility of the professional early childhood educator.

adults are calm, encouraging, and knowledgeable, children are reassured. In time, some fears subside and disappear, new fears emerge, and new coping strategies become a part of the child's behavior repertoire.

## TRANSITIONAL OBJECTS

Although the importance of transitional objects varies from child to child, transitional objects continue to represent an important part of the psychosocial development of children ages 4 through 5. The duration of attachments to transitional objects also varies. For some children, the attachment is long-lived; for others, the attachment may be brief, perhaps even transitory from one object to another for varying periods of time. Affection for the transitional object(s) can be quite deep and openly expressed. At the same time, the object(s) can become the target of aggressive and serious mistreatment as children fantasize or work through emotional and social conflicts.

The need for the transitional object recedes as children shift their energies and attentions from themselves to others and from fantasy to real-life tasks. The child may then choose to carry the object in the car en route to school, but leave it there for "reunion" when the school day is over. Or the child may wish to carry it into the classroom, only to stuff it into a cubbyhole to be "visited" on occasion during the day. Sometimes symbolic substitutes signal a more mature approach. A symbolic substitute can take the form of a photograph of the child with the transitional object or a family photograph carried in the child's backpack or lunch box. Often classroom teachers provide bulletin board space for children's photographs of themselves and their families.

Children themselves must make the decision to give up the transitional object. Coercion, disparaging remarks, ridicule, or other attempts to separate the child from the transitional object only serve to intensify the child's resolve to cling to it (Jalongo, 1987). Adults must accept the child's right to refuse to share the transitional object with others. Sometimes the child's maturity in other areas leads adults to believe that the child should have outgrown the need for the transitional object, but it does not necessarily signal a readiness to abandon it.

Jeremy's interest in astronomy has found support in books provided for him by his parents and teachers. Though beyond the expected reading abilities for his years, Jeremy reads his astronomy books with some facility. Each morning his backpack is carefully prepared for school with one or two of his current favorite astronomy books *and* his well-worn teddy bear. For the duration of kindergarten, Jeremy carries his teddy bear to school with him, carefully tucked into his backpack. Wisely, neither his parents nor his teachers discourage this practice. ■

## SOCIAL COMPETENCE IN THE YOUNG CHILD AGES 4 THROUGH 5

Jeremy has brought to kindergarten a large, multiple-color water painting set that was purchased for him the preceding day. He proudly shows it to some of his classmates. Many of them offer to play with him if he will share the water paints. Since the water paints are still new to him, Jeremy emphatically replies, "No, not now! No one can use my paint set." He then retreats to a table to work alone with his paints. One or two persistent classmates follow him to the table and continue to beg and prod. Finally, Jeremy capitulates, "OK, Madeline, you can paint with me, but Joey, you can't paint with us. Maybe tomorrow I will let you paint."  ■

Frequently toys from the sociodramatic center are finding their way into the restroom and remaining there until the teacher retrieves them. In addition to becoming soiled, the toys are "lost" and unavailable to others who want to play with them. Angela's teacher convenes a class meeting to discuss the situation. After explaining her concerns about the availability and cleanliness of the toys, she asks the class to help her find a solution to this problem.

Thomas asserts that whoever is doing that should get a spanking. Geraldo insists that if the toys are really lost or too dirty to play with, his daddy will buy another one. Katie suggests that if they get dirty, her mommy can wash them. Rashid implores the teacher to throw the toys away, as they might be "really, really, really dirty!"

Sensing the direction the discussion is going, the teacher attempts to bring the children back to the central issue: responsibility for the care of classroom materials. "You have made some interesting suggestions and have been very thoughtful; we all appreciate that. However, I am still wondering if there is something we ourselves can do right here in our classroom and not involve people who are not here with us every day."

Carson suggests, "We could wash our own toys in the sand-water table."

Then Angela, after moments of musing and listening and with a look of earnest contemplation, suggests, "We can put a sign on the toilet door that says 'No toys allowed' to remind everybody not to take toys in there." Her classmates agree and talk about who will make the sign.

The teacher further enlists the children: "Is there anything else we can do?"

Angela, her problem-solving abilities taxed to the limit, asserts, "They will just have to remember not to do that."  ■

Each of these vignettes illustrates different levels of emerging social competence. How would you characterize a socially competent person? Does that person demonstrate any of these characteristics: positive self-regard, self-confidence, curiosity, spontaneity, humor, warmth, reliability, sense of right and wrong, self-discipline, morally responsible behaviors, awareness of the needs of others, positive interactions with others, genuineness, friendliness, cooperation, problem-solving ability, adaptability, helpfulness, and/or ability to give and receive praise? We could list many more characteristics describing the socially competent person. Which of these or other descriptors did Jeremy display? What characteristics describe Angela's social competence?

While we can describe social competence and certainly appreciate its value in social interactions, a concrete definition has been difficult for theorists to construct, particularly in terms of measuring social competence achievement (Raver & Zigler, 1991). However, for the most part, experts agree on the origins or antecedents of social competence:

1. Social competence emerges from *social development*, in which the child exhibits a growing awareness of others and chooses to interact or not to interact with them. Social development includes establishing a repertoire of strategies for initiating interactions and ways to sustain them. Feelings and

responses evoked by social interactions determine the extent (or the persistence) to which the child is motivated to pursue further social interactions.

2. The *socialization processes* and *sociocultural contexts* in which children grow and learn impose values, beliefs, customs, and social skills that have been transmitted to children from one generation to the next and teach them the expectations of their families and cultural groups. Consequently, children in different cultural groups develop unique social abilities and understandings that allow them to succeed in a particular sociocultural context. Parents are generally the primary socializing agents; other socializing agents include siblings and other extended family members, family friends, and neighbors. The socialization of young children is also influenced by out-of-home experiences such as those in church preschool, observing other people in many different places and contexts, and the media.

3. *Social cognition* refers to the ability to make social judgments on the basis of what one perceives to be the viewpoints and expectations of others. It is characterized in part by a growing awareness of the effects of one's own behaviors on others. Thus, aggressive behavior may be self-controlled through an awareness of how aggression hurts others. On the other hand, a child learns that empathic behaviors evoke warm and friendly responses from others.

With this introductory information about social competence, let us now explore some aspects of growth and development that precede and lead to greater social competence in young children. Egocentric behaviors, prosocial development, positive self-concept, gender understandings, self-control, moral development, and awareness of diversity and individual differences all influence the development of social competence and the child's emerging abilities to make, sustain, and benefit from positive interactions with others.

## EGOCENTRIC BEHAVIOR

Few kindergarten teachers would disagree that 4- and 5-year-old children exhibit egocentric behaviors. Fifteen 4- or 5-year-olds in a group often present 15 or more competing requests for the teachers's attention:

- In the middle of a finger-play, Jeremy discovers a hangnail on one of his fingers, leaves his seated position, and climbs over the group to show his injured finger to the teacher.

- Upon arrival at kindergarten, Angela tempts her teacher with "Do you want to see what I brought in my lunch today?"

- During the school nurse's demonstration of handwashing, Kari interjects, "You know what? My daddy washed his new car last night."

- Lawanda shouts from across the room, "Teacher, Shannon is sitting in *my* chair."

Egocentrism in 4- and 5-year-olds is characterized by the belief that others are experiencing the world as they are. However, through social interactions in preschool groups, children experience the needs and wishes of others and are exposed to a variety of points of view. Peer group interactions provided by preschools and kindergartens offer unlimited opportunities for children to experience the perspectives of others. Perspective taking is a skill that emerges through social interactions and assists children in becoming less egocentric.

During sociodramatic play, pretending promotes perspective taking. As the child engages in a variety of role-taking experiences ("You be the nurse, and I'll be sick"), awareness of others' roles emerges. In attempting to play out a sociodramatic scenario, the child becomes aware of discrepancies between her or his own intentions and those of playmates. In adjusting the sociodrama to the wishes of others, the child's perspective taking abilities are enhanced.

In their review of research on social perspective taking in young children, Rubin and Everett (1982) identified three forms of perspective taking: (1) cognitive perspective taking, which includes the ability to consider others' thoughts and intentions; (2) affective perspective taking, or the ability to take into account the feelings and emotions of others; and (3) spatial perspective taking, or the ability to consider the other person's physical view of the world. A child who attempts to organize a game may be exhibiting cognitive perspective taking. A child who attempts to comfort a crying playmate may be exhibiting affective perspective taking, an awareness of the child's distress or its cause. A child who removes an obstacle from the path of another, thus preventing an accident, is demonstrating spatial perspective taking.

## PROSOCIAL DEVELOPMENT

As with perspective taking, prosocial behaviors also demonstrate emerging social competence. Prosocial behaviors include empathy and altruism. *Empathy* is the ability to recognize the feelings of others, such as distress, anxiety, or delight, and to vicariously experience those feelings. **Altruism** is defined as behavior intended to help another without expectation of reward. In young children, a number of factors influence prosocial behaviors. Among these factors are age, level of cognitive functioning, perspective-taking abilities, individual personality, family interactions, disciplinary strategies, and role models.

*altruism: intentions to help others without the expectation of reward*

Studies have shown that when children observe prosocial models, they generally become more prosocial themselves (Bandura, 1977; Radke-Yarrow, Zahn-Waxler, & Chapman, 1983). This is particularly true when the child and the model have had a warm relationship and the child has experienced nurturing from the model (Yarrow, Scott, & Zahn-Waxler, 1973).

Jeremy's friend Shaun has just recovered from chicken pox and is finally available for a visit. Ann greets Shaun upon his arrival and hustles the two children off to Jeremy's room to play. Jeremy's delight in seeing his absent friend is somewhat overshadowed by his observation of his mother's greeting. Nevertheless, he leads Shaun to his room, and the two become involved in a new and rather difficult puzzle. Stumped in putting the puzzle together, Jeremy runs to another room to summon his mother's assistance. Walking back to his room together, Jeremy engages his mother in his concern: "You didn't tell Shaun you were sorry." Confused, his mother inquires, "Sorry? About what, Jeremy?" "About he's been sick," Jeremy responds.

*Opportunities to interact with others in intergenerational contexts assist young and old alike in developing a sense of mutual caring and of continuity across the life span.*

Jeremy's own previous experiences with being sick were accompanied by expressions of concern such as "I am so sorry you are not feeling well"; "I am really glad you feel better today." Also, he had observed his parents convey similar concern with others. Thus, through observation, Jeremy has learned to verbally express concern for others and felt some incongruence when such concern wasn't made evident on this happy occasion with Shaun—an unintentional oversight on his mother's part. ■

Studies of discipline maintain that when **inductive discipline** strategies are employed, prosocial behaviors are more likely to emerge (Baumrind, 1972; Hoffman, 1975; Moore & Eisenberg, 1984). Inductive discipline is characterized by respect, reason, warmth, affection, and clear expectations.

*inductive discipline: a positive, nonpunitive form of discipline that relies on reasons and rationales to help children control their behaviors*

In addition to role models and disciplinary techniques, prosocial development is fostered by

1. Experiences that promote positive self-concepts. There is some evidence that positive feelings about oneself are related to higher frequencies of cooperative behaviors among 4- and 5-year-old children (Cauley & Tyler, 1989)

2. Assignment of age-appropriate responsibilities whereby children come to feel they are a contributing part of the family, class, or other group (Whiting & Whiting, 1975)

3. Opportunities to interact with other children and to engage in sociodramatic play that enhances role taking and perspective taking (Rubin & Everett, 1982)

4. Opportunities to participate in noncompetitive, cooperative games (Orlick, 1981)

5. Exposure to literature, television programs, toys, and computer and video games that project prosocial themes (Coates, Pusser, & Goodman, 1976; Moore & Eisenberg, 1984).

## SELF-CONCEPT

According to Erikson (1963), autonomy facilitates new discoveries and the acquisition of new skills and leads to an activity-based self-concept appropriate to the emergence of a sense of initiative. With autonomy in place, the 4- to 5-year-old describes herself or himself according to skills being mastered. The self-concept is based mostly on the child's perceptions of his or her physical attributes and possessions (Damon & Hart, 1982). A self-description based on perceptions of physical attributes is evident in statements such as "I am bigger"; "I can tie my shoes"; and "Watch me skip." The child also uses self-descriptions related to age and possessions to affirm the sense of self, for example, "I'm going to be four on my birthday," or "I have a new bicycle with training wheels." A positive self-concept provides the sustenance for self-confidence and one's expectations that mastering life's challenges is possible. A well-established sense of one's worth as an individual is protective in that frustrating obstacles and failures are less likely to be followed by the perception of oneself as incapable (Stipek, Recchia, & McClintic, 1992).

Some children have difficulty forming positive self-concepts due to a variety of reasons, including parental and child caring methods that militate against the development of a positive self-concept. Limited opportunities to use and enhance emerging physical/motor abilities, lack of affection and appropriate attention, harsh and punitive discipline, family stress, or excessive negative responses to the child are examples of factors that preclude effective development of self-awareness, self-concept, and self-esteem.

## GENDER IDENTITY AND GENDER-ROLE DEVELOPMENT

An integral part of the self-concept is an awareness of one's gender. Since parents and caregivers tend to respond differently to males and females from birth, socialization and the gender-role expectations placed on the child during early development influence both gender identity and development of gender-role behaviors. Parents often provide gender-typed toys for their children, such as dolls for girls

*Androgenous play behaviors are common as young children grow in awareness of the various roles each gender might assume.*

and trucks for boys (Huston, 1983). From infancy, boys are encouraged to be more physically active than girls (Frisch, 1977; Smith & Loyd, 1978). Parents are more inclined to encourage boys to explore and learn about the environment and encourage girls to remain dependent and helpless (Fagot, 1978). Parental treatment with respect to freedom and independence seems to favor boys (Block, 1973, 1983; Saegert & Hart, 1976).

There is some evidence that parents interact in quantitatively different ways with boys and girls, providing more attention to girls (Fagot, 1978). As a rule, boys receive more pressure than girls to assume gender-typical behaviors. Mothers do not seem to get as disturbed over "gender-inappropriate" play behaviors as do fathers (Langlois & Down, 1980). Some of this anxiety on the part of parents stems from confusion about how gender identity and gender-role development occur.

Kohlberg (1966) proposed a cognitive stage sequence for the development of gender roles:

1. Gender identity, wherein the child can provide a label for himself or herself as either a boy or a girl. This is usually achieved by age 3.
2. Gender stability, wherein the child realizes that boys grow up to be men and girls grow up to be women.
3. Gender constancy, wherein the child realizes that changes in hairstyle or clothing do not alter a person's sex. Gender constancy emerges between ages 5 and 7.

Prior to achievement of gender stability, children's pretend play is quite androgenous; boys can be mothers, and girls can be fathers. Child development researchers find little cause for concern in these play behaviors of young children, for these behaviors represent opportunities for children to affirm their own gender identities and gender roles. Honig (1983) asserts that children need role models who encourage a wide spectrum of expressions of feelings and behaviors. Role models who are comfortable with their own gender assist children in developing healthy gender identities and gender-role behaviors.

## AWARENESS OF DIVERSITY AND INDIVIDUAL DIFFERENCES

As noted earlier, self-concept emerges as children become aware of their distinguishing physical characteristics, gender, and abilities. Also related to the emerging sense of self is the child's awareness of race. Between ages 3 and 5, children become aware of differences among people. When young children discover racial differences, the disturbance in their own tenuous self-identification may cause them to respond with rejection or hostility toward others with different racial characteristics (Stevenson, 1967). Children at this phase are not forming generalized negative attitudes toward other races but are dealing with their own self-concepts and racial identities. There are now discrepancies between self-perceptions and what the child is seeing in others.

With this discovery, young children behave in a variety of curious, prosocial, and sometimes negative ways toward one another. They feel one another's hair, compare skin colors, and ask questions about their differences. They may verbally experiment with names of racial groups. There is some evidence that children from minority groups develop racial awareness earlier than other children (Katz, 1982). Further, young children seem to be particularly vulnerable to racial stereotyping (Thurman & Lewis, 1979). Sensitive and positive support of these early encounters among young children provides the scaffolding for the positive relationships that generally emerge among young children.

From birth onward, child rearing occurs in a cultural context that instills in the child concepts and attitudes about race, cultural identities, values, and expectations. Cultural contexts include the language spoken in the home, modes of expression, celebrations, holidays, family traditions, family cohesion, disciplinary techniques and authority relationships, food and clothing preferences, family goals and values, achievement orientations, and choices and opportunities in education, work, and recreation. Children's concepts, understandings, and attitudes about race—their own and those of others—derive first from the cultural contexts of home and family.

Early child care, preschool, and kindergarten experiences support and extend the child's growing sense of membership in a particular cultural or racial group. Early childhood programs support multicultural perspectives by

- Enhancing self-concept development and cultural identity
- Helping children develop the social skills of perspective taking, communicating, cooperating, and conflict resolution
- Broadening children's awareness of other lifestyles, languages, points of view, and ways of doing things through enriched multicultural curriculums (Ramsey, 1982).

Still another factor is the provision of antibias curriculas (see Box 12.2), materials, activities, and performance expectations.

## SELF-ESTEEM

The journey from self-awareness and self-recognition in infancy, to a reasonably accurate and positive self-concept in early childhood, to healthy self-esteem is punc-

---

❏❏❏   **BOX 12.2**         **TEACHING CHILDREN TO RESPECT DIVERSITY**

Children deserve the best we can give them. ...They deserve to live in a world free of discrimination and to receive an education that will help them be respectful and appreciative of the diversity around them. ...

What children learn about the wide variety of people in the world around them will significantly influence the way they grow and what kind of adults they will become. It will determine whether they develop into confident, secure members of society who respect and appreciate diversity or into adults who view others with hostility and fear because of ignorance. ...

Education about our differences reduces young people's fear and replaces it with curiosity and acceptance. Helping young people to explore why others look, dress, speak, and act differently can help turn their mistrust into understanding and appreciation of the rich diversity that makes up our world.

*Source*: Excerpted from Gwendolyn Calvert Baker, President and CEO, United States Committee for UNICEF (1994). "Teaching Children to Respect Diversity." *Childhood Education*, 71(1), 33–35. Reprinted by permission of the Association for Childhood Education.

tuated with evaluative events in which children assess themselves against the responses of others. Along the way, children take in and process information about their own physical attributes, gender, race, family, friends, and cognitive and social abilities. From this information, children draw conclusions about their worthiness, thus forming impressions that may or may not be accurate and may or may not be positive or self-affirming. A child who has experienced positive and self-affirming relationships with parents, caregivers, siblings, and peers feels competent, worthy, accepted, loved, and valued. This self-evaluative information provides the underpinnings for healthy self-esteem and enhanced interactions with others.

Interactions with the child need to be supportive, positive, and nurturing and must convey acceptance of the child's uniqueness, age, stage, and capabilities. Expectations must be age and developmentally appropriate to ensure a cumulative history of successes. As the child gets older, peer reactions become important and, for a time, may surpass those of adults in influencing the child's self-evaluations.

## SELF-CONTROL, COMPLIANCE, AND DISCIPLINE

Studies of child-rearing practices have provided insights into the kinds of adult-child interactions that are most likely to result in child behaviors that are cooperative, self-controlled, and compliant. Infant attachment studies emphasize the importance of the infant-mother attachment in later development of compliance (Matas, Arend, & Stroufe, 1978). When infants and toddlers have developed a warm, mutually affectionate relationship with their caregivers, they are more inclined to obey requests. Toddlers whose mothers are affectionate, verbally stimulating, and responsive and use positive methods of control are more compliant (Olson, Bates, & Bayles, 1984).

Conversely, children whose parents have used arbitrary commands, physical control, or coercive strategies to bring children into compliance are less inclined to cooperate with other adults, regardless of how gentle or friendly those adults are (Londerville & Main, 1981; Main & Weston, 1981). The implications for these children as they enter preschool and kindergarten are clear. Caregivers and early childhood teachers may encounter challenges with such children in establishing rapport and in engendering a spirit of cooperation and compliance within the group.

Guidance and disciplinary techniques are often classified into three types: inductive, power assertive, and permissive. Inductive discipline, as discussed earlier, uses a teaching mode in which children are provided reasons and rationales for expectations imposed on them. Inductive discipline sets logical limits for behavior and includes reasonable and logical consequences for noncompliance.

*power assertive discipline:*
*a form of discipline in which the power of the adult is used to coerce, deprive of privileges or material goods, or use physical punishment to modify a child's behavior*

**Power assertive** strategies, on the other hand, use coercion in the form of unreasonable and illogical threats (e.g., withdrawal of love), deprivation of material objects and privileges, belittling remarks, and physical force or punishment. Permissive strategies tend to ignore inappropriate behaviors and generally fail to teach appropriate ones.

The consequences of these styles of discipline have been the subject of numerous studies. Inductive discipline results in more cooperative, compliant, and self-

---

**FIGURE 12.2**
**Discipline or Punishment?**

*Children are disciplined when ...*
they are shown positive alternatives rather than just told "no";
they see how their actions affect others;
good behavior is rewarded;
adults establish fair, simple rules and enforce them consistently.

*Children are punished when ...*
their behavior is controlled through fear;
their feelings are not respected;
they behave to avoid a penalty or get a bribe;
the adult only tells the child what not to do.

*Children who are disciplined ...*
learn to share and cooperate;
are better able to handle their own anger;
are more self-disciplined; feel successful and in control of themselves.

*Children who are punished ...*
feel humiliated;
tend to be angry and aggressive;
fail to develop control of themselves.

---

*Source:* Miller, C. S. (1984). Building Self-Control: Discipline for Young Children. *Young Children, 40,* 15-19. Reprinted with permission from the National Association for the Education of Young Children.

controlled behaviors and has been associated with more positive relationships and popularity with peers (Hart et al., 1990; Hart, Ladd, & Burleson, 1990; Maccoby & Martin, 1983). It has also been associated with advanced moral development (Hoffman, 1975). See Figure 12.2 for a comparison of discipline and punishment.

Diana Baumrind (1967, 1971, 1972) contrasted the behaviors of three groups of nursery school children and the child-rearing practices of their parents. She later observed these same children and their parents when the children were 8 to 9 years old. Baumrind identified three patterns of parental control, each with corresponding patterns of child behaviors:

1. Parents who used **authoritative discipline** combined control with positive encouragement of autonomy and independence in their children. These parents directed their children's activities, but in a rational, reasoned manner. They valued verbal give-and-take and self-expression in their children and respected their interests and individual capabilities. Children of authoritative parents were self-reliant, self-controlled, explorative, and content. They tended to be more responsible, friendly, cooperative, and achievement oriented. In addition, they appeared more curious, more cheerful, and better able to handle stress.

2. Parents who used **authoritarian discipline** were detached, controlling, and less warm toward their children. These parents attempted to shape and control their children's behavior and attitudes according to a set standard of conduct that was often absolute and theologically motivated. Obedience,

*authoritative discipline: a child-rearing style in which child behavior is directed through rational and reasoned guidance from the adult*

*authoritarian discipline: a child-rearing style in which parents apply rigid standards of conduct and expect unquestioning obedience from the child*

FIGURE 12.3
Supporting Compliance and Self-Control in 4- and 5-Year-Olds

1. Provide an environment in which the child's growing sense of initiative can flourish. Such an environment includes
   - Adequate space for the child to use and pursue toys, equipment, creative materials, and realia
   - Developmentally appropriate and culturally inclusive play items and activities through which children can experience success and enhanced self-confidence and self-esteem
   - Low, open shelves for personal work and play materials
   - Engaging, enriching play items that encourage decision making, sharing, and cooperating
   - Safe and sturdy furnishing, play items, and surroundings

2. Provide an atmosphere in which it is not only physically but also psychologically safe to explore, experiment, and ask questions. Such an atmosphere includes
   - Rich interactional opportunities that encourage dialogue
   - Answers to questions and encouragement of further curiosities

3. Provide opportunities to interact with other children and to participate in peer groups. This allows children to
   - Share and problem solve with age-mates
   - Engage in sustained sociodramatic play with other children

4. Establish a predictable daily schedule to help children develop a sense of time and anticipate and respond appropriately to regular events. Such a schedule
   - Meets the child's physiological needs for food, water, rest, and exercise
   - Adjusts activities and expectations to the child's short but expanding attention span
   - Provides advance notice of a need to change from one event to another
   - Allows time for the completion of tasks once started
   - Avoids long waiting times

5. Involve children in the setting of rules, limits, and standards for behavior.
   - Set simple rules that are few in number, truly necessary, and focused on the most crucial behaviors first. Perhaps the three *D*s of discipline is a good starting point: Set rules that help children recognize things that are Dangerous, Destructive, and/or Disturbing or hurtful to others. However, rules should always be stated in a positive way, telling children *what* to do rather than *what not* to do.
   - Explain the reasons behind rules, and engage children in conversations about logical consequences and the need for reciprocity.
   - Assign age-appropriate chores and responsibilities with adult assistance if needed. Chores can include returning personal items to assigned places, tidying room or toy shelves, watering certain houseplants, or caring for a pet.

respect for authority, respect for work and for the preservation of order and tradition were valued. Verbal give-and-take was not encouraged, and children were expected to accept the parents' word as right. Often punitive and forceful methods of discipline were used. Children of authoritarian parents tended to be distrustful, discontent, and withdrawn. These children exhibited more moodiness, unhappiness, and annoyance and were inclined to be passively hostile, vulnerable to stress, aimless, and unfriendly.

3. Parents who used **permissive discipline** were noncontrolling and nondemanding, yet relatively warm. While these parents were accepting and affirming in their behavior, they made few demands for responsibility and orderly behavior. Children were allowed to regulate their own behaviors and were expected to use the parent as a resource to be sought as they wished. Children of permissive parents were found to be the least self-reliant, explorative, and self-controlled of the three groups. They exhibited more impulsive, aggressive, and rebellious behaviors, were less self-reliant and self-controlled, were often aimless, and were lower achievers.

*permissive discipline: a noncontrolling, nondemanding form of discipline in which the child, for the most part, is allowed to regulate his or her own behavior*

Young children gain self-control from their interactions with the environment and other children. Figure 12.3 provides suggestions for helping children gain self-control through their use of time, space, materials, and interactions with other children.

## MORAL DEVELOPMENT

Piaget's (1932/1965) studies of moral development focused on how children develop a respect for rules and a sense of justice. He studied the former by quizzing children about rules as he engaged them in marble play. To assess childhood conceptions of social justice, he used moral dilemma stories with children, followed by questions concerning punishment, or appropriateness of certain behaviors. From these studies, Piaget proposed a stage/sequence of moral development consisting of (1) a premoral stage, (2) a stage of **moral realism**, and (3) a stage of **moral relativism**.

*moral realism: a morality that focuses on rules and the seriousness of the consequences of an act rather than on the intentions behind the act*

Children below age 6 are thought to be in a premoral stage of morality because of an absent or limited concern for rules. For instance, play groups exhibit an assortment of rules and behavior expectations, making rules up as play proceeds and altering them arbitrarily and unilaterally. Awareness of the use of or reasons for rules is minimal.

Toward the end of this stage, around age 6, children begin to exhibit characteristics of Piaget's second stage, moral realism. During this stage, children become quite rule-bound, believing that rules are unalterable and set forth by "all-knowing" authority figures (God, parent, teacher). They believe one's behavior is judged to be "right" or "wrong" based on having followed the rules or on the seriousness of the consequences. This stage is often referred to as a **heteronomous** stage of morality in that the child's behaviors are governed by others rather than by the self, as would be true of autonomous behaviors.

*moral relativism: a morality that focuses on the judgment of situations and intentions underlying individual behavior rather than focusing solely on the consequences of an act*

*heteronomous morality: a morality that is governed by others rather than by oneself*

Due to the characteristic egocentrism of this age, the child believes others are subject to the same rules and perceive rules in the same way. In addition, the magnitude of the consequences of a deed determines for the child whether the deed is right or wrong. For instance, breaking a large but very inexpensive item would be judged to be more serious than breaking a small but expensive one. Moreover, any deed that is punished is viewed as wrong.

At this stage of morality, children perceive punishment as it relates to breaking the rule, usually without regard for the rule breaker's intentions. For these young moralists, punishment should be quickly forthcoming when rules are broken. Their suggestions for punishment do not necessarily relate to the misdeed. Some children at this stage may believe that injury or misfortune following their own misdeeds is deserved punishment for having broken a rule. Sometimes, unable to control the rule conformity of playmates, older preschoolers seek the assistance of an adult through "tattling." One should view this behavior as a natural part of the child's emerging sense of rules and rule infringement and not necessarily as an attempt to be unkind to a playmate. In this regard, tattling might be viewed as a positive aspect of psychosocial development.

## KOHLBERG'S DEVELOPMENTAL SEQUENCE OF MORAL THINKING

Lawrence Kohlberg (1968, 1984) expanded and modified Piaget's theory by proposing an invariant developmental sequence consisting of three levels of moral thinking: premoral (or preconventional), conventional, and postconventional, the end product of which is a sense of justice. Children are believed to pass through each of the stages, though perhaps at different rates. Each stage incorporates the developments of the preceding stage and builds on them. The premoral and conventional levels are summarized here.

### Premoral Level

*Stage 1: Punishment and obedience orientation*—The child's moral behaviors are oriented toward punishment and exhibit unquestioning deference to superior power. The physical consequences of action, regardless of their human meaning or value, determine goodness or badness.

*Stage 2: Naive instrumental hedonism*—The child views right actions as those which instrumentally satisfy her own needs and occasionally the needs of others. Elements of fairness, reciprocity, and equal sharing are present, but they are always interpreted in a physical, pragmatic way. Reciprocity is a matter of "you scratch my back and I'll scratch yours," not of loyalty, gratitude, or justice.

### Conventional Level

*Stage 3: Morality of conventional role conformity*—At this level, we see a "good boy/good girl" orientation. Good behavior is that which pleases or helps others and is approved by them. There is much conformity to stereotypical images of what is majority or "natural" behavior. Behavior is often judged by intention; "He means well" becomes important for the first time and is often overused. One seeks approval by being "nice."

*Adults who use authoritative means of helping children resolve conflicts assist them in understanding not only their own needs and wishes but also those of others.*

*Stage 4: Authority-maintaining morality*—The child's behaviors are oriented toward authority, fixed rules, and the maintenance of the social order. Right behavior consists of doing one's duty, showing respect for authority, and maintaining the social order for its own sake. One earns respect by performing dutifully.*

Kohlberg's third level, postconventional moral thinking, is characterized by "a major thrust toward autonomous moral principles which have validity and application apart from authority of the groups or persons who hold them and apart from the individual's identification with those persons or groups" (Kohlberg, 1968, p. 63).*

Four and 5-year-old children exhibit Kohlberg's stages 2 and 3. As children are better able to ascertain intentions, take another person's perspective, and understand reciprocity, they make the transition from premoral thinking and behaviors to the conventional level of thinking and behaving.

Contemporary research continues to examine various aspects of moral development. Topics such as the child's abilities to understand intentions, moral emotions, notions of negligence, responsibility, and restitution, and role taking are elaborating on the theories of Piaget and Kohlberg and increasing our knowledge of moral development in children (Hoffman, 1988; Krebs & Gillmore, 1982; Nunner-Winkler & Sodian, 1988; Shultz, Wright, & Schliefer, 1986; Surber, 1982).

*Excerpts from *The Psychology of Moral Development* by Lawrence Kohlberg. Copyright © 1984 by Lawrence Kohlberg. Reprinted by permission of Harper & Row, Publishers, Inc.

## FRIENDSHIPS

In Miriam Cohen's (1967) sensitive children's book *Will I Have a Friend?*, Jim asks his father on the way to his first day at preschool, "Will I have a friend?" His father answers, "I think you will." This worried question is quite typical for children entering preschool or new play groups. It signals a very important aspect of psychosocial development: establishing and maintaining friendships.

Social knowledge and skills emerge from early experiences in the home (Damon, 1988; Hart, Ladd, & Burleson, 1990; Barth & Parke, 1993) and are often enhanced through sibling interactions (Dunn & Munn, 1986; Lamb, 1978a, 1978b); however, the peer group is a particularly significant contributor to childhood social development (Hartup, 1977, 1983; Hartup & Moore, Howes, 1988; 1990).

Some studies have contrasted the effects of home care and preschool experiences on the development of social competence in young children. These studies suggest that children who have been enrolled in regular play groups, preschool, or child care programs exhibit more social competence with peers than do their age-mates who have been cared for at home with fewer opportunities to interact with other children (Harper & Huie, 1985; Roopnarine, 1985).

Relating effectively with others is an important goal for early childhood. Becoming socially competent with peers involves the development of certain social skills: (1) initiating interactions, (2) maintaining ongoing relations, and (3) resolving interpersonal conflicts (Asher, Renshaw, & Hymel, 1982).

Some children are more adept than others at initiating interactions, such as a newcomer finding a way into the kindergarten class or joining a group of children already at play. According to Asher et al. (1982), children who tend to be popular with their peers initiate interactions by suggesting a joint activity or engaging others in talk. These children seem to have a better sense of timing, waiting for an opportunity to join in, perhaps during a natural break in an ongoing activity. These children are also less obtrusive and create fewer disruptions in the play in progress. In contrast, unpopular children are more uncertain about how to initiate interactions and use vague strategies such as smiling or tactics that call attention to themselves rather than integrating themselves into the ongoing activity.

Friendships in 4- and 5-year-old children have their own characteristics, which are indicative of increasing cognitive and social development. Friendships in early childhood tend to be transient; that is, today's "best friend" may not be so tomorrow or perhaps even this afternoon! As children reach ages 4 and 5, friendships become more durable. Yet during play sequences, conflict may arise over the use of a toy or how a shared activity should proceed, and a friendship can be promptly terminated, only to be reinstated soon thereafter.

As a rule, friendships at this age are dependent on proximity, shared activities or toys, and physical attributes (Selman, 1981). This differs from the friendships of a later age, which are more often based on shared values, perceived virtues, and common interests. In young children, neither bartering for friendships ("I'll be your friend if you'll let me hold your doll") nor threatening ("If you don't give me one of those trucks, I won't ever, ever be your friend!") is uncommon.

Once successfully initiated, social interactions teeter precariously on the edge of conflict. Young children lack the social behavior strategies, facility with language, and social knowledge needed to manage friendships well. Conflicts are frequent and can be quite intense.

For friendship maintenance and conflict resolution skills to emerge, young children need to experience peers in a variety of contexts—as visitors in their homes, in preschool settings, in neighborhood play groups, in family gatherings, and so on. Charlesworth and Hartup (1967) suggest that children need opportunities to interact with a minimum of adult interference to experience peer feedback and reinforcement for their developing social skills. Through such experiences, children may experiment with various strategies for interacting and may come to reuse successful ones and modify or discard less successful attempts.

## FRIENDSHIPS AND PLAY

Play provides an essential medium for the development of social knowledge, skills, and competence and for the establishment of friendships. According to Parten's (1933) descriptions of play patterns, 4- and 5-year-olds exhibit *associative* and/or *cooperative* play behaviors. The onlooker, solitary, and parallel play of previous ages continues to be observed in older children, however.

In **associative play**, children may share and converse about materials and activities, but each will explore and use the materials in individual ways. Associative play may involve following another child around or imitating the play behaviors of others; yet one's own play preferences supersede those of the other child or children.

*associative play: a loosely organized form of social play characterized by overt social behaviors indicating common activities, shared interests, and interpersonal associations*

**Cooperative play**, on the other hand, signals the child's growing ability to acknowledge the ideas of others and to incorporate those ideas into his or her own play behaviors. This play is characterized by planning, sharing, and organizing play scenarios around goals or themes. Group membership is decided by certain members of the group and can be inclusive or quite restrictive.

Recall the social skills necessary for developing social competence: initiating interactions, maintaining relations, and resolving interpersonal conflicts. Could it be that associative play is a form of experimentation with initiating interactions? William Corsaro (1985) suggests that friendship is a device children use to gain access into play groups and to initiate social interactions during free play. Further, he describes social interactions during play activities as means by which young children protect not only their toys or their play equipment but also the ecological area in which the social exchanges occur (p. 125). Perhaps through associative play, some friendships effectively "connect" through subtle verbal negotiations and physical posturing. Cooperative play allows children to experience the interests and wishes of others and counterbalance them with their own to prevent or resolve conflict. The value of play in friendships, peer relationships, and social competence continues to be an important area of research (Ladd, 1990; Hart, Ladd, & Burleson, 1990).

*cooperative play: a well-organized form of social play characterized by well-defined social roles within play groups, influential peer leaders, and shared materials and equipment used to pursue a well-understood group play theme*

## FACTORS INFLUENCING PSYCHOSOCIAL DEVELOPMENT

A number of factors can be attributed to healthy psychosocial development. Among them are the child's own personality and unique developmental pathways, the nature of familial and extrafamilial interactions and caregiving strategies, sibling and peer relationships, and television and other media. Let's look briefly at each of these factors in turn.

## THE CHILD'S PERSONALITY AND UNIQUE DEVELOPMENTAL PATHWAYS

In previous chapters, we explored the role of individual temperaments, which children seem to innately possess, and the effects of the "goodness-of-fit" relationships proposed by Chess and Thomas (1987). Additional studies of the reciprocal relationship between the personalities of children and their caregivers expand on this theory.

In their studies, Bell and Chapman (1986) proposed a "control system model" of how parents and children regulate each other's behaviors. The model suggests that both parent and child have behavioral repertoires that elicit predictable responses in each other. Both parent and child are said to have upper and lower limits of tolerance for the intensity, frequency, and situational appropriateness of behaviors exhibited by the other.

In addition to temperament and control systems, other characteristics of children influence the types of responses they get from others. Physical appearance, notions of attractiveness or unattractiveness, health, vitality, cleanliness, and grooming produce behaviors that can be either positive and prosocial or negative and difficult. A study by Langlois and Down (1979) found that social behaviors of attractive and unattractive children at age 3 did not differ appreciably, but by age 5 unattractive children exhibited more aggression toward their peers, suggesting a behavior response to being perceived as unattractive. The manner in which others respond to a child determines, to a great extent, the child's reciprocal responses.

Contemporary studies are finding that a child's temperament has a strong impact on adjustment to preschool and how children are perceived by their teachers (Mobley & Pullis, 1991). It is apparent that the child both influences and is influenced by the behaviors and responses of others. Recognizing this, adults should be aware of their own behaviors and expectations and assess the possible effects those behaviors are having on the child. It is the adult who manages the "equilibrium/disequilibrium" dimensions of the adult-child relationship. The supportive adult both accepts the uniqueness of the child's personality and capabilities and adapts her or his own responses to that uniqueness. The adult's goal is to help the child learn to manage relationships in positive and mutually accepting and respecting ways.

## NATURE OF FAMILIAL AND EXTRAFAMILIAL INTERACTIONS AND CAREGIVING STRATEGIES

Although 4- through 5-year-olds are becoming more independent, self-sufficient, and eager for social interactions with their peers, they continue to depend on adults for support and guidance as they explore an ever-widening social world. As during infancy and the toddler period, children ages 4 through 5 continue to seek intimacy and affection, communication and companionship, encouragement and assistance, and assurances and affirmation from those who care for them. Children also look to adults to protect them from harm, provide reasoned guidance and leadership, and teach them or help them discover acceptable and effective social behaviors and emotional outlets. As children attempt to understand their own feelings and desires and strive to govern their behaviors and interactions, they take many of their cues from the behaviors of those around them.

> Angela is setting the table in the home-living center at kindergarten. Her friend Jason joins her and proceeds to pour water in the cups for "hot chocolate." The two seat themselves and begin to sip, when Angela interrupts and reprimands Jason, "You have to put your napkin in your lap first." To which Jason queries, "Why?" Angela responds, "Because that's the way my Mama does it." ■

Young children carefully observe the interactions and responses, both verbal and nonverbal, of adults who care for them. Young children are particularly cognizant of the words and actions of those with whom they have close and warm relationships (Bandura, 1977; Grusec & Abramovitch, 1982). These observations often become incorporated into the child's behavior and have the potential to become internalized and lasting.

In addition to the impact of the adult model on psychosocial development, adults (parents, caregivers, preschool teachers) influence psychosocial development through the quality of the support system they provide for the child's emerging sense of self, self-esteem, and self-confidence. The nurturing dimensions of their relationships with children are critical. Guidance and disciplinary strategies, developmentally appropriate (or inappropriate) expectations, and the degree to which adults attempt to coach children in social skills are all determinants of positive or negative outcomes for psychosocial development.

## SIBLING RELATIONSHIPS

Siblings influence one another's psychosocial development in reciprocal ways. Though the quality of sibling relationships varies from family to family and depends on a variety of factors, including the number and ages of siblings in the family, children learn from interactions with their siblings. Children learn family rules and values, and how to play with others of different ages, from their siblings. They learn to share family time, space, and resources. They learn about gender and gender-role behaviors. They learn to communicate their needs and to respond to the needs of others. They learn to disagree and to resolve disagreements. They learn about individual differences and individual rights, and about loyalty and mutual caring.

Older siblings may be called on to care for younger ones. In this role, the older sibling becomes playmate, teacher, and disciplinarian. Children sometimes form attachment relationships with their older siblings (Stewart, 1983). While older siblings may focus on the parent as the role model, younger ones focus on the older sibling (Baskett, 1984). In times of family grief or trauma, siblings may rely on one another for support and comfort (Bank & Kahn, 1982b; Chess & Thomas, 1987), or they may suffer a deteriorated peer relationship (Hetherington, Cox, & Cox, 1982).

Sibling rivalry, a common occurrence in families, receives considerable attention in both popular and scholarly literature. Yet studies are beginning to show that kindness and affection are more common in sibling relationships than are the antagonistic and rivalrous behaviors so often discussed (Abramovitch et al., 1986; Baskett & Johnson, 1982).

Sibling rivalry is generally a response to feelings of jealousy or loss of attention or nurturing. Changes in family structure due to divorce, remarriage, blended or reconstituted families, a new baby, or the illness of a family member may give rise to these feelings. Rivalry can occur when perceived favoritism, inconsistent child-rearing practices, or sex stereotyping within the family causes the allocation of affection, assignment of chores, and expectations of certain behaviors and achievements to differ according to the sex of the child.

Teachers and child caregivers must recognize the positive and supportive nature of sibling relationships for children. Four- and 5-year-olds want to talk about their younger and older siblings. They also enjoy having a sibling visit their classroom, showing them around, and introducing them to friends. In school and child care settings where siblings may be attending in other classrooms, sensitive adults allow brothers and sisters to visit with one another when possible. It is particularly comforting for younger siblings to locate the older one's classroom to have a mental picture of where a brother or sister is while they are separated. This is often true for the older sibling as well. In times of illness or distress at school, siblings can provide a measure of security until parents can be summoned.

## PEER RELATIONSHIPS

Young children enjoy the company of their peers. The amount and types of peer interactions children have experienced by 4 or 5 years of age vary widely. Some children have experienced age-mates from infancy through child care arrangements; others may have had few peer group interactions before enrollment in kindergarten at age 5.

From peers, children learn both appropriate and inappropriate behaviors. As models, peers often serve as frames of reference for self-evaluation. Experience with prosocial peer models may encourage prosocial imitative behaviors. Aggressive models encourage experimentation with aggressive forms of behavior. Peer groups may be viewed as a testing ground for the child to explore and experience social interactions. While peers serve to enhance and enlarge the child's social awareness at ages 4 and 5, adults remain the source of greatest influence. Later peers will become increasingly influential in the social lives of children.

## TELEVISION AND OTHER MEDIA

Today's children enjoy the products of an ever-changing and expanding electronics industry. Television, the most common and readily available electronic medium, has been a topic of concern and research for decades. Much of the literature relating to television's influence on the minds and behaviors of children has addressed violence and aggression, inadequate and inappropriate gender and cul-

*A child's limited ability to separate fantasy and reality often makes the content of television shows and video games confusing, misleading, and frightening.*

tural role models, and the effects of advertising directed at young consumers. Other studies have attempted to identify the positive influences of television on such aspects of development as language, literacy, cognition, and prosocial behaviors. The more recent technologies of computers, video equipment, and other electronic toys and devices are finding their way into more and more American homes, and like television, are coming under the scrutiny of child development and early education researchers.

The effects of television, video games and the newer electronic toys, and devices on psychosocial development depends on a number of factors, including the amount of time used and taken from other healthy and productive activities, the content and quality of the programs and games, and the attitudes and values surrounding the use of these technologies.

The amount of time children devote to television continues to be of concern to psychologists, educators, and health care experts. By some estimates, young children view 28 hours of television per week and will have watched 22,000 hours of television by age 18. Time spent watching television precludes physical activities needed to enhance motor development. The reduced opportunities to engage in focused interactions with playmates, parents, and others interfere with healthy psychosocial development.

It is believed that children learn best through interactive processes. Because children seek feedback from manipulated objects, and from events and people to help them make sense of their experiences, excessive television viewing is considered disruptive to this process. Moreover, the child's limited abilities to separate fantasy from reality and the emerging sense of rules and their applications often make the content of television and video games confusing and misleading.

Concern over bias, violence, aggression, vulgarity, and explicit sex in television programs has prompted numerous studies on their long-term effects and child advocacy efforts through state legislatures and Congress to curtail programming known to result in imitative and desensitized behaviors. One study estimated that by the time children finish elementary school, they will have seen 8,000 murders and 100,000 other acts of violence (American Psychological Association, 1992). The number of violent acts per hour a decade ago was estimated to be 18.6; today the estimate is 26.4 violent acts per hour (Gerbner & Signorielli, 1990). Responding to increasing concern over violence in the media, the Governing Board of the National Association for the Education of Young Children has published a position statement and teachers' guide (NAEYC, 1990, 1995) condemning violent television programming, movies, videotapes, computer games, and other forms of media to which young children are exposed.

Bronfenbrenner (1970, 1986) expressed concern about the effects of television on family interactions when he suggested that "[it is] not so much in the behavior it produces as the behavior it prevents" (1970, p. 170). Family interactions, including talking, arguing, playing games, and taking part in family festivities, are among the forgone opportunities Bronfrenbrenner sees as essential for learning and the formation of character.

On the other hand, a number of programs do promote prosocial behaviors and understandings, and child and family viewing can be guided toward them. Regular exposure to such programming has been shown to positively influence the behaviors of children (Coates, Pusser, & Goodman, 1976; Freidrich & Stein, 1975). However, viewing alone does not presuppose such behaviors. Children need adults to help them verbalize their understandings (and misunderstandings) of program topics and role models and to encourage them to role play and utilize prosocial behaviors of admired characters in their own daily interactions. David England (1984) describes his concern over television's potential influence on his daughter Jessica's life:

> From the beginning, there is television. Though she did not know it immediately, TV was a conspicuous part of the world our youngest daughter first entered five years ago. Jessica's home was not unlike most of the others around it. An entire room, appropriately referred to as "The TV Room," was dominated by a gray-faced deceptive piece of furniture around which other furniture was arranged. Within hours of Jessica's first coming into our home, that box clamored for someone's attention, beguiling us with a colorful and noisy life of its own. Very early on, then, my wife and I had to decide whether TV would raise Jessica, be her best friend, broaden her experience, or steal her youth. (p. 7)

## CHILDREN WITH SPECIAL NEEDS

Children with special needs are at heightened risk for socialization problems. Self-concept, self-esteem, prosocial behaviors, and the development of friendships may be particularly vulnerable areas. Some examples of socialization problems children with delayed development, chronic diseases, or handicapping conditions may experience include problems in learning how to initiate friendships and activities (Bryan, Sonnefeld, & Greenberg, 1981) and shyness and withdrawal, and the accompanying difficulty with reciprocal interactions. Hearing-impaired children tend to have difficulties in this area and are often misinterpreted by others as unfriendly (Lerner, 1985). A lack of social comprehension skills is not uncommon in children with learning disabilities (Weiss, 1984), who frequently misread the social cues of others and consequently use inappropriate means of initiating contacts and making friends. These children may also have difficulty in perspective taking, preventing them from taking others' feelings and views into consideration (Bryan & Bryan, 1986). Visually impaired children may fail to provide facial cues of friendliness and other nonverbal cues that encourage interactions with others (Van Hasselt, 1983).

Special-needs children may benefit from direct instruction in the social skills they need to interact successfully with others. Lerner, Mardell-Czudnowski, & Goldenberg (1987) suggest that role playing, peer assistance, and adult models can be employed to teach needed social skills. This assistance is readily available in well-planned, developmentally appropriate early childhood classrooms in which teachers are sensitive and supportive to the needs of individuals.

Helping children accept and interact with special-needs children provides both groups with learning experiences. Because young children are curious and often quite frank, teachers will want to provide reassuring and accurate information about the special-needs child, but should avoid labeling or otherwise embarrassing him or her. The teacher should provide opportunities for all children to interact, with as little adult interference as possible. Teachers can assist all children in learning how to initiate activities and friendships and provide playmates who model social competence for children who need help in this area.

---

## Role of the Early Childhood Professional

### Enhancing Psychosocial Development of Children Ages 4 Through 5

1.  Support the child's continuing need for nurturance and security.
2.  Support the child's emerging sense of self, and provide experiences and interactions that enhance self-esteem.
3.  Model prosocial behaviors.
4.  Facilitate initiative while providing safe, reasonable limits.
5.  Help children understand and cope with their fears.
6.  Understand the young child's moral development and egocentric behaviors.
7.  Provide inductive, authoritative discipline.

8. Encourage interaction with other children.

9. Facilitate positive sibling relationships.

10. Respond to the child's questions about gender, race, and family with focused interest and helpful and forthright answers.

11. Provide media experiences that focus on prosocial themes. ■

## KEY TERMS

| | | |
|---|---|---|
| altruism | heteronomous morality | permissive discipline |
| associative play | inductive discipline | power assertive |
| authoritarian discipline | initiative | discipline |
| authoritative discipline | moral realism | |
| cooperative play | moral relativism | |

## REVIEW STRATEGIES AND ACTIVITIES

1. Review the key the terms in this chapter individually or with a classmate.

2. Visit a developmentally appropriate prekindergarten or kindergarten classroom in your local public school.
   a. Observe and record teacher behaviors that model social skills for children, including empathy and altruism, initiating conversations and friendships, accepting and understanding others, and perspective taking, prosocial behaviors, and the cultural perspectives of teachers and parents.
   b. Observe and record attempts to teach social skills to children.

3. At another time in this same classroom, observe and record anecdotal accounts of associative and cooperative play behaviors among the children. What types of activities promoted cooperative play behaviors?

4. Interview several parents of 4- and 5-year-old children. Ask what kinds of limits they set for their children. Which ones do they emphasize most often? Why? How do they enforce these limits at home? What did you learn about behavior priorities of parents?

5. Interview several prekindergarten or kindergarten teachers. What kinds of limits do they set for children in the classroom? Why? How do they enforce these limits? What did you learn about behavior priorities of teachers? In what ways are teachers and parents the same or different in this respect?

6. Watch three popular children's television shows several times over a period of three weeks. Record the prosocial events that take place in each. Compare the different programs. Were there differences in the specific prosocial behaviors emphasized by the different programs? Were you aware of any violent or aggressive models? How did the commercials communicate with young viewers?

7. With your classmates, develop a list of television programs that might be considered developmentally appropriate for 4- and 5-year-olds.
8. Discuss with your classmates the role of adults in helping children use modern technology to enhance psychosocial development.

## FURTHER READINGS

Comer, J. P., & Poussaint, A. F. (1992). *Raising black children.* New York: Penguin Books.

Curry, N. E., and Johnson, C. N. (1990). *Beyond self-esteem: Developing a genuine sense of human value.* Research Monograph of the National Association for the Education of Young Children. Washington, DC: NAEYC.

Garbarino, J., Dubrow, N., Kostelny, K., & Pardo, C. (1992). *Children in danger: Coping with the consequences of community violence.* San Francisco: Jossey-Bass.

McGinnis, E., & Goldstein, A. P. (1990). *Skill-streaming in early childhood: Teaching prosocial skills to the preschool and kindergarten child.* Champaign, IL: Research Press Company.

National Association of State Boards of Education. (1991). *Caring Communities: Supporting young children and families: A report of the National Task Force on School Readiness.* Alexandria, VA: Author.

Slaby, R. G., W. C. Roedell, D. Arezzo and K. Hendrix (1995). Early Violence Prevention: Tools for teachers of young children. Washington, DC: National Association for the Education of Young Children.

Spodek, B., & Saracho, O. N. (1994). *Dealing with individual differences in the early childhood classroom.* New York: Longman.

Stipek, D., Recchia, S., & McClintic, S. (1992). Self-evaluation in young children. *Monographs of the Society for Research in Child Development, 57* (1, Serial No. 226).

Trawick-Smith, J. (1994). *Interactions in the classroom: Facilitating play in the early years.* Columbus, OH: Merrill.

Vold, E. B. (Ed.) (1992). *Multicultural education in each childhood classroom.* Washington, DC: National Education Association.

# CHAPTER THIRTEEN

*Was it not then that I acquired all that now sustains me? And I gained so much and so quickly that during the rest of my life I did not acquire a hundredth part of it. From myself as a five-year-old to myself as I now am there is only one step. The distance between myself as an infant and myself at five years is tremendous.*

Leo Tolstoy

# Cognitive, Language, and Literacy Development Ages 4 Through 5

After studying this chapter, you will demonstrate comprehension by:

- Describing cognitive development in children ages 4 and 5.
- Describing oral language development in children ages 4 and 5.
- Describing literacy development in children ages 4 and 5.
- Identifying special needs and sociocultural concerns relating to cognitive, language, and literacy development in children ages 4 and 5.
- Defining the role of adults in promoting cognitive, language, and literacy development in children ages 4 and 5.

## MORE ON PIAGET'S PREOPERATIONAL STAGE

Piaget's research indicated that children under age 6 or 7 are not capable of mental operations; hence the term *preoperational*. From Piaget's perspective, this means children cannot yet form accurate internal representations of actions because thought is still dependent on the young child's perception (Piaget & Inhelder, 1969).

Piaget came to his conclusions about children's thinking during the preoperational stage after conducting a number of conservation experiments. **Conservation** is the understanding that the physical attributes of an object or substance remain the same even if its appearance changes. Figure 13.1 depicts some of Piaget's conservation tasks. The results of these experiments generally suggest that children generally do not conserve until they are in the stage of concrete operations (Piaget, 1963).

Piaget's explanation of this lack of ability to conserve was based on young children's behaviors in a number of his experiments. For example, he noted that preoperational children tended to focus on specific events of a situation rather than on the process of **transformation**, that is, attending to all states or stages of an event from beginning to end. For example, preoperational children had difficulty representing the in-between successive stages of a pencil falling. According to Piaget, young children's thought is transductive in that it is centered on specific

*conservation: the understanding that physical attributes (e.g., mass and weight) stay the same even if appearance changes*

*transformation: attending to all the states of an event from the beginning to the final stage*

327

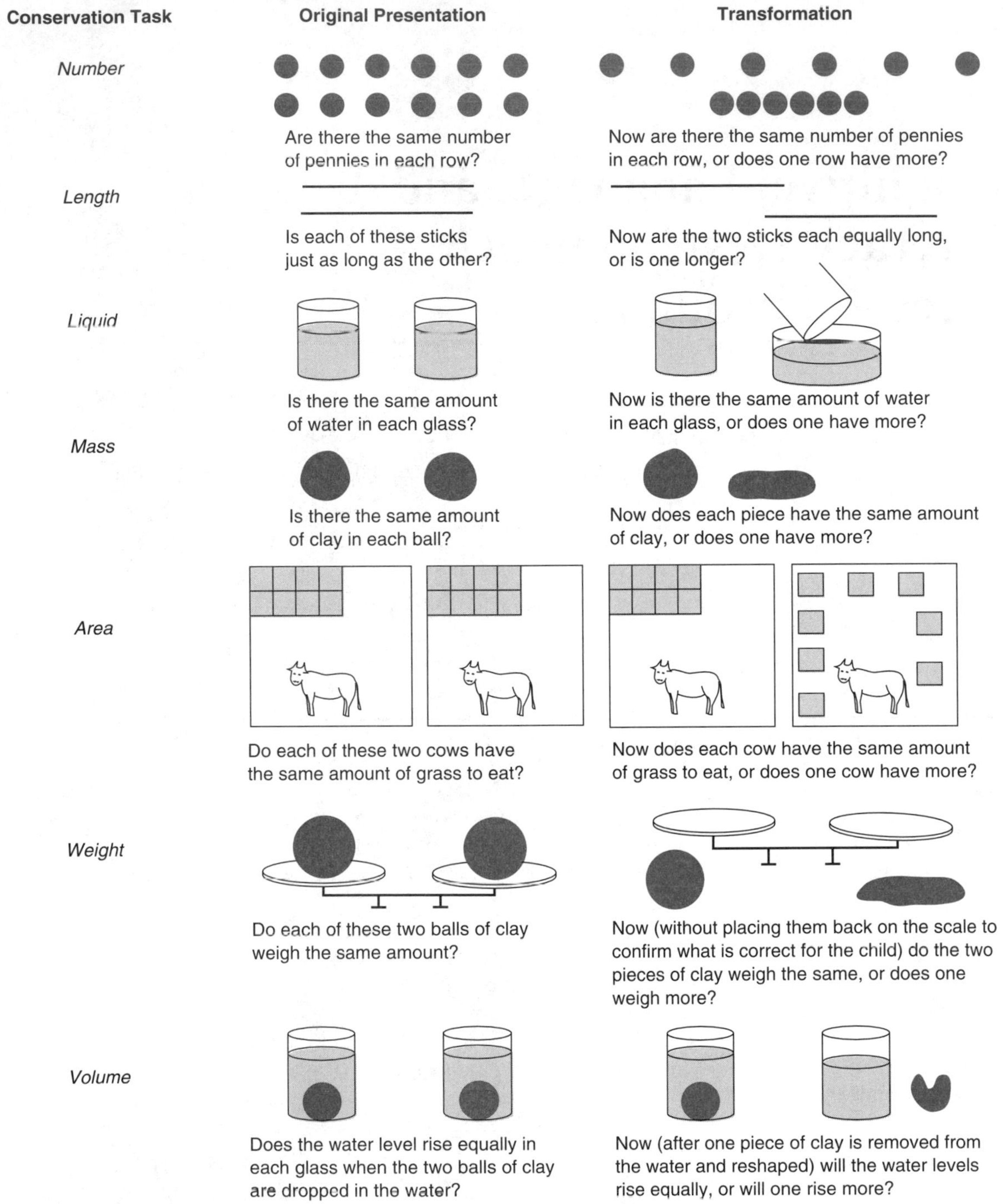

| Conservation Task | Original Presentation | Transformation |
|---|---|---|

**Number**

Are there the same number of pennies in each row?

Now are there the same number of pennies in each row, or does one row have more?

**Length**

Is each of these sticks just as long as the other?

Now are the two sticks each equally long, or is one longer?

**Liquid**

Is there the same amount of water in each glass?

Now is there the same amount of water in each glass, or does one have more?

**Mass**

Is there the same amount of clay in each ball?

Now does each piece have the same amount of clay, or does one have more?

**Area**

Do each of these two cows have the same amount of grass to eat?

Now does each cow have the same amount of grass to eat, or does one cow have more?

**Weight**

Do each of these two balls of clay weigh the same amount?

Now (without placing them back on the scale to confirm what is correct for the child) do the two pieces of clay weigh the same, or does one weigh more?

**Volume**

Does the water level rise equally in each glass when the two balls of clay are dropped in the water?

Now (after one piece of clay is removed from the water and reshaped) will the water levels rise equally, or will one rise more?

**FIGURE 13.1**
Piaget's conservation experiments indicated that preoperational children had difficulty with these tasks. (From *Child Development* 3/e (p. 238) by L. E. Berk. Copyright © 1994 by Allyn & Bacon, Inc. Reprinted by permission.)

events of a situation rather than on a perception of the relationship among all the parts of that situation. Piaget indicated that young children lack the ability to reason inductively—to proceed in their thinking from the specific to the general. Conversely, they cannot reason deductively—move from the general to the specifics of a situation (Flavell, 1963).

Piaget also explained preoperational thought as occurring because children between ages 2 and 7 are **perceptually bound**. In other words, their explanations of certain phenomena are largely dependent on their perceptions. This behavior is most often documented by Piaget's experiment with water poured from a tall, narrow container into a short, wide container (Inhelder, 1960). Preoperational children state that there is less water in the short wide container than in the tall, narrow container because it "looks" that way according to their perceptions.

*perceptually bound: young, preoperational children's explanations for certain phenomena (because it "looks" that way)*

A third characteristic of preoperational thinking is **centration**, in which young children center on one aspect of a situation. According to Piaget, if young children are asked to compare two rows, with one containing a lesser number of objects but spread farther apart, they usually state that this row has "more" objects. In other words, young children center on the length of the row and do not attend to the number of objects in each row (Inhelder, 1960).

*centration: the preoperational child's inclination to attend to one aspect of a situation*

**Irreversibility**, according to Piaget (1963), is the most distinguishing difference between the thinking of preoperational children and the thinking of older children and adults. Irreversibility refers to the inability of very young children to reverse their thinking and return to the beginning point of their thought. This characteristic of preoperational thinking can be explained in a variation of the row experiment described earlier. This time, the same number of objects are placed in each row and the rows are the same length. Then, as children watch, the objects in one row are spread out so that they appear in a wider array than the other row. When asked which row has more objects, preoperational children point to the longer row. Children's inability to reverse their thinking to the beginning of the experiment, where there were two rows with the same number of objects of the same length, prevents them from understanding that both rows contain the same number of objects.

*irreversibility: the inability of preoperational children to reverse their thinking and to return to their original point of thought*

## CHANGES FROM EARLY STAGES OF PREOPERATIONAL THINKING

If children ages 2 to 3 are asked to group objects that belong together, they are generally unable to do so. Sometime between ages 4 and 6, children can classify objects on the basis of their attributes. However, their efforts are not systematic, and they often forget the attribute to which they were originally attending. Late in the preoperational period, children can systematically classify objects based on attributes. However, they cannot deal with **class inclusion**, or the hierarchies of classification. This behavior is most often explained by the flower experiment (Flavell, 1985). Children are presented with an array of flowers, most of them red and a few white. The children are asked whether there are "more red flowers or more flowers." The usual response of the preoperational child is that there are more red flowers. This experiment illustrates the preoperational child's inability to

*class inclusion: understanding the relationship between class and subclass; occurs during the period of concrete operational thought*

*This young child is learning underlying geometry and physics principles regarding spatial relationships, weight, mass, and balance.*

**transivity:**
*the ability to seriate, or order, according to size; usually occurs in the period of concrete operational thought*

focus on the whole class—flowers—and the tendency to center on certain aspects of a situation.

Another distinguishing feature between the thought of early and later preoperational children is **transivity,** or the ability to seriate (order) according to size. Children ages 2 to 3 generally cannot arrange a series of objects from shortest to longest. Older preoperational children can arrange objects in order. However, they cannot seriate representationally. This ability to order mentally, without the use of concrete objects, appears later in the development of thought (Piaget & Inhelder, 1956).

A third feature of the evolution of thought that develops during the preoperational stage is identity constancy. **Identity constancy** is the understanding that the characteristics of a person or species remain the same even though its appearance can be altered through the use of masks or costumes. Younger preoperational children do not demonstrate identity constancy. Children around ages 5 and 6 seem to understand that identity remains constant even though physical appearance is changed (DeVries, 1969; Harris et al., 1986). A change in identity constancy can be observed in the following vignette.

**identity constancy:**
*the understanding that a person or species remains the same, even though appearance is changed through masks or costumes; occurs during the late preoperational stage*

*Shortly after Jeremy turned 3, Ann's mother came to visit for several weeks. It was close to Halloween, and Grandma wanted to help make Jeremy's costume. Jeremy* decided he wanted to be a ghost. Ann found an old white sheet, and Grandma began to make Jeremy's costume. At first, Jeremy seemed quite enthusiastic about being a ghost for Halloween. However, as time went on, he seemed increasingly reluctant to be fitted for his costume. When Ann and her mother picked up Jeremy at school on the day of the Halloween party, they asked Jeremy's teacher if he had worn his costume during the parade. Ms. Buckley said he had. Ann then described the change in Jeremy's behavior while the costume was being made. Jeremy's teacher then explained that at this age, reality and fantasy are not clearly defined in the young child's mind. Jeremy was probably fearful that he might actually become a ghost if he wore the costume. The ghost costume was put in a toy box, but Jeremy did not play with it. Shortly after Jeremy's fourth birthday, he was taking all the toys out of his toy box. He discovered the ghost costume, put it on, and ran around the house shouting, "Boo!" From then on, Jeremy would play "ghost" occasionally. Ann thought about what Ms. Buckley had said. She also noted that when they were reading, Jeremy was beginning to talk about whether the story could "really happen." These behaviors seemed to indicate that Jeremy was achieving identity constancy and was becoming increasingly able to differentiate between reality and fantasy. ■

## BEYOND PIAGET'S THEORY

Chapter 10 reported a great deal of new research regarding Piaget's theory. This recent information indicates that even early in the preoperational stage, children are more advanced in their cognitive development than Piaget suggested. Similarly, research with older preoperational children concludes that Piaget's ideas probably need some modification. Following is an overview of some of this research as summarized by Berk (1989).

Gelman and Shatz (1978) found that children at 4 years of age use simpler speech when talking to 2-year-olds than when talking with adults. Gelman (1979) also found that 4-year-olds indicated through their speech behaviors that they were aware adults knew more than they did. Gelman suggests that this adjusting of speech to younger children and adults could not take place if preoperational children were truly egocentric.

Additional research also suggests that both 3- and 4-year-olds are capable of attending to transformations and can reverse their thought (Bullock & Gelman, 1979; Gelman, Bullock, & Meck, 1980). Other studies indicate that when the number of items in conservation of number tasks is reduced from six or seven to three, children ages 3, 4, and 5 are able to conserve (Fuson, Secada, & Hall, 1983; Gelman, 1972). Other researchers, however, argue that true conservation should occur without reducing the number of items. In addition, these researchers believe that true conservation occurs only when children can reverse a transformation internally without actual counting or matching (Halford & Boyle, 1985).

In summary, there appears to be a growing belief that younger preoperational children may be perceptually bound in their approach to conservation problems. However, as children move through the preoperational stage, their reliance on perceptual strategies to solve problems decreases. Gradually, they begin to solve conservation problems through counting and pairing. They learn to solve problems containing a large number of items, and later in the elementary school years they

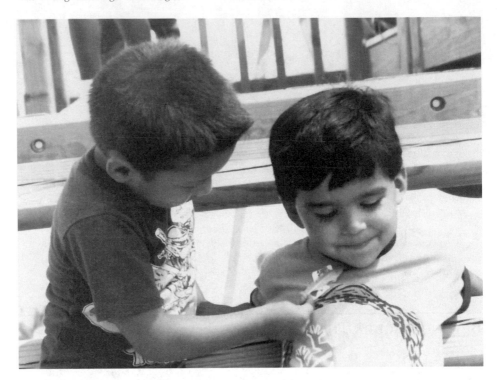

*Research indicates that preoperational children use simplified language when talking to younger children, suggesting that 4-, 5-, and 6-year-olds are not as egocentric as Piaget theorized.*

do not have to rely on concrete experiences to solve conservation problems (Siegler, 1981; Siegler & Robinson, 1982).

Studies within the past two decades have yielded evidence suggesting that young children's thought is more sophisticated and evolving than Piaget indicated. However, Piaget's notion that true understanding of conservation of number, length, liquid, and mass is probably not possible until age 6 and after is probably accurate (Flavell, 1985). In addition, the effects of training in the development of logical operations in the preoperational child appear to be influenced by age (Beilin, 1980). Older preoperational children seem much better able to generalize to situations outside the training context (Field, 1981; Siegler, 1981).

One group of **neo-Piagetians**—researchers who have modified Piaget's ideas—believes that research may eventually identify global stages that can be applied to all areas related to cognitive development, such as language, the arts, and mathematics (Case et al., 1986; Case, 1992).

*neo-Piagetians: researchers who support Piaget's ideas, but are updating his theory according to recent findings about cognitive development*

## INFORMATION PROCESSING AND LEVELS OF PROCESSING

While Piaget's theory provides us with a sense of how a child thinks at different points in growth and development, the information-processing model of child

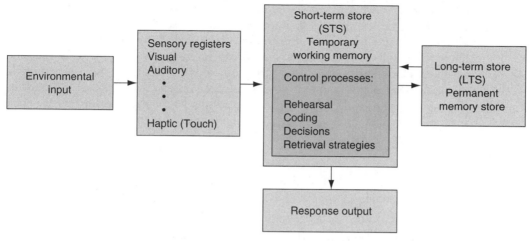

**FIGURE 13.2**

The information-processing approach compares cognitive development to the way a computer works. (From *The Development of Children* 2/e (p. 333) by Michael Cole and Sheila R. Cole. Copyright © 1993 by Michael Cole, Sheila R. Cole, and Judith Boies. Reprinted with permission by W. H. Freeman and Company.)

cognition represents a systematic approach to cognitive development that differs from Piaget's invariant stage-sequence theory, and is often compared to the way a computer works. This perspective on cognitive development is illustrated in Figure 13.2.

As this model suggests, an individual receives information from the environment through the senses (vision, hearing, touch, taste, and smell). This information then enters the STS (short-term memory storage) file, a place where the mind can work on this information. How does one cognitively "work" on this temporary information? According to the information-processing model, certain cognitive events occur that either result in placing this information in long-term memory or discarding it. Such events including attending; such as "rehearsal" which employs repeating a thought or concept over and over until it can be understood, or perhaps retrieved from long-term memory; coding features of the concept to form mental images or representations; making decisions about certain features of the input that make it worth remembering; and employing problem solving and retrieval strategies.

Certain processes flow from these cognitive activities and mental strategies: drawing further information from the environment to process, and/or drawing further information from the LTS (long term memory) file to assist in interpreting, classifying, and modifying this new information so that one can use the information, respond to it, and/or simply store it in the LTS file.

In the past, children's cognitive development and thinking processes were explored in terms of their lack of sustained attention (Vurpillot, 1968; Zinchenko, Chzhi-Tsin, & Tarakanov, 1963). Limited ability to store information in long-term and short-term memory and to apply it was viewed as problematic for young children (Case & Khanna, 1981; Chi & Klahr, 1975; Siegler, 1986). However, many parents and early childhood professionals have observed that young children can indeed hold information in short-term and long-term memory and, in certain contexts, can demonstrate extended attention spans. Consider the number of 4- and 5-year-olds with long-term memory and extended attention spans when dealing with the subject of dinosaurs. Indeed, investigation has demonstrated that both short- and long-term memory appear to vary more widely than previously thought (Siegler, 1983). Consequently, some researchers have modified the memory-store-information processing approach by proposing a **levels of processing theory**. This idea suggests that one's attention is not limited by memory constraints but is influenced by:

*levels of processing theory:*
*an information-processing model that focuses on the depth of attention rather than aspects of memory in explaining levels of cognitive performance*

- the child's increasingly effective use of strategies in local, meaningful circumstances which are easier to process than global or general situations,

- the child's interests,

- the extent of the child's background knowledge and experience,

- amount of freedom and time to mentally combine and consolidate previous ideas or generate new ones, and

- the manner in which information is presented.

When information is presented appropriately, levels of attention and cognitive performance increase, and at times surpass, the performance of less knowledgeable adults and older children (Craig & Tulving, 1975; Vygotsky, 1987; Beddard & Chi, 1992). Information that is processed meaningfully and linked with other background information is retained and can be demonstrated by the young child. Information presented in a superficial way is soon forgotten and cannot be used by the child. Early childhood professionals should assist young children in observing and attending to environmental stimuli and provide interesting and meaningful experiences that develop background information on which to draw when confronted with new information. Early childhood professionals will continue to derive improved practices from emerging research and discussion of various models of cognitive development. Detailed models of information processing/levels of processing are still being formulated. Many researchers believe development is a continuous process while others take a Piagetian point of view.

In the last decade, Case (1992) has attempted to portray a model of cognitive development that integrates both stage/sequence theory with recent research relating to specific tasks, developmental domains, and sociocultural dimensions of cognitive development. Case's theory is an attempt to unite Piagetian and information-processing theories. Case asserts that research data support the concept of general stages in cognitive development, however, this concept can constrain our thinking about cognitive operations in all areas of development.

Other groups of neo-Piagetians continue to maintain that differences in cognitive development among and within same-age subjects is the rule rather than the exception (Gelman & Baillargeon, 1983; Keating & MacLean, 1988; Kuhn, 1992). These investigators believe children do learn through assimilation and accommodation. However, they suggest that each domain or area of learning has its own stages and that no global stage applies to all domains. They also believe that there is little carryover from what a child learns in one situation to another. Thus, a stage in learning language differs from stages in learning mathematics, or drawing.

While Piaget's theory has formed the cornerstone for thinking, research, and practice for over 40 years, more contemporary research identifying weaknesses in Piaget's theory has provided additional ways to view childhood thinking and learning. Information-processing models and information levels of processing models continue to be formulated. Like growth and development, this research process is a continuous one and promises further enlightenment with each new revelation.

## OTHER EXPLANATIONS FOR COGNITIVE DIFFERENCES IN YOUNG CHILDREN

Another explanation for the differences in young children's thinking compared with the thought of older children and adults is addressed in the **biological model**, which focuses on the processes of growth and development in the brain. The **sociocultural model** takes into account the child's experiences in the various layers of the ecosystem (Bronfenbrenner, 1979), which promote cognitive development through scripts. This section provides information regarding biological and sociocultural influences on cognitive development in young children.

*biological model: the explanation of cognitive development as influenced by biological processes of growth and development in the brain*

Chapter 8 discussed the rapid brain growth in young children. You will remember that by age 6, the brain has developed about 90 percent of its adult weight (Tanner, 1978). Along with this weight gain, myelination occurs. During myelination, fatty tissue covers the nerve cells, facilitating the sending of impulses along the neurons (see Figure 13.3). Rapid growth and myelination in the brain coincide with the development of the auditory system, rapid language development, and increased processing of visual, spatial, and temporal (or time) information. Simultaneously, these increased connections promote better processing of information, and their presence in the speech center of the brain facilitates the development of symbolization and communication. Gains in short-term memory and small motor skills are also attributed to the rapid myelination occurring during ages 4 and 5 (Cole & Cole, 1989).

*sociocultural model: the explanation of cognitive development as influenced by various sociocultural experiences within the family, the community, and society*

Another explanation for children's differences in cognitive development concerns the influence of the sociocultural experiences within the family, community, and society on the formation of scripts. Recall from Chapter 10 that as young children repeatedly participate in routine events with adults over a period of time, they develop ideas about the roles people play in certain situations, the objects or materials used, and the order of events in the situation. This information is called a *script*. As children experience certain contexts over a period of time, they develop more complete scripts.

Children at 4 and 5 years of age generally demonstrate more knowledge of certain scripts than do most 3-year-olds (Nelson, 1986; Nelson & Gruendel, 1981). When playing restaurant, they take time to decide on the roles: who will be the "cooker," the server, and the diners. Then children enact these various roles, demonstrating knowledge of behaviors and sequences of events such as entering restaurants, ordering, eating, paying for the food, and leaving the restaurant. Four and 5-year-old children often use appropriate materials to facilitate script enactment.

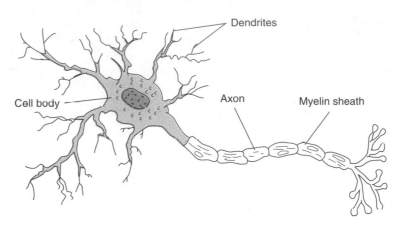

FIGURE 13.3
The growth of myelin, or fatty tissue, around the nerve cells of the brain coincides with development of the auditory system, rapid language development, and increased processing of visual, spatial, and temporal information.

They may use menus, ordering pads, pencils, dishes, pots and pans, tables, chairs, and cash registers. They may wear aprons and chef's hats. Thus, as children mature, their increased cognitive awareness of the culture is reflected in their scripts.

The idea of scripts can also help explain some of the differences in cultural behaviors of young children (Childs & Greenfield, 1980). For example, children from some Asian cultures become very skilled at eating with chopsticks, origami (the art of paper folding), and other small motor tasks because adults in the culture provide many opportunities for them to practice these skills. These skills may not be important to the scripts or contexts of other cultures. Therefore, children from other cultures do not have the opportunity to repeatedly practice the same small motor tasks and thus are less advanced in their small motor development than children from some Asian cultures.

These various attempts to explain young children's cognitive development are not complete when considered alone. Until a more complete theory is developed, the suggestions of Piaget, the neo-Piagetians, the information-processing model, the biological model, and the sociocultural model should be considered as possible pieces to the puzzle of cognitive development. Cole and Cole (1989, pp. 333–338) provide an interesting example of how all of these approaches can be used to facilitate the understanding of a cognitive behavior such as drawing. This example is partially summarized in the following section.

## THE DEVELOPMENT OF DRAWING

### STAGE PERSPECTIVE

Cross-cultural research suggests that children all over the world move through similar stages in the development of their drawing (Gardner, 1980; Kellogg,

**FIGURE 13.4**
Angela's first representational picture of a witch with face, hair, eyes, and two legs protruding from the head is an example of the stage perspective in the development of drawing.

1969). This information supports Piaget's notion that development proceeds in stages. The first stage is scribbling.

Angela had seen her mother write while doing her homework. Cheryl would give her paper and pencil, and Angela would then scribble. Angela makes no attempt to label these spontaneous scribbles. Rather, her scribbling is uncontrolled, and she engages in this activity for the pleasure of movement and to observe the marks her movements make. ■

Around age 3, children develop more small motor control. They also begin to realize that lines can be used to make representations of objects that interest them. The month after Angela turns 3, she brings home her first representational picture. It is October, and Angela's class in the child care center has been talking about Halloween. Her interest in this special day is reflected in her picture of a witch (see Figure 13.4). Gradually, Angela's drawings become stereotyped repetitions with radiating suns, rainbows, and square houses with triangular roofs. She then begins to draw pictures of both people and objects, reflecting a variety of experiences and interests. At around age 6, Angela, like other children of this age, will begin to become more realistic in her drawing.

## INFORMATION-PROCESSING PERSPECTIVE

Cole and Cole (1993, p. 347) use the child's gradual ability to draw a three-dimensional house as an example of how the information-processing perspective relates to the development of drawing. Over a period of time, children gradually learn the drawing rules for creating objects in the third dimension. They remember that all three spatial coordinates—length, width, and depth—must be used in their drawings (see Figure 13.5).

## BIOLOGICAL PERSPECTIVE

The biological perspective views the mind as having the ability to focus on particular kinds of environmental information. While most children seem to develop drawing ability in the stages previously described, there appear to be some interesting deviations from these patterns. A well-known exception to the typical stages of drawing was described by Selfe (1977). An autistic child named Nadia began to exhibit well-developed perspective and coordination in her drawings at age 3½. In other situations, her hand movements were uncontrolled. Selfe (1977) and Gardner (1980) suggest that a few individuals possess mental modules or mental computational devices, which cause advanced development in certain isolated areas. Nadia had very coordinated movements in her drawing but not in other areas of small motor behavior.

## SOCIOCULTURAL PERSPECTIVE

The sociocultural perspective takes the view that the content of the child's drawings reflects the traditions of the culture. In addition, children generally absorb adult and cultural expectations about what it means to draw a picture.

Shortly after Jeremy turned 3, Ann asked him to tell her about his drawing, shown in Figure 13.6 (see page 340). Jeremy said it was a cricket. Jeremy's scribbled picture is not at all representational of a cricket. He probably did not plan to draw a cricket and lacked the motor control needed to draw an identifiable cricket. Yet he is beginning to understand that marks he makes can be named and that he is expected to produce in his drawings objects that can be named. Children at 4 and 5 years of age gradually come to understand adult requests to "draw a picture." ■

The preceding examples adapted from Cole and Cole (1989) should help you understand that different theories should not necessarily be viewed as competing.

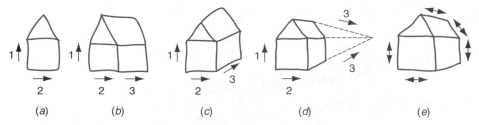

(a)         (b)         (c)         (d)         (e)

**FIGURE 13.5**

The increasing ability of school-age children to remember to represent all three spatial coordinates of length, width, and depth in a three-dimensional drawing is an example of the application of the information-processing model to the development of drawing. (From *The Development of Children* 2/e [p. 347] by Michael Cole and Sheila R. Cole. Copyright © 1993 by Michael Cole, Sheila R. Cole, and Judith Boies. Reprinted with permission by W. H. Freeman and Company.)

Rather, different perspectives considered together can present a more complete picture of development, including typical patterns and explanations for exceptions to the patterns.

## LANGUAGE DEVELOPMENT

By age 4, young children's communication skills appear to be adultlike. However, research indicates that children continue to develop in the area of language into the elementary school years (Menyuk, 1988; Pflaum, 1986).

## INTELLIGENCES AND CULTURE

As mentioned previously, Gardner's (1983) theory of multiple intelligences is culturally sensitive in that "an intelligence must be valued by a culture in order to be considered a true intelligence" (Armstrong, 1994, p. 161). While all cultures make use of the seven intelligences, the value placed on particular intelligences and the ways they are used vary greatly. Armstrong (1994, p. 161) cites the following examples.

In the South Sea Islands, the Puluwat culture places high value on spatial intelligence for the purpose of navigating to and from several hundred islands. Children are taught from an early age to identify the constellations, the islands in the horizon, and textual differences on the surface of the water that pinpoint geographic information. In this society, individuals with major navigational responsibilities have more prestige than the political leaders.

Other cultures prize highly musical intelligence. For example, children of the Anang tribe in Nigeria know hundreds of dances and songs by the time they are 5 years of age. In Hungary, children are expected to learn and read musical notation due to the influence of the composer Kodaly. Armstrong (1994) emphasizes that

**FIGURE 13.6**
Jeremy names this picture "a cricket," indicating that he has become aware of
sociocultural expectations to name and label pictures.

all cultures have and use the seven intelligences. He cautions that educators therefore should exercise great caution and not refer to certain racial or ethnic groups
in terms of only one intelligence (e.g., "Blacks are musical," "Asians are logical").

## INTERACTION BETWEEN THOUGHT AND LANGUAGE

As mentioned previously, the child's developing cognitive ability to remember
more information seems to facilitate language development. In addition, as children have more experiences, they internalize more scripts and language that is
appropriate to those scripts. This common knowledge of scripts and sequencing of
events results in a new event in the development of language: sustained dialogue
between children (Nelson & Gruendel, 1981). This sustained dialogue is often
observed as children play out the scripts with which they have become familiar,
such as "going to the doctor," "eating out," or "grocery shopping."

   Despite this developing competence, young children at 4 and 5 years of age still
have a great deal to sort out in terms of language and exactly what it means. For
example, one evening, as Ann helped Jeremy out of the tub and was drying his
feet, she noticed how much his feet were shaped like Bill's. She said, "Jeremy, you

sure have your daddy's feet." Jeremy replied, "I do not have Daddy's feet. These are my feet!" Ann's **indirect speech act,** or speech that infers more than the actual utterance, was not comprehended by Jeremy.

*indirect speech act: speech that infers more than the actual words uttered*

Children begin to understand indirect speech around ages 4 and 5. At first, all young children take others' speech literally. Humor and lying are two indirect speech acts that appear during the early childhood years. Children around 5 years of age begin to be interested in riddles and jokes. They often create "jokes" that have no humorous element to older children and adults. Yet when young children provide the punch line, they laugh uproariously. They have the notion of the form of jokes or riddles, and they know it is appropriate to laugh. However, most young children around age 5 have yet to internalize the idea that words can have double meanings (Sutton-Smith, 1975). Young children also gradually become aware of lying. They are usually not very proficient at lying because they cannot take into account all the attributes of the addressee, the relationship between the addressor and the addressee, and the context (Menyuk, 1988).

As discussed in Chapter 10, the scaffolding of adults and older children can help younger children develop in their thought and language. In addition, adults need to provide many experiences for children to develop meaning. Thus, the ideas of activity and interaction continue to be important for the language development of 4- and 5-year-olds, just as they are for children 2 through 3 years of age.

## DEVELOPMENT OF SYNTAX

As children enter the fourth year, conjunctions with *and* begin to appear ("I want cookies *and* milk). Later connectives such as *then, because, so, if, or,* and *but,* appear. Use of *when, then, before,* and *after* develop still later (Bowerman, 1979, p. 287). Embedded sentences, tag questions, indirect object–direct object constructions, and passive sentence forms also begin to appear during ages 4 and 5. (For examples of these forms of language, see Figure 13.7.) By the end of the fifth year, most children also have a broader understanding of pronouns. For example, they know that a pronoun does not always refer to the name of another person in the sentence, as in "*She* said Sally was sick." During the fifth and into the sixth year, children begin to incorporate irregular inflections into their speech (Menyuk, 1964). At this time, they may include both the irregular forms and the overgeneralization within the same sentence: "We gocd/we went/we wented to my grandma's house last night." These behaviors indicate that children are becoming aware that there are some exceptions to the regularities of inflectional endings and are trying to incorporate these irregularities into their speech.

## SOUND PRODUCTION

Many children become considerably more proficient in the production of various sounds between ages 4 and 5. However, a number of children are still learning to produce some sounds even into the elementary school years. Table 13.1 (shown on pp. 343–344)indicates the approximate ages at which sounds are learned. Ingram (1986) suggests that some children can hear contrasting sounds but cannot produce them. Teachers of 4- and 5-year-olds need to be aware of the relative ages for

---

**Figure 13.7**
**The Emergence of Grammatical Forms and Usage during Ages 4, 5, and 6**

1. **Conjunctions**
   a. Using *and* to connect whole sentences:
      "My daddy picked me up at school *and* we went to the store."
      "We ate breakfast *and* we ate doughnuts, too!"
   b. Later expressing relations between clauses using *because* and *if:*
      "I can't hold my cup *because* I'm just little."
      "I'll play with my new truck *if* my daddy will bring it."

2. **Embedded Sentences**
   "I *want to hold it* myself!"
   "I *want to go to sleep* in my big boy bed."
   "My mommy said *she could fix it.*"

3. **Tag Questions**
   "I can do it myself, can't I?"
   "Caitlin is crying, isn't she, Mommy?"
   "Mommy, this shoe is too small, isn't it Daddy?"

4. **Indirect Object–Direct Object Constructions**
   "My Mommy showed Daddy her new briefcase."
   "I gave Nikki my new toy just to share."
   "Ms. Gray called me on her telephone!"

5. **Passive Sentence Forms**
   "The car was chased by the dog."
   "My toy was broken by the hammer."
   "The page was ripped by a ghost, Daddy!"

---

the development of various sounds so that they can detect delays. In addition, this knowledge can help alleviate fears of parents who are concerned that their children may need speech therapy.

Ann was concerned about Jeremy's inability to pronounce the *th* sound. Ann asked about Jeremy's speech at the spring conference with Ms. Buckley. Ms. Buckley showed Bill and Ann a chart (similar to Table 13.1) indicating that the production of *th* is expected to develop in the seventh year. Ms. Buckley reassured Bill and Ann that at this stage of Jeremy's language development, there was no need to be concerned. ■

## DIVERSITY IN CULTURAL COMMUNICATION STYLES

As discussed in Chapter 10, while young children are expanding their vocabularies and learning how to express their thoughts through oral language, they are also gaining interactional competence. Interactional competence refers to the child's knowledge of the uses of language, appropriate nonverbal behavior, and awareness of conversational conditions and constraints. Grammatic and interactional competence interact to create the child's communicative competence.

Some teachers who come from European American cultures, which tend to be highly verbal, may interpret some children's nonverbal, less verbal, or silent

**TABLE 13.1**
**Phonologic Development**

| Age* | Behavior |
|---|---|
| Birth | Crying |
| 1 week | 92% of front vowels present—/i/, /ɪ/, /e/, /ɛ/, /æ/ |
| | 7% of middle vowels present—/ɜ/, /ə/, /ʌ/, /ə/ |
| | No back vowels present—/u/, /U/, /o/, /ɔ/, /a/ |
| 1 month | Reflexive vocalization (undifferentiated vocalizations) |
| | One-half of the vowels and a few consonants present—/æ/, /ɛ/, /ʌ/, /ɪ/, /e/, /u/, /l/, /h/, /k/, /g/, /m/, /n/ |
| 2 months | Vocal play and babbling (differentiated vocalizations) |
| | Perceptual development begins |
| | Behaviors up to and including this level are derivative of chewing, sucking, and swallowing movements |
| | Vowel distribution—front vowels, 73%; middle vowels, 25%; back vowels, 2% |
| | Consonants present—/m/, /b/, /g/, /p/, /j/, /w/, /l/, /r/ |
| | Occasional diphthongs are heard |
| 3 months | Sounds added—/ɛ/, /j/, /ŋ/ |
| | Increased vocal play and babbling |
| 4 months | Sounds added—/t/, /v/, /z/, /θ/, /ɔ/, /o/ |
| | Vowel distribution—front vowels, 60%; middle vowels, 26%; back vowels, 14% |
| 5 months | Syllable repetition |
| | Sixty-three variations of sounds present |
| 6 months | Lalling begins |
| | Imitation of sounds |
| | Vowel distribution—front vowels, 62%; middle vowels, 24%; back vowels, 14% |
| 7 months | Syllables and diphthongs continue to develop |
| 8 months | Marked gain in back vowels and front consonants |
| | Babbling peaks |
| 9 months | Echolalia appears |
| | Continued imitation of sounds |
| | Jargon (jabber) |
| | More back vowels, central vowels, and consonants appear |
| 10 months | Invention of words |
| | Continued imitation of sounds and words |
| 11 months | First true word may appear |
| 12 months | Vowel distribution—front vowels, 62%; middle vowels, 16%; back vowels, 22% |
| | Consonants begin to develop faster than vowels |
| | Diphthongs continue to develop |
| | Word simplification begins |
| | Reduplication occurs |
| 16–24 months | Intelligibility is 25% |
| | Deletion of unstressed syllables |
| | Word combinations begin to develop |
| | Use of holophrastic words |
| | Diphthongs continue to develop |
| | Better production of some sounds now than later |

TABLE 13.1
(continued)

| Age* | Behavior |
|---|---|
| 24–30 months | 90% of all vowels and diphthongs are learned |
| | Mean length of utterance—three and one-half words |
| | Articulation is intelligible 60% of the time |
| | Front consonants continue to develop |
| 30–36 months | All vowels are learned except /ɝ/ and /ɚ/ |
| | All rising diphthongs—/aɪ/, /aʊ/, /oʊ/, /eɪ/—are learned except /ju/ |
| | Consonants /p/, /b/, /m/, /w/ are learned |
| | Articulation is intelligible 75% of the time |
| | Mean length of utterance—five words |
| 36–54 months | Centering diphthongs develop /iɚ/, /ɛɚ/, /aɚ/, /ɔɚ/, /uɚ/ |
| | Some stops are substituted for fricatives |
| | Consonants /n/, /ŋ/, /j/, /t/, /d/, /k/, /g/ are learned |
| | Mean length of utterance—six words |
| 54–66 months | Consonants /f/, /v/, /j/, /θ/, /ð/, /l/ are learned |
| 66–78 months | Consonants /r/, /s/, /z/, /tʃ/, /dʒ/, /ʃ/, /ʒ/ are learned |
| | The remaining middle vowels, /ɝ/ and /ɚ/, are learned as well as all centering diphthongs |
| 84 months | All consonant clusters are learned, and articulation is completely normal; morpho-phonemic rules continue developing to age 12 years |

*It should be noted that whereas many vowels and consonants are used by the infant in the first weeks or months of life, they are not actually "learned" or used consistently and meaningfully, not usually for the purpose of communication, but are random vocalizations and babbling. These sounds are gradually refined (learned) and assume semantic significance. It is interesting that a number of consonants, which are relatively late to be "learned," such as /l/, /r/, /t/, /v/, /z/, and /θ/, are used very early by the infant but often do not reappear until the child is ready to learn them and use them for purposeful communication.

*Source:* From *Clinical Management of Articulation Disorders* by C. E. Weiss, H. S. Lillywhite, and M. D. Gordon. Copyright 1980 by the C. V. Mosby Company. Reprinted by permission.

behaviors as strange or rude (Menyuk, 1988, p. 55). Trawick-Smith (1994, pp. 317–322) cites these examples:

- Some Mexican American children tend to use touch and physical cues in their interactions.

- Some Western Apache children have been observed to be somewhat less verbal in their interactions.

- Some Chinese American children often use silence to avoid conflict or threatening situations.

- Brazilian and Peruvian children frequently acknowledge guests with silence (respect).

- Arab children may use silence to indicate a wish for privacy.

- Some Japanese American children may use a smile to hide embarrassment, anger, or sorrow.
- African American, Puerto Rican, and Mexican American children may avoid direct eye contact to demonstrate respect for persons in authority.
- Japanese American children and their families may be less likely to touch others, particularly those of a different gender.
- Puerto Rican and African American children generally stand close to conversation partners and touch one another in their interactions.
- Some African American, Hawaiian, Puerto Rican, and Jewish families engage in simultaneous talk rather than turn taking in conversation.

## LITERACY DEVELOPMENT

As indicated in Chapter 10, virtually all young children have the opportunity to interact with a variety of forms of print, including business logos, print on familiar products used in the home or seen in stores, and environmental signs. However, young children need more than environmental print experiences to learn about reading and writing. They need to understand that reading and writing are tools that can help them (1) achieve goals and meet needs, (2) communicate with others, and (3) increase knowledge and understanding.

## INTERACTION AMONG THOUGHT, LANGUAGE, AND LITERACY

Children at ages 4 and 5 are very observant and demonstrate increased awareness that drawing and writing communicate thought (Dyson, 1982, 1983, 1985; Teale & Sulzby, 1986). As 4- and 5-year-olds encounter more drawing and print contexts, they become increasingly aware that the thoughts they have and share with others can be drawn or written down and read by others. This notion evolves over a period of time and in a variety of contexts. In addition, the development of small motor skills encourages these drawing and writing behaviors. If children ages 4 and 5 are provided with paper and drawing or writing tools, they usually begin to draw about experiences that are meaningful to them. As they think about these experiences and represent them through drawing, they often talk to themselves or with others who are nearby about their thoughts and drawings (Dyson, 1990). These thoughts are often incorporated into the drawings via print. An adult may say, "Tell me about your picture," or "Let me write down what you said." As children observe adults writing down their thoughts and verbalizations, they begin to understand that thoughts can be expressed not only through words and pictures but also through print. They may then begin to incorporate print into their drawings or produce "written" products themselves.

James, Cheryl, and Angela have decided to celebrate James's pay raise by going out to eat. Some friends join the celebration. Angela becomes restless while waiting for their food. One of Cheryl's friends gives Angela a pencil, and she begins to write

*Adults serve as scaffolders in young children's literacy development by answering their questions about print, taking advantage of literacy opportunities, and providing writing tools and print materials.*

lines imitating adult cursive on her paper placemat. Suddenly she tugs at Cheryl's arm, points to her writing, and says, "This says 'double cheeseburger.' This says 'Coke.' This says 'fries.'" Angela's behavior indicates an awareness of how print is used to make a request. She has observed and been thinking and deciding what she and others want to eat. These decisions were discussed and then given to the server, who wrote down what they thought and said regarding the food they wanted to eat. Thought, oral language, and written language were all used in an interactive way to get what they wanted: food. ■

Ann and Jeremy are at the greeting card store in the mall. Five-year-old Jeremy knows it is close to Ann's birthday and tells her he wants to get her a card. Ann asks Jeremy how much money he has in his Mickey Mouse billfold. He tells her, "four dollars." Ann shows Jeremy how the price is marked on the back of the card and helps him decide whether he has enough money. Jeremy begins looking at cards and selects one that has pretty flowers on it. Ann looks at it and tells him that it is a get-well card. She then directs Jeremy to the birthday cards for mothers. Jeremy finds one he likes and checks with Ann to see if he has enough money. Finding he has enough money, he takes the card to the cash register and pays for it. As soon as they get home, Jeremy goes to a basket on his toy shelf, which has pencils and felt pens. He selects a red pen and writes "4 U" on the envelope. Inside the card he writes, "I ♡ U ᒑEREMY." Jeremy's behavior indicates that he knows about cards and how thoughts are written on cards to help celebrate birthdays. He uses thought, drawing, and written language to convey his birthday greeting to his mother. ■

## AWARENESS OF PRINT AS A FORM OF COMMUNICATION

The two vignettes indicate the varied contexts in which young children continue to learn about how to talk about and write down their thoughts. These examples also demonstrate how adults continue to serve as scaffolders in promoting literacy development. Adults help children write their thoughts down, provide experiences for them to participate in literacy events, help them become aware of appropriate literacy behaviors, and provide the tools for them to practice their developing literacy awareness. Thus, four major behaviors on the part of adults ensure the continuation of print awareness in young children. The first is alertness to opportunities for literacy development in the home, school, and community (Schickedanz, 1986). Appropriate scaffolding and providing answers to children's questions also help children become more aware of print. Adults can also provide time and tools for children to engage in the act of writing. Finally, adults need to continue to provide opportunities for children to experience books and literature. Just as children need to hear oral language to learn to talk, they need to hear written language to learn how to write. Following is a discussion of how early writing and reading behaviors emerge and the importance of the interrelationship between reading and writing experiences in promoting literacy development.

## EARLY WRITING BEHAVIOR

Young children appear to first consider drawing and writing as being the same. At some point during the fourth or fifth year, most children begin to realize that drawings usually represent objects and persons within the environment and that writing represents the words for objects, persons, or thoughts. However, some young children in the primary grades continue to incorporate drawings into their writing to help them convey meaning (Davis, 1990; Dyson, 1990). Jeremy's "I ♡ U" is such an example. Occasionally, letters and numerals are also combined to express thought, for example, "I 8 ic krem" ("I ate ice cream").

Children's first attempts at writing may include imitation of adult cursive, their names or various configurations of the letters in their names, and other letters of the alphabet that they recognize and can reproduce (Clay, 1975). Just as young children experiment with blocks and paint, they play and experiment with letters (see Figure 13.8). Through this experimentation and opportunity to explore

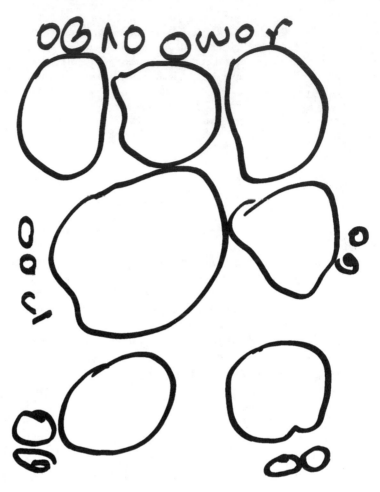

**FIGURE 13.8**
Four-year-old Jon has "labeled" the rocks in his drawing. He has used various letterlike shapes and configurations of the letters in his name, such as Os and inverted or partial Js and Ns.

writing, children begin to learn about the organization of written language
(Ferrerio & Teberosky, 1982). This is a complex process that takes time and
support from adults. Adults often forget that developmental tasks such as learning
to walk and talk take place over a period of months and years. Likewise, literacy
develops over a period of years. However, parents and teachers are not always
patient and encouraging. Adults often convey to young children that they expect
conventional or mature reading and writing behaviors within a relatively short
time. Pressuring young children to conform to adult conventions of writing and
reading can lead to problems in reading and writing with a potential long-term
impact (Holdaway, 1979). Thus, emerging-literacy researchers caution adults to
be patient, supportive, and aware of developmentally appropriate experiences.

At first, children's use of print is not always horizontal. Gradually they internalize the notion that print should proceed from left to right (Clay, 1975). At times letters are inverted, sideways, or in an unconventional position. One major concept young children have to learn about print is **constancy of position in space**. For example, a shoe is a shoe regardless of what position it is in. The same is true for a hamburger, a glass, a towel, and most other objects in the environment. This is not so for letters of our alphabet. Change the position of *b* and it is no longer a *b*. It can become a *d*, a *p*, or a *q*.

In addition, young children may reverse certain letters, words, or phrases. These **reversals**, or backward printing of letters, often cause parents to become concerned that their child has **dyslexia**, a general term for reading disorders. Teachers of 4- and 5-year-olds need to reassure parents that these reversals are a normal developmental behavior. Only if the behavior is still frequent by the end of first grade or if other developmental concerns arise should teachers refer a child for evaluation based on reversals of letters.

One explanation for these reversals, or "mirror writing," is based on the nature of various letters of the alphabet. Certain letters, for example, *J* and *S*, end in a right-to-left orientation. Thus, it is probably somewhat natural for children who have names beginning with these letters to continue writing from right to left rather than left to right. As children use these letters in their writing and work to understand the principles of directionality, reversals of these letters also appear. Jeremy signed his name on Ann's card by reversing the *J*. This behavior suggests that he is working on the left-to-right principle of print, but has not yet sorted out letters that end in the opposite direction. Sorting out these irregularities of written language can be compared to young children's sorting out irregularities in oral language ("We goed to Grandma's" rather than "We went to Grandma's").

In addition, it is difficult for children to attend to spacing concerns. They may run out of space and finish part of a word by starting another line of print below the first. Or a picture may take up most of the space and the word is written in a vertical or other unconventional position. Another common writing behavior in young children is to omit spaces between words. Explanations for this behavior include lack of knowledge about the concept that a word is a group of letters printed in close proximity. Children may also not be aware that in our language system, there are spaces between words. Some language systems use no spacing between words. Laotian print has spacing between sentences but not between words. A third explanation is that children may not think about the needs of the reader of their writing, that is, that using spaces between words is a convention that makes it easier for others to read writing. Finally, since writing is a complex task, it is difficult for young children to think about what they want to write, how to make the letters represent the sounds in the words, and at the same time remember to leave spaces between words. Some children may use their own markers, such as a dash between words, when they realize a need to separate words.

At some point, most children realize that each letter represents a sound or phoneme in our language system. If children are encouraged by supportive adults, they will often begin to invent their own forms of spelling at this point. This **invented spelling** (*bs* for *bus*, *mi* for *my*, *snac* for *snake*) may concern adults who long ago learned conventional spelling and most of its idiosyncracies. In reality,

*constancy of position in space:*
*the notion that letters of the alphabet must have fixed positions to maintain their identity*

*reversals:*
*printing letters or words in reverse*

*dyslexia:*
*a general term for the condition affecting the auditory and visual processes that cause print to be perceived with distortion*

*invented spelling:*
*spelling that young children create based on their own knowledge of sound-symbol relationships and that over a period of time evolves into conventional spelling behaviors*

close examination of these spellings often reveals very logical processing of speech in terms of articulation features on the part of young children. In fact, the more closely adults examine these invented spellings, the more respect they often have for the young language learner. Read (1971) did an extensive investigation of young children's spellings. His research documents that these invented spellings are reasonable based on similarity in articulation features and the substitution of one short vowel for another. Usually young children's invented spelling first contains consonant sounds, perhaps only the initial consonant sound, such a *b* for *bus*. Later final and medial sounds may appear with long vowel sounds, such as *bs* for *bus* and *lik* for *like*. Short vowel sounds usually appear later and are often substituted for one another, for example, *git* for *get*.

*public spelling:*
*conventional spelling*
*that children learn over*
*a period of time during*
*the schooling process*

Adults should not insist that young children spell conventionally. Encouraging them to use their private spelling facilitates their active involvement in the writing process. Young children can be told that there is **public spelling**, the spelling that everyone learns over a long time. There is also **private spelling**, which is their own way of spelling words. Adults can remind children that learning to spell conventionally takes time just like learning to walk, talk, or play soccer.

*private spelling:*
*invented spelling or*
*spelling that young chil-*
*dren create to meet*
*their personal commu-*
*nication needs before*
*they learn public or*
*conventional spelling*

A print-rich environment based on usefulness and meaning in young children's lives helps them to gradually become aware of conventional spellings. Interaction with the print in favorite books, environmental print, print in the classroom such as signs, labels, charts, stories accompanying artwork, and the placing of relevant print in various learning centers all encourage young children's gradual awareness of conventional spelling (Fields, Spangler, & Lee, 1991).

As young children encounter various print situations, their knowledge of various forms of print is reflected in their writing. Recipes are in list order, newspapers have columns, letters take letterlike forms, and stories appear in connected print format.

## EARLY READING BEHAVIOR

As mentioned in Chapters 7 and 10, adults need to begin reading to children very early. Early reading on a consistent basis is the most reliable factor in successful literacy development (Clark, 1976; Doake, 1981; Durkin, 1977; Wells, 1981). Reading to children ages 4 and 5 promotes oral language development by introducing them to new vocabulary words (Robbins & Ehri, 1994). Reading to young children also promotes other important behaviors that facilitate literacy development.

*book-handling*
*knowledge:*
*knowledge of fronts*
*and backs of books,*
*where the story begins,*
*left-to-right progres-*
*sions of the pages, and*
*differences between*
*print and illustrations*

Young children who have many story-reading experiences learn **book han-dling-knowledge**, or how to use a book. They learn that a book has a front and a back and that the story does not begin on the title page. They learn about reading one page and then going to the next, page turning, and the general left-to-right progression of pages. While young children often indicate that the illustrations tell the story, the scaffolding behavior of adults can help them realize that the print actually tells the story. Discussions about the title of the book and the names of the author and illustrator, telling and showing the child, "This is where the words are that tell me what to read to you," and casually pointing to the words can help young children get the notion that print conveys information about the book, the title, and the author as well as the story (Clay, 1979).

*Young children acquire book-handling knowledge through story-reading experiences in a variety of contexts.*

Using **predictable books,** books with repeated patterns and predictable text, facilitates print awareness (Rhodes, 1981). Repeated readings of these books encourage children to internalize the story lines. Because the illustrations in a good predictable book support the text on that page, young children often become aware of the text and how it works on that particular page. Early on, many children think each letter represents a word. Attempts to match the predictable text with the letters in a word may not work. Children eventually figure out that each cluster of letters represents a word. Or adult behaviors can help young children scaffold to the relationship of words to story line. Pointing to the text with a finger or a pointer when reading a predictable book also helps children understand the relationship between speech and print. In this early stage of literacy development, pointing is helpful in establishing the one-to-one relationship between speech and text (Holdaway, 1979).

Continuous reading to 4- and 5-year-olds helps develop other important ideas that facilitate literacy development. Just as young children need to hear oral language to learn to talk, they need to hear written language to develop ideas about how to read and write. Oral language differs from written language. Spoken language often relies on the immediate context of the situation to provide needed meaning, while written language must be more formal and complete so that the

*predictable books: books that have repeated patterns and predictable text*

reader can comprehend the meaning. In addition, as children interact with books, they see the meanings that stories can have for them in their own lives. They can see that in one book, Alexander has "terrible, horrible, no good, very bad days" just as they do. They find it interesting to learn that a triceratops has three horns. They discover that books can provide information, comfort, and joy in their lives.

Studies indicate that interaction in the form of interruptions, questions, and comments between adults and children while stories are being read facilitates children's comprehension of the stories and also of school dialogue patterns (Heath, 1983; Mehan, 1982). For example, the questions adults ask very young children about a story are similar to the kinds of questions teachers ask children in the more formal environment of the elementary school years.

## RELATIONSHIP BETWEEN READING AND WRITING

Chapter 10 indicated that in the past, reading was thought to develop first, followed by learning to write. It is now widely accepted that children can learn about reading and writing at the same time and at earlier stages than previously thought. However, this does not suggest that children at ages 4 and 5 should be expected to read and write like older children and adults. Even though it is now recognized that children learn about reading and writing earlier than previously believed, this process takes time. Furthermore, early reading and writing behaviors differ in many ways from those of older children and adults. Invented spelling and the use of fingers to match the text with verbal language are two such examples.

An awareness of the apparent interrelationship between reading and writing is important in facilitating literacy development. The previous discussion about the importance of books and reading to young children provided information about how young children gradually become aware that words, not letters, match with the oral text of the story. If young children are also provided with opportunities to write or to have their thoughts written down, they can also begin to develop concepts about what a word is. Learning to write their names, developing their own vocabulary cards, and having adults who talk about what letters are in words and what words say all help children learn to read as well as write. In addition, if children have thoughts that they want to write about, this motivates them to read what they have written. Thus, experiences in writing help provide the young child with information about reading, and vice versa.

## THE ROLE OF PLAY IN PROMOTING COGNITIVE, LANGUAGE, AND LITERACY DEVELOPMENT

Piaget (1962) suggests that children follow a developmental pattern of stages that is a unique interplay between innate human characteristics and the environment. Typically, 4- and 5-year-old children's play activities correspond to their level of cognitive development. Preschoolers frequently engage in sociodramatic and fantasy play activities. Sociodramatic play activities are characterized by a group of children assuming roles and engaging in loosely coordinated "performances."

These sociodramatic "plays" represent common daily events in children's lives, such as going to the store, playing house, or going to the hospital. The play scripts are based on reality, and as children engage in social play more frequently, they expect their peers to be knowledgeable about the details of particular roles or social contexts. Early in the preoperational stage, these enactments are one-dimensional, easily understood, and generally simplistic by adult standards. However, these early attempts to integrate a body of social knowledge and to allow these ideas to dictate their role play is rather remarkable for an egocentric, preoperational child. As children's cognitive abilities develop, their sociodramatic play incorporates more detailed information and more peer participants. However, children are less reliant on play objects to facilitate their activities. During the latter period of the preoperational stage, children begin to engage in fantasy play activities. Fantasy play is characterized by multifaceted characterizations and dynamic, intense physical activities. Surprisingly, with more abstract social information, more peer participants, and a heightened level of activity, older preschool children perform the task of coordinating fantasy play. Concrete objects that were used in sociodramatic play are no longer a necessity. Fantasy roles are constantly shifting, changing focus, and adding new characteristics at the whim of the participants. Fantasy play activities incorporate new themes and new participants to suit the desires of the entire play group or the play group leader (Bell, 1989).

According to Johnson & Yawkey (1988) and Yawkey (1988) the development of language, shared meaning, and basic literacy is greatly influenced by the development of decentralization; that is, the ability to comprehend a peer's point of view in social situations. The integration of social knowledge into a common, consistent, and unified body of information is essential to the development of social relationships among young children. Johnson, Christie, and Yawkey (1987) suggest a close relationship between group sociodramatic play and perspective taking. During the initiation and development of group play activities, an understanding of others' perspectives among participants is essential. Further, they suggest that during dramatic play, two styles of communication occur. First, pretend communication takes place and is acted out "in character" in a way that is generally consistent with the social parameters of the dramatic activity. Second, metacommunications (or communicating about their talk and scripts) occur when children break the play script and comment on the play activity as a matter of play theme management. Both Garvey (1977) and Rubin (1980) suggest that these shifts between fantasy and reality are responsible for the positive effects of sociodramatic and fantasy play on young children's cognitive, language, literacy, and social development.

## SPECIAL NEEDS IN THE DEVELOPMENT OF COGNITION, LANGUAGE, AND LITERACY

Earlier chapters have emphasized the importance of early identification of special learning needs of young children. If these needs can be identified early and

FIGURE 13.9
The Deficit Paradigm versus the Growth Paradigm in Special Education

| Deficit Paradigm | Growth Paradigm |
|---|---|
| • Labels the individual in terms of specific impairment(s) (e.g., ED, BD, EMR, LD). | • Avoids labels; views the individual as an intact person who happens to have a special need. |
| • Diagnoses the specific impairment(s) using a battery of standardized tests; focuses on errors, low scores, and weaknesses in general. | • Assesses the needs of an individual using authentic assessment approaches within a naturalistic context; focuses on strengths. |
| • Remediates the impairment(s) using a number of specialized treatment strategies often removed from any real-life context. | • Assists the person in learning and growing through a rich and varied set of interactions with real-life activities and events. |
| • Separates the individual from the mainstream for specialized treatment in a segregated class, group, or program. | • Maintains the individual's connections with peers in pursuing as normal a life pattern as possible. |
| • Uses an esoteric collection of terms, tests, programs, kits, materials, and workbooks that are different from those found in a regular classroom. | • Uses materials, strategies, and activities that are good for *all* children. |
| • Segments the individual's life into specific behavioral/educational objectives that are regularly monitored, measured, and modified. | • Maintains the individual's integrity as a whole human being when assessing progress toward goals. |
| • Creates special education programs that run on a track parallel with regular education programs; teachers from the two tracks rarely meeting except in IEP meetings. | • Establishes collaborative models that enable specialists and regular classroom teachers to work hand in hand. |

*Source:* From Armstrong, T. (1994). *Multiple intelligences in the Classroom.* Alexandria, VA: Association for Supervision and Curriculum Development. By permission of the Association for Supervision and Curriculum Development and the author.

appropriate programming planned, any negative, long-term impact can be eliminated or reduced.

Identification of special learning needs in young children usually includes **primary disabilities**, involving attention, memory, and perception, and **secondary disabilities**, which focus on thinking and oral language (Kirk & Chalfant, 1984). These disabilities can create the need for special learning environments for young children. It is critical that the early childhood professional be aware of normal development in young children. As previously discussed, adults who lack knowledge of how young children develop can interpret the common reversal of letters as an indication of dyslexia. Similarly, some adults who are not knowledgeable about the development of young children may label a young child as "hyperactive" when in reality the child is demonstrating the curiosity and motor behaviors exhibited by normal, active young children. As discussed previously, early childhood professionals realize that attention span depends on the child's interest in an activity, the appropriateness of the activity, and the child's background of experience for the activity. Two- and 3-year-old children have been observed to attend to interesting activities for periods of 30 to 45 minutes. Therefore, adults need to provide children with interesting and appropriate activities.

Armstrong (1994) argues that the notion of multiple intelligences brings an enlightened perspective to the area of special education in that it places so called "disabilities" in a broader context. He notes that the history of special education documents the "disturbing tendency," with the exception of gifted education, to operate from a deficit approach, that is, focusing on what students cannot do to help them succeed in school. Terms such as "speech pathology," "mental retardation," and "attention deficit disorder" reflect this negative viewpoint. In contrast, these developmental deficiencies can be viewed from the more positive growth paradigm, which encompasses a wider spectrum of abilities. Figure 13.9 contrasts these differing perspectives.

Early childhood development professionals need to observe children carefully to determine their more highly developed intelligences so that an alternative route can be used to address their special needs. Frequently this process of *cognitive bypassing* can be used as an alternative symbol system in an unimpaired intelligence (for example, braille for the seeing challenged or sign language for the hearing challenged) or as an alternative technology or special learning tool (Gardner, 1983, pp. 388–392).

According to Armstrong (1994, pp. 143–144), this broadened perspective and the cultivation of other intelligences to address special needs has a number of effects, including

- Fewer referrals to special education classes to facilitate inclusion
- A changing role for the special education teacher from a "pull-out" or special class teacher to a special multiple-intelligences consultant to the regular classroom teacher
- A greater emphasis on identifying strengths using qualitative and authentic measures of assessment rather than standardized diagnostic measures
- Increased self-esteem among more children within the school setting

*primary disabilities: learning disabilities involving attention, memory, and perception*

*secondary disabilities: learning disabilities involving thinking and oral language*

- Increased understanding and appreciation of students, helping to make full integration into the classroom a reality.

Nevertheless, McCollum and Bair (1994) assert that research suggests that young children with disabilities often have not only delays in development but also differences in development, thereby influencing how development is structured. They suggest that knowledge of normal development and the processes that facilitate it may be inadequate if used as the only guide to understanding and providing for the learning and development of children with special needs. They suggest that scaffolding, or the appropriate balance between support and challenge for children with disabilities, may look quite different from the child who frequently initiates and independently pursues interaction with objects, persons, and events. McCollum and Bair (1994) stress a need for more research to recognize developmentally appropriate adaptations to improving the quality of instruction as well as creating a better match between the individual child and the particular task.

McCollum and Bair suggest that the concept of developmentally appropriate practices needs to reflect the fact that children with special learning needs may require alternative methods of instruction. In particular, they may need more direct instruction. In this regard, Donaldson (1992) expresses concern regarding the notion that spontaneous, informal learning is the ideal model for all learning and that children should never be systematically taught. On the contrary, she thinks direct teaching is appropriate in certain contexts. This perspective should be extended to all young children and their opportunities for learning.

Rose and Smith (1993) state, "Both regular- and special-education personnel need to be prepared through preservice and in-service training to become a part of a new school community, a community that recognizes that all children learn, all children contribute and all children belong" (p. 62). They cite research by Guskey (1986) suggesting that staff-development can ultimately change teacher attitudes through implementing appropriate classroom practices and resulting child outcomes. These improved child outcomes, in turn, can facilitate changes in teachers' beliefs and attitudes regarding inclusion.

Many early childhood programs such as Head Start include children with disabilities in the regular classroom as the least restrictive environment. The least restrictive environment provides children with disabilities with programming that is as normal as is possible.

The term *special needs* usually brings to mind children who are identified as being at risk because they come from families with low incomes. It is important to caution against stereotyping children who come from these environments as inevitably having learning problems. Low-income 4- and 5-year-old children who have had limited or different home literacy experiences than middle-income children demonstrate continued literacy learning if they are in supportive literacy environments in the school setting (Taylor & Dorsey-Gaines, 1988; Teale, 1986). Thus, attitudes of early childhood professionals and the learning environments they create are critical in facilitating the development of young children's concepts about literacy and about themselves as learners.

Another special-needs area that has begun to receive more attention concerns gifted young children. Wolfle states, "Every child deserves a developmentally appropriate education, not just 'average' children and children who are 'behind'"

(1989, p. 47). **Gifted** children are identified as "children who give evidence of high performance capability in areas such as intellectual, creative, artistic, leadership capacity, or academic fields who require services or activities not ordinarily provided by the school in order to fully develop such capabilities" (Education Consolidation and Improvement Act, 1981, Sec. 582). Identification of young gifted children can be difficult. It is important to use multiple means of identifying and to use parents as important sources of information.

*gifted:*
*children who give evidence of high performance in various areas of development*

Teachers need to remember that the development of gifted young children may be quite uneven. One child who demonstrates advanced abilities in math may have motor development quite typical as that of a child of the same age. At times, this child may become frustrated with other children because she or he can't understand that they do not know all this child does in the area of math. Teachers need to remember that a gifted young child should be treated as a *young* child, not as an older child or a miniature adult (Wolfle, 1989). Early childhood professionals also need to be aware of gifted young children with disabilities and those who come from low-income or culturally different backgrounds. Karnes and Johnson (1989) caution that attention to this population is virtually nonexistent.

Providing a variety of activities in learning areas from which children can self-select is one approach that can help the early childhood teacher serve gifted children as well as children with other learning and developmental needs. Identifying the areas that interest children and providing materials and experiences in these areas can help support the learning needs of gifted 4- and 5-year-olds. Using parents, the community, and older child volunteers to engage in special activities and projects with gifted young children is another approach (Wolfle, 1989). Using community resources both inside and outside the classroom is still another. Finally, just as teachers of young children need to be aware of possible negative attitudes toward children who are at risk, they need to be conscious of possible prejudices against gifted young children. Wolfle (1989) comments, "There is a great deal of teacher prejudice against gifted children. Is it fair? Is it professional?" (p. 48).

## SOCIOCULTURAL FACTORS IN PROMOTING COGNITIVE, LANGUAGE, AND LITERACY DEVELOPMENT

It is important that early childhood teachers create classrooms in which all children and parents feel accepted. An **antibias curriculum** helps children become more aware of prejudice, stereotyping, and bias, as well as facilitating an awareness of the commonalities among all groups of people and the differences among cultural groups (Derman-Sparks & A.B.C. Task Force, 1989). Related sociocultural factors include the nature of support for children from diverse sociolinguistic backgrounds within the school setting.

*antibias curriculum:*
*an active approach to challenging prejudice, stereotyping, bias, and the isms (sexism, racism, etc.)*

According to Genishi, Dyson, and Fassler (1994), a great deal of controversy still surrounds bilingual education in both the public sector and the educational community. They report that statistical data seem to support "late exit" (throughout the elementary years) bilingual classrooms as opposed to "early exit" (through second grade). However, the data do not reveal significant academic differences across programs. Other programming efforts to assist students from diverse sociolinguistic backgrounds include ESL (English as a second language), immersion, structured immersion, and submersion.

Approximately three-fourths of all students who need language support are concentrated in six states. However, one-sixth of the counties in 47 states have substantial numbers of children with programmatic needs in the English language (U.S. General Accounting Office, 1994, p. 5). Challenges to providing adequate programmatic support include (1) more languages for which it is difficult to find teachers fluent in that particular language, (2) a shortage of trained bilingual teachers, (3) a lack of appropriate instructional materials, and (4) difficulties in assessing language proficiency and academic achievement. Related issues include competence in the first-language system, student transiency, parent involvement, cultural barriers, emotional needs, and overcrowding of schools (U.S. General Accounting Office, 1994, pp. 51–79).

Genishi, Dyson, and Fassler (1994) suggest that the background and qualifications of teachers, parental involvement, and willingness of staff to learn about instructional innovations may be factors related to effective bilingual programs. Learning about the culture of children's home communities helps teachers conceive a literacy program that builds on children's identities and previous knowledge, and subsequently encourages children to value and explore both of their worlds. This process increases their understanding of the dual connection and mastery of their first- and second-language systems (Perez & Torres-Guzman, 1992).

Promising approaches to helping students expand their second-language acquisition include (1) the use of objects and activities related to real life, including pictures, charts, and regalia; (2) frequent checking for student comprehension and adjusting the pacing of questions and answers; and (3) providing for a variety of response modes, including written, pictorial, and translation by other students. Other effective strategies include peer tutoring, cooperative learning, and the use of instructional aides who are fluent in the students' native languages (U.S. General Accounting Office, 1994, p. 40).

Similar issues arise concerning children who come to school with a dialect that differs from the language used within the school setting. Phillips (1994) reports on how African American children appear to respond during the first years of school. She notes that one of three outcomes generally occur: (1) children respond by continuing to use Ebonics and an African American learning style, (2) children completely immerse themselves in the demands of school and relinquish the African American style completely, or (3) children learn to operate in both school and African American styles. According to Phillips, children who learn to operate in both school and African American styles become able to switch language and behavioral styles and develop "the capability for powerful interactions both in school and in their families and community . . . the potential for transforming relationships both within and between settings" (pp. 147–148). For this third outcome to be realized, teachers need to

- Acquire an in-depth understanding of the cultural styles of African American children

- Adopt behaviors that create good rapport with students, including warmth, verbal interplay during instruction, rhythmic styles of speech, and distinctive intonation patterns
- View children and their parents as sources of information about African American learning styles
- Consult literature from reliable sources (e.g., the *Journal of Negro Education* and the *Journal of Black Psychology*)
- Examine their role as teachers in the social and political ecosystem and the role institutions can play in perpetuating discrimination against various groups in the population
- Help children to understand and develop strategies for dealing with opposing demands of school, community, and home

Williams (1994, p. 160) also cautions teachers that another sociocultural factor in promoting cognitive, language, and literacy development is the process by which knowledge is constructed. In Native American cultures, knowledge is not so much individually constructed as it is socially constructed. The process is still active in nature but is different in engagement. Consequently, providing opportunities for the observation of a model and then individual practice may be more appropriate than child initiation in facilitating learning and development.

 ## Role of the Early Childhood Professional

### Promoting Cognitive, Language, and Literacy Development in Children Ages 4 through 5

1. Provide opportunities for individual and social construction of knowledge that takes into account children's intelligences, sociocultural backgrounds, and special learning needs, including equipment and materials.
2. Provide opportunities for language development that accommodate children with special language needs and diverse sociolinguistic backgrounds: (Trawick-Smith, 1994, pp. 317-326)
   - If children indicate they are overwhelmed by the teacher's comments or questions, the teacher may need to moderate the degree of verbal behavior and to respond with smiles or touches or be in close proximity to the children.
   - Avoid criticizing children who are not used to turn taking in conversation, and provide opportunities for incorporating other strategies.
   - Use a peripheral gaze when talking with children who are sensitive to direct eye contact.
   - Be aware of children's physical touch and personal space preferences.

- Show appreciation for all languages and dialects.
- Avoid criticizing or correcting children's language.
- Encourage cross-linguistic conversation.
- Facilitate second-language acquisition.

3. Provide opportunities for literacy development that accommodate children with special needs and children from diverse sociolinguistic backgrounds.
   - Develop an awareness of appropriate practices that meet the backgrounds of children with special needs and children from diverse cultural groups.
   - Make sure learning is culturally relevant and connected.
   - Provide authentic tasks.
   - Engage in the role of scaffolder.

4. Instill an antibias curriculum in the classroom.

5. Make parent participation essential, and ensure that parents play an active role in their children's learning experiences. ■

## KEY TERMS

| | | |
|---|---|---|
| antibias curricula | gifted | primary disabilities |
| biological model | identity constancy | private spelling |
| book-handling | indirect speech act | public spelling |
| knowledge | invented spelling | reversals |
| centration | irreversibility | secondary disabilities |
| class inclusion | levels of processing | sociocultural model |
| conservation | theory | transformation |
| constancy of position | neo-Piagetians | transitivity |
| in space | perceptually bound | |
| dyslexia | predictable books | |

## REVIEW STRATEGIES AND ACTIVITIES

1. Review the key terms in this chapter individually or with a classmate.
2. Conduct traditional Piagetian conservation experiments with young children, and write your results. Next, conduct modified conservation experiments using more appropriate oral language, materials, and experimental settings. Write your results and compare your findings from both sets of experiments. Were you results the same or different? Why?
3. Observe children in the sociodramatic area of the classroom or in learning areas. Document the following areas:
   a. Children's knowledge of scripts
   b. Possible cultural differences in play behaviors
4. Collect samples of young children's writing. Analyze them for children's concepts about print, including

a. Meaning
b. Use of space
c. Knowledge of directionality
d. Concept of word
e. Invented spelling

5. Interview early childhood professionals in inclusive classroom settings. Ask them to describe how they provide cognitive, language, and literacy experiences for children with developmental needs and diverse sociocultural backgrounds.

6. Ask early childhood professionals to discuss parent participation in their children's learning experiences.

## FURTHER READINGS

Derman-Sparks, L., & A.B.C. Task Force. (1989). *Anti-bias curriculum: Tools for empowering young children.* Washington, DC: National Association for the Education of Young Children.

Donaldson, M. (1992). *Human minds: An exploration.* London: Penguin.

Edwards, C., Gandini, L., & Forman, G. (Eds.). (1993). *The hundred languages of children.* Norwood, NJ: Ablex.

Ollila, L. O., & Mayfield, M. I. (Eds.). (1992). *Emerging literacy: Preschool, kindergarten and primary grades.* Boston: Allyn & Bacon.

Perez, B., & Torres-Guzman, M. E. (1992). *Learning in two worlds: An integrated Spanish/English biliteracy approach.* White Plains, NY: Longman.

Siegler, R. (1991). *Children's thinking,* 2nd ed. (1991). Englewood Cliffs, NJ: Prentice-Hall.

# PART SIX

# The Young Child
# Ages 6 Through 8

# CHAPTER FOURTEEN

*Children are, after all, growing organisms whose development shows an organization, pattern, and direction that is characteristic of the species.*

David Elkind

# Physical and Motor Development Ages 6 Through 8

After studying this chapter, you will demonstrate comprehension by:

- Outlining expected patterns of physical and motor development in children ages 6 through 8.

- Describing landmarks in large and small motor development in children ages 6 through 8.

- Describing perceptual-motor development in children ages 6 through 8.

- Describing body and gender awareness in children ages 6 through 8.

- Identifying major factors influencing physical and motor development in children ages 6 through 8.

- Suggesting strategies for enhancing physical and motor and perceptual-motor development in children ages 6 through 8.

## PHYSICAL/MOTOR COMPETENCE OF THE YOUNG CHILD 6 THROUGH 8 YEARS OLD

### GENERAL PHYSICAL CHARACTERISTICS

The expected height of a 6-year-old is about 45 inches. Over the next 2 or 3 years, increases in height average 2 to 3 inches each year. Individual heights can range 2 to 2½ inches on either side of the average of 45 inches. Children's heights are closely related to the heights of their parents, though children today seem to "top out" at an average of 1 to 2 inches taller than their parents. This is thought to be due to improved nutrition and health care for children over the past 50 years.

Gross deviations from the average may be cause for concern. Unusual variations in height and growth rates could be a result of illness, malnutrition, thyroid or pituitary gland dysfunction, or some inherited anomaly. As well, the failure to thrive syndrome mentioned in Chapter 8, associated with severe lack of emotional security, may be a contributing factor. Once the cause or causes are identified, appropriate treatment may set the growth rate back on course. However, for the most part, growth patterns and rates are genetically programmed.

Weight graphs of boys and girls reveal similar trends. While boys are usually heavier than girls at birth, girls catch up with them, and by age 8, boys and girls weigh about the same. The weight of 6-year-old boys at the 50th percentile on the growth chart is around 45.5 pounds. Boys gain an average of about 5 pounds per year over the next three years. The weight of girls at the 50th percentile position on the growth chart is slightly less than that of boys at 6 years old (42.9 pounds), but by age 8 there is little difference in their weights, with girls weighing around 54.6 pounds and surpassing boys in weight by age 10 to 12.

Variations in weight are due to many of the same factors as those associated with variations in height. Differences may be attributed simply to differences in body build, but may also be due to over- and undernutrition. Activity levels and metabolic disorders are often related to weight deviations in children. Efforts to remedy weight problems in children should always be guided by a physician familiar with the individual child's health history and current health status.

Body proportions change with increases in height as slender legs and arms continue to grow longer in proportion to the trunk. Muscles of the arms and legs are small and thin; the hands and feet continue to grow more slowly than the arms and legs. The abdomen becomes flatter, shoulders more square, and chest broader and flatter. The trunk is slimmer and more elongated, and posture is more erect. The head is still proportionally large, but that top-heavy look of younger bodies is diminishing. Facial features are also changing. The forehead is more proportionate to the rest of the face, and the nose is growing larger. The most dramatic change to facial features during this period are those brought on by the shedding of deciduous (baby) teeth and the eruption of permanent teeth. Figure 14.1 shows the approximate ages at which the permanent teeth erupt.

**Recent Findings.**   Physical growth is generally believed to proceed at a slow but steady pace, with a slight decline in rate of growth during the 6-to-10-year age period, followed by a growth spurt during puberty and early adolescence. However, in what may come to be viewed as breakthrough research on growth patterns, Dr. Michelle Lampl (1994), a growth researcher at the University of Pennsylvania suggests a different pattern. While additional studies are needed to answer a number of questions arising from her findings, her research challenges traditional assumptions about how children grow. Lampl's research found that rather than growing at a gradual, regular pace, children grow in short, dramatic spurts, with starts and stops. Some children grew as much as 1/2 inch in a day, followed by a period of no growth at all for several days and sometimes weeks and even months. This researcher also noted that children exhibited distinct behaviors before and during growth pulses, including irritability, sleeping more, and greater hunger than usual. These new findings spark a need for additional studies relating to the cell division process, hormonal influences on growth, and the biochemical process(es) that trigger growth pulses. Lampl's research, along with continuing studies of the growth hormone (GH),

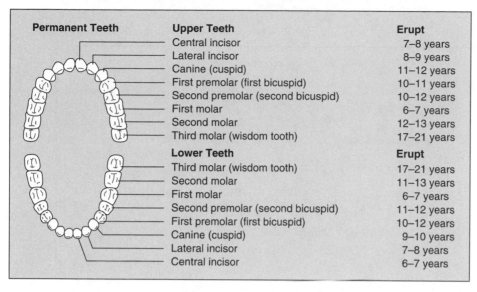

| Permanent Teeth | Upper Teeth | Erupt |
|---|---|---|
| | Central incisor | 7–8 years |
| | Lateral incisor | 8–9 years |
| | Canine (cuspid) | 11–12 years |
| | First premolar (first bicuspid) | 10–11 years |
| | Second premolar (second bicuspid) | 10–12 years |
| | First molar | 6–7 years |
| | Second molar | 12–13 years |
| | Third molar (wisdom tooth) | 17–21 years |
| | **Lower Teeth** | **Erupt** |
| | Third molar (wisdom tooth) | 17–21 years |
| | Second molar | 11–13 years |
| | First molar | 6–7 years |
| | Second premolar (second bicuspid) | 11–12 years |
| | First premolar (first bicuspid) | 10–12 years |
| | Canine (cuspid) | 9–10 years |
| | Lateral incisor | 7–8 years |
| | Central incisor | 6–7 years |

**FIGURE 14.1**
Facial features change dramatically during the period from ages 6 to 8 with the shedding of (a) deciduous teeth and the eruption of (b) permanent teeth. (From American Dental Association (1995). *CDT-1 First Edition (1990-1995): A User's Manual.* With permission from the American Dental Association.)

released by the pituitary gland, may enable future treatments for children with growth disorders that are more accurate and more predictive of outcomes at maturity.

Such research may help scientists to discover the unique growth pulse characteristics of individuals that result in very short or very tall stature at maturity. Growth hormone treatments for children with growth deficiencies have been available for many years and have improved expected growth attainments in certain of these children. Such treatment has been used in very limited cases and under strict medical supervision. At present, researchers believe there is little evidence that GH treatment will make a healthy short child a taller adult (Saenger, 1991). Such questions of ethics surrounding potential abuse in manipulation of the growth process have arisen. For instance, consider a child who is expected to reach a mature height of 6 feet but whose parents want him to be taller so that he can play basketball some day and urge professionals to manipulate the child's growth pulses. Who makes such a decision? Is this decision in the best interest of the child? What might be the long-term physiological, psychological, and social consequences for the child? How should the medical profession respond? It will be interesting to follow this issue.

## LARGE MOTOR DEVELOPMENT

Motor development affects all facets of a child's life. The importance of coordinated large motor abilities was stressed in earlier chapters. Such coordination facilitates

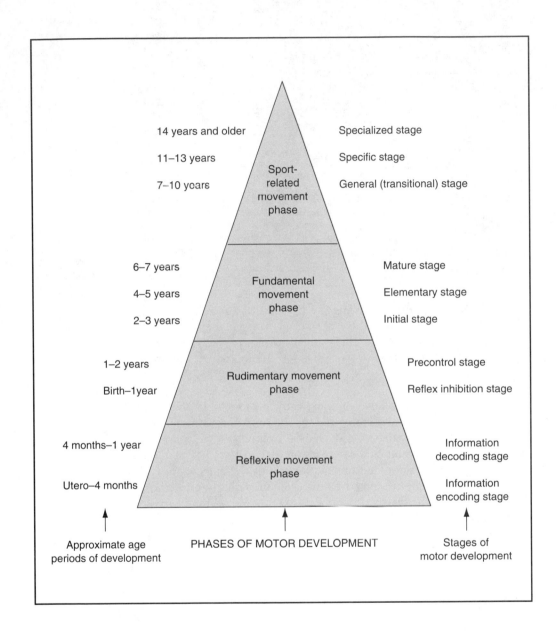

**FIGURE 14.2**
Gallahue (1982) outlines the progression of motor development from prebirth to adolescence. (Reprinted with permission of Simon and Schuster, Inc. from the Merrill/Prentice Hall text *Developmental Movement Experiences for Children* by David L. Gallahue. Copyright © 1982 by Prentice Hall, Inc.)

**fundamental movements** of running, walking, jumping, climbing, kicking, and reaching. Facility with fundamental movements paves the way for the acquisition of more complex coordinations and movements involved in typical games and sports of the 6- through 8-year-old: chasing, dodgeball, catching, and throwing.

Figure 14.2 shows the phases of motor development as outlined by Gallahue, (1982) from reflexive movements of prenatal and infant development, to rudimentary movements of the toddler, to fundamental movements during the 3- through 7-year-old period, and then to the sports-related movement abilities of the 7- to 14-year-old. The latter two phases are important to our discussion of the 6- through 8-year-old, as a number of implications can be drawn about developmentally appropriate and inappropriate physical activities and expectations for this age group.

*fundamental movements: coordinations that are basic to all other movement abilities*

## ORGANIZED GAMES AND SPORTS

Motor skills advance with increasing age and are enhanced by opportunities to use emerging abilities in active, unstructured play and child-initiated games. Should children be given instruction in specific skill areas, such as dance, gymnastics, or

*Opportunities to engage in spontaneous and organized games enhance both fundamental movements and game-related skills.*

swimming? If so, is there an optimal time to begin such instruction? Is there a period in development when such instruction could hinder further development or curtail interest?

Figure 14.2 suggests that there may be optimal periods for instruction in specific skill areas. Gallahue (1982, p. 23) asserts that fundamental movement abilities must not only be present but must also be refined before the introduction of specific skill training. Gallahue identified the following fundamental abilities as prerequisites to such training:

- *Basic locomotion:* walking, running, leaping, jumping, hopping
- *Locomotion combinations:* galloping, sliding, skipping, climbing
- *Propulsive manipulation:* throwing, kicking, punting, striking, volleying, bouncing, rolling
- *Absorptive manipulations:* catching, trapping
- *Axial stability:* bending, stretching, twisting, turning, swinging
- *Static and dynamic postures:* upright balances, inverted balances, rolling, starting, stopping, dodging, floating

According to Gallahue, these skills do not automatically emerge with maturation but rely on some guidance and planned opportunities for development. However, not until these coordinations are refined will children benefit from instruction and participation in such formalized activities as baseball, hockey, tumbling, track, swimming, wrestling, racquet games, dance, and so on. Preschool and primary-grade children are developing and refining these fundamental movements. Opportunities to use these abilities should be provided in both informal and guided ways through rhythm and movement activities, well-designed and well-constructed outdoor play equipment, simple games, and guided practice. Children can be assisted with such activities as aiming for a target when throwing a ball or bean bag, jumping specified distances, hopping on one foot and then the other for a specified count, catching balls thrown from various distances, kicking a ball to a target, balancing on balance beams, and walking with facility on the balance beam forward, backward, and sideways.

Based on the foregoing information, organized sports training and competition may not be desirable for children 6 and 7 or younger, since their fundamental coordinations are not sufficiently refined. For the 8-year-old, such organized activities must be encouraged with an understanding of the specific motor capabilities and interests of the individual child. Consideration must be given not only to the physiological ramifications of early specific skill training but also to social, emotional, and cognitive aspects. Individual children bring to any kind of formal instruction their own interests, aptitudes, motivations, and perceptual-motor and cognitive abilities. In addition, as children enter the school years, peer group acceptance becomes a critical goal in their lives. Success with a particular sport confers status on the child, while failure can be embarrassing and sometimes socially ostracizing. Parental expectations and disappointments strain the child's efforts to achieve and tax the child's sense of autonomy, initiative, industry, and self-esteem. Prematurely imposing formal training and competition on young children places them at risk for injury, diminished interest in participation, lowered self-esteem and self-confidence, and unnecessary social and emotional pressures.

## SMALL MOTOR DEVELOPMENT

By ages 6, 7, and 8, prehension is exhibited in the ability to hold a pencil or other writing implement, select and pick up the small pieces of a jigsaw puzzle, squeeze glue from a plastic bottle, and use scissors. Dexterity is revealed in assembling models and other small constructions, playing jacks with facility, shuffling and sorting playing cards, and using household tools such as a hammer or screwdriver with reasonable efficiency. Managing clothes and food packaging, unlocking a door with a key, turning the pages of a book, and folding paper along straight lines all require dexterity and are generally exhibited by the early primary grades.

As children enter the primary grades, handwriting becomes an important skill. Since small motor coordinations are dependent on fairly well-established large motor coordinations, most first-graders do not exhibit strong drawing and handwriting skills. Children who have difficulty with handwriting may be given additional opportunities to refine their large motor skills. Additional large motor activities, along with a variety of manipulative games and activities, enhance small-muscle development and eye-hand coordination.

Mastery of drawing and handwriting skills is dependent on both large and small motor development and coordination. Adults who are cognizant of the emerging small motor skills needed for handwriting will provide opportunities for children to use these skills in both guided and unguided endeavors. Lamme (1979) lists the following prerequisites to skilled handwriting:

1. Small-muscle development
2. Eye-hand coordination
3. Ability to hold a writing tool
4. Ability to make basic strokes
5. Letter perception
6. Orientation to printed language

In addition to ongoing large motor activities and a variety of manipulative games and activities, opportunities to use the tools of reading and writing assist children in eye-hand coordination and visual/perceptual refinements. An assortment of writing implements such as felt markers, pencils, ballpoint pens, and a variety of papers encourage children to use their emerging handwriting skills. Experiences with print, such as story reading and environmental print, and opportunities to write notes, lists, and stories enhance the visual/perceptual abilities necessary for later skilled drawing and handwriting.

*Children need varied opportunities to use emerging small motor skills in both guided and unguided endeavors.*

## PERCEPTUAL-MOTOR DEVELOPMENT

At ages 6, 7, and 8, children have fairly well-organized perceptual abilities (Bornstein, 1988). These abilities continue to be refined as children combine sensory and motor activities with cognitively challenging endeavors. Perceptual-motor development is dependent on both maturation and experience.

Recall that the components of perceptual-motor development include both sensory abilities and kinesthetic sensitivity. The sensory components of perceptual-motor abilities include visual (depth, form, and figure perception), auditory (discrimination and memory), and tactile (discrimination and memory) perception. Kinesthetic abilities include body, spatial, and directional awareness, and temporal awareness relating to rhythm, sequence, and synchrony (Gallahue, 1982).

Some important perceptual abilities during this period include recognizing and adjusting to one's own and others' personal space and spatial and directional awareness needed for effective participation in games. Following directions in school (e.g., "Please walk in a single line on the right side of the hallway.") requires perceptual abilities, as does developing **figure-ground discrimination** (the ability to focus on the dominant figure in a picture without being distracted by elements in the background). Figure-ground discrimination is dependent on size, shape, and form perceptions, which are helpful in forming letters and numbers.

*figure-ground discrimination: the ability to focus on the dominant figure in a picture without being distracted by elements in the background*

Visual memory assists the child in following written instructions, and auditory memory facilitates carrying out verbal instructions.

Perceptual-motor abilities at this age are fostered through both large and small motor activities. Games and activities that require visual-motor coordinations, such as tossing a beanbag to a target (large motor) and manipulating puzzle pieces (small motor), foster visual-perceptual development. Auditory-motor coordinations are fostered through rhythm and dance activities (large motor) and listening in order to match pairs of tone bells (small motor). Tactile discriminations occur when children attempt to tear, rather than cut, shapes from art paper. Kinesthetic awareness is fostered by playing games such as walking through a maze or traversing an obstacle course.

The relationship between these abilities and school success is interesting to scholars. Refined perceptual motor abilities enhance the child's ability to meet the expectations of the school experience. Visual, auditory, tactile, and kinesthetic perceptions, integrated with refined motor coordinations, enhance all types of learning.

## RELATIONSHIP BETWEEN PHYSICAL/MOTOR DEVELOPMENT AND PSYCHOSOCIAL DEVELOPMENT

### SELF-CONCEPT, SELF-CONFIDENCE, AND INTERACTIONS WITH OTHERS

Whereas the younger child's self-concept is based on general physical characteristics, a more abstract, less physically based concept emerges during the early school years. Children at this age have the ability to compare themselves with others and also have an awareness of their own unique abilities, traits, and the roles they play within various family and social groups. At this age, young children may become self-critical and, perhaps, critical of others, engaging in putting down or teasing others, or making self-deprecating remarks. They are becoming sensitive to what others think of them and whether or not they are included in social groupings.

Toward the end of the 6- through 8-year period, children may begin to assess themselves against some internalized measure relating to some self-imposed expectation. They may exaggerate or diminish their own attributes and the attributes of others. Their levels of aspiration may not be synchronized with their actual abilities. Their internalized measures are expressed in interests and efforts and are verbalized in remarks such as "I can't draw pictures"; "I'm so clumsy"; "You should have seen me at my recital; I didn't make one single mistake!"; "Next year, my daddy is going to teach me to ride a motorcycle!"

Self-criticism can lead to an unwillingness to take part in group games and self-consciousness about the child's abilities to perform physical/motor tasks. On the other hand, attributing greater skill to themselves than exists may lead children to take physical risks such as climbing to a high tree branch, riding a bicycle at breakneck speed, attempting to lift something quite heavy, and so on. One of the goals in early childhood is to help children accurately assess their own abilities and accept individual uniqueness: their own and that of others. At this point, the appropriateness of competitive classroom games and sports is called into question.

Positive and affirming interactions with others, particularly parents and teachers, assist young children in developing reasonable expectations for themselves and positive regard for their own physical characteristics and abilities. Providing opportunities to enhance motor skills that are appropriate to their capabilities assists children in formulating positive self-concepts.

## GENDER IDENTITY AND ROLE EXPECTATIONS

Unlike one's sex, which is biologically determined, one's gender is psychologically and socially constructed. Different cultures label various behaviors or expectations as *feminine* or *masculine* and may vary these labels and expectations over time relative to context- and age-expected behaviors (Wood, 1994). In most cultures in the United States, young children know their sex by ages 6 through 8 and have some understanding of society's gender expectations. This sense of gender is acquired through interactions with others: parents, siblings, peers, teachers, and other individuals whom the child admires, and the media (Basow, 1992; Sedney, 1987; Sheldon, 1990). From infancy onward, children imitate the behaviors of those important to them and eventually internalize many of those behaviors, particularly those that result in positive feedback and affirmation.

From a very early age, parents influence the play behaviors of children through the selection and provision of gender-typed toys (e.g., dolls for girls, trains for boys) (Brooks-Gunn & Matthews, 1979). Through the kinds of behaviors condoned or expected, boys may be encouraged to be independent, aggressive, and exploratory, while girls may be protected, cuddled, and hugged (Fagot, 1982; Fagot & Kronsberg, 1982; Fagot et al., 1985). These early gender-typed experiences influence the perceptions children form about themselves and their gender, and about gender-role expectations held by persons important to them. In turn, from ages 6 through 8, choices of play themes, physical activities, and friends emerge that reflect these perceptions. In a study of children's toy requests in letters to Santa Claus, Richardson and Simpson (1982) found that toy preferences for children ages 5 to 9 were quite stereotypical. Boys requested such items as toy race cars, sports equipment, construction sets and bicycles, while girls requested dolls, domestic accessories, and stuffed animals. Girls requested "opposite-sex" items more often than boys did. Such experiences, coupled with increased attention to role models, influence the child's gender awareness and gender-role preferences. Gender awareness and role preferences influence play choices and encourage or impede physical activity essential to healthy and sound motor development.

Another development in gender awareness and gender-role expectations is the child's emerging interests in topics related to sex and procreation. Six- and 7-year-olds whose earlier questions about anatomy and "where babies come from" have been answered frankly for them are more likely to continue such dialogue with their parents. However, television, books, and peers will augment the child's knowledge in this area. Sometimes the information derived from these other sources is accurate and helpful. Often, however, television depicts human sexuality and reproduction in sensational, distorted, and perhaps sordid and frightening ways. Also, information shared among friends can be inaccurate and misleading.

As children get older, their sexual curiosity becomes more disguised. The frank and open questions and unrestrained curiosities of an earlier age are less evident. Interests tend to focus on pregnancies and babies—how long the baby will be in mother's tummy, how the baby will get out, and the role father plays in reproduction. The 6- to 8-year-old does not, however, seek as much information as one might think. Children need simple and accurate information from adults who understand what the child is really asking and are sensitive to the child's developmental abilities to understand. At times, asking the child what she or he thinks about a question asked can provide the adults with background information regarding what the child is really asking, reveal possible misinformation, and give clues about how to respond to the child's questions.

During this age period, self-consciousness associated with modesty begins to emerge. Dressing, undressing, and toileting in the presence of others are fiercely avoided. The "bathroom" talk of earlier ages decreases, though occasionally it is used to shock or insult others. Adults who provide an atmosphere of rapport and respect for children assist children in becoming comfortable with their own sexuality and accepting of their own anatomies.

## RELATIONSHIP BETWEEN PHYSICAL/MOTOR DEVELOPMENT AND COGNITIVE DEVELOPMENT

From preceding chapters, you have learned that perspectives on cognitive development are changing from predominantly Piagetian to enlarged and modified neo-Piagetian models. These new perspectives have given rise to research on the influence of physical and motor development on cognition. From a Piagetian point of view, children acquire concepts and increasing knowledge as they physically interact with objects and people in their environments. Through sensorimotor activity and concrete operations, young children build on prior experience to construct new concepts and new knowledge. For many children this process indeed occurs, but let's explore it from another perspective: that of the child with physical disabilities.

Neo-Piagetians have challenged the prevailing view of cognitive development by citing the cognitive development of children who are visually or hearing impaired or have motor impairments. In a review of research, Bebko et al., (1992) argue that children with various disabilities attain normal concept development despite their inability to physically and motorically explore and manipulate objects in the environment in traditional ways. These authors identified three models for describing early cognitive development and the role of physical/motor activity: the Piagetian model, the neo-Piagetian model, and the perceptual analysis model. The latter two models are supported by the fact that mental representations and concepts have been exhibited in children as young as $3\frac{1}{2}$ to $5\frac{1}{2}$ months of age, a period that precedes the onset of coordinated motor movements (Baillargeon, 1987). The perceptual analysis model, proposed by Mandler (1988, 1992), argues that children are born with a capacity to engage in perceptual analysis, a mental process by which one perception is actively compared with another. External sensorimotor activity may provide input to this analysis, but the analysis is not necessarily dependent on it. From their review of the research, Bebko et al. (1992) conclude,

*other-mediated action: an action, originated by a child who is physically unable to act directly on objects in the environment, that can be carried out by some other person or agent.*

> The literature on children with severe physical handicaps suggests that motor activity and the ability to directly manipulate the environment may not be necessary conditions for development. Rather, it is interaction with the environment that seems critical, but interaction defined in the broadest sense, making use of both direct and **other-mediated action** and encompassing input from any sensory system or action by any kinesthetic organ. Information from these varied sources allows for the coordination of schemes, the verification or disconfirmation of hypotheses and subsequent cognitive growth. (p. 238)

It would appear that given these different points of view, a new and more eclectic theory of cognitive development has emerged. In view of changing theoretical perspectives, the early childhood professional must not only address the needs of non-impaired children in providing physical/motor opportunities but must also consider the capabilities of children with various disabilities to formulate concepts and new knowledge by way of various modalities.

## FACTORS INFLUENCING PHYSICAL AND MOTOR DEVELOPMENT

A major goal of early childhood development is the promotion and protection of the general health and well-being of children. A number of factors influence this goal. Certainly the genetic makeup of the child sets limits on growth and development and determines the presence or absence of certain disabilities. In addition, environmental factors influence the extent to which optimal growth and development can be achieved. Proper nutrition, medical and dental care (including timely immunizations and other protections from disease), adequate rest, sleep, and physical/motor activity, protection from accidents and injury, and emotional and social support are necessary for optimal growth and development. Because many of these factors were discussed in previous chapters, this chapter will address only certain topics relating to the 6- through 8-year-old.

## HEALTH AND WELL-BEING ISSUES

### NUTRITION

**Overnourishment (Obesity).** There is evidence that the number of obese children in the United States is increasing (Gortmacher, et al., 1987). Some reports suggest an increase of 54 percent among 6- to 11-year-olds over the past 15 to 20 years. It is estimated that 30 percent of males and 25 percent of females in the 6- to 10-year-old age group are obese (Dietz, 1986). It is also estimated that at least 40 percent of children ages 5 through 8 show at least one heart disease risk factor such as high blood pressure, elevated cholesterol, or obesity (Williams, 1990). The fact that children are becoming obese at earlier ages (Gortmacher et al., 1987) and that the tendency toward childhood obesity persists into the adult years (American Academy of Pediatrics, 1993) makes this an important topic to address.

The obese child faces physiological and psychological penalties. Adults hoping to prevent these adverse effects of obesity look for causes. Obesity has many possible causes, including

1. Inactivity and poor habits of physical exercise
2. Television viewing, which interferes with more active pursuits and may also encourage snacking
3. Overeating, associated with boredom and psychological needs for self-comfort or self-reward
4. Parenting styles that use food to reward or to relieve parental anxiety or guilt; parents who judge their success as parents on how well their children are fed
5. Inherited body types that predispose some children toward obesity (Pipes, 1989)

Children prone to obesity should be under a physician's supervision. With the physician's guidance, parents and teachers will need to monitor growth rates, nutrient and calorie intake, exercise and other physical activity, and psychosocial health. The family may need nutrition counseling and to modify eating and exercise habits. Responses of those who care for the child must be sensible and sensitive. Only medically approved diets should be implemented, since the child's nutritional needs remain basically the same as those for all children the same age. Failure to adequately meet the child's nutritional needs places the child at risk for complications associated with malnutrition, decreased resistance to disease, and failure to grow in height.

Sensitivity to the child's emotional and social needs is particularly important. Care must be taken to affirm the child's dignity and worth. The child may need help finding acceptance within the peer group and realizing her or his own special attributes. The child's need for acceptance and belonging, self-esteem, initiative, and industry must be supported and encouraged.

**School Meal Programs.** Begun in 1946 and expanded and modified over the years, the National School Lunch, School Breakfast, and special milk programs are made available to public and some nonprofit schools, child care programs, and residential care programs for children through the U. S. Department of Agriculture (USDA). The Food and Nutrition Service, an agency within the USDA, administers the program, which provides cash assistance to states to provide free and reduced-price meals for eligible children. State education agencies in conjunction with local school districts administer the program at the local level. More than 92,000 schools and residential child care institutions take part in the program, which

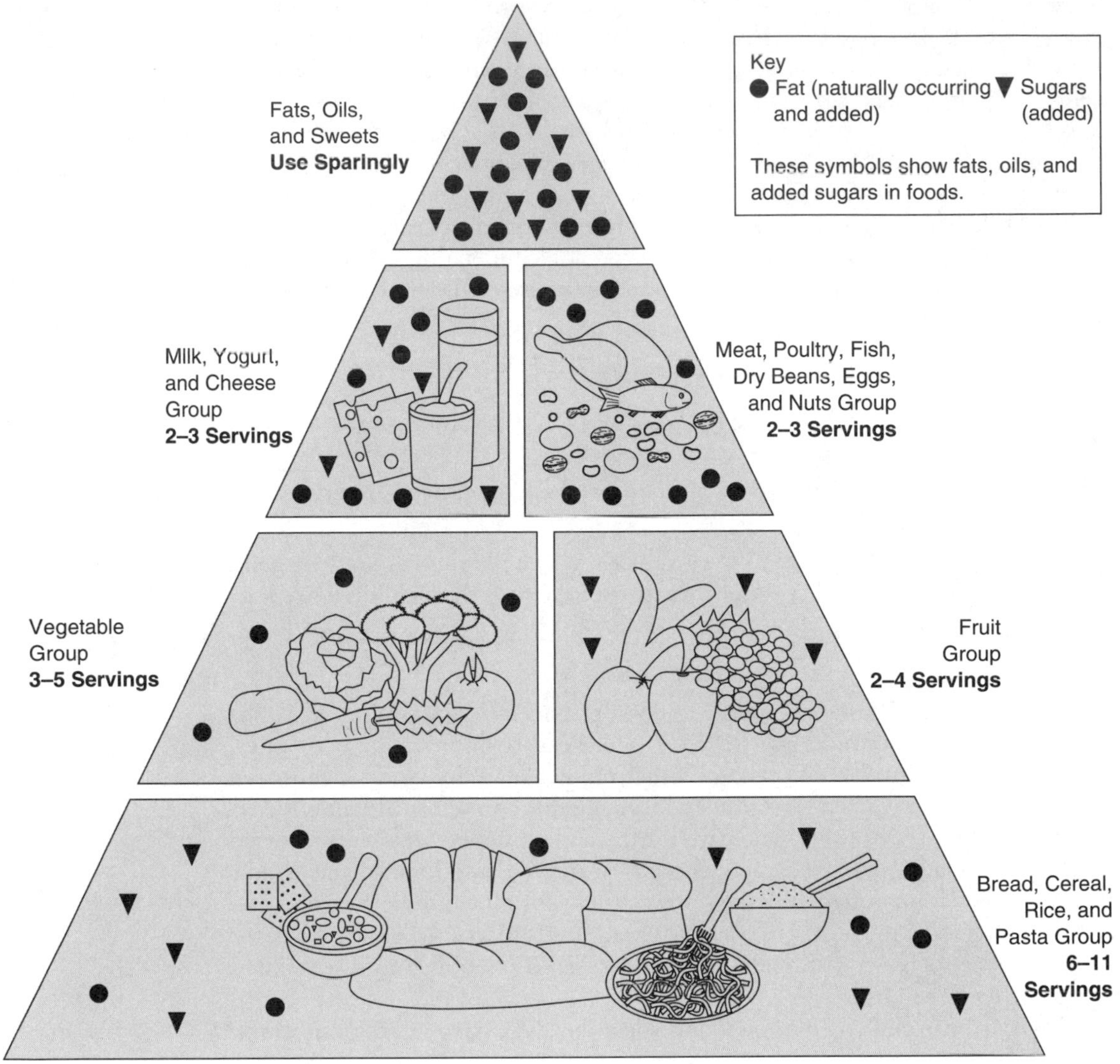

**FIGURE 14.3**
Food Guide Pyramid – A Guide to Daily Food Choices (*Source:* United States Department of Agriculture, 1985.)

serves 25 million children each school day (United States Department of Agriculture, 1993).

Currently, to qualify for free meals, a child must live in a family with an income at or below 130 percent of the poverty level; a child whose family income is between 130 and 185 percent of the poverty level is eligible for reduced-price meals. Children over the 185 percent of poverty level pay the full price. These figures may change as economic conditions change.

Schools receiving funds from the National School Lunch or School Breakfast Programs must provide meals that meet the U.S. dietary guidelines for Americans released in 1990. These guidelines specify menu composition and serving sizes commensurate with the Food Guide Pyramid (see Figure 14.3). Whereas in the past school lunches tended to be high in carbohydrates and fats, sugars and fats are reduced and grains, fruits, and vegetables increased when meal planners follow the Food Guide Pyramid. In addition to modifying menus for children, attention is being given to food service strategies that promote interest in nutritious meals, appealing presentation of foods, and educational programs that enhance knowledge of the importance of good nutrition.

**Nutrition and School Performance.** Evidence suggests that skipping breakfast affects a student's performance in school. In one study, late-morning problem-solving ability was shown to be impaired in children who skipped breakfast (Pollitt, Leibel, & Greenfield, 1981). Poor performance on arithmetic tasks on days when breakfast was skipped was documented in another study (Kruesi & Rapoport, 1986). When children do not eat breakfast they do not attend well, they are lethargic and irritable, and energy required for learning is diminished.

Recent reports on school participation in the National School Breakfast Program have raised concerns among nutritionists and early childhood professionals. According to a report of the Food Research and Action Center (FRAC), a nutrition advocacy group, and the U. S. Department of Agriculture (1992), millions of children across the United States begin the school day hungry despite the fact that the number of schools offering breakfast increased between 1990 and 1991. Many schools do not apply (or are unable to apply) for federal funds for school breakfast programs for a variety of reasons, including community opposition or religious beliefs and cultural practices. Busing schedules and staffing for before-school supervision may also impede utilization of the school breakfast program. With fewer than 50 percent of eligible schools offering breakfast (Food Research and Action Center, 1992), the impact on children's general health and well-being and on school learning could prove to be more costly in the long run than resolving the issues surrounding the choice to forgo participation in the National School Breakfast Program.

## SAFETY AND THE 6- THROUGH 8-YEAR OLD CHILD

Children ages 6 through 8 are subject to many of the same hazards younger children are, and some of these risks increase as they begin to expand their activities beyond the home and classroom. Their ability to explore the neighborhood, visit with friends, and play in groups or playgrounds, their interest in physically active games and sports, and spontaneous rough-and-tumble play, their beginning use of bicycles, roller blades, and other sports equipment all subject them to additional hazards.

As children get older, they may be away from home more frequently and have less direct adult supervision. They are eager to do things for themselves and are often willing to try anything to "go along" with their friends. Common hazards for this age group are organized sports, such as Little League, particularly where performance expectations are developmentally inappropriate and rules about wearing appropriate gear and using age-appropriate equipment are not enforced, (see "Organized Games and Sports" earlier in this chapter); inappropriate use of toys and playground equipment and inadequate supervision of children using them; traffic and pedestrian accidents; swimming pools and other bodies of water; flammable agents; tools and home appliances; toxic substances; and firearms.

Some recreational items are particularly dangerous. The time-honored bicycle poses very serious safety concerns. Bicycle-related deaths exceed deaths from accidental poisonings, falls, and firearm accidents combined. Yet the use of bicycle safety helmets can reduce the risk of head trauma and brain injury by as much as 88 percent (Storo, 1993). Children must be taught the importance of bicycle helmet usage and safe bicycling practices. Safety helmets should have a sticker indicating that they meet the safety standards of the American National Standards Institute or the Snell Memorial Foundation. Helmets should fit the wearer snugly and be free of dents.

Children using roller blades, skateboards, ice skates, and similar equipment must also wear helmets to prevent head injury. Some communities have laws and ordinances restricting or banning the use of such equipment in certain locations and prescribing proper safety gear and use. With regard to skateboarding, Nanko (1994) advises that well into adolescence, parental supervision is essential to ensure child safety:

> Parents should know where, when, and how their children are riding, what messages and pressures they are getting from their friends, and what kind of behavior is being encouraged in skateboarding magazines and videos. They must insist that riders are properly trained, wear safety gear at all times, and obey all local laws regarding skateboards. They must sometimes be available to transport them to areas which are safe for riding.

We suggest that the same precautions be applied to the other "wheel" activities of school-age children. The U.S. Consumer Product Safety Commission recommends that children not be allowed to roller-blade in traffic, at night, or on rough surfaces and not wear anything that can obstruct their vision or hearing. Appropriate gear for this sport must include helmets, wrist guards with palm protection, and elbow and knee pads, and participants should be given lessons on proper use and safety (American Academy of Pediatrics, Larson, 1994).

Accident and injury prevention includes both setting rules and boundaries for and with children and teaching them about hazards and how to protect themselves. Table 14.1 lists typical hazards at this age and suggests topics to discuss with children. In addition to the safety issues addressed in Table 14.1, adults must be aware of children's play themes and cognizant of the influences of television, movies, and video games on these themes and the quality of child play resulting from them. Some violent behaviors have been shown to relate to media events and heroes. Violence in children's lives is discussed further in the next section.

Another safety concern is the young child who is in "self-care," or the "latchkey child" (so named for the key children wear on a string around their necks or pinned inside their clothing to allow them to enter their homes after school and care for themselves until a parent returns). Children in self-care are

TABLE 14.1
Preventing Accidents in the School-Age Child

| Accident | Preventive Measure |
|---|---|
| Motor vehicle accidents | Encourage children to use seat belts in a car; role model their use. |
| | Teach street-crossing safety; stress that streets are no place for roughhousing, pushing, or shoving. |
| | Teach bicycle safety, including advice not to take "passengers" on a bicycle and to use a helmet. |
| | Teach parking lot and school bus safety (do not walk in back of parked cars, wait for crossing guard, etc.). |
| Community | Teach to avoid areas specifically unsafe, such as train yards, grain silos, back alleys. Teach not to go with strangers (parents can establish a code word with child; child does not leave school with anyone who does not know the word). |
| | Teach to say "no" to anyone who touches them whom they do not wish to do so, including family members (most sexual abuse is by a family member, not a stranger). |
| Burns | Teach safety with candles, matches, campfires—fire is not fun. |
| | Teach safety with beginning cooking skills (remember to include microwave oven safety such as closing door firmly before turning on oven; not using metal containers). |
| | Teach not to climb electric poles. |
| Falls | Teach that roughhousing on fences, climbing on roofs, etc. is hazardous. |
| | Teach skateboard safety. |
| Sports injuries | Wearing appropriate equipment for sports (face masks for hockey, knee braces for football, batting helmets for baseball) is not babyish but smart. |
| | Teach not to play to a point of exhaustion or in a sport beyond physical capability (pitching baseball or toe ballet for a grade-school child). |
| | Teach to use trampolines only with adult supervision to avoid serious neck injury. |
| Drowning | Children should learn how to swim and that dares and rough-housing when diving or swimming are not appropriate. |
| | Teach not to swim beyond limits of capabilities. |
| Drug | Teach to avoid all recreational drugs and to take prescription medicine only as directed. |
| Firearms | Teach safe firearm use. Parents should keep firearms in locked cabinets with bullets separate from gun. |
| General | Teach school-agers to keep adults informed as to where they are and what they are doing. |
| | Be aware that the frequency of accidents increases when parents are under stress and therefore less attentive. Special precautions must be taken at these times. |
| | Some children are more active, curious, and impulsive and therefore more vulnerable to accidents than others. |

*Source:* From Pillitteri, A. (1992). *Maternal and child health nursing: Care of the childbearing and childrearing family.* Philadelphia: J. B. Lippincott Co. Reprinted with permission by the author.

especially vulnerable to physical danger such as strangers, sexual abuse, household accidents, toxic substances, experimentation with unsecured medicines or drugs, alcohol, tobacco, and firearms. Their television watching is unsupervised and therefore subject to misperception and imitation. These children need specific guidance on how to be safe when home alone and how to protect themselves and seek help in an emergency. An additional concern for children in self-care is restrictions on play and exercise after school until adults are present. Early childhood professionals must strive to find ways to provide safe and healthy before- and after-school programs for these children, as well as for children who are ill and unable to attend school or their child care centers and may be left in self-care by parents who lack access to other options.

## VIOLENCE IN THE LIVES OF CHILDREN

Violence in the lives of children has become so pervasive in recent years that education and health care professionals, along with law enforcement agencies, are launching various campaigns, educational programs, and research in an attempt to understand and curtail its continuing rise. The American Academy of Pediatrics convened a major conference on violence and published the proceedings and recommendations in a supplement to the journal *Pediatrics* entitled "The Role of the Pediatrician in Violence Prevention" (American Academy of Pediatrics, 1994a). Professional early childhood associations have formed committees and task forces to explore the role of the early childhood professional in addressing this national concern. For example, the Association for Childhood Education International devoted a theme issue of its journal, *Childhood Education* (1994), entitled Creating Safer Environments for Children in the Home, School, and Community, to address violence issues. The Children's Defense Fund, a child advocacy organization, engaged religious groups around the country to launch the "National Observance of Children's Sabbaths" to raise awareness of this serious threat and encourage greater community participation in combating it.

Violence crosses all socioeconomic boundaries and locales—urban, suburban, and rural. Professionals in early childhood care and education need to learn more about how violent behavior is learned and reinforced in children at home and at school, in their neighborhoods, and through the media. The emerging collaborations among various professional, religious, and civic groups can help identify strategies for reducing violence in children's lives. Following are some strategies suggested by the American Academy of Pediatrics (1994a):

- Direct attention to the content of children's media experiences by helping to educate parents and pressing for strong implementation of the Children's Educational Television Act (1990).

- Help educate parents and other adults about the harmful effects of corporal punishment.

- Educate ourselves and others about child development and behavioral consequences for children who witness domestic violence.

**TABLE 14.2**
**Family Characteristics That Affect Children's Use of Drugs**

| Drug Abuse Is More Likely in These Families | Drug Abuse Is Less Likely in These Families |
|---|---|
| Family members feel lonely, isolated, frustrated. Parents and children communicate poorly, particularly fathers and sons. Parents demonstrate little sense of ethics. Parents and children lack self-esteem. Parents drink heavily. Children feel rejected. Parents have low expectations for children. Family follows rigid, stereotyped sex roles. Family management is inadequate. Parents excessively dominate and control their children. Parents use negative discipline measures (either extremely strict or too permissive). Adults fight about discipline and other issues. | Family members have warm, positive relationships. Parents are committed to education. Parents believe in society's general values. Family attends religious services. Household tasks are distributed among all family members. Families have high aspirations for children's success. Strong kinship networks exist in the family. The family is proud of children's accomplishments. Affectionate, supportive parent-child relationships meet the children's emotional needs. Children derive a great deal of satisfaction from their families. Parents use a reasoned, democratic discipline style. |

*Source:* From "Drug Abuse Prevention Begins in Early Childhood" by U. J. Oyemade and V. Washington, 1989, *Young Children, 44,* p. 11. Copyright 1989 by NAEYC. Reprinted by permission of the authors.

- Collaborate with community leaders and violence prevention researchers to develop and support community violence prevention programs.

- Encourage parents to remove guns from the home (or keep them unloaded and locked away), limit children's viewing of gun violence in the media and play with toy guns and video games featuring guns, be alert to early signs of aggressive behaviors, and advocate for laws restricting the availability of guns.

## THE ROOTS OF DRUG ABUSE

There is some evidence that the roots of drug abuse are found in early childhood (Oyemade & Washington, 1989). Child-rearing practices, family life patterns and trauma, and role model attitudes and behaviors contribute to later propensities toward drug abuse. Table 14.2 describes family characteristics that could increase the likelihood of drug abuse in children.

 *Role of the Early Childhood Professional*

## *Enhancing Physical and Motor Development in Children Ages 6 Through 8*

1. Provide safe and healthy surroundings for children.
2. Provide for the child's nutritional needs.
3. Oversee health care through immunizations and other protections from exposure to disease.
4. Oversee regular dental examinations.
5. Establish healthy routines for rest, sleep, play, and activity.
6. Provide opportunities to refine perceptual-motor abilities.
7. Provide age- and developmentally-appropriate games, play equipment, and sports activities.
8. Ensure the child's safety through adequate planning, rules, supervision, and education.
9. Facilitate satisfying and supportive psychosocial interactions with peers, family, and others.
10. Encourage a sense of responsibility for one's own health maintenance and safety. ■

## KEY TERMS

| figure-ground discrimination | fundamental movements | other-mediated action |

## REVIEW STRATEGIES AND ACTIVITIES

1. Review the key terms individually or with a classmate.
2. Locate several children ages 6 to 8. Ask them what three gifts they would like to receive for their birthdays. Compare the boys' and the girls' preferences. How many of the items are gender stereotypical? How many are not gender specific? How many are opposite-gender items? Compare your survey with that of a classmate. What trends do you see in gender-related toys or gift preferences of boys and girls in this age range?
3. Visit a physical education class in which physically challenged children participate. What kinds of activities are planned for these children? What physical and motor benefits can be realized from these activities? How do these activities differ from traditional physical education requirements?

4. Attend an organized sports event for children in the 6-to-8 age range. Are the expectations developmentally appropriate? Does each child have an opportunity to participate? Is the coach sensitive to individual differences? Are children's needs for rest and refreshments met? Are children required to wear and use appropriate safety gear and equipment? Is winning or participation and fun stressed more?

5. Collect a month's supply of public school breakfast and lunch menus. Compare them for child appeal, adherence to the food pyramid guide, variety, and estimated calorie content.

## FURTHER READINGS

Association for Childhood Education International. (1994). *Childhood Education: Theme issue 1994: Creating safer environments for children in the home, school and community*. Wheaton, MD: Author.

Endres, J. B., and Rockwell, R. E. (1994). *Food, nutrition and the young child* (4th ed.). New York: Macmillan.

Jones, E., and Reynolds, G. (1994). *The play's the thing: Teachers' roles in children's play*. New York: Teachers College Press.

Keda, J., and Naworski, P. (1992). *Am I fat? Helping young children accept differences in body size*. Santa Cruz, CA: ETR Publishers.

Kozloff, M. A. (1994). *Improving educational outcomes for children with disabilities: Guidelines and protocols for practice*. Baltimore: Paul H. Brookes.

Levin, D. E. (1994). *Teaching young children in violent times: Building a peaceable classroom*. Cambridge, MA: Educators for Social Responsibility.

# CHAPTER FIFTEEN

*If you see a child without a smile, give him yours.*

**Talmud**

# Psychosocial Development
# Ages 6 Through 8

After studying this chapter, you will demonstrate comprehension by:

- Describing the psychosocial development of the 6- through 8-year-old child.
- Listing major social and emotional milestones in psychosocial development during this period.
- Identifying factors that influence psychosocial development during this period.
- Describing the role of adults in healthy psychosocial development of 6- through 8-year-olds.

In a popular U. S. Children's Bureau booklet from the 1960s, the 6- to 8-year-old is described as a "commuter to the wonderful outside world of middle childhood," traveling "back and forth between the outside world and the smaller more personal one of [the] family." The child's travels are said to start with short trips at age 6, becoming longer trips away from the family's "home station" with increasing age (Chilman, 1966, p. 5).

As this metaphor implies, the psychosocial world of the 6- through 8-year-old is expanding rapidly beyond the home and family. By age 6, children are growing less dependent on their parents and are now encountering an ever-widening array of extrafamilial interactions. New psychosocial challenges ensue.

During the first part of this age period, the child is characterized as highly active, boisterous, sometimes verbally aggressive, and teasing. Boys enjoy rough-and-tumble play, and both boys and girls enjoy creative projects and playing games with rules. Children at this age are inclined to dawdle and are talkative, boastful, impatient, and competitive. They are also sensitive and affectionate, and enjoy playful interactions that employ humor, jokes, and riddles. Giggling is also characteristic.

Around age 7, children exhibit more brooding behaviors and become sensitive, private, and moody. The child is growing more reflective and more concerned about the reactions of others. Expressions of self-confidence are not quite as verbose as before, and the child is as inclined to listen as to talk. While the 6-year-old are described as quite active and talkative, the 7-year-old is more introspective and contemplative.

Helpfulness and consideration of others are present. Enjoyment of friends often over-rides time with family.

By the end of this age period, we again see behaviors that are outgoing and interactive. Interests are outward bound and spurred by curiosity. The child is self-confident and self-aware, yet self-critical and self-conscious. The child reacts with both interest and hostility toward the opposite sex, is peer oriented, independent, and for the most part dependable. Interest in the adult world is marked by listening to adult conversations and seeking to be included in more "adultlike" activities.

What do these behavioral descriptions tell us about the processes of psychoso-cial development? In this chapter, we explore major areas of psychosocial devel-opment and explain how 6- through 8-year-olds acquire these characteristics.

## INDUSTRY VERSUS INFERIORITY

*industry:*
*Erikson's psychosocial*
*stage during which the*
*child is mastering social*
*and academic skills nec-*
*essary to feel self-*
*assured; the opposite*
*result of this "nuclear*
*crisis" is a sense of*
*inferiority*

Between ages 6 and 11, the child is in Erikson's fourth stage of psychosocial devel-opment, developing a sense of **industry**. The fantasy and make-believe of earlier years begin to defer to more reality-based perceptions. Children at this stage are eager to learn how things work and want to master "real" tasks. Whereas process characterized the efforts of previous stages, products are now important as children begin to take pride in their abilities to create and to produce. Art projects, blocks and other constructions, cooking, and participating in household chores become sources of pride and accomplishment. The child's activities are, in a word, industrious.

At this time, formal schooling takes on new importance to the child, setting goals and expectations, imposing limits on behaviors and activities, and multiply-ing social interactions. Eager to learn the "real" skills that school can teach, the child's sense of competence becomes vulnerable to the influences of classmates, teachers, curriculums, and grades. Success with school tasks fosters a sense of competence, self-worth, and industry. However, the child who experiences too many failures in school, academic or social, develops a sense of inferiority. As a result, confidence and self-worth suffer.

During the industry/inferiority stage of psychosocial development, individual skills and interests become evident. Aspirations emerge, though levels of aspirations often outpace capabilities. Children find their skill areas as they explore a variety of interests and enjoy the products of their own labors that emerge from these explo-rations. The fifth stage of psychosocial development, developing a sense of identity (versus role confusion), has its origins in these early skill discoveries.

## EMOTIONAL DEVELOPMENT

### EFFECTS OF EARLIER ATTACHMENTS

As children reach ages 6, 7, and 8, attachment behaviors of earlier ages change dramatically. Children seek increasing independence and pursue relationships that reach well beyond attachment persons and the immediate family. An expanding social world tests the child's sense of self, autonomy, initiative, and social competence. Success in these developmental challenges can be traced to the quality of early attachments that occurred in infancy, toddlerhood, and the preprimary years (Lyons-Ruth, Alpern, & Repacholi, 1993). Table 15.1 illustrates findings of a study by Main and Cassidy (1988) regarding the relationship between early attachments and later behaviors.

At 6, 7, and 8, relationships with parents are still dependent and affectionate; however, these relationships are often punctuated with oppositional behaviors and challenges to parental authority. Attention-getting behaviors, perhaps a form of proximity seeking, appear. The child employs behaviors known to irritate in an apparent attempt to sustain parental attentions (arguing, teasing, shocking, bragging, name calling). Such behaviors reveal the child's ambivalence about his or her emerging independence and, to some extent, the child's growing recognition of the inequality of the adult-child relationship (Elkind, 1994).

The parent's role shifts from that of protector to facilitator and to "program director" as the child's itinerary expands to include out-of-home activities. The parent also becomes the child's advocate. The child's perspective, the parent's role as an "all-knowing" source of information diminishes as teachers increasingly become the source of "all" knowledge. Despite these redefinitions, however, children still need their parents to be nurturing, predictable, and supportive, and to provide parameters for often out-of-bounds behaviors (Wenk et al., 1993; Ahmeduzzaman, M. & Roopnarine, 1992).

## FEARS

The close relationship between fears and cognitive development is evidenced by the changes in causes of and responses to fears as children get older. Cognitive development results in increasing abilities to perceive meanings not previously perceived and to relate those meanings to oneself. With increasing experiences and understandings during the 6- to 8-year period, fear becomes less specific (fear of dogs, fear of the dark) and more general (fear of not being liked at school). The ability to imagine, empathize, and to take the perspectives of others changes the nature of children's fears. Table 15.2 summarizes the way children's fears change as they get older.

Unlike the toddler, whose fear responses are often vociferous, the older child responds in less intense or overt ways when frightened. Older children may repress or mask their fears. Their behaviors bespeak their discomfort: nail biting, inattention or distractibility, changed eating or sleeping patterns, heightened emotionality, increased dependency, or feigned illness. They may deny that they are afraid or boast of their bravery.

Previous experiences and life circumstances influence what children fear and how they respond: family life trauma, accidents and illnesses, loss of a parent to death or divorce, severe punishments, frightening movies or television programs,

## TABLE 15.1
### Four Forms of Attachment Organization Observed at 12 Months and at 6 Years of Age

| Attachment Organization/Age | Description |
| --- | --- |
| **Insecure-avoidant** [a] | |
| 12 months | Actively avoids and ignores parent on reunion, looking away, and remaining occupied with toys. At extremes, moves away from parent and ignores parent's efforts to communicate. |
| 6 years | Minimizes and restricts opportunities for interaction with parent on reunion, looking and speaking only briefly and minimally as required and remaining occupied with toys or activities. At extremes, moves away but subtly, with rationale such as retrieving a toy. |
| **Secure** | |
| 12 months | Seeks interaction, proximity, physical contact or any combination therefore, with the parent on reunion, often actively attempts to maintain physical contact. Readily soothed after distress by parent and returns to exploration and play. |
| 6 years | Initiates conversation and pleasant interaction with the parent on reunion or is highly responsive to parent's own initiations. May subtly move into proximity or physical contact with parent, usually with rationale such as seeking a toy. Remains calm throughout episode. |
| **Insecure-ambivalent** | |
| 12 months | Distress because of separation is not effectively soothed by parent, although infant seems to want proximity and contact. Overt to subtle signs of anger toward the parent are often present (e.g., child may seek proximity and contact, then resist it). |
| 6 years | In movements, posture, and tones of voice child appears to attempt to exaggerate intimacy, with the parent as well as dependency on the parent. May seek proximity or contact, but shows some resistance or ambivalence (e.g., lying on parent's lap while wriggling uncomfortably). Moderately avoidant, often subtle signs of hostility are sometimes present. |
| **Insecure-controlling** [b] | |
| 12 months | Child shows one or several signs of disorganization (e.g., crying for parent at door, then moving sharply away when door opens; approaching parent with head averted) or disorientation (e.g., stilling or freezing movement for a few seconds) during the Strange Situation. |
| 6 years | Seems partially to assume a parental role toward parent. Attempts to control and direct the parent's behavior, either through punitive behavior (directing, embarrassing, or humiliating the parent) or through overbright/caregiving behavior (exhibiting extreme enthusiasm for reunion, solicitous behavior to parent, or careful attempts to guide and direct parent). |

[a]Descriptions of reunion behavior used to classify infant attachment organization at 12 months are taken from Ainsworth, Blehar, Waters, and Wall, 1978.
[b]Sixth-year classification title is used for general title. There is no controlling category for infancy; in infancy these children were identified as disorganized/disoriented.
*Source:* Main, M., & Cassidy, J. (1988). Categories of response to reunion with a parent at age 6. *Developmental Psychology, 24,* 420. Copyright © 1988 by the American Psychological Association. Reprinted by permission of the authors.

TABLE 15.2
Changes in Children's Fears from Infancy Through Age 8

| Infants | Toddlers | Children Ages 4 to 5 | Children Ages 6–8 |
|---|---|---|---|
| Loud noises<br>Loss of support | Heights<br>Separation<br>Strangers<br>Sudden surprise, e.g.,<br>jack-in-the-box toy | Noises<br>Imaginary creatures<br>Punishment<br>Dogs, small animals<br>Storms<br>Supernatural<br>(ghosts, witches) | Dark<br>Being left alone<br>Scoldings<br>Physical injury, sickness<br>Ridicule, failure<br>Criticism<br>Being different in clothes, hairstyles, etc.<br>Worries (what could be): nuclear war,<br>hurricane, family safety, death of<br>family member<br>Parental or teacher rejection |

adult conversations not fully comprehended, violence, and so on. School-age children typically fear being different from their peers, and in school they fear teacher rejection. Physical and psychological well-being also influence fear responses. As with adults, discomfort such as hunger, fatigue, illness, and stress cause children to exaggerate events, real or imagined, and respond in disproportionate ways.

Peers influence children's fears. Playmates may share frightening experiences, fabricate or exaggerate scary stories, or spread unsubstantiated rumors among other children. Peers who say that a certain teacher "never lets you go to the bathroom," that the principal "locks those who misbehave in a closet," that there is "a volcano under the school building," and so on are exhibiting fabrications that, even when unbelievable, can leave a measure of doubt in the listener. By the same token, peers often serve as models for coping with a fear. Thus, peers can influence childhood responses to fear in both positive and negative ways.

Gender differences in fear responses are sometimes exhibited. Girls are often allowed to be more fearful; they may squeal at crawling things and run away from pretend monsters. In our society, real and pretend fear responses are socially permissible for girls but often ridiculed in boys. Boys are expected to be stoic in the face of fearful events and are often discouraged from overtly expressing fears.

As with fears of earlier years, children at this stage need adults to talk with them about their fears and help them find ways to cope with and control feared situations. Adults should allow children to bring up subjects that concern them and explore with them topics of concern in an authoritative and unemotional way. In addition, adults should provide accurate information about topics such as nuclear war, severe weather, fire, and other fearful subjects; talk about what individuals can do to protect themselves; and deal with the subject of death forthrightly and honestly, yet with gentle understanding of the anxiety this topic evokes. It is important to accept children's fears and worries as real and show respect for the child's concerns, even if they seem unrealistic to the adult.

## TRANSITIONAL OBJECTS

Attachment to transitional objects of earlier years may well persist into the period from ages 6 through 8, and possibly beyond. By age 7, a child who still clings to a transitional object may do so in more private and subtle ways, perhaps preferring its comfort only at bedtime or during times of stress or illness. Soon other sentimental objects will compete for the child's attentions, and the need for the original transitional object may wane. For some children, however, discarding the transitional object altogether is out of the question. The teddy bear may remain on the shelf well into adolescence; the worn special blanket may be safely tucked away in a drawer to remain there indefinitely. No attempt should be made to dispose of transitional objects, since they represent the child's continuing need to find self-comforting strategies. The affection for the transitional object continues, and only the child should decide what to do with it when it is no longer in use.

## COLLECTIONS

Related to the transition object is an interest in collecting. During the early school years, children find enjoyment in objects to collect: baseball and football cards, rocks, seashells, matchbox cars, insects, postcards, jewelry, doll clothes and accessories, stuffed toys, candy wrappers, comic books, and so on. Sometimes trading and bartering go along with these collections, with some children becoming avid collectors through this process. Children also enjoy perusing toy and electronics catalogs and thumbing through junk mail for hidden "treasures." Making lists is another form of collecting: "What I want for Christmas," telephone numbers, addresses, birthdays, and so on.

Collections and hobbies enhance children's sense of self and their abilities, interests, and aspirations and expand their knowledge of certain objects or topics. Collections and hobbies engage the child in identifying, sorting, ordering, classifying, and researching tasks; they expand the child's knowledge and awareness and enhance cognitive development. They provide focus and entertainment during moments of self-imposed privacy, as well as a medium for initiating contacts with others. To adults, some childhood collections may seem valueless and trivial. However, these collections, and others yet to come, may spark an interest that will endure and grow into other, related interests. Some represent the origins of what may someday become an occupation or a career.

## SELF-CONCEPT

Self-concept is more stable at ages 6 to 8, due at least in part to gender constancy and to realizations about the permanence of racial and cultural group memberships. Self-concept during this period begins to include not only what children themselves think but also what they believe others think about them. This period

*Collections and hobbies enhance the child's sense of self.*

is marked by self-criticism and comparison of self with others. Home, school, peers, and organized groups all provide experiences that engender self-appraisals.

Through his work in counseling and psychotherapy, Carl Rogers (1961) became interested in how the unique self evolves and what it means to be a "fully functioning person." Rogers' *self-theory* proposes that each individual responds to countless events in his or her ever-changing world. Perceptions of each experience are subjective and private, holding special meanings for the individual. The self-concept emerges as a result of these subjective interactions.

Rogers asserted that each individual strives to become a fully functioning person. Such a person is self-accepting, governed by his or her own expectations rather than the expectations of others, and open to new experiences. She or he has no need to mask or repress unpleasant thoughts, feelings, or memories. The fully functioning person accepts others as separate and different individuals and can tolerate those behaviors not preferred for himself or herself.

Adults help children become fully functioning individuals when they

1. Recognize and accept their own feelings and recognize the role these feelings and attitudes play in their relationships with children

2. Establish relationships with individual children characterized by acceptance, rapport, mutual support, and recognition

3. Recognize and accept the child's feelings (both positive and negative) and help the child to find constructive emotional outlets

4. Enlist a helping process through which genuine understanding and empathy are effectively communicated to the child

5. Support the child's growing sense of self by helping the child to recognize and build on his or her strengths and capabilities

Research on the self-concept consistently reports a relationship between the self-concept and achievement. Since the development of a sense of industry is a major psychosocial task of this period, and feelings of competence and self-confidence are necessary for the development of a sense of industry, school plays a critical role in the child's sense of competence or incompetence. Children who perceive themselves as capable show little hesitance in trying new tasks and often succeed in them. On the other hand, children who feel they are incapable often experience reduced success in new tasks. Successes at this stage, then, are paramount; failures are damaging and can lead the child to a self-perception of inadequacy and inferiority, the polar opposite of Erikson's sense of industry.

*defense mechanism: a psychological response to ego threat, frustration, or failure*

When children feel inadequate, they often employ coping strategies known to psychologists as **defense mechanisms**. A variety of defense mechanisms exist. Defense mechanisms begin to emerge during the school years. Freud was among the first to suggest that during these years, defense mechanisms emerge to protect the ego from frustration and failure. Defense mechanisms serve to relieve anxiety when a person anticipates or experiences failures, mistakes, or mishaps. Their positive functions lie in their ability to at least temporarily relieve distress or embarrassment.

However, when defense mechanisms are relied on excessively, the individual is unduly attempting to escape reality. In such cases, parents and teachers must assess the expectations and stresses being placed on the child to ascertain the origins of the child's defense mechanisms. Failure to respond to this behavioral cue places the child at risk for social and emotional problems. Perhaps the child is experiencing excessive teasing or ridicule from an older sibling; the child's school experiences may involve too much competition or developmentally inappropriate expectations; perhaps the child fears parental disappointment or anger over his or her inadequacies or failures; or the child may be fearful and want to be in control. These are but a few of the underlying reasons for defense mechanisms. Table 15.3 lists a number of common defense mechanisms.

## GENDER IDENTITY AND GENDER-ROLE DEVELOPMENT

As children reach ages 6 through 8, gender identity and gender-role behaviors are evident in their mannerisms, occasional sexist language, play choices, and friendships. Having formed gender-role stereotypes, children now have rather inflexible

**TABLE 15.3**
**Common Defense Mechanisms**

| Defense Mechanism | Description | Example |
|---|---|---|
| Regression | Returning to earlier, less mature behaviors | Bed wetting; thumb sucking; wanting to be carried in arms |
| Repression | Inhibiting uncomfortable, frightening memories and storing them in the unconscious | Child abuse victim's inability to name abuser |
| Projection | Attributing to others one's own thoughts, motives, and traits | Seeking a cookie for oneself, asserting that a playmate needs it |
| Reaction formation | Behavior opposite from true feelings | Jealous sibling's exaggerated show of affection for newborn brother or sister |
| Displacement | Shifting feelings or emotions from something that is threatening to a substitute | Premature weaning and adult disapproval of thumb sucking leads to child's nail biting or chewing on a toy |
| Rationalizing | Attempting to provide a logical excuse for one's own disappointments, failures, or shortcomings | Person who was not invited to a party saying, "I didn't want to go to her birthday party, anyway—parties are boring." |
| Denial | Refusing to accept or acknowledge the reality of a situation | Clinging to Santa Claus myth after learning the truth |
| Fixation | Serious conflict or trauma at one age or stage that arrests further development | Prolonged separation anxiety resulting from traumatic event associated with an earlier separation |
| Sublimation | Channeling of psychological energies (e.g., aggression) into other outlets | Overachieving in school, sports, and hobbies |
| Escape/withdrawal | Avoiding a situation by physically or psychologically removing oneself from it | Nonparticipation in classroom discissions; avoiding eye contact with others lest they intrude |
| Compensation | Finding a satisfying substitute for inadequate abilities | Pursuing hobbies or collections when social interactions are difficult |

ideas about girl/boy expectations, attributing to gender certain behaviors, clothing, hairstyles, play and school activities, home chores, and adult occupations.

Children's stereotypes are learned from those around them and are sometimes imposed on them by their families and cultures. School experiences particularly influence gender identity and gender-role development. There is some evidence of gender bias on the part of classroom teachers. A study by Myra and David Sadker (1985) showed that teachers engage in more conversations, assistance, and praise with boys than they do with girls. They also respond to boys' questions with more precision and often answer girls' questions with bland or diffused responses. Following is an example exchange from their research (Sadker & Sadker, 1985, p. 166):

Teacher:  "What is the capital of Maryland? Joel?"
Joel:  "Baltimore."
Teacher:  "What's the largest city in Maryland, Joel?"
Joel:  "Baltimore."

Teacher:   "That's good. But Baltimore isn't the capital. The capital is also the
     location of the U.S. Naval Academy. Joel, do you want to try again?"
Joel:   "Annapolis."
Teacher:   "Excellent. Anne, what's the capital of Maine?"
Anne:   "Portland."
Teacher:   "Judy, do you want to try?"
Judy:   "Augusta."
Teacher:   "Ok."
(Reprinted with permission from *Psychology Today* magazine. Copyright © 1985
Sussex Publishers, Inc.).

This teacher was probably not aware of the different responses given to male and female students. Such stereotyping is often unconscious and subtle, though its potential for perpetuating stereotypes in children is great. Stereotypes imposed on girls and boys, such as attributing aggression, independence, and mathematical skills to boys and verbal, dependent, and passive behaviors to girls, may persist well into adult life (Richardson, 1981).

Scholars are encouraging an increasingly androgynous view of gender identity and gender roles. From this perspective, an individual may possess characteristics that are both masculine and feminine. Some studies suggest that androgynous individuals show greater self-esteem and enjoy better psychological health than do more gender-typed individuals (Whitley, 1985).

According to Kohlberg (1966), once the child has established gender-role constancy between ages 5 and 7, she or he becomes increasingly interested in observing and imitating the gender-role behaviors of others. Parents and teachers become powerful role models, as do other individuals the child admires, such as siblings, relatives, friends, and media personalities, athletes, or other celebrities.

Studies of gender-role development emphasize gender schema in which young children organize and internalize information about what is typical or appropriate for males and females in their particular sociocultural contexts (Levy & Carter, 1989; Martin & Halverson, 1981, 1987). According to these studies, such schemas do not necessarily depend on the emergence of gender constancy but derive from a variety of developmental and experiential sources from infancy onward. While Kohlberg's stage descriptions emphasize the importance of the child's notion of gender constancy as a point at which the child becomes more aware of gender-related attributes, these recent theories emphasize an information-processing perspective. This point of view proposes that each person may possess internal motivations (schemas) to conform to sociocultural gender-role expectations and stereotypes.

## AWARENESS OF DIVERSITY AND INDIVIDUAL DIFFERENCES

*socioccentric:*
*the inability to take or*
*accept as valid the*
*perspectives of the*
*group*

As cognitive development moves from preoperational thinking to concrete operational thinking, differences emerge in the way children view diversity. As children begin to decenter and become less egocentric, their awareness of groups emerges. Around age 5 they begin to use categories to define these groups. Children at this age are said to be **sociocentric**, that is, while they have formed a repertoire of group categories, they nevertheless are unable to take or accept the perspectives of other groups as valid. This declines after age 7 when children can focus more on individuality than on group categories and characteristics. Children's feelings about their own racial or cultural group identity are tested when they experience diverse groups of people, some of whom may exhibit stereotypes and bias.

Aboud (1988) believes that prejudice has origins in cognitive changes. Taking a social-cognitive developmental point of view, Aboud believes that ethnic attitudes spring from two overlapping sequences of development. The first sequence relates to developmental processes that flow from affect (feelings) to perceptions and then to cognition. The second sequence flows from one's self-concerns, to awareness of and attention to cultural groups, to individuals within groups. A child's responses to ethnic groups are determined by the child's developmental placement in these sequences and are most heavily influenced by information and guidance that fit the child's level of racial awareness development (p. 23). Following is a summary of Aboud's descriptions of the affect/perception/cognition sequence:

Step 1

- Wariness of strangers
- Wariness of people who are different and unpredictable
- Happiest with people who supply their wants and meet their needs

Step 2

- Perceptions rather than cognition dominate
- Perceptions are relative to oneself
- Aware of similar/dissimilar people
- Dominated by observable qualities: language, skin color, clothing, and so on
- Ethnic self-identification
- Modifies preferences to bring them into line with self-perceptions

Step 3

- Cognitive understandings
- Begins to understand that ethnicity is based on ancestry, not on observable identifiers
- Decentering helps child to accept another's preferences and perceptions

In Aboud's theory, children at step 3 should be most susceptible to information and interventions that build positive relationships with others. At this point, children can appreciate the fact that ethnicity doesn't change, that there are individual internal qualities to be appreciated, and that differences among groups are reconcilable. Aboud called this development the *focus of attentions sequence* and noted the following progression:

Step 1

- Egocentrism

Step 2

- Preoccupation with groups and the differences between one's own and other groups
- Exaggerates contrasts between groups, which can lead to pro- or anti-perspectives
- Later becomes aware of similarities as well as differences between one's own and other groups

Step 3

- Focuses on individuals and unique personalities
- Likes or dislikes people on the basis of personal rather than ethnic group qualities
- Some ethnic group stereotypes continue

As in the development of self-concept and gender identity, the child's growing acceptance and appreciation of his or her own ethnicity pave the way for acceptance of the uniqueness of others. Individuals who are comfortable with their ethnicity have little difficulty building relationships with members of other groups, and do so without feelings of conflict or insecurity (Aboud, 1988).

Parents and early childhood professionals must take an active role in fostering an appreciation for diversity in children. As adult role models, we must be aware that word, deed, and demeanor form the underpinnings of the child's developing appreciation and acceptance of human diversity. If antibias attitudes and feelings are to develop, young children need many informative, positive, self-affirming, and perspective-taking experiences.

## SELF-ESTEEM

Maslow (1968, 1970) described a hierarchy of human needs leading to self-esteem and self-actualization. Individuals are said to progress from lower needs to higher needs on the way to becoming self-actualized. Lower and higher needs differ in the degree to which they are "species specific"; that is, the lower physiological needs for food and water are common to all living things, the need for love might be shared with higher apes of the animal kingdom, but the needs for self-esteem and self-actualization are uniquely human and shared with no other animals. Figure 15.1 illustrates Maslow's hierarchy.

The first and lowest, yet most potent, of the five levels in Maslow's hierarchy of needs is the physiological needs such as hunger and thirst. All other needs are superseded by these needs. Classroom teachers are well aware that children who come to school hungry are not motivated to learn. According to Maslow, their energies and innermost thoughts are directed toward satisfying this physiological need.

Level two, safety needs, include security, stability, dependency, freedom from fear, anxiety and chaos; and the need for structure, order, law, limits, protection, and strength in a protector (Maslow, 1970). As mentioned frequently throughout this text, predictable routines help children feel safe. Unpredictable adults and rou-

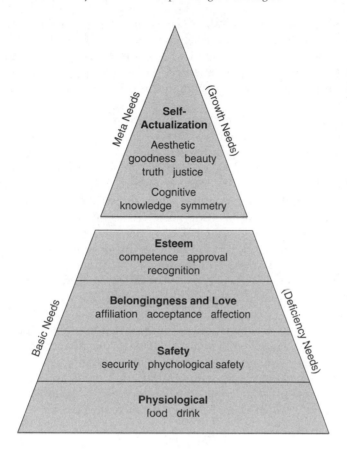

**FIGURE 15.1**
In Maslow's hierarchy of needs, the needs at the lowest level have the most potency—they must be fulfilled before a person is motivated to try to fulfill higher needs. (From *Psychology For Teaching: A Bear Always Usually Sometimes Faces the Front*, 3/e by Guy R. LeFrancois. © 1979 by Wadsworth Publishing Co., Inc. Reprinted by permission of the publisher.)

tines are unsettling to children. Chaotic and uncontrolled classroom behaviors elicit fear and a wish that the teacher (protector) were in greater control. Children need adults to provide safe, secure surroundings and enough structure to assure them of their boundaries, both physical and psychological.

At level three, belongingness and love needs are evident when the person feels the need for others. Hungering for love, affection, and acceptance, the child seeks a place in the family, play or school group, or other social entity. Parents and teachers must seek to assure children of their place within the family or school and their value to the group.

At level four, esteem needs emerge. According to Maslow, a need for a stable and firmly based positive self-evaluation is prevalent in all individuals. The need for self-respect and the esteem of others is central to healthy personality development. Self-esteem includes feelings of self-confidence, self-worth, and capability, and feelings of being wanted and needed. Individuals who lack self-esteem feel helpless, weak, discouraged, and unneeded. These feelings can lead to compensatory behaviors such as the defense mechanisms described earlier and possibly to neurotic tendencies.

Maslow cautions that true self-esteem derives from authentic accomplishments or deserved respect, not from contrived or trivial praise, popularity, or fame. An individual must come to base his or her self-esteem on real competence and adequacy in a task rather than on the opinions of others. This raises the question about the often overused classroom management technique in which the teacher praises inconsequential behaviors with "I like the way Maria is sitting" ". . . holding her pencil," or ". . . using a soft voice" (Curry & Johnson, 1990).

Of level five, Maslow (1970) says, "What a man can be, he must be" (p. 46). The self-actualized person is seeking to meet her or his potential. The individual has interests, talent, and abilities to be pursued, fostered, and mastered. The desire to be the best one can be, to be self-fulfilled, is the dominant theme of this level. It can be achieved only when the preceding lower-level needs have been satisfied.

During the 6-through-8 age period and beyond, self-appraisals find their verification in both home and school. Frequent successes, positive results from efforts, and teachers and peers who respond in helpful and accepting ways enhance children's good feelings about themselves. On the other hand, frequent failures or repeated negative responses undermine the development of self-esteem and impede the child's progress toward becoming a self-actualized person.

## MORAL DEVELOPMENT

Recall that Piaget's stage-sequence theory of moral development cites three stages: (1) premoral, (2) moral realism, and (3) moral relativism. Earlier chapters discussed stage 1 in describing the moral behaviors of children under 6. Children in the 6-through-8 age group exhibit characteristics of Piaget's stage 2 level of moral development, that of moral realism. Moral realism is characterized by rule-bound thinking and behaving. Children at this stage of moral development believe

1. Rules are rules, regardless of intentions.
2. Rules are unalterable.
3. Rules have been set by an all-knowing and powerful authority figure (God, parent, teacher).
4. The importance of a rule is in direct proportion to the severity of the punishment.
5. Obedience to rules means one is good; disobedience means one is bad.
6. Punishment is a necessary result of breaking a rule.

The term *heteronomy* describes this stage, for it implies that individuals are other-governed rather than autonomous or self-governed. Parents, teachers, and other authoritative adults impose a variety of rules and expectations to which children must comply. Many children comply with adult rules without question, believing in the absolute authority of the adult. With the emergence of autonomy, initiative, and curiosity, the child begins to challenge adult rules.

With these developments, children begin to encounter and distinguish different kinds of rules: social conventional rules and moral rules (Turiel, 1980). *Social conventional* rules are social regulations such as modes of dress for certain occasions, which side of the street to drive on, how to address the classroom teacher, and so on. Such rules are arbitrary in that they do not generalize to all situations, places or cultures; they are not universal. *Moral* rules, on the other hand, are rules relating to generalized values such as honesty, fairness, justice, and so on. According to Turiel, children as young as 6 years are able to distinguish between conventional rules and rules of morality and justice.

Children imitate the social conventions and moral values of adults who are important to them. Through these imitations during their own social interactions, children become increasingly aware of moral rules and values. However, adults can be misled by some of these behaviors, believing that verbalized values and imitated social conventions indicate understanding and internalized behaviors. On the contrary, children are in the process of understanding, and such behaviors must be practiced and the consequences observed or experienced before internalized moral behavior can occur.

At this age, sociodramatic play continues to be a powerful source for moral understandings. Imitations of adult moral and social conventions and transgressions can be explored in the safe context of pretend play. Moreover, role-taking abilities increase through sociodramatic play, as does experiencing competing points of view. These experiences are necessary precursors to solving moral dilemmas later on.

As children move from preoperational thinking to concrete operations during this period, they can compare, classify, and draw logical conclusions. These abilities assist the child in making the shift from rule-bound morality to the realization that there are many sources of rules (parents, teachers, and laws). In addition, children have decentered and become less egocentric and are becoming aware that others have needs, intentions, feelings, and expectations and that others' needs may be more important than their own from time to time. This represents stage 3 of Kohlberg's sequence of moral development.

Kohlberg refers to this stage as the "good boy/good girl" stage, wherein children seek approval. They are more inclined to conform to be perceived as "good." The desire to please peers as well as adults is evident in this phase. Often children find themselves in situations where they must choose between family and peer group rules. They may go along with the peer group despite known prohibitions. These behaviors are not necessarily deliberate, nor resistive of established rules or authority; they simply preempt previous constraints. Parents who respond to these transgressions with reason and an attempt to understand the child's motivations help children develop a conscience and facilitate the development of inner controls, which can guide behaviors in the absence of authority figures.

## DEVELOPMENT OF CONSCIENCE

Conscience generally emerges out of the child's identification with his or her parents (Mussen, 1979; Snyder, Snyder, & Snyder, 1980). Discipline that maintains supportive and affectionate relationships is more readily associated with the development of a conscience than are other forms of discipline. Fear of loss of love from a parent appears to underlie this development. Inductive discipline techniques, which elicit perspective taking, empathy, altruism, and other prosocial attitudes and behaviors, are closely associated with the development of conscience. Power-assertive strategies, on the other hand, provide little impetus for the development of conscience.

Children who have internalized standards of right and wrong from their earlier family experiences fall back on these standards when confronted with discrepancies and temptations outside the family. While self-control may not always be present in these situations, the conscience is. The conscience becomes a "stand-in" for the parent and attempts to guide behaviors along internalized family expectations.

## FRIENDSHIPS

The peer group emerges as a powerful socializing force in the child's life during the early school years. The child has shifted from seeking interactions with adults more than with children to seeking interactions with children more than with adults. Peer group acceptance becomes paramount to the child.

Friendships begin to segregate along gender lines during the 6- through 8-year period. The beginnings of this segregation are seen in the preprimary years, but by the time children are 7 or 8 years old, the preference for same-sex peer groups becomes the rule rather than the exception. In another year or so, same-sex peer group preference will reach its peak.

Friendships are now less transient than they were in previous years. It has become somewhat more difficult to make friends, and dissolved friendships can be quite emotionally unsettling. The circle of friends is smaller than in previous years. As children become somewhat choosy, not only gender but also culture and economic background influence friendship choices (Hartup, 1983). Choices become based on attributes ("She is real nice"), rather than possessions or situational factors, as with younger children ("I like him because he has a Lego set to play with") (Boggiano, Klinger, & Main, 1986). One can see that the social competence skills of initiating, maintaining, and resolving conflicts become important skills to have mastered by early school age.

Participation in games and activities involving rules brings children into frequent conflicts as rules become debatable and children discover that each player may perceive the rules differently. Through conflict encounters such as these, children's points of view compete and their negotiating skills are tested. Lever (1976) found a difference in the amount of conflict engaged in by boys and girls. Boys' games tended to result in more conflict, while girls were more inclined to engage in turn-taking behaviors. Girls were also found to be more inclined to try to diffuse conflict situations. Boys were more likely to use heavy-handed persuasion to get what they wanted. Boys were shown to use these tactics whether in conflict with boys or

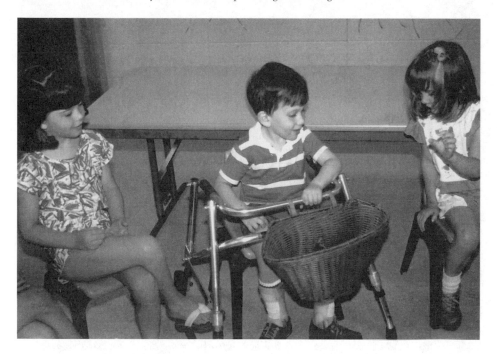

*The peer group emerges as a powerful socializing force during the 6- through 8-year period.*

with girls. Interestingly, girls tended to use heavy-handed tactics with boys but seldom with girls (Miller, Danaher, & Forbes, 1986). Some of these differences may be explained by the expectation that boys will behave more aggressively than girls (Maccoby & Jacklin, 1974/1980). There is also the expectation that girls prefer social harmony and therefore provoke less conflict (Gilligan, 1982).

Cooperation emerges through these early friendships and sustains them (Hartup, 1989). Through friendships children derive companionship, emotional security and support, enhanced feelings of self-worth, interpersonal relationship skills, and knowledge about cultures and social conventions.

## CHILDREN WITH SPECIAL NEEDS

Children with special needs face greater psychosocial challenges as they begin to move through the elementary grades. They share needs for acceptance, belonging, and self-esteem with their age-mates. The extent to which they have had opportunities to develop the social skills of initiating and maintaining friendships and resolving conflicts through inclusive programs and activities will influence their successes with interpersonal relationships and peer acceptance. By the same token, the extent to which other children have learned to understand and relate to their peers with disabilities also influences the climate for acceptance and participation in inclusive groups.

FIGURE 15.2
Cooperation versus Competition

Compared with competitive and individualistic learning situations, working cooperatively with peers:
1. Will create a pattern of promotive interaction, in which there is
    a. more direct face-to-face interaction among students;
    b. an expectation that one's peers will facilitate one's learning;
    c. more peer pressure toward achievement and appropriate classroom behav-
       ior;
    d. more reciprocal communication and fewer difficulties in communicating
       with each other;
    e. more actual helping, tutoring, assisting, and general facilitation of each
       other's learning;
    f. more open-mindedness to peers and willingness to be influenced by their
       ideas and information;
    g. more positive feedback to and reinforcement of each other;
    h. less hostility, both verbal and physical, expressed toward peers.

2. Will create perceptions and feelings of
    a. higher trust in other students;
    b. more mutual concern and friendliness for other students, more attentiveness
       to peers, more feelings of obligation to and responsibility for classmates, and
       desire to win the respect of other students;
    c. stronger beliefs that one is liked, supported, and accepted by other students,
       and that other students care about how much one learns and want to help
       one learn;
    d. lower fear of failure and higher psychological safety;
    e. higher valuing of classmates;
    f. greater feelings of success.

*Source:* D. Johnson and R. Johnson, "Classroom Learning Structure and Attitudes toward
Handicapped Students in Mainstream Settings: A Theoretical Model and Research Evidence," in
R. L. Jones (Ed.), *Attitudes and Attitude Change in Special Education: Theory and Practice* (Reston,
Va.: The Council for Exceptional Children, 1984). Reprinted with permission.

A common challenge for special-needs children regardless of type of disability
is the feeling of being different from other children. The self-concepts of many
children with disabilities may center too heavily on their disabilities. Teachers who
seek positive and successful psychosocial experiences for children with special
needs will find effective ways to promote group understandings and acceptance.
Teachers will structure both the physical and psychosocial environments to
encourage social interactions among all children.

Teachers should be aware that any emphasis on competition among children can
be particularly detrimental to the psychosocial development of children with special
needs. Instead, arranging for more cooperative group endeavors assists all children in the development of social skills and social competence (see Figure 15.2).

# FACTORS INFLUENCING PSYCHOSOCIAL DEVELOPMENT

## SOCIOCULTURAL INFLUENCES

As children enter school, concerns for healthy cultural experiences emerge. Often teachers are from different cultural groups than those of their students. Classroom populations often include children from several cultures. Adults who are knowledgeable about differences among and within cultural groups and understand the impact on children of language backgrounds are better equipped to provide positive antibias experiences and promote productive and satisfying social interactions among classmates. Teachers who understand differences in parenting styles and in expectations and goals parents have for their children are able to foster positive and supportive home-school relationships. Andrews (1981) lists four basic cultural needs of young children and their families: (1) self-esteem, (2) belonging, (3) achievement, and (4) dignity. According to Andrews, all children, regardless of ethnic or racial background, have these same basic cultural needs.

Among the factors contributing to healthy psychosocial development in the 6- to 8-year-old are the child's sociocultural context, the child's own personality, the nature and quality of adult-child relationships, experiences beyond school in before- and after-school child care settings, sibling relationships, increasing social interactions, stress, and television.

## THE CHILD'S PERSONALITY

From previous chapters, we have seen that children have distinctive temperamental characteristics that are probably genetically derived but are also influenced in a variety of ways by the child's environment. The concept of temperament refers to a number of behavioral aspects: activity level, regularity of behavior, distractibility, approach and withdrawal in new experiences, adaptability to change, attention span/persistence, intensity of reactions to stimuli, response threshold (amount of stimulation needed to evoke a response), and mood (Chess & Thomas, 1987; Thomas et al., 1963).

The social contexts in which these variable temperament qualities are exhibited determine the effects these qualities will have on others and how others will respond to the child. For instance, a child with a very high activity level could be viewed in positive terms ("energetic," "lively") or negative terms ("jumpy," "restless"). Such views influence the person's responses and interactions with the child. The child, then, is subjected to a variety of responses of others based on how others perceive his or her temperament.

Differences in personality at ages 6 through 8 have their roots in these early and continuing perceptions and interactions. Recent studies have attempted to ascertain the relationship between early personality traits and later psychosocial adjustment. Some traits have been found to persist. For instance, highly aggressive children have been found to remain relatively more aggressive than others as they get older (Huesmann et al., 1984). Other studies have suggested that negative emotional behaviors such as aggressiveness, being hard to please, undercompliance, and difficulties with peers are fairly stable over the course of childhood and affect later adjustment. Children who have been socially rejected during their earliest elementary years may be at greater risk for social difficulties in adolescence and early adulthood (Hymel et al., 1990).

The complex social interactions of children ages 6 through 8 encompass the family, school, peer groups, organized activity groups, and myriad incidental social encounters. This complex network of interactions expands the child's insights into the personalities of others and into her or his own developing personality. Though self-awareness has been emerging since infancy, self-perceptions during this age period are becoming more acute. Maturing social perceptions also help children to appreciate the needs of others and engage in cooperative activities.

## NATURE OF ADULT-CHILD RELATIONSHIPS

As previously discussed, qualities of early experiences such as attachment, parenting styles, nonparental child care and reactions to individual temperament have been associated with various psychosocial outcomes. Certain aspects of the relationship between the parent and the child have also been related to the child's psychosocial development. A recent study observed playful mother-child and father-child interactions and correlated them with the child's adaptation to peers (MacDonald & Parke, 1984). The findings suggest that boys who were competent with their peers had fathers who were physically playful and affectionate. The fathers of competent girls engaged their daughters in stimulating verbal exchanges. Certain maternal behaviors have been found to influence social acceptance with peers. Children whose mothers used positive verbal interactions, such as polite requests and suggestions, and were less demanding of and disagreeable with their children were found to be less abrasive and more positive in their peer interactions (Putallaz, 1987).

It is generally believed that social skills necessary for later successful peer group interactions are learned through early experiences in the family (Petit, Dodge, & Brown, 1988). But the quality of parent-child interactions is not the only influence on psychosocial development. By providing opportunities for peer group interaction, encouraging and facilitating friendships, and monitoring children's relationships for positive outcomes, parents provide the scaffolding essential to the development of social competence.

## BEFORE- AND AFTER-SCHOOL CARE

As we have seen, the need for child care has increased appreciably in recent years, as has the availability and utilization of before- and after-school care arrangements. Children's experiences in these programs influence their psychosocial development. The need for adults in these settings to be good role models—to be nurturing and supportive of growth and development—is crucial. The expectations placed on children in child care situations must be scrutinized carefully. As with developmentally appropriate schooling experiences discussed in previous chapters, child care programs must meet the physical/motor and social/emotional needs of children as well as their cognitive needs.

For some school children, the out-of-home day may be as long as 10 to 13 hours. Long days are tiring and stressful. The daily before-school/school/after-school routine may involve two or more different settings, perhaps in two or more locations; different sets of adult authorities with different levels of education and training; different teaching and discipline styles; different behavior and performance expectations; and different modes of interacting with individual children. There may also be different peer groups with different group configurations and interactional dynamics. Clearly, children in these situations are called on to be flexible, resilient, and adaptable, not to mention physically hearty!

For some children, these demands present no problems. For others, adapting to multiple authority figures and different peer groups can be stressful and difficult. Parents, caregivers, and classroom teachers must be sensitive to the physical and psychological demands of these routines. When a balanced schedule that includes rest, relaxation, play, self-directed activities, outdoor and indoor activities, and group and solitary moments, along with structured and adult-directed activities, is provided, the child's day can be productive and enjoyable. However, emphasis on group participation, schoolwork, and academic endeavors before, during, and after school would tax any child.

Teachers and caregivers need to provide space (both physical and psychological) for children to distance themselves from the group from time to time. Schedules in both the school and the child care program need to be sensitive to the physiological needs for nourishment, physical exercise, rest, spontaneous play, and informal interactions with friends and siblings. After-school programs need to resist the urge to "help" with schooling by insisting on additional schoolwork activities. Likewise, schools and teachers must resist the temptation to defer practice and reinforcement activities to after-school times. This, of course, opens the debate on whether or not homework should be regularly assigned. This topic, while critical, is beyond the intent of this discussion. The points here are that:

1. Long days with repeated structured activities may impede school learning by causing fatigue, frustration, and burnout.

2. Children's physical and motor needs (addressed in Chapters 11 and 14) must be met for children to be physically and neurologically healthy.

3. Sound psychosocial development relies on warm, nurturing, supportive, and meaningful adult-child relationships.

4. Social competence, including social problem-solving skills, perspective-taking abilities, and prosocial abilities, depends on opportunities to interact with friends in meaningful ways and be reasonably free from adult interference.

*Siblings typically move in and out of their close relationships with one another.*

Before- and after-school child care can play a positive and supportive role in psychosocial development. When children are allowed to experience autonomy and control in the use of their time and energies and are provided with activities over which they can have a sense of mastery, adaptability to the routines of child care and school is facilitated (Bryant, 1985).

Programs that provide for the safety and nurturing needs of children offer a valuable support system for families. When parents feel secure and confident about the experiences their children are having while they are at work, family relationships are enhanced. Relieved of the worry and stress associated with unpredictable or latchkey arrangements, parents are able to pursue their own work in a more productive manner. Emerging prescriptions for child care will include greater coordination among family, school, and child care and more efforts to meet a variety of family support service needs (Kagan, 1989; NASBE, 1988).

## SIBLING RELATIONSHIPS

The positive and constructive relationships siblings enjoy have received far less attention in the media and research than have sibling rivalry and jealousy. Yet studies reveal that siblings are nurturing, protective, and cooperative with one another and are more likely to be so with one another than with unrelated children (Dunn & Kendrick, 1982b).

The sense of self derives in part from the relationships a child has with siblings. Yet siblings face a variety of self-concept issues relating to their close or distant relationships with brothers and sisters, their feelings of acceptance or rejection of one another, and their feelings of being similar or different from one another (Bank & Kahn, 1982b). These relationships and the perceptions that accompany them play a complex role in the child's developing sense of self as a unique and separate individual and also as part of a broader identity that includes brothers and sisters.

Rivalrous behavior at ages 6 through 8 is often an indication of the child's emerging sense of identity. Children at this age compare themselves with others in an attempt to affirm their self-worth. In families, brothers and sisters become objects for comparison as children seek to distinguish similarities and differences between themselves and others. At the same time, siblings begin to identify with one or more of their siblings, who are often powerful role models.

It is difficult to establish a comfortable and separate identity when parents dress siblings alike, provide the same enrichment opportunities (swimming, piano, ballet, or tennis lessons) or group memberships (Little League, scout troops), or adopt an "if it is done for one, it must be done for the other" approach to child rearing. Each child's unique needs, interests, and capabilities need nurturing and support. Self-confidence and self-esteem emerge from finding one's own attributes, separate and apart from those of others, particularly those of siblings.

Parents who project their own unfulfilled ambitions (to play baseball, master the violin, or be at the top of the class) on one or more of the siblings place all of the children at risk on several fronts. The full realization of one's own interests and capabilities are thwarted in the child on whom these projections are imposed. The child grows to believe that success in the parent-selected pursuit will bring favor to him or her over others and failure will bring serious disappointment to the parent and perhaps lead to retribution. The sibling excluded from these particular expectations perceives herself or himself as being less important and/or less competent, to the parent, even if the child is not interested in the activities in question. The sibling relationship is undermined by feelings of rejection, envy, competition, and other negative responses to the parent's insensitive expectations. The parent-child relationship is undermined in both cases.

Classroom teachers and other adults with whom the child interacts often compare one sibling to another, both favorably and unfavorably. This also impedes self-concept development and undermines sibling relationships. Where sibling relationships are at risk or already strained, differential treatment by parents, teachers, or others can exacerbate the situation for the siblings.

## INCREASED SOCIAL INTERACTIONS

As children get older, an expanding social circle, from parents and family to individuals and groups outside of the family, brings additional influences on the child's psychosocial development. Social interactions include incidental encounters (sharing the "sights" of the toy aisle at the supermarket with an acquaintance); informal interactions with individuals (riding bicycles with a special friend) and with loosely formed groups (neighborhood play groups); and formal or organized activities (Pee-Wee and Little League).

At this age, children establish and maintain close friendships with one or more age-mates and enjoy visiting in one another's homes, sometimes overnight. Such friendships help children to grow in independence and social interaction skills. Through these friendships, children learn the importance of "give and take" and gain a sense of loyalty.

Children enlarge their friendship circles through loosely formed social groups. As a rule, these groups simply "play around" with one another. However, their organization may take on the elements of a club or gang, with leaders and followers, membership preferences, rules, and sometimes a name. Adults can harness the energy and enthusiasm that emerges from these friendship groups.

Jeremy is a member of the Walla Street Club. This group includes the 7-year-old boy next door, the two brothers (8 and 9) who live across the street, a 7-year-old from several doors down the street, and another 6-year-old from a block away. Girls are not admitted to the "club," though two of the members have younger sisters who are allowed to participate in their games on rare occasions. They spend as much time together after school or on weekends as they can. These boys seem to have an insatiable desire to be together and boundless energy when engaged in play.

Jeremy's dad has initiated a weekend project for the boys: building a clubhouse in the backyard. The design, collection of building materials and tools (some borrowed from other members' parents), and the construction of the house have been going on for about two months. The boys plan each step with energy and enthusiasm. Their wills occasionally clash: which board should go where, where the door will be, who is going to bring more nails. At home the boys draw pictures of their clubhouse, gather items to furnish it, and brag to their siblings about their own private place. They talk about the fun or complain about the conflicts with their parents. Together they anticipate their meetings and what they will do, who will come, and who can never come into the clubhouse. It is a dynamic and ongoing "avocation" in their current lives. ■

What do children gain from experiences like these? What about a child excluded from the play group? In these loosely formed groups, children experience leading and following, negotiating and compromising, rule setting, rule changing, and rule constraints. They become aware of the needs and wishes of others, and they practice perspective taking and diplomacy. They experience loyalty and disloyalty, democracy and autocracy. Their sense of industry is tapped, and their sense of belonging is reinforced. Their confidence and self-esteem are enhanced.

Despite all the positive influences of these social groupings, there can be difficulties associated with membership. Children ages 6 through 8 measure themselves against their perceptions of others, and in so doing are self-critical and critical of others. When group expectations are at odds with the child's abilities and desires, conflicts occur and group membership may become detrimental. Treating others unkindly, expecting members to engage in mischief or forbidden activities, setting standards for dress, imposing undesired rivalry and competition, excluding a valued friend, and devaluing one's other activities (e.g., piano lessons, participation in scouting or a family picnic) are influences that can strain the child's abilities to negotiate. Adults need to be aware of these problems and sensitive to the child's dilemma. Guidance and support are needed, and in some instances so will intervention and coaching.

These informal groups, which are often based on proximity and accessibility, may also define their memberships arbitrarily along age, gender, socioeconomic, cultural, or religious lines. Children who are excluded are subjected to feelings of rejection and lowered self-esteem. Sensitive adults will need to provide positive guidance for handling these situations when they arise. Adult intervention is needed to guide the group toward more prosocial goals and inclusive and antibiased behaviors. Here again, adults serve as social role models and coaches for children.

In addition to informally structured social groupings, children ages 6 through 8 are exposed to a variety of other extrafamilial social interactions. Now more predictable and dependable, children are included in various celebrations and recreational events—weddings, graduation ceremonies, football games, concerts. Children often join their parents in religious services on a more regular basis than in previous years. These opportunities broaden the child's social awareness and provide additional role models. The developmental appropriateness of special lessons or sports training for a particular child should be a concern. Athletic training can be physically risky and should be pursued on the advice of the individual child's physician. Participation in athletic teams should be viewed with the same caution, since these activities can place the child at risk for physical injury and can be emotionally and socially taxing for the child.

## STRESS

Children, like adults, experience stress from time to time. Unlike adults, young children lack sufficient knowledge and experience to understand their stressors and a repertoire of strategies for dealing with stress.

The causes of stress in young children are many and varied. Honig (1986) categorized stressor variables as (1) *personal*, including prematurity, sex, temperament, neurological sturdiness, age of child, and intellectual capacity; (2) *ecological*, including characteristics of living environments such as neighborhood crime, antisocial role models, unaesthetic surroundings, household density, individual privacy requirements, and inadequate play space; (3) *socioeconomic status*; (4) *catastrophes and terrors*, including hospitalization, societal disasters, threat of nuclear war and terrorism; and (5) *family events*, including birth of siblings, death of parent or sibling, separation and divorce, and blended families.

Pressures to perform tasks or to achieve beyond one's years and developmental capacities, changes in school or child care arrangements, and childhood social events such as birthday parties and school field trips may also be stressful. Obviously, a great number of potential stressors exist for young children. Certainly not all of these events cause anxiety or stress in all children. Responses to stress are as varied as the stressors themselves and may be physiological (headache, stomachache, loss of appetite, sleep disturbances) or psychological (crying, nightmares, regression, irritability, increased dependency).

Responses to stress are based on temperament, cognitive styles, and social support networks (Owens-Stively, 1987). Characteristics often associated with stress-related personalities, such as competitiveness, impatience, aggressiveness, low frustration tolerance, hostility, and high achievement orientation, have been found in very young children. The child's ability to appraise a stressful situation influences the extent to which the child will cope. Children need adults to help them identify their stressors and to evaluate them with a goal toward either eliminating the stressors when possible or finding constructive ways to deal with stress.

Jeremy's second-grade teacher invited his parents to a conference. His usual classroom performance had deteriorated since the beginning of the school year, and she was concerned. Jeremy's behaviors in school were off-task and disruptive. He teased his classmates, antagonized his project partners, and resorted to name calling when they protested. When the teacher intervened, he withdrew, became sullen, and often cried.

In conference, Ann and Bill revealed that similar behaviors were occurring at home, and they did not know what to do. Their individual work commitments, church work, and social life were consuming larger and larger amounts of their time and energies. In addition, Ann's mother recently underwent surgery and needed Ann's assistance during her recovery.

The teacher asked them to focus on Jeremy's routines. What did he do before and after school and on the weekends? Jeremy's schedule included regular before- and after-school care at a child care center near the school. In addition, he was taking piano lessons early each Monday morning, had karate lessons on Wednesday afternoon, and played Pee-Wee League baseball on Saturday mornings.

Clearly all members of the family had become overcommitted and overprogrammed. The stress of such scheduling, the logistics of transportation and attendance, and the reduced opportunities for family interaction and mutual support were beginning to take their toll on each member. Jeremy's behavior in school was a clue to the stress he was encountering.

A reassessment of their commitments, goals, and priorities led Bill and Ann to conclude that each member of the family would benefit from a change. Jeremy was encouraged to talk about the extracurricular activities in which he was enrolled, and was allowed to decide which one or ones were most important to him and most enjoyable. Ann and Bill did the same assessment of their own activities. From this exercise, each family member eliminated all but the most pressing and important activities. Jeremy chose to drop the piano and karate lessons. Maybe later he will want to pursue those lessons; for now, he feels relieved. With commitments and extracurricular activities returned to a manageable level, Jeremy and his parents have more time and energy to respond to one another and to interact with focused attention. ■

## TELEVISION

The amount of time school-age children spend viewing television is a major concern to parents, educators, child advocacy groups, and government officials. The following research statements support this concern:

> More time is spent watching television in the first 15 years of life than going to school; in fact, by the time a child reaches age 18, more time will have been spent watching television than any other single activity besides sleeping. (Liebert, Sprafkin, & Davidson, 1982, p. ix)
>
> The average high school graduate will have spent 22,000 hours in front of a television set, and will have been exposed to 350,000 commercials. (Adler et al., 1980, p. 1)

Clearly television plays a major role in the socialization and culturalization of children. Children learn from television, and their behaviors are influenced by what they learn. Studies of violence and aggression on television have overwhelmingly concluded that television has a measurable impact on behavior. Concern over this issue continues. Studies of gender and of racial and cultural groups on television have pointed out misrepresentations in television programming and the potential deleterious effects of stereotyping. Studies of commercials have likewise suggested that childhood values and attitudes may be distorted and that commercials exploit children for financial gains.

Programs with prosocial themes and role models have also been shown to influence behavior, although the impact of these programs is thought to be less potent than that of violence and aggression (Radke-Yarrow, Zahn-Waxler, & Chapman, 1983). Contemporary studies of the impact of television on children's lives are attempting to determine to what extent children actually attend to television when the set is on, what types of program events or program attributes attract and hold the child's attention (e.g., other children, puppets, unusual voices, animation, rhyming, laughing, and repetition), and to what extent children comprehend what they view on television.

Large amounts of television watching interfere with psychosocial development in the following ways:

1. Physical activity and outdoor play are curtailed. Lack of exercise impedes physical motor development and sound physical and mental health.

2. Interaction with other children is reduced. As we have seen, children at this age need the social experiences that peer group interaction affords. Without these experiences, children are deprived of opportunities to gain social knowledge and social competence.

3. Children who are unskilled in social interaction with peers or are unpopular and rejected by playmates find escape in television viewing, further reducing their interactions with others and further impeding their psychosocial development.

4. Parent-child conversations and interactions are interrupted. Both children and parents forgo dialogue and in-depth conversations when television viewing dominates their free time. Opportunities to address issues of concern to the

child and to provide needed emotional and social guidance are often irretrievably lost.

5. Opportunities to discover one's own interests and unique capabilities or talents are reduced. Children at this age, who are developing initiative, industry, self-concept, and self-esteem, need to explore and experience a variety of endeavors and interests on the way to self-discovery.

Based on the assumption that school-age children can be taught to use critical viewing skills, child development experts are developing programs and strategies to be used in classrooms and perhaps at home (Dorr, Graves, & Phelps, 1980). The objectives of these programs include

- Decreasing the belief that TV programs are real
- Increasing the child's tendency to compare what is seen on TV with other sources of information
- Decreasing television's credibility by teaching children about the economic and production aspects of television
- Teaching children to evaluate the content of television programming.

At home, adults can practice critical viewing skills with children by pointing out how television provides both worthwhile and objectionable programs. Family values can be conveyed in these comparisons. Role playing and pantomime illustrate that characters on television are actors playing a particular role. Adults can help children compare these roles with individuals in similar roles in real life, perhaps individuals the child knows personally. Adults can watch and listen with children for special effects such as laugh tracks, sounds, lighting, and fast-sequenced photos; listen to background music for familiar tunes or specific instruments; converse about the story just viewed; retell the story with a "better" ending; answer questions about the story while they are fresh in the child's mind; critique a program for both its good qualities and its shortcomings; and help children identify implied messages by pointing out how commercials use loud, fast talk and flashy colors and music to capture the viewer's attention. Together parents and children can make a list of famous people who make commercials to illustrate how the industry uses these people to promote products; compare products advertised with the ones the family already prefers; and, when shopping, make price and quality comparisons, helping children draw conclusions about the feasibility of purchasing an advertised product.

Parents and teachers have important roles to play in facilitating the positive effects of television for children. The amount of time children spend viewing television can be curtailed in favor of more physically and mentally challenging activities and increased social interactions with others. Wise program choices can result when children are taught to evaluate the offerings. In addition, children need adults to talk with them about the content of programs they see and to help them become discerning viewers.

 *Role of the Early Childhood Professional*

### Enhancing Psychosocial Development in Children Ages 6 Through 8

1. Support the child's continuing need for nurturance and security.

2. Enhance the child's self-esteem through positive and supportive interactions.

3. Model prosocial and moral behaviors; help children understand the need and rationales for rules.

4. Support the child's sense of industry through opportunities to participate in meaningful activities.

5. Understand the child's increasing needs for social interactions, and encourage and facilitate a variety of social interactions.

6. Provide positive, inductive, authoritative discipline.

7. Recognize the child's continuing need for boundaries and guidance.

8. Respond to the child's changing interests in gender with acceptance and respect.

9. Assist the child in accepting and appreciating others.

10. Provide appropriate media experiences, and help the child to become a critical evaluator of media programs. ◼

## KEY TERMS

defense mechanism
industry
sociocentric

## REVIEW STRATEGIES AND ACTIVITIES

1. Review the key terms individually or with a classmate.

2. Develop an annotated bibliography of children's books that address the issues children confront in making and maintaining friendships.

3. Observe a developmentally appropriate third-grade classroom. How is social interaction encouraged? Are informal social groups evident? Observe these friendship groups on the playground at recess. What are the compositions of the groups? How do they interact with one another? Is there a leader? What rules seem to be evident? How do the children respond to nongroup members?

4. Engage in a dialogue with a member of a different ethnic background. Discuss similarities and differences in your child rearing with regard to school achievement, respect for authority, independence, responsibilities to family, choice of friends, gender role, and racial identity.

5. With a partner, brainstorm ways to promote and facilitate the developing sense of industry in young school-age children.

6. Discuss with your classmates the meaning of inclusion practices in the lives of young children.

---

## FURTHER READINGS

Aboud, F. (1988). *Children and prejudice*. New York: Basil Blackwell, Inc.

Cottle, T. J. (1990). *Children's secrets*. Reading, MA: Addison-Wesley.

Cowles, M., & Aldridge, J. (1992). *Activity-oriented classrooms*. Washington, DC: National Education Association.

Curry, N., & Johnson, C. (1990). *Beyond self-esteem: Developing a genuine sense of human value*. Washington, DC: National Association for the Education of Young Children.

DeVries, R., & Zan, B. (1994). *Moral classrooms, moral children: Creating a constructivist atmosphere in early education*. New York: Teachers College Press.

Derman-Sparks, L. (1989). *Anti-bias curriculum: Tools for empowering young children*. Washington, DC: National Association for the Education of Young Children.

Derman-Sparks, L. D., Gutierrez, M., & Phillips, C. B. (1991). *Teaching young children to resist bias: What parents can do*. Washington, DC: National Association for the Education of Young Children.

Dimidjian, V. J. (Ed.), (1992). *Play's place in public education for young children*. Washington, DC: National Education Association.

Dolinar, K., Boser, C., & Holm, E. (1994). *Learning through play: Curriculum and activities for the inclusive classroom*. Albany, NY: Delmar.

Dunn, J., & Plomin, R. (1992). *Separate lives: Why siblings are so different*. New York: Basic Books.

Edelman, M. W. (1992). *The measure of our success: A letter to my children and yours*. Boston, MA: Beacon Press.

Eisenberg, N. (1992). *The caring child*. Cambridge, MA: Harvard University Press.

Frost, J. L. (1992). *Play and playscapes*. Albany, NY: Delmar.

Garbarino, J. Scott, M. & Faculty of the Erikson Institute. (1992). *What children can tell us: Eliciting, interpreting and evaluating critical information from children*. San Francisco: Jossey-Bass.

Katz, L., & McClellan, D. (1991). *The teacher's role in the social development of young children*. Urbana, IL: Clearinghouse on Elementary and Early Childhood Education.

Korczak, J. (1993). *The child's right to respect*. Lantham, MD: University Press of America.

Kozloff, M. A. (1994). *Improving educational outcomes for children with disability: Guidelines and protocols for practice*. Baltimore, MD: Paul H. Brooks.

McCracken, J. B. (1993). *Valuing diversity: The primary years*. Washington, DC: National Association for the Education of Young Children.

*Newsletter: School Age Notes* (Bimonthly newsletter for teachers and directors of programs for school-age children).

Patillo, J., & Vaughn, E. (1992). *Learning centers for child-centered classrooms*. Washington, DC: National Education Association.

Rogers, Carl R. (1994). *Freedom to learn* (3rd ed.). Columbus, OH: Merrill/ Macmillan.

Young, R. D. (1991). *Risk-taking in learning, K–3*. Washington, DC: National Education Association.

# CHAPTER SIXTEEN

*Continual interaction with materials in the classroom supports the construction of knowledge and meaning for the learner. No cut off age of six exists for such interaction. . . . During all the early childhood years the search for meaning is facilitated or impeded by the nature of the environment: opportunities for exploration, discovery, and the integration of learnings are essential.*

Evelyn Weber

# Cognitive, Language, and Literacy Development Ages 6 Through 8

After studying this chapter, you will demonstrate comprehension by:

- Describing the continuum in development and learning throughout *all* of the early childhood years.
- Describing the cognitive development of children ages 6 through 8.
- Describing the oral language development of children ages 6 through 8.
- Describing the literacy development of children ages 6 through 8.
- Identifying special needs and sociocultural information relating to the cognitive, language, and literacy development of children ages 6 through 8.
- Defining the role of adults in promoting cognitive, language, and literacy development in young children ages 6 through 8.

## CONTINUITY IN DEVELOPMENT AND LEARNING THROUGHOUT THE EARLY CHILDHOOD YEARS

It is in the spring of Jeremy's kindergarten year. Ms. Buckley, Jeremy's teacher, has sent several letters about the first-grade year to the parents of the children in her class. One letter tells of a first-grade open house in the evening for kindergarten children and their parents. As Ann, Bill, and Jeremy discuss their upcoming visit, Jeremy indicates that he already knows much about the first grade in his school. Throughout the year, there have been many opportunities for the kindergarten children to interact with the first-grade children and their teachers. Class books have been exchanged. Informal plays of nursery rhymes and fairy tales have been shared at both grades. Visits to see special displays have occurred. The kindergarten and first-grade classes have gone to the park together for nature scavenger hunts. Both classes have worked cooperatively cleaning up the playground once a month. They have eaten popcorn and sung songs together. Thus, Jeremy has been in the first-grade classrooms, he knows the teachers, and he has interacted with first-graders. He feels comfortable about going to first grade for these reasons and also because he knows he will continue to see his kindergarten teacher and from time to time will be in his "old room."

After returning from the visit of the first-grade classes, Bill remarks that these classrooms sure look different from his first-grade classroom. The desks are clustered in fours so that the children can interact while they are learning. There are learning centers throughout the room. Bill also notes that much of the children's writing was displayed around the room. The writing contained invented spellings and was not corrected by the first-grade teachers. Bill thinks times certainly have changed. Because of Jeremy's involvement and the teacher's orientation in which she explained the importance of the transition between kindergarten and first grade, Bill feels relatively comfortable with these changes.

The principal and the kindergarten and first-grade teachers were aware that many parents, based on their own experience, would think that first-graders learn only in quiet classrooms where the desks are arranged in rows, with the teacher conducting reading groups and other instruction from the front of the classroom. To help the parents understand the need for continuity in learning experiences between the kindergarten and first-grade years, the professionals at Jeremy's school provided written information, plan meetings and open houses for the parents of future first-graders. ■

In reality, the unification of kindergarten and the primary grades is not a new idea. Weber (1984) says,

> Early specialists of kindergarten education worked not just for more kindergartens, but also for the extension into the primary grades of the principles and the philosophy of the education they espoused so heartily. Those staunch reformers believed their "new" educational design ensured a more child-centered curriculum that employed different methods and procedures for early learning. They also believed that the nature of children of five, six, and seven years of age was similar; in social, emotional, and intellectual characteristics they were much alike. So adult leaders strove toward the unification of kindergarten-primary education. (pp. 198–199)

Today, there is much renewed interest in providing continuity among programs for children in the early years. Bredekamp (1987) indicates that when young children move from one early childhood program to another, adjustments must be made. Teachers, administrators, and parents can work cooperatively to promote successful adjustment in the transition from one early childhood environment to another.

In October 1988, the National Association of State Boards of Education (NASBE) Task Force on Early Childhood Education issued a report entitled *Right From the Start*. This report calls for a restructuring of the early years of the elementary school based on child development knowledge and curriculum from successful preprimary programs, that is, programs for children before first grade. The recommendations include the creation of early childhood units in elementary schools for children ages 4 through 8. In addition, increased cooperation among schools, parents, and other programs and services is proposed. Thus, continuity from one early childhood program to another is important throughout all of the early years, including the primary grades. Mixed-age grouping is an attempt to promote continuity of learning in the early years of schooling (Friedman & Koeppel, 1990; Katz, Evangelou, & Hartman, 1990; Nachbar, 1989).

Another type of continuity that is important in working with young children is the continuity between home and school. Trawick-Smith (1994) suggests that children can benefit from a moderate amount of home-school discontinuity in that they may acquire skills of capability and adaptability. However, if teachers do not understand the culture of the child and his or her family, home-school discontinuity may become problematic (Powell, 1989, 1994). Sources of discontinuity can include

- *Parenting beliefs and practices*. In some cultures adult-child relationships are very formal, with children expected to be very compliant with and respectful of adults. In other cultural groups, adult-child relationships are very informal.
- *Parenting styles*. These can vary across cultures and should be interpreted as differences, not deficits, when compared with European American parenting styles.
- *Differences in styles of parenting and teaching*. Parenting styles may differ greatly from teaching styles. Children's achievement can improve when learning environments are adapted to resemble home environments (Au & Kowakami, 1991).
- *Differences in priorities placed on school*. Parents of all cultures view learning as important, but differences exist in how school is valued in relationship to family and other aspects of life. Lack of attendance at school functions may be a result of cultural values, with family responsibilities taking priority. Differences also exist concerning the role of parents in the education process. Steward and Steward (1974) reported that Chinese mothers tended to view teaching as a primary role of parenting, European American mothers thought teaching was a small part of parenting, and Mexican American mothers considered themselves solely as parents and not teachers.

Teachers of young children can promote smooth home-school transitions by understanding the cultures of the children in their classrooms through reading and engaging in parent discussions and meetings (Powell, 1994). Powell (1994) also emphasizes the importance of perspective taking on the part of staff in the development of effective partnerships with parents. He advocates specialized preparation in areas concerning parenting, parent development, and family life.

Parents must be involved in educational decisions regarding their children (Delpit, 1988; Gandini, 1993; Puckett & Black, 1994; Powell, 1994). Debates have occurred over issues involving direct teaching versus informal learning contexts and skills versus process approaches and the extent of parental input on these educational decisions. These issues will be revisited later in this chapter in the section on literacy development.

Transition classrooms have been established in an effort to promote continuity and achievement among early childhood educational settings. However, data on these programs do not support these assumptions (Dennebaum & Kulberg, 1994). Some form of extra support in the regular classroom may be more appropriate.

While this chapter discusses the differences and changes in development that occur during the primary-grade years, it is important to remember that the years from 6 through 8 are still part of early childhood. Therefore, many of the same experiences that facilitate cognitive, language, and literacy development earlier in life also contribute to these areas of development in 6-, 7- and 8-year-olds. Before you read the next section, reread the quote at the beginning of this chapter, which sets the stage for our final discussion of how young children develop cognition, language, and literacy in the primary grades. Notice how the word *interaction* is used in the quotation. Where have you read about this before?

## COGNITIVE DEVELOPMENT

Piaget's research indicated that young children develop concepts about the world through active physical and sensorimotor interactions with the environment. This is in contrast to the quiet, more passive learning of older children and adults. Piaget's research also suggested that young children cannot be directly taught a body of knowledge as can older children and adults, but learn by constructing their own knowledge. For example, a young boy who is playing with sand may pour sand from one container to another, feel the sand in his hands, or put the sand in his mouth. Through actions like these, young children discover and construct their knowledge of sand: what it does, how it feels, and how it tastes. The child cannot construct accurate knowledge about sand unless he acts on the sand. Adults cannot simply tell a child that sand feels gritty. This is the process by which young children develop physical knowledge (Wadsworth, 1984, pp. 22–23).

The second type of knowledge Piaget identified was what he called *logical-mathematical knowledge*. Here the child thinks about, constructs, or invents knowledge from his or her actions on objects. However, in this type of learning, the objects serve merely as a means of permitting the construction of knowledge to occur. For example, a little girl plays with a set of six buttons. She puts them in a row and counts them. Then she puts them in a circle and counts them. Next, she puts them in a stack and counts them. Through active experiences like these, she eventually constructs the concept that the number of objects in a set remains the same regardless of the arrangement of the individual elements. As experiences are repeated in different settings with different materials, the concepts become more refined. Like physical knowledge, logical-mathematical knowledge is *not* acquired from reading or listening to teachers talk. It is constructed or invented in the child's mind (Wadsworth, 1984, pp. 23–24).

This section first discusses the transition from the preoperational stage to the stage of concrete operations. Next, it presents Piaget's ideas regarding cognitive processing during concrete operations. Finally, it introduces more recent thought regarding cognitive development in children ages 6 through 8.

## TRANSITION FROM PREOPERATIONAL TO CONCRETE OPERATIONAL STAGE

Chapter 10 indicated that some researchers think that children in the preoperational stage give evidence of some concrete operational behaviors (Fuson, Secada, & Hall, 1983; Gelman, 1979; Gelman, Bullock, & Meck, 1980; Gelman & Shatz,

1978). As mentioned previously, some of these investigations suggest that there may not be stages of cognitive development. However, Piaget asserts that between ages 5 and 7, most young children undergo dramatic changes in their cognitive processing, indicating a new stage of development, the **concrete operational stage** (Piaget & Inhelder, 1956). Some children begin to move into more concrete operational stage behaviors at age 5. Other children provide little evidence of concrete operational behavior until around age 7 (Gardner, 1978). The wide age range involved in this transition is an important reason for maintaining a continuum of experiences between the preprimary and primary grades.

## PIAGET'S STAGE OF CONCRETE OPERATIONS

Piaget viewed the shift from the preoperational stage to the stage of concrete operations as a major milestone in the development of cognition. Children in this stage are no longer perceptually bound in their thinking. They can now perform mental operations if the physical objects are present. According to Piaget, the ability to perform mental operations without concrete objects, to think abstractly, and to reflect develops in adolescence during the stage of **formal operations** (Inhelder & Piaget, 1958; Piaget & Inhelder, 1956).

Children in the stage of concrete operations gradually master a variety of conservation tasks. (Refer to Chapter 13 for a review of these tasks.) Piaget and others have determined that conservation of number occurs first, followed by conservation of length, mass and liquid, and finally of weight and volume (Brainerd, 1978; Brainerd & Brainerd, 1972; Gruen & Vore, 1972). This increasing ability to conserve helps children's thinking become more logical and flexible. Children can now return to their original point in thought and can think about alternative ways to solve problems. Elkind (1978a,b) noted that children in the stage of concrete operations gradually become aware of more aspects of a problem.

This ability to see more aspects of a situation appears to promote the gradual awareness of views of other children and adults (Krauss & Glucksberg, 1969; Rubin, 1973; Shatz, 1983). The decline of egocentric behavior also causes children to think about how others perceive their behavior (Selman, 1976, 1980). This improved ability to see the viewpoints of others results in increased proficiency in games with rules and team sports.

Jeremy has gradually changed in his behaviors at his soccer games. At age 6, when playing goalie, he easily became distracted, often looking at the ground or hunting bugs in the grass. But at age 8, he consistently focuses on the game and actively positions himself to block the soccer ball.

Jeremy also likes baseball. He has become an avid collector of baseball cards. From time to time, he classifies the cards in various ways: teams, player positions, leagues, batting averages, and other statistics. ■

Jeremy's ability to create multiple classifications also reflects the differences in cognitive processing between preoperational and concrete operational children. Thus, the changes in intellectual processing described in Piaget's viewpoint differ substantially from those of preoperational children and warrant the designation of another stage: the stage of concrete operations. However, Chapter 10 indicated

*concrete operational stage:*
*according to Piaget, the stage in which children, approximately 7 to 11 years of age, can use logical reasoning (rather than relying on perceptions) in situations that are concrete, that is, involve objects and events in the child's immediate environment*

*formal operations:*
*according to Piaget, the fourth and final stage of cognitive development, which occurs during adolescence, when mental operations can be performed without concrete objects and abstract thinking begins*

that some theorists and researchers think that the development of cognition occurs over a period of time in varying domains rather than in separate stages. The following discussion considers cognitive development during ages 6 through 8 from this perspective.

## BEYOND PIAGET: RECENT IDEAS ABOUT COGNITIVE DEVELOPMENT IN 6- TO 8-YEAR-OLDS

Some researchers suggest that children around ages 6, 7, and 8 begin to develop the ability to hold information in short-term memory (White & Pillemer, 1979). Changes in children's intellectual functioning at these ages are thought to be the result of more efficient mental processing (Case, 1985). Rehearsal techniques and improved memory organization appear to increase children's ability to store and retrieve information in an organized and systematic manner (Kail, 1984; Weissburg & Paris, 1986). Another suggested reason for improved cognitive abilities during this time is that children of 6, 7, and 8 years of age simply have had more time than preprimary-age children to establish a knowledge base or a background of information to apply in new contexts (Chi, 1978; Chi & Koeske, 1983; Beddard & Chi, 1992).

Finally, 7- and 8-year-olds demonstrate that they have increased knowledge about the process of remembering, or **meta memory**, and **metacognition**, an understanding of their own cognitive processes (Flavell, Friederichs, & Hoyt, 1970). This increased awareness of their own memory processes appears to facilitate more sophisticated cognitive processing. Some of these new ideas are reflected in current thinking regarding the development of mathematical concepts in young children.

*meta memory: an awareness or knowledge of how one's memory processes work*

*metacognition: an awareness or knowledge of how one processes information and thought*

## NEW IDEAS ABOUT THE DEVELOPMENT OF MATHEMATICAL CONCEPTS: INFORMATION PROCESSING AND COGNITIVE SCIENCE

Price (1989) reports that researchers and theorists in the area of mathematical development are currently revising Piaget's ideas in relation to information-processing theory and the cognitive science perspective. According to Price's (1989) review of research, the information-processing theory suggests that the limitations on short-term memory can create problems for young children as they attempt basic mathematical tasks such as counting and simple mental addition. Moreover, unfamiliarity can put an additional load on short-term memory. Implications from research suggest that it is important for teachers to provide opportunities for young children to develop ways to cope with the simultaneous demands of short-term memory when counting (Baroody, 1984). In addition, it is important for teachers to create situations where young children can gain familiarity with counting or recognizing numbers through practice in meaningful and socially natural situations without "even remotely resembling drill" (Price, 1989).

*cognitive science: the investigation of the knowledge and strategies used in the cognitive process that distinguish expert cognitive processes from novice cognitive processes*

Cognitive science is a second perspective on explaining the development of math in young children. **Cognitive science** examines the strategies and knowledge that separate experts from novices. According to Price (1989), experts possess knowledge special to a particular domain, and expertise in a particular domain, such as counting, apparently can be taught. Skill in counting involves (1) tagging or touching each object, (2) learning that tagging must occur in order, and (3) making the connection between the process of counting and the concept of number.

A second area of expertise in young children involves addition and subtraction in word problems. According to Price (1989), research in this area has revealed some differences among types of word problems in terms of difficulty for young children. While these differences may seem minor to adults, they are very real to young children. The four basic kinds of addition and subtraction problems are join problems, separate problems, combine problems, and compare problems. Join problems and separate problems involve action. The action of *adding* or *joining* elements to the set with which one started is representative of join problems. The action in separate problems requires *subtracting* elements from the set with which one started. In both join and separate problems, three quantities are involved: (1) the *start*, or the amount before the action; (2) the *change*, or the amount involved in the action; and (3) the *result*, or the amount after the action. Price says, "Teachers and curriculum designers unfamiliar with this research are likely to favor one of these types—typically, Result Unknown Join Problems—and omit others" (Price, 1989, p. 56). Some of these categories of problems contain several types. Awareness of the differences among these categories of problems has enabled some first-grade teachers to create more developmentally appropriate instructional strategies (Carpenter, Carey, & Kouba, 1990; Carpenter et al., 1988; Carpenter et al., 1989; Fennema, Carpenter, & Peterson, 1990).

The concept of place value and learning the appropriate notation of place value are difficult for young children. One reason they are so difficult is that the procedures for writing numbers vary from the procedures for writing print. For example, children ages 6 and 7 often write *23* as *203*, thinking that *20* represents twenty (Ginsburg, 1977). Children are used to the left-right orientation in reading and writing and therefore find it difficult to remember that in math, place value dictates an orientation from right to left. Such processing produces approximations such as

$$\begin{array}{r} 1\ 1 \\ +\ 1 \\ \hline 2\ 1 \end{array}$$

Close examination of children's math approximations usually reveals that they are applying knowledge in a logical way based on their prior experience (Kamii, 1985, 1985a and 1985b, 1989). Comprehending place value and representing it accurately are tasks that usually take several years to master, from the primary-grade years and beyond.

While some mathematical concepts appear to be gradually internalized over a period of years, there is some indication that children in the primary or earlier grades are capable of solving more challenging problems involving a range of operations. Carpenter and Fennema (1993) studied kindergartners from a wide range of ethnic and socioeconomic groups. The children were asked to demonstrate how they would solve word problems involving addition, subtraction, mul-

*Counting experiences with concrete objects, including children's use of their fingers, continue to help children ages 6 to 8 develop the concept of numbers.*

tiplication, and division by using counters, their fingers, or other objects. These children had little difficulty responding appropriately, and actually performed better than older students in previous studies.

Price (1989) does not make specific recommendations for teachers for helping children develop their cognition in the area of math. However, he suggests that teachers should (1) "not put math down," (2) "take pains to not make math seem difficult," and (3) "not discourage child invented problem solving techniques that work and 'feel right'—such as counting on one's fingers" (Price, 1989, p. 57). Specific recommendations for teaching mathematics to young children have been developed by the National Council of Teachers of Mathematics (1989). Consult the Further Readings section at the end of the chapter for more information.

In conclusion, whether viewing children's cognitive development from a Piagetian stage perspective or from the information-processing perspective, children ages 6 through 8 appear to differ from preprimary-age children and from adolescents and adults. However, primary-age children still need continued interaction with materials and people. The availability of concrete experiences continues to promote cognitive development.

## ORAL LANGUAGE DEVELOPMENT

Children at 6, 7, and 8 years demonstrate many competencies in the area of language development. In fact, they appear very adultlike in many oral language contexts. However, studies indicate that there are still some aspects of language development that children continue to acquire through the elementary school years, into adolescence, and throughout life (Clark & Clark, 1977). The following section discusses the relationship between thought and language and the continuing development of syntax, vocabulary, and interactional competence during the primary-grade years.

### INTERACTION BETWEEN THOUGHT AND ORAL LANGUAGE DEVELOPMENT

The shift in children's cognitive development during ages 6, 7, and 8 is reflected in their oral language in several ways. Children gradually become aware of the meanings of metaphors. For example, the metaphor "She eats like a bird" is no longer interpreted literally as a girl eating worms or pecking at food in a birdlike manner. Rather, this metaphor is gradually understood as meaning that a person eats sparingly. Children understand metaphors before they actually produce them (Green, 1985; Winner, Rosenstiel, & Gardner, 1977).

Children of primary-grade age also demonstrate increasing awareness of puns and jokes because of their ability to think about the multiple meanings of words, the relationships among words, and the structure of narratives (Menyuk, 1988). They also become more proficient liars, both because they can now think about events simultaneously and because of their broader knowledge base. The use of "white lies" and of lying to prevent hurting another's feelings also appears to be due to children's increased social and cognitive awareness (Menyuk, 1988).

Another area of increased understanding of language is reflected in the comprehension and use of sarcasm. Ackerman (1982) determined that first-graders were able to interpret sarcasm if the context was evident before the sarcastic remark was made. However, third-graders were able to detect sarcastic remarks in an increasing variety of situations.

**Metalinguistic awareness**, or the ability to consciously think about the meanings and forms of language, becomes more evident as children mature. Researchers have determined that around age 7, children begin to separate words from phrases (Tunmer, Bowey, & Grieve, 1983). Around 8, children can identify the phonemes in words that are spoken aloud (Tunmer & Nesdale, 1982).

*metalinguistic awareness: the ability to think about the forms and meanings of language*

Menyuk (1976, 1985, 1988) suggests that metalinguistic abilities do not develop suddenly. Rather, the awareness of various aspects of language develops at different times for different categories and relationships in language. However, the process by which metalinguistic awareness develops appears to have a definite pattern. First, children incorporate new structures on an unconscious level. Then they develop the ability to recognize appropriate or inappropriate uses of the structure. Finally, children become able to talk about the structure (Bialystok, 1986; Menyuk, 1983; deVilliers & deVilliers, 1992).

As young children's cognitive abilities continue to develop, language increasingly becomes an independent symbol system. That is, children gradually begin to talk more about topics that are not in their immediate context. Bloom (1975) says, "This transition from maximum dependence in contextual support to speech which is independent of the states of affairs in which it occurs is the major accomplishment in the school years" (pp. 283–284).

Another area that demonstrates the interrelationship between language and thought is primary-grade children's use of pronouns. The understanding of pronominal references appears to increase with age. Seven-year-olds use more referenced pronouns in their stories than 6-year-olds do (Solan, 1983). The degree of metalinguistic awareness in first-graders appears to be a statistically significant predictor of reading comprehension in both third- and fifth-graders (Dreher & Zenge, 1990).

## DEVELOPMENT OF SYNTAX

Development of syntax also continues through the primary-grade years. One grammatical development that occurs during this period is the ability to understand infinitive phrases. At age 5, children do not relate the grammatical subject with the agent role. For example, when presented with a blindfolded doll and asked, "Is the doll easy or hard to see?", their response is "Hard to see." By age 10, the response changes to "Easy to see" (Chomsky, 1969; Karmiloff-Smith, 1979). Understanding the passive voice ("The ball was hit by Joe" rather than "Joe hit the ball") also takes place over an extended period of time and is not achieved until the end of the elementary school years (Bever, 1970; Sudhalter & Braine, 1985). According to Menyuk (1971), virtually all morphological indicators of plurals, possession, and past tense are acquired between ages 6 and 8. Menyuk (1964, 1983) suggests that children first become "aware" of a new structure and use it in an unconscious manner. Their knowledge is tentative at this point. Children use both old and new forms from time to time and may use both forms within the same utterance. In time, the earlier form disappears and is replaced by the conventional form.

## VOCABULARY DEVELOPMENT

Vocabulary development continues to expand with increased cognitive development, experience, and formal education (Carey, 1986). Children 6, 7, and 8 years of age use their vocabularies in more accurate and conventional ways. Lindfors (1987) describes how new experiences influence the school-age child's vocabulary: "Overextensions continue to disappear as six, seven, and eight year olds develop new vocabulary to accommodate new cognitive structures" (1980, p. 151). For example, a child may not just use the word *doggie* anymore, but may talk about *poodles, German shepherds, mutts,* and *puppies,* indicating increased cognitive awareness of the various categorical labels under the general class *dogs.* Menyuk (1988) states that "continued development of the meaning of words can take place over a lifetime, since meanings change as a function of wide experiences" (Menyuk, 1988, p. 153).

## INTERACTIONAL COMPETENCE

Children at ages 6, 7, and 8 have an increasing number of experiences in new environments and with different people. Upon entering first grade, children learn not only about their own teacher and classroom but also about other teachers and classrooms; about expected behaviors in the lunchroom, in the library, and on the playground; and about special classes such as art, physical education, and music. In addition, many school-age children visit friends' homes, join Scouts, take lessons, and participate in religious activities. Based on their interactions with other children and adults who serve as scaffolders, they gradually learn the scripts, or behaviors and language appropriate to each context. Participation in these varied contexts promotes increased interactional competence in 6-, 7-, and 8-year-old children. For example, Dorval and Eckerman (1984) noted that second-graders took turns in their conversations. Other researchers (e.g., Wanska & Bedrosian, 1985) have observed that children between ages 5 and 9 increasingly use the technique of **shading** to change topics of conversation. Younger children usually change topics abruptly, while older children change topics gradually.

*shading: gradually changing the topic of conversation*

Primary-grade children also demonstrate an increasing awareness of the intent of many utterances. A second-grader knows that when mother says, "This room is a disaster area," she or he had better get the room cleaned up right away. In addition, children ages 6, 7, and 8 indicate an increasing awareness of **registers,** or the speech variations needed in different social situations. For example, Ervin-Tripp, O'Connor, and Rosenberg (1984) found that children of primary-grade age exhibit deference when making requests of adults who appear busy and preoccupied. Language development in 6-, 7-, and 8-year-olds continues to mature and expand due to increasing cognitive development and increasing interactions with people in new and varied contexts. Children enter first grade knowing a great deal about oral language and how it works. This knowledge can be extended by helping the child engage in experiences that add to this knowledge. Activities that encourage the child to plan, remember, and learn promote further language development (Vygotsky, 1962).

*registers: variations in the style of speech according to the particular social setting*

Nevertheless, some investigators have noted that language used in the home can be quite different from language used in the school setting (Heath, 1983; Wells, 1981). Frequently, children entering the primary grades are expected to listen and engage in little verbal interaction with other children and teachers. Much verbal interaction with teachers consists of children responding with a *yes* or a *no* and a single-word answer to teacher questions. These contexts may be outside the zone of proximal development for some children. Thus, it is important that teachers in the primary grades continue oral language experiences from the prekindergarten and kindergarten years: opportunities to talk with other children in a

*Meaningful real-life experiences are essential to the acquisition of concepts and vocabulary.*

variety of settings, including learning centers; discussing stories and tapes; giving dictation; interviewing; sharing information in group sharing times; role playing; storytelling; and improvisation (Flood & Salus, 1984). Teachers need to be aware of the linguistic backgrounds of their children and gradually introduce children to other means of communicating and more formal ways of acquiring knowledge (Wells, 1981). In addition, as children 6, 7, and 8 years of age develop their metalinguistic awareness, teachers can help them bring their intuitive knowledge into conscious awareness. Such scaffolding helps primary-grade children strengthen and extend their knowledge of oral language. Such experiences can play a role in the acquisition of written language. The following section on the development of literacy addresses this important relationship.

## LITERACY DEVELOPMENT

Our discussion of literacy development in the primary grades will focus on three themes: the holistic nature of the development of literacy, the continuity of literacy experiences between the preprimary and primary grades, and the need for opportunities to interact with adults and children in meaningful print contexts.

# INTERACTION AMONG THOUGHT, LANGUAGE, AND LITERACY DEVELOPMENT

Chapters 10 and 13 provided background information on current thinking regarding the development of literacy in young children. In review, recent information suggests that (1) young children learn about reading and writing in the early years of life, certainly well before first grade; (2) in many ways, young children's reading and writing differ from the reading and writing of older children and adults; and (3) meaningful experiences seem to facilitate learning about reading and writing in young children.

In many primary-grade classrooms, literacy learning is very different from prekindergarten and kindergarten classroom experiences (Kamii, 1985a). First-graders are often asked to focus on parts of words, memorize phonics rules, and sound out words. Writing experiences may consist of copying teacher-printed material from the chalkboard, with emphasis on making letters properly and staying on the lines. This concentration on the form rather than the meaning of written language can create several problems for young children (Holdaway, 1979).

First, if children cannot make sense out of learning experiences, they begin to doubt themselves as learners. Their self-concepts and self-esteem can be affected in negative ways. Second, children can develop distorted concepts about the processes of reading and writing. First-graders who are in classrooms in which reading is done mainly in reading groups emphasizing sounding out words and oral reading without mistakes probably do not perceive reading as a meaningful experience (Holdaway, 1979).

Both the Piagetian and information-processing perspectives note age shift in cognitive development from ages 5 to 7. As previously discussed, Piaget (Piaget & Inhelder, 1956) suggests that many children are not yet able to focus on more than one part of a situation. The information-processing theorists suggest that short-term memory is still developing (White & Pillemer, 1979). For these reasons, asking first-graders to remember phonics rules, read without error, and sound out words—all at the same time—makes it very difficult for children to also think about the meaning of the story or text.

Likewise, copying teacher writing from the chalkboard does not give children the opportunity to develop the concept that writing is communication. Rather, children may tend to view writing at school as lacking in meaning and even as a painstaking, laborious process (Black & Martin, 1982). Thus, the teaching of reading and writing from the perspective of form is usually not related to thought or meaning.

Recent literacy research suggests that young children learn about reading and writing best in a holistic manner in which thought, oral language, and written language are interrelated (Goodman, 1986; Watson, 1994). The following vignette demonstrates the holistic nature of literacy development.

Six-year-old Angela was playing with several neighborhood children in her garage. One of the children discovered a tarantula crawling across the cement floor. The children discussed what they should do and whether tarantulas were really dangerous. Finally, one of the children suggested killing the tarantula with "bug spray." The tarantula was sprayed and sprayed. Finally, it died. The children used a garden tool to turn the tarantula over and then closely examined it. Next, they scooped it up, put it in a plastic container, and went on a tour of the neighborhood, showing

We had a big tarantula
We killed it by bug-spray
We had a black wasp in
 our house.
We were scared to death.

**FIGURE 16.1**
Long words with meaning, such as *tarantula*, are easier for young children to identify than shorter words without meaning, such as *the* and *what*.

the tarantula to other children. The tarantula episode was the main topic at the family dinner table that evening.

   The next day, Angela went to her classroom composed of 4-, 5-, and 6-year-olds. She painted a picture and then dictated the story (see Figure 16.1) to one of the teachers in her classroom. The spelling of *tarantula* was checked by using the dictionary. Angela's picture and story (consisting of 23 words) were hung on the classroom wall at the children's eye level. One of the teachers found some books about tarantulas to read to interested children. They discovered, among other things, that tarantulas are really not all that dangerous. Several days later, Angela and a teacher were looking at her picture/story and talking about her experience with the tarantula. The teacher asked Angela if she could find the word *tarantula*. Without any hesitation, Joanie pointed to the exact location of the word. ■

   This vignette demonstrates the powerful relationships among thought, experience, oral language, and literacy. Angela had a very meaningful experience. It was

**FIGURE 16.2**
**Whole Language**

| What Is Whole Language? | What Is Not Whole Language? |
| --- | --- |
| It's real and natural. | It's artificial. |
| It's whole. | It's broken into bits and pieces. |
| It's sensible. | It's nonsense. |
| It's interesting. | It's boring. |
| It's relevant. | It's irrelevant. |
| It belongs to the learner. | It belongs to somebody else. |
| It has social utility. | It has no social value. |
| It has purpose for the learner. | It has no discernible purpose. |
| The learner chooses to use it. | It's imposed by someone else. |
| It's accessible to the learner. | It's inaccessible to the learner. |
| The learner has the power to use it. | The learner is powerless. |
| THIS IS EASY! | THIS IS HARD! |

Whole language programs get it all together: the language, the culture, the community, the learner, and the teacher.

When schools break language into bits and pieces, sense becomes nonsense, and it's always hard for kids to make sense out of nonsense.

*Source: What's Whole in Whole Language?* by Ken Goodman. (p. 8). Reprinted by permission of Scholastic Canada Ltd.

talked and read about with others in several contexts: in the neighborhood, at the family dinner table, and at school. The experience was shared symbolically through Angela's painting and through oral language. It was translated into written language, which was read by Angela, her teacher, and other children. The interaction among thought, oral language, and written language in this vignette demonstrates how the wholeness of language can promote the development of literacy. Angela knew where the long word *tarantula* was located among 23 other words! Figure 16.2 provides a definition of *whole language*.

## RELATIONSHIP BETWEEN READING AND WRITING

Chapter 13 discussed the relationship between reading and writing. As the vignette about Angela and the tarantula indicates, reading and writing appear to be interrelated and to facilitate the development of literacy. Children learn to read by reading what they write and by reading print that is important to them. They learn to write if they believe they have thoughts and messages that are important enough to be shared with others in a written context (Chomsky, 1971; Goodman & Goodman, 1983).

Both Jeremy's and Angela's first-grade teachers see the teaching of reading and writing as inseparable. They do not relegate reading and writing to separate time slots during the day; rather, both reading and writing are taught throughout the day in many contexts and in interrelated ways. Both teachers continue many of the literacy experiences Angela and Jeremy encountered in their preprimary classrooms.

Jeremy's and Angela's primary-grade classrooms are organized to promote interaction with materials and with other children. Abundant print materials are located throughout the classroom and in learning centers. These materials include calendars, several kinds of charts (helper charts, charts with pen pal names, charts written by the children with spelling strategies, strategies for figuring out words, strategies listing the steps in the writing process, and charts of science experiment results), recipes for apple sauce and pancakes, the Pledge of Allegiance, the weekly schedule, a story about the author of the week, children's artwork and written reports, learning center signs describing the learning that takes place in the center, books, and magazines. Paper and writing tools are located in each center. The class library is stocked with a wide variety of books: class-made books, individually made books, big books, and many patterned or predictable books. There are a variety of centers in the classrooms: art, publishing/writing, computer, math, science, listening, and a display area. There are animals and plants to observe and to draw and write about. Both teachers display children's writing on attractive bulletin boards. Desks are clustered in groups of four to promote interaction. Children are encouraged to talk as they engage in their learning activities, and they do so for much of the day.

The schedule in Jeremy's room reflects the teacher's plan to emphasize the interaction and integration of reading and writing in all learning activities. Basal readers are used when they seem appropriate and not on a daily basis or in a sequential order. See Figure 16.3 for a typical daily schedule in Jeremy's classroom. ■

The preceding descriptions of materials, organization of the classroom environment, and daily schedule illustrate how reading and writing develop in an interrelated and holistic manner. The following two sections discuss the teaching of reading and writing separately for the purpose of documenting how children learn about the form or skills of reading and writing, even though the emphasis is on meaning.

## WRITING IN CHILDREN AGES 6, 7, AND 8

Ms. Wood continues many of the writing and print experiences of Jeremy's kindergarten in her first-grade classroom. She models writing for the children and facilitates purposeful opportunities for them to write in a variety of situations, from thank-you notes to stories to lists of needed classroom supplies. Ms. Wood allows children to freely explore their writing. She provides ample time for the rehearsal stage of writing, in which the children can draw or talk about their writing. This talking and drawing help to organize children's thoughts so they can write.

Ms. Wood also continues to read to the children. Hearing the written language helps children learn about writing. They learn how to write fairy tales, dialogue, narratives, and other forms of literature. Ms. Wood also carefully observes children and acts as a scaffolder to move them into new awareness of the processes of reading and writing.

Early in the school year, the PTA at Jeremy's school invites a children's book author to visit for a day. Through this experience, children learn about the editing process and what it means to be an author. Approximately once a month, Jeremy's class publishes a class book. Ms. Wood serves as the editor and helps the children with revisions. Suggested revisions are made in pencil, and then the children recopy their stories for the published book. The final edition is read to other classes and

---

**FIGURE 16.3**
**Daily Schedule for Jeremy's First Grade Class**

---

**8:15–8:30 Opening**   Children mark the calendar, weather, and lunch count. The class shares information and announcements.

**8:30–9:00 Music**   The class goes to the music classroom.

**9:00–9:30 Journal writing**   When children return from the music classroom, they write in their journals. Ms. Wood and the classroom assistant write in their own personal journals as well.

**9:30–10:15 Reading and writing**   The children read the story, *Case of Clyde Monster*. In the story, specific words are missing. Each cluster of children works on this together and decides what words need to go in the blank. They work together or write out some answers to questions after they have read the story.

**10:15–10:30 Outdoor activity**

**10:30–11:15 Learning centers**   Children go to learning centers to work on various projects.

**11:15–11:45 Sharing time**   Children share books they have produced or favorite books from the library and information about special projects and upcoming events.

**11:45–12:15 Lunch**

**12:15–12:30 Sustained silent reading**   Children and Ms. Wood read books of their choice.

**12:30–1:00 Math**   Lesson is on coupons. The children use real coupons and work on assignments together in their clusters.

**1:00–1:30 Science**   Each cluster works or experiments to determine if air is matter. They write their conclusions on a chart.

**1:30–2:00 Physical education**

**2:00–2:30 Teacher reading**   Ms. Wood reads a chapter from *Charlotte's Web*.

**2:30–2:45 Closing**   Announcements and reminders for the children.

---

then is placed in the school library for a period of time before becoming part of the classroom library. This experience introduces Jeremy and the other first-grade children to the editing process. Ms. Wood does no other correcting of the children's writing in her first-grade classroom. She wants the children to feel competent about their writing, and she knows that invented spellings, reversals, inattention to spacing, and lack of punctuation are developmentally appropriate behaviors. Figure 16.4 shows a typical first-grade attempt at writing.

**FIGURE 16.4**
A 6-year-old wrote this letter to his grandparents during holiday time.

Just as it takes time for infants and toddlers to learn to walk and talk, it takes time for young children to learn to read and write. Early childhood professionals are patient with young readers and writers and appreciate their approximations in spacing, spelling, handwriting, and punctuation. Analysis of this letter written by a 6-year-old demonstrates developmentally appropriate writing behaviors.

| | |
|---|---|
| Spacing | Some words run together (*niespesnts = nice presents*). Sometimes it is difficult to write in a linear fashion (*icsiting = exciting*). |
| Spelling | Sometimes it is convention (*you, and, love*). Sometimes it is invented (*HIO = hello, hv = have, icsiting = exciting, gbl = gobble, git = get, sam = some, nys = nice, pesnt = presents, em = am, giting = getting, abowt = about, ckaming = coming*. Note that both *c* and *k* are used here, indicating the child's awareness that *c* and *k* can represent the same sound.) |
| Handwriting | Reversals: *dring* for *bring*. |
| Punctuation | Used sometimes. Question mark at end of question "Have you been doing anything exciting?" Periods appear in various places. |
| Editing | Evidence of beginning attempts at editing are seen in the *g*, which was crossed out before the question mark and also after *abowt*. |
| Translation | "Hello. Have you been doing anything exciting? Gobble, gobble, gobble. Get some nice presents. I am getting (excited) about you coming. Bring some nice presents and — for us. Love Jon XOXOXO" |

Ms. Wood shares her reasons for not correcting children's papers at the parent orientation sessions and conferences. Showing examples of how writing develops throughout the first-grade year also enables parents to see that children will make progress in their written language without those traditional red corrections. If parents need further information, Ms. Wood shares articles from professional journals and books concerning the development of young children's writing. She also helps parents to understand that they can help their children to write at home by providing writing materials, taking advantage of opportunities to write, and being supportive of children's efforts to write at home.

The ability to write varies greatly among the children in Ms. Wood's class. The children want to write and have others read their writing. Mailboxes, pen pals, and message boards facilitate this communication process. Through writing that is meaningful to the children, they gradually learn about the forms of writing, including spelling and punctuation. They discover that the spelling of some words makes sense, but a number of words are spelled in ways that do not. Jeremy says that *egg* should have an *a* in it, not an *e*. First-graders struggle with the silent *e*, and try to understand how the same letter can be used for different sounds, such as the *g* in *giant* and *gate*.  ◾

Invented spelling provides a meaningful way for children to learn about sound-symbol relationships, or **phonics**, and other word recognition skills (Willert & Kamii, 1985). Through children's observation of print in many contexts, their own reading, discussions with classmates about how to spell, and teacher-peer scaffolding, children gradually become more aware of conventional spellings during the course of the primary grades.

*phonics:*
*the sound-symbol relationship of a language system*

As children communicate through their writing, they not only become more aware of conventional spelling but also learn about other forms of written language: handwriting, spacing between words, and punctuation. It is not unusual to see young children's writing with no spaces between words, filled with repeated exclamation marks and periods inserted here and there as children try to learn what a sentence really is and where it ends.

By the end of the first-grade year, the children in Ms. Wood's room have learned much about writing. The environment has been supportive, meaningful, and rich with print experiences. Jeremy's story about dinosaurs reveals that he is most confident in himself as a writer (see Figure 16.5). He organizes and presents his thoughts in a logical manner. He demonstrates no hesitancy in spelling long dinosaur names. He indicates that he has learned much about handwriting, spacing, and punctuation, and he gives evidence of moving into conventional spelling.  ◾

As children progress through the primary grades, many changes appear in their written language (Lamme, 1984). Their spelling becomes more conventional. Maturing small motor development makes handwriting more readable, and eventually children move into cursive writing. Reversals decline and appear only occasionally. Children also become more adept at writing in a variety of forms: jokes and riddles, newspaper, plays, and reports. Second- and third-graders can learn the process of writing from the modeling of their teachers.

Mr. Rodriguez is Angela's third-grade teacher. Angela and the other children use the computer to write lengthy stories and reports. Before the children begin to write, they engage in prewriting activities. Talking, drawing, and making lists about what

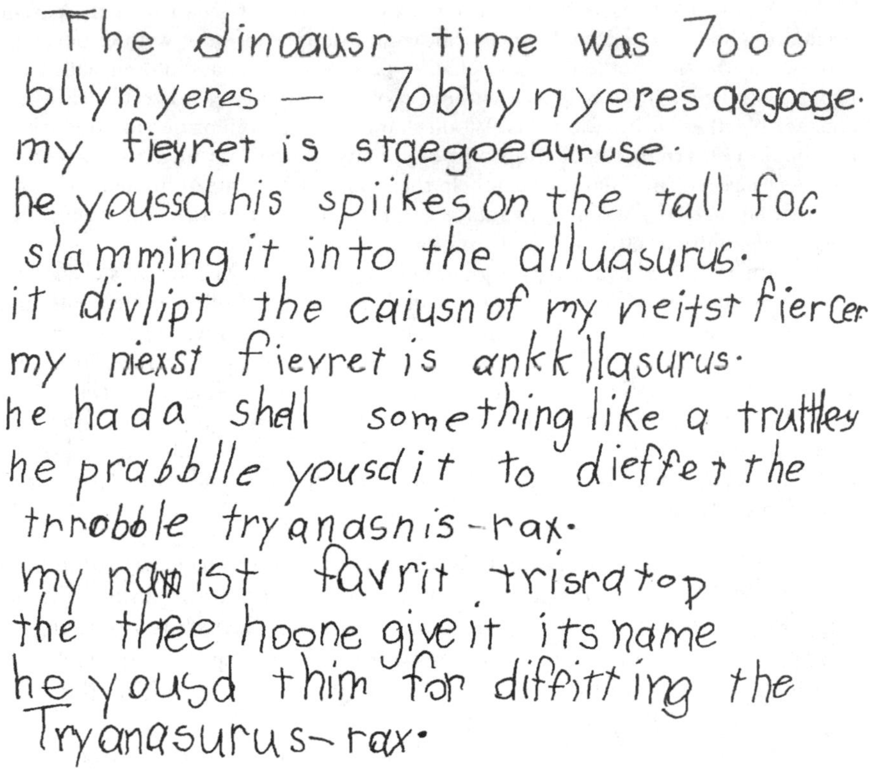

The dinoausr time was 7000
bllyn yeres — 7obllyn yeres aegooge.
my fieyret is staegoeauruse.
he youssd his spiikes on the tall foc.
slamming it into the alluasurus.
it divlipt the caiusn of my neitst fiercer
my niexst fievret is ankkllasurus.
he hada shdl something like a truttley
he prabblle yousdit to dieffet the
throbble tryanashis-rax.
my nawist favrit trisratop
the thee hoone give it its name
he yousd thim for diffitting the
Tryanasurus-rax.

**FIGURE 16.5**
Jeremy's story about dinosaurs, written in first grade, reveals that he is most
confident in himself as a writer.

they want to write helps them prepare the "fast write" or first draft. Angela shares
her writing with other children, who help her edit her writing, first for meaning and
then for spelling, grammar, punctuation, and paragraphs. Reading aloud what she
has written helps Angela and her peers decide whether pauses require commas or
inflections of the voice indicate a need for exclamation marks. After the editing
process, Angela returns to the word processor and revises her writing and prints it
out. If the computer is not available, Angela tries to be very neat and uses her best
handwriting for her final copy. Mr. Rodriguez helps the children understand that the
editing process is used only when writing for an intended audience. Journal writing,
list making and other forms of writing for individual use generally do not require
editing. As Angela has become more aware of the viewpoints of others, her ability to
take her audience into account in the writing process has increased. ■

Given supportive environments, children in the primary years can develop positive attitudes about writing as well as knowledge about the functions of writing.
These experiences in writing also facilitate competence in reading.

*Opportunities for young children to talk with other children in a variety of settings within the classroom promote communicative competence.*

## READING IN CHILDREN AGES 6, 7, AND 8

When children read for meaning, they gradually internalize the skills related to reading. However, if young readers are encouraged to focus on skills before meaning, it can be difficult for them to develop comprehension. **Sight words** or words that young children recognize immediately, are helpful to young readers. Knowledge of sight words helps children feel successful as they begin to read and provides them with a basis for learning about phonics and word analysis skills.

*sight words: words that young children recognize immediately*

Angela's first-grade teacher, Mr. Bray, does not use word lists that have been developed commercially. Isolated words in a list have no meaning. Only through words in context can children focus on the real purpose of reading: getting meaning from print. Therefore, Mr. Bray uses a variety of meaningful experiences to help children build their own banks of sight words, written on 3" x 5" cards and stored in recipe file boxes.

The most important sight word to young children is their name. Mr. Bray has all the children's names displayed on the helper's board. He also has poster board strips with each child's name on them in the writing center. Mr. Bray is amazed at how quickly first-graders learn one another's names. One day Angela saw a drawing with Charles's name on it. She commented that it was Charlotte's drawing. Charlotte quickly told Angela that it was not her drawing. "My name is longer than Charles's," she said. She took Angela to the writing center, found the name cards with her name and Charles's name on them, and showed them to Angela.

Through dictations, signs, labels, class and individual books, predictable books, and reading their own writing, the children have begun to recognize frequently used words and can point them out to Mr. Bray and their classmates. Mr. Bray also has the children select words that are important to them from their journal writing to go into the children's individual word banks. The children frequently use and refer to these special words in their writing. Mr. Bray scaffolds by calling attention to words that he knows the children encounter repeatedly. Mr. Bray uses the children's interests and writing rather than workbooks or ditto papers because he knows children learn better when they are interested. In many instances, word lists in workbooks or on worksheets have little or no meaning for young children. ■

Mr. Bray knows that larger words with specific meanings are frequently easier for young children to learn (remember Angela and *tarantula*?). Often the short, simple words used in preprimers and primers, the beginning books in the basal reading series, are more difficult to remember. Some of these short words are **service words,** or words that hold sentences together. They may lack specific meanings to which young children can relate. Many service words look like other words and are confusing to young children, for example, *the, then, they, there, them,* and *those.* If children are in learning environments that encourage them to share their thoughts with others through writing, they will use these words in their own dictation and writing. Actual use of these words in their own stories and writing encourages children to pay attention to the subtle differences among them (Holdaway, 1979). These kinds of experiences help children learn not only sight words but also phonics (Graves, 1983). Recent literacy research suggests that young children learn about phonics from meaningful reading and writing experiences, rather than learning reading and writing from phonics (Graves, 1983; Teale & Sulzby, 1986).

Mr. Bray explains this global-to-specific, or whole-to-part, learning of young children to their parents. Parents often think phonics is the best way to learn to read. Mr. Bray helps parents understand that phonics is a part of reading but should not be the primary focus. He reassures parents that children do not have to know all the sounds in a word to learn to read. ■

Actually, children need to understand the concept of *word* before they can understand phonics. Early in their literacy development, young children often think that each letter in a word represents a separate word. Using word banks, taking dictation so that children can see their own words, pointing to words in big books, and drawing children's attention to spacing between words help them develop the notion that a word is composed of clusters of letters that represent the sounds of that word.

Mr. Bray knows his first-graders will find the regular consonants at the beginnings and ends of words the easiest to recognize. Later they will recognize the consonants in the middle of words. Long vowel sounds are easy for children to detect; short vowel sounds are more difficult. Mr. Bray knows most first-graders often substitute one short vowel sound for another, for example, "*git*" for "*get*." As children progress through the primary grades, their development in phonics moves from the global to the specific. They begin to become more aware of phonics in general, of short vowels, and of various consonant combinations. In addition, their increasing physiological maturity enables them to more accurately hear and reproduce the sounds. Take another look at the chart of sound production from Chapter 13. Notice that it indicates that some sounds do not develop in young

**FIGURE 16.6**
"The Wndrfl Fgin A dat burds." Children ages 6 to 8 are still developing their
physiological ability to hear and reproduce sounds.

children until they are 6 or 7 years of age. Jeremy still substitutes *f* for *th* during
most of the first grade. He makes a book entitled *The Wndrfl Fgin A dat Burds
(The Wonderful Things About Birds)*, shown in Figure 16.6. He also spells *birthday* as *brfday,* since he cannot hear or articulate *th.* This auditory processing and
verbal production of sound is reflected in his spelling. Yet he is progressing normally as a young reader. In short, children do not have to know all the sounds in
a word to learn how to read. Formal phonics instruction is not necessary for a
child to be a successful reader in first grade.

As children ages 6, 7 and 8 write rhyming poems, they often discover similar word
patterns. Children delight in finding relationships among words. Questions by Mr.
Bray also help children develop **word analysis skills**. Looking for words that have
similar patterns on charts, lists, recipes, familiar songs, and poems help children
learn about the parts of words. Angela's first-grade teacher has a flip chart full of
favorite finger plays, poems, and songs, and a big book of nursery rhymes. As the
children recite these charts and songs, Mr. Bray or one of the children points to the
words. While the children engage in the various activities, they often stop and read
these poems and chants to themselves or with a classmate, using a yardstick to
point at each word. In this process, they discover similarities among many of the
words. Mr. Bray made small versions of these poems and chants with cards of the
individual words so the children can match the similar words with the actual text of
the poem, finger play, or nursery rhymes.

Mr. Bray also helps the children develop strategies for reading by encouraging
them to look at the **configuration**, or overall shape, of the word. Angela's
teacher's comment about the length of the word *tarantula* probably helped her
remember that word.

*word analysis skills:
the ability to analyze
words using a variety of
strategies, such as
rhyming words*

*configuration:
the general shape or
outline of a word*

Mr. Bray helps Angela to become an independent reader by encouraging her to read silently. He does not have large reading groups on a regular basis, but has individual or small groups of children read to him from a variety of materials, both commercial or child-made, at various times throughout the day. He encourages children to read in pairs or in their desk clusters. Children are encouraged to incorporate a number of strategies if they do not know a word, such as rereading the sentence, looking at the illustrations, asking a friend, or substituting a word that makes sense. Rather than always asking the children to sound out words, Mr. Bray helps them use a variety of strategies to focus on the meaning of what they are reading. If the children are reading with him, he allows them about seven seconds to respond. This allows the children time to explore various strategies for selecting an appropriate word that relates the meaning of the text to the form of the word. ■

*comprehension: understanding the meaning of print*

Both Jeremy's and Angela's first-grade teachers know that if children in their classes are to become truly literate, **comprehension** or understanding of the text is essential. Fields, Spangler, and Lee (1991) suggest that literacy development is "a process in which reading involves *interacting* with the thoughts someone else has expressed in writing, in which writing is perceived as recording one's own thoughts, and in which thinking is basic" (p. 133). Reading aloud both quality fiction and nonfiction trade books encourages the development of critical thinking and problem solving, as well as flexibility in reading, for young children (Doiron, 1994).

As children continue to develop in their reading ability in second and third grades, it is important to keep the focus on the meaning of print and the wholeness of language. Third grade is usually the year in which children are expected to deal with more content knowledge in the areas of science, health, and social studies. Specific textbooks are often introduced at this grade level, and children are expected to read for meaning and be accountable for the material through tests. If literacy experiences during the first and second grades have been meaning based, children will have the critical mindset that print has a message for them. This concept will help them as they continue to learn throughout their school years. On the other hand, if young children view reading as an isolated performance activity, comprehending content material and reading independently may be a problem as they progress through the elementary school grades.

If primary-grade teachers have students who do not seem to be comprehending or thinking about what they are reading, they may want to do an analysis of children's concepts about reading. If the results indicate that these children have distorted concepts about the reading act and limited strategies for reading, teachers need to help them learn that (1) reading is getting meaning from print; (2) good readers sometimes read quickly and sometimes read slowly, depending on the purpose for reading; and (3) good readers make mistakes in reading, but they can use a number of strategies to help them identify and correct their mistakes.

In summary, children ages 6, 7, and 8 learn most effectively about reading and writing if the emphasis is on meaning. Through meaningful opportunities in which they can engage in reading and writing, they will also learn about the skills used in reading and writing.

## SPECIAL NEEDS AND SOCIOCULTURAL INFLUENCES

The reader must remember that while there may be overall patterns to development, individual differences and variations in development also exist. Dyson (1987) notes this in her research on young children's writing. If teachers of 6-, 7-, and 8-year-old children do not take into account individual differences and the need for continuity of learning environments through the primary grades, young children fail to develop positive attitudes about themselves as learners. It is essential that teachers of young children not misinterpret differences in cognition, language, and literacy behaviors as deficits. For example, research on story schemata, or knowledge of the structure of stories, indicates that some minority children do not lack story schemata; rather, they have different story schemata (Michaels, 1981).

It is also important that teachers of young children be aware of possible stereotypical attitudes about young children in their classrooms and the effects of these attitudes on young children's cognitive, language, and literacy development. At times, teachers may consider a particular income level, race, or ethnicity an indicator of inability to learn, read, and write. Taylor and Dorsey-Gaines (1988) refute this notion in their in-depth study of African American children from urban low-income homes who were growing up literate. In addition, Rhodes and Dudley-Marling (1988) and Spears, Carpenter, and Burstein (1994) challenge the assumption that students with learning disabilities can become literate only through a skills-based approach. They indicate that whole language strategies facilitate language and literacy development with young children in special education settings.

Genishi, Dyson, and Fassler (1994) suggest several ideas for promoting language development in children from diverse sociolinguistic backgrounds:

- Develop a classroom climate in which children are free to code switch, or alternate between languages, to communicate their message.

- Provide opportunities for social interaction and negotiating shared meaning.

- Provide a wide variety of activities and materials that encourage communication for authentic purposes.

They conclude that "the overriding goal for language education throughout the preschool and school years should not be the mastery of one genre or dialect but the capacity to negotiate among contexts, to be socially and politically astute in discourse use" (p. 264).

As mentioned earlier in this chapter, teachers who work with young children from diverse backgrounds need to be sensitive to parents and their educational goals for their children. Delpit (1988) states that at times teachers from middle-class backgrounds insist on process approaches to the exclusion of skills that minority parents often view as critical to accessing mainstream culture. She challenges teachers and parents to open their eyes, ears, hearts, and minds to one another even though doing so may be "painful" (p. 296).

## MEDIA AND TECHNOLOGY

Two other influences on cognitive, language, and literacy development in young children are television and computers.

### TELEVISION

*television literacy:*
*understanding the spe-*
*cialized symbolic code*
*conveyed through the*
*medium of television*

Anderson and Smith (1984) suggest that young children must develop **television literacy,** or the understanding of the special symbolic way in which television conveys information. They indicate that it takes time for children to develop an understanding of the medium of television.

To become television literate, young children must understand the distinction between reality and fantasy. Research by Dorr (1983) indicates that even 7- and 8-year-old children are still confused regarding the television and real-life relationships and behaviors of performers. In addition, studies indicate that young children do not grasp many television production techniques before age 8. Because young children have difficulty inferring and relating past events to the present and future, they often fail to understand story lines and view scenes without obvious transitions as separate incidents (Collins et al., 1978). Young children gradually learn to understand techniques such as fades (Anderson & Smith, 1984) and instant replays (Rice, Huston, & Wright, 1986). However, fast-paced programs that lack clearly defined continuity between scenes are still not understood by 9- and 10-year-olds (Wright et al., 1984). Adult comments and explanations can help young children better understand and evaluate television programs (Ball & Bogatz, 1973; Collins, 1983; Watkins et al., 1980).

Television can help children learn. However, there is still no clear consensus about the best format to promote learning. The research on *Sesame Street* appears to confirm that children do learn from this fast-paced program (Ball & Bogatz, 1972). However, Singer and Singer (1979) indicate that programs with a slower pace allow children time to reflect. Thus, programs such as *Mr. Roger's Neighborhood* may be more effective in stimulating thinking in young children than *Sesame Street.* Lesser (1979) suggests that there may not be one type of television programming that is best for all children. He recommends that a variety of types of programming be available to meet young children's individual differences and learning styles. Parent and teacher co-viewing and discussion of educational programming with children appear to facilitate more learning than occurs if adults are not present and no discussion takes place (Abelman, 1984; Ball & Bogatz, 1973; Corder-Bolz, 1980; Salomon, 1977; Houston et al., 1992).

Too much television viewing takes time away from other activities that promote learning and creativity (Singer & Singer, 1981, 1983). Extensive television viewing can also deny children the opportunity to engage in reading, play, oral language, and other activities that promote thinking, concentration, and attention spans (Peterson, Peterson, & Carroll, 1986).

In conclusion, it appears that television can promote young children's cognitive, language, and literacy development if (1) programming is appropriate to young children's cognitive development, (2) adults are involved in the viewing process and discuss the program with children, and (3) children have opportunities to engage in other activities that promote cognitive, language, and literacy development.

## COMPUTERS

Initial research regarding the effects of computers on young children's cognitive, language, and literacy development indicates that there can be some benefits. However, these benefits depend on the quality of the software, the attitudes and behaviors of the teacher, the nature of the physical and social environment of the classroom, and the accessibility of the computer (Campbell & Fein, 1986).

Young children can learn about computers and how they work. Interaction with computers in contexts similar to learning centers, where children are free to explore and discover, helps children learn about the nature of computers and develop positive attitudes toward technology (Hofmann, 1986; Kull, 1986).

Computer experiences can be highly sociable, promoting oral language and interaction with both adults and other children (Borgh & Dickson, 1986; Genishi, McCollum, & Strand, 1985; Newman, 1988). Teachers appear to facilitate this interaction by encouraging group participation rather than individual activity and through their availability to children. In addition, teachers can encourage children to use one another as resources. Knowledge of developmentally appropriate software programs can help teachers determine when their assistance is warranted.

Computer experiences also seem to facilitate divergent and creative thinking. Programs such as Logo provide opportunities for children to express their own learning styles (Kull, 1986). Word-processing software can be designed to interface with all of the seven intelligences (Armstrong, 1994, pp. 158–159). Two examples are word-processing software, which requires linguistic intelligence, and drawing and painting software, which calls for spatial intelligence. Another interesting application of technology involving multiple intelligences is in the area of hypertext. Through the multiple stacking of "cards" in a program stored on a CD-ROM disk, a project that incorporates word text (linguistic), illustrations (spatial), sound score (musical or linguistic), and video data (bodily-kinesthetic and other intelligences) can be developed (Armstrong, 1994, p. 59). In addition, such a process involves intrapersonal intelligence and, if the project is cooperative, interpersonal intelligence as well. The CD-ROM disks can serve as "electronic portfolios" that document children's learning.

Computer experiences can also allow young children to make discoveries about learning. One study demonstrated that second-graders discovered orthographic and phonetic principles (Hofmann, 1986). Children have also learned about mathematical concepts such as subtraction while using computers (Hofmann, 1986; Kull, 1986).

Computers can also help children develop their writing abilities. Word processing can assist children in more in-depth composing by freeing them from the small motor task of handwriting. The process of revision is also facilitated, since word processing makes it easier for children to edit their compositions (Bruce, Michaels, & Watson-Gegeo, 1985; Hoot & Silvern, 1989).

Teachers need to be cautious in selecting software for young children. Just because a program is fun does not always mean it is a developmentally appropriate or worthwhile learning activity (Burns, Goin, & Donlon, 1990; Clements, 1985). Drill should not be confused with thinking and learning. Teachers must

*Early childhood professionals need to make certain that computer software is developmentally appropriate for young children.*

evaluate software for ineffective approaches to instruction for young children, such as isolated drills and activities that resemble workbooks (Fields, Spangler, & Lee, 1991; Kasmoski, 1984). Fields, Spangler, & Lee (1991) caution against high-pressure sales techniques by publishers that encourage schools to spend large amounts of money on inappropriate programs and recommend that teachers carefully evaluate all software programs for their developmental appropriateness (see Figure 16.7 for general criteria).

Computers demonstrate the potential to promote learning in young children. However, their use must be closely monitored by early childhood professionals. As new information is discovered about young children and computers, more definitive recommendations for facilitating young children's development will become available.

## THE ROLE OF PLAY IN PROMOTING COGNITIVE, LANGUAGE, AND LITERACY DEVELOPMENT IN 6-, 7-, AND 8-YEAR-OLDS

Children in the primary grades begin to demonstrate cognitive abilities indicative of concrete operations and emerging social understandings. They are becoming more comfortable with a wide range of social situations and the cognitive, language, and social demands placed on them in contexts such as school, home, playground, athletic teams, and community organizations. Piaget (1962), Bruner (1983), and Sutton-Smith (1979, 1986) state that play is significant in the development of children's

FIGURE 16.7
**Criteria for Developmentally Appropriate Software for Young Children**

1. Are children able to boot up the software program independently?
2. Do children understand the initial directions? Are the directions presented using both auditory and visual senses—(i.e., words and graphics)?
3. Is the vocabulary used in the program appropriate to the children's developmental level?
4. Are children informed about whether their responses are correct or incorrect? Are approximations acknowledged or rewarded at appropriate levels?
5. Are the program keyboard functions too complex for young children? Are the participants required to strike one, two, or three keys at one time?
6. Are the program graphics complimentary, appropriate, or distracting?
7. Does the program have an audio component? Are the sound levels appropriate for the learning environment (too loud, too soft)? Is the audio component of the program accurate? (Does a bird sound like a bird in the computer program?)
8. Does the program offer children choices? If so, how many? Are the choices appropriate, too simple, or too complex?
9. Do the program and computer system foster independence in children or reliance on teacher direction and assistance?
10. Is the computer program congruent with the content and scope of the classroom curriculum, or is "computing" viewed as an isolated learning experience?

cognitive abilities to function in novel situations and the development of skills relating to flexibility and adaptability. More recently, Dyson (1990) characterized young children as eloquent and inventive users of symbols during the primary school years. She suggests that children use a wide range of expressive activities to convey their understanding to peers during social exchanges. At no time in a young child's life are there more opportunities to use language in unique and exciting situations.

Primary-grade children have not yet abandoned fantasy play as a means of socialization, communication, and cognitive stimulation among peers. Meanwhile, they are confronted with new educational challenges in formal and informal settings. Opportunities to use symbols in various contexts appear to be limitless. Six-, 7-, and 8-year-old children regularly express their need to communicate with age-mates during creative play situations. However, the increasing complexity of their ideas and occasional misunderstandings between peers require that they develop ingenious and resourceful communication strategies to foster their social relationships.

Children in the primary grades should be encouraged to use any means possible to express themselves to adults and age-mates. Combinations of drawings and various art media, printed words, spoken language, gestures, and movements provide young children with a wide range of communicative expression. The use of these various media and expressive methods should not be restricted to formal classroom settings. Play situations provide primary-grade children with exciting opportunities to enhance their symbolic repertoire through extemporaneous social experiences. During these makeshift social exchanges, primary-grade children can interact with age-mates regarding games, play events, and shared learning experiences. Young children are capable of sharing social information and basic knowledge in a manner that is sensitive to the listener and the social context (Corsaro, 1985). When shared social interests exist among peers, young children are capable of expressing their understanding about the texture of wet sand, a colorful butterfly, a new soccer ball, and their anticipation of the climax of a new book.

Pellegrini and Glickman (1990) suggest that playgrounds and play activities provide young children with the best opportunities for peer interactions independent of adult influences. From their study of lower and middle socioeconomic children at play, they suggest that the most reliable means of assessing primary-grade children's cognitive abilities, communicative skills, and social competence occur during spontaneous play activities. Further, they believe that children who engage in social games with rules and related verbal exchanges with peers are more intellectually competent than children who tend to be socially passive. During the primary grades, children develop social skills and communicative abilities that foster positive cognitive, linguistic, and social patterns of behavior. The cognitive and communicative experiences that occur during spontaneous play extend young children's social skills, deepen their empathy toward their friends, and foster their ability to express their understanding of their world.

---

## Role of the Early Childhood Professional

### Enhancing Cognitive, Language, and Literacy Development in Children Ages 6 Through 8

1. Provide for continuity of learning experiences from kindergarten to first grade and through the primary grades, involving families.

2. Allow for individual differences to promote children's self-esteem and positive attitudes toward school.

3. Provide learning experiences that are concrete, whole, and integrated rather than experiences that are abstract, are isolated, or emphasize separate subject matter areas.

4. Provide learning experiences that allow children to interact with materials, other children, and adults.

5. Provide opportunities for child-initiated learning.

6. Be patient and accept developmentally appropriate behaviors such as invented spelling, reversals, and counting with fingers.

7. Demonstrate curiosity and interest in learning.

8. Model oral, written, and computer language. Read to children.

9. Engage parents as partners in the learning process.

10. Provide appropriate technological and media experiences.

11. Continue to scaffold children's learning.  ∎

## KEY TERMS

| | | |
|---|---|---|
| cognitive science | metacognition | service words |
| comprehension | metalinguistic | shading |
| concrete operational | awareness | sight words |
| stage | meta memory | television literacy |
| configuration | phonics | word analysis skills |
| formal operations | registers | |

## REVIEW ACTIVITIES AND STRATEGIES

1. Review the key terms individually or with a classmate.

2. Interview principals and kindergarten and primary-grade teachers in several school districts to determine what is being done to provide a continuum of experience between kindergarten and the primary grades, including parent participation.

3. Conduct Piagetian conservation experiments with several 6-, 7-, and 8-year olds. Write up your results.
   a. Note how these children compare with 4- and 5-year-olds.
   b. Note differences among the 6-, 7-, and 8-year-olds.

4. Examine some of the curricular materials and software written for first, second, and third grades. Analyze them using the criteria in Figure 16.7. Also consider (a) gender bias, (b) cultural diversity, and (c) special learning needs.

5. Collect samples of children's writing from first, second, and third grades. Analyze it according to (a) content, (b) form, and (c) developmental progression.

6. Read an article about young children's television-viewing habits. Discuss it with your class.

## FURTHER READINGS

Allen, J., & Mason, J. (Eds.). (1989). *Risk makers, risk takers, risk breakers: Reducing the risks for young literacy learners*. Portsmouth, NH: Heinemann.

Bredekamp, S., & Rosengrant, T. (Eds.). (1992) *Reaching Potentials: Appropriate curriculum and assessment for young children*, Vol. I. Washington, DC: National Association for the Education of Young Children.

Derman-Sparks, L., & the ABC Task Force (1989). *Anti-bias curriculum: Tools for empowering young children*. Washington, DC: National Association for the Education of Young Children.

Fields, M. V., & Spangler, K. L. (1995). *Let's begin reading right: Developmentally appropriate beginning literacy* (3rd ed.). Englewood Cliffs, NJ: Prentice Hall.

Gandini, L. (1993). Fundamentals of the Reggio Emilia approach to early childhood education. *Young Children, 49*, 1, 4–8.

Gardner, Howard (1993). *Multiple Intelligences: The theory in practice*. New York: Basic Books.

Gardner, Howard (1991). *The unschooled mind: How children think and how schools should teach*. New York: Basic Books.

Gibbs, J. R. & Huang, L. N. & Associates (1989). *Children of color: Psychological interventions with minority youth*. San Francisco, CA: Jossey-Bass.

Hong, M. (1993). *Growing up Asian American*. New York: Avon Books.

Houston, A. C., Donnerstein, E., Fairchild, H., Feshback, H. D., Katz, P. A., Murray, J. P., Rubenstein, E. A., Wilcox, B. L., & Zuckerman, D. (1992). *Big world, small screen*. Lincoln, NE: University of Nebraska Press.

Puckett, M. B., & Black, J. K. (1994). *Authentic assessment of the young child: Celebrating development and learning*. New York: Macmillan.

Shepard, L. A., & Smith, M. L. (1989). *Flunking Grades: Research and policies on retention*. New York: Falmer Press.

# PART SEVEN

# A Brief Look Beyond the Early Years: The Effects of Early Development on Later Development

# CHAPTER SEVENTEEN

*Good teaching, like good parenting, is hard work. There are simply no easy ways to help children grow and develop into independent, self-confident and responsible adults.*

*When we instruct children in academic subjects, or in swimming, gymnastics, or ballet at too early an age, we miseducate them; we put them at risk for short-term success and long-term personality damage for no useful purpose. There is no evidence that such early instruction has lasting benefits, and considerable evidence that it can do lasting harm.*

David Elkind

# Later Childhood and Adolescence

After studying this chapter, you will demonstrate comprehension by:

- Describing the major aspects of development in later childhood and adolescence.
- Citing research evidence documenting the effects of quality experiences in the early years on later childhood, adolescence, and young adulthood.
- Identifying factors in the early years that can adversely affect development in later childhood and adolescence.
- Describing the role of adults in facilitating the development of older children and adolescents.

As Jeremy and Angela move into the later years of childhood and adolescence, what can we expect? What will their development be like? Jeremy has had an almost ideal early childhood. He has had loving and supportive care provided by parents, caregivers, and teachers who are knowledgeable about young children and their developmental needs. He lives in a family free of economic stress. Angela has had a different family experience, although it too has been full of love and care. Her parents, James and Cheryl, have done the best they could under adverse social and economic circumstances. Even though Angela's birth and first years of life were difficult, the services and support systems available prevented many problems. These services and the love and care of the extended family provided Angela with a good start in life. ■

## AN OVERVIEW OF LATER CHILDHOOD AND ADOLESCENCE

The following sections provide a brief description of what to expect in the years of later childhood and adolescence.

### LATER CHILDHOOD

**Later childhood** refers to the period from ages 9 through 11. This period is generally characterized by somewhat slower physical development, more even

*later childhood:*
*the period of development between the early childhood years and adolescence (ages 9 through 11)*

social and emotional behavior than in the early childhood years and later adolescence, and the consolidation of cognitive skills emerging early in the elementary school years.

During the fourth, fifth, and sixth grades, peers become increasingly important (Hartup, 1983). Children are usually seen in pairs or small groups. Their position in the peer group becomes important (Damon, 1983). Likewise, children become more aware of labels and status within the community and larger society. Involvement in various groups outside the school setting is common. Children in this age group are frequently involved in sports activities, engage in the visual and performing arts, and participate in Scout and religious activities. Their closest friends are generally of the same gender (Huston, Carpenter, & Atwater, 1986). While their interest in sex continues, it is usually hidden from adults during this period of development.

Even though the peer group has an increasing influence on children in later childhood, the home and family are still important (Furman & Buhrmester, 1985). The home can provide a refuge from the problems encountered within the peer group. Parents also continue to serve as a source of useful social information. Fights with siblings are common during this period; yet most children of later childhood age are quick to defend their brothers and sisters if others verbally or physically threaten them (Bryant, 1982). Efforts on the part of parents to prepare young children in advance for the birth of a sibling appear to promote positive long-term sibling relationships (Dunn & Kendrick, 1982a, 1982b).

During their ninth through eleventh years, children consolidate their growing skills in the area of cognitive development (Inhelder & Piaget, 1958; Moshmon & Timmons, 1982). They master the symbol systems in reading and math. Their developing reasoning abilities permit them to solve increasingly complex problems. While they are becoming more objective, at times their emotions can control their thinking. They seek more knowledge about the world in general and become more aware of life, death, bodily processes, and social issues. Moral judgment becomes more flexible (Kohlberg, 1984).

School performance and peer group position contribute to self-concept. Erikson (1963) describes this time as part of the industry versus inferiority stage. Thus, it is important to older children's psychosocial well-being to develop feelings of competence and productivity during this time. Appropriate tasks at home and school that require independent action and behavior can facilitate feelings of competence and industry.

Physical development usually slows down during this period (Tanner, 1989). Torsos lengthen, and many children become slender in appearance. Other children may gain weight and become pudgy. This extra weight gain often sets the stage for rapid growth in height during adolescence. Generally, motor abilities become more refined, as reflected in increasing participation in sports and musical activities. Changes in physical development indicating the coming of adolescence can begin during this time. The onset of **puberty** is usually earlier for girls than for boys. It can begin as early as age 8 and generally occurs by age 14. For boys, the age range is from 9 to 15 (Shonkoff, 1984).

*puberty:*
*the biological developments that result in the ability to produce children*

*During Erikson's stage of industry versus inferiority, it is important that children continue to have opportunities to engage in and successfully complete various tasks and projects.*

## ADOLESCENCE

**Adolescence** is a period of dramatic change in all areas of development, generally including the years between ages 12 and 16. Several major changes occur during this period, including rapid growth in height and weight and sexual development (Tanner, 1989). Wide individual differences in growth patterns occur during adolescence, and both early- and late-maturing adolescents can have difficult adjustments (Peskin, 1967; Simmons & Blyth, 1987; Brooks-Gunn & Petersen, 1992).

A major task of adolescence is to establish a personal identity. Erikson (1968) calls this stage of psychosocial development *identity versus role confusion* (see Figure 17.1). During this time, teenagers attempt to sort out their various roles: gender, racial, familial, religious, peer, and student. Efforts to develop this identity also involve trying on various behaviors of well-known or admired persons.

Adolescents continue to work on establishing a place in the peer group and separating from their parents (Coleman, 1980). Peer influences can be both positive and negative (Brown, Lohn, & McClenghan, 1986). Children whose parents are authoritative rather than authoritarian or permissive are less prone to be influenced by peers (Baumrind, 1991). Some studies indicate that the separation process may not be less volatile than previously thought (Kandel & Lesser, 1972; Youniss & Smollar, 1985). Parents are also working on separating from their adolescents. Acknowledging the adolescent's increasing independence and sexual maturity often forces parents to deal with their own progression through the life span.

The need for independence and freedom often goes unmet because sociocultural freedoms, with the exception of driving, are usually not given until ages 18 or 21

*adolescence:
the time of rapid development between the later childhood years and adulthood*

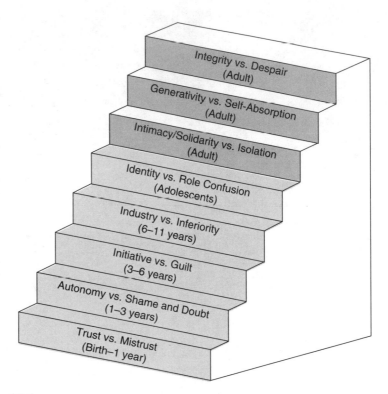

**FIGURE 17.1**
During later childhood and adolescence, industry versus inferiority and identity versus role confusion are two psychosocial tasks to be resolved.

(Kett, 1977). Definite ideas and attitudes toward religion, politics, and racial and ethnic groups often appear during adolescence. These can reflect similar attitudes of parents or, in an effort to express independence, can be very different from those of parents (Chand, Crider, & Willits, 1975; Kelley, 1972). At times, some teens are very concerned about social issues. They blame adults for world problems and propose idealistic solutions (Kohlberg, 1984).

The dominant theory of cognitive development for adolescents is Piaget's stage of formal operations as described in Chapter 1. Research suggests that the development of formal operations is influenced by culture (Dasen & Heron, 1981; Rogoff, 1990). The onset and development of formal operations may be delayed or even absent in societies that do not emphasize symbolic skills or provide formal educational experiences.

Intellectually, adolescents are now able to take on the perspectives of others (Inhelder & Piaget, 1958). They view peers, parents, and teachers in a critical manner. This critical view of others also causes them to look critically at themselves (Elkind, 1978, 1994). As a result, they are highly preoccupied with their own behavior, personality, and physical appearance.

Adolescents can now deal with more abstract concepts and can consider and construct multiple alternatives (Keating, 1980). They can distinguish between fact and hypothesis and between realism and idealism. They begin to think about and plan for the future, often moving from idealistic to more realistic career goals. School takes on a broader dimension. It is now not only a place to learn but is often the primary place to socialize with the peer group (Simmons & Blyth, 1987).

The social pressures as well as the financial and intrinsic rewards are often cited as reasons for drug use by teenagers from all backgrounds (Santrock, 1984). Findings of a study commissioned by the National Institute on Drug Abuse (1994) indicate that drug use among high school students is up after a period of decline. In terms of drug trafficking, a recent study reported that only 41 percent of adolescents involved in this activity expected to continue (Xiaoming & Feigelman, 1994). This finding suggests that drug trafficking by adolescents may be experimental in nature rather than a long-term involvement. Nevertheless, drug trafficking and related gang participation appear to be major factors in the increased use of weapons and the resulting violence and deaths in communities.

A recent study reports that 85 percent of adolescents arrested for violent crimes and 65 percent of the victims are high school dropouts (Menninga, 1994). Other suggested causes of violence include inward and outward anger, lack of strategies for dealing with aggression, greater availability of weapons, adult acceptance of violence, and media portrayals of violence.

A survey of adolescents' health-related concerns revealed that the top 10 issues were schoolwork, dental health, abuse, sexually transmitted disease, acne, sex, adults, pregnancy, friends, and drugs (Joffe & Radius, 1991).

Coming to terms with sexual development and the need for peer acceptance presents today's adolescents with different issues than those faced by adolescents of earlier years. The epidemic of AIDS, the dramatic increase in teenage pregnancy, and the general adolescent attitude of "it will never happen to me" create challenges for parents and other adults who work with teens to encourage responsible sexual behavior (National Research Council, 1987).

Other adolescent behaviors that are attributed to societal pressures and **separation-individuation** problems include anorexia and bulimia. Both of these conditions affect mostly females. Approximately 3 percent of teenagers suffer from anorexia, a life-threatening condition brought on by an obsession with losing weight (Shlevar, 1987). Suggested causes of this condition are inadequate separation-individuation and excessive protectiveness on the part of one or both parents. Anorexia appears to be an attempt to get release from parental control while maintaining rigid control of one's emerging adult body.

*separation-individuation: the realization in infancy that others are separate entities and not extensions of themselves*

Bulimia tends to emerge later in adolescence. This condition is characterized by self-induced vomiting on a regular basis or following an eating binge. Bulimia is also attributed to an unsuccessful resolution of Mahler's (1986) separation-individuation process in that this behavior is thought to be a response to maternal underinvolvement.

While many changes occur during later childhood and adolescence, continuity in development is usually the pattern. Thus, in general, children who have done well socially and academically in the early childhood years continue to do well in the later childhood and adolescent years. Positive foundations built in the early years of childhood usually continue through later childhood and adolescence. This phenomenon has been documented through longitudinal research and is one of the major reasons quality early experiences are important.

# RESULTS OF LONGITUDINAL RESEARCH ON QUALITY EARLY CHILDHOOD PROGRAMS

In the early 1960s, three important discoveries laid the groundwork for the development of new programming for young children. First, Hunt (1961) reported that the nature of environments in the early years has a profound and long-term effect on learning. Second, Bloom (1964) analyzed previously published studies on learning and concluded that as much as 70 percent of intellectual aptitude as measured by IQ tests and about 50 percent of the reading skill of young adults had been established between ages 4 and 9. Third, the research of Piaget documented that young children's cognitive systems and intellectual processing differ from those of older children and adults. These three developments, coupled with an increasing awareness of the negative effects of adverse social conditions, provided the impetus for the creation of a number of early childhood programs in the 1960s. Examples of these programs are Head Start, Follow-Through, the Perry Preschool Project, and the Tuscon Model of Early Childhood Education.

*washout effect: the decline of gains in intelligence and achievement scores several years after the termination of an intervention program for young children*

The research on these programs after the first several years looked promising. However, as children who had been in these programs moved into the third and fourth grades, a **washout effect** was observed in that there was no significant difference in performance between children who had been in these preschool programs and those who had not (Cicerelli, Evans, & Schiller, 1969). Politicians and others protested further funding of these programs. Fortunately, a number of scholars suggested that the final chapter on the real benefits of these programs might not be written until years later, after these children were adolescents or young adults (Berrueta-Clement et al., 1984; Lazar & Darlington, 1982). These farsighted advocates of early childhood education called for and helped implement longitudinal research on the effects of these programs.

Following is a summary of the identified benefits of preschool programs (Schweinhart, Barnes, & Weikart, 1993).

## Effects on School Performance

- Program participants exhibited significantly higher intellectual performance than nonparticipants during the program and for a year or two after.
- Significantly fewer program participants than nonparticipants in a matched control group were placed in special education classes.
- Significantly fewer program participants were retained in-grade compared with program nonparticipants.
- Female participants in the program had significantly higher high school graduation rates than female nonparticipants.

## Effects on Community Behavior

- Male program participants had significantly higher monthly earnings at age 27 than nonparticipants.
- Eighty percent of female program participants were employed at age 27, compared to only 55 percent of nonparticipants.

- Significantly more program participants than nonparticipants owned their own homes and second cars.

- Significantly fewer program participants than nonparticipants received welfare assistance or other social services.

- Significantly more female program participants were married at age 27 than nonparticipants.

- Significantly more out-of-wedlock births occurred among female nonparticipants than among participants.

**Return on Investment.**  Expressed in constant 1992 dollars discounted annually at 3 percent, the program returned $88,433 per participant from the following sources:

- Savings in schooling costs due to reduced need for special education classes and services

- Higher taxes paid by program participants due to their higher earnings

- Savings in welfare assistance

- Savings to the criminal justice system and to potential victims of crimes

According to Schweinhart, Barnes, and Weikart (1993), these longitudinal studies indicate that high-quality programs produce significant long-term benefits for three reasons:

- High-quality programs *empower children* by encouraging them to initiate their own learning activities, solve problems, and learn to control their environment.

- High-quality programs *empower parents* through working with teachers in supporting children's development and learning.

- High-quality programs *empower teachers* by providing them with inservice curriculum training and supportive supervision that encourages practices that support children and their families.

---

 *Role of the Early Childhood Professional*

## Promoting Positive Long-Term Development in Children and Adolescents

1. Help parents, other educators, and policymakers become aware of developmentally appropriate practices for young children.

2. Help parents, other educators, and policymakers become aware of the negative short-term effects of developmentally inappropriate practices.

3. Help parents, other educators, and policymakers become aware of the negative long-term effects of developmentally inappropriate practices on older children and adolescents. ■

## KEY TERMS

| | | |
|---|---|---|
| adolescence | puberty | washout effect |
| later childhood | separation-individuation | |

## REVIEW STRATEGIES AND ACTIVITIES

1. Review the key terms individually or with a classmate.
2. Think back to your teenage years.
   a. Make a list of the pressures you encountered.
   b. What were some of the competencies you developed during your adolescence?
   c. What foundations were laid during your childhood years that helped you in later childhood and adolescence?
2. Make a list of ways you can inform others about the long-term benefits of quality early childhood programs.
3. Design a program for teenagers that emphasizes preparation for parenting.

## FURTHER READINGS

Frymier, J. (1992). *Growing up is risky business, and schools are not to blame.* Bloomington, IN: Phi Delta Kappa.

Garbarino, J., F. M. Stott, & the Faculty of The Erikson Institute (1992). *What children can tell us.* San Francisco: Jossey-Bass Publishers.

Gibbs, J. T., Huang, L. N., and Associates (1989). *Children of color: Psychological interventions with minority youth.* San Francisco: Jossey-Bass Publishers.

Hamburg, D. A., M. D. (1994). *Today's Children: Creating a future for a generation in crisis.* New York: Times Books.

Hong, M. (Ed.) (1993). *Growing up Asian American.* New York: Avon Books.

Sadker, M., & D. Sadker (1994). *Failing at fairness: How our schools cheat girls.* New York: Simon & Schuster.

Sanders, B. (1994). *A is for ox: Violence, electronic media and the silencing of the written word: America's youth is dying not to read.* New York: Pantheon Books.

Schweinhart, L. J., Barnes, A. V., & Weikart, D. P. (1993). *Significant benefits: The High/Scope Perry Preschool Study through age 27.* Monographs of the High/Scope Educational Research Foundation, 10. Ypsilanti, MI: High/Scope Press, PS 021 998.

UNICEF (1995). *The state of the world's children.* New York: Oxford University Press.

# CHAPTER EIGHTEEN

*The power to animate all of life's seasons is a power that resides within us.*

**Gail Sheehy**

*Early childhood careers can successfully develop using a "path" model of diverse personal growth experiences linked by commitment and concern. Traditional career ladder models are often too rigid.*

*Political activity . . . [must be] the very foundation of our work. . . . [It] can benefit young children, their families, ourselves, and all humankind.*

**Janna Dresden and Barbara Kimes Myers**

# Developing Adults in the Lives of Developing Young Children

After studying this chapter, you will demonstrate comprehension by:

- Describing how dynamics of adult behavior can promote self-understanding and facilitate the understanding of other adults in professional relationships: parents, teachers, administrators, and other support staff.
- Identifying general adult developmental patterns and the factors that appear to influence adult behaviors.
- Describing the importance of understanding professional development.
- Outlining the process of professional development.
- Describing the role of professional responsibility and ethics in assisting other adults in understanding the unique development and learning styles of young children.
- Describing the relationship between professionalism and advocacy for young children and their families.
- Describing the rewards of becoming a competent early childhood professional by helping young children develop positive self-concepts and attitudes toward learning.

The concept that a person's development extends over the entire life span is relatively recent (Erikson, 1963). For many years, researchers assumed that development stops once one becomes an adult despite changes in physical appearance. Nevertheless, cognitive potential was assumed to be fixed and unchanging through the life span. However, the notion that intelligence continues to develop and change throughout adulthood is now widely accepted (Baltes, Dittman-Kohli, & Dixon, 1984). In addition, little thought was given to the ongoing social and emotional development of adults until Erikson developed his concept of the eight stages of human development (1963). While a number of researchers support developmental stages throughout the **life span** (Erikson, 1963; Levinson, 1986; Sheehy, 1976; Vaillant, 1977), recent research suggests more complex theories. Before we present these ideas, you may find it helpful to think about why it is important for an early childhood professional to know about the development of adults.

*life span:*
*the idea that development is a lifelong process and is influenced by biological, environmental, and historical causes*

## THE IMPORTANCE OF UNDERSTANDING THE DYNAMICS OF ADULT DEVELOPMENT

An awareness of the dynamics of adult development can promote self-understanding. Early childhood professionals need knowledge about the growth and development of young children to be competent professionals. They also need to understand themselves. Self-understanding promotes responsibility and healthy functioning in adults, and adults must possess positive personalities to work effectively with young children.

Helen Pope returned to teaching when her children started school. After her eight-year absence from the classroom, Helen is surprised to find that teaching now takes more time due to increased recordkeeping and paperwork. She also tries to continue doing all the household chores she did when she was at home all day. Pressure and stress mount, and she realizes that her family and the children in her classroom are affected by her behavior. Helen comes to realize that she now has two full-time jobs and that changes need to be made. Including her family in household chores, readjusting the family budget to provide money for meals outside the home, and modifying some of her classroom procedures so that the children are more responsible and independent help to relieve stress for Helen, her family, and her students. ■

In addition to self-understanding, an awareness of the dynamics affecting adult behavior and development can help early childhood professionals understand the actions and reactions of other adults in the professional relationship. These adults include parents, other teachers, administrators, and support staff. Understanding others' behavior can foster more empathetic, positive, and productive relationships. Lack of understanding can produce negative and hostile relationships. Consider the following vignette.

Ms. Schwartz, the kindergarten teacher had previously encouraged Kathleen's mother to stay in the classroom until Kathleen adjusted to coming to school. Ms. Schwartz's knowledge of child development and the nature of the separation process was quite helpful in that situation. Her knowledge of adult behavior patterns in the separation process proved invaluable in another incident. When Ms. Bealer came to pick up her daughter Beth from kindergarten one afternoon, Ms. Schwartz asked Ms. Bealer how things were going. In a defensive tone, Ms. Bealer said, "Well you have become the new authority in our house. All Beth says is 'Ms. Schwartz this' and 'Ms. Schwartz that.'" Ms. Schwartz' knowledge of the feelings and behaviors of many parents regarding their children's entry into school helped her understand Ms. Bealer's somewhat hostile remarks. Ms. Schwartz knows that Beth is the first child in the Bealer family to attend school and that this is Beth's first extended time away from the home. It is not unusual at this time for parents to feel they are being replaced in their child's life by another important adult, the teacher. Ms. Schwartz realizes that the developmental milestone of a child entering school can also heighten parental awareness of their own progression in the life span. Parents too are getting older and now must learn new roles and responsibilities as parents of a school-age child. Ms. Schwartz is aware that school entry is a time of new adjustments for the family and that this transition can cause an increased stress level. Consequently, Ms. Schwartz does not take Ms. Bealer's comments personally. Nor does she respond to Ms. Bealer in a negative way or allow the comment to affect her long-term relationship with Ms. Bealer. ■

## TRENDS AND FACTORS INFLUENCING ADULT BEHAVIORS

Erik Erikson was the first researcher to promote the concept of sequential stages of adult development (1963). The last three stages of his eight stages of human development deal with adult development (see Figure 18.1). Erikson also believed that success in each stage depends on the successful resolution of the challenges of the preceding stage. The investigations of Levinson (1986) and Vaillant (1977) supported Erikson's notion. Their research was the basis for Gail Sheehy's book *Passages* (1976), which popularized the idea of predictable age-related stages for adults. Sheehy also wrote a sequel entitled *Pathfinders* (1982), which explores life stages that she categorized as the Freestyle Fifties, the Selective Sixties, the Thoughtful Seventies, and the Proud-to-Be Eighties.

More recently, various investigators have suggested there is great variation in adults at particular ages (Elder, 1982). Therefore, specific stages of adult development may not be reliable indicators of behavior for all adults in particular age ranges. This **life course** approach suggests the following ideas about adult development:*

- During adolescence, most people develop ideas about major events in their life cycle, including the timetable for the unfolding of these events. They plan to assume an occupation, marry, have a family, and retire.

- Great variation occurs among individual adults as they move through adult life. Some men enter the work force at age 18; others take over a decade to prepare to enter their chosen occupation. Some women become mothers in their mid-teens; others spend a number of years establishing a career and then choose to become mothers; still others become mothers first, get their children into school, and then focus on career goals. Some parents combine career development and raising a family, others focus on working at home, and some choose not to marry or have children.

- Societal changes, often involving economics, affect the timetable for various groups of people in a particular age range and how they live their adult lives. Those people who grew up during the Depression often have lived out their lives differently than the adult baby boomers.

- Chance events and opportunities can cause wide variation in adult lives. Early retirement, the premature death of a spouse or parent, and the early or unplanned birth of children are chance events to which people respond in a variety of ways.

- People who believe they are not progressing according to their individual social clocks may find their lives more stressful.

- People who find themselves among the first group to be influenced by changing societal and economic forces may perceive themselves as being stressed. Two-income families who must find adequate child care for young children and juggle parenting, household, and career responsibilities are under stress due to traditional male-female role expectations, lack of quality child care options, and the failure of many employers to accommodate demands on families.

*life course:*
*the idea that views development and behavior from birth to death as being influenced by major life events rather than by well-defined stages*

*Adapted from Rosenfeld, A., & Stark, E. (1987). The prime of our lives. *Psychology Today, 21*(5), 62–72. Reprinted with permission from Psychology Today Magazine copyright © 1987 Sussex Publishers Inc.

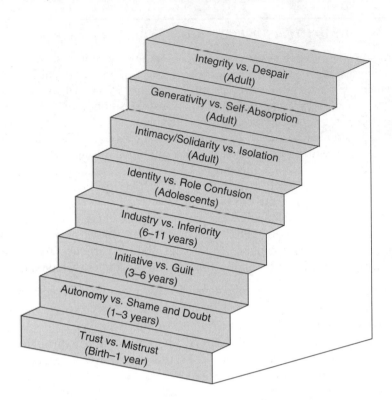

**FIGURE 18.1**
The last three of Erikson's eight stages deal with adult development.

- It appears that not all adults undergo a "midlife crisis." Some investigators have reinterpreted this event by terming it "mid-life consciousness," in that this is a time for an awakening of thought about the meaning of life and one's place in the life cycle.

- The idea that an adult must successfully resolve the crisis of one developmental stage before moving on to the next stage is no longer universally accepted.

- Attention must also be paid to cultural variation in expectations regarding the life cycle. Roles and timetables may be gender specific and differ from mainstream thinking about society at large.

In conclusion, it appears that expectations of traditional life events still exist for many adults. However, due to a number of complex factors, both societal and individual, the timetable for these events is more varied than in the past. These variations can create options and freedom for some people; for others, they can cause stress and crisis.

An awareness of life events and their impact on parents, other teachers, staff, and administrators is important if the early childhood professional is to establish effective cooperative relationships. The following vignette demonstrates how knowledge of the impact of various events on the life course can promote understanding among adults in professional relationships.

*During the teen years, most people develop individual timetables regarding when they would like the major events in their lives to occur. Unpredictable life situations may change their plans.*

Three first-grade teachers had enjoyed positive, cooperative professional relationships for several years. Linda, who had always been dependable and helpful, began to demonstrate inconsistent and unpredictable behaviors. Elena and Tim could not figure out what was happening. Finally, one day after school, Linda confided that her husband had lost his job and that the family was under great emotional and financial stress. Linda's oldest daughter was planning to start college next year, and now it seemed this would not be financially possible. The impact of Linda's husband's unemployment on their life plans and those of their daughter had adversely affected Linda's professional behavior. Sharing her problems with Elena and Tim, and their awareness and support, helped Linda to cope. As a result, their working relationships improved. If Tim and Elena had not been aware of the stress caused by the disruption of their co-worker's life, they could have reacted with hostility toward Linda, undermining their positive professional relationship. Eventually, this compounded stress could have affected the nature of Linda's interactions with the children in her classroom. ∎

An awareness of the factors influencing the development and behaviors of adults in the life course can serve to foster understanding of self and others and preserve professional relationships. Ultimately, this understanding of the dynamics affecting adults can influence the quality of adult interactions with young children and the nature of the learning environment.

A major theme throughout this book is the dynamic nature of development, which occurs not only in the early childhood years but throughout the life span. Chapter 17 presented a brief overview of the continuing development of older children and adolescents. The first part of this chapter discussed the development of adults. We will now discuss the ongoing development of early childhood professionals.

## THE IMPORTANCE OF UNDERSTANDING THE DEVELOPING EARLY CHILDHOOD PROFESSIONAL

An awareness of how teachers develop professionally can also facilitate professional self-awareness and understanding of other professionals. Understanding oneself and others in the professional context can promote more productive relationships and working environments. Cooperative professional relationships among adults promote positive climates in which young children can develop and learn (Berger, 1991). Thus, knowledge of professional development is an important component of promoting the development of young children. Following is a discussion of several interrelated ideas that appear to influence the developing professional.

## THE DEVELOPING PROFESSIONAL

Some theorists (Erikson, 1963; Havighurst, 1972) have suggested that an important aspect of young adulthood is securing a full-time job. From this perspective, it appears that young early childhood professionals encounter unique problems and concerns that older or experienced professionals may not. Other researchers propose that professionals progress through a sequence of stages (Fuller, 1969; Katz, 1972, 1977). Katz (1972) is one of the few researchers who have examined the development of teachers of young children and has identified four stages: survival, consolidation, renewal, and maturity.*

The *survival* stage may last throughout the first full year of teaching. At this stage, the teacher focuses on how to get through each day and week. Teachers in their early professional development not only are learning basic instructional and management skills but are also concerned about acceptance by colleagues and by the parents of the children in their classrooms. Discrepancies between the perceived ideal classroom and the realities that emerge can produce anxieties.

*Adapted with permission from "Developmental Stages of Preschool Teachers" by L. G. Katz, 1972, *The Elementary School Journal*, 23, pp. 50–54. Copyright 1972 by The University of Chicago Press.

According to Katz, teachers at this stage need on-site classroom assistance, comfort, guidance, and instruction in specific skills.

Teachers then move into the next stage, *consolidation*. In this stage, teachers' ideas and learning during the survival stage are consolidated. Teachers can begin to focus on the needs of individual children in their classrooms. Teachers in this stage need on-site consultants or experienced teachers to help them strengthen and consolidate their knowledge. Sharing of ideas and information about individual children with these resource people is also helpful during this time.

Katz found that teachers who were in their third or fourth year of teaching often became bored with their past routine of activities in their classrooms. They felt a need for new ideas and different ways of teaching. This stage of *renewal* finds teachers attending conferences and workshops, reading professional magazines and journals, and visiting other classrooms in search of new ideas.

Katz suggests that the last stage, *maturity*, varies from teacher to teacher. Some teachers reach this stage by their third year of teaching, while others take five or more years. Teachers who have reached the maturity stage need more in-depth information pertaining to the historical and philosophical basis of the field. They seek out more information about the nature of learning and about the profession. Teachers in the maturity stage frequently pursue advanced degrees, attend conferences and seminars, read extensively about the field, and interact with other mature professionals.

Other researchers (e.g., Swick, Brown, & Guddemi, 1986) have determined that personality orientation affects the development of teaching behaviors. Flexible teachers with high self-esteem seem to have fewer discipline problems than teachers who are rigid, are introverted, and have low self-esteem.

A more encompassing view (Heck & Williams, 1984; Lieberman & Miller, 1984) suggests that the development of teacher behaviors is affected by many factors. As Figure 18.2 shows, this ecological perspective takes into account teachers' past experiences, including their own classroom encounters from the early childhood years through teacher training. The environment of the schools in which they teach, the overall school system, the community, and wider societal perspectives on learning influence teachers and their behaviors. Ost (1989) indicates that teachers are continually learning about the subculture of teaching. Like the culture at large, the subculture of teaching is always changing.

While Katz's four developmental stages of teachers end with reaching the maturity stage at around the fifth year of teaching, a more recent notion suggests that the development of teachers can be viewed from a long-term or **career perspective**. According to Kohl (1984), this career perspective of teaching takes the following into account:

**career perspective:** *the theory that development of early childhood professionals continues throughout their careers and is unique to each person*

- Each teacher's life space, or experiences and background, is unique, just as each child's is.

- Teacher development does not end at one year or five years, but is a long-term process that continues throughout the career.

- The roles of teachers broaden as they develop and may include serving as mentors to younger teachers or assuming other leadership positions.

- Teacher development is facilitated when guided by a plan.

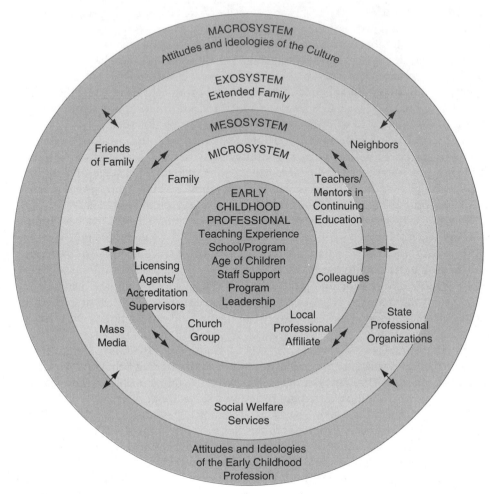

**FIGURE 18.2**

The development of teachers' behaviors is affected by many factors, including prior classroom experiences from the early years of schooling through teacher training, the schools in which they teach, the overall school system, the community, and wider societal perspectives on learning.

*career ladder:*
*the idea that the profes-*
*sional's career advance-*
*ment involves moving*
*up from position to*
*position and that each*
*step up involves*
*increased authority and*
*rewards*

*career path:*
*the idea that profession-*
*al development can*
*involve moving to a dif-*
*ferent position, which*
*provides new opportu-*
*nities for learning and*
*growth, rather than*
*increased authority*

Gehrke (1987) also takes a long-term view of the development of teachers and identifies five stages of teaching: choosing, beginning, learning, continuity, and leaving. Dresden and Myers (1989) suggest that the current emphasis on the **career ladder** may be somewhat limiting. Whereas the career ladder theory implies moving up in the organizational pattern with increased authority and greater renumeration, Dresden and Myers (1989) propose the idea of a **career path**. A career path does not focus on increased authority but emphasizes the notion of moving to another position that offers opportunities for additional learning and growth (Dresden & Myers, 1989). According to Cunningham (1985), effective schools and professional settings plan for and support the continuing development and renewal of teachers.

## OPPORTUNITIES FOR CONTINUED PROFESSIONAL DEVELOPMENT

Much of the recent attention to school reform has focused on teachers (Carnegie Task Force on Teaching as a Profession, 1986; Holmes Group, 1986). The recognition of the first years of teaching as important to teacher effectiveness and retention in the classroom has prompted some states and school districts to mandate induction and orientation programs for beginning teachers. These programs often provide knowledge about various procedures of the school setting and classroom management, and may include support teams or individual mentors who advise and guide beginning teachers (Hawk, 1987; Hawk & Robards, 1987; Huling-Austin, 1986; Lasley, 1986).

Beginning teachers who find themselves in settings that do not have a formalized support system may want to identify more mature early childhood professionals who can serve as **mentors** and provide needed support. Mentors may be other teachers within or outside the beginning teacher's immediate professional setting. College or university instructors or advisors in early childhood education can also help beginning teachers. In addition, contact with other beginning professionals helps create an awareness of the commonality of concerns and problems most beginning teachers encounter. Sharing with others who are in similar circumstances also provides support.

*mentor:*
*an experienced early childhood professional who provides support and guidance to a beginning teacher*

Choosing a teaching position with a school district that is part of a **professional development center** can also facilitate ongoing professional development. In professional development centers, preservice and inservice teachers, along with teacher education professionals affiliated with a college or university, collaborate to provide continued mutual professional development. Such centers encourage and facilitate the reflecting-in-action and teacher-as-researcher perspectives described in Chapter 2.

*professional development center:*
*an organization, usually established within a public elementary school, in which professional development of preserve and inservice classroom teachers and other professionals is pursued collaboratively*

One of the emerging trends mentioned in Chapter 1 was increased efforts in credentialing or certifying teachers. One such effort is certification by the National Board for Professional Teaching Standards (NBPTS). The board is in the process of developing teaching certification standards and assessments around five central concepts:

- Teachers are committed to students and their learning.
- Teachers know the subjects they teach and how to teach those subjects to students.
- Teachers are responsible for managing and monitoring student learning.
- Teachers think systematically about their experience and learn from experience.
- Teachers are members of learning communities. (National Board for Professional Teaching Standards, 1991, p. 4)

*Maintaining membership in professional organizations provides the opportunity for continued professional development and establishes a network of colleagues.*

These standards and assessments are being developed in more than 30 fields, including early childhood. The following education policy reform issues have been identified as priority areas:

- Creating a more effective environment for teaching and learning in schools
- Increasing the supply of high-quality entrants into the profession, with special emphasis on minorities
- Improving teacher education and continuing professional development (National Board for Professional Teaching Standards, 1991, p. 8)

Maintaining membership in professional organizations provides another opportunity for further professional development. Professional magazines, journals, and position statements provide developing professionals with current thinking and ideas for their classrooms. Professional organizations also provide conferences, workshops, and seminars, which can be sources of support and continuing education. Serving on professional organization committees and making presentations can develop leadership skills.

Another opportunity for continuing professional development is additional training at the graduate level. Information obtained from advanced instruction at a college or university can promote the development of **master teachers**, those recognized as outstanding teachers of young children. In addition, teachers who seek

*master teachers:*
*early childhood professionals who are recognized as outstanding in implementing developmentally appropriate practice*

advanced training may enter leadership positions that influence policymaking regarding the development and learning of young children. In short, true professionals continue to learn throughout their careers and consciously seek ways to ensure their ongoing professional development.

## PROFESSIONAL RESPONSIBILITY AND ETHICS

In 1989, the NAEYC approved the Code of Ethical Conduct and Statement of Commitment (Feeney & Kipnis, 1992) (see Figure 18.3). Several of the ideas and principles contained in this code of **ethics** are particularly relevant to the early childhood professional's responsibility in promoting developmentally appropriate practices. Consider the following statement:

*ethics:*
*a set of standards describing a professional's responsibilities in terms of behaviors and conduct*

> Above all, we shall not harm children. We shall not participate in practices that are disrespectful, degrading, dangerous, exploitative, intimidating, psychologically damaging, or physically harmful to children. **This principle has precedence over all others in this code.** (P–1.1)

In addition, the code states the following responsibilities of the early childhood professional:

> To be familiar with the knowledge base of early childhood education and to keep current through continuing education and in-service training. (I–1.1)

> To base program practices upon current knowledge in the field of child development and related disciplines and upon particular knowledge of each child. (I–1.2)

> To interpret each child's progress to parents within the framework of a developmental perspective and to help families understand and appreciate the value of developmentally appropriate early childhood programs. (I–2.5)

> To help family members improve their understanding of their children and to enhance their skills as parents. (I–2.6)

## PROFESSIONAL RESPONSIBILITY AND ADVOCACY

The NAEYC Code of Ethical Conduct (Feeney & Kipnis, 1992) also addresses the early childhood professional's ethical responsibilities to community and society. Some of these responsibilities pertaining to **advocacy** include:

*advocacy:*
*actively taking a position that promotes the quality of life for young children and their families*

> To work through education, research, and advocacy toward an environmentally safe world in which all children are adequately fed, sheltered and nurtured. (I–4.3)

FIGURE 18.3
The National Association for the Education of Young Children Statement of Commitment

As an individual who works with young children, I commit myself to furthering the values of early childhood education as they are reflected in the NAEYC Code of Ethical Conduct.

To the best of my ability I will:

- Ensure that programs for young children are based on current knowledge of child development and early childhood education.
- Respect and support families in their task of nurturing children.
- Respect colleagues in early childhood education and support them in maintaining the NAEYC Code of Ethical Conduct.
- Serve as an advocate for children, their families, and their teachers in community and society.
- Maintain high standards of professional conduct.
- Recognize how personal values, opinions, and biases can affect professional judgment.
- Be open to new ideas and be willing to learn from the suggestions of others.
- Continue to learn, grow, and contribute as a professional.
- Honor the ideals and principles of the NAEYC Code of Ethical Conduct.

*Source:* Reprinted by permission of the National Association for the Education of Young Children. Note: The Statement of Commitment expresses those basic personal commitments that individuals must make to align themselves with the profession's responsibilities as set forth in the NAEYC Code of Ethical Conduct.

To work through education, research, and advocacy toward a society in which all young children have access to quality programs. (I–4.4)

To promote knowledge and understanding of young children and their needs. To work toward greater social knowledge of children's rights and greater social acceptance of responsibility for their well-being (I–4.5)

To support policies and laws that promote the well-being of children and families. To oppose those that impair their well-being. To cooperate with other individuals and groups in these efforts. (I–4.6)

These ethical behaviors form the basis for early childhood advocacy. Goffin and Lombardi (1989) state that

advocacy on behalf of children needs to become a part of our professional— and even ethical—responsibilities. Early childhood educators can serve as models of advocacy for those still unaware that the interests of children and society are mutually supportive. Advocacy is a critical vehicle for actualizing our commitment to children. Our caring cannot be restricted to our classrooms or offices if we truly want to improve the lives of children. (p. 2)

Policies affecting children are made at the local, state, and national levels. Early childhood professionals must become knowledgeable about issues as well as share their professional expertise. The media, professional organizations, and appropriate policy- and decision makers can help keep early childhood professionals informed. Goffin and Lombardi (1989) suggest six ways in which early childhood professionals can promote advocacy:

- Sharing knowledge
- Sharing professional experiences
- Redefining the "bottom line" for children
- Standing up for the profession
- Activating parental power
- Expanding the constituency for children (pp. 3–5)

In summary, true professional behavior is based on a code of ethical responsibility that requires professionals to not only provide children with developmentally appropriate opportunities to develop and learn but also educate other adults about young children's development and developmentally appropriate practice. In addition, early childhood professionals advocate for improvement in the lives of young children and their families in arenas outside the classroom and office. Promoting developmentally appropriate practice and advocating for young children require that the early childhood professional pursue continual development and learning. Katz & Ward (1978) says, "Knowing my capacity to continue to learn throughout life, I shall vigorously pursue knowledge in early childhood education by informal and formal means" (p. 21).

## KNOWLEDGE OF HOW YOUNG CHILDREN DEVELOP AND LEARN

Katz (1978) says, "Our understanding of the nature of development helps us to answer the *when* questions in curricular planning" (p. 91). Early childhood professionals recognize that development is interrelated, and therefore they provide for developmentally appropriate experiences that contribute to young children's growth in all areas: social, emotional, cognitive, language, literacy, and motor. Early childhood professionals who are well grounded the variations in development and culture continue to learn about, from, and with children and their families.

## THE REWARDS OF WORKING WITH YOUNG CHILDREN

Knowing how young children develop and learn, how to implement developmentally appropriate education that is sensitive to diversity and is inclusive, and how to articulate this information to other adults helps the early childhood professional support the development of young children's healthy self-concepts and their sense of empowerment as learners, providing the foundation for successful and productive lives.

*Advocacy on behalf of children needs to be part of the teacher's professional and ethical responsibilities.*

Recall the quote at the beginning of Chapter 1: "There are two lasting gifts we can give our children—one is roots, the other is wings." Knowledge of how children grow and learn helps early childhood professionals promote the development of positive self-concepts, a positive attitude toward learning, and a sense of control in young children—the gifts of roots and wings. The challenge of being an early childhood professional is great, but the rewards of facilitating the development of healthy and productive human beings are even greater. We authors hope this text has provided you with the foundation for becoming a competent early childhood professional and a knowledge of how young children develop and learn. Best wishes as you continue your development as an early childhood professional!

*Early childhood education professionals* can *influence legislative outcomes.*

## Role of the Early Childhood Professional

### Continuing to Develop as a Professional

1. Be aware of the importance of knowledge of the life course and its influence on self-understanding and the understanding of adults in personal and professional relationships.
2. Be aware of the importance of adult life course events and their impact on the interrelationships of adults and children in the home and in the learning environment.
3. Be aware of the dynamic process of becoming an early childhood professional.
4. Be aware of professional ethics and responsibility in promoting developmentally appropriate practices for young children.
5. Be aware of professional ethics and responsibility in educating other adults about developmentally appropriate education.
6. Be aware of professional ethics and responsibility in becoming an advocate for improving the lives of young children and their families beyond the classroom and the workplace. ▪

*The challenge of being an early childhood professional is great, but the rewards of facilitating the development and learning of healthy and productive human beings are greater.*

## KEY TERMS

| | | |
|---|---|---|
| advocacy | ethics | mentor |
| career ladder | life course | professional |
| career path | life span | development center |
| career perspective | master teacher | |

## REVIEW STRATEGIES AND ACTIVITIES

1. Review the key terms individually or with a classmate.

2. Recall the life cycle events you envisioned during your adolescence. Have these events occurred according to your timetable? Why or why not? What kinds of stress have resulted? How have you handled this stress?

3. Interview some early childhood professionals about stressors in their professional lives. How do they cope?

4. Interview several early childhood professionals who have varying amounts of experience. Ask them about their interests and concerns at various times during their career: first year, second year, third through fifth years, and beyond the fifth year.

5. Invite the public policy chairperson of your local early childhood organization or teacher organization to discuss the advocacy process in your community, your state, or the nation.

6. Make a list of ways you will help your colleagues, parents, and policymakers become more aware of developmentally appropriate, inclusive practices.

## FURTHER READINGS

Abdal-Hagg, I. (Ed.). (1993). *Professional development schools: A directory of projects in the United States.* Washington, DC: Clinical Schools Clearing House.

Anderson, C. R. (Ed.). (1993). *Voices of change: A report of the clinical schools project.* Washington, DC: Ford Foundation.

Dresden, J., & Myers, B. K. (January 1989). Early childhood professionals: Toward self-definition. *Young Children, 44(2),* 62–66.

Feeney, S., & Kipnis, K. (1992). *The National Association for the Education of Young Children Code of Ethical Conduct and Statement of Commitment.* Washington, DC: National Association for the Education of Young Children.

Goffin, S. G., Lombardi, J. (1989). *Speaking out: Early childhood advocacy.* Washington, DC: National Association for the Education of Young Children.

Jensen, M. A., & Chevalier, L. W. (1990). *Issues and advocacy in early childhood education.* Boston: Allyn & Bacon.

National Association for the Education of Young Children (1995). *Guidelines for preparation of early childhood professionals: Associate, Baccalaureate, and Advanced Levels.* Washington, DC: Author.

National Association for the Education of Young Children. (n. d.). *Guiding principles for the development, analysis, and implementation of early childhood legislation.* Washington, DC: Author.

National Board for Professional Teaching Standards. (1991). *Toward high and rigorous standards for the teaching profession: Initial policies and perspectives of the National Board for Professional Teaching Standards.* (2nd ed.). Detroit: Author.

*Standards for quality programming for young children: Early childhood education and the elementary school principal.* (1990). Alexandria, VA: National Association of Elementary School Principals.

# GLOSSARY

**abortion:** the ending of a pregnancy, usually during the first trimester

**accommodation:** the cognitive process by which patterns of thought (schemata) and related behaviors are modified to conform to new information or experience (Piaget)

**achievement test:** a test that measures what children have learned as a result of instruction

**acquired immunodeficiency syndrome (AIDS):** a virus that can be transmitted from the mother to the fetus/embryo via the placenta and attacks the immune system, causing death from illnesses that the immune system cannot prevent

**adaptation:** the process by which one adjusts to changes in the environment

**adipose:** the name for tissue in which there is an accumulation of connective tissue cells, each containing a relatively large deposit of fat

**adolescence:** the time of rapid development between the later childhood years and adulthood

**advocacy:** actively taking a position that promotes the quality of life for young children and their families

**afterbirth:** the placenta after it moves from the uterus and is expelled

**alphafetoprotein test (AFP):** a blood test that can identify disorders in the brain or spinal column in the fetus

**altruism:** intentions to help others without the expectation of reward

**amniocentesis:** a technique that involves extracting amniotic fluid from the uterus for the purpose of detecting all chromosomal and over 100 biomedical disorders

**anecdotal record:** a type of narrative observation that describes in detail an incident after it occurs

**anemia:** a condition caused by a lack of red blood cells

**anomaly:** a deviation from the norm

**anorexia:** a severe disorder, usually seen in teenage girls, characterized by self-starvation

**anoxia:** the condition that is caused by the lack of oxygen in the brain of an infant during labor and delivery and can cause brain damage

**antibias curriculum:** an active approach to challenging prejudice, stereotyping, bias and the *isms*: (sexism, racism, etc.)

**Apgar score:** a score that rates the physical condition of newborns in the areas of appearance, pulse, grimace, activity, and respiration

**apnea:** absence of breathing for a period of up to 20 seconds

**approximations:** children's attempts at conventional oral or written language, which, when produced, are not quite conventional

**assimilation:** the process of incorporating new motor or conceptual learning into existing schemata (Piaget)

**associative play:** a loosely organized form of social play that is characterized by overt social behaviors indicating common activities, shared interests, and interpersonal associations

481

**at-risk:** children who have been or are in prebirth or afterbirth environments that do not promote typical physical/motor, psychosocial, cognitive, language, and literacy development

**attachment:** a strong emotional relationship between two persons, characterized by mutual affection and a desire to maintain proximity

**authentic assessment:** the ongoing, continuous, context-based observation and documentation of children's behavior used to make decisions about extending children's learning and development

**authoritarian discipline:** a child rearing style in which parents apply rigid standards of conduct and expect unquestioning obedience from the child

**authoritative discipline:** a child-rearing style in which child behavior is directed through rational and reasoned guidance from the adult

**autonomy:** a sense of independence or self-government

**balance:** a body awareness component in which postural adjustments prevent one from falling

**behavioral theory:** the theory that emphasizes the importance of directly observable behavior as influenced by the environment rather than genetic factors or other unobservable forces such as motivation

**biological model:** the explanation of cognitive development as influenced by biological processes of growth and development in the brain

**body awareness:** one's cognizance of one's body and its parts and one's internal and external controls over the body's capabilities

**bonding:** a complex psychobiological connection between parent and infant

**book-handling knowledge:** knowledge of fronts and backs of books, where the story begins, left-to-right progression of pages, and differences between print and illustrations

**botulism:** an often fatal form of food poisoning

**breech birth:** a birth in which a part other than the head presents itself for delivery first, usually the buttocks, feet, or in some cases the umbilical cord

**bulimia:** a severe disorder, usually seen in teenage girls, characterized by binging and then self-induced vomiting

**career ladder:** the idea that the professionals' career advancement involves moving up from position to position and that each step up involves increased authority and rewards

**career path:** the idea that professional development can involve moving to a different position that provides new opportunities for learning and growth, rather than increased authority

**career perspective:** the idea that development of early childhood professionals continues throughout their careers and is unique to each person

**centration:** the preoperational child's inclination to attend to one aspect of a situation

**cephalocaudal:** refers to the head to tail or long axis of the body

**cerebral cortex:** the outer layer of the cerebral hemisphere, made up of gray tissue that is mostly responsible for higher nervous functions

**cervix:** the opening of the uterus

**cesarean:** a surgical procedure during which an incision is made through the abdominal and uterine walls of the mother to deliver the baby

**checklist:** a list of developmental behaviors that the observer identifies as present or absent

**chorionic villus test (CVT):** a test that analyzes samples of the hairlike projections (chorionic villi) of tissue in the placenta to determine chromosomal disorders (can be done earlier than amniocentesis)

**chromosomes:** ordered groups of genes within the nucleus of a cell

**classical conditioning theory:** the first idea regarding behavior theory, based on Pavlov's experiment in which repeated pairing of two events conditioned the same response to either event

**class inclusion:** understanding the relationship between class and subclass, which occurs during the period of concrete operational thought

**clostridium botulinum:** the bacterium that causes botulism

**cognitive development:** the aspect of development that deals with thinking, problem solving, intelligence, and language

**cognitive science:** the investigation of the knowledge and strategies used in the cognitive process that distinguish expert cognitive processes from novice cognitive processes

**cognitive theory:** the theory that explains the development of learning in terms of how children think and process information; usually associated with Piaget and, more recently, the information process theorists

**colostrum:** the first fluid secreted by the mammary glands soon after childbirth

**comprehension:** understanding the meaning of print

**concept clusters:** organization of the tools of the world into categories or patterns of thinking (Vygotsky)

**concrete operational stage:** according to Piaget, the stage in which children, approximately 7 to 11 years of age, can use logical reasoning (rather than relying on perceptions) in situations that are concrete, that is, involve objects and events in the child's immediate environment

**configuration:** the general shape or outline of a word

**congenital malformations:** skeletal or body system abnormalities caused by defective genes within the chromosomes that usually affect the developing embryo during the first eight weeks of pregnancy

**conservation:** the understanding that physical attributes (e.g., mass and weight) stay the same even if appearance changes

**constancy of position in space:** the notion that letters of the alphabet must have fixed positions to maintain their identity

**contraction:** the movement of the muscles of the uterus that forces the baby through the cervical opening and into the birth canal

**cooperative play:** a well-organized form of social play characterized by well-defined social roles within play groups, influential peer leaders, and shared materials and equipment used to pursue a well-understood group play theme

**correlational study:** research that attempts to determine a relationship between two or more sets of measurements

**creative vocabulary:** young children's creation of new words to meet the need for words they have not learned, have forgotten, or for which no word in the language system exists

**critical period:** a time of physiological and/or psychological sensitivity during which the normal development of a major organ or structural system must take place or permanent damage to body structure and/or behavior will result

**cross-sectional study:** research that studies subjects of different ages at the same time

**deciduous teeth:** the first set of teeth, which erupts during infancy; often called *temporary* or *baby teeth*; will later be replaced by a set of 36 permanent teeth

**defense mechanism:** a psychological response to ego threat, frustration, or failure

**deferred imitation:** the child's ability to imitate behaviors observed at an earlier time or another place; occurs near the end of the sensorimotor stage

**descriptive study:** research collected by observing and recording behavior and providing a description of the observed behavior

**developmentally appropriate:** pertains to (1) age appropriateness, the universal and predictable patterns of growth and development that occur in children from birth through age 8; and (2) individual appropriateness, the individual rates and patterns of physical/motor, psychosocial, cognition, language and literacy development, personality and learning style, and family and cultural background of each young child

**developmentally inappropriate:** pertains to adult expectations that are not age appropriate or individually appropriate for children from birth through age 8

**developmental milestones:** significant events during the course of growth and development

**developmental screening test:** a test that determines if a child is developing normally

**dexterity:** quick, precise movements and coordination of the hands and fingers

**diagnostic test:** a test that identifies a child's strengths or weaknesses in a certain area of development

**dialects:** different forms of language used by various ethnic groups or by people who live in certain geographic regions

**dilation:** the gradual opening of the cervix, which occurs in the first stage of labor

**directionality:** the perceptual awareness of direction

**disequilibrium:** the imbalance in thinking that leads the child to assimilate or accommodate (Piaget)

**DNA:** deoxyribonucleic acid, the substance in genes containing the information that causes the formation of chains of protein that stimulate the development of tissue and organs and affects other genes and physiological functions

**dyslexia:** a general term for the condition affecting the auditory and visual processes that causes print to be perceived with distortions

**early childhood development:** the study of the physical/motor, psychosocial, cognitive, language, and literacy development in children from prebirth through age 8, including those from developmentally and culturally diverse backgrounds

**echolalia:** the infant's repetitive babbling of one sound

**ecological systems theory:** the theory that argues that a variety of social systems influence the development of children (Brofenbrenner)

**egocentrism:** the tendency to view the world from one's own perspective; the inability to see another point of view

**electronic fetal monitor:** a device used during labor that is attached to the abdomen of the pregnant woman or the scalp of the fetus to determine the fetal heart rate

**embryonic stage:** weeks 3 through 8 of pregnancy, during which the major organ systems are formed

**empathy:** experiencing the feelings or emotions that someone else is experiencing

**environment:** the experiences, conditions, objects, and people that directly or indirectly influence the development and behavior of a child

**episiotomy:** an incision sometimes made in the opening of the vulva to prevent its tearing during birth

**equilibration:** the process of establishing a balance in thinking (Piaget)

**ethics:** a set of standards describing professional responsibilities in terms of behaviors and conduct

**event sampling:** an observation technique for recording when certain events occur

**expansions:** responses to young children's use of overgeneralizations by using the conventional form in the conversational context

**experimental study:** research that involves treating each of two or more groups in different ways to determine cause-and-effect relationships

**extensions:** responses to children's language that extend the meaning of their language

**extensors:** muscles that act to stretch or extend a limb

**extinguish:** stopping a behavior or response by not reinforcing it over a period of time

**extrafamilial:** actions and behaviors occurring outside the immediate family

**extrafamilial relationships:** those relationships that include people outside the immediate or extended family

**failure to thrive:** a condition in which an apparently healthy infant fails to grow normally

**family child care home:** a private residence that provides child care for a small number of children

**fast mapping:** children's rapid learning of language by relating a word to an internalized concept and remembering it after only one encounter with that word

**fatherese:** modification in the father's speech when talking with young children; can differ from motherese

**fetal alcohol syndrome (FAS):** the physical and mental abnormalities found in babies whose mothers consumed excessive amounts of alcohol during pregnancy

**fetal stage:** the stage that begins after the first eight weeks of pregnancy and continues until birth

**fetus:** the developing human from nine weeks after conception until birth

**figure-ground discrimination:** the ability to focus on the dominant figure in a picture without being distracted by elements in the background

**flexors:** muscles that act to bend a joint

**fontanelles:** membranous space between the cranial bones of the fetus and infant

**forceps:** a surgical instrument, similar to tongs, that is applied to the head of the fetus to speed delivery

**formal approach:** refers to information gathered about young children, usually through standardized tests

**formal operations:** according to Piaget, the fourth and final stage of cognitive development, which occurs during adolescence, when mental operations can be performed without concrete objects and abstract thinking begins

**fraternal twins:** twins whose development began by the fertilization of two ova (eggs) by two sperm, causing both twins to have different genetic codes

**fundamental movements:** coordinations that are basic to all other movement abilities

**gender:** the maleness or femaleness of the zygote as determined by the kind of sperm fertilizing the ovum (Y sperm—genetically male; X sperm—genetically female)

**gender awareness:** one's understanding that one is (biologically) male or female

**gender constancy:** the realization that one's gender remains the same regardless of age or changes in clothing, hairstyles, or other outward characteristics

**gender role:** the public expression of one's gender identity

**genes:** molecules of DNA that store and transmit the characteristics of past generations

**genetic counseling:** information provided to parents or prospective parents regarding the possibility and nature of genetic disorders in their offspring

**genotype:** the combination of genes inherited from both parents and their ancestors

**gifted:** children who give evidence of high performance in various areas of development

**glial cells:** supporting and connecting cells in the nervous system

**heredity:** the inherited characteristics of humans carried by genes

**heteronomous morality:** a morality that is governed by others rather than by oneself

**holophrasic:** refers to the infant's use of one word to convey a phrase or sentence

**human immunodeficiency virus (HIV):** a virus that attacks the central nervous system and is particularly harmful to the fetus when contracted through the infected mother

**hypotheses:** hunches about the development of young children, usually examined through research

**identical twins:** twins whose development began when the zygote split into two identical halves, thus ensuring that both twins have the identical genetic code

**identity constancy:** the understanding that a person or species remains the same, even though appearance is changed through masks or costumes; occurs during the late preoperational stage

**idiosyncratic concepts:** ideas of the preoperational child, based on personal experience and overgeneralized to other situations

**inclusion:** the principle of including children who are developmentally and culturally diverse in integrated settings; refers to theoretical and curricular means for ensuring that all children are fully accepted members of the learning communities in which they participate

**indirect speech act:** speech that infers more than the actual words uttered

**inductive discipline:** a positive, nonpunitive form of discipline that relies on reasons and rationales to help children control their behaviors

**industry:** Erikson's psychosocial stage during which the child is mastering social and academic skills necessary to feel self-assured; the opposite result of this "nuclear crisis" is a sense of inferiority

**infant mortality:** deaths during the first year of life

**informal approach:** refers to information gathered about young children through approaches other than standardized tests

**information-processing theory:** a theory of cognitive development that suggests that the mind is similar to the information-processing system of a computer and, unlike Piaget, emphasizes similarities in the thinking of children and adults

**initiative:** the third of Erikson's psychosocial stages, in which the child pursues ideas, individual interests, and activities; when thwarted, the child becomes self-critical and experiences guilt

**inservice:** individuals who have completed teacher training programs and accepted jobs teaching or serving young children

**intelligence test:** a test that measures those abilities designated as signs of intelligence

**interactional competence:** the repertoire of behaviors that help young children communicate effectively with others

**interactionist perspective:** derived primarily from the works of Jean Piaget, refers to the interactive influences of heredity and environment

**interview:** asking the child predetermined questions on a one-to-one basis to find out more about the child

**intrafamilial:** actions and behaviors occurring within the immediate family

**invented spelling:** spelling that young children create based on their own knowledge of sound-symbol relationships and that over a period of time evolves into conventional spelling behaviors

**irreversibility:** the inability of preoperational children to reverse their thinking and to return to their original point of thought

**isolette:** a small crib that provides a controlled environment for newborns who are considered at risk

**kinesthetic:** the sensation of body, presence, position, and movement

**labor:** the three stages of the birth process: dilation, birth of the baby, and discharge of the placenta

**Lamaze method:** a method developed by Fernand Lamaze that involves training the prospective mother and a partner/coach in breathing and relaxation techniques to be used during labor

**language acquisition device (LAD):** an innate mental mechanism that some theorists believe make language development possible

**later childhood:** the period of development between the early childhood years and adolescence (ages 9 through 11)

**lateralization:** the process whereby certain skills and competencies become localized in one or the other hemisphere of the brain

**Leboyer method:** a technique used during childbirth to help the baby in the transition from life inside to outside the uterus; characterized by warm delivery rooms, muted lighting, soothing music, a warm bath, etc.

**left/right dominance:** occurs when one or the other side of the body takes the lead in motor coordination activities such as eating or writing

**levels of processing theory:** an information-processing model that focuses on the depth of attention rather than aspects of memory in explaining levels of cognitive performance

**life course:** the idea that views development and behavior from birth to death as being influenced by major life events rather than by well-defined stages

**life span:** the idea that development is a lifelong process and is influenced by biological, environmental, and historical causes

**locomotor:** the ability to move independently from place to place

**logico-mathematical knowledge:** knowledge that is constructed primarily from children's actions on and interpretations of objects

**longitudinal study:** research that collects information about the same subjects at different ages over a period of time

**low birthweight:** a weight at birth of less than 5 pounds or 2,500 grams

**low-risk:** children who have been and continue to be in settings that facilitate normal physical/motor, psychosocial, cognitive, language, and literacy development

**master teachers:** early childhood professionals who are recognized as outstanding in implementing developmentally appropriate practice

**mental symbols:** the behaviors that occur at the beginning of the preoperational stage, including speech, imitation of others, and using one object to represent another

**mentor:** an experienced early childhood professional who provides support and guidance to a beginning teacher

**metabolic:** pertains to the body's complex chemical conversion of food into substances and energy necessary for maintenance of life

**metacognition:** an awareness or knowledge of how one processes information and thought

**metalanguage:** talk about language itself

**metalinguistic awareness:** the ability to think about the forms and meanings of language

**meta memory:** an awareness or knowledge of the ways one's memory processes work

**moral behavior:** the ability to consider the needs and well-being of others and exhibit appropriate behaviors consistent with a set of standards or value orientation

**moral realism:** a morality that focuses on rules and the seriousness of the consequences of an act rather than on the intentions behind the act

**moral relativism:** a morality that focuses on the judgment of situations and intentions underlying individual behavior rather than focusing solely on consequences of an act

**morpheme:** the smallest unit of meaning in oral or written language

**motherese:** modification in the mother's speech when talking with young children

**motor fitness:** a physical state in which motor coordination facilitates speed, agility, power, and balance

**multicultural education:** learning experiences that help young children become more aware of and appreciate the commonalities as well as the diversity of various cultural and ethnic groups

**myelinization:** a process in which nerve fibers are coated with a fatty sheath (myelin) that facilitates the transmission of messages across synapses

**narrative observation:** a written observation of behavior as it occurs

**Neonatal Behavioral Assessment Scale (NBAS or Brazelton Scale):** an assessment of 16 reflexes, responsiveness, state changes, and ability to calm itself in the newborn

**neonatal period:** the first four weeks of extrauterine life

**neo-Piagetians:** researchers who support Piaget's ideas, but are updating his theory according to recent findings about cognitive development

**neuron:** a nerve cell responsible for transmitting information in the brain

**nonmaternal care:** child care provided by someone other than the child's mother

**nonparental care:** child care provided by someone other than the child's parent

**norms:** the average age of developmental behaviors or average scores on tests that, according to statistical procedures, should be based on large samples representative of the whole population

**object permanence:** the realization that objects and people continue to exist even though they may not be visible or detected through other senses

**operant conditioning:** Skinner's term for the voluntary change or modification in behavior as a result of reinforcement or punishment

**ossify:** to convert cartilage or membrane to bone

**other-mediated action:** an action, originated by a child who is unable to act directly on object, that is carried out by some other person or agent

**overextension:** occurs when young children use a word to refer to a similar but different object, situation, or category

**overgeneralized speech:** the use of a single word or label to represent an entire category of objects similar in use or appearance

**parallel play:** activities in which two or more children play near one another while engaged in independent activities

**peers:** other children who are the same age as a particular child

**percentile:** a statistical measure that ranks subjects from lowest to highest based on a common characteristic or results of an assessment

**perception:** the physiological process by which sensory input is interpreted

**perceptually bound:** young, preoperational children's explanations for certain phenomena (because it "looks" that way)

**perceptual-motor:** interrelationship between perception and motor abilities

**permissive discipline:** a noncontrolling, nondemanding form of discipline in which the child, for the most part, is allowed to regulate his or her own behavior

**perspective taking:** the ability to understand one's own or another's viewpoint and an awareness of the coordinated and interrelated sets of ideas and actions that are reflected in behavior

**phonics:** the sound-symbol relationship of a language system

**phonology:** the speech sounds of a particular language system

**physical fitness:** a physical state in which muscular strength, endurance, flexibility, and the circulatory-respiratory systems are all in optimal condition

**physical knowledge:** knowledge of physical characteristics of objects and events gained through sensorimotor interactions

**placenta:** the organ attached to the wall of the uterus that transmits nutrients from the mother to the embryo/fetus and filters wastes from the embryo/fetus to the mother

**polymerase chain reaction (PCR):** the process used to identify disease-causing genes in an eight-cell embryo

**portfolio:** a collection of children's products, e.g., art, written work, and related materials, all of which are dated and used to document development and learning over a period of time

**postpartum depression:** a period of depression that affects most mothers for a few days and in some cases for weeks and months after childbirth

**power assertive discipline:** a form of discipline in which the "power" of the adult is used to coerce, deprive of privileges or material goods, or use physical punishment to modify a child's behavior

**predictable books:** books that have repeated patterns and predictable text

**prehension:** the coordination of fingers and thumb to permit grasping

**premoral:** the period in early childhood when the child is unaware of moral rules or values

**prenatal:** the time from conception until birth, an average of 266 days or 38 weeks

**preoperational:** the second of Piaget's stages of cognitive development, in which children from ages 2 to approximately 8 develop the ability to internally represent sensorimotor actions, but cannot engage in the operational or logical thinking of older children and adults

**preprimary:** the time in young children's lives before they enter the primary (first, second, or third) grades

**preservice:** individuals who are in training to teach or serve young children

**preterm:** infants born several weeks before the full term (38 weeks) of pregnancy

**primary child caregiver:** the person from whom the child receives nonparental care and with whom a warm relationship can form

**primary circular reactions:** simple, pleasurable, repetitive acts centered on the infant's body

**primary disabilities:** learning disabilities involving attention, memory, and perception

**primitive reflexes:** reflexes, controlled by subcortical structures in the brain, that gradually disappear during the first year of life

**private speech:** speech to oneself that helps direct one's own behavior or communication with oneself

**private spelling:** invented spelling or spelling that young children create to meet their personal communication needs before they learn public or conventional spelling

**professional development center:** an organization, usually established within a public elementary school, in which professional development of pre service and inservice teachers and other professionals is pursued collaboratively

**professionals:** individuals who have internalized the evolving knowledge base of their particular fields and implement this knowledge in appropriate practice

**prosocial behavior:** behavior that benefits others, such as helping, sharing, comforting, and defending

**proximity seeking:** the child's attempts to maintain nearness and contact with the attachment person

**proximodistal:** refers to the direction from the body's center outward to the extremities

**psychoanalytic theory:** the ideas of personality development as presented in Freud's psychosexual and Erikson's psychosocial theories

**psychological state:** pertains to conditions of arousal and alertness in infancy

**psychosexual theory:** Freud's theory that suggests that sexual drives play an important role in personality development

**psychosocial theory:** Erikson's theory that argues that social interactions are more important than sexual drives in personality development

**puberty:** the biological developments that result in the ability to produce children

**public spelling:** conventional spelling that children learn over a period of time during the schooling process

**random:** assigning children to experimental and control groups so that each child has the same chance of being selected

**rating scale:** a scale with various traits or categories that allows the observer to indicate the importance of the observed behaviors

**readiness test:** a test that measures what beginning skills children have to predict whether they will succeed in a new learning task, e.g., reading

**recessive gene:** a gene that carries a trait that may not appear unless a gene for the same trait is inherited from both parents

**reflecting-in-action:** thinking about and analyzing one's professional behavior and children's or parents' behaviors while engaged or acting in contexts for purposes of assessment and evaluation

**reflex:** an unlearned, involuntary response to stimuli

**registers:** variations in the style of speech according to the particular social setting

**reliability:** the consistency with which various research methods produce the same or relatively similar results for each individual from one assessment administration to the next

**representative sample:** a sample of subjects from approximately the same proportions that are in the population as a whole regarding age, gender, racial and ethnic background, geographic location, and socioeconomic level

**resource persons:** persons outside the educational setting, usually from health-related fields, who can provide information about young children's development and learning

**reversals:** printing letters or words in reverse

**Rh factor:** a condition in the mother that produces antibodies that destroy the red blood cells of her second baby and subsequent babies

**rich interpretation:** acknowledging that young children know more than they can verbally express and use nonverbal behaviors to communicate

**rubella:** a virus that can cause birth disorders if the mother contracts it during the first three months of pregnancy (also known as *German measles*)

**running record:** a type of narrative observation that records all behavior as it occurs

**satiety:** the feeling of having had sufficient food to satisfy hunger

**scaffolding:** according to Vygotsky, the process of adults or more skilled children facilitating concept development or classification in young children by providing verbal information categories

**schemata:** mental concepts or categories; plural for *schema* (Piaget)

**scripts:** the knowledge of a social procedure or event, which includes sequence of events and of roles, often observed in young children in play contexts

**secondary circular reactions:** simple, pleasurable, repetitive acts centered on external objects

**secondary disabilities:** learning disabilities involving thinking and oral language

**self-actualization:** according to Maslow, the process of having basic physical and social/emotional needs met so that individuals can become creative, contributing members of society and feel positive about themselves

**self-awareness:** refers to infant's perception of himself or herself as distinct and separate from other people and objects

**self-concept:** one's sense of oneself as separate and unique from others

**self-control:** the ability to govern one's own behavior

**self-definition:** the criteria by which the self is defined, such as age, size, and physical and mental abilities

**self-esteem:** refers to one's positive or negative self-evaluation

**self-recognition:** refers to the infant's ability to recognize his or her image in a mirror, photograph, or other representation

**semantics:** the meaning of language

**sensorimotor:** learning that occurs through the senses and motor activities

**separation anxiety:** fear of being separated from the attachment person

**separation individuation:** the realization in infants that others are separate entities and not extensions of themselves

**service words:** words that help hold a sentence together, such as *the* and *to*

**shading:** gradually changing the topic of conversation

**sight words:** words that young children recognize immediately

**signs:** internalized representations that are later associated with tools of the world (Vygotsky)

**simultaneous bilingualism:** learning two languages at the same time, beginning at birth

**skeletal age:** a measure of physical development based on examination of skeletal X rays

**social cognition:** the ability to understand the thoughts, intentions, and behaviors of oneself and of others

**social learning theory:** a behavioral theory that argues that learning can also occur through observing others, thus emphasizing the role modeling of other persons the child observes directly and in various media

**sociocentric:** the inability to take or accept as valid the perspectives of another group

**sociocultural model:** the explanation of cognitive development as influenced by various sociocultural experiences within the family, the community, and society

**specimen record:** a type of narrative observation that provides detailed information about a particular event, child, or time of day

**standardized test:** a test that is administered and scored according to set procedures and whose scores can be interpreted according to statistical measures representative of the group for which the test was designed

**stranger anxiety:** fear of strangers characterized by avoidance, crying, or other distress signals

**subcortical:** the portion of the brain just below the cerebral cortex responsible for controlling unlearned and reflexive behavior

**successive bilingualism:** learning a second language after acquiring proficiency in a first language

**support staff:** other persons within the educational setting who support the learning and development of young children, e.g., nurses, social workers, diagnosticians, psychologists, secretaries, cooks, and custodians

**survival reflexes:** reflexes that are essential to sustaining life

**synapse:** the point of contact between nerve fibers

**syndrome:** a group of combined symptoms that characterize a physiological or psychological disorder

**syntax:** the grammar or structure of a particular language system

**teacher-as-learner:** the process by which teachers continue to learn from children, parents, other professionals, and the changing professional research and literature throughout their careers

**teacher-as-researcher:** the process by which early childhood professionals, through their perspective taking and reflecting-in-action, acquire and demonstrate the behaviors of a researcher

**telegraphic speech:** children's early speech which, like a telegram, includes only words necessary to understanding meaning

**television literacy:** understanding the specialized symbolic code conveyed through the medium of television

**temperament:** an individual's biologically based behavior style

**teratogens:** environmental factors, such as viruses and chemical substances, that can cause abnormalities in the developing embryo or fetus

**tertiary circular reactions:** reactions in children between 12 and 18 months of age that indicate that toddlers are experimenting to develop knowledge of the environment around them (Piaget's substage 5 in the sensorimotor period)

**theories:** ideas that are organized in a systematic manner based on observations or other kinds of evidence and are used to explain and predict the behaviors and development of young children, older children, and adults

**time sampling:** an observation technique for recording how often certain behaviors occur over time

**toilet learning:** a gradual maturational process in which the child gains control over elimination

**tools of the world:** the language and objects of the external world (Vygotsky)

**toxemia:** a disease of unknown cause that occurs in the last trimester of pregnancy and can cause death to both mother and child

**toxoplasmosis:** an infection that can be transmitted from cat droppings or raw meat to the mother and to the fetus or embryo via the placenta, causing birth disorders

**transactional model:** the give-and-take model of hereditary and environmental influences on growth and development

**transductive reasoning:** according to Piaget, reasoning that occurs in the preoperational stage and involves the young child's attention to the specifics of the immediate situation rather than all aspects of it

**transformation:** attending to all the states of an event from the beginning to in-between to final stage

**transitional object:** an object, usually a soft, cuddly item, to which a child becomes attached

**transivity:** the ability to seriate, or order, according to size; usually occurs in the period of concrete operational thought

**trimester:** the first, second, or third three months of pregnancy

**ultrasound:** a technique using sound frequencies that can detect structural disorders in the fetus and the approximate week of pregnancy

validity: the degree to which an instrument or a procedure measures what it is intended to measure

vernix caseosa: the oily covering that protects the skin of the fetus

vocables: early sound patterns used by infants that approximate words

washout effect: the decline of gains in intelligence and achievement scores several years after the termination of an intervention program for young children

word analysis skills: the ability to analyze words using a variety of strategies, such as rhyming words

zone of proximal development: according to Vygotsky, the level of concept development that is too difficult for the child to accomplish alone but can be achieved with the help of adults or more skilled children

zygote: the first cell resulting from the fertilization of the ovum by the sperm

# REFERENCES

**Abel-Hagg, I.** (Ed.) (1993). *Professional development schools: A directory of projects in the United States.* Washington, DC: Clinical Schools Clearing House.

**Abelman, R.** (1984). Children and TV: The ABC's of TV literacy. *Childhood Education, 60,* 200–205.

**Aboud, F.** (1988). *Children and prejudice.* Cambridge, MA: Basil Blackwell.

**Abramovitch, R., Corter, C., Pepler, D. J., & Stanhope, L.** (1986). Sibling and peer interaction: A final follow-up and a comparison. *Child Development, 57,* 217–229.

**Ackerman, B.** (1982). Contextual integration and utterance interpretation: The ability of children and adults to interpret sarcastic utterances. *Child Development, 53,* 1075–1083.

**Ackerman-Ross, S., & Khanna, P.** (1989). The relationship of high quality day care to middle-class 3-year-olds' language performance. *Early Childhood Research Quarterly, 4,* 97–116.

**Adair, R., Baucher, H., Philipp, B., Levenson, S., & Zuckerman, B.** (1991). Night waking during infancy: Role of parental presence at bedtime. *Pediatrics 87*(4), 500–504.

**Adamson, L. B., & Bakeman, R.** (1985). Affect and attention: Infants observed with mothers and peers. *Child Development, 56,* 582–593.

**Adler, R. P., Lesser, G. S., Meringoff, L. K., Robertson, T. S., Rossiter, J. R., & Ward, S.** (1980). *The effects of television advertising on children.* Lexington, MA: Heath.

**Ahmeduzzaman, M., & Roopnarine, J. L.** (1992). Sociodemographic factors, functioning styles, social support, and fathers' involvement with preschoolers in African-American families. *Journal of Marriage and the Family 54*(3) 699–707.

**Ainsworth, M. D. S.** (1962). The effects of maternal deprivation: A review of findings and controversy in the context of research strategy. In World Health Organization, *Deprivation of maternal care: A reassessment of its effects* (Public Health Paper No. 14, pp. 97–165). Geneva: Author.

**Ainsworth, M. D. S.** (1967). *Infancy in Uganda: Infant care and the growth of love.* Baltimore: The John Hopkins Press.

**Ainsworth, M. D. S.** (1973). The development of infant-mother attachment. In B. M. Caldwell & H. N. Ricciuti (Eds.), *Review of child development research* (Vol. 3, pp. 1–94). Chicago: University of Chicago Press.

**Ainsworth, M. D. S., Bell, S. M., & Stayton, D. J.** (1974). Infant-mother attachment and social development: Socialization as a product of reciprocal responsiveness to signals. In M. P. M. Richards (Ed.), *The integration of the child into a social world* (pp. 99–135). London: Cambridge University Press.

**Ainsworth, M. D. S., Blehar, M. C., Waters, E., & Wall, S.** (1978). *Patterns of attachment: A psychological study of strange situations.* Hillsdale, NJ: Erlbaum.

**Ainsworth, M. D. S., & Wittig, B. A.** (1969). Attachment and the exploratory behavior of one-year-olds in a strange situation. In B. M. Foss (Ed.), *Determinants of infant behavior* (Vol. 4, pp. 113–136). London: Methuen.

**American Academy of Pediatrics.** (1986). *Report of the Committee on Infectious Diseases* (20th ed.). Elk Grove Village, IL: Author.

**American Academy of Pediatrics.** (1987). Neonatal anesthesia. *Pediatrics, 80,* 446.

**American Academy of Pediatrics.** (1993). *Pediatric nutrition handbook.* Elk Grove Village, IL: Author.

American Academy of Pediatrics. (1994). The role of the pediatrician in violence prevention. *Pediatrics, 94*(4) (Supp., part 2 of 2), 577–651.

American Academy of Pediatrics Committee on Genetics. (1994). Prenatal genetic diagnosis for pediatricians. *Pediatrics 93*(6), 1010–1015.

American Academy of Pediatrics, Committee on Nutrition. (1979). Commentary on breast feeding and infant formulas, including proposed standards for formulas. In American Academy of Pediatrics, *Nutrition handbook* (pp. 119–138). Evanston, IL: Author.

American Academy of Pediatrics Committee on Nutrition. (1983). Toward a prudent diet for children. *Pediatrics, 77*(1), 78–80.

American Academy of Pediatrics Committee on Nutrition. (1986). Prudent life style for children: Dietary fat and cholesterol. *Pediatrics, 78*(1), 521–525.

American Academy of Pediatrics Committee on Nutrition. (1992). Statement on cholesterol. *Pediatrics, 90*(3), 469–473.

American Academy of Pediatrics Task Force on Circumcision. (1989). Report of the Task Force on Circumcision. *Pediatrics, 84*(2), 388–391.

American Psychological Association, Committee on Ethical Standards in Psychological Research. (1972, May). Ethical standards for research with human subjects. *APA Monitor*, pp. I–XIX.

American Psychological Association. (1985). *Standards for educational and psychological testing.* Washington, DC: Author.

American Public Health Association and American Academy of Pediatrics. (1992). *Caring for our children: National health and safety performance standards: Guidelines for out-of-home child care.* Washington, DC, and Elk Grove Village, IL: Author.

Ames, L. B., Gillespie, C., Haines, J., & Ilg, F. L. (1979). *The Gesell Institute's child from one to six.* New York: Harper and Row.

Ammann, A. J. (1994). Human immunodeficiency virus infection / AIDS in children: The next decade. *Pediatrics, 93* (8), 930–935.

Anastasi, A. (1958). Heredity, environment, and the question: How? *Psychological Review, 65*(4), 197–208.

Anderson, C.R. (Ed.). (1993). *Voices of change: A report of the clinical school project.* Washington, DC: Ford Foundation.

Anderson, D. R., & Smith, R. (1984). Young children's TV viewing: The problem of cognitive continuity. In F. J. Morrison & D. P. Keating (Eds.), *Applied developmental psychology* (Vol. 1, pp. 115–163). Orlando, FL: Academic Press.

Andrews, P. (1981). Children and families: Some basic cultural needs. *Dimensions, 10,* 149–151.

Anselmo, S. (1987). *Early childhood development: Prenatal through age eight.* Columbus, OH: Merrill.

Anthony, J., & Benedek, T. (Eds.). (1975). *Depression and human existence.* Boston: Little, Brown.

Apgar, V. A. (1953). A proposal for a new method of evaluation in the newborn infant. *Current Research in Anesthesia and Analgesia, 32,* 260–267.

Arend, R., Gove, F. L., & Stroufe, L. A. (1979). Continuity of individual adaptation from infancy to kindergarten: A predictive study of ego-resiliency and curiosity in preschoolers. *Child Development, 50,* 950–959.

Armstrong, T. (1994). *Multiple intelligences in the classroom.* Alexandria, VA: Association for Supervision and Curriculum Development.

Arnold, D. H., Lonigan, C. J., Whitehurst, G. J., & Epstein, J. N. (1994). Accelerating language development through picture book reading: Replication and extension to a videotape training format. *Journal of Educational Psychology, 86*(2), 235–243.

Aronson, S. (1991). *Health and safety in child care.* New York: HarperCollins.

Asher, S. R., Renshaw, P. D., & Hymel, S. (1982). Peer relations and the development of social skills. In S. G. Moore & C. R. Cooper (Eds.), *The young child: Reviews of research* (Vol. 3, pp. 137–158). Washington, DC: National Association for the Education of Young Children.

Association for Childhood Education International Exchange. (1990). Breastfeeding safeguards infants' health. Synopsis of findings from a UNICEF and WHO international conference, Breastfeeding in the 1990s: A Global Initiative, Florence, Italy.

Au, K. H., & Kowakami, A.J. (1991). Culture and ownership: Schooling minority students. *Childhood Education, 67*(5), 280–284.

Au, K. H., & Mason, J. M. (1983). Cultural congruence in classroom participation structures: Achieving a balance of rights. *Discourse Processes, 6*(2), 145–167.

Bailey, D. B., Jr., & Wolery, M. (1989). *Assessing infants and preschoolers with handicaps.* Columbus, OH: Merrill.

Baillargeon, R. (1987). Object permanence in 3 1/2 and 4 1/2 month old infants. *Developmental Psychology, 23*(5), 655–664.

Baker, G. C. (1994). Teaching children to respect diversity. *Childhood Education, 71*(1), 33–35.

Ball, S., & Bogatz, G. A. (1972). Summative research of *Sesame Street:* Implications for the study of preschool children. In A. D. Pick (Ed.), *Minnesota symposium on child psychology* (Vol. 6, pp. 3–17). Minneapolis: University of Minnesota Press.

Ball, S., & Bogatz, G. A. (1973). *Reading with television: An evaluation of Electric Company.* Princeton, NJ: Educational Testing Service.

Baltes, P. B., Dittman-Kohli, F., & Dixon, R. A. (1984). New perspectives on the development of intelligence in adulthood: Toward a dual-process conception and a model of selective optimization with compensation. In P. B. Baltes & O. G. Brim, Jr. (Eds.), *Life-span development and behavior* (Vol. 6, pp. 33–76). New York: Academic Press.

Bandura, A. (1965). Influence of models' reinforcement contingencies on the acquisition for imitative responses. *Journal of Personality and Social Psychology, 1,* 587–595.

Bandura, A. (1977). *Social learning theory*. Englewood Cliffs, NJ: Prentice-Hall.

Bandura, A. (1986). *Social foundation of thoughts and actions: A social cognitive theory*. Englewood Cliffs, NJ: Prentice Hall.

Bank, S. P., & Kahn, M. D. (1982a). Intense sibling loyalties. In M. E. Lamb & B. Sutton-Smith (Eds.), *Sibling relationships: Their nature and significance across the life span* (pp. 251–284). Hillsdale, NJ: Erlbaum.

Bank, S. P., & Kahn, M. D. (1982b). *The sibling bond*. New York: Basic Books.

Barbero, G. J., & Shaheen, E. (1967). Environmental failure to thrive: A clinical view. *Journal of Pediatrics, 71,* 639–644.

Barness, L. A. (Ed.). (1993). *Pediatric nutrition handbook*. Elk Grove Village, IL: American Academy of Pediatrics Committee on Nutrition.

Baroody, A. J. (1984). The case of Felicia: A young child's strategies for reducing memory demands during mental addition. *Cognition and Instruction, 1,* 109–116.

Bar-Tal, D., Raviv, A., & Goldberg, M. (1982). Helping behavior among children: An observational study. *Child Development, 53,* 396–402.

Barth, J. M., & Parke, R. D. (1993). Parent-child relationship influences on children's transition to school. *Merrill-Palmer Quarterly, 39*(2), 173–195.

Baskett, L. M. (1984). Ordinal position differences in children's family interactions. *Developmental Psychology, 20,* 1026–1031.

Baskett, L. M., & Johnson, S. M. (1982). The young child's interaction with parents versus siblings: A behavioral analysis. *Child Development, 53,* 643–650.

Basow, S. A. (1992). *Gender stereotypes and roles* (3rd ed.). Pacific Grove, CA: Brooks/Cole.

Baumrind, D. (1967). Child care practices anteceding three patterns of preschool behavior. *Genetic Psychology Monographs, 75,* 43–88.

Baumrind, D. (1971). Current patterns of parental authority. *Developmental Psychology Monographs, 4* (No. 1, Pt. 2).

Baumrind, D. (1972). Socialization and instrumental competence in young children. In W. W. Hartup (Ed.), *The young child: Reviews of research* (Vol. 2, pp. 202–224). Washington, DC: National Association for the Education of Young Children.

Baumrind, D. (1991). The influence of parenting style on adolescent competence and substance use. *Journal of Early Adolescence 1,* 56–95.

Bayley, N. (1969). *Bayley scales of infant development*. New York: Psychological Corporation.

Beaty, J. J. (1990). *Observing the development of the young child* (2nd ed.). Columbus, OH: Merrill.

Bebko, J. M., Burke, L., Craven, J., & Sarlo, N. (1992). The importance of motor activity in sensorimotor development: A perspective from children with physical handicaps. *Human Development, 35*(4), 226–240.

Beddard, J. R., & Chi, M. T. H. (1992). Expertise. *Current Directions in Psychological Science, 1,* 135–139.

Behrman, R. E., & Vaughan, V. C. (1987). *Nelson textbook of pediatrics* (13th ed.). Philadelphia: Saunders.

Beilin, H. (1980). Piaget's theory: Refinement, revision, or rejection? In R. Kluwe & H. Spada (Eds.), *Developmental models of thinking* (pp. 245–261). New York: Academic Press.

Bell, M. J. (1989). Peer leadership and its influence on the outdoor activities of preschool play groups (Doctoral dissertation, The University of Texas at Austin). *Dissertation Abstracts International, 50,* 1554A.

Bell, R. Q., & Chapman, M. (1986). Child effects in studies using experimental or brief longitudinal approaches to socialization. *Developmental Psychology, 22,* 1353–1354.

Bell, S. M., & Ainsworth, M. D. S. (1972). Infant crying and maternal responsiveness. *Child Development, 43,* 1171–1190.

Belsky, J. (1988). The effects of infant day care reconsidered. *Early Childhood Research Quarterly, 3,* 235–272.

Belsky, J., & Rovine, M. (1988). Non-maternal care in the first year of life and the security of infant-parent attachment. *Child Development, 59*(1), 157–167.

Bench, J. (1978). The auditory response. In V. Stave (Ed.), *Perinatal physiology*. New York: Plenum Press.

Benn, R. (1985, April). *Factors associated with security of attachment in dual career families*. Paper presented at the biennial meeting of the Society for Research in Child Development, Toronto.

Ben-Zeev, S. (1977). The influence of bilingualism on the cognitive strategy and cognitive development. *Child Development, 48,* 1009–1018.

Berg, W. K., Adkinson, C. D., & Strock, B. D. (1973). Duration and frequency of periods of alertness in neonates. *Developmental Psychology, 9,* 434.

Berger, E. (1991). *Parents as partners in education: The school and home working together* (3rd ed.). Columbus, OH: Merrill.

Bergstrom, J. M. (1984). *School's out—now what: Creative choices for your children*. Berkeley, CA: Ten Speed Press.

Berk, L. E. (1984). Development of private speech among low-income Appalachian children. *Developmental Psychology, 20,* 271–286.

Berk, L. E. (1985). Why children talk to themselves. *Young Children, 40*(5), 46–52.

Berk, L. E. (1986a). Relationship of elementary school children's private speech to behavioral accompaniment to task, attention and performance. *Developmental Psychology, 22,* 671–680.

Berk, L. E. (1986b, May). Private speech: Learning out loud. *Psychology Today*, pp. 34–42.

Berk, L. E. (1989). *Child Development*. Boston: Allyn & Bacon.

Berk, L.E. (1994). *Infants and children: Prenatal through middle childhood*. Boston: Allyn & Bacon.

Berner, E. S. (1971). *Private speech and role-taking abilities in preschool children*. Unpublished doctoral dissertation, Harvard University.

Bernstein, B. (1972). A critique of the concept of compensatory education. In C. B. Cazden, V. P. John, & D. Hymes (Eds.), *Functions of language in the classroom* (pp. 135–151). New York: Teachers College Press.

Berreuta-Clement, J. R., Schweinhart, L. J., Barnett, W. S., Epstein, A. S., & Weikart, D. P. (1984). Changed lives: The effects of the Perry Preschool Program on youths through age 19. *Monographs of the High/Scope Educational Research Foundation, 8*. Ypsilanti, MI: High/Scope Press.

Bever, T. G. (1970). The cognitive basis for linguistic structure. In J. R. Hayes (Ed.), *Cognition and the development of language* (pp. 279–362). New York: Wiley.

Bialystok, E. (1986). Factors in the growth of linguistic awareness. *Child Development, 57*, 498–510.

Bijou, S., & Baer, D. (1961). *Child development: Vol. 1. A systematic and empirical theory*. Englewood Cliffs, NJ: Prentice-Hall.

Birch, L. L., Johnson, S. L., Graciela, A., Peters, J. C., & Schulte, M. C. (1991a). The variability of young children's energy intake. *The New England Journal of Medicine, 324*(4), 232–235.

Birch, L. L., Johnson, S L., Graciela, A., Peters, J. C., & Schulte, M.C. (June, 1991b). (to the editor). *The New England Journal of Medicine, 324*(25), 1817.

Bissex, G. (1980). *GYNS at work: A child learns to read and write*. Cambridge, MA: Harvard University Press.

Black, J. K. (1981). Are young children really egocentric? *Young Children, 36* (6), 51–55.

Black, J. K. (1984). Beginning readers and beginning teachers. In J. F. Baumann & D. D. Johnson (Eds.), *Reading instruction and the beginning teacher* (pp. 95–120). Minneapolis: Burgess.

Black, J. K., & Martin, R. (1982). Children's concepts about writing at home and school. In J. A. Niles & L. A. Harris (Eds.), *New inquiries in reading research and instruction* (pp. 300–304). Rochester, NY: National Reading Conference.

Black, J. K., & Puckett, M. (1987). Informing others about developmentally appropriate practice. In S. Bredekamp (Ed.), *Developmentally appropriate practice in early childhood programs serving children from birth through age 8* (pp. 83–87). Washington, DC: National Association for the Education of Young Children.

Block, J. H. (1973). Conceptions of sex-role: Some cross-cultural and longitudinal perspectives. *American Psychologist, 28*, 512–526.

Block, J. H. (1983). Differential premises arising from differential socialization of the sexes: Some conjectures. *Child Development, 54*, 1335–1354.

Bloom, B. (1964). *Stability and change in human characteristics*. New York: Wiley.

Bloom, L. (1970). *Form and function in emerging grammars*. Cambridge, MA: MIT Press.

Bloom, L. (1975). Language development review. In F. D. Horowitz (Ed.), *Review of child development research* (Vol. 4). Chicago: University of Chicago Press.

Blosch, N., Tabachnick, B. R., & Espinosa-Dulanto, D. (1994). Teacher perspectives on the strengths and achievements of young children: Relationship to ethnicity, language, gender and class. In B. L. Mallory & R. S. New (Eds.), *Diversity and developmentally appropriate practices* (pp. 223–249). New York: Teachers College Press.

Boggiano, A. K., Klinger, C. A., & Main, D. S. (1986). Enhancing interest in peer interaction: A developmental analysis. *Child Development, 57*, 852–861.

Borgh, H., & Dickson, W. P. (1986). Two preschoolers sharing one microcomputer: Creating pro-social behavior with hardware and software. In P. Campbell & G. Fein (Eds.), *Young children and microcomputers* (pp. 37–44). Englewood Cliffs, NJ: Prentice-Hall.

Borich, G. D. (1994). *Observation skills for effective teaching* (2nd ed.). New York: Merrill/Macmillan.

Borke, H. (1983). Piaget's mountains revisited: Changes in the egocentric landscape. In M. Donaldson, R. Grieve, & C. Pratt (Eds.), *Early childhood development and education: Readings in psychology* (pp. 254–259). New York: Guilford Press.

Bornstein, M. H. (1984). A descriptive taxonomy of psychological categories used by infants. In C. Sophian (Ed.), *Origins of cognitive skills. The eighteenth annual Carnegie Symposium on Cognition* (pp. 313–338). Hillsdale, NJ: Erlbaum.

Bornstein, M. H. (1985). Human infant color vision and color perception. *Infant Behavior and Development, 8*, 109–113.

Bornstein, M. H. (1988). Perceptual development across the life cycle. In M. H. Bornstein & M. E. Lamb (Eds.), *Developmental psychology: An advanced textbook* (2nd ed., pp. 151-204). Hillsdale, NJ: Erlbaum.

Bornstein, M. H., & Lamb, M. E. (1992). *Development in infancy: An introduction* (3rd ed.). New York: McGraw-Hill.

Bower, T. G. R. (1982). *Development in infancy* (2nd ed.). New York: Freeman.

Bowerman, M. (1979). The acquisition of complex sentences. In P. Fletcher & M. Garman (Eds.), *Language acquisition* (pp. 285–305). Cambridge, England: Cambridge University Press.

Bowlby, J. (1969/1982). *Attachment and loss: Vol. 1. Attachment* (2nd ed.). New York: Basic Books.

Bowlby, J. (1973). *Attachment and loss: Vol. 2. Separation: Anxiety and anger*. New York: Basic Books.

Bowlby, J. (1980). *Attachment and loss: Vol. 3. Loss: Sadness and depression*. New York: Basic Books.

Bowman, B. T., & Stott, F. M. (1994). Understanding development in a cultural context: The challenge for teachers. In B. L. Mallory & R. S. New (Eds.), *Diversity and developmentally appropriate practices*. New York: Teachers College Press.

Bradshaw, J. (1989). *Hemispheric specialization and psychological function*. New York: Wiley.

Brainerd, C. J. (1978). *Piaget's theory of intelligence.* Englewood Cliffs, NJ: Prentice-Hall.

Brainerd, C. J., & Brainerd, S. H. (1972). Order of acquisition of number and liquid quantity conservation. *Child Development, 43,* 1401–1405.

Brazelton, T. B. (1973). *Neonatal Behavioral Assessment Scale* (Clinics in Developmental Medicine No. 50, Spastics International Medical Publication). Philadelphia: Lippincott.

Brazelton, T. B. (1984). *To listen to a child: Understanding the normal problems of growing up.* Reading, MA: Addison-Wesley.

Brazelton, T. B., Koslowski, B., & Tronick, E. (1971). Neonatal behavior among urban Zambians and Americans. *Journal of Child Psychiatry, 15,* 97–107.

Brazelton, T. B. (1987). *Working and caring.* Menlo Park, CA: Addison-Wesley.

Brazelton, T. B., & Yogman, M. W. (Eds.). (1986). *Affective development in infancy.* Norwood, NJ: Ablex.

Brecht, M. C. (1989). The tragedy of infant mortality. *Nursing Outlook, 37,* (18).

Bredekamp, S. (Ed.). (1987). *Developmentally appropriate practice in early childhood programs serving children from birth through age 8* (Exp. ed). Washington, DC: National Association for the Education of Young Children.

Bredekamp, S. (Ed.). (1991). *Accreditation criteria and procedures of the National Academy of Early Childhood Programs.* Washington, DC: National Association for the Education of Young Children.

Bredekamp, S., & Rosegrant, T. (Eds.). (1992). *Reaching potentials: Appropriate curriculum and assessment for young children* (Vol. 1). Washington, DC: National Association for the Education of Young Children.

Bredekamp, S., & Shepard, L. (1989). How best to protect children from inappropriate school expectations, practices, and policies. *Young Children, 44* (3), 14–24.

Bretherton, I., & Walters, E. (Eds.). (1985). Growing points in attachment theory and research. *Monographs of the Society for Research in Child Development, 50* (1–2, Serial No. 209).

Bronfenbrenner, U. (1970, November). *Who cares for America's children?* Keynote address delivered at the Annual Conference of the National Association for the Education of Young Children, Boston.

Bronfenbrenner, U. (1977). Toward an experimental ecology of human development. *American Psychologist, 32,* 513–531.

Bronfenbrenner, U. (1979). *The ecology of human development.* Cambridge, MA: Harvard University Press.

Bronfenbrenner, U. (1986). Ecology of the family as a context for human development: Research perspectives. *Developmental Psychology, 22,* 723–742.

Brooks-Gunn, J., & Lewis, M. (1982). The development of self-knowledge. In C. Kropp & J. Krakow (Eds.), *The child: Development in a social context* (pp. 333–387). Reading, MA: Addison-Wesley.

Brooks-Gunn, J., & Matthews, W. S. (1979). *He and she: How children develop their sex-role identity.* Englewood Cliffs, NJ: Prentice-Hall.

Brooks-Gunn, J., & Petersen, A. C. (1992). Studying the emergence of depression and depressive symptoms in adolescence. *Journal of Youth and Adolescence, 22,* 115–120.

Brown, A. L., Bransford, J. D., Ferrara, R. A., & Campione, J. C. (1983). Learning, remembering, and understanding. In J. H. Flavell & E. M. Markman (Eds.), *Handbook of child psychology: Vol. 3. Cognitive development* (4th ed., pp. 75–166). New York: Wiley.

Brown, B.B., Lohn, M. J., & McClenghan, E. L. (1986). Early adolescents' perceptions of peer pressure. *Journal of Early Adolescence, 6,* 139–154.

Brown, D. (1979). *Mother tongue to English: The young child in the multicultural school.* New York: Cambridge University Press.

Brown, R. (1973). *A first language: The early stages.* Cambridge, MA: Harvard University Press.

Brown, R. & Fraser, C. (1963). The acquisition of syntax. In C. N. Cofer & B. S. Musgrave (Eds.), *Verbal behavior and learning: Problems and processes* (pp. 158–209). New York: McGraw-Hill.

Bruce, B., Michaels, S., & Watson-Gegeo, K. (1985). How computers can change the writing process. *Language Arts, 62,* 143–149.

Bruner, J. (1975). The ontogenesis of speech acts. *Journal of Child Language, 3,* 1–19.

Bruner, J. (1983). The acquistion of pragmatic commitments. In R. M. Golinkoff (Ed.), *The transition from prelinguistic to linguistic communication* (pp. 27–42). Hillsdale, NJ: Erlbaum.

Bryan, J. H., Sonnefeld, J., & Greenberg, F. (1981). Children's and parents' views about integration tactics. *Learning Disability Quarterly, 4,* 170–179.

Bryan, T. H., & Bryan, J. H. (1986). *Understanding learning disabilities.* Palo Alto, CA: Mayfield.

Bryant, B. (1982). Sibling relationships in middle childhood. In M. E. Lamb & B. Sutton-Smith (Eds.), *Sibling relationships: Their nature and significance across the life span* (pp. 87–122). Hillsdale, NJ: Erlbaum.

Bryant, B. K. (1985). The neighborhood walk: Sources of support in middle childhood. *Monographs of the Society for Research in Child Development, 50* (3, Serial No. 210).

Bullock, M., & Gelman, R. (1979). Preschool children's assumptions about cause and effect: Temporal ordering. *Child Development, 50,* 89–96.

Burgess, D. M., & Streissgoth, A. P. (1992). Fetal alcohol syndrome and fetal alcohol effects: Principles for educators. *Phi Delta Kappan,(1),* 24–29.

Burns, S., Goin, L., & Donlon, J. (1990). A computer in my room. *Young Children, 45* (2), 62–67.

Campbell, P., & Fein, G. (Eds.). (1986). *Young children and microcomputers.* Englewood Cliffs, NJ: Prentice Hall.

Campos, J. J., Barrett, K. C., Lamb, M. L., Goldsmith, H. H., & Stenberg, C. (1983). Socioemotional development. In M. M. Haith & J. J. Campos (Eds.), *Infancy and developmental psychobiology* (pp. 783–915). New York: Wiley.

Campos, J. J., & Stenberg, C. R. (1981). Perception appraisal and emotion: The onset of social referencing. In M. E. Lamb & L. R. Sherrod (Eds.), *Infant social cognition: Empirical and theoretical considerations* (pp. 273–314). Hillsdale, NJ: Erlbaum.

Carey, S. (1978). The child as word learner. In M. Halle, J. Bresnan, & G. Miller (Eds.), *Linguistic theory and psychological reality* (pp. 264–293). Cambridge, MA: MIT Press.

Carey, S. (1986). Are children fundamentally different kinds of thinkers and learners than adults? In S. F. Chipman, J. W. Segal, & R. Glaser (Eds.), *Thinking and learning skills: Current research and open questions* (Vol. 2, pp. 485–517). Hillsdale, NJ: Erlbaum.

Carle, E. (1979). *The very hungry caterpillar.* New York: Collins.

Carlson-Paige, N., & Levin, D. E. (1985). *Helping children understand peace, war, and the nuclear threat.* Washington, DC: National Association for the Education of Young Children.

Carnegie Corporation. (1994). *Starting points: Meeting the needs of our youngest children: The report of the Carnegie Task Force on Meeting the Needs of Young Children.* New York: Author.

Carnegie Task Force on Teaching as a Profession. (1986). *A nation prepared: Teachers for the 21st century.* New York: Carnegie Corporation.

Caron, A. J., Caron, R. F., & MacLean, D. (1988). Infant discrimination of naturalistic emotional expressions: The role of face and voice. *Child Development, 59,* 604–616.

Carpenter, T. P., Carey, D. A., & Kouba, V. L. (1990). Developing concepts of operations: A problem-solving approach. In J. Payne (Ed.), *Learning mathematics in early childhood.* Reston, VA: National Council of Teachers of Mathematics.

Carpenter, T. P., Fennema, E., Peterson, P. L., & Carey, D. (1988). Teacher's pedagogical content knowledge in mathematics. *Journal of Research in Mathematics Education, 19,* 345–357.

Carpenter, T. P., Fennema, E., Peterson, P. L., Chiang, C. P., & Loef, M. (1989). Using knowledge of children's mathematical thinking in classroom teaching: An experimental study. *American Educational Research Journal, 26,* 499–531.

Carpenter, T., & Fennema, E. (1993). *Journal of Mathematics Education.* Cited by D. Viadero and P. West (Column authors), "Curriculum." In *Education Week,* January 19, 1994, p. 6.

Case, R. (1978). Intellectual development from birth to adulthood: A neo-Piagetian approach. In R. S. Siegler (Ed.), *Children's thinking: What develops?* (pp. 37–71). Hillsdale, NJ: Erlbaum.

Case, R. (1984). The process of stage transition: A neo-Piagetian view. In R. J. Sternberg (Ed.), *Mechanisms of cognitive development* (pp. 19–44). New York: Freeman.

Case, R. (1985). *Intellectual development: A systematic reinterpretation.* New York: Freeman.

Case, R. (1987). Neo-Piagetian theory: Retrospect and prospect. In A. Demetriou (Ed.), *The neo-Piagetian theories of cognitive development. Toward an integration.* Amsterdam: North Holland.

Case, R. (1992). *The mind's staircase: Exploring the conceptual underpinnings of children's thought and knowledge.* Hillsdale, NJ: Erlbaum.

Case, R., & Khanna, F. (1981). The missing links: Stages in children's progression from sensorimotor to logical thought. In K. W. Fischer (Ed.), *Cognitive development* (New Directions for Child Development No. 12, pp. 21–32). San Francisco: Jossey-Bass.

Case, R., Marini, Z., McKeough, A., Dennis, S., & Goldberg, J. (1986). Horizontal structure in middle childhood: Cross domain parallels in the course of cognitive growth. In I. Levin (Ed.), *Stage and structure: Reopening the debate* (pp. 1–39). Norwood, NJ: Ablex.

Cassidy, J., & Berlin, L. J. (1994). The insecure/ambivalent patterns of attachments: Theory & research. *Child Development, 65*(4), 971–991.

Cauley, K., & Tyler, B. (1989). The relationship of self-concept to prosocial behavior in children. *Early Childhood Research Quarterly, 4,* 51–60.

Ceci, S. J., & Bronfenbrenner, U. (1985). "Don't forget to take the cupcakes out of the oven": Prospective memory, strategic time monitoring and context. *Child Development, 56*(1), 152–164.

Center for Disease Control. (1988). Measles in HIV-infected children in the United States. *MMWR, 37,* 185–186.

Center for Disease Control. (1992). Retrospective assessment of vaccination coverage among school-aged children—selected United States cities, 1991. *MMWR, 41,* 103–107.

Chance, N. (1984). Growing up in a Chinese village. *Natural History, 93,* 78–81.

Chand, I. P., Crider, D. M., & Willits, F. K. (1975). Parent-youth disagreement as perceived by youth: A longitudinal study. *Youth and Society, 6,* 365–375.

Charlesworth, R. (1989). "Behind" before they start? Deciding how to deal with the risk of kindergarten "failure." *Young Children, 44* (3), 5–13.

Charlesworth, R. & Hartup, W.W. (1967). Positive social reinforcement in the nursery school peer group. *Child Development, 38,* 993–1002.

Chess, S. (1967). Temperament in the normal infant. In B. Straub & J. Hellmuth (Eds.), *Exceptional infant: Vol. 1. The normal infant* (pp. 143–162). Seattle, WA: Special Child Publications.

Chess, S., & Thomas, A. (1987). *Origins and evolution of behavior disorders from infancy to early adult life.* Cambridge, MA: Harvard University Press.

**Chi, M. T. H.** (1978). Knowledge structures and memory development. In R. S. Siegler (Ed.), *Children's thinking: What develops?* (pp. 73–96). Hillsdale, NJ: Erlbaum.

**Chi, M. T. H., & Klahr, D.** (1975). Span and rate of apprehension in children and adults. *Journal of Experimental Child Psychology, 19*, 434–439.

**Chi, M. T. H., & Koeske, R. D.** (1983). Network representation of a child's dinosaur knowledge. *Developmental Psychology, 19*, 29–39.

**Child Abuse Prevention and Treatment Act of 1975.** 42, U. S. Code 501.

**Children's Defense Fund.** (1989). *A vision for America's future: An agenda for the 1990's: A children's defense budget.* Washington, DC: Author.

**Children's Defense Fund.** (1994a). States bolster pre-K initiatives. *Children's Defense Fund Reports, 15*(10), 1–2.

**Children's Defense Fund.** (1994b). *The State of America's Children: Yearbook 1994.* Washington, DC: Author.

**Children's Educational Television Act of 1990,** U. S. Code 1988, Title 47, Section 394, 397, October 18, 1990, (P.L. 101–437), 104 Stat. 996 Title 2.

**Childs, C. P., & Greenfield, P. M.** (1980). Informal modes of learning and teaching: The case of Zinacanteco learning. In N. Warren (Ed.), *Studies in cross-cultural psychology* (Vol. 2). New York: Academic Press.

**Chilman, C. S.** (1966). *Your child from 6 to 12.* Washington, DC: Children's Bureau, U.S. Department of Health, Education, and Welfare.

**Chomsky, C.** (1968). *Language and mind.* San Diego, CA: Harcourt Brace Jovanovich.

**Chomsky, C.** (1969). *The acquisition of syntax in children from five to ten.* Cambridge, MA: MIT Press.

**Chomsky, C.** (1971). Write first, read later. *Childhood Education, 47*, 296–299.

**Chomsky, N.** (1980). *Rules and representations.* New York: Columbia University Press.

**Christian, J. L., & Gregor, J. L.** (1988). *Nutrition for living* (2nd ed.). Menlo Park, CA: Benjamin/Cummings.

**Cicerelli, V. G., Evans, J. W., & Schiller, J. S.** (1969). *The impact of Head Start: An evaluation on the effects of Head Start on children's cognitive and affective development* (Vols. 1–2). Athens, OH: Westinghouse Learning Corporation and Ohio University.

**Cicourel, A.** (1972). Cross-modal communication: The representational context of sociolinguistic information processing. In R. Shuy (Ed.), *Monograph Series on Language and Linguistics: Twenty-third Annual Round Table* (pp. 187–222). Washington, DC: Georgetown University Press.

**Clark, E. V.** (1978). Strategies for communicating. *Child Development, 49*, 977–987.

**Clark, E. V.** (1983). Meanings and concepts. In J. H. Flavell & E. M. Markman (Eds.), *Handbook of child psychology: Vol. 3. Cognitive development* (4th ed., pp. 787–840). New York: Wiley.

**Clark, G.** (Asst. Ed.). (1994). Childhood tuberculosis cases escalate. *American Academy of Pediatrics News, 10*(5), 1 8, 9, 11.

**Clark, M. M.** (1976). *Young fluent readers.* London: Heinemann.

**Clark, R., & Clark, E.** (1977). *Psychology and language.* New York: Harcourt Brace Jovanovich.

**Clarke-Stewart, K. A.** (1973). Interactions between mothers and their young children: Characteristics and consequences. *Monographs of the Society for Research in Child Development, 38* (6–7, Serial No. 153).

**Clay, M.** (1975). *What did I write?* Auckland, New Zealand: Heinemann.

**Clay, M.** (1979). *Sand (concepts about print test).* Auckland, New Zealand: Heinemann.

**Clements, D.** (1985, April). *Implications of media research for the instructional application of computers with young children.* Paper presented at the annual meeting of the American Educational Research Association.

**Clyman, R. B., Emde, R. N., Kempe, J. E., & Harmon, R. J.** (1986). Social referencing and social looking among 12-month-old infants. In T. B. Brazelton & M. W. Yogman (Eds.), *Affective development in infancy* (pp. 75–94). Norwood, NJ: Ablex.

**Coates, B., Pusser, H. E., & Goodman, I.** (1976). The influence of "Sesame Street" and "Mister Rogers' Neighborhood" on children's social behavior in the preschool. *Child Development, 47*, 138–144.

**Cohen, M.** (1967). *Will I have a friend?* New York: Macmillan.

**Cole, M., & Cole, S.** (1989, 1993). *The development of children.* New York: Freeman.

**Coleman, J.** (1980). Friendship and the peer group in adolescence. In J. Adelson (Ed.), *Handbook of adolescent psychology* (pp. 408–431). New York: Wiley.

**Collins, W. A.** (1983). Children's processing of television content: Implications for prevention of negative effects. *Prevention in Human Services, 2*, 53–56.

**Collins, W. A., Wellman, H., Keniston, A. H., & Westby, S. D.** (1978). Age-related aspects of comprehension and inference from a televised dramatic narrative. *Child Development, 49*, 389–399.

**Colon, P. A., & Colon, A. R.** (1989). The health of America's children. In F. J. Macchiarola & A. Gartner (Eds.), *Caring for America's children. Proceedings of the Academy of Political Science, 37* (Vol. 2, pp. 45–57). New York: The Academy of Political Science.

**Comer, J. P., & Poussant, A. F.** (1992). *Raising black children.* New York: Penguin Books.

**Corder-Bolz, C. R.** (1980). Mediation: The role of significant others. *Journal of Communication, 30*, 106–118.

**Cornell, E. H., & McDonnell, P. M.** (1986). Infants' acuity at twenty feet. *Investigative Ophthalmology and Visual Science, 27*, 1417–1420.

Corsaro, W. A. (1985). *Friendship and peer culture in the early years.* Norwood, NJ: Ablex.

Council for Early Childhood Professional Recognition. (1992). *Child Development Associate assessment and competency standards.* Washington, DC: Author.

Craig, S. E. (1992). The educational needs of children living with violence. *Phi Delta Kappan, 74*(1), 67–71.

Craik, F. I. M., & Tulving, E. (1975). Depth processing and the retention of words in episodic memory. *Journal of Experimental Psychology: General, 104*, 268–294.

Crain-Thoreson, C., & Dale, P. S. (1992). Do early talkers become early readers? Linguistic precocity, preschool language and emergent literacy. *Developmental Psychology, 28*(3), 421–429.

Cratty, B. J. (1986). *Perceptual and motor development in infants and children.* Englewood Cliffs, NJ: Prentice Hall.

Cross, T. G. (1978). Mother's speech and its association with rate of linguistic development in young children. In N. Waterson & C. E. Snow (Eds.), *The development of communication* (pp. 199–216). New York: Wiley.

Cunningham, L. (1985). Leaders and leadership: 1985 and beyond. *Phi Delta Kappan, 67*, 17–20.

Curry, N., & Johnson, C. (1990). *Beyond self-esteem: Developing a genuine sense of human value.* Washington, DC: National Association for the Education of Young Children.

Damon, W. (1983). *Social and personality development.* New York: Norton.

Damon, W. (1988). *The moral child: Nurturing children's natural moral growth.* New York: The Free Press.

Damon, W., & Hart, D. (1982). The development of self-understanding from infancy through adolescence. *Child Development, 53*, 841–864.

Danziger, S. K., & Danziger, S. (1993). Child poverty and public policy: Toward a comprehensive anti-poverty agenda. *Daedalus, 122*, 57–58.

Darwin, C. (1936). *The origin of species.* New York: Modern Library. (Original work published 1859)

Dasen, E. P., & Heron, A. (1981). Cross-cultural tests of Piaget's theory. In H. C. Triandis & A. Heron (Eds.), *Handbook of cross-cultural psychology: Developmental psychology* (Vol. 4). Boston: Allyn & Bacon.

Davis, C. M. (1938). The self-selection of diet experiment: Its significance for feeding in the home. *Ohio State Medical Journal, 34*, 862.

Davis, D. L. (Ed.). (1989). *Biological markers in reproductive and developmental toxicity.* Washington, DC: National Academy of Science Press.

Davis, R. (1990). *A comparison of the reading and writing performance of children in a whole language pre-first grade class and a modified traditional first grade class.* Unpublished doctoral dissertation, University of North Texas, Denton.

Dean, A. L. (1994). Instinctual affective focus in the internalization process: Contributions of Hans Loewald. *Human Development, 37*, 42–57.

DeBoysson-Bardies, B., Sagart, L., & Durand, C. (1984). Discernible differences in the babbling of infants according to target language. *Journal of Child Language, 11*, 1–16.

DeCasper, A. J., & Fifer, W. P. (1980). Of human bonding: Newborns prefer their mothers' voices. *Science, 208*, 1174–1176.

DeCasper, A. J., & Spence, M. J. (1986). Prenatal maternal speech influences newborn's perception of speech sounds. *Infant Behavior and Development, 9*, 133–150.

DeCasper, A. J., & Spence, M. (1992). Auditorily mediated behavior during the perinatal period: A cognitive view. In *Newborn attention: Biological constraints and the influence of experience.* Norwood, NJ: Ablex.

DeHaas-Warner, S. (1994). The role of child care professionals in placement and programming decisions for preschoolers with special needs in community based settings. *Young Children, 45*(5), 76–78.

Delpit, L. D. (1988). The silenced dialogue: Power and pedagogy in educating other people's children. *Harvard Educational Review, 58*(3), 280–298.

Demos, V. (1986). Crying in early infancy: An illustration of the motivational function of affect. In T. B. Brazelton & M. W. Yogman (Eds.), *Affective development in infancy* (pp. 39–73). Norwood, NJ: Ablex.

Dennebaum, J. M., & Kulberg, J. M. (1994). Kindergarten retention and transition classrooms: Their relationship to achievement. *Psychology in the Schools, 11*(1), 5–12.

Derman-Sparks, L. (1989). *Anti-bias curriculum: Tools for empowering children.* Washington, DC: National Association for the Education of Young Children.

deVilliers, P.A., & deVilliers, J. G. (1992). Language development. In M. E. Lamb & M. H. Bornstein (Eds.), *Developmental psychology: An advanced textbook* (3rd ed.). Hillsdale, NJ: Erlbaum.

DeVries, R. (1969). Constancy of generic identity in the years three to six. *Monographs of the Society for Research in Child Development, 34* (3, Serial No. 127).

Diamond, J. (1990). War babies. *Discover, 11*(12), pp. 70–75.

Diaz, R. M. (1985). Bilingual cognitive development: Addressing three gaps in current research. *Child Development, 56*, 1376–1378.

Dietz, W. H. (1986). *Prevention of childhood obesity.* Philadelphia: Pediatric Clinics of North America/Saunders.

Dixon, J. (1992, February 13). Too few schools serve breakfast (based on Food Research and Action Center Report). *Denton (TX) Chronicle.*

Doake, D. (1981). *Book experience and emergent reading in preschool children.* Unpublished doctoral dissertation, University of Alberta, Edmonton.

Dobbing, J. (1984). Infant nutrition and later achievement. *Nutrition Reviews, 42*, 1–7.

Doiron, R. (1994). Using nonfiction in a read-aloud program: Letting the facts speak for themselves. *The Reading Teacher, 47*(8), 616–624.

Dollaghan, C. (1985). Child meets word: "Fast mapping" in pre-school children. *Journal of Speech and Hearing Research, 28*, 449–454.

Donaldson, M. (1979). *Children's minds.* New York: Norton.

Donaldson, M. (1983). Children's reasoning. In M. Donaldson, R. Grieve, & C. Pratt (Eds.), *Early childhood development and education: Readings in psychology* (pp. 231–236). New York: Guilford Press.

Donaldson, M. (1992). *Human minds: An exploration.* London: Penguin.

Dorr, A. (1983). No shortcuts to judging reality. In P. E. Bryant & S. Anderson (Eds.), *Watching and understanding TV: Research on children's attention and comprehension.* New York: Academic Press.

Dorr, A., Graves, S., & Phelps, E. (1980). Television literacy for young children. *Journal of Communication, 30*, 71–83.

Dorval, B., & Eckerman, C. (1984). Developmental trends in the quality of conversation achieved by small groups of acquainted peers. *Monographs of the Society for Research in Child Development, 49* (2, Serial No. 206).

Dreher, M. J., & Zenge, S. D. (1990). Using metalinguistic awareness in first grade to predict reading achievement in third and fifth grades. *Journal of Educational Research, 84*(1), 13–21.

Dresden, J., & Myers, B. K. (1989). Early childhood professionals: Toward self-definition. *Young Children, 44* (2), 62–66.

Duncan, B., Holberg, E. J., Wright, A. L., Martinez, F. D., & Taussig, L. M. (1993). Exclusive breastfeeding for at least 4 months protects against otitus media. *Pediatrics, 91*(5), 867–872.

Dunn, J. (1984). *Sisters and brothers.* Cambridge, MA: Harvard University Press.

Dunn, J. (1993). *Young children's close relationships: Beyond attachment.* Newbury Park, CA: Sage.

Dunn, J., & Kendrick, C. (1982a). Siblings and their mother: Developing relationships within the family. In M. E. Lamb & B. Sutton-Smith (Eds.), *Sibling relationships: Their nature and significance across the lifespan* (pp. 39–60). Hillsdale, NJ: Erlbaum.

Dunn, J., & Kendrick, C. (1982b). *Siblings: Love, envy, and understanding.* Cambridge, MA: Harvard University Press.

Dunn, J., & Munn, P. (1986). Siblings and the development of prosocial behavior. *International Journal of Behavioral Development, 9*, 265–284.

Durkin, D. (1966). *Children who read early.* New York: Teachers College Press.

Dyson, A. H. (1981). *A case study examination of the role of oral language in writing processes of kindergartners.* Unpublished doctoral dissertation, The University of Texas at Austin.

Dyson, A. H. (1982). The emergence of visible language: Interrelationships between drawing and early writings. *Visible Language, 16*, 360–381.

Dyson, A. H. (1983). The role of oral language in the early writing processes. *Research in the Teaching of English, 17*, 1–30.

Dyson, A. H. (1985). Puzzles, paints and pencils: Writing emerges. *Educational Horizons, 64*, 13–16.

Dyson, A. H. (1987). Research currents: The emergence of children's written voices. *Language Arts, 64*, 648–658.

Dyson, A. H. (1990). Symbol makers, symbol weavers: How children link play, pictures, and print. *Young Children, 45* (2), 50–57.

Earls, F., & Carlson, M. (1993). Towards sustainable development for American families. *Daedalus, 122*(1), 93–121.

Eaton, W. O., Chipperfield, J. G., & Singbeil, C. E. (1989). Birth order and activity level in children. *Developmental Psychology, 25*, 668–672.

Eaton, W. O., & Von Bargen, D. (1981). Asynchronous development of gender understanding in preschool children. *Child Development, 52*, 1020–1027.

**Education Consolidation and Improvement Act of 1981.** U.S. Code 1982 Title 20, § 3801 et. seq. Aug. 13, 1981 PL 97–35 STAT. 357, § 551–596.

**Education for All Handicapped Children Act of 1975.** U.S. Code 1976, Title 20, § 1232, 1401, 1405, 1406, 1411 to 1420, 1433, November 29, 1975 (P.L. 94–142), Stat. 773.

**Education of All Handicapped Act Amendments of 1986.** U.S. Code 1988, Title 20, § 1401, 1471, October 6, 1986, (P.L. 99–457), 100 Stat. 1143.

**Education of All Handicapped Act Amendments of 1990.** U.S. Code 1988, Title 20, § 1401, 1471, October 1990, (P.L. 101–476), 104 Stat. 1103.

Eichorn, D. (1979). Physical development: current foci of research. In J. D. Osofsky (Ed.), *Handbook of infant development* (pp. 253–282). New York: Wiley.

Elder, G. H., Jr. (1982). Historical experiences in the later years. In T. K. Hareven & K. J. Adams (Eds.), *Aging and life course transitions: An interdisciplinary perspective* (pp. 75–107). New York: Guilford Press.

Elkind, D. (1978a). *The child's reality: Three developmental themes.* Hillsdale, NJ: Erlbaum.

Elkind, D. (1978b) *A sympathetic understanding of the child 6 to 16.* Boston: Allyn & Bacon.

Elkind, D. (1978c). Understanding the young adolescent. *Adolescence, 13*, 127–134.

Elkind, D. (1987). *Miseducation: Preschoolers at risk.* New York: Knopf.

Elkind, D. (1994). *A sympathetic understanding of the child, birth to 16* (3rd ed.). Boston: Allyn & Bacon.

Emde, R. N., & Harmon, R. J. (1972). Endogenous and exogenous smiling systems in early infancy. *Journal of the American Academy of Child Psychiatry, 11*, 177–200.

England, D. A. (1984). *Television and children* (Fastback Series No. 207). Bloomington, IN: Phi Delta Kappa Educational Foundation.

Entwisle, D. R., & Alexander, K. L. (1987). Long term effects of cesarean delivery on parents' beliefs and children's schooling. *Development Psychology, 23*, 676–682.

Epstein, A. S. (1993). Training for quality: Improving early childhood programs through systematic in-service training. *Monographs of the High/Scope Educational Research Foundation, 9.* Ypsilanti, MI: High/Scope Press.

Erhardt, R. P. (1973). Sequential levels in the development of prehension. *The American Journal of Occupational Therapy, 28,* 592–596.

Erickson, M. F., Stroufe, L. A., & Egeland, B. (1985). The relationship between quality of attachment and behavior problems in preschool in a high risk sample. In I. Bretherton & E. Waters (Eds.), Growing points of attachment theory and research. *Monographs of the Society for Research in Child Development, 50* (1–2, Serial No. 209, pp. 147–166).

Erikson, E. (1963). *Childhood and society* (2nd ed.). New York: Norton.

Erikson, E. (1968). *Identity: Youth and crisis.* New York: Norton.

Ervin-Tripp, S., O'Connor, S., & Rosenberg, J. (1984). Language and power in the family. In J. deWit & W. W. Hartup (Eds.), *Determinants and origins of aggressive behavior* (pp. 347–380). The Hague: Mouton.

Evans, H. J. (1981). Abnormalities and cigarette smoking. *Lancet, (1),* 627–634.

Eveleth, P., & Tanner, J. (1976). *World wide variation in human growth.* Cambridge, England: Cambridge University Press.

Fagot, B. I. (1974). Sex differences in toddlers' behavior and parental reaction. *Developmental Psychology, 10,* 554–558.

Fagot, B. I. (1978). The influence of sex of child on parental reactions to toddler children. *Child Development, 49,* 459–465.

Fagot, B. I. (1982). Sex role development. In R. Vasta (Ed.), *Strategies and techniques of child study* (pp. 273–303). New York: Academic Press.

Fagot, B. I., Hagan, R., Leinback, M. D., & Kronsberg, D. (1985). Differential reactions to assertive and communication acts of toddlers boys and girls. *Child Development, 56*(6), 1499–1505.

Fagot, B. I., & Kavanagh, K. (1990). The prediction of antisocial behaviors from avoidant attachment classifications. *Child Development, 61*(3), 863–873.

Fagot, B. I., & Kavanagh, K. (1993). Parenting during the 2nd year: Effects of children's age, sex, and attachment classification. *Child Development, 64*(1), 258–271.

Fagot, B. I., & Kronsberg, S. J. (1982). Sex differences: Biological and social factors influencing the behavior of young boys and girls. In S. G. Moore & C. R. Cooper (Eds.), *The young child: Reviews of research* (Vol. 3, pp. 193–210). Washington, DC: National Association for the Education of Young Children.

Fantz, R. L. (1961). The origin of form perception. *Scientific American, 204,* 66–72.

Farber, E. A., & Egeland, B. (1982). Developmental consequences of out-of-home care for infants in a low income population. In E. Zigler & E. Gordon (Eds.), *Day care:*

*Scientific and social policy issues* (pp. 102–125). Boston: Auburn House.

Fecter, L., & Mactutos, C. (1983). Carbon monoxide and fetal memory. *Science News, 124,* 387.

Federal Motor Vehicle Safety Standard Act of 1980. 213 U.S.C. (1981).

Feeney, S., & Kipnis, K. (1992). *The National Association for the Education of Young Children Code of Ethical Conduct and Statement of Commitment.* Washington, DC.: National Association for the Education of Young Children.

Fein, G. (1978). *Child development.* Englewood Cliffs, NJ: Prentice Hall.

Fein, G., Gariboldi, A., & Boni, R. (1993). The adjustment of infants and toddlers to group care: The first 6 months. *Early Childhood Research Quarterly, 8*(1), 1–14.

Fennema, E., Carpenter, T. P., & Peterson, P. L. (1990). Learning mathematics with understanding: Cognitively guided instruction. In J. E. Brophy (Ed.), *Advances in research on teaching* (Vol. 1). Greenwich, CT: JAI Press.

Ferguson, C. A. (1977). Learning to pronounce: The earliest stages of phonological development in the child. In F. D. Minifie & L. L. Lloyd (Eds.), *Communicative and cognitive abilities: Early behavioral assessment* (pp. 141–155). Baltimore: University Park Press.

Fernald, A. (1993). Approval and disapproval: Infant responsiveness to vocal affect in familiar and unfamiliar languages. *Child Development, 64*(3), 657–674.

Fernald A., & Morikawa, H. (1993). Common themes and cultural variations in Japanese and American mothers' speech to infants. *Child Development, 64*(3), 637–656.

Ferrerio, E., & Teberosky, A. (1982). *Literacy before schooling.* Exeter, NH: Heinemann.

Fields, D. (1981). Can preschool children really learn to conserve? *Child Development, 52,* 326–334.

Fields, M., & Lee, D. (1987). *Let's begin reading right: A developmental approach to beginning literacy.* Columbus, OH: Merrill.

Fields, T. M. (1979). Differential behavioral & cardiac responses of 3-month-old infants to a mirror and a peer. *Infant Behavior and Development, 2,* 179–184.

Fields, T. M. (1982). Individual differences in the expressivity of neonates and young infants. In R. Feldman (Ed.), *Development of nonverbal behavior in children* (pp. 279–298). New York: Springer-Verlag.

Fields, T. M., Schanberg, S. M., Scafidi, F, Bauer, C. R., Vegalahr, N., Garcia, R., Nystrom, J., & Kuhn, C. M. (1986). Effects of tactile/kinesthetic stimulation on preterm neonates. *Pediatrics, 77,* 654–658.

Fields, T. M., Vega-Lahr, N., & Jagadish, S. (1984). Separation stress of nursery school infants and toddlers graduating to new classes. *Infant Behavior and Development, 7,* 277–284.

Fields, M. V., & Spangler, K. L. (1995). *Let's begin reading right: Developmentally appropriate beginning literacy* (3rd ed.). Englewood Cliffs, NJ: Prentice Hall.

Fields, M. V., Spangler, K. L., & Lee, D. M. (1991). *Let's begin reading right: Developmentally appropriate beginning literacy.* (2nd ed.). New York: Macmillan.

Fike, R. D. (1993). Personal relationship-building between fathers and infants. Association for Childhood Education International Theme Issue: Focus on Infancy. *Childhood Education, 5*(4), 1–2.

Fisher, J. J. (Ed.). (1988). *From baby to toddler.* New York: Pergee Books.

Fivush, R. (1984). Learning about school: The development of kindergartners' school scripts. *Child Development, 55,* 1697–1709.

Flavell, J. H. (1963). *The developmental psychology of Jean Piaget.* New York: Nostrand.

Flavell, J. H. (1985). *Cognitive development* (2nd ed.). Englewood Cliffs, NJ: Prentice Hall.

Flavell, J. H., Frederichs, A. G., & Hoyt, J. D. (1970). Developmental changes in memorization processes. *Cognitive Psychology, 1,* 324–340.

Fleege, P. O. (1990). Stress begins in kindergarten: A look at behavior during standardized testing (Doctoral dissertation, Louisiana State University). *Dissertation Abstracts International, 51,* 3628A.

Fleege, P. O., Charlesworth, R., Burts, D. C., & Hart, C. H. (1992). Stress begins in kindergarten: A look at behavior during standardized testing. *Journal of Research in Childhood Education, 7*(1), 20–26.

Fleishman, D. (n.d.). Cultural sensitivity: *Developing programs for the people who will use them* (AAP Special Report). Elk Grove Village, IL: American Academy of Pediatrics.

Flood, J., & Salus, P. (1984). *Language and the language arts.* Englewood Cliffs, NJ: Prentice Hall.

Fogel, A. (1979). Peer vs. mother directed behavior in 1- to 3-month-old infants. *Infant Behavior and Development, 2,* 215–226.

Forman, G., & Kuschner, D. (1983). *The child's construction of knowledge: Piaget for teaching children.* Washington, DC: National Association for the Education of Young Children.

Forman, M. A., Hetznecker, W. H., & Dunn, J. M. (1983). Psychosocial dimensions of pediatrics: Gender identity and role. In R. E. Behrman & V. C. Vaughn, III (Eds.), *Nelson textbook of pediatrics* (12th ed., pp. 56–58). Philadelphia: Saunders.

Fraiberg, S. (1976). Intervention in infancy: A program for blind infants. In E. Resford, L. Sander, & T. Shapiro (Eds.), *Infant psychiatry: A new synthesis* (pp. 264–284). New Haven, CT: Yale University Press.

Freedman, D. G., & Freedman, N. (1969). Behavioral differences between Chinese-Americans and European-American newborns. *Nature, 224,* 1227.

Freidrich, L. K., & Stein, A. H. (1975). Prosocial television and young children: The effect of verbal labelling and role-playing on learning and behavior. *Child Development, 46,* 27–38.

Freud, S. (1905/1930). *Three contributions to the theory of sex.* New York: Nervous and Mental Disease Publishing. (Original work published 1905)

Freud, S. (1933). *New introductory lectures on psychoanalysis.* New York: Norton.

Freud, S. (1938). The history of the psychoanalytic movement. In A. A. Brill (Ed. and Trans.), *The basic writing of Sigmund Freud* (pp. 931–977). New York: Modern Library.

Friedman, J., & Koeppel, J. (1990). Pre-K and first grade children: Partners in a writing workshop. *Young Children, 45* (4), 66–67.

Frisch, H. L. (1977). Sex stereotypes in adult-infant play. *Child Development, 48,* 1671–1675.

Frost, J. L. (1992a). *Play and playscapes.* Albany, NY: Delmar.

Frost, J. L. (1992b). Reflections on research and practice in outdoor play environments. *Dimensions, 20*(14), 6–10.

Frost, J. L., & Wortham, S. C. (1984). Frost and Wortham Developmental Checklist. In S. C. Wortham, *Organizing instruction in early childhood.* Boston: Allyn & Bacon.

Frymier, J. (1992). Growing up is risky business, and schools are not to blame. Bloomington, IN: Phi Delta Kappa.

Fuller, F. F. (1969). Concerns of teachers. *American Educational Research Journal, 6,* 207–226.

Furman, W., & Buhrmester, D. (1985). Children's perceptions of the qualities of sibling relationships. *Child Development, 56,* 448–461.

Furstenberg, F. F., Jr., Brooks-Gunn, J., & Chase-Lansdale, L. (1989). Teenage pregnancy and child bearing. *American Psychologist, 44*(1), 313–320.

Furth, H. G. (1992a). The developmental origin of human societies. In H. Beilin and P. B. Pufall (Eds.), *Piaget's theory: Prospects and possibilities.* Hillsdale, NJ: Erlbaum.

Furth, H. G. (1992b). Life's essential—The story of mind over body: A review of "I raise my eyes to say yes: A memoir by Ruth Sienkiewicz-Mercer & S.B. Kaplan. *Human Development, 35*(2), 254–261.

Furth, H. G.(1992c). Commentary on Bebko, Burke, Craven & Sarlo (1992): The importance of sensorimotor development: A perspective from children with physical handicaps. *Human Development, 36*(4), 226–240.

Fuson, K. C., Secada, W. G., & Hall, J. W. (1983). Matching, counting, and conservation of numerical equivalence. *Child Development, 54,* 91–97.

Gabbard, C., Dean, M., & Haensly, P. (1991). Foot preference behavior during early childhood. *Journal of Applied Developmental Psychology, 12*(1), 131–137.

Galinsky, E., Howes, C., Kontos, S., & Shinn, M. (1994). *The study of children in family child care and relative care: Highlights of findings.* New York: Families and Work Institute.

Gallahue, D. L. (1982). *Developmental movement experiences for children.* New York: Wiley.

Galler, J. R., Ramsey, F., & Solimano, G. (1984). The influence of early malnutrition on subsequent development: 3. Learning disabilities as a sequel to malnutrition. *Pediatric Research, 18,* 309.

Galler, J. R., Ramsey, F., & Solimano, G. (1985). A follow-up study of the effects of early malnutrition on subsequent development: 2. Fine motor skills in adolescence. *Pediatric Research, 19,* 524.

Gandini, L. (1993). Fundamentals of the Reggio Emilia approach to early childhood education. *Young Children, 49*(1), 4–8.

Garbarino, J. (1977). The human ecology of child maltreatment: A conceptual model for research. *Journal of Marriage and the Family, 39,* 731–736.

Garbarino, J., Dubrow, N., Kostelny, K., & Pardo, C. (1992). *Children in danger: Coping with the consequences of community violence.* San Francisco: Jossey-Bass.

Garbarino, J., Kostelny, K., & Dubrow, N. (1991). *No place to be a child: Growing up in a war zone.* Lexington, MA: Lexington Press.

Garcia-Coll, C. T. (1990). Developmental outcomes of minority infants: A process-oriented look into our beginnings. *Child Development, 61*(2), 270–289.

Gardner, H. (1978). *Developmental psychology: An introduction.* Boston: Little, Brown.

Gardner, H. (1980). *Artful scribbles: The significance of children's drawings.* New York: Basic Books.

Gardner, H. (1983). *Frames of mind: Theory of multiple intelligences.* New York: Basic Books.

Gardner, H. (1991a). Assessment in context: The alternative to standardized testing. In B. R. Gifford & M. C. O'Connor (Eds.), *Changing assessments: Alternative views of attitude, achievement and instruction.* Boston: Kluwer Publishers.

Gardner, H. (1991b). *The unschooled mind: How children think and how schools should teach.* New York: Basic Books.

Gardner, H. (1993). *Multiple intelligences: The theory in practice.* New York: Basic Books.

Gardner, R. A. (1979). *Understanding children.* Cresskill, NJ: Creative Therapists.

Garrett, P., Ferron, J., Ng'Andu, N., Bryant, D., & Harbin, G. (1994). A structural model for the developmental status of young children. *Journal of Marriage and the Family, 56*(1), 147–163.

Garvey, C. (1977). *Play.* Cambridge, MA: Harvard University Press.

Geber, M. (1958). The psychomotor development of African children in the first year and the influence of maternal behavior. *Journal of Social Psychology, 47,* 185–195.

Gehrke, N. J. (1987). *On being a teacher.* West Lafayette, IN: Kappa Delta Pi Publications.

Gelles, R. J., & Edfeldt, A. W. (1990). Violence toward children in the United States and Sweden. In M. A. Jensen & Z. W. Chevalier (Eds.), *Issues and advocacy in early education* (pp. 133–140). Boston: Allyn & Bacon.

Gelles, R. J., & Straus, M. A. (1988). *Intimate violence.* New York: Simon & Schuster.

Gelman, R. (1972). Logical capacity of very young children: Number invariance rules. *Child Development, 43,* 75–90.

Gelman, R. (1979). Preschool thought. *American Psychologist, 34,* 900–905.

Gelman, R., & Baillargeon, R. (1983). A review of some Piagetian concepts. In P. H. Mussen (Ed.), *Handbook of child psychology: Vol. 3. Cognitive development* (pp. 167–230). New York: Wiley.

Gelman, R., Bullock, M., & Meck, E. (1980). Preschooler's understanding of simple object transformation. *Child Development, 51,* 691–699.

Gelman, R., & Gallistel, C. R. (1983). The child's understanding of number. In M. Donaldson, R. Grieve, & C. Pratt (Eds.), *Early childhood development and education: Readings in psychology* (pp. 185–203). New York: Guilford Press.

Gelman, R., & Shatz, M. (1978). Appropriate speech adjustments: The operation of conversational constraints on talk to two-year-olds. In M. Lewis & L. A. Rosenblum (Eds.), *Interaction, conversation, and the development of language,* (pp. 27–61). New York: Wiley.

Genishi, C. (1988). Children's language: Learning words from experience. *Young Children, 44*(1), 16–23.

Genishi, C. (Ed.). *Ways of assessing children and curriculum: Stories of early childhood practice.* New York: Teachers College Press.

Genishi, C., & Dyson, A. H. (1984). *Language assessment in the early years.* Norwood, NJ: Ablex.

Genishi, C., Dyson, A. H., & Fassler, R. (1994). Language and diversity in early childhood: Whose voices are appropriate? In B. L. Mallory & R. S. New (Eds.), *Diversity and developmentally appropriate practices.* New York: Teachers College Press.

Genishi, C., McCollum, P., & Strand, E. (1985). Research currents: The interactional richness of children's computer use. *Language Arts, 62,* 526–532.

Gerbner, G., & Signorielli, N. (1990). *Violence profile 1967 through 1988–89: Enduring trends.* Philadelphia: University of Pennsylvania, Annenberg School of Communication.

Gesell, A. (1930). *Guidance of mental growth in infant and child.* New York: Macmillan.

Gesell, A., & Amatruda, C. S. (1941). *Developmental diagnosis: Normal and abnormal child development.* New York: Hoeber.

Gesell, A., & Ilg, F. L. (1949). *Child development.* New York: Harper and Row.

Gesell, A., & Thompson, H. (1929). Learning and growth in identical infant twins: An experimental study by the method of co-twin control. *Genetic Psychology Monographs, 6,* 1–125.

Ghazvini, A. S., & Readdick, C. A. (1994). Parent-caregiver communication and quality of care in diverse child care settings. *Early Childhood Research Quarterly, 9*(2), 207–222.

Gilligan, C. (1982). *In a different voice*. Cambridge, MA: Harvard University Press.

Ginsburg, H. (1977). *Children's arithmetic*. New York: Van Nostrand.

Ginsburg, H. (1982). The development of addition in the contexts of culture, social class, and race. In T. P. Carpenter, J. M. Moser, & T. A. Romberg (Eds.), *Addition and subtraction: A cognitive perspective* (pp. 191–210). Hillsdale, NJ: Erlbaum.

Ginsburg, H., & Opper, S. (1979). *Piaget's theory of intellectual development* (2nd ed.). Englewood Cliffs, NJ: Prentice Hall.

Gleason, J. (1975). Fathers and other strangers: Men's speech to young children. In D. Dato (Ed.), *Developmental Psycholinguistics* (pp. 289–297). Washington, DC: Georgetown University Press.

Glover, B. & Shepherd, J. (1980). *The family fitness handbook*. New York: Penguin USA.

Glover, B., & Shepherd, J. (1989). *Speaking out: Early childhood advocacy*. Washington, DC: National Association for the Education of Young Children.

Goffin S. G., & Lombardi, J. (1989). *Speaking out: Early childhood advocacy*. Washington, DC: National Association for the Education of Young Children.

Golinkoff, R. M. (1983). The preverbal negotiation of failed messages: Insights into the transition period. In R. M. Golinkoff (Ed.), *The transition from prelinguistic to linguistic communication* (pp. 57–75). Hillsdale, NJ: Erlbaum.

Goodman, K. (1986). *What's whole in whole language?* Portsmouth, NH: Heinemann.

Goodman, K., & Goodman, Y. M. (1983). Reading and writing relationships: Pragmatic functions. *Language Arts, 60*, 590–599.

Goodman, Y. (1980). The roots of literacy. In M. P. Douglass (Ed.), *Claremont Reading Conference forty-fourth yearbook*. Claremont, CA: Claremont Graduate School.

Gordon, A. M., & Browne, K. W. (1985). *Beginnings and beyond*. Albany, New York: Delmar.

Gordon, J. S., & Haire, D. (1981). Alternatives in childbirth. In P. Ahmed (Ed.), *Pregnancy, childbirth and parenthood*. New York: Elsevier.

Gortmacher, S. L., Dietz, W. H., Sobol, A. M., & Wehler, C. A. (1987). Increasing pediatric obesity in the United States. *American Journal of Diseases of Children, 141*, 535–540.

Gottfried, A. (1984). Touch as an organizer of human development. In C. Brown (Ed.), *The many facets of touch* (pp. 114–120). Skillman, NJ: Johnson and Johnson.

Grace, K., Shores, E. F., Brown, M., Arnold, F. D., Graves, S. B., Jambor, T., & Neill, M. (1991). *The portfolio and its use*. Little Rock, AR: Southern Early Childhood Association.

Graves, D. (1983). *Writing: Teachers and children at work*. Exeter, NH: Heinemann.

Green, J. A., Jones, L. E., & Gustafson, G. E. (1987). Perception of cries by parents and nonparents: Relation to cry acoustics. *Developmental Psychology, 23*, 370–382.

Green, M. (1985). The development of metaphoric comprehension and preference (Doctoral dissertation, Boston University). *Dissertation Abstracts International, 46*, 1264A.

Greenspan, S., & Greenspan, N. T. (1985). *First feelings*. New York: Penguin.

Gregorchik, L. A. (1992). The cocaine exposed children are here. *Phi Delta Kappan, 73*(9), 709–711.

Griffith, D. P. (1992). Prenatal exposure to cocaine and other drugs: Developmental and educational prognosis. *Phi Delta Kappan, 74*(1), 30–34.

Grossmann, K. E., & Grossmann, K. (1990) The wider concept of attachment in cross-cultural research. *Human Development, 33*: 31–37.

Grossmann, K., Grossmann, K. E., Spangler, G., Suess, G. L., & Unzner, L. (1985). Maternal sensitivity and newborns' orientation responses as related to quality of attachment in Northern Germany. In I. Bretherton & E. Waters (Eds.), Growing points of attachment theory and research. *Monographs of the Society for Research in Child Development, 50* (1–2, Serial No. 209, pp. 233–256).

Gruen, G. E., & Vore, D. A. (1972). Development of conservation in normal and retarded children. *Developmental Psychology, 6*, 146–157.

Grusec, J. E., & Abramovitch, R. (1982). Imitation of peers and adults in a natural setting: A functional analysis. *Child Development, 53*, 636–642.

Guskey, T. R. (1986). Staff development and the process of teacher change. *Educational Researcher, 15*(5), 5–12.

Haith, M. M. (1966). The response of human newborns to visual movement. *Journal of Experimental Child Psychology, 3*, 235–243.

Halford, G. S., & Boyle, F. M. (1985). Do young children understand conservation of number? *Child Development, 56*, 165–176.

Hall, G. S. (1893). *The contents of children's minds*. New York: Kellogg.

Hall, M., Moretz, S., & Statom, J. (1976). A study of early writing. *Language Arts, 53*, 582–585.

Harlap, S., & Shlono, P. H. (1980). Alcohol, smoking, and incidence of spontaneous abortion in the first and second trimester. *Lancet, 2*, 173–176.

Harper, L. V., & Huie, K. S. (1985). The effects of prior group experience, age and familiarity on the quality and organization of preschoolers' social relationships. *Child Development, 56*, 704–717.

Harris, P. L., Donnelly, K., Huz, G. R., & Pitt-Watson, R. (1986). Children's understanding of the distinction between real and apparent emotion. *Child Development, 57*, 895–909.

Hart, C. H., DeWolf, D. M., Royston, K. E., Burts, D. C., & Thomasson, R. H. (1990, Spring). Maternal and paternal disciplinary styles: Relationships to behavioral orientations and sociometric status. Paper presented at the annual conference of the American Educational Research Association, Boston.

Hart, C. H., Ladd, G. W., & Burleson, B. R. (1990). Children's expectations of the outcomes of social strategies: Relations with sociometric status and maternal disciplinary styles. *Child Development, 61,* 127–137.

Hartup, W. W. (1977). Peer relations: Developmental implications and interaction in same- and mixed-age situations. *Young Children, 32* (3), 4–13.

Hartup, W. W. (1983). Peer relations. In E. M. Hetherington (Ed.), *Handbook of child psychology: Vol. 4. Socialization, personality and social development* (4th ed., pp. 103–196). New York: Wiley.

Hartup, W. W. (1989). Behavioral manifestations of children's friendships. In T. J. Berndt & G. W. Ladd (Eds.), *Peer relationships in child development* (pp. 46–70). New York: Wiley.

Hartup, W. W., & Moore, S. G. (1990). Early peer relations: Developmental significance and prognostic implications. *Early Childhood Research Quarterly, 5*(1), 1–17.

Havighurst, R. J. (1972). *Developmental tasks and education.* New York: McKay.

Hawk, P. (1987). Beginning teacher programs: Benefits for the experienced educator. *Action in Teacher Education, 8* (4), 59–63.

Hawk, P., & Robards, S. (1987). Statewide teacher induction programs. In D. Brooks (Ed.), *Teacher induction: A new beginning* (pp. 33–44). Reston, VA: Association of Teacher Educators.

Hay, D. F. (1979). Cooperative interactions and sharing between very young children and their parents. *Developmental Psychology, 15,* 647–653.

Hay, D. R., Nash, A., & Pederson, J. (1983). Interaction between six-month-old peers. *Child Development, 54,* 557–562.

Head Start Reauthorization Act of 1994. P.L. 103–252.

Healy, J. M. (1987). *Your child's growing mind.* Garden City, NY: Doubleday.

Heath, D. C. (1977). *Maturity and competence: A transcultural view.* New York: Gardner Press.

Heath, S. (1982). What no bedtime story means: Narrative skills at home and school. *Language in Society, 11,* 49–76.

Heath, S. B. (1983). *Ways with words: Language life and work in communities and classrooms.* Cambridge, MA: Cambridge University Press.

Heck, S., & Williams, C. R. (1984). *The complex roles of the teacher: An ecological perspective.* New York: Teachers College Press.

Hellige, J. B. (1990). Hemispheric asymmetry. *Annual Review of Psychology, 41.* Palo Alto, CA: Annual Review.

Hetherington, E. M., Cox, M., & Cox, R. (1982). Effects of divorce on parents and children. In M. E. Lamb (Ed.), *Nontraditional families* (pp. 233–288). Hillsdale, NJ: Erlbaum.

Hiebert, E. H. (Ed.). (1991). *Literacy for a diverse society: Perspectives, practices and policies.* New York: Teachers College Press.

Hofferth, S. L., Brayfield, A., Deich, S. G., & Holcomb, P. (1991). *The national child care survey, 1991.* Washington, DC: The Urban Institute.

Hoffman, M. L. (1975). Altruistic behavior and the parent-child relationship. *Journal of Personality and Social Psychology, 31,* 937–943.

Hoffman, M. L. (1988). Moral development. In M. H. Bornstein & M. E. Lamb (Eds.), *Developmental psychology: An advanced textbook* (2nd ed., pp. 497–548). Hillsdale, NJ: Erlbaum.

Hofmann, R. (1986). Microcomputers, productive thinking, and children. In P. Campbell & G. Fein (Eds.), *Young children and microcomputers* (pp. 87–101). Englewood Cliffs, NJ: Prentice Hall.

Holdaway, D. (1979). *The foundations of literacy.* Sydney: Ashton Scholastic.

Holder-Brown, L.. & Parette, P., Jr. (1992). Children with disabilities who use assistive technology: Ethical considerations. *Young Children, 47*(6), 73–77.

Holmes Group. (1986). *Tomorrow's teachers: A report of the Holmes Group.* East Lansing, MI: Author.

Honig, A. S. (1983). Research in review: Sex role socialization in early childhood. *Young Children, 38*(6), 57–70.

Honig, A. S. (1986). Research in review: Stress and coping in children (Part I). *Young Children, 41*(4), 50–63.

Hooker, D. (1952). *The prenatal origin of behavior.* Lawrence: University of Kansas Press.

Hoot, J. L., & Roberson, G. (Guest Eds.). (1994). Creating safer environments for children in the home, school, community. *Childhood Education 70*(5), 258–318. Wheaton, MD: Association for Childhood Education International.

Hoot, J. L., & Silvern, S. (Eds.). (1989). *Writing with computers in the early grades.* New York: Teachers College Press.

Hopkins, J., Marcus, M., & Campbell, S. (1984). Postpartum depression: A critical review. *Psychological Bulletin, 95,* 498–515.

Householder, J., Matcher, R., Burnes, W., & Chasnoff, I. (1982). Infants born to narcotic-addicted mothers. *Psychological Bulletin, 92,* 453–468.

Houston, A. C., Donnerstein, E., Fairchild, H., Feshbach, N. D., Katz, P. A., Murray, J. P., Rubenstein, E. A., Wilcox, G. L., & Zuckerman, D. (1992). *Big world, small screen.* Lincoln, NE: University of Nebraska Press.

Howes, C. (1987). Quality indicators in infant and toddler child care: The Los Angeles study. In D. A. Phillips (Ed.), *Quality in child care: What does research tell us?* (pp. 81–88). Washington, DC: National Association for the Education of Young Children.

Howes, C. (1988). Peer interaction of young children. *Monographs of the Society for Research in Child Development, 53*(1, Serial No. 217).

Howes, C., & Hamilton, C. E. (1993). The changing experience of child care: Changes in teachers and in teacher-child relationships and children's social competence with peers. *Early Childhood Research Quarterly, 8*(1), 15–32.

Hudson, J., & Nelson, K. (1983). Effects of script structure on children's story recall. *Developmental Psychology, 19*, 525–635.

Huesmann, L. R., Eron, L. D., Lefkowitz, M. M., & Walder, L. O. (1984). Stability over time and generations. *Developmental Psychology, 20*, 1120–1134.

Hughes, M., & Donaldson, M. (1983). The use of hiding games for studying coordination of points. In M. Donaldson, R. Grieve, & C. Pratt (Eds.), *Early childhood development and education: Readings in psychology* (pp. 245–253). New York: Guilford Press.

Hughes, M., & Grieve, R. (1983). On asking children bizarre questions. In M. Donaldson, R. Grieve, & C. Pratt (Eds.), *Early childhood development and education: Readings in psychology* (pp. 104–114). New York: Guilford Press.

Huling-Austin, L. (1986). Teacher induction programs: What can and cannot reasonably be expected from teacher induction programs. *Journal of Teacher Education, 37*(1), 2–5.

Hunt, C. E., & Brouillette, R. T. (1987). Sudden infant death syndrome: 1987 perspective. *Journal of Pediatrics, 110*, 669–678.

Hunt, J. McV. (1961). *Intelligence and experience.* New York: Ronald Press.

Hunziker, U. A., & Barr, R. G. (1986). Increased carrying reduces infant crying: A randomized controlled trial. *Pediatrics, 77*, 641–648.

Hurwitz, E. S., Gunn, W.J., Pinsky, P. F., & Schonberger, L. B. (1991). "Respiratory illness and day care attendance" *Pediatrics, 87*(1), 62–69.

Huston, A. C. (1983). Sex-typing. In E. M. Hetherington (Ed.), *Handbook of child psychology: Vol. 4. Socialization, personality and social development* (4th ed., pp. 387–467). New York: Wiley.

Huston, A. C., Carpenter, C. J., & Atwater, J. B. (1986). Gender, adult structuring of activities, and social behavior in middle childhood. *Child Development, 57*, 1200–1209.

Hymel, S., Rubin, K., Rowden, L., & LeMare, L. (1990). Children's peer relationships: Longitudinal prediction of internalizing and externalizing problems from middle to late childhood. *Child Development, 61*, 2004–2021.

Hymes, D. (1971). Competence and performance in linguistic theory. In R. Huxley & E. Ingram (Eds.), *Language acquisition: Models and methods* (pp. 5–28). London: Academic Press.

Individuals with Disabilities Education Act Amendments of 1991. U.S. Code 1988, Title 20, § 1401, October 7, 1991 (P.L. 102–119), 105 Stat. 587.

Ingram, D. (1986). Phonological development: Production. In P. Fletcher & M. Garman (Eds.), *Language acquisition* (2nd ed., pp. 223–239). Cambridge, England: Cambridge University Press.

Inhelder, B. (1960). Criteria of stages of mental development. In J. M. Tanner & B. Inhelder (Eds.), *Discussions on child development* (pp. 75–86). New York: International Universities Press.

Inhelder, B., & Piaget, J. (1958). *The growth of logical thinking from childhood to adolescence.* New York: Basic Books.

Isabella, R. A. (1993). Origins of attachment: Maternal interactive behavior across the first year. *Child Development, 64*(2), 605–621.

Isabella, R. A., Belsky, J., & von Eye, A. (1989). Origins of infant-mother attachment: An examination of interaction synchrony during the infant's first year. *Developmental Psychology, 25*, (12–21).

Izard, C. E., & Buechler, S. (1986). Theoretical perspectives on emotions in developmental disabilities. In M. Lewis & L. Taft (Eds.), *Developmental disabilities: Theory, assessment, and intervention.* New York: Medical and Scientific Books.

Jalongo, M. R. (1987). Do security blankets belong in preschool? *Young Children, 42*(3), 3–8.

Jensen, M. A., & Chevalier, Z. W. (1990). *Issues and advocacy in early education.* Boston: Allyn & Bacon.

Jensen, W. A., Heinrich, B., Wake, D. B., & Wake, M. H. (1979). *Biology.* Belmont, CA: Wadsworth.

Jersild, A. T., & Holmes, F. B. (1935a). *Children's fears.* New York: Teachers College Press.

Jersild, A. T., & Holmes, F. B. (1935b). Methods of overcoming children's fears. *Journal of Psychology, 1*, 75–104.

Joffe, A., & Radius, S. M. (1991). Health counseling of adolescents. *Pediatrics in Review, 12*(11), 344–351.

Johnson, D., & Johnson, R. (1984). Classroom learning structure and attitudes toward handicapped students in mainstream settings: A theoretical model and research evidence. In R. L. Jones (Ed.), *Attitudes and attitude change in special education: Theory and practice* (pp. 118–142). Reston, VA: Council for Exceptional Children.

Johnson, J., & McCraken, J. B. (Eds.). (1994). *The early childhood career lattice: Perspectives on professional development.* Washington, DC: National Association for the Education of Young Children.

Johnson, J. E., Christie, J. F., & Yawkey, T. D. (1987). *Play and early childhood development.* Glenview, IL: Scott, Foresman.

Johnson, J. E., & Yawkey, T. D. (1988). Play and integration. In T. D. Yawkey & J. E. Johnson (Eds.), *Integrative processes and socialization: Early to middle childhood* (pp. 97–117). Hillsdale, NJ: Erlbaum.

Jones, E. (Ed.). (1993). *Growing teachers; Partnerships in staff development.* Washington DC: National Association for the Education of Young Children.

Jones, H. E., & Jones, M. C. (1928). A study of fear. *Childhood Education, 5*, 136–143.

Jones, K. L. (1988). *Smith's recognizable patterns of human malformation.* Philadelphia: Saunders.

Jusczyk, P. W., Cutler, A., & Redanz, N. J. (1993). Infants' preference for the predominant stress patterns of English words. *Child Development, 64*(3), 675–687.

Kagan, J. (1971). *Change and continuity in infancy.* New York: Wiley.

Kagan, J. (1982). *Psychological research on the human infant: An evaluative summary.* New York: W. T. Grant Foundation.

Kagan, S. L. (1989). The care and education of America's young children: At the brink of a paradigm shift. In F. J. Macchiarola & A. Gartner (Eds.), Caring for America's children. *Proceedings of the Academy of Political Science, 37* (Vol. 2, pp. 70–83). New York: The Academy of Political Science.

Kail, R. (1984). *The development of memory in children* (2nd ed.). New York: Freeman.

Kamii, C. (1982). *Number in preschool and kindergarten.* Washington, DC: National Association for the Education of Young Children.

Kamii, C. (1985a). Leading primary education toward excellence—beyond worksheets and drill. *Young Children, 40*(6), 3–11.

Kamii, C. (1985b). *Young children reinvent arithmetic.* New York: Teachers College Press.

Kamii, C. (1989). *Young children continue to invent arithmetic: 2nd grade.* New York: Teachers College Press.

Kamii, C. (1990). *Achievement testing in the early grades: The games grown-ups play.* Washington, DC: NAEYC Publications.

Kamii, C., & DeClark, G. (1985). *Young children reinvent arithmetic: Implications of Piaget's theory.* New York: Teachers College Press.

Kamii, C., & DeVries, R. (1978). *Physical knowledge in preschool education.* Englewood Cliffs, NJ: Prentice Hall.

Kandel, G., & Lesser, G. (1972). *Youth in two worlds: U.S. and Denmark.* San Francisco: Jossey-Bass.

Karmel, M. (1959). *Thank you, Dr. Lamaze: Painless childbirth.* Philadelphia: Lippincott.

Karmiloff-Smith, A. (1986). Stage-structure versus phase-process in modeling linguistic and cognitive development. In I. Levin (Ed.), *Stage and structure: Reopening the debate* (pp. 164–190). Norwood, NJ: Ablex.

Karnes, M. B., & Johnson, L. J. (1989). Training for staff, parents, and volunteers working with gifted young children, especially those with disabilities from low income homes. *Young Children, 44*(3), 49–56.

Kasmoski, K. (1984). Educational computing: The burden of ensuring quality. *Phi Delta Kappan, 66,* 244–248.

Katcher, A. L., & Haber, J. S. (1991). The pediatrician and early intervention for the developmentally disabled or handicapped child. *Pediatrics in Review, 12*(10), 305–312.

Katz, L. G. (1972). Develomental stages of preschool teachers. *The Elementary School Journal, 23,* 50–54.

Katz, L. G. (1977a). *Talks with teachers.* Washington, DC: National Association for the Education of Young Children.

Katz, L. G. (1977). Early childhood programs and ideological dispute. In L. C. Katz (Ed.), *Talks with teachers.* Washington, DC: National Association for the Education of Young Children.

Katz, L. G., & Chard, S. (1988). *Engaging children's minds: The project approach.* Norwood, NJ: Ablex.

Katz, L. G., Evangelou, D., & Hartman, J. (1990). *The case for mixed-aged grouping in early education.* Washington, DC: National Association for the Education of Young Children.

Katz, P. A. (1976). The acquisition of racial attitudes in children. In P. A. Katz (Ed.), *Towards the elimination of racism* (pp. 125–154). New York: Pergamon Press.

Katz, P. A. (1982). Development of children's awareness and intergroup attitudes. In L. G. Katz (Ed.), *Current topics in early childhood education* (Vol. 4, pp. 17–54). Norwood, NJ: Ablex.

Kaufman, N. (1985). Review of Gesell School Readiness Test. In J. V. Mitchell, Jr. (Ed.), *Ninth mental measurements yearbook* (Vol. 1, pp. 607–608). Lincoln, NE: Buros Institute of Mental Measurements.

Keating, D. P. (1980). Thinking processes in adolescence. In J. Adelson (Ed.), *Handbook of adolescence psychology* (pp. 211–246). New York: Wiley.

Keating, D. P. (1990). Charting pathways to the development of expertise. *Educational Psychologist, 25,* 243–267.

Keating, D. P., & MacClean, D. J. (1988). Reconstruction in cognitive development: A poststructuralist agenda. In P. B. Baltes, D. L. Reatherman, & R. M. Lerner (Eds.), *Life-span development and behavior.* Hillsdale, NJ: Erlbaum.

Kelley, R. K. (1972). The premarital sexual revolution: Comments on research. *Family Coordinator, 21,* 334–336.

Kellogg, R. (1969). *Analyzing children's art.* Palo Alto, CA: National Press Books.

Kelly, D. H., & Shannon, D. C. (1982). Sudden infant death syndrome and near sudden infant death syndrome: A review of the literature, 1964–1982. In W. Oh (Ed.), *The pediatric clinics of North America* (Vol. 29, pp. 1241–1262). Philadelphia: Saunders.

Kendall, F. E. (1983). *Diversity in the classroom: A multicultural approach to the education of young children.* New York: Teachers College Press.

Kendall, E. D., & Moukaddem, V. E. (1992). Who's vulnerable in infant child care centers? *Young Children, 47*(5), 72–78.

Kendrick, A. S., Kaufmann, R., & Messenger, K. P. (Eds.). *Healthy young children: A manual for programs.* Washington, DC: National Association for the Education of Young Children.

Kerwin, M. L. E., & Day, J. D. (1985). Peer influences on cognitive development. In J. B. Pryor & J. D. Day (Eds.), *The development of social cognition* (pp. 211–218). New York: Springer.

Kett, J. F. (1977). *Rites of passage: Adolescence in America 1790 to the present.* New York: Basic Books.

Kirk, R. (1990). Abortion: The Hispanic perspective. *Vista, 1,* 6–8.

Kirk, S., & Chalfant, J. C. (1984). *Academic and developmental learning disabilities.* Denver: Love.

Kisker, E. E., Hofferth, S. L., Phillips, D. A., & Farquhar, E. (1991). *A profile of child care settings: Early education and care in 1990.* Washington, DC: United States Department of Education.

Kitano, M. (1989). The K-3 teacher's role in recognizing and supporting young gifted children. *Young Children, 44* (3), 57–63.

Klahr, D., & Wallace, J. G. (1976). *Cognitive development: An information processing view.* Hillsdale, NJ: Erlbaum.

Klaus, M. H., & Kennell, J. H. (1982). *Parent-infant bonding* (2nd ed.). St. Louis: Mosby.

Kleinman, A. S. (1974). The use of private speech in young children and its relation to social speech (Doctoral dissertation, University of Chicago). *Dissertation Abstracts International, 36,* 472B.

Klerman, L. V. (1991). *Alive and well? A research and policy review of health programs for poor young children.* New York: National Center for Children in Poverty, Columbia University School of Public Health.

Kohl, H. (1984). *Growing minds: On becoming a teacher.* New York: Harper and Row.

Kohlberg, L. (1966). A cognitive-developmental analysis of children's sex-role concepts and attitudes. In E. E. Maccoby (Ed.), *The development of sex differences* (pp. 82–173). Stanford, CA: Stanford University Press.

Kohlberg, L. (1968, September). The child as a moral philosopher. *Psychology Today,* pp. 63–67.

Kohlberg, L. (1984). *Essays on moral development: Vol. 2. The psychology of moral development.* San Francisco: Harper and Row.

Kohlberg, L., Yaeger, J., & Hjertholm, E. (1968). Private speech: Four studies and a review of theories. *Child Development, 39,* 691–736.

Korner, A. F. (1989). Infant stimulation: The pros and cons in historical perspective. *Bulletin of National Center for Clinical Infant Programs, 10,* 11–17.

Korner, A. F., Zeanah, C. H., Linden, J., Berkowitz, R. I., Kraemer, H. C., & Agras, W. S. (1985). The relation between neonatal and later activity and temperament. *Child Development, 56,* 38–42.

Kostelny, K. (1994). Witnessing violence damages development. *American Academy of Pediatric News, 10*(5), 1 & 12–13.

Krashen, S. (1981). *Second language acquisition and second language learning.* Elmsford, New York: Pergamon Press.

Krashen, S. D. (1991). *Bilingual education: A focus on current research.* Washington, DC: National Clearinghouse for Bilingual Education.

Krauss, R. M., & Glucksberg, S. (1969). The development of communication: Competence as a function of age. *Child Development, 40,* 255–266.

Krebs, D., & Gillmore, J. (1982). The relationship among the first stages of cognitive development, role-taking abilities and moral development. *Child Development, 53,* 877–886.

Kreutzer, M. A. & Leonard, C., & Flavell, J. H. (1975). An interview study of children's knowledge about memory. *Monographs of the Society for Research in Child Development, 40* (1, Serial No. 159).

Kruesi, M. J., & Rapoport, J. L. (1986). Diet and human behavior: How much do they affect each other? *Annual Reviews of Nutrition, 6,* 113–130.

Kuhn, D. (1992). Cognitive development. In M. H. Borstein & M. E. Lamb (Eds.), *Developmental psychology: An advanced textbook.* Hillsdale, NJ: Erlbaum.

Kull, J. A. (1986). Learning and Logo. In P. Campbell & G. Fein (Eds.), *Young children and microcomputers* (pp. 103–128). Englewood Cliffs, NJ: Prentice Hall.

Kunjufu, J. (1980). Nutrition for child development. *Black Child Journal, 1,* 6–13.

Laboratory of Comparative Human Cognition (1983). Culture and cognitive development. In W. Kessen (Ed.), *Handbook of child psychology: Vol I, History, theory, and methods* (14th ed.), (pp. 295–356). NY: Wiley.

Labov, W. (1970). The logic of nonstandard English. In F. Williams (Ed.), *Language and poverty* (pp. 153–189). Chicago: Markham.

Labov, W. (1972). *Language in the inner city: Studies in the black English vernacular.* Philadelphia: University of Pennsylvania.

Ladd, G. W., & Golter, B. S. (1988). Parents' management of preschooler's peer relations: Is it related to children's social competence? *Developmental Psychology, 24,* 3–7.

Lamb, M. (1977). The development of mother-infant attachments in the second year of life. *Developmental Psychology, 13,* 639–649.

Lamb, M. E. (1978a). The development of sibling relationships in infancy: A short-term longitudinal study. *Child Development, 49,* 1189–1196.

Lamb, M. E. (1978b). Interactions between 18-month-olds and their preschool-aged siblings. *Child Development, 49,* 51–59.

Lamb, M. E. (1981). The development of father-infant relationships. In M. E. Lamb (Ed.), *The role of the father in child development* (rev. ed., pp. 1–73). New York: Wiley.

Lamb, M. E., Morrison, D. C., & Malkin, C. M. (1987). The development of infant social expectations in face-to-face interaction: A longitudinal study. *Merrill-Palmer Quarterly, 33,* 241–254.

Lamme, L. L. (1979). Handwriting in an early childhood curriculum. *Young Children, 35* (1), 20–27.

Lamme, L. L. (1980). Reading with an infant. *Childhood Education, 56,* 285–290.

Lamme, L. L. (1984). *Growing up writing.* Washington, DC: Acropolis Books.

Lamme, L. L., Cox, V., Matanzo, J., & Olson, M. (1980). *Raising readers: A guide to sharing literature with young children.* New York: Walker.

Langlois, J. H., & Down, C. A. (1980). Mothers, fathers, and peers as socialization agents of sex-typed play behavior in young children. *Child Development, 51,* 1237–1247.

Larson, J., & Robinson, C. (1989). Latter effects of preschool on low risk children. *Early Childhood Research Quarterly* (Vol. 4, No.1, pp. 133–144).

Larson, L. (News Writer), (June, 1994). *AZT reduces maternal AIDS transmission.* In American Academy of Pediatrics Health Briefs, (p..2). Elk Grove Village, IL.

Larson, L. (News Writer), (August, 1994). In-line skating injuries double. In *American Academy of Pediatrics News Health Briefs,* 10 (8), 2. Elk Grove Village: IL: American Academy of Pediatrics.

Lasley, T. (Ed.). (1986). Teacher induction: Programs and research [Special issue]. *Journal of Teacher Education,* 37 (1).

Lazar, I., & Darlington, R. (1982). Lasting effects of early education: A report from the Consortium for Longitudinal Studies. *Monographs of the Society for Research in Child Development,* 47(2–3, Serial No. 195).

Le Francois, G.R. (1979). *Psychology of teaching: A bear always usually, sometimes faces the front,* (3rd. Ed.). Belmont, CA: Wadsworth Publishing Co., Ind.

Leahy, R. L., & Shirk, S. R. (1984). The development of classifactory skills and sex trait stereotypes in children. *Sex Roles,* 10, 281–292.

Leboyer, F. (1975). *Birth without violence.* New York: Knopf.

Loewald, H. (1988). *Sublimation: Inquiries into theoretical psychoanalysis.* New Haven, CT: Yale University Press.

Lerner, J. W. (1985). *Learning disabilities: Theories, diagnosis, and teaching strategies* (4th ed.). Boston: Houghton Mifflin.

Lerner, J. W., Mardell-Czudnowski, C., & Goldenberg, D. (1987). *Special education for the early childhood years* (2nd ed.). Englewood Cliffs, NJ: Prentice Hall.

Lesser, G. S. (1979, March). Stop picking on Big Bird. *Psychology Today,* pp. 57, 60.

Leung, E. H., & Rheingold, H. L. (1981). Development of pointing as a social gesture. *Developmental Psychology,* 17, 215–220.

Lever, J. (1976). Sex differences in games children play. *Social Problems,* 23, 478–487.

Levinson, D. J. (1986). A conception of adult development. *American Psychologist,* 41, 3–13.

Levy, G. D., & Carter, D. B. (1989). Gender schema, gender constancy, and gender role knowledge: The roles of cognitive factors in preschoolers' gender-role stereotype attributions. *Developmental Psychology,* 25, 444–449.

Lewis, M., & Brooks, J. (1978). Self-knowledge and emotional development. In M. Lewis & L. Rosenblum (Eds.), *The development of affect* (pp. 205–226). New York: Plenum Press.

Lewis, M., & Brooks-Gunn, J. (1979). *Social cognition and the acquisition of self.* New York: Plenum Press.

Lewis, M.D. (1994). Reconciling stage and specificity in neo-Piagetian theory: Self organizing conceptual structures. *Human Development,* 37 (3) 143–169.

Liben, L. S., & Signorella, M. L. (1980). Gender-related schemata and constructive memory in children. *Child Development,* 51(1), 11–18.

Lickona, T. (1983). *Raising good children: Helping your children through the stages of moral development—from birth through the teenage years.* New York: Bantam.

Lieberman, A., & Miller, L. (1984). *Teachers, their world, and their work: Implications for school improvement.* Alexandria, VA: Association for Supervision and Curriculum Development.

Liebert, R. M., Sprafkin, J. N., & Davidson, E. S. (1982). *The early window: Effects of television on children and youth.* (2nd ed.). New York: Pergamon Press.

Lindfors, J. (1980). *Children's language and language learning.* Englewood Cliffs, NJ: Prentice Hall.

Lindfors, J. (1987). *Children's language and language learning* (2nd ed.). Englewood Cliffs, NJ: Prentice Hall.

Linehan, M. F. (1992). Children who are homeless: Educational strategies for school personnel. *Phi Delta Kappan,* 74(1), 61–66.

Linn, S., Schoenbaum, S., Monson, R., Rosner, B., Stubblefield, R., & Ryan, K. (1982). Coffee and pregnancy. *New England Journal of Medicine,* 306, 141–145.

Lipton, M. A., & Mayo, J. P. (1983). Diet and hyperkinesis: An update. *Journal of the American Dietetic Association,* 83, 132.

Little Soldier, L. (1992). Working with Native American children. *Young Children,* 47(6), 15–21.

Locust, C. (1988). Wounding the spirit: Discrimination and traditional American Indian belief systems. *Harvard Educational Review,* 58(3), 315–329.

Loewald, H. (1988). *Sublimation: Inquiries into theoretical psychoanalysis.* New Haven: Yale University Press.

Londerville, S., & Main, M. (1981). Security attachment, compliance, and maternal training methods in the second year of life. *Developmental Psychology,* 17, 289–299.

Lucariello, J., & Nelson, K. (1985). Slot-filler categories as memory organizers for young children. *Developmental Psychology,* 21, 272–282.

Lyons-Ruth, K., Alpern, L., & Repacholi, B. (1993). Disorganized infant attachment classification and maternal psychosocial problems as predictors of hostile-aggressive behavior in the preschool classroom. *Child Development,* 64(2), 572–585.

Maccoby, E., & Jacklin, C. N. (1974/1980). Sex differences in aggression: A rejoinder and a reprise. *Child Development,* 51, 964–980.

Maccoby, E. E., & Martin, J. A. (1983). Socialization in the context of the family: Parent-child interaction. In E. M. Hetherington (Ed.), *Handbook of child psychology: Vol. 4. Socialization, personality and social development* (4th ed., pp. 1–101). New York: Wiley.

MacDonald, K., & Parke, R. D. (1984). Bridging the gap. Parent-child play interaction and peer interactive competence. *Child Development,* 55, 1265–1277.

MacDonald, L. L., Danila, R. N., & Osterholm, M. T. (1985). Infection with human T-lymphotropic virus types III/lymphadenopathy-associated virus. *MMWR,* 37, 183–186.

MacFarlane, A. (1977). *The psychology of childbirth.* Cambridge, MA: Harvard University Press.

MacLaughlin, B. (1978). *Second language learning in children.* Hillsdale, NJ: Erlbaum.

Mahler, M. (1968). *On human symbiosis and the vicissitudes of individuation.* New York: International Universities Press.

Main, M., & Cassidy, J. (1988). Categories of response to reunion with parent at age 6: Predictable from infant attachment classification and stable over 1-month period. *Developmental Psychology, 24,* 415–426.

Main, M., & Solomon, J. (1990). Procedures for identifying infants as disorganized/disoriented during the Ainsworth strange situation. In M. Greenberg, D. Cicchetti, & E. M. Cummings (Eds.), *Attachment in the preschool years: Theory, research, and intervention.* Chicago: University of Chicago Press.

Main, M., & Weston, D. R. (1981). The quality of the toddler's relationship to mother and father: Related to conflict behavior and the readiness to establish new relationships. *Child Development, 52,* 932–940.

Makin, J. W., & Porter, R. H. (1989). Attractiveness of lactating females' breast odors to neonates. *Child Development, 60,* 803–810.

Mallory, B. L. & New, R. S. (Eds.).(1994). *Diversity and developmentally appropriate practices* New York: Teachers College Press.

Mandler, J. M. (1988). How to build a baby: On the development of an accessible representational system. *Cognitive Development, 3,* 113–136.

Mandler, J. M. (1990). A new perspective on cognitive development in infancy. *American Scientist, 78*(3), 236–243.

Mandler, J. M. (1992). Commentary on Bebko, Burke, Craven and Sarlo (1992): The importance of sensorimotor development: A perspective from children with physical handicaps. *Human Development, 36*(4), 226–240.

Mange, A., & Mange, E. (1990). *Genetics: Human aspects.* Sunderland, MA: Sinauer Associates.

Maratsos, M. (1983). Some current issues in the study of the acquisition of grammar. In J. H. Flavell & E. M. Markman (Eds.), *Handbook of child psychology, Vol. 3. Cognitive development* (4th ed., pp. 707–786). New York: Wiley.

Marcus, D. E., & Overton, W. E. (1978). The development of cognitive gender constancy and sex-role preference. *Child Development, 49,* 434–444.

Marion, M. (1991). *Guidance of young children* (3rd ed.). Columbus, OH: Merrill.

Marsden, D. B., Meisels, S. J., & Jablon, J. R. (1993). *The work sampling system: Preschool through grade three.* Ann Arbor, MI: University of Michigan Center for Human Growth and Development.

Martin, C. L., & Halverson, C. F. (1981). A schematic processing model of sex-typing: Theory and research. *Child Development, 52,* 1119–1132.

Martin, C. L., & Halverson, C. F. (1987). The role of cognition in sex role acquisition. In D. B. Carter (Ed.), *Current conceptions of sex roles and sex typing: Theory and research* (pp. 123–137). New York: Praeger.

Maslow, A. (1968). *Toward a psychology of being* (2nd ed.). Princeton, NJ: Van Nostrand.

Maslow, A. (1970). *Motivation and personality* (2nd ed.). New York: Harper and Row.

Masur, E. F., & Gleason, J. B. (1980). Parent-child interaction and the acquisition of lexical information during play. *Developmental Psychology, 16,* 404–409.

Matas, L., Arend, R. A., & Stroufe, L. A. (1978). Continuity of adaptation in the second year: The relationship between quality of attachment and later competence. *Child Development, 49,* 547–556.

Mayhall, P., & Norgard, K. (1983). *Child abuse and neglect.* New York: Wiley.

McAfee, O., & Leong, D. (1994). *Assessing and guiding young children's development and learning.* Boston: Allyn & Bacon.

McCracken, J. B. (1992). *Keeping healthy: Parents, teachers, and children* (brochure). Washington, DC: National Association for the Education of Young Children.

McCollum, J. A., & Bair, H. (1994). Research in parent-child interaction: Guidance to developmentally appropriate practice for young children with disabilities. In B. L. Mallory & R. S. New (Eds.), *Diversity and developmentally appropriate practices.* New York: Teachers College Press.

McDonald, R., & Avery, D. (1983). *Dentistry for the child and adolescent* (4th ed.). St. Louis: Mosby.

McNally, R. J., & Saugh, P. A. (1993). On the distinction between traumatic simple phobia and post traumatic distress disorder. In J. R. T. Davidson & E. B. Foa (Eds.), *Post traumatic stress disorder: DSM-IV and beyond* (pp. 207–212). Washington, DC: American Psychiatric Press.

McNeill, D. (1970). *The acquisition of language.* New York: Harper and Row.

Mead, M., & Newton, N. (1967). Cultural patterning of perinatal behavior. In S. Richardson & A. Guttmacher (Eds.), *Childrearing: Its social and psychological aspects.* Baltimore: Williams and Wilkins.

Medina, Z., & Neill, D. M. (1988). *Fallout from the testing explosion: How 100 million standardized exams undermine quality and excellence in America's public schools.* Cambridge, MA: National Center for Fair and Open testing.

Mehan, H. (1982). The structure of classroom events and their consequences for student performance. In P. Gilmore & A. A. Glatthorn (Eds.), *Children in and out of school: Ethnography and education* (pp. 59–87). Washington, DC: Center for Applied Linguistics.

Mehler, J. (1985). Language related dispositions in early infancy. In J. Mehler & R. Fox (Eds.), *Neonate cognition: Beyond the blooming buzzing confusion* (pp. 7–28). Hillsdale, NJ: Erlbaum.

Meisels, S. J. (1987). Uses and abuses of developmental screening and school readiness testing. *Young Children. 42*(2), 68–73.

Meisels, S. J. (1989). *Developmental screening in early childhood: A guide* (3rd ed.). Washington, DC: National Association for the Education of Young Children.

Meltzoff, A. N., & Moore, M. K. (1983). Newborn infants imitate adult facial gestures. *Child Development, 54* (3), 702–709.

Menninga, B. (1994). Violence in schools: No single cause, no simple solutions. *The Wingspread Journal, 16*(2), 3.

Menyuk, P. (1964). Alternation of rules in children's grammar. *Journal of Verbal Learning and Verbal Behavior, 3,* 480–488.

Menyuk, P. (1971). *The acquisition and development of language.* Englewood Cliffs, NJ: Prentice Hall.

Menyuk, P. (1976). That's another funny, awful way of saying it. *Journal of Education, 158,* 25–38.

Menyuk, P. (1983). Language development and reading. In T. Gallagher and C. Prutting (Eds.), *Pragmatic assessment and intervention issues in language* (pp. 151–170). San Diego, CA: College Hill Press.

Menyuk, P. (1985). Wherefore metalinguistic skills? A commentary on Bialystok and Ryan. *Merrill-Palmer Quarterly, 31,* 253–259.

Menyuk, P. (1988). *Language development: Knowledge and use.* Glenview, IL: Scott, Foresman.

Merewood, A. (1991). Sperm under siege. *Health, 23*(3), 53–57, 76–77.

Meyerhoff, M. K. (1994, March). Perspective on parenting: Crawling around. *Pediatrics for Parents,* pp. 8, 9.

Michaels, S. (1981). Sharing time: Children's narrative styles and differential access to literacy. *Language in Society, 10,* 49–76.

Michel, G. L. (1981). Right-handedness: A consequence of infant supine head orientation preference? *Science, 212,* 685–687.

Miller, C. S. (1984). Building self-control: Discipline for young children. *Young Children, 40*(1), 15–19.

Miller, N. E., & Dollard, J. (1941). *Social learning and imitation.* New Haven, CT: Yale University Press.

Miller, P. M., Danaher, D. L., & Forbes, D. (1986). Sex-related strategies for coping with interpersonal conflict in children aged five and seven. *Developmental Psychology, 22,* 543–548.

Minkoff, H., Deepak, N., Menez, R., & Fikrig, S. (1987). Pregnancies resulting in infants with Acquired Immune Deficiency Syndrome or AIDS related complex: Follow-up of mothers, children and subsequently born siblings. *Obstetrics and Gynecology, 69,* 288–291.

Mobley, C. E. & Pullis, M. E. (1991). Temperament and behavioral adjustments in preschool children. *Early Childhood Research Quarterly, 6*(4), 577–586.

Moore, B. S., & Eisenberg, N. (1984). The development of altruism. In G. Whitehurst (Ed.), *Annals of child development* (Vol. 1, pp. 107–174). Greenwich, CT: JAI Press.

Moore, K. L. (1983). *Realities in childbearing.* Philadelphia: Saunders.

Moore, K.L. (1986). *Before we are born* (3rd ed.). Philadelphia: Saunders.

Morgan, H. (1976). Neonatal precocity and the black experience. *Negro Educational Review, 27,* 129–134.

Morphett, M. V., & Washburne, C. (1931). When should children begin to read? *The Elementary School Journal, 31,* 496–503.

Moshmon, D., & Timmons, M. (1982). The construction of logical necessity. *Human Development, 25,* 309–323.

Motta, R.W. (1994). Identification of characteristics and causes of childhood post traumatic stress disorder. *Psychology in the Schools, 31*(1), 49–56.

Musick, J. S., & Householder, J. (1986). *Infant development: From theory to practice.* Belmont, CA: Wadsworth.

Mussen, P. (1979). *The psychological development of the child* (3rd ed.). Englewood Cliffs, NJ: Prentice Hall.

Myers, B. J. (1982). Early intervention using Brazelton training with middle-class mothers and fathers of newborns. *Child Development, 53,* 462–471.

Nachbar, R. (1989). A K/1 class can work—wonderfully! *Young Children, 44*(5), 67–71.

Nanko, M. J. (1994, March). Keeping your skateboarder alive and well. *Pediatrics for Parents,* pp. 2–3.

National Academy of Early Childhood Programs. (1984). *Accreditation criteria and procedures.* Washington, DC: National Association for the Education of Young Children.

National Association for the Education of Young Children. (1988). *Position statement on standardized testing of young children 3 through 8 years of age.* Washington, DC: NAEYC Publications.

National Association for the Education of Young Children. (1990). *Position statement on media violence in children's lives.* Washington, DC: Author.

National Association for the Education of Young Children. (1991). *Early childhood teacher education guidelines: Basic and advanced* (a position statement). Washington, DC: Author.

National Association for the Education of Young Children, & National Association of Early Childhood Specialists in State Departments of Education. (1992). *Guidelines for appropriate curriculum content and assessment in programs serving children 3 through 8 years of age.* Washington, DC: National Association for the Education of Young Children.

National Association for the Education of Young Children. (1992). Announcing . . . Child Care Aware: A partnership for quality child care. *Young Children, 47*(5), 82–83.

National Association for the Education of Young Children. (n.d.). *Guiding principles of the development, analysis, and implementation of early childhood legislation* (brochure no. 590). Washington, DC: Author.

National Association for the Education of Young Children. (1994). Public policy report: Starting Points: Executive Summary of the report of the Carnegie Corporation of New York Task Force on meeting the needs of young children. *Young Children, 49*(5), 58–61.

**National Association for the Education of Young Children.** (1995). Guidelines for preparation of early childhood professions: Associate, baccalaureate, and advanced. Washington, DC: Author.

**National Association of Elementary School Principals.** (1990). *Standards for quality programming for young children: Early childhood education and the elementary school principal.* Alexandria, VA: Author.

**National Association of State Boards of Education.** (1988). *Right from the start: The report of the NASBE Task Force on Early Childhood Education.* Alexandria, VA: Author.

**National Board for Professional Teaching Standards** (2nd ed.). (1991). *Toward high and rigorous standards for the teaching profession: Initial policies and perspectives of the National Board for Professional Teaching Standards.* Detroit, MI: Author.

**National Center for Children in Poverty.** (1994, Summer). *Strengthening families in need—models and commitments, 4*(2), 1–3.

**National Cholesterol Education Program.** (1992). Report of the Expert Panel on Blood Cholesterol in Children and Adolescents. *Pediatrics, 89,* (Supp.), 525–584.

**National Council of Teachers of Mathematics.** (1989). *Curriculum and evaluation standards for school mathematics.* Reston, VA: Author.

**National Institute on Drug Abuse Michigan's Institute for Social Resource.** (nd).

**National Research Council.** (1987). Panel on adolescent pregnancy and childbearing. In C. Hayes (Ed.), *Risking the future: Adolescent sexuality, pregnancy and childbearing.* Washington, DC: National Academy Press.

**National Research Council.** (1993). *Understanding and preventing violence.* Washington, DC: National Academy Press.

**Needleman, H. L.** (1992). Childhood exposure to lead: A common cause of school failure. *Phi Delta Kappan, 74*(1), 35–37.

**Nelson, K.** (1973). Structure and strategy in learning to talk. *Monographs of the Society for Research in Child Development, 38* (1–2, Serial No. 149).

**Nelson, K.** (1979). The role of language in infant development. In M. H. Bornstein & W. Kessen (Eds.), *Psychological development from infancy: Image to intention* (pp. 307–338). Hillsdale, NJ: Erlbaum.

**Nelson, K.** (1980). *Children's language* (Vol. 1). New York: Gardener Press.

**Nelson, K.** (1981). Individual differences in language development: Implications for development and language. *Developmental Psychology, 17,* 170–187.

**Nelson, K.** (1986). *Event knowledge.* Hillsdale, NJ: Erlbaum.

**Nelson, K., Carskaddon, G., & Bonvillian, J. D.** (1973). Syntax acquisition: Impact of experimental variation in adult verbal interaction with the child. *Child Development, 44,* 497–504.

**Nelson, K., & Gruendel, J.** (1981). Generalized event representations: Basic building blocks of cognitive development. In M. Lamb & A. Brown (Eds.), *Advances in development psychology* (Vol. 1, pp. 131–158). Hillsdale, NJ: Erlbaum.

**Nelson, K. & Lucariello, J.** (1985). The development of meaning in first words. In M. Barrett (Ed.), *Children's single word speech.* New York: Wiley.

**Nevin, M. M.** (1988). Dormant dangers of DES. *The Earadian Nurse, 84,* 17–19.

**New, R. S.** (1994). Culture, child development, and developmentally appropriate practices: Teachers as collaborative researchers. In B. L. Mallory & R. S. New (Eds.), *Diversity and developmentally appropriate practices* (pp. 65–83). New York: Teachers College Press.

**Newell, A., & Simon, H. A.** (1972). *Human problem solving.* Englewood Cliffs, NJ: Prentice Hall.

**Newman, J.** (1988). On line: Logo and the language arts. *Language Arts, 65,* 598–605.

**Nickolls, K. B., Cassel, J., & Kaplan, B. H.** (1972). Psychosocial assets, life crisis, and the prognosis of pregnancy. *American Journal of Epidemiology, 95,* 431–441.

**Ninio, A., & Bruner, J.** (1978). The achievements and antecedents of labelling. *Journal of Child Language, 5,* 1–16.

**Nizel, A. E.** (1977). Preventing dental carries: The nutritional factors. In C. Neumann & D. B. Jelliffe (Eds.), *The pediatric clinics of North America* (Vol. 24, pp. 141–155). Philadelphia: Saunders.

**Nord, C. W., Moore, K. A., Morrison, D. R., Brown, B., & Myers, D.** (1992). Consequences of teen-age parenting. *Journal of School Health, 62*(7) pp. 310–318.

**Nowakowski, R. S.** (1987). Basic concepts of central nervous system development. *Child Development, 58*(3), 568–595.

**Nunner-Winkler, G., & Sodian, B.** (1988). Children's understanding of moral emotions. *Child Development, 59,* 1323–1338.

**Ogbu, J. U.** (1981). Origins of human competence: A cultural ecological perspective. *Child Development, 52*(2), 413–429.

**Olney, R., & Scholnick, E.** (1976). Adult judgments of age and linguistic differences in infant vocalizations. *Journal of Child Language, 3,* 145–156.

**Olson, S. L., Bates, J. E., & Bayles, K.** (1984). Mother infant interaction and the development of individual differences in children's cognitive competence. *Developmental Psychology, 20,* 166–179.

**Omer, H. & Everly, B. S.** (1988). Psychological factors in preterm labor: Critical review and theoretical synthesis. *American Journal of Psychiatry, 195,* 1507–1513.

**Oppenheim, J. F.** (1987). *Buy me, buy me! The Bank Street guide to choosing toys for children.* New York: Pantheon.

**Orlick, T. D.** (1981). Positive socialization via cooperative games. *Developmental Psychology, 17,* 426–429.

**Ost, D. H.** (1989). The culture of teaching: stability and change. *The Educational Forum, 53,* 163–181.

Osterholm, M. T., Klein, J. O., Aronson, S. S., & Pickering, L. K. (Eds.). (1986). *Infectious diseases in child day care: Management and prevention* (pp. 9–14). Chicago: University of Chicago Press.

Owens-Stively, J. (1987). Stress and coping in children. In S. Moore & K. Kolb (Eds.), *Reviews of research for practitioners and parents* (No. 3, pp. 21–33). Minneapolis: University of Minnesota.

Oyemade, U. J., & Washington, V. (1989). Drug abuse prevention begins in early childhood. *Young Children, 44*(5), 6–12.

Paley, V. (1988). *Bad guys don't have birthdays: Fantasy play at four.* Chicago: Unversity of Chicago Press.

Palkovitz, R. (1984). Parental attitudes and fathers' interactions with their 5-month old infants. *Developmental Psychology, 20,* 1054–1060.

Parke, R. D., & Sawin, D. B. (1977, November). Fathering: It's a major role. *Psychology Today,* pp. 109–112.

Parke, R. D., & Sawin, D. B. (1981). Father-infant interaction in the newborn period: A re-evaluation of some current myths. In E. M. Hetherington & R. D. Parke (Eds.), *Contemporary readings in child psychology* (2nd ed., pp. 229–234). New York: McGraw-Hill.

Parten, M. B. (1933). Social participation among preschool children. *Journal of Abnormal Psychology, 27,* 243–269.

Paul, A. S. (1992). American Indian (Native American) influences. In L. R. Williams & D. P. Fromberg (Eds.), *Encyclopedia of early education* (pp. 11–13). New York: Garland Publishing.

Pederson, F. A., Zaslow, M., Cain, R., & Anderson, B. J. (1981). Cesarean childbirth: Psychological implications for mothers and fathers. *Infant Mental Health Journal, 2,* 257–263.

Pellegrini, A.D. & C.D. Glickman (1990). Measuring Kindergartners' Social Competence. *Young Children, 45*(4), 40–44.

Perez, B., & Torres-Guzman, M. E. (1992). *Learning in two worlds: An integrated Spanish/English biliteracy approach.* White Plains, New York: Longman.

Perrin, J. M. (1990). Children with special health needs: A United States perspective. In Child Health in 1990: The United States compared to Canada, England and Wales, France, The Netherlands, and Norway. *Pediatrics, 86*(6) (Supp., part 2 of 2), 1120–1121.

Peskin, H. (1967). Pubertal onset and ego functioning. *Journal of Abnormal Psychology, 72,* 1–15.

Peterson, C. C., Peterson, J. L, & Carroll, J. (1986). Television viewing and imaginative problem solving during preadolescence. *Journal of Genetic Psychology, 147,* 61–67.

Petit, G. S., Dodge, K. A., & Brown, M. M. (1988). Early family experience, social problem solving patterns, and children's social competence. *Child Development, 59,* 107–120.

Pflaum, S. W. (1986). *The development of language and literacy in young children.* (3rd ed.). Columbus, OH: Merrill.

Phillips, C. B. (1994). The movement of African-American children through sociocultural contexts: A case of conflict resolution. In B. L. Mallory & R. S. New (Eds.), *Diversity and developmentally appropriate practices.* New York: Teachers College Press.

Phillips, D. A. (Ed.). (1987). *Quality in child care: What does research tell us?* Washington, DC: National Association for the Education of Young Children.

Phillips, D. A., & Howes, C. (1987). Indicators of quality child care: Review of research. In D. A. Phillips, (Ed.), *Quality in child care: What does research tell us?* (pp. 1–19). Washington, DC: National Association for the Education of Young Children.

Piaget, J. (1926). *The language and thought of the child.* New York: Harcourt, Brace and World.

Piaget, J. (1929). *The child's conception of physical casualty.* New York: Harcourt, Brace and World.

Piaget, J. (1952). *The origins of intelligence in children.* New York: Norton.

Piaget, J. (1954). *The construction of reality in the child.* New York: Basic Books.

Piaget, J. (1962). *Play, dreams and imitation in childhood.* New York: Norton.

Piaget, J. (1963). *The psychology of intelligence.* Paterson, NJ: Littlefield, Adams.

Piaget, J. (1965). *The moral judgment of the child.* New York: Norton. (Original work published 1932)

Piaget, J. (1969). *Six psychological studies.* New York: Vintage.

Piaget, J., & Inhelder, B. (1956). *The child's conception of space.* London: Routledge and Kegan Paul.

Piaget, J., & Inhelder, B. (1969). *The psychology of the child.* New York: Basic Books.

Pianta, R. C. (Ed.). (1992). *Beyond the parent: The role of other adults in children's lives.* San Francisco: Jossey-Bass.

Pillitteri, A. (1992). *Maternal and child health nursing: Care of the childbearing and childrearing family.* Philadelphia: J. B. Lippincott.

Pipes, P. L. (1989). *Nutrition in infancy and childhood* (4th ed.). St. Louis: Times Mirror/Mosby.

Poest, C. A., Williams, J. R., Witt, D. D., & Atwood, M. E. (1989). Physical activity patterns of preschool children. *Early Childhood Research Quarterly, 4,* 367–376.

Pollitt, E., Leibel, R. L., & Greenfield, D. (1981). Brief fasting stress and cognition in children. *American Journal of Clinical Nutrition, 34,* 1526–1533.

Porter, F. L., Miller, R. H., & Marshall, R. E. (1986). Neonatal pain cries: Effect of circumcision on acoustic features and perceived urgency. *Child Development, 57,* 790–802.

Powell, D. R. (1989). *Families and early childhood programs.* Washington, DC: National Association for the Education of Young Children.

Powell, D. R. (1994). Parents, pluralism, and the National Association for the Education of Young Children statement on developmentally appropriate practice. In B. L. Mallory & R. S. New (Eds.), *Diversity and developmentally appropriate practices.* New York: Teachers College Press.

Powell, G. J., Yammamoto, J., Romero, A., & Morales, A. (Eds.). (1983). *The psychosocial development of minority children.* New York: Brunner/Mazel.

Press, B., & Greenspan, S. (1985). Ned and Dan: The development of a toddler friendship. *Children Today, 14,* 24–29.

Price, G. G. (1989). Mathematics in early childhood. *Young Children, 44*(4), 53–58.

Province, S., & Lipton, R. C. (1962). *Infants in institutions.* New York: International Universities Press.

Puckett, M. B., & Black, J. K. (1994). *Authentic assessment of the young child: Celebrating development and learning.* New York: Merrill/Macmillan.

Pucynski, M., Rademaker, D. D., & Gatson, R. (1983). Burn injury related to improper use of microwave oven. *Pediatrics, 72*(5), 714–715.

Putallaz, M. (1987). Maternal behavior and children's sociometric status. *Child Development, 58,* 324–340.

Radke-Yarrow, M., Zahn-Waxler, C., & Chapman, M. (1983). Children's prosocial dispositions and behavior. In E. M. Hetherington (Ed.), *Handbook of child psychology: Vol. 4. Socialization, personality and social development* (4th ed., pp. 469–545). New York: Wiley.

Raikes, H. (1993). Relationship duration in infant care: Time with a high ability teacher and infant-teacher attachment. *Early Childhood Research Quarterly, 8*(3), 309–325.

Ramirez, J. D., Yuen, S. D., & Ramey, D. R. (1991). *Longitudinal study of structural English immersion strategy, early-exit and late-exit transitional bilingual education programs for language-minority children. Final report to the United States Department of Education, Executive Summary and Volumes 1 and 2.* San Mateo, CA: Aquirre International.

Ramsay, D. S. (1980). Onset of unimanual handedness in infants. *Infant Behavior and Development 3,* 377–385.

Ramsey, P. G. (1982). Multicultural education in early childhood. *Young Children, 37*(2), 13–24.

Ramsey, P. G. (1987). *Teaching and learning in a diverse world: Multicultural education for young children.* New York: Columbia University Press.

Raver, C. C., & Zigler, E. F. (1991). Three steps forward, two steps back: Head Start and the measurement of social competence. *Young Children, 46*(4), 3–8.

Read, C. (1971). Pre-school children's knowledge of English phonology. *Harvard Educational Review, 41,* 1–34.

Reich, P. A. (1986). *Language development.* Englewood Cliffs, NJ: Prentice Hall.

Reilly, T. W., Entwisle, D. R., & Doerling, S. G. (1987). Socialization into parenthood: A longitudinal study of the development of self evaluations. *Journal of Marriage and the Family, 49*(2), 295–308.

Rescorla, L. A. (1980). Category development in early language. *Journal of Child Language, 8,* 225–238.

Resnick, M. B., Stralka, K., Carter, R. L., Arret, M., Bucciarelli, R.L., Evass, R. R., Curran, J. S., & Ausbon, W. W. (1990). Effects of birth weight and socio-demographic variables on mental development of neonatal intensive care unit survivors. *American Journal of Obstetrics and Gynecology, 162*(2), 374–378.

Restak, R. (1984). *The brain.* New York: Bantam Books.

Rhodes, L. (1981). I can read: Predictable books as resources for reading and writing activities. *The Reading Teacher, 34,* 511–518.

Rhodes, L. K., & Dudley-Marling, C. (1988). *Readers and writers with a difference: A holistic approach to teaching learning disabled and remedial students.* Portsmouth, NH: Heinemann.

Ricciardelli, L. A. (1993). Creativity and bilingualism. *Journal of Creative Behavior, 26*(4), 242–254.

Ricciuti, H. N. (1980). Developmental consequences of malnutrition in early childhood. In E. M. Hetherington & R. D. Parks (Eds.), *Contemporary readings in child psychology* (2nd ed., pp. 21–25). New York: McGraw-Hill.

Rice, M. L., Huston, A. C., & Wright, J. C. (1986). Replays as repetitions: Young children's interpretation of television forms. *Journal of Applied Developmental Psychology, 7,* 61–76.

Richardson, J. G., & Simpson, C. H. (1982). Children, gender, and social structure: An analysis of the contents of letters to Santa Claus. *Child Development, 53,* 429–436.

Richardson, L. W. (1981). *The dynamics of sex and gender* (2nd ed.). Boston: Houghton Mifflin.

Riley, S. S. (1984). *How to generate values in young children: Integrity, honesty, individuality, self-confidence, and wisdom.* Washington, DC: National Association for the Education of Young Children.

Rizzo, T., Corsaro, W., & Bates, J. E. (1992). Ethnographic methods and interpretive analysis: Expanding the methodological options of psychologists. *Developmental Review, 12,* 101–123.

Robbins, C., & Ehri, L. C. (1994). Reading storybooks to kindergartners helps them learn new vocabulary words. *Journal of Educational Psychology, 86*(1) 54–64.

Rogers, C. R. (1961). *On becoming a person.* Boston: Houghton Mifflin.

Rogers, C., & Freiberg, H. J. (1994). *Freedom to learn* (3rd. ed.). New York: Merrill/Macmillan.

Rogoff, B. (1990). *Apprenticeship in thinking: Cognitive development in social context.* New York: Oxford University Press.

Rogoff, B., & Waddell, K. J. (1982). Memory for information organized in a scene by children from two cultures. *Child Development, 53*(5), 1224–1228.

Roopnarine, J. L. (1985). Changes in peer-directed behaviors following preschool experience. *Journal of Personality and Social Psychology, 48,* 740–745.

Rose, D. F., & Smith, B. J. (1993). Preschool mainstreaming: Attitude barriers and strategies for addressing them. *Young Children, 48*(4), 59–62.

Rosen, H. (1994). Commentary. *Human Development, 37*(1). 58–60.

Rosen, M. (1981). *The rise in caesareans.* Paper presented at the First International Symposium on Computers in Prenatal Medicine, Cleveland, OH.

Rosenfield, A., & Stark, E. (1987, May). The prime of our lives. *Psychology Today,* pp. 62–72.

Rosenholtz, S. J., & Rosenholtz, S. H. (1981). Classroom organization and the perception of ability. *Sociology of Education, 54,* 132–140.

Rosenthal, M. K. (1982). Vocal dialogues in the neonatal period. *Developmental Psychology, 18,* 17–21.

Rosett, H. L., Synder, P., Sander, L. W., Lee, A., Cook, P., Weiner, L., & Gould, J. (1979). Effects of maternal drinking on neonate state regulation. *Developmental Medicine and Child Neurology, 27,* 464–473.

Ross, H. W. (1992). Integrating infants with disabilities? Can "ordinary" caregivers do it? *Young Children, 47*(3), 65–71.

Rowe, D. C., Vazonyi, A.T., & Flannery, A. J. (1994). No more than skin deep: Ethnic and racial similarity in developmental process. *Psychological Review, 101*(3), 396–413.

Rubin, K. H. (1973). Egocentrism in childhood: A unitary construct? *Child Development, 44,* 102–110.

Rubin, K. H. (1982). Nonsocial play in preschoolers: Necessarily evil? *Child Development, 53,* 651–657.

Rubin, K. H., & Everett, B. (1982). Social perspective-taking in young children. In S. G. Moore & C. R. Cooper (Eds.), *The young child: Reviews of research* (Vol. 3, pp. 97–113). Washington, DC: National Association for the Education of Young Children.

Rubin, K. H., Watson, K. S., & Jambor, T. W. (1978). Free play behaviors in preschool and kindergarten children. *Child Development, 49,* 534–536.

Rubin, Z. (1980). *Children's friendships.* Cambridge, MA: Harvard University Press.

Ryan, C. A., & Finer, N. N. (1994). Changing attitudes and practices regarding local analgesia for newborn circumcision. *Pediatrics, 94*(2), 230–233.

Sadker, M., & Sadker, D. (1985, March). Sexism in the schoolroom of the '80's. *Psychology Today,* pp. 54–57.

Saegert, S., Hart, R. (1976). The development of sex differences on the environmental competence of girls and boys. In P. Burnett (Ed.), *Women in society.* Chicago: Maaroufa Press.

Saenger, P. (1991, June). Use of growth hormone in the treatment of short stature: Boon or abuse? *Pediatrics in Review 12*(12), 355–363.

Salk, L. (1974). *Preparing for parenthood.* New York: Bantam Books.

Salkind, N. J., & Ambron, S. R. (1987). *Child development* (5th ed.). New York: Holt, Rinehart and Winston.

Salomon, G. (1977). Effects of encouraging mothers to co-observe "Sesame Street" with their five year olds. *Child Development, 48,* 1146–1151.

Sameroff, A. & Chandler, M.J. (1975). Reproductive risk and the continuum of caretaking casualty. In F. D. Horowitz (Ed.), *Review of child development research, (Vol. 4).* Chicago: University of Chicago Press.

Samuels, C. A. (1985). Attention to eye contact opportunity and facial motion by three-month-old infants. *Journal of Experimental Child Psychology, 40,* 105–114.

Samuels, M., & Samuels, N. (1986). *The well pregnancy book.* New York: Summit.

Santrock, J. (1984). *Adolescence.* Dubuque, IA: Wm. C. Brown.

Sapon-Shevin, M. (1983). Teaching children about differences: Resources for teaching. *Young Children, 38* (2), 24–31.

Sawhill, I. V. (1992). *Young children in families. In setting domestic priorities: What can government do?* Washington, DC: The Brookings Institute.

Schank, R. C., & Abelson, R. P. (1977). *Scripts, plans, goals, and understanding.* Hillsdale, NJ: Erlbaum.

Schickedanz, J. A. (1986). *More than ABC's: The early stages of reading and writing.* Washington, DC: National Association for the Education of Young Children.

Schoevar, G. P. (1987). Anorexia nervosa and bulima. In H. L. Field & B. B. Domamgus (Eds.), *Eating disorders throughout the life span* (pp. 31–47). New York: Praeger.

Schweinhart, L. J., Barnes, A. V., & Weikart, D. P. (1993). Significant benefits: The High/Scope Perry Preschool Study through age 27. *Monographs of the High/Scope Educational Research Foundation, 10.* Ypsilanti, MI: High/Scope Press. PS 021–998.

Schweinhart, L., & Weikart, D. P. (1985). Evidence that good early childhood programs work. *Phi Delta Kappan, 66,* 545–551.

Sedney, M. A. (1987). Development of androgyny: Parental influences. *Psychology of Women Quarterly, 11*(3), 311–326.

Segan, C. (1994, March 6). Literacy—the path to a more prosperous, less dangerous America. *Parade Magazine,* (4–7).

Seidel, J. F. (1992). Children with HIV-related difficulties. *Phi Delta Kappan, 74*(1) 38–40.

Selfe, L. (1977). *Nadia: A case of extraordinary drawing ability in an autistic child.* New York: Academic Press.

Selman, R. L. (1976). Social cognitive understanding. In T. Lickona (Ed.), *Moral development and behavior: Theory, research, and social issues* (pp. 219–240). New York: Holt, Rinehart and Winston.

Selman, R. L. (1980). *The growth of interpersonal understanding: Developmental and clinical analysis.* New York: Academic Press.

Selman, R. L. (1981). The child as friendship philosopher. In S. R. Asher & J. M. Gottman (Eds.), *The development of children's friendships* (pp. 242–273). Cambridge, MA: Cambridge University Press.

Sepkowski, C. (1985). Maternal obstetric medication and newborn behavior. In J. W. Scanlon (Ed.), *Prenatal anesthesia*. London: Blackwell.

Sexton, D. (1990). Quality integrated programs for infants and toddlers with special needs. In E. Surbeck & M. F. Kelley (Eds.). *Personalizing care of infants, toddlers and families* (pp. 41–50). Wheaton, MD: Association for Childhood Education International.

Shaffer, H. R. (1971). *The growth of stability*. London: Penguin.

Shapiro, J. (1987, January). The expectant father. *Psychology Today*, pp. 36–42.

Shatz, M. (1983). Communication. In P. H. Mussen (Ed.), *Handbook of child psychology: Vol. 3. Cognitive development* (pp. 841–889). New York: Wiley.

Sheehy, G. (1976). *Passages: Predictable crises of adult life*. New York: Dutton.

Sheehy, G. (1982). *Pathfinders*. New York: Bantam Books.

Sheldon, A. (1990). "Kings are royaler than queens": Language and socialization. *Young Children, 45*(2), 4–9.

Shelov, S. P., & Hannemann, R. E. (1993). *Caring for your baby and young child: Birth to age 5: The complete and authoritative guide*. New York: Bantam Books.

Shepard, L. A., & Smith, M. L. (1986). Synthesis of research on school readiness and kindergarten retention. *Educational Leadership, 44*(3), 78–86.

Shepard, L. A., & Smith, M. L. (1987). Effects of kindergarten retention at the end of first grade. *Psychology in the School, 24*, 346–357.

Shirley, M. M. (1961). *The first two years: A study of twenty-five babies*. Minneapolis: University of Minnesota Press.

Shlono, P. H., Klebanoff, M. A., Graubard, M. A., Berendes, H. W., & Rhoads, G. G. (1986). Birth weight among women of different ethnic groups. *Journal of the American Medical Association, 255*, 48–52.

Shonkoff, J. P. (1984). The biological substrate and physical health in middle childhood. In W. A. Collins (Ed.), *Development during middle childhood: The years from six to twelve* (pp. 24–69). Washington, DC: National Academy Press.

Shriffin, R. M., & Atkinson, R. C. (1969). Storage and retrieval processes in long-term memory. *Psychological Review, 76*, 179–193.

Shultz, T. R., Wright, K., & Schleifer, M. (1986). Assignment of moral responsibility and punishment. *Child Development, 57*, 177–184.

Siegler, R. S. (1981). Developmental sequences within and between concepts. *Monographs of the Society for Research in Child Development, 46*(2, Serial No. 189).

Siegler, R. S. (1983). Information processing approaches to development. In W. Kesson (Ed.), *Handbook of child psychology: Vol. 1 History, theory and methods* (4th ed., pp. 129–211). New York: Wiley.

Siegler, R. S. (1986). *Children's thinking*. Englewood Cliffs, NJ: Prentice Hall.

Siegler, R. S., & Robinson, M. (1982). The development of numerical understandings. In H. W. Reese & L. P. Lipsitt (Eds.), *Advances in child development and behavior* (Vol. 16, pp. 241–312). New York: Academic Press.

Siegler, R. (1991). *Children's thinking* (2nd. ed.). Englewood Cliffs, NJ: Prentice Hall.

Simmons, R., & Blyth, D. (1987). *Moving into adolescence: The impact of pubertal change and school context*. New York: Aldine/Hawthorne.

Singer, J. L., & Singer, D. G. (1979, March). Come back, Mr. Rogers, come back. *Psychology Today*, pp. 56, 59–60.

Singer, J. L., & Singer, D. G. (1981). *Television, imagination, and aggression: A study of preschoolers*. Hillsdale, NJ: Erlbaum.

Singer, J. L., & Singer, D. G. (1983). Psychologists look at television. *American Psychologist, 38*, 826–834.

Skinner, B. F. (1938). *The behavior of organisms*. Englewood Cliffs, NJ: Prentice Hall.

Skinner, B. F. (1948). *Walden two*. New York: Macmillan.

Skinner, B. F. (1957). *Verbal behavior*. East Norwalk, CT: Appleton-Century-Crofts.

Skinner, B. F. (1974). *About behaviorism*. New York: Knopf.

Skinner, B. F. (1979). *The shaping of a behaviorist*. New York: Knopf.

Sleeter, C. (1994). White racism. *Multicultural Education, 1*(4), 5–8, 39.

Smilansky, S. (1968). *The effects of sociodramatic play on disadvantaged preschool children*. New York: Wiley.

Smith, B., & Strain, P. (1988). *Does early intervention help?* (Report No. R188062207).

Smith, C., & Loyd, B. (1978). Maternal behavior and perceived sex of infant: Revisited. *Child Development, 49*, 1263–1266.

Smith, C. A., & Berenberg, W. (1970). The concept of failure to thrive. *Pediatrics, 46*, 661.

Snow, C. E., & Ferguson, C. (Eds.). (1977). *Talking to children: Language input and acquisition*. New York: Cambridge University Press.

Snow, C. E., & Ninio, A. (1986). The contracts of literacy: What children learn from learning to read books. In W. H. Teale & E. Sulzby (Eds.), *Emergent literacy: Writing and reading* (pp. 116–138). Norwood, NJ: Ablex.

Snow, C. E. (1983). Literacy and language: Relationships during the preschool years. *Harvard Educational Review, 53*, 165–189.

Snow, C. W. (1989). *Infant development*. Englewood Cliffs, NJ: Prentice Hall.

Snyder, M., Snyder, R., & Snyder, R., Jr. (1980). *The young child as person: Toward the development of healthy conscience*. New York: Human Sciences Press.

Society for Research in Child Development, Ethical Interest Group. (1975). *Ethical standards for research with children*. Chicago: Society for Research in Child Development.

Solan, L. (1983). *Pronominal reference: Child language and theory of grammar*. Dordreeht, Holland: Reidel.

Spangler, G. & Grossman, K. E. (1993). Biobehavioral organization in securely and insecurely attached infants. *Child Development, 64:* 1439–1450.

Spears, S., Carpenter, C., & Burstein, N. (1994). Meaningful reading instruction for learners with special needs. *The Reading Teacher, 47*(8), 632–638.

Sperry, R. (1970). Perception in the absence of neocortical commissures. In *Perception and its disorders* (Research Publication, Vol. 48). New York: Association for Research in Nervous and Mental Disease.

Spock, B. (1988). *Dr. Spock on parenting.* New York: Simon and Schuster.

Stechler, G., & Halton, A. (1982). Prenatal influences on human development. In B. B. Wollman, G. Stricker, S. J. Ellman, P. Keith-Spiegel, & D. S. Palermo (Eds.), *Handbook of developmental psychology.* Englewood Cliffs, NJ: Prentice Hall.

Stein, N. L., & Glenn, C. G. (1979). An analysis of story comprehension in elementary school children. In R. O. Freedle (Ed.), *Advances in discourse processing* (Vol. 2, pp. 53–120). Norwood, NJ: Ablex.

Steiner, J. E. (1979). Human facial expressions in response to taste and smell stimulation. In H. Reese & L. Lipsitt (Eds.), *Advances in child development and behavior* (Vol. 13, pp. 257–295). New York: Academic Press.

Sternberg, R. J. (1985). *Beyond IQ: A triarchic theory of human intelligence.* New York: Cambridge University Press.

Stevens, L. J., & Price, M. P. (1992). Meeting the challenge of educating children at risk. *Phi Delta Kappan, 74*(1), 18–23.

Stevenson, H. W. (1967). Studies of racial awareness in young children. In W. W. Hartup & N. L. Smothergill (Eds.), *The young child: Reviews of research* (pp. 206–213). Washington, DC: National Association for the Education of Young Children.

Steward, M. S., & Steward, D. S. (1974). Effect of social distance on teaching strategies of Anglo-American and Mexican-American mothers. *Developmental Psychology, 10*(6), 797–807.

Stewart, R. B. (1983). Sibling attachment relationships: Child infant interactions in the strange situation. *Developmental Psychology, 19,* 192–199.

Stewart, R. B., Mobley, L. A., Van Tuyl, S. S., & Salvador, M. A. (1987). The firstborn's adjustment to the birth of a sibling: A longitudinal assessment. *Child Development, 58,* 341.

Stipek, D., Recchia, S., & McClintic, S. (1992). Self-evaluation in young children. Monographs of the Society for *Research in Child Development, 57*(1) (Serial No. 226.), 1–98.

Storo, W. (1993). Role of bicycle helmet in bicycle related injury prevention. *Clinical Digest Series, 4*(3), 23. (Reprinted from *Clinical Pediatrics* (1992), *31:* 421–427).

Streissguth, A. P., Martin, D. C., Barr, H. M., & Sandman, B. H. (1984). Intrauterine alcohol and nicotine exposure: Attention and reaction time in 4-year old children. *Developmental Psychology, 20,* 533–541.

Strong, M. (1982). Social styles and second language acquisition of Spanish-speaking kindergarteners. *TESOL Quarterly, 17,* 2.

Stroufe, L. A. (1979). Socioemotional development. In J.D. Osofsky (Ed.), *Handbook of infant development* (pp. 462–516). New York: Wiley.

Stroufe, L. A. (1983). Infant caregiver attachments and patterns of adaptation in preschool: The roots of maladaptation and competence. In M. Perlmutter (Ed.), *Minnesota symposium on child psychology* (Vol. 16, pp. 41–81). Hillsdale, NJ: Erlbaum.

Stroufe, L. A. (1985). Attachment classification from the perspective of infant-caregiver relationships and infant temperament. *Child Development, 56,*(1), 1–14.

Stroufe, L. A. (1988). A developmental perspective on day care. *Early Childhood Research Quarterly, 3,*(3), 283–291.

Stroufe, L. A., Fox, N. E., & Pancake, V. R. (1983). Attachment and dependency in developmental perspective. *Child Development, 54,* 1615–1627.

Stroufe, L. A., Schork, E., Motti, F., Lawroski, N., & LaFreniere, P. (1984). The role of affect in social competence. In C. E. Izard, J. Kagan, & R. Zajonc (Eds.), *Affect, cognition and behavior* (pp. 289–319). New York: Plenum Press.

Sudhalter, V., & Braine, M. D. S. (1985). How does comprehension of passives develop? A comparison of actional and experiential verbs. *Journal of Child Language, 12,* 453–470.

Sugarman, S. (1987). *Piaget's construction of the child's reality.* Cambridge, England: Cambridge University Press.

Surbec, E., & Kelley, M. F. (Eds.). (1990). *Personalizing care with infants, toddlers, and families.* Wheaton, MD: Association for Childhood Education International.

Surber, C. F. (1982). Separable effects of motives, consequences, and presentation order of children's moral judgments. *Developmental Psychology, 18,* 257–266.

Sutton-Smith, B. (1967). The role of play in cognitive development. *Young Children, 22,* 361–370.

Sutton-Smith, B. (1975). A developmental structural account of riddles. In B. Kirschenblatt-Gimblett (Ed.), *Speech play* (pp. 111–119). The Hague: Mouton.

Sutton-Smith, B. (1979). *Play and learning.* New York: Wiley.

Sutton-Smith, B. (1986). The spirit of play. In G. G. Fein & M. Rivkin (Eds.), *The young child at play* (pp. 3–15). Washington, DC: National Association for the Education of Young Children

Swick, K., Brown, M., & Guddemi, M. (1986). *Personality dimensions of effective teachers.* Columbia: University of South Carolina.

Tanner, J. M. (1973). The regulation of human growth. In F. Rebelsky & L. Dorman (Eds.), *Child development and behavior.* New York: Knopf.

Tanner, J. M. (1978). *Fetus into man: Physical growth from conception to maturity.* Cambridge, MA: Harvard University Press.

Tanner, J. M. (1989). *Fetus into man: Physical growth from conception to maturity* (rev. & ed.). Cambridge, MA: Harvard University Press.

Task Force on Early Childhood and Elementary Education. (1994, January). *First impressions/Primeras impressiones.* Austin, TX: Texas Education Agency.

Taylor, D. (1986). Creating a family story. In W. H. Teale & E. Sulzby (Eds.), *Emergent literacy: Writing and reading* (pp. 139–155). Norwood, NJ: Ablex.

Taylor, D., & Dorsey-Gaines, C. (1988). *Growing up literate: Learning from inner-city families.* Portsmouth, NH: Heinemann.

Teale, W. H. (1981). Parents reading to children: What we know and need to know. *Language Arts, 58,* 902–912.

Teale, W. H. (1984). Reading to young children: Its significance for literacy development. In H. Goelman, A. Oberg, & F. Smith (Eds.), *Awakening to literacy* (pp. 110–121). Portsmouth, NH: Heinemann.

Teale, W. H. (1986). Home background and young children's literacy development. In W. H. Teale & E. Sulzby (Eds.), *Emergent literacy: Writing and reading* (pp. 173–206). Norwood, NJ: Ablex.

Teale, W. H., Estrada, E., & Anderson, A. B. (1981). How preschoolers interact with written communication. In M. L. Kamil (Ed.), *Directions in reading: Research and instruction. Thirtieth yearbook of the National Reading Conference* (pp. 257–265). Washington, DC: National Reading Conference.

Teale, W. H., & Sulzby, E. (Eds.). (1986). *Emergent literacy: Writing and reading.* Norwood, NJ: Ablex.

Templin, M. C. (1957). Certain skills in children: Their development and interrelationships. *University of Minnesota Institute of Child Welfare Monographs, 26.*

Thain, W. S., Casto, G., & Peterson, A. (1980). *Normal and handicapped children: A growth and development primer for parents and professionals.* Littleton, MA: PSG Publishing.

The Goals 2000, Educate America Act (P.L. 103–227).

Thomas, A., & Chess, S. (1977). *Temperament and development.* New York: Brunner/Mazel.

Thomas, A., Chess, S., & Birch, H. G. (1968). *Temperament and behavior disorders in children.* New York: New York University Press.

Thomas, A., Chess, S., Birch, H. G., Hertzig, M. E., & Korn, S. (1963). *Behavioral individuality in early childhood.* New York: New York University Press.

Thomas, A., Chess, S., & Korn, S. (1982). The reality of difficult temperament. *Merrill-Palmer Quarterly, 28,* 1–20.

Thompson, J. S., & Thompson, M. W. (1986). *Genetics in medicine.* Philadelphia: Saunders.

Thurman, S. K., & Lewis, M. (1979). Children's responses to differences: Some possible implications for mainstreaming. *Exceptional Children, 45,* 468–470.

Trawick-Smith, J. (1994). *Interactions in the classroom: Facilitating play in the early years.* New York: Macmillan.

Tronick, E. Z., Cohn, J., & Shea, E. (1986). The transfer of affect between mother and infant. In T. B. Brazelton & M. W. Yogman (Eds.), *Affective development in infancy* (pp. 11–25). Norwood, NJ: Ablex.

Tunmer, W. E., Bowey, J. A., & Grieve, R. (1983). The development of young children's awareness of the word as a unit of spoken language. *Journal of Psycholinguistic Research, 12,* 567–594.

Tunmer, W. E., & Nesdale, A. R. (1982). The effects of digraphs and pseudo-words on phonemic segmentation in young children. *Journal of Applied Linguistics, 3,* 299–311.

Turiel, E. (1980). The development of social-conventional and moral concepts. In M. Windmiller, N. Lambert, & E. Turiel (Eds.), *Moral development and socialization* (pp. 69–106). Boston: Allyn & Bacon.

Tyler, R. (1992). Prenatal drug exposure: An overview of associated problems and intervention strategies. *Phi Delta Kappan, 73*(9), 705–708.

United States Congress, Senate Committee on Human Resources Research. (1978). *Obstetrical practices in the U.S.* Washington, DC: U.S. Government Printing Office.

United States Consumer Product Safety Commission (1981). *A handbook for public playground safety. Vols I & II: Technical guidelines for equipment and surfacing.* Washington, DC: U.S. Government Printing Office.

United States Consumer Product Safety Commission (1991). *Handbook for public playground safety.* Washington, DC: Government Printing Office.

United States Department of Agriculture. (1992). *Human Nutrition Information Service* (Leaflet # 572). Pueblo, CO: U.S. Superintendent of Documents.

United States Department of Agriculture. (1993, October). *Food Program Facts* (fact sheet). San Francisco: Food and Nutrition Service, USDA.

United States Department of Education. (1991). *America 2000: Educate America* (rev. ed.). Washington, DC: Author.

United States Department of Health and Human Services. (1990). *The health consequences of smoking for women: A report of the Surgeon General.* Rockville, MD: Author.

United States Department of Labor, Secretary's Commission on Achieving Necessary Skills (SCANS). (1992). *Learning a living: A blueprint for high performance.* Washington, DC: U.S. Government Printing Office.

United States General Accounting Office Report to the Chairman, Committee on Labor and Human Resources, U.S. Senate. (1994). *Limited English proficiency: A growing and costly educational challenge facing many school districts.* Washington, DC: U.S. General Accounting Office.

Vaillant, G. E. (1977). *Adaptation to life.* Waltham, MA: Little, Brown.

Vandell, D., & Mueller, E. (1980). Peer play and friendships during the first two years. In H. Foot, A. Chapman, & J. Smith (Eds.), *Friendship and social relations in children* (pp. 181–208). New York: Wiley.

Van Hasselt, V. C. (1983). Social adaptation in the blind. *Clinical Psychology Review, 3,* 87–102.

Vaughn, V. C., III, & Litt, I. F. (1987). The newborn infant. In R. E. Behrman & V. C. Vaughn (Eds.), *Nelson textbook of pediatrics* (13th ed., pp. 7–17). Philadelphia: Saunders.

Vogel, F., & Motulsky, A. G. (1979). *Human genetics: Problems and approaches.* New York: Springer.

Volpe, J. J. (1987). *Neurology of the newborn,* (2nd ed.). Philadelphia: Saunders.

Vorhees, C. V., & Mallnow, E. (1987). Behavior teratogenesis: Long-term influences on behavior. In J. D. Osofsky (Ed.), *Handbook of infant development* (2nd ed., pp. 913–971). New York: Wiley.

Vurpillot, E. (1968). The development of scanning strategies and their relation to visual differentiation. *Journal of Experimental Child Psychology, 6,* 632–650.

Vygotsky, L. S. (1962). *Thought and language.* Cambridge, MA: MIT Press. (Original work published 1934)

Vygotsky, L. S. (1978). *Mind in society: The development of higher mental processes.* Cambridge, MA: Harvard University Press.

Vygotsky, L. S. (1987). Thinking and speech. In N. Minick (Trans.), *The collected works of L. S. Vygotsky: Vol. 1. Problems in general psychology.* New York: Plenum Press.

Wadsworth, B. (1984). *Piaget's theory of cognitive and affective development.* New York: Longman.

Wald, E. R., Dahefsky, B., & Byers, C. (1988). Frequency and severity of infections in day care. *Journal of Pediatrics, 112,* 5400–5406.

Wallis, C. (1986, January 20). Cocaine babies. *Time,* p. 50.

Wanska, S. K., & Bedrosian, J. L. (1985). Conversational structure and topic performance in mother-child interaction. *Journal of Speech and Hearing Research, 28,* 579–584.

Ward, E. H. (1978). A code of ethics: The hallmark of a profession. In L. G. Katz & E. H. Ward (Eds.), *Ethical behavior in early childhood education* (pp. 17–26). Washington, DC: National Association for the Education of Young Children.

Watkins, B., Calvert, S., Huston-Stein, A., & Wright, J. C. (1980). Children's recall of television material: Effects of presentation mode and adult labeling. *Developmental Psychology, 16,* 672–674.

Watson, D. J. (1994). Whole language: Why bother? *The Reading Teacher, 48*(8), 600–607.

Watson, J. B. (1924). *Behaviorism.* New York: Norton.

Watson, J. B. (1928). *Psychological care of infant and child.* New York: Norton.

Watson, J. B., & Rayner, R. (1920). Conditioned emotional reactions. *Journal of Experimental Psychology, 3,* 1–14.

Weber, E. (1984). *Ideas influencing early childhood education.* New York: Teachers College Press.

Webster, L., Wood, R., Eicher, C., & Hoag, C. (1989). A preschool language tutoring project: Family support— The essential factor. *Early Childhood Research Quarterly, 4,* 217–224.

Weir, R. (1962). *Language in the crib.* The Hague: Mouton.

Weisner, T. (1982). Sibling interdependence and child caretaking: A cross cultural view. In M. E. Lamb & B. Sutton-Smith (Eds.), *Sibling relationships.* Hillsdale, NJ: Erlbaum.

Weiss, C. E., Lillywhite, H. S., & Gordon, M. D. (1980). *Clinical management of articulation disorders.* St. Louis: Mosby.

Weiss, E. (1984). Learning disabled children's understanding of social interactions with peers. *Journal of Learning Disabilities, 17,* 612–615.

Weissburg, J. A., & Paris, S. G. (1986). Young children's remembering in different contexts: A reinterpretation of Istomina's study. *Child Development, 57,* 1123–1129.

Wells, G. (1981). *Learning through interaction: The study of language development.* Cambridge, MA: Cambridge University Press.

Wenk, D. A., Hardesty, C. L., Morgan, C. S., & Blair, S. E. (1994). The influence of parental involvement on the well-being of sons and daughters. *Journal of Marriage and the Family, 56*(1), 229–243.

Werner, E. E. (1979). *Cross-cultural child development: A view from the planet earth.* Monterrey, CA: Brooks/Cole.

Werner, E. E., & Smith, R. S. (1982). *Vulnerable but invincible: A longitudinal study of resilient children and youth.* New York: McGraw-Hill.

Werner, E. E. (1989). Children of the garden island. *Scientific American, 260,* 107–111.

Wertsch, J. V., & Tulviste, D. (1992). L. S. Vygotsky and contemporary developmental psychology. *Developmental Psychology, 28*(4), 548–557.

White, B. (1985). *The first three years of life.* Englewood Cliffs, NJ: Prentice Hall.

White, S. H., & Pillemer, D. B. (1979). Childhood amnesia and the development of a socially accessible memory system. In J. F. Kihlstrom & F. J. Evans (Eds.), *Functional disorders of memory* (pp. 29–73). Hillsdale, NJ: Erlbaum.

Whiting, B. B., & Whiting, J. W. M. (1975). *Children of six cultures: A psychocultural analysis.* Cambridge, MA: Harvard University Press.

Whitley, B. E. (1985). Sex role orientation and psychological well-being: Two meta-analyses. *Sex Roles, 12,* 207–215.

Wilcox, A., & Russell, I. (1990). Why small black infants have a lower mortality rate than small white infants: The case for population specific standards for birth weight. *Pediatrics, 116*(1), 7–10.

Willert, M. K., & Kamii, C. (1985). Reading in kindergarten: Direct vs. indirect teaching. *Young Children, 40* (4), 3–9.

Williams, J. E., & Moreland, J. K. (1976). *Race, color, and the young child.* Chapel Hill: University of North Carolina Press.

Williams, L. (1990, March 22). Growing up flabby in America. *The New York Times.*

Williams, L. R. (1994). Developmentally appropriate practice and cultural values: A case in point. In B. L. Mallory & R. S. New (Eds.), *Diversity and developmentally appropriate practices.* New York: Teachers College Press.

Wilson, J. G. (1977). Current status of teratology. In J. G. Wilson & F. C. Fraser (Eds.), *Handbook of teratology* (Vol. 1), New York: Plenum Press.

Winick, B. (1981). Food and the fetus. *American Scientist, 1,* 76–81.

Winick, M. (1976). *Malnutrition and brain development.* New York: Oxford University Press.

Winner, E., Rosenstiel, A. K., & Gardner, H. (1977). The development of metaphoric understanding. *Journal of Learning Disabilities, 10,* 147–149.

Winnicott, D. W. (1953). Transitional objects and transitional phenomena. *International Journal of Psycho-Analysis, 34,* 1–9.

Winnicott, D. W. (1971). *Playing and reality.* London: Tavistock Publications.

Winnicott, D. W. (1977). *The piggle.* New York: International Universities Press.

Wishart, J. G., & Bower, T. G. R. (1985). A longitudinal study of the development of the object concept. *British Journal of Developmental Psychology, 3,* 243–258.

Wolfe, D. A., & Korsch, B. (1994). Witnessing domestic violence during childhood and adolescence. Implications for pediatric practice. *Pediatrics, 94*(4) (Supp. A, part 2 of 2), 594–599.

Wolff, P. (1963). Observation on the early development of smiling. In B. Foss (Ed.), *Determinants of infant behavior* (Vol. 2, pp. 113–138). London: Methuen.

Wolff, P. H. (1966). The causes, controls, and organization of behavior in the neonate. *Psychology Issues, 5*(1, Serial No. 17).

Wolfle, J. (1989). The gifted preschooler: Developmentally different but still 3 or 4 years old. *Young Children, 44*(3), 41–48.

Wong-Fillmore, L. (1976). *The second time around: Cognitive and social strategies in second language acquisition.* Unpublished doctoral dissertation, Stanford University.

Wong-Fillmore, L. (1981). *Language minority students and school participation: What kind of English is needed?* Paper presented at the Conference on Literacy and Language Use, University of Southern California, Los Angeles.

Wong-Fillmore, L. (1991). Language and cultural issues in early education. In S. L. Kagan (Ed.), *The care and education of America's young children: Obstacles and opportunities* (Part I). (pp. 30–49). The 90th Yearbook for the National Society for the Study of Education. Chicago: National Society for the Study of Education.

Wood, J. T. (1994). *Gendered lives.* Belmont, CA: Wadsworth.

Wortham, S. C. (1984). *Organizing instruction in early childhood.* Boston: Allyn & Bacon.

Wortham, S. C. (1990). *Tests and measurement of early childhood education.* Columbus, OH: Merrill.

Wright, J. C., Huston, A. C., Ross, R. P., Calvert, S. L., Rolandelli, D., Weeks, L. A., Raeissi, P., & Potts, R. (1984). Pace and continuity of television programs: Effects on children's attentions and comprehension. *Developmental Psychology, 20,* 653–666.

Wyden, B. (1971, December 17). Growth: 45 crucial months. *Life,* pp. 93–95.

Xiaoming, L., & Feigelman, S. (1994). Recent and intended drug trafficking among male and female urban African-American early adolescents. *Pediatrics, 93*(8), 1044–1049.

Yaffee, S. (1980). *Safe sedatives and pregnancy.* Paper presented at the American Association for the Advancement of Science, Washington, DC.

Yarrow, L. (1961). Maternal deprivation: Toward an empirical and conceptual re-evaluation. *Psychological Bulletin, 58,* 459–490.

Yarrow, M. R., Scott, P. M., & Zahn-Waxler, C. Z. (1973). Learning concern for others. *Developmental Psychology, 8,* 240–260.

Yarrow, M. R., & Zahn-Waxler, C. Z. (1977). The emergence and functions of prosocial behaviors in young children. In R. C. Smart & M. S. Smart (Eds.), *Readings in child development and relationships* (2nd ed., pp. 77–81). New York: Macmillan.

Yawkey, T., & Johnson, J. E. (1988). *Integrative processes and socialization: Early to middle childhood.* Hillsdale, NJ: Erlbaum.

Yip, R., Zhu, L., & Chong, W. H. (1991). Race and birth weight: The Chinese example. *Pediatrics, 87*(5), 688–693.

Youniss, J., & Smollar, J. (1985). *Adolescent relations with mothers, fathers, and friends.* Chicago: University of Chicago Press.

Zahn-Waxler, C., Radke-Yarrow, M., & King, R. A. (1979). Child rearing and children's prosocial initiations toward victims of distress. *Child Development, 50,* 319–330.

Zaslow, M. J., & Pedersen, F. A. (1981). Sex role conflicts and the experience of childbearing. *Professional Psychology, 12* (1), 47–55.

Zinchenko, V. P., Chzhi-Tsin, V., & Tarakanov, V. V. (1963). The formation and development of perceptual activity. *Soviet Psychology 2,* 3–12.

Zuravin, S. J. (1987). Unplanned pregnancies, family planning problems and child maltreatment. *Family Relations, 36*(2), 136–139.

# AUTHOR INDEX

# SUBJECT INDEX